Psychological Problems

Psychological Problems

The Social Context

Edited by
Philip Feldman
Department of Psychology
University of Birmingham
Birmingham

and

Jim Orford
Department of Psychology
University of Exeter/Exe Vale Hospital
Exeter

JOHN WILEY & SONS
Chichester · New York · Brisbane · Toronto

British Library Cataloguing in Publication Data:

Psychological problems.
1. Social psychology
2. Mental illness
I. Feldman, Philip
II. Orford, Jim
301.1 HM291

ISBN 0 471 27741 X

Typeset by Computacomp (UK) Ltd,
Fort William, Scotland, and printed in the
United States of America by
Vail-Ballou Press, Inc., Binghamton, N.Y.

Contributors

Michael Argyle	*Department of Experimental Psychology, University of Oxford, England.*
Raymond Cochrane	*Department of Psychology, University of Birmingham, England.*
Mark Cook	*Department of Psychology, University of Swansea, Wales.*
Emory L. Cowen	*Department of Psychology, University of Rochester, U.S.A.*
Steve Duck	*Department of Psychology, University of Lancaster, England.*
Philip Feldman	*Department of Psychology, University of Birmingham, England.*
Martin Herbert	*School of Social Work, University of Leicester, England.*
William J. McGuire	*Department of Psychology, Yale University, U.S.A.*
Clifford R. O'Donnell	*Department of Psychology, University of Hawaii, U.S.A.*
Jim Orford	*Department of Psychology, University of Exeter, England.*
Geoff Shepherd	*Department of Psychology, Institute of Psychiatry, London, England.*
Michael P. Sobol	*Department of Psychology, University of Guelph, Canada.*
William Yule	*Department of Psychology, Institute of Psychiatry, London, England.*

Contents

Preface

For many years the experimental psychology of learning was the major area of 'basic psychology' upon which it was possible to draw for an explanation for psychological problems and for models for the psychological therapies. More recently, social psychology has made a major and growing contribution, and this collection of chapters is an attempt to represent some aspects of this development. Without denying the key roles of biological and learning events it is our conviction that social variables also play a major part in the occurrence of psychological problems, in their effective management, and, most important of all, in their prevention.

This volume has two major sections. The main emphasis of the first is on basic theory and research findings in social psychology with current or future implications for the solution of psychological problems. The second concentrates more on the practical applications of social and community psychology in changing either the behaviour of individuals or the environment in which they live.

Chapter 1, by Jim Orford, is concerned with the family, one of the key social settings for the acquisition of attitudes and behaviours, and the focus of considerable recent research which has begun to do justice to the subtleties of family interactions. Illustrating his thesis with reference to research on drinking problems, child abuse, and psychiatric disorder, he argues for the relevance of the concept of the cohesive group in social psychology.

In the second chapter, Martin Herbert focuses more specifically on child-rearing methods and skills, the family's physical resources, and the consequences of these for the development by children of socially and personally positive, or damaging, behaviours.

In the next three chapters Steve Duck, Mark Cook, and Michael Argyle explore the complexities of interpersonal perception and social behaviours outside the family setting. Cook discusses what determines social perception and judgements and draws some implications for the development of clinically relevant behaviours. The field covered by Duck, that of intimate personal relationships, is a relatively new one and includes basic research and theory on love and romance as well as on close friendships, together with the personal consequences of failures in such relationships. Argyle lists the components of competent social performance, pointing out the widespread occurrence of deficits in social skills and the consequences of such problems for many areas of personal life.

In the last chapter of this section Ray Cochrane and Michael Sobol discuss in detail the importance for psychological problems of a wide range of life events. This area has considerable implications for the large-scale social planning of environments which promote, rather than hinder, effective coping behaviours, implications which are taken up in several chapters of the second section.

In Chapter 7, the first of the second section, Philip Feldman reviews the social experiences which increase the probability of criminal behaviours and the attempts which are being made to reduce the initial or repeated occurrence of such behaviours. These attempts may have an effect quite opposite to that intended and it is clear that current penal policy is largely ineffective. In the next two chapters William Yule and Geoff Shepherd focus on special groups—the handicapped and those in residential care settings. Yule describes the difficulties of children with several forms of demonstrable handicap when faced with the particular demands of particular social settings. He also reviews various forms of effective social intervention. Shepherd both reinforces the importance of satisfactory social relationships for psychological wellbeing and discusses attempts at retraining, in a wide range of social skills, those confined to residential institutions for long periods. He focuses on the importance of the institutional environment, staff behaviours, and the crucial issue of generalization to the natural environment.

Three chapters then take up the theme of large-scale social action, both in managing psychological problems and, more importantly, in preventing them. Cliff O'Donnell conveys the essential message that small is beautiful for all kinds of planned social environments, from hospitals to places of work. The implications of his approach to environmental design extend from the prevention of psychological problems to the prevention of crime. This emphasis on prevention, rather than intervention, is again strong in Cowen's review of community psychology, which he distinguishes sharply from mental health facilities which are merely sited 'in the community' rather than in hospitals. Cowen reviews several large-scale projects on prevention which have used para-professionals, volunteers, and self-help groups, all of great importance in the current, and probable future, context of severe constraints on public funding for the helping professions. In the final chapter, McGuire takes us even further into the theme of a shift from costly interventions after the problem has occurred to large-scale field programmes aimed at prevention in advance. He reviews both the literature on social influence and several fascinating attempts to use mass-media methods to apply these findings to socially beneficial ends, for example, in heart-disease prevention.

In our final chapter we bring together the main themes of our contributors and draw some conclusions for the training of psychologists, emphasizing particularly the interdependence of all branches of psychology, both of research and of professional application.

We hope that this book will be of scientific interest and of practical value to all those engaged in research into the development, management, and prevention of psychological problems, to the wide range of professionals engaged in management and prevention and to students in several social science disciplines.

Finally, we are most grateful to our contributors for their patient and helpful responses to our editorial efforts and to the many secretaries too numerous to mention by name.

Philip Feldman and Jim Orford
1980

PART I

Social settings and social processes

The Social Psychology of Psychological Problems
Edited by P. Feldman and J. Orford

1

The Domestic Context

JIM ORFORD

I. PSYCHOLOGICAL FUNCTIONS OF THE FAMILY

Homo sapiens and his ancestors have mostly lived in small 'family' groups since the middle of the Pleistocene period—500,000 years ago (Washburn, 1961). It is difficult to imagine that such groups do not constitute one of the most important contexts, perhaps the most important, for an understanding of the nature of psychological problems. If the social environment is in any way responsible for the origin or maintenance of a psychological problem, or if such a problem has any impact upon the social environment, then we may reasonably expect to find evidence of such influence and impact within the family group.

It is in fact much more difficult to define 'the family' precisely than might be supposed. Critics of family studies which assume that the nuclear family is the norm can point to the importance of extended kin in living groups in various parts of the world (Fox, 1967), and in modern western society also (Young and Willmott, 1957). Although a disproportionate amount of relevant research has been carried out on intact, nuclear, seemingly normal families, in this chapter I shall try to have in mind a broader concept of a 'family' which includes any close-knit co-living group whether or not based upon ties of blood or marriage. It is, of course, normal to live away from a kinship or marriage family at certain periods of life, especially at times of status passage, and perhaps particularly at times when psychological problems occur. Even so-called nuclear families go through developmental changes—the family life-cyle—the childless couple, a couple with an infant child or children, an ageing couple whose children have left home, etc. (e.g. Rollins and Feldman, 1970). Many people live in institutions, live at their place of work, look after other people's children for periods of time, or opt for alternative domestic arrangements even though their life stage would qualify them for membership of a nuclear family (e.g. Rigby, 1974). It is probably counterproductive to attempt a formal definition of the family conceived broadly in this way. There is a host of characteristics which crudely differentiate family relationships from other types of relationship. For example, family members are more likely to see one another daily or at least very often, to have close knowledge of one another, to use terms of endearment amongst one another, to share meals, to share material resources, to live under the same roof, and to think of themselves as part of the same family. But no one criterion applies universally even to members of the most clear-cut nuclear families, and each criterion used alone would encompass relationships that would not normally be thought of as family relationships even when the family is defined broadly. The family, however, is probably most readily understood as a group of people who live together, interact much, and who think of themselves as 'a family'.

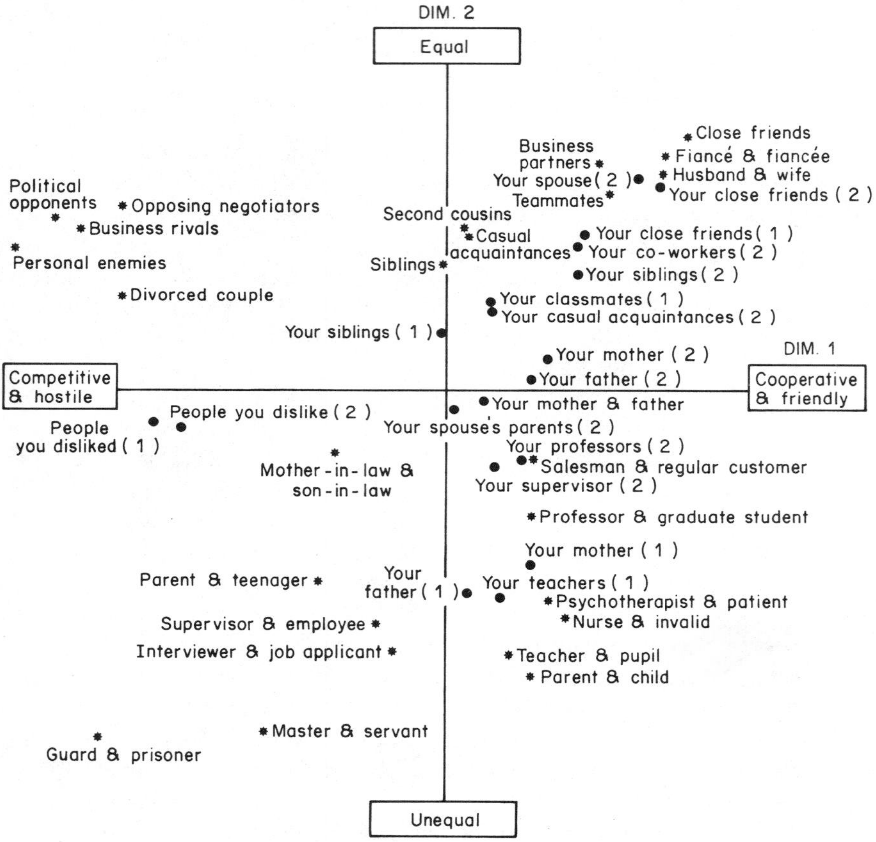

* Denotes a typical dyadic relation between the designated individuals.

● Denotes a relation between the subject and the designated individual. The subject's childhood relations are indicated by A (1), while the subject's current relations are indicated by A (2).

Figure 1.1 The first two dimensions used by subjects in the study by Wish *et al.* to discriminate between different relationships. (From Wish *et al.*, 1976, p. 413, figure 1. Copyright 1976 by the American Psychological Association. Reprinted by permission.)

Although family studies have a long tradition in anthropology and sociology, family life has only relatively recently begun to command the attention in psychology that it deserves. Many of the ideas that have been put forward are subtle and complex, and methods of investigation in psychology are incapable of doing them justice at present. Others are evidently oversimple but point the way for future study. Amongst the latter are Wish's analyses of the way in which people describe a range of different relationships which they experience in their everyday lives (Wish, 1976; Wish *et al.*, 1976). The subjects of his studies appeared to use four basic dimensions—those shown in Figures 1.1 and 1.2. Amongst other things, the diagrams show how, for these subjects, relationships with close kin and marriage partners stand out on the intensity and socioemotional–informal dimensions, but

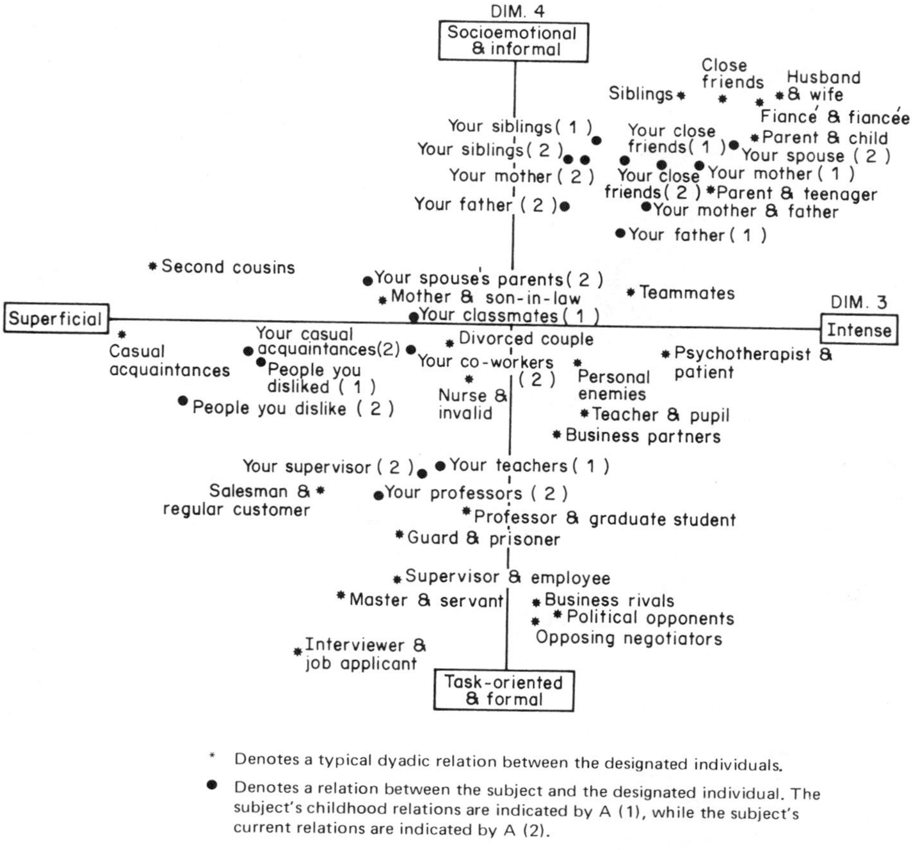

Figure 1.2 The third and fourth dimensions used by subjects in the study by Wish *et al.* to discriminate between different relationships. (From Wish *et al.*, 1976, p. 414, figure 2. Copyright 1976 by the American Psychological Association. Reprinted by permission.)

vary and are on average not easily distinguishable from many other types of relationship in terms of friendliness and equality. Although other relationships may rival family ones for equality and friendliness, family relations perhaps constitute the majority of 'intense but informal' bonds for most people.

Wish's analysis sets the scene for psychological studies of the family. The very fact that getting together in close living groups or 'families' is such a universal preoccupation suggests, as do Wish's intensity and informality dimensions, that the family serves some very basic psychological functions for its members. Weiss (1974) and Caplan and Killilea (1976) are amongst the many who have speculated about the nature of these functions. Caplan in particular has discussed the family as a principal support system, and under the term 'support' has subsumed the following functions: the collection and dissemination of information about the world; feedback and guidance about members' behaviour; the provision of a system of beliefs, values and codes of behaviour; guidance and mediation in problem-solving; the provision of practical service and concrete aid; the provision of a haven for rest and recuperation; the provision of a reference and control group; a validation of a member's self-identity; and assistance in emotional mastery. Several of these functions would be exercised especially at times of crisis. Weiss, on the basis of his research experience with couples and with self-help groups, has argued that the functions served by the family reduce to two basic provisions: the fostering of, firstly, a feeling of security, and, secondly, a sense of capability, self-esteem or self-worth. These basic 'needs' are not always met by the family, but the family is their most likely source and other sources can compensate for the family's deficiency in providing them only to a limited degree.

Certainly there is evidence that having a family, in the one limited sense of being married, is associated with a lower than average prevalence of psychological problems—at least recorded 'official' psychological problems such as treated psychiatric disorder (Bloom *et al.*, 1978); also that being married is associated with a relatively good prognosis for the same sorts of psychological problem (Clum, 1975). There are, of course, several logically distinct explanations for such a correlation between social facts, but one possibility is that being married and in a family carries the psychological advantages listed above and that the family serves a preventive function—either preventing the occurrence of identifiable problems in the first place, or if they occur preventing them from getting worse. Recently there have been a number of attempts to move beyond this necessarily superficial examination. Three important studies in particular (Brown and Harris, 1978; Henderson *et al.*, 1978; and Tolsdorf, 1976) support the general hypothesis that the existence of quite severe psychological problems, such as depression or other diagnosed psychiatric complaint, will tend to be associated with a departure from the ideal close affectional relationships between family members which are suggested by the descriptions of Wish's subjects and by Caplan's list of positive family functions.

Henderson *et al.* (1978) interviewed 50 psychiatric patients who had non-psychotic psychological disorder, and 50 matched control subjects, using a social interaction schedule designed to examine a person's primary group interactions (30 and 31 people in the two groups respectively were currently married). Patients and controls on average reported spending a very similar amount of time in the previous week with members of their household, but patients reported that a significantly greater proportion of this contact time was 'unpleasant' (between 7 and 8 hours unpleasant interaction compared with just over 1 hour in the week for control subjects). Interviewees were also asked to identify their 'principal attachment figure' (the person they felt they needed most or to whom they felt closest and most attached), plus other attachment figures. The patient group had significantly fewer attachment figures, described a significantly smaller number of people as 'good friends', and reported significantly fewer contacts with people outside their own household in the previous week. They also obtained a lower score on an 'index of perceived social support' which included such items as, 'People don't come to visit me as often as I would like', and, 'I don't have anyone I can confide in'. Clearly there are a number of possible interpretations of such findings, but they at least show that shortly after referral to a psychiatrist for the types of psychological problem experienced by Henderson *et al.*'s patient sample, people are very likely to describe deficient social contact with their 'nearest and dearest'. It appears that this deficiency is partly one of quality as well as quantity, and may concern relationships with friends as well as close kin. Miller and Ingham (1976) have also found that people with these types of diagnosed psychological problem report having fewer friendship contacts than other people, and Mayo (1968) found that women without any obvious psychological problem reported more self-disclosure toward 'the person to whom they felt closest' than either women who had a diagnosed psychiatric disorder of the 'neurosis' type, or women who reported such problems but who were not receiving any treatment for them.

A second recent study is of particular interest because of its explicit use of a social network model (Bott, 1957) and its use of indices for summarizing a person's social network. Tolsdorf (1976) conducted an interview, lasting between 2 and 7 hours, with ten people with serious psychological problems (all had a psychiatric diagnosis of 'schizophrenia') and ten matched people with medical problems. All subjects were male. They were asked to describe their whole social network—in fact subjects described between nine and 54 other people with whom they had definite relationships of one kind or another. The size of the network was itself one variable examined, others being 'adjacency density' (a measure of the degree to which a subject's contacts had relationships with each other), the number of a subject's 'multiplex' relationships (relationships that cover more than one of the following content areas—primary kin, secondary kin, primary friend, secondary friend, economic, recreational, political, religious, sexual, fraternal, mutual aid, service), 'relationship density' (the number of a subject's content areas covered per relationship), the number and overall percentage of links with kin members, and the number and percentage of relationships with 'functional' people (people serving one or more of three basic functions: support, advice, or feedback on performance).

Whilst there were not many differences between the two groups in network size, the medical control subjects reported many more multiplex relationships (16.6 versus 5.4 on average), a higher relationship density, a lower overall proportion of kin members in the network, and fewer functions served per person in the network. However, the most statistically significant finding, and certainly the most telling, was that the ten people with problems reported that they themselves *provided* fewer functions on average for other people in their network than did medical subjects, and that as a consequence they had many fewer 'symmetrical' functional relationships, i.e. relationships in which they gave as much support, advice or feedback as they got (2.0 versus 7.5 such relationships on average). Tolsdorf summarizes these findings as follows:

> psychiatric subjects reported fewer intimate relationships ... in a network that was more heavily dominated by family members, where functional people were in a more controlling and dominant position, and where overall there were relatively fewer but relatively more powerful functional people in the network. (p. 412)

This study is on a small scale but raises many fundamental matters to do with the nature of close intimate relationships and psychological disorder. Particularly intriguing is the notion of symmetry, or equity, in relationships (see Duck's chapter in this volume) and the possibility that one qualitative abnormality associated with psychological disorder may be asymmetry in the provision of social support. It would be easy to lose sight of the vital reciprocal aspect of relationships, and treat social support as a provision that is received but not given (or vice versa). Tolsdorf's subjects with psychological problems may have been experiencing rather severe and long-term problems, and it is interesting that Mayo (1968) found that the women in her study who had diagnosed (but probably less severe) psychiatric problems reported 'giving' more self-disclosure about themselves than they 'received' in return from others.

The third study to be mentioned in this introductory section is the recent but already much quoted study reported by Brown and Harris (1978) in their book *The Social Origins of Depression* (and in Brown *et al.*, 1975). The study of close relationships of the women in their study was in fact only a small part of an investigation which was largely concerned with the relationship between stressful life events or difficulties on the one hand and depression on the other (see Cochrane and Sobol in this volume). The main interest of their study in the present context lies in the vulnerability factors which they found moderated the link between life stress and depression. Amongst these was the lack of an intimate relationship with a husband or other close male attachment figure. Women without an intimate confiding relationship of this kind were more likely than others to be depressed if they had experienced life stress or difficulty. The rating of intimacy was admittedly a simple one, but again it points the way to an important area for future investigation. It appears from Brown and Harris's description that their simple intimacy scale principally tapped the degree to which a woman felt she could confide, and share her problems. This is of the utmost practical and theoretical importance, both because it connects with an important area in social psychology to do with self-disclosure, interpersonal attraction and intimacy (e.g. Jourard, 1959; Taylor and Altman, 1966; Duck, in this volume), and because of the important place of self-disclosure in studies of psychotherapy process (e.g. Shapiro, 1969; Schauble, 1973).

These three studies all concern adults who have already developed identifiable psychological problems. Demonstrating a link between qualities of care-taking relationships in childhood and subsequent psychological problems in adolescence or adulthood is, of course, a much more difficult research exercise (Orford, 1976). There is, however, evidence of some association between apparent absence of parental warmth or nurturance in childhood and lack of social competence in children, relatively lower self-esteem amongst adolescents, and psychological problems of an anti-social nature in adolescence and adulthood (see Rollins and Thomas, 1975; and the chapter by Herbert in this volume, for reviews of some of this literature).

This chapter will now proceed to a consideration of three specific areas of psychological problem, each of major practical and theoretical importance, in order to illustrate a number of themes which have been the focus of family studies in the context of psychological problems. These themes will then be drawn together in an attempt to outline a model of family functioning based upon the idea of the cohesive group in social psychology.

II. EXCESSIVE DRINKING AND THE FAMILY

Government departments responsible for health both in the UK and the USA recognize the excessive drinking of alcohol as one of their nations' major health and social problems. Furthermore, there seems good evidence that we are currently witnessing an international upswing both in drinking and problem drinking (Royal College of Psychiatrists, 1979). Most people who drink excessively are family members, and problem drinking is a very frequent concomitant of family disharmony.

Family stress

One of the most straightforward ways of conceiving of excessive drinking in relation to the family, is to view the excessive drinking of one family member as a noxious agent, or life difficulty. An excessive drinker, because of his/her condition, is thus the *agent*, and other family members bear the *impact* and must adjust or *cope* as they may. For example, a number of investigators have tried to assess the degree of 'hardship' to which a spouse (almost always a wife married to an excessively drinking husband in these studies) has been exposed as a result of the partner's alcoholism. For instance, Bailey *et al.* (1962) asked women married to men with identified drinking problems, whether their husbands had lost jobs as a result, and if so how many; whether they were concerned about their husband's job and economic security; whether their husbands had been unfaithful; whether they had been involved with the police; whether there had been physical violence in the family; and whether their social contacts had been reduced. Jackson and Kogan (1963) and Orford *et al.* (1976) adopted similar strategies, asking in addition about violence in the family, embarrassment of family members, financial strain, failure to keep up personal appearances, rows and quarrels, damage to household objects or furniture, and possessiveness and jealousy directed towards the wife. There can be little doubt from these and related studies that married people in this predicament very often describe a great deal of severe, and often long-standing, hardship. It is also clear, however, that this hardship is variable in quantity and that the likelihood of a spouse using any of a variety of coping reactions or strategies is roughly proportional to the extent of hardship reported.

Much publicity has been given recently to the apparent disproportionate increase in the number of women with drinking problems, and there is now a small literature on the problems faced by, and the reactions of, men who are married to excessive drinkers (Jacob *et al.*, 1978).

A considerable amount has also been written on the impact upon children of having an excessively drinking parent (Jacob *et al.*, 1978; Wilson and Orford, 1978). Amongst the hardships described by such children are frequent witnessing of the parent in an intoxicated state, witnessing parents rowing and possibly fighting, having to intervene themselves in scenes of family argument or violence, chronic feelings of fear and apprehension about the drinking parent's state and the effects of drinking, and unhappiness about an absence of fun and a state of tension in the family atmosphere. Repeatedly noted in this literature, and perhaps of particular importance because of its key role in the development of social maturity, is inhibition of the development of friendship links on account of a child's embarrassment, fear, or guilt.

Coping

There has now been a number of studies, largely confined to wives of excessively drinking husbands, of self-reported attempts to cope with this particular form of family stress. The procedure adopted by the present author and his colleagues was to construct a questionnaire from statements about their coping strategies made informally by individual wives. Use of this questionnaire in two quite separate studies in two different countries has shown quite clearly that the extent of coping, i.e. the number of separate reactions that a wife reports having tried, is proportional to the degree of hardship she has experienced (Orford *et al.*, 1975; James and Goldman, 1971).

Factor analysis of this questionnaire shows that the items can be grouped into a number of factors that appear to represent types of reaction of a quite different quality. Although each, without exception, was positively associated with degree of hardship, some may be much more effective than others in modifying the drinker's behaviour. Reactions which appeared to indicate avoidance, withdrawal, or action designed to protect the rest of the family, were predictive of a poor outcome for the husband's drinking over the following few months. On the other hand, 'competition' (e.g. getting drunk herself, trying to make him jealous), 'assertion' (e.g. hitting him, trying to make him feel ridiculous, rowing with him when he gets drunk, *not* making him comfortable when he gets drunk), and 'anti-drink' action (hiding his drink or pouring it away), carried a more favourable prognosis. This led Orford *et al.* (1975) to speculate that a style of 'engaged but discriminated' coping action might be the best to advise. Avoidance strategies would not be recommended but rather a style of engaged coping involving punishing drinking rather than the drinker. Interestingly, the questionnaire contained scarcely any items that could be construed as providing the drinker with positive reward for appropriate behaviour, but this could be due to a failure to recognize such behaviour as 'coping' behaviour at all, even when it occurs.

There has been no similar systematic study of the way in which children cope, but informal observations suggest that they use a very similar range of reactions, and that their scope for avoidance, at least in the case of adolescent children, is greater than for a marital partner.

Family resistance

Clinical practitioners have, for a long time, had difficulty in working exclusively within a simple disease–stress–coping model of drinking problems and families. They were struck, as have been clinicians working in quite other areas, by the apparent resistance of other family members to change in the member with the identified problem. There were many anecdotal accounts of spouses themselves breaking down when 'the patient' gave up excessive drinking (the so-called 'decompensation' hypothesis), and of spouses sabotaging treatment efforts. Evidence for decompensation as a general phenomenon is, in fact, thin (Paolino and McCrady, 1977; Orford, 1975), but individual cases continue to be compelling.

What is interesting here is the way that fashions of thinking based upon ideas of individual psychopathology have dominated this field in the absence of other unifying perspectives. Until recently, with the advent of systems models of the family, the only alternative to viewing the drinker as the source of a family's problems and all else as secondary, appears to have been to scapegoat an alternative member of the family (usually the spouse) and to regard her as the real villain. Clinicians and researchers have had as much difficulty in attributing cause and effect as have family members themselves in attributing blame.

Even within the research literature, which is almost exclusively based upon grouped data and an individual psychopathology framework, there are a number of findings which are difficult to incorporate within a simple model. These include the following:

1. that a large proportion of couples recall that the drinker was drinking excessively at the time of their marriage;

2. that in a large minority of cases roles were non-egalitarian and non-ideal in the first year of marriage;
3. that wives married for a relatively short period of time to excessively drinking husbands describe abnormally high levels of anxiety, and significantly higher levels than wives married to excessively drinking husbands for longer periods of time;
4. that these anxiety scores increase very slightly (non-significantly) rather than decrease over a period of 12 months in which the drinker's excessive drinking decreases markedly;
5. that spouses often describe the drinker unfavourably even when 'sober' and these perceptions remain remarkably stable even when excessive drinking stops;
6. that a spouse's self-reported current level of psychological problems, her report of recently experienced personal stress in marriage, *and* her perception of abnormality in her own childhood were all higher in marriages complicated by alcoholism than in control marriages, and that all three variables were positively intercorrelated (these findings are all discussed in detail elsewhere—Orford, 1975).

A complete understanding of marriages (let alone whole families) complicated by this particular psychological problem clearly requires a consideration of the total history of the family group with a detailed consideration of the nature of relationships, and an understanding of the function which excessive drinking plays in the total picture.

One line of research which has begun to take part of this formulation seriously, although it is still limited to family dyads, is that pursued by Steinglass and his colleagues (1977). Their research is in the growing tradition of experimental intoxication studies in the field of alcohol problems, but is the first research programme to extend it into a family context. Their early work involved a father and son and also two pairs of brothers, but a recent report concerns ten husband–wife pairs in which one partner (and in one case both partners) was the heavy problem-drinker. Their procedure involves a simultaneous hospital admission of both husband and wife for a few days, and drinking is encouraged and observed during this time. Observations and videotape recordings are fed back to the couple. This procedure has resulted in rich individual material, and it is difficult to reach general conclusions. On the whole it was observed that interactional behaviour became relatively stereotyped during intoxication and that the quality of interaction was quite different during intoxication and during sobriety. For a number of couples described, changes were particularly apparent in assertive or dominant behaviours, couples often showing a reversal of their normal relationship when one or both had been drinking. In other cases drinking appeared to alter the display of affectionate behaviour, in some cases apparently for the better. In the case of dominance, these preliminary findings are in keeping with Orford's (1976) finding that both drinking-problem husbands and their wives, as groups, ascribed less-than-ideal levels of dominance to the husband 'when sober', but ascribed more ideal levels of dominance to husbands 'when drinking'. The area of dominace conflicts in marriage, a very general theme in clinical family studies (e.g. Dicks, 1967), would appear to be a very important one in the study of alcohol and the family also.

Person perception and attribution

A number of investigators have tried to go beyond the disease–stress model by asking family members what qualities they attribute to other members. Several have used adjective check lists, such as Leary's (LaForge and Suczek, 1955), for this purpose. A variation of this procedure is to use a standardized personality questionnaire, and amongst other things to ask family members to complete it as they think another family member (e.g. their spouse) would do (e.g. Drewery and Rae, 1969). Several studies have used the analytic technique of computing discrepancy scores in an attempt to capture aspects of interpersonal sensitivity, understanding or communication. For example, Drewery and Rae (1969) found a number of significantly larger discrepancies in person perception among drinking-problem husbands and their wives than among a control group of couples. Larger discrepancies in the problem group were apparent at the level of spouse perceptions (e.g. a comparison of what W thinks of H with what H thinks of himself) and at the level of 'meta-perceptions' (e.g. a comparison of what H thinks of W with what W thinks H thinks about her). However, by a detailed analysis Drewery and Rae were able to show that these differences could be attributed to the stronger operation of a male 'stereotype response set' in the control group and not necessarily to any greater sensitivity or understanding on the part of control husbands and wives in their own marriages.

Kogan and Jackson (1961) asked women in their studies to describe their husbands both 'when sober' and 'when drinking'. These two sets of perceptions were markedly different in some cases but by no means in all. Perceptions of husbands 'when drinking' were fairly uniformly negative, but the variance for 'when sober' perceptions was far greater. The result was that whilst some women made a clear distinction between the two conditions, others did not, their husbands being described unfavourably under both. Kogan and Jackson considered this high frequency of unfavourable attribution, whether drinking or sober, to be surprising and suggested the implication was that drinking was no more than a secondary issue, and that the marriage problems might be little changed by the cessation of drinking in such cases. Orford *et al.* (1976) confirmed Kogan and Jackson's findings and extended them by showing that unfavourable 'when sober' perceptions were predictive of a relatively poor outcome for the drinking problem over the subsequent 12 months.

This aspect of person perception studies, raised by the work of Kogan and Jackson (1961), may be related to a general issue originally identified by Jackson (1954) in her early Al-Anon study. She argued, on the basis of her extensive interview material, that a major problem for family members was the making of clear *attribitions* about the nature of the circumstances in which they found themselves. Many women went through a lengthy period of uncertainty about the 'correct' interpretation of their husbands' behaviour as 'normal', 'a problem', or an 'illness', along with uncertainty about the interpretation of their own behaviour and feelings as well as those of other members of their families. It may be that a set of person perceptions in which a clear distinction is made between the Jekyll and Hyde, the sober and the drunk, is part of an understanding of the family predicament which places emphasis upon the drinking problem, whereas a set of negative perceptions in which this distinction is not made clear is part of an understanding which stresses deviant character or personality.

III. VIOLENCE TOWARDS CHILDREN IN THE FAMILY

The problem of violence by parents towards their children in the home has a number of features in common with the problem of excessive alcohol use. Each is recognized to be a frequently occurring problem, often very serious in its consequences; often presented to welfare and helping agencies in a disguised form, and hence often 'missed', and each carries a high risk of relapse or repetition. Available statistics on each problem show a quite marked sex difference (with men much more likely to be officially diagnosed as 'alcoholics' and women much more likely to be designated officially as perpetrators of violence towards their children), but in each case statistics are based upon admittedly biased agency-contact samples, and sex ratios vary widely depending upon the particular sample examined. There is a further link between the two psychological problems on account of the facilitating effect of alcohol upon violence of all sorts and because of the specific suggestion that a person with a drinking problem who is also a parent is more at risk of committing violent acts against their children (Belsky, 1978). In the present context the most important similarity is that each may be viewed as a problem of individual psychopathology, or may be viewed in family interactional terms (or indeed may be viewed as a cultural product without reference to individual psychopathology or family interaction).

Much of the research that has been carried out on child abuse has involved small clinical samples, and it is relatively rare to find control groups employed. Hence, many of the ideas to be discussed below have the status of unverified hunches, albeit based upon sensitive and often extensive clinical experience.

The individual contributions of parent and child

As in the alcohol-problems literature, a great deal of attention has been focused upon the psychopathology, personality or background of the individual child-abusing parent. As several reviewers have pointed out (e.g. Allan, 1978; Belsky, 1978), suggestions made about characteristics of parents are inconsistent, and where standard questionnaires have been employed the results are often based upon very small and select samples. Early research and discussion in this field appears to have suffered from the homogeneity assumption which has similarly bedevilled research on alcoholism and personality in the past, as it has research in many other fields (for example the search for 'the epileptic personality'). The likely result of treating child-abusing parents as a single group is that findings will be very general and difficult to interpret; for example the NSPCC study (1976) finding that both mothers and fathers had unusually high anxiety scores on the 16 Personality Factor questionnaire (16 PF).

As with alcohol problems, the view is widely held that the violent parent is predisposed to child abuse on account of aspects of his or her own childhood upbringing. In particular it has been reported on a number of occasions that abusive parents are very likely to recall being the victims of physical violence from a parent during their own childhood, and this has led to the view that child abuse is transmitted within the family from generation to generation. The evidence for this association between violence to children in one generation and the next within the same families is, however, not incontrovertible (Belsky, 1978) and in any case cannot account for more than a proportion of cases.

There appear to be three major contenders as explanations for intergenerational transmission, if such exists. One is based on *modelling* of violience by a parent, leading to observational learning which results in the performance of violent acts when the child finds herself/himself in the role of parent later in life. The second explanation is based on an operant conditioning model (Belsky, 1978), and suggests that family members unwittingly reinforce a child's violent attitudes and behaviour, thus predisposing him/her to later violence as a parent. The third, less specific explanation comes in various forms but is based upon some notion of emotional deprivation in childhood (Allan, 1978). For example, one suggestion is that abusive parents have an 'inability to empathize' as a result of their own dependency needs having been frustrated in childhood (Steele and Pollock, 1968; Melnick and Hurley, 1969).

Just as it may be supposed that some people are driven to drink by their families, so it has been suggested that some parents are driven to violent acts by the provocation of their particulary 'difficult' children. This may be because the child is handicapped in some way (Gil, 1971), or because the child has a temperament that makes him/her frustrating to care for. There certainly appears to be evidence that abused children are more likely than others to have been premature and of low birthweight (Maden and Wrench, 1977). These suggestions about the contribution of individual child differences appear to have avoided some of the one-sidedness of some of the literature on 'wives of alcoholics'. There appears to be an awareness of the reciprocally contingent nature of social interaction between parent and child and a willingness to believe that individual differences in both parent and child may make a contribution.

Problems in dyadic relationships

A consideration of the role of the child in child abuse leads naturally to concepts of abnormality in the *relationship* between the child and the abusing parent. Avoidance of the parent by the child (which could have its parallel in neglect of, or indifference to, the child by the parent) is one theme here, as it is in the literature on the coping behaviour of spouses of problem drinkers. Hyman has produced evidence, both from simulated observation (Hyman, 1978), and from application of the Bene–Anthony test of family relationships (NSPCC, 1976), that battered children tend to be uncomfortable with their mothers, are less interested in being reunited with them when separated, and make relatively little reference to interaction with them, and that mothers are relatively unsuccessful in initiating interaction with them. As with many studies in this particular field, it is very difficult to know whether to interpret these findings as representing the effects of violent incidents or as characteristics of a relationship predisposing to violence.

More specific hypotheses such as that of 'bonding failure' (Klein and Stern, 1971), have proposed an early disturbance of attachment between mother and child, possibly brought about by the practice of separating mother and newborn baby for intensive medical care on account of low birthweight, prematurity or other problems. This particular hypothesis has been criticized for being oversimple and for failing to take account of the continuing development of parent–child relationships (Allan, 1978).

The other dyadic relationship that has been the focus of many suggestions about the origins of child abuse, has been the relationship between the abusing parent and her/his spouse or partner. Whilst there have been numerous suggestions that this is a vital causative factor, there has been scarcely any hard evidence on the subject. About the only relevant research finding is that of the NSPCC (1976) who reported a significantly greater degree of marital stress amongst parents suspected of child abuse in comparison with a control group of parents of children who had suffered accidents. Most suggestions have focused upon general marital discord or lack of cohesion (a high rate of separation often with later reunion, a high rate of complaints by wives about their husbands, partners not satisfying the abusive parent's dependency needs, etc.), but there have been alternative suggestions. These have included the possibility that the abusive parent is highly dominant and the more submissive partner collusive; that the husband is 'pathologically jealous' of his wife and displaces his aggression onto a child; or that the non-abusive parent is highly denigrating of the abusive parent and his or her abilities. It is probably faulty to assume homogeneity of dyadic relationships in the context of child abuse, as it is faulty to assume homogeneity of individual character; each of these suggestions will perhaps find application in a minority of couples. Whether each is any more prevalent in families where violent incidents involving children occur, than in other families, remains to be tested rigorously.

Stress and coping

A rather different approach is to view the caring of a young child at home as a normal but potentially stressful set of circumstances. Several authors have put forward the view that situational factors making for frustration and anger can trigger aggressive acts and may be as important as, if not more important than, predisposing factors (e.g. Gil, 1971; Goldstein, 1975; Frude, 1978). Quite a substantial proportion of all parents may feel themselves to be at risk of greater or lesser degrees of violence to their children at some time or another and may be aware of using self-control to inhibit such impulses (Frude, 1978).

Taking care of young children is likely to be more stressful for some parents than for others on account of circumstances. Identified child-abusing parents are more than usually likely to be under 20 at the birth of their first child, to have a relatively large number of children, and at least one study has reported that mothers frequently complain of impatience, lack of understanding and unhelpfulness from their husbands (Ounsted *et al.*, 1975). Brown and Harris (1978) found that having three or more children under the age of 14 at home, and lacking an intimate confiding relationship with a husband or close male friend, were two factors putting women at risk of responding to life stress and difficulty with depression. A link between depression and child abuse has been suggested (Elmer, 1967).

If circumstances make care-taking particularly stressful, it may be all the more important to possess coping skills adequate to the task in hand. Although a young child's behaviour may be normal for its age, the behaviour of young children in the home can be very disruptive and frustrating. It may not be too fanciful to draw a parallel between coping with the difficult behaviour of an excessively drinking adult partner (developmentally non-normal) and coping with the often disruptive behaviour of an infant (developmentally normal). There have been a number of suggestions made that abusive parents may lack good child-handling skills. For example, Allan (1978) has hypothesized that the use of physical punishment from an early age may increase the likelihood of aggressive behaviour in the child, thus leading to a spiral of unpleasant interaction which increases the risk of violence from parent to child. A related hypothesis is that the parent may lack the skill to induce compliance following disciplinary action and that the child's defiance or non-compliance leads to an escalation in the level of parental controlling action (Parke, 1974, cited by Belsky, 1978). Differences in child temperament may clearly contribute to this scenario.

Perception and attribution

It has been said that part of the cause may lie in faulty parental perceptions of the child and his or her behaviour. One form of this theory is 'role reversal' (Morris and Gould, 1963). This theory proposes that abusive parents lack the capacity for the largely one-sided giving of nurturance which is necessary to the role of parent of young children. Possibly because of some fault in their own child-rearing, some parents look inappropriately to their young children for responses which on account of their age the latter are unable to give. Related to this idea is the observation that some abusive parents quite inappropriately attribute negative intent to the frustrating behaviour of their young children (NSPCC, 1976), and may have quite unrealistic expectations of the children through lack of knowledge of developmental norms. However, one study of ordinary non-abusive adolescent couples showed how little knowledge of basic developmental norms they possessed (deLissovoy, 1973), and Belsky cites an unpublished study by Stultz (1975) suggesting that abusive parents had no higher expectations for their children's performance than did parents of handicapped children or parents of children in day care.

Social isolation

Social isolation is a theme in all three of the problem areas considered specifically in this chapter (see also the chapter by Yule in this volume for a consideration of social isolation amongst parents of handicapped children). Although there have been no systematic studies of social networks along the detailed lines of Tolsdorf's research cited in the introduction to this chapter, there has been a number of studies reporting abusive parents having fewer associations outside the home than other parents (Elmer, 1967), being less likely to have a telephone, and perceiving neighbours more negatively (Newberger *et al.*, 1975), and abusive mothers feeling more alientated from their extended families and receiving less assistance in caring for their children (Green *et al.*, 1974; Green, 1976). Belsky (1978) offers two explanations for the relationship between child abuse and social isolation. Either deviant child care-taking behaviour is more likely when parents have fewer contacts and therefore less surveillance of their behaviour, or alternatively the stress of child care-taking is greater without an adequate social support network. A further contribution may be made by feelings of guilt and shame on account of previous abusive acts, or on account of other social problems, such as unemployment, which child-abusing parents appear to be more likely to suffer than most people.

IV. PSYCHIATRIC DISORDER

The category 'psychiatric disorder' or 'mental illness' is an exceedingly broad and heterogeneous one, and there is great dispute over the value of using such a category and the diagnostic sub-catergorizations within it (e.g. Clare, 1976). Nevertheless, like 'alchoholism' and 'child abuse', psychiatric disorder* may be said to be a social fact in that psychiatric services exist in most countries (extensively in areas like the USA and UK) and very large numbers of people annually are referred to and treated by them. There has been a very large number of family studies using identified psychiatric patients as the 'way in' to family study, and this research and its findings involve many themes, some of which overlap considerably with those identified above.

* Psychological problems: any difficulties concerning behaviour, thought, or feeling, usually non-physical in origin. Only a very small proportion of people with such difficulties will receive help from a psychiatrist. Psychiatric problems or disorders: any such problems, when diagnosed and treated within the mental health services, often by psychiatrists.

Impact and attribution

One of the few detailed studies of the impact of 'mental illness' upon the family was that of Clausen and Yarrow (1955). In the report of their intensive study of the illness and hospitalization of 33 married men, they place particular emphasis, as did Jackson (1954) in the case of problem drinking, upon the spouses' attempts, often over a considerable period of time, to understand and make sense of their husbands' behaviour. Most wives found it impossible to pinpoint the exact start of the problems and their initial interpretations varied widely. Very few 'realized' early on that their husband had a serious 'illness'. The majority began by interpreting the husband's behaviour in terms of a physical problem or in terms of 'character' weakness and 'controllable' behaviour. Still others thought that the behaviour was just a normal response to crisis and would change with circumstances. Rather less than half the wives in this study altered their interpretations towards an 'illness' attribution as time went on. However this was by no means always a non-judgemental or non-evaluative construction on behaviour.

Vaughn and Leff (1978) have recently suggested, on the basis of a detailed analysis of recordings of interviews with close relatives of psychiatric patients, that the attribution of blame by a key relative may be a crucial factor in prognosis. Attributing blame to an 'illness' condition, or accepting handicap without rancour, they suggest, are associated with a relatively supportive domestic environment. On the other hand, relatively unsupportive home environments may be associated with the attribution of blame to relatively long-standing aspects of the patient's character, doubting the validity of the patient's 'illness', and questioning the degree to which behaviour is beyond his/her control.

As in the alcohol problems field, a number of studies have examined person perception amongst couples who are self-admittedly unhappy or who are undergoing marital counselling, and have compared them with 'happy' or non-counselled couples. The most general finding from these studies is that spouses in the former group tend to describe *both* themselves and their partners in relatively unfavourable terms, using a higher proportion of descriptive terms indicative of hostility or unpleasantness, or of excessive dominance or assertiveness (e.g. Luckey, 1964; Murstein and Glaudin, 1966). Control couples use a preponderance of favourable terms in describing themselves and their partners—terms implying affection or pleasantness, and other terms implying a moderate or appropriate degree of assertiveness.

Before leaving the issue of person perception in the family, it may be worth pausing to reflect upon the nature of 'dominance', a term which has been much used in family role studies. It seems that this construct has a variety of overlapping meanings. It has already been pointed out, for example, that to dominate the carrying out of tasks in a family is by no means the same thing as to dominate decision-making (and presumably much finer distinctions need to be made between different tasks and different areas of decision-making). Role dominance of these different varieties may have quite different effects upon attributions of 'dominance'. Furthermore, it has also been pointed out that, 'dominance' can be a good or a bad thing depending upon circumstances. Some dominance attributions are favourable (e.g. 'respected', 'assertive', 'advises others') whilst others are decidedly unfavourable (e.g. 'bossy', 'domineering'). Concordance between different measures of dominance is therefore hardly to be expected, and in fact lack of concordance does appear to be the rule (Cromwell and Olson, 1975).

Hence theories of family behaviour and psychological problems which concern dominance in any way have to be more precise in their specification of what dominance is. This would apply for example to the influential theory of Lidz *et al.* (1957) who suggested that many families in which an adolescent or young adult child developed schizophrenic symptoms were characterized by the undue dominace of one parent over the other, a relationship they termed 'marital skew'.

Affection and cohesiveness

Influenced by the suggestions of authors such as Lidz *et al.* (1957) who wrote of the importance of marital 'schism' and marital 'skew' in the marriages of parents of young people with schizophrenic symptoms, there has now been a very large number of investigations of family interaction patterns where one family member or another is experiencing some psychological problem, often a diagnosed psychiatric complaint. For example work of this kind was carried out by Farina and his colleagues (Farina and Holzberg, 1967, 1968) comparing families with sons diagnosed as suffering from schizophrenia and control families. Their work was typical of much of the research in this area. Family members would be observed for a limited period of time discussing a set topic (sometimes a general issue about which they had already been shown to disagree—the 'revealed differences technique'), and indices of their interactional behaviour would be computed. For example, the total amount of time a family member spoke might be used as an index of 'dominance', and the number of times family members disagreed as an index of 'conflict'.

This work has been reviewed by Fontana (1966), Hirsch and Leff (1975) and most comprehensively by Jacob (1975). Jacob's overall conclusion was that, '... family interaction studies, although based on a potentially sound methodological strategy, have not yet isolated family patterns that reliably differentiate disturbed from normal groups' (p. 56). However, some interesting trends were revealed by breaking down the studies reviewed into different diagnostic groups and different indices employed. First of all Jacob divided subject groups into those where the identifying problem was one of schizophrenia, versus all others (a very large and mixed group containing a number of studies where the identified problem was the deliquency of one family member). Secondly he divided the areas of interest into four groups: conflict, dominance, affect, and communication clarity. Studies of dominance produced no very consistent findings, although a number did find fathers to be more influential in control than in problem families, and mothers to be more dominant when the problem took the form of schizophrenia. Interestingly, Jacob also discerned a trend for power structures to be more often hierarchical than egalitarian in control than in non-schizophrenic problem families. Findings for conflict were largely inconsistent as were those for communication clarity (except for a tendency for problem families with schizophrenia to communicate with less clarity and accuracy than control families). Disappointingly, some of the apparently more objective indices such as talking time (assumed to be a measure of dominance) and number of interruptions (assumed to be a measure of conflict) produced particularly inconsistent results.

The clearest results by far involved measures of affect in families where the diagnosis was other than schizophrenia (results for families with schizophrenia were quite inconsistent). Of 33 such comparisons, 17 produced significant group differences and 15 of these concerned expressions of affect that were rated as definitely positive (supportive, affectionate, warm, involving laughter) or definitely negative (defensive, hostile, anxious involvement, rejection). Five indicated more positive affect in control than in problem families, and ten indicated more negative affect in problem as opposed to control families. These results represent the most consistent set of findings upon which to base a model of family functioning and psychological problems. A warning is in order, however. Jacob points out that all affect measures were based upon observer ratings and although he takes the possibility of unreliability and bias in ratings into account, such results must be viewed critically. More importantly, it is possible that affect produces the most consistent results because affective expression is a simple response to the demand characteristics of the research setting, which are arguably very different for identified problem families than for control families without problems. Conceivably, the most telling aspects of family interaction lie in areas such as dominance, conflict and communication clarity but their elucidation may be beyond the capacity of present research methods.

A particularly intriguing and influential concept which appears largely to have evaded satisfactory operational definition and systematic quantitative research (Sluki and Ransom, 1976) is that of the 'double-bind' (Bateson *et al.*, 1956). First noted by Bateson *et al.* in the communication patterns of families containing one member with schizophrenia, this concept is a highly complex and easily misunderstoood one. As Sluki and Ransom make clear the concept refers both to the quality of ongoing family interaction and the nature of particular incidents which occur within the context of that relationship. Whilst paradoxically double-binding communications involving conflicting messages on different levels (perhaps the verbal and non-verbal levels) may occur in the setting of many types of relationship, it is the repeated occurrence of such incidents within an emotionally key, inescapable and tense relationship which it is suggested confers its particular pathological impact. The concept is thus a highly sophisticated one, involving both a behavioural specification and a quality of relationships specification. Not surprisingly, attempts to quantify the double-bind have failed because they are unreliable or trivial, often neglecting the ongoing relationship component altogether.

Family factors in the prediction of relapse

A line of research which is potentially of great practical value, and at the same time of social psychological importance, concerns the prediction, from family relationship factors, of the outcome of psychological problems following psychiatric hospitalization.

Of the small number of prospective studies on this topic those that have produced the clearest and most consistent results are the series of studies reported by Brown and his colleagues (Brown *et al.*, 1962, 1972) and more recently by Vaughn and Leff (1976). The findings that have emerged from this series of studies can be summarized as follows. The short-term (9 months) post-hospital clinical prognosis of patients hospitalized with 'schizophrenia' (defined strictly and in accordance with UK rather than US conventions) who return to the family home, can be partially predicted from the sentiments which a very close relative expresses about the patient. The greater the emotion expressed when talking about the patient the worse the prognosis. In particular, prognosis is relatively poor if trained interviewer/raters subsequently count a large number of *critical remarks* (fairly subtle non-verbal aspects being necessary elements) or rates the relative as having been relatively *hostile*, or alternatively rates the relative as having indicated a high degree of *emotional over-involvement* with the patient. The last-mentioned ingredient of high expressed emotion is important because it can exist in the absence of the more obviously negative aspects of criticism or hostility, yet it adds considerably to the prediction of relapse. Vaughn and Leff (1976) have also shown that criticism, measured in the same way, was predictive when the patients concerned were diagnosed as having 'neurotic depression', although in this case the number of critical remarks necessary to place a patient in a group with a high probability of relapse was fewer than was the case for 'schizophrenia', and other aspects of expressed emotion were not predictive.

Three other studies reported respectively by Morrow and Robins (1964), Cheek (1965), and by Lorei (1967), differed from the series already discussed in a number of respects. For example Morrow and Robins used standard questionnaires and rating scales rather than interviews, and of these, four produced a significant prediction of post-hospital adjustment. The most significant prediction came from a short four-item scale completed by wives (the patients) in which each was asked the extent to which her husband had more say in making important family decisions, made important family decisions without consulting his wife, pressured his wife into doing things she did not want to do, and in general got his way more often. 'Non-subordination of wife' was predictive of a good outcome.

Cheek (1965) employed the 'revealed differences' family discussion technique referred to above. Interpretation of Cheek's findings is difficult because a large number of variables was examined, only some of which were significant. The most important predictors of a poor follow-up adjustment appear to have been high levels of family activity and tension, high levels of disagreement, hostility and tension relief on the part of mothers, descriptions of the patients by mothers as actively rebellious and unconforming, and parental self-descriptions suggesting low support-permissiveness and high role-enforcement and withdrawal. Lorei (1967) obtained information on relatives' attitudes by means of a postal questionnaire and these data were combined with others in a large factor analysis. Of a number of factors predictive of re-hospitalization, one, with high loadings virtually confined to relatives' attitude items, was termed 'depreciation of the patient'.

My own study of prognosis for married men (Orford *et al.*, 1976) with drinking problems can be included here because it is similar in design to these studies of psychiatric problems. The study contrasted marriages which were highly cohesive despite an identified drinking problem with very non-cohesive, but formally intact families at the other end of a continuous spectrum. Indications of low cohesion included reports of relatively little affection either given to or received from the spouse, reports of relatively low husband involvement in family tasks, negative person perceptions by W of H 'when sober', and pessimism about the future survival of the marriage. Cohesion, as defined by these indices, was found to be a very variable quantity within this sample of marriages complicated by drinking problems, and in addition it was found to be a predictor of 12-month drinking problem outcome, with high marital cohesion carrying a relatively favourable prognosis.

This list of studies excludes a considerable number (reviewed by Clum, 1975) predicting outcome from demographic or family structure variables. Probably the most ambitious of these, Freeman and Simmons (1963), found the patient role in the family to be of great importance. Patients who returned from hospital to live with parents did relatively badly in the community, whilst others did relatively better, particularly if they were the chief or only family breadwinner (males), or when there were relatively few other full-time workers in the home (males and females). Differences between the two diagnostic groups studied by Vaughn and Leff (1976) may be related to differences in family structure. The 'schizophrenia' group consisted predominantly of young adult patients living with their parent(s), whereas the 'neurotic depression' group was composed largely of married patients living with their spouses. This could certainly explain the absence of prediction on the basis of the relatives' over-involvement in the latter group. Over-involvement may more often be a parental than marital failing (see Herbert's chapter in this volume), and indeed it was more often found in 'parental' than 'marital' families in Vaughn and Leff's study (Kuipers, personal communication).

Each of these studies has to contend with the problems of disentangling the influences of a number of correlated variables and of interpreting findings in terms of cause-and-effect relationships. Certainly each of them has found the supposedly crucial relative or family variable to be correlated with variables derived from the identified patient, and has found the latter to be predictive, sometimes equally if not more predictive, of outcome. For example, Brown *et al.* (1962) found that the patient's hostility towards the relative correlated with the relative's hostility, and both were predictive. Orford *et al.* (1976) found the patient's occupational status and self-esteem to be predictive, and both correlated with cohesion. Further complexity is added when it is realized that each of these studies has really only concerned dyads within the family, and in many of these studies the question of how the 'key' relative is chosen for inclusion in the study is little discussed. These considerations argue for the position that many would now adopt, which is that of considering the whole family as the proper unity of analysis.

V. A DESCRIPTIVE MODEL FOR DOMESTIC SETTINGS

These three short reviews of specific problem areas each shows ways in which the family can fall far short of the ideal of an intimate domestic setting serving for its members the crucial functions outlined by Caplan and Killilea (1976) and Weiss (1974). Nevertheless, despite some evident similarities between the themes emerging from research and discussion of these three problem areas, there is no unifying social psychological framework for describing the family factors involved. The purpose of this section is to discuss a number of separate approaches to describing the family, and then to attempt to piece them together into a model which might have utility in the study of a range of psychological problems in the family, including excessive drinking, child abuse, and psychiatric disorder. The intention is to provide a bridge between clinical insights and social psychological theory. To this end three approaches derived from clinical practice and research will be discussed first, and they will be followed by a discussion of the concept of group cohesiveness in social psychology.

The Stuart–Patterson system

This system represents an extension of behavioural ideas, in particular operant conditioning ideas, and has largely though not entirely been confined in its application to marital interaction (Stuart, 1969; Patterson *et al.*, 1975). The essential idea is that family relationships that are unsatisfying are usually so because they involve a relatively low rate of reward for the participants. As a result interaction becomes unattractive or generally 'unrewarding'. This leads to the use of one or other, or both, of two major classes of interpersonal strategy (or coping reaction, to bring terminology in line with that used earlier); namely coercion and withdrawal. Coercion, in essence, means making life unpleasant, or threatening to do so, if A doesn't get what he/she wants from B, or if B does not behave as A wishes. Withdrawal speaks for itself. If the relationship is to continue, neither is adaptive: coercion is likely to lead to a spiral of negative interaction and perhaps eventually to withdrawal, and withdrawal itself does nothing to increase the rewardingness of interaction and may itself be unrewarding if the expectation of the relationship is for intimacy (as is usually the case for families).

Simple though this description is, it is attractive for at least two quite separate reasons. One is that it makes sense of some of the findings in the specific problem areas already discussed. The majority of 'coping' behaviours reported by family members with a problem drinker in the family appear to correspond with these two general classes of reaction, and research has suggested that neither is particularly effective in modifying the drinker's behaviour. The behaviour of abusive parents towards their children may be analyzable in the same terms. The possibility that the parent–child relationship may be unrewarding for the parent—and that this may lead to a greater use of coercion and perhaps to a spiral of unpleasant and sometimes violent interactions, and furthermore that the parent–child relationship is often one of avoidance by the time the family comes to the notice of a social agency—were both discussed in the section on child abuse, above.

The second attractive feature of this descriptive system is its use of ideas familiar to social psychologists. Stuart's (1969) description of this approach employs concepts such as social power, attribution, exchange, and reciprocity or equity. In the case of coercion, A uses his/her power to punish B in attempts at control. Alternative, and probably more effective, sources of power are the ability to provide rewards for B, A's expertise, A's legitimate authority, and B's identification with A (French and Raven, 1959). Attribution is relevant because each participant tends to attribute causal significance to the other's behaviour and justifies his/her own behaviour as a reaction to the other's action. From a quite different tradition of family research, Watzlawick *et al.* (1968) call this phenomenon 'punctuating the sequence of interactional events'. Whereas objectively the sequence of interaction has no beginning and no end and can be depicted as: →A→B→A→B→, A punctuates this continuous sequence and describes events as: B→A (in other words if A is coercive or avoiding, this is only because B behaved in a way which demanded it). On the other hand, B describes: A→B. The idea of exchange of reward for reward is essential to this system, and the type of marital therapy proposed by Stuart rests upon the equitable use of reward power. The vicious cycle of increasing coercion and withdrawal is broken by requiring each participant to specify aspects of the relationship which they find rewarding, and arrangements are made for these to be exchanged on an equitable basis.

The Gibb–Alexander system

Based on his observations, particularly of families of delinquent youths, and the theorizing of Gibb (1961), Alexander (1973) has suggested that interpersonal communications in the family can be divided into two broad groups; those that are 'supportive' and those that are 'non-supportive' or 'defensive'. The major types of supportive and non-supportive communication which Alexander rated in his own studies are shown in Table 1.1.

This scheme shares with the Stuart–Patterson system the simplicity of dividing interactional events into those that are negative and those that are positive, rewarding or unrewarding, supportive or non-supportive. Although this may strike some readers as over-simple, Jacob's (1975) review, Henderson *et al.*'s (1978) recent findings, and much of the literature on psychiatric disorder and problem drinking in the family suggest that such an evaluative dimension may be a particularly important discriminator of troubled and trouble-free families.

Table 1.1 Defensive and supportive communications in the Gibb–Alexander System

Defensive communications	*Supportive communications*
Judgemental—dogmatism	Genuine information-seeking/giving
Control and strategy	Spontaneous problem-solving
Indifference	Empathic understanding
Superiority	Equality

A number of the Gibb–Alexander categories tie in with other work. For example, there are obvious similarities between their category 'judgemental dogmatism' and the variable 'critical remarks' found to be predictive of relapse amongst psychiatric patients by Brown *et al.* (1972) and Vaughn and Leff (1976). With this and other categories, Alexander stresses the importance of non-verbal aspects of communication (intonational, paralinguistic and kinesic). Brown *et al.* (1972) have equally emphasized the importance of 'tone of voice' (intonational and paralinguistic) in the rating of criticism, but their method rules out a consideration of kinesic aspects as their ratings are based upon audio-only tape recordings. 'Control and strategy' and 'superiority' look like the unacceptable or unrewarding aspects of dominance in another guise (reminiscent of Morrow and Robins' (1964) 'subordination' and Brown *et al.*'s (1962, 1972) 'over-involvement'), and 'indifference' looks like the communicational equivalent of the avoidance and withdrawal which appear in one form or another in the context of almost every psychological problem in the family.

Although, as presented here, this scheme is largely a static descriptive one, there was an element of prediction of change in Gibb's (1961) formulations. Supportive behaviours are also termed by him 'system-integrating' and non-supportive behaviours as 'system-disintegrating'. He proposed as a general rule that systems displaying a predominance of supportive communications amongst its members were tending towards closer integration and longer life, while systems displaying a predominance of non-supportive behaviours were tending towards disintegration and breakdown.

Before leaving the Gibb–Alexander system it should be pointed out that there is nothing in their suggestions which need limit their application to families. In this sense their scheme is akin to general systems theory because it focuses upon aspects of social systems that are common and not unique to a social system of a particular kind. On the other hand, neither this nor the Stuart–Patterson scheme can be said to be systems theories of the family, because they make no allowance for feedback, or for decisions based on feedback, nor do they make predictions about the relative likelihood of homeostasis or change in the family (Straus, 1973).

The Leary–Benjamin system

The system proposed by Leary (1957), and the very similar system more recently proposed by Benjamin (1974, 1977), lay the social psychological basis for a more dynamic account of family behaviour (other similar models are those proposed by Bierman, 1969, and by Sprenkle and Olson, 1978). Both take the view that interpersonal behaviour can be depicted in the form of a circumplex such as those shown in Figures 1.3 and 1.4.

The similarity between the two systems is apparent. For present purposes the most important feature of their proposals concerns predictions about contingencies between different types of interpersonal behaviour. Leary's proposal was that behaviour elicited *similar* behaviour along horizontal axes (hostile behaviour eliciting hostile behaviour from others; affectionate behaviour eliciting affection, etc.), whilst along any vertical line drawn through the circumplex, behaviour elicited *opposite* behaviour (dominant behaviour tending to elicit submissive behaviour and vice versa, for example). A certain amount of research has tended to confirm these hypotheses in a general way (e.g. Heller *et al.*, 1963; Shannon and Guerney, 1973).

Although basically very similar, Benjamin's (1977) system departs from Leary's in a number of significant respects. In particular it may be noted that Benjamin's scheme requires two diagrams, one for actions and one for reactions, whilst Leary uses one diagram for both. This creates particular complications for the vertical, dominance or control axis, which has always been a source of major difficulty for social theoreticians. Benjamin's scheme allows for 'giving autonomy' as an action, but only makes provision for 'submissiveness' as a reaction. Leary's scheme, on the other hand, allows 'submissiveness' to be both an action and a reaction but has no place for the 'giving of autonomy'. The difference may partly be understood when it is realized that Benjamin's scheme was designed to account for non-reciprocal parent–child interaction. Her first diagram may be thought of as portraying parent-like behaviour and the second as portraying child-like behaviour. Shannon and Guerney (1973), who used Leary's model for the basis of their own research, concluded that the contingencies between one behaviour and the next in a social sequence would very probably depend upon the role-relationships of the interactants. Hence a whole set of action and reaction diagrams may be necessary to even begin to account for contingencies in different types of relationship.

For present purposes it is interesting to note that behaviours described as supportive and system-integrating in the Gibb–Alexander scheme correspond closely with several of the items in the NE quadrant of Benjamin's action diagram which involves a combination of affectionateness and the allowing of freedom (fair exchange, exploring in a friendly way, showing empathic understanding, etc.). According to Benjamin, social action departs from this ideal in one of two major directions: either by moving through neglect and avoidance towards hostility and attack (it may be more correct to think of these as two separate forms of departure from the ideal—corresponding respectively to withdrawal and coercion in the

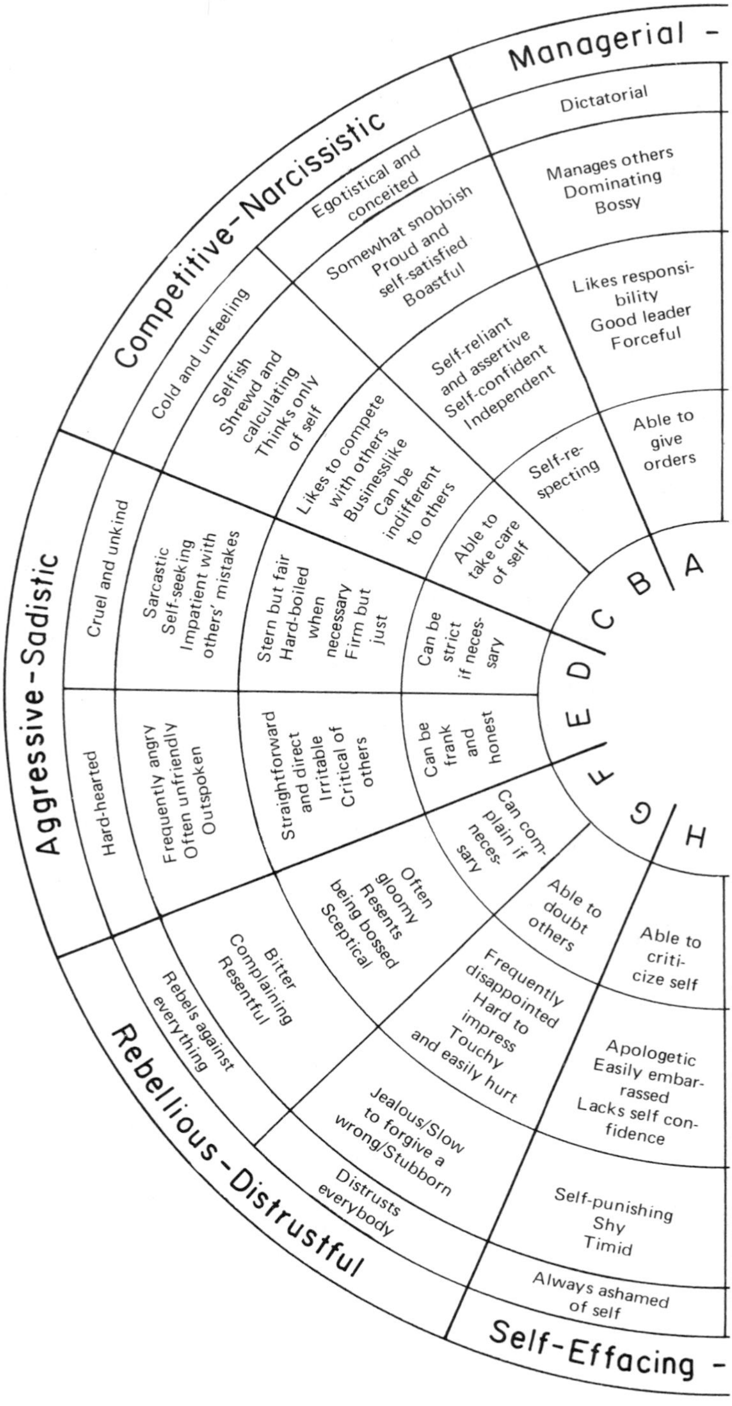
Managerial -
Dictatorial
Manages others
Dominating
Bossy
Likes responsibility
Good leader
Forceful
Able to give orders
Competitive-Narcissistic
Egotistical and conceited
Somewhat snobbish
Proud and self-satisfied
Boastful
Self-reliant and assertive
Self-confident
Independent
Self-respecting
Cold and unfeeling
Selfish
Shrewd and calculating
Thinks only of self
Likes to compete with others
Businesslike
Can be indifferent to others
Able to take care of self
Aggressive-Sadistic
Cruel and unkind
Sarcastic
Self-seeking
Impatient with others' mistakes
Stern but fair
Hard-boiled when necessary
Firm but just
Can be strict if necessary
Hard-hearted
Frequently angry
Often unfriendly
Outspoken
Straightforward and direct
Irritable
Critical of others
Can be frank and honest
A
B
C
D
E
F
G
H
Rebellious-Distrustful
Rebels against everything
Bitter
Complaining
Resentful
Often gloomy
Resents being bossed
Sceptical
Can complain if necessary
Distrusts everybody
Jealous/Slow to forgive a wrong/Stubborn
Frequently disappointed
Hard to impress
Touchy and easily hurt
Able to doubt others
Self-Effacing -
Always ashamed of self
Self-punishing
Shy
Timid
Apologetic
Easily embarrassed
Lacks self confidence
Able to criticize self

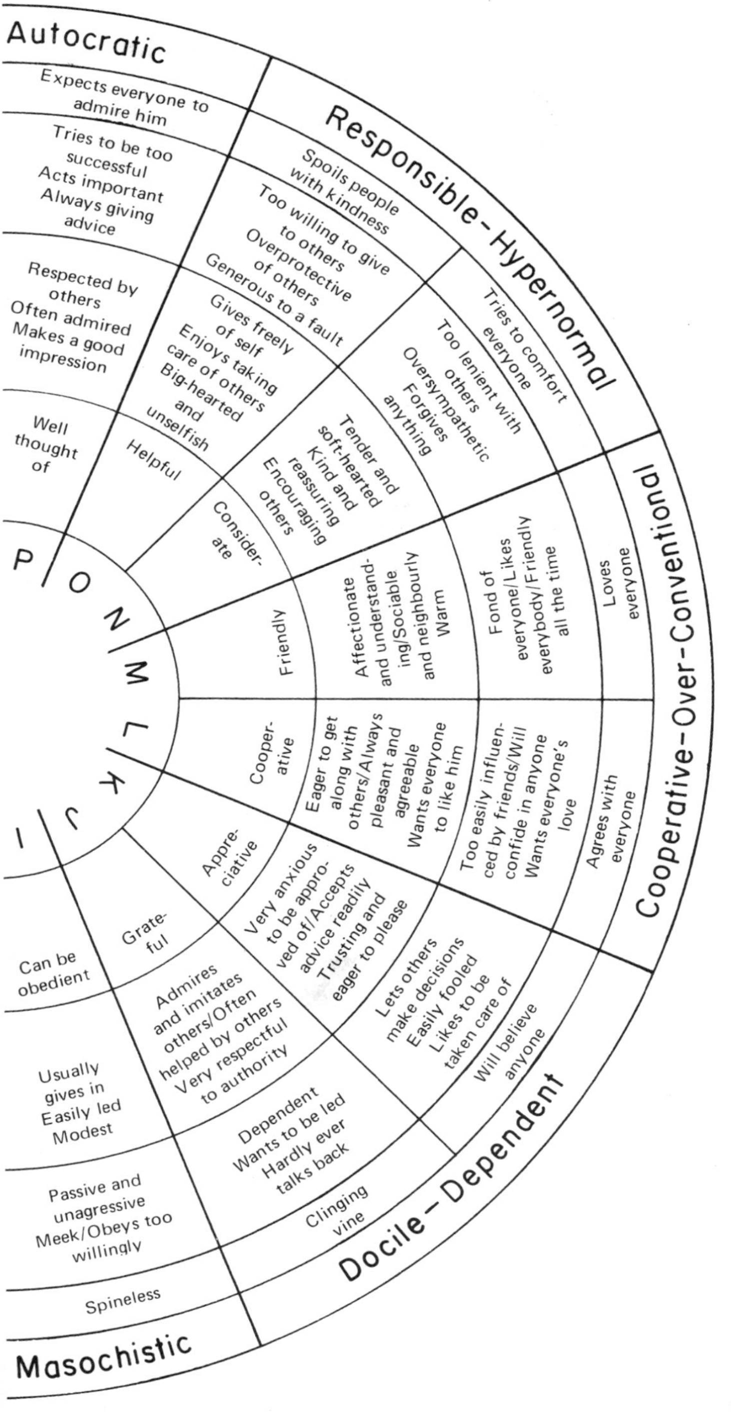

Figure 1.3 Leary's proposal for an interpersonal behaviour circumplex. (From Leary, 1957, p. 135, figure 6.)

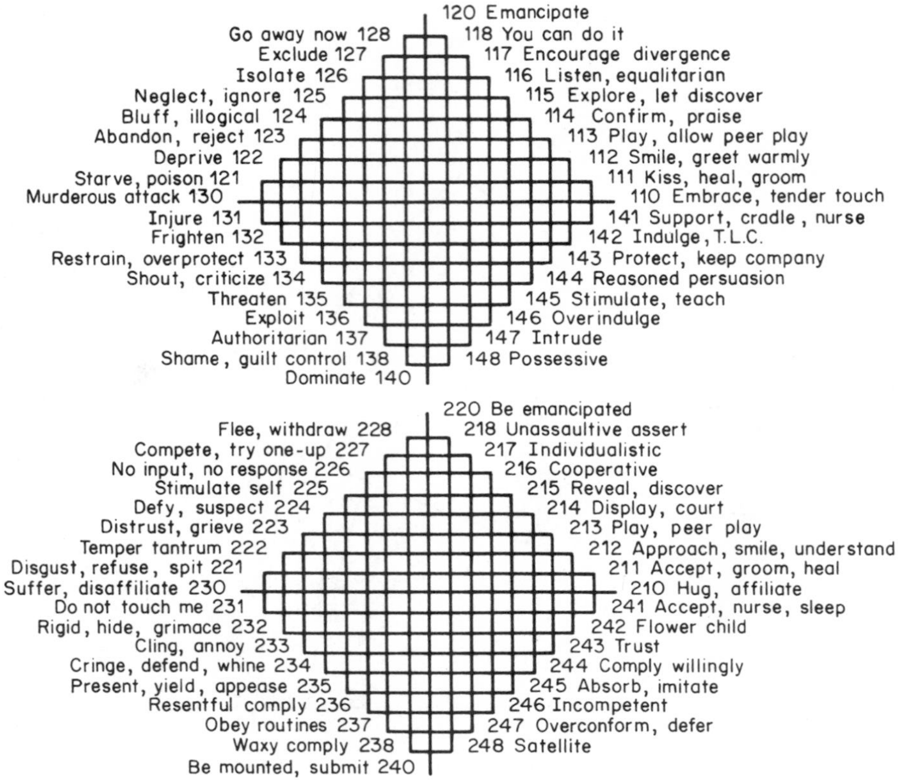

Figure 1.4 Benjamin's charts of social behaviour. The upper chart describes parent-like behaviours or actions; the second, child-like behaviours or reactions. (Reprinted, with permission, from Benjamin, 1973, p. 220.)

Stuart–Patterson model); or alternatively by moving through overindulgence towards managerial control.

Leary's model does not allow for choice which according to Straus (1973) is necessary for an adequate systems model of the family. This scheme inevitably leads to spiralling hostility (or affection) and to a static but skewed dominance–submissiveness relationship. Benjamin, however, introduces the possibility of choice through her concept of the 'antidote'. She argues that every reaction, as well as having a complementary action most likely to provoke it, also has its antidote or action most likely to elicit its opposite. For example, authoritarian action (code 137) is depicted in Benjamin's scheme as complementary to obeying routines (237). Hence we would expect to find some couples within families enmeshed in a relationship characterized by a great deal of authoritarian control by one partner and a great deal of obedience by the other. The former has the choice of breaking this reciprocal pattern by employing the opposite of authoritarian control, namely encouraging divergence (117), which is likely to provoke individualistic behaviour from the partner (217). Unlike Leary's scheme, which makes no distinction between actor and reactor, Benjamin gives the actor the choice but does not make it clear whether the reactor in this case could break the cycle of complementary behaviour by behaving individualistically. Common sense suggests that children can force parents to encourage divergence by themselves being stubbornly individualistic even in the face of authoritarian control.

Each of the two circumplex schemes so far described are two-dimensional and reduce to the familiar orthogonal axes warm–hostile and control–autonomy. Although these are the most frequently recurring themes in analyses of interpersonal behaviour, it is not altogether clear how adequate a picture they provide. There is some evidence, for example from empirical analyses of parental behaviour, that dominance may be subdivided into restrictiveness and firmness (their opposites being giving autonomy and laxness respectively), and that these two aspects of dominance have quite different effects on the socialization process (see the chapter by Herbert in this volume). Nor is it clear that disengagement, avoidance, or withdrawal, which appear to be so much a feature of family behaviour associated with psychological problems, are adequately represented. Benjamin's model allows for isolating, neglecting and ignoring behaviour at a position intermediate between attack and emancipate, but some other models allow for separate dimensions for activity, engagement, involvement, or intensity of relationship (Bierman, 1969; Mehrabian, 1971; Wish, 1976).

Whatever the deficiencies of the circumplex models of interpersonal behaviour, and there can be little doubt that they are deficient in many respects, they do contain two principal insights upon which a descriptive model can be built. These are: first, that interpersonal behaviour in the family (and probably elsewhere) has a roughly predictable structure to it with departures from the warmly egalitarian ideal which take the form of over-control, hostility, or indifference; and secondly, that such behaviour follows a law of complementary contingency, so that there is a greater than chance expectancy that certain types of interpersonal behaviour will be followed by certain others.

The cohesive family group

The foregoing models of family behaviour are all clinically derived, and employ similar and overlapping concepts. Each focuses upon behaviour, and makes little mention of perceptions or feelings. It is my view that there is considerable advantage to be had by incorporating the clinical insights of these models into the well-established and more general concept of the cohesive group in social psychology.

Group cohesiveness can be an elusive concept (Fraser, 1978), but it has proved indispensable in accounting for variation in the productivity and satisfaction of members of *ad hoc* groups in social psychological studies. Amongst the characteristics of the cohesive group, listed by Collins and Raven (1969), are the following:

1. a high level of participation in shared activities, and persistence in working towards group goals;
2. full and accurate communication amongst members;
3. members evaluate other members' behaviour favourably, and also perceive other members as being similar to themselves;
4. a high level of satisfaction and morale;
5. relatively much interpersonal influence within the group.

This concept of group cohesiveness goes a considerable way towards integrating work that has been carried out in the three specific problem fields reviewed above, and also the clinically derived models of the family which have been outlined. The first factor corresponds to a very basic dimension of engagement versus withdrawal in social relationships. This is a dimension of importance in all of the models discussed (whether in the form of 'withdrawal', 'indifference' or 'avoidance'), and appears to be important to an understanding of marital relationships in families complicated by drinking problems and to an understanding of parent–child bonds in cases of child abuse. Solidarity, bonding, attachment or closeness are seen as key attributes of family relationships, which mark them off from other relatively superficial social contacts (Wish *et al.*, 1976). Avoidance, withdrawal and disengagement are therefore the very antitheses of family cohesion, and carry the most obvious threat to the maintenance of family functions.

Communication ability is a crucial part of a number of family theories and has been a focus of examination in a very large number of family studies (Jacob, 1975). However the results of these studies have been inconsistent and communication *per se* has not been a major focus of studies in the drinking-problems or child-abuse areas. It may be that family studies of communication have examined accuracy of communicating under circumstances where some form of communication is forced (as in a laboratory discussion task). Conceivably they may have missed the most obvious source of variation in communication, namely full communication versus *avoidance* of communication. Furthermore, some family theories of communication, such as the theory of the double bind, are extremely subtle and difficult to test.

The significance of negative and critical perceptions of other family members emerged strongly from reviews of the literature on problem drinking, child abuse and psychiatric disorder. The models discussed are largely behavioural, and therefore make no particular mention of person perception variables. Nevertheless attitudes are implicit in a number of the Gibb–Alexander categories and in the circumplex systems.

Interpersonal influence has been an underlying theme, rather than a particular focus of attention, in the relevant family studies. The power of the family to influence its members for good is reflected in the functions attributed to the family by Caplan and Killilea (1976).

Satisfaction and morale, as global subjective elements of group cohesion, have rarely been the particular focus of studies of the family and psychological problems. An exception is the work of Moos and his colleagues (e.g. Moos and Moos, 1976) using the Family Environment Scale which assesses the perceived social environments of families along a number of dimensions. The first of these scales is termed by Moos cohesion, and is defined as: the extent to which family members are concerned and committed to the family and the degree to which they are helpful and supportive to each other. Families low in cohesion are particularly likely to be high on a further dimension also; that of conflict, which is defined as: the extent to which the open expression of anger and aggression and generally conflictual interactions are characteristic of the family. From his own research, it appears that families containing a member who drinks excessively are particularly likely to be in this low-cohesion conflict-oriented group.

Table 1.2 The syndrome of cohesion in families—hypothesised to be associated with the psychological well-being of group members

1. More time spent in shared activity.
2. Less withdrawal, avoidance and segregated activity.
3. A higher rate of warm interactions, and a lower rate of critical or hostile interactions amongst members.
4. Fuller and more accurate communication between members.
5. A more favourable evaluation of other members; a lower level of criticalness of other members.
6. More favourable meta-perceptions; i.e. members more likely to assume that other members have a favourable view of them.
7. A higher level of perceived affection between members.
8. A higher level of satisfaction and morale, and greater optimism about the future stability of the family group.

To summarize the position taken in this chapter, it may be said that family cohesion is a core construct which serves to link work in otherwise separated problem areas, and to link applied family studies within the body of social psychology. The chief characteristics of a cohesive family are listed in Table 1.2. Families which display these characteristics tend to enhance the psychological well-being of their members. Families which lack these characteristics, on the other hand, put their members at risk of experiencing psychological distress. Particularly vulnerable will be those family members who are already at risk for other reasons—the young, the elderly, those experiencing other forms of stress, those recovering from some illness or other trauma or stress, or those genetically predisposed to some psychiatric or psychosomatic disorder. When family cohesion is high, members are more likely, for example, to cope with the stress of caring for a number of very young children without abusing them, to overcome such problems as alcohol-dependence, or to make a successful adjustment after a period in a psychiatric hospital. The link between cohesion and well-being, it may be hypothesized, is mediated by the satisfactory exercise of the positive family functions outlined by Caplan and Killilea (1976) and by Weiss (1974). The cohesive family provides its members with information about the world, guides its members' behaviour, provides a set of values, helps problem-solve, provides practical aid and a place of sanctuary, validates members' self-identities, assists in emotional mastery and in general fosters feelings of security and competence.

This has been an admittedly theoretical chapter, and it is not the place to begin to consider the nature or success of family therapy or family-based prevention programmes. Nevertheless, the idea may be put forward that the rich variety of forms of family therapy now being discussed in the literature has a common theme. Each works, perhaps, if and when it brings about an increment in family cohesion.

REFERENCES

Alexander, J. F. (1973). Defensive and supportive communications in family systems. *Journal of Marriage and the Family*, **35,** 613–617.

Allan, L. J. (1978). Child abuse: a critical review of the research and the theory. In: J. P. Martin (Ed.), *Violence and the Family*. (Chichester: Wiley.)

Bailey, M. B., Haberman, P. W., and Alksne, H. (1962). Outcomes of alcoholic marriages; endurance, termination or recovery. *Quarterly Journal of Studies on Alcohol*, **23,** 610–623.

Bateson, G., Jackson, D. D., Haley J., and Weakland, J (1956). Toward a theory of schizophrenia. *Behavioural Science*, **1,** 251–264.

Belsky, J. (1978). Three theoretical models of child abuse: a critical review. *Child Abuse and Neglect*, **2,** 37–50.

Benjamin L. S. (1973). A biological model for understanding the behaviour of individuals. In: J. Westman (Ed.), *Individual Differences in Children*. (New York: Wiley.)

Benjamin, L. S. (1974). Structural analysis of social behaviour. *Psychological Review*, **81,** 392–425.

Benjamin, L. S. (1977). Structural analysis of a family in therapy. *Journal of Consulting and Clinical Psychology*, **45,** 391–406.

Bierman, R. (1969). Dimensions of interpersonal facilitation in psychotherapy and child development. *Psychological Bulletin*, **72,** 338–352.

Bloom, B. L., Asher, S. J., and White, S. W. (1978). Marital disruption as a stressor: a review and analysis. *Psychological Bulletin*, **85,** 867–894.

Bott, E. (1957). *Family and Social Network*. (London: Tavistock.)

Brown, G. W., Birley, J. L. T., and Wing, J. K. (1972). Influence of family life on the course of schizophrenic disorders: a replication. *British Journal of Psychiatry*, **121,** 241–258.

Brown G. W., Bhrolchain, M. N., and Harris, T. (1975). Social class and psychiatric disturbance among women in an urban population. *Sociology*, **9,** 225–254.

Brown, G. W. and Harris, T. (1978). *Social Origins of Depression: A Study of Psychiatric Disorder in Women*. (London: Tavistock.)

Brown, G. W., Monck, E. M., Carstairs, G. M., and Wing, J. K. (1962). Influence of family life on the course of schizophrenic illness. *British Journal of Preventive and Social Medicine*, **16**, 55–68.

Caplan, G. and Killilea, M. (1976). *Support Systems and Mutual Help: Multidisciplinary Exploration*. (New York: Grune & Stratton.)

Cheek, F. E. (1965). Family interaction patterns and convalescent adjustment of the schizophrenic. *Archives of General Psychiatry*, **13**, 138–147.

Clare, A. (1976). *Psychiatry In Dissent: Controversial Issues in Thought and Practice*. (London: Tavistock.)

Clausen, J. A. and Yarrow, M. R. (1955). The impact of mental illness on the family. *Journal of Social Issues*, **11**, 3–65.

Clum, G. A. (1975). Intrapsychic variables and the patient's environment as factors in prognosis. *Psychological Bulletin*, **82**, 413–431.

Collins, B. E. and Raven, B. H. (1969). Groups structure: attraction, coalitions, communication and power. In: G. Lindzey and E. Aronson (Eds.), *The Handbook of Social Psychology*, 2nd edn, vol. 4. (Reading, Mass.: Addison-Wesley.)

Cromwell, R. E. and Olson, D. H. (1975). *Power in Families*. (New York: Sage.)

DeLissovoy, V. (1973). Highschool marriages: a longitudinal study. *Journal of Marriage and the Family*, **35**, 245–255.

Dicks, H. (1967). *Marital Tensions: Clinical Studies Towards a Psychological Theory of Interaction*. (London: Routledge & Kegan Paul.)

Drewery, J. and Rae, J. B. (1969). A group comparison of alcoholic and nonalcoholic marriages using the interpersonal perception technique. *British Journal of Psychiatry*, **115**, 287–300.

Elmer E. (1967). *Children in Jeopardy: A Study of Abused Minors and Their Families*. (Pittsburgh: University of Pittsburgh Press.)

Farina, A. and Holzberg, J. D. (1967). Attitudes and behaviours of fathers and mothers of male schizophrenic patients. *Journal of Abnormal Psychology*, **72**, 381–387.

Farina, A. and Holzberg, J. D. (1968). Interaction patterns of parents and hospitalized sons diagnosed as schizophrenic or non-schizophrenic. *Journal of Abnormal Psychology*, **73**, 114–118.

Fontana (1966). Familial etiology of schizophrenia: is a scientific methodology possible? *Psychological Bulletin*, **66**, 214–227.

Fox, R. (1967). *Kinship and Marriage: An Anthropological Perspective*. Harmondsworth, Middlesex: Penguin.)

Fraser, C. (1978). Small groups. In: H. Tajfel and C. Fraser (Eds.), *Introducing Social Psychology*. (Harmondsworth, Middlesex: Penguin.)

Freeman, H. E. and Simmons, O. G. (1963). *The Mental Patient Comes Home*. (New York: Wiley.)

French, J. R. P. and Raven, B. H. (1959). The bases of social power. In: D. Cartwright (Ed.), *Studies in Social Power*. (Ann Arbor, Michigan: University of Michigan Press.)

Frude, N. (1978). Abuse as aggression. Paper presented at the Annual Conference of the British Psychological Society, York, 6–10 April.

Gibb, J. R. (1961). Defensive communications. *Journal of Communication*, **3**, 141–148.

Gil, D. (1971). Violence against children. *Journal of Marriage and the Family*, **33**, 639–648.

Goldstein, H. H. (1975). *Aggression and Crimes of Violence*. (New York: Oxford University Press.)

Green, A. (1976). A psychodynamic approach to the study and treatment of child abusing parents. *Journal of the American Academy of Child Psychiatry*, **15**, 414–420.

Green, A. H., Gaines, R. W., and Sandgrun, A. (1974). Child abuse: pathological syndrome of family interaction. *Americal Journal of Psychiatry*, **131**, 882–886.

Heller, K., Myers, R. A., and Kline, L. V. (1963). Interviewer behaviour as a function of standardized client role. *Journal of Consulting Psychology*, **27,** 117–122.

Henderson, S., Byrne, D. G., Duncan-Jones, P., Adcock, S., Scott, R., and Steel, G. P. (1978). Social bonds in the epidemiology of neurosis: a preliminary communication. *British Journal of Psychiatry*, **132,** 463–466.

Hirsch, S. and Leff, J. P. (1975). *Abnormality in Parents of Schizophrenics: A Review of the Literature and an Investigation of Communication Defects and Deviancies.* (Oxford: Oxford University Press.)

Hyman, C. (1978). Mother–child interaction in abusive and non-abusive families. Paper presented at the Annual Conference of the British Psychological Society, York, 6–10 April.

Jackson, J. K. (1954). The adjustment of the family to the crisis of alcoholism. *Quarterly Journal of Studies on Alcohol*, **15,** 562–586.

Jackson, J. K. and Kogan, K. L. (1963). The search for solutions: help-seeking patterns of families of active and inactive alcoholics. *Quarterly Journal of Studies on Alcohol*, **24,** 449–472.

Jacob, T. (1975). Family interaction in disturbed and normal families: a methodological and substantive review. *Psychological Bulletin*, **82,** 33–65.

Jacob, T., Favorini, A., Meisel, S. S., and Anderson, C. M. (1978). The alcoholic's spouse, children and family interactions: substantive findings and methodological issues. *Journal of Studies on Alcohol*, **39,** 1231–1251.

James, J. E. and Goldman, M. (1971). Behavior trends of wives of alcoholics. *Quarterly Journal of Studies on Alcohol*, **32,** 373–381.

Jourard, S. M. (1959). Self-disclosure and other-cathexis. *Journal of Abnormal and Social Psychology*, **59,** 428–431.

Klein, M. and Stern, L. (1971). Low birth weight and the battered child syndrome. *American Journal of Disorders of Childhood*, **122,** 15–18.

Kogan, K. L. and Jackson, J. K. (1961). Some role perceptions of wives of alcoholics. *Psychological Reports*, **9,** 119–124.

LaForge, R. and Suczek, R. F. (1955). The interpersonal dimensions of personality: an interpersonal checklist. *Journal of Personality*, **24,** 94–106.

Leary, T. (1957). *Interpersonal Diagnoses of Personality: A Functional Theory and Methodology for Personality Evaluation.* (New York: Ronald.)

Lidz, T., Cornelison, A., Fleck, S., and Terry, D. (1957). The intrafamily environment of schizophrenic patients: II. Marital schism and marital skew. *American Journal of Psychiatry*, **114,** 241–248.

Lorei, T. W. (1967). Prediction of community stay and employment for released psychiatric patients. *Journal of Consulting Psychology*, **31,** 349–357.

Luckey, E. B. (1964). Marital satisfaction and its concommitant perceptions of self and spouse. *Journal of Counselling Psychology*, **11,** 136–145.

Maden, M. F. and Wrench, D. F. (1977). Significant findings in child abuse research. *Victimology*, **II,** 196–224.

Mayo, P. R. (1968). Self-disclosure and neurosis. *British Journal of Social and Clinical Psychology*, **2,** 140–148.

Mehrabian, A. (1971). Nonverbal communication. In: J. K. Cole (Ed.), *Nebraska Symposium on Motivation*, Vol. 19. (Nebraska: University of Nebraska Press.)

Melnick, B. and Hurley, J. (1969). Destructive personality attributes of child abusing mothers. *Journal of Consulting and Clinical Psychology*, **33,** 746–749.

Miller, P. M. and Ingham, J. G. (1976). Friends confidants and symptoms. *Social Psychiatry*, **11,** 51–58.

Moos, R. H. and Moos, B. S. (1976). A typology of family social environments. *Family Process*, **15,** 357–371.

Morris, M. and Gould, R. (1963). Role reversal: a necessary concept in dealing with the battered child syndrome. *American Journal of Orthopsychiatry*, **33,** 298–299.

Morrow, W. R. and Robins, A. J. (1964). Family relations and social recovery of psychotic mothers. *Journal of Health and Human Behaviour*, **5,** 14–24.

Murstein, B. I. and Glaudin, V. (1966). The relationship of marital adjustment to personality: a factor analysis of the interpersonal check list. *Journal of Marriage and the Family*, **28,** 37–43.

National Society for the Prevention of Cruelty to Children (1976). *At Risk: An Account of the Work of the Battered Children's Research Department.* (London: Routledge & Kegan Paul.)

Newberger, E., Reed, R., Daniel, J., Hyde, N., and Kotelchuck, M. (1975). Paediatric Social Illness: Toward an Aetiologic Classification. Paper presented at the Biennial Meeting of the Society for Research in Child Development, Denver.

Orford, J. (1975). Alcoholism and marriage: the argument against specialism. *Journal of Studies on Alcohol*, **36,** 1537–1563.

Orford, J. (1976). *The Social Psychology of Mental Disorder.* (Harmondsworth, Middlesex: Penguin.)

Orford, J. (1976). A study of the personalities of excessive drinkers and their wives, using the approaches of Leary and Eysenck. *Journal of Consulting and Clinical Psychology*, **44,** 534–545.

Orford, J., Guthrie, S., Nicholls, P., Oppenheimer, E., Egert, S., and Hensman, C. (1975). Self-reported coping behaviour of wives of alcoholics and its association with drinking outcome. *Journal of Studies on Alcohol*, **36,** 1254–67.

Orford, J. Oppenheimer, E., Egert, S., Hensman, C., and Guthrie, S. (1976). The cohesiveness of alcoholism—complicated marriages and its influence on treatment outcome. *British Journal of Psychiatry*, **128,** 318–339.

Ounsted, C., Oppenheimer, R., and Lindsay, J. (1975). The psychopathology and psychotherapy of the families: aspects of bonding failure. In: A. Franklin (Ed.), *Concerning Child Abuse.* (Edinburgh: Churchill Livingstone.)

Paolino, T. J. and McCrady, B. S. (1977). *The Alcoholic Marriage: Alternative Perspectives.* (New York: Grune & Stratton.)

Parke, R. (1974). Rules, roles and resistance to deviations in children: explorations in punishment, discipline and self-control. In: A. Pick (Ed.), *Minnesota Symposium on Child Psychology*, Vol. 8. (Minneapolis: University of Minnesota Press.)

Patterson, G. R., Hops, H. and Weiss, R. L. (1975). Interpersonal skills training for couples in early stages of conflict. *Journal of Marriage and the Family*, **37,** 295–303.

Rigby, A. (1974). *Communes in Britain.* (London: Routledge & Kegan Paul.)

Rollins, B. C. and Feldman, H. (1970). Marital satisfaction over the family life cycle. *Journal of Marriage and the Family*, **32,** 20–28.

Rollins, B. C. and Thomas, D. L. (1975). A theory of parental power and child compliance. In: R. E. Cromwell and D. H. Olson (Eds.), *Power in Families.* (New York: Sage.)

Royal College of Psychiatrists. (1979). *Alcohol and Alcoholism: The Report of the Special Committee.* (London: Tavistock.)

Schauble, P. G. (1973). Facilitating conditions: basic dimensions for psychological growth and effective communication. In: R. H. Woody and J. D. Woody (Eds.), *Sexual, Marital and Family Relations: Therapeutic Interventions for Professional Helping.* (Springfield, Illinois: Charles Thomas.)

Shannon, J. and Guerney, B. (1973). The interpersonal effects of interpersonal behavior. *Journal of Personality and Social Psychology*, **26,** 142–150.

Shapiro, D. A. (1969). Empathy, warmth and genuineness in psychotherapy. *British Journal of Social and Clinical Psychology*, **8,** 350–361.

Sluki, C. E. and Ransom, D. C. (Eds.) (1976). *Double bind: the foundation of the*

Communicational Approach to the Family. (New York: Grune & Stratton.)

Sprenkle, D. H. and Olson, D. H. (1978). Circumplex model of marital systems: an empirical study of clinic and non-clinic couples. *Journal of Marriage and Family Counseling*, **4,** 59–74.

Steele, B. and Pollock, C. (1968). A psychiatric study of parents who abuse infants and small children. In: R. Helfer and C. H. Kempe (Eds.), *The Battered Child*. (Chicago: University of Chicago Press.)

Steinglass, P., Davis, D. I., and Bevenson, D. (1977). Observations of conjointly hospitalized 'alcoholic couples' during sobriety and intoxication: implications for theory and therapy. *Family Process*, **16,** 1–16.

Straus, M. A. (1973). A general systems theory approach to a theory of violence between family members. *Social Science Information*, **12,** 105–125.

Stuart, R. B. (1969). Operant interpersonal treatment for marital discord. *Journal of Consulting and Clinical Psychology*, **33,** 675–682.

Stultz, S. (1975). A controlled investigation of the child rearing attitudes of abusive mothers. Unpublished doctoral dissertation. (Cotnell Universty, Ithaca, New York.)

Taylor, D. A. and Altman, I. (1966). Intimacy-scaled stimuli for use in studies of interpersonal relations. *Psychological Reports*, **19,** 729–730.

Tolsdorf, C. C. (1976). Social networks, support, and coping: an exploratory study. *Family Process*, **15,** 407–417.

Vaughn, C. and Leff, J. P. (1976). The influence of family and social factors on the course of psychiatric illness: a comparison of schizophrenic and depressed neurotic patients. *British Journal of Psychiatry*, **129,** 125–137.

Vaughn, C. and Leff, J. P. (1978). Interaction characteristics in families of schizophrenic patients. Pre-Publication Manuscript.

Washburn, S. L. (Ed.) (1961). *The Social Life of Early Man*. (Chicago: Aldine)

Watzlawick, P., Beavin, J. H., and Jackson, B. D. (1968). *Pragmatics of Human Communication: A Study of Interactional Patterns, Pathologies and Paradoxes*. (London: Faber & Faber.)

Weiss, R. S. (1974). The provisions of social relationships. In: Z. Rubin (Ed.), *In Doing Unto Others: Joining, Molding, Conforming, Helping, Loving*. (Englewood Cliffs, New Jersey: Prentice Hall.)

Wilson, C. and Orford, J. (1978). Children of alcoholics: report of a preliminary study and comments on the literature. *Journal of Studies on Alcohol*, **39,** 121–142.

Wish, M. (1976). Comparisons among multidimensional structures of interpersonal relations. *Multivariate Behavioural Research*, **11,** 297–324.

Wish, M., Deutsch, N. and Kaplan, S. J. (1976). Perceived dimensions of interpersonal relations. *Journal of Personality and Social Psychology*, **33,** 409–420.

Young, M. and Willmott, P. (1957). *Family and Kinship in East London*. (London: Routledge & Kegan Paul.)

The Social Psychology of Psychological Problems
Edited by P. Feldman and J. Orford

2

Socialization for Problem Resistance

MARTIN HERBERT

The search for the specific and crucial conditions in the child's cumulative experience with his family, and other agents of socialization, is an ancient one. Here is a couplet which contains an ironic comment on child-care practices; it expresses concern over the adequacy with which children are reared:

> Come listen now to the good old days when children,
> strange to tell,
> Were seen not heard, led a simple life, in short,
> were brought up well.

This is not a modern grandmother bemoaning, in verse, the passing of Victorian childrearing practices. The lines are from Aristophanes and date back to the fifth century B.C.

In part, the scientific inquiry into childhood arises out of a conviction about the extensive power and reach of early experience; a belief that optimal care and training of children during the impressionable years of life, will function as a kind of vaccination—inoculating them against the future problems of adolescence and adulthood. As such, it has all the pathos of the researches of those early alchemists, seeking a formula to transform base metal into pure gold. Sadly the base metal today is our meagre supply of knowledge—mainly ambiguous correlations and fragile generalizations hedged around with a multitude of qualifications—about the social influences on child development.

Yet 'experts' in child-care have not been shy to come forward with confident, indeed, precise, advice about whether to breast-feed or bottle-feed, when to wean and toilet train—for the good of the child's adjustment and personality. Fashions in such advice have come and gone (Sears, 1975; Vincent, 1951).

Perhaps it is not all that surprising that such confidence should abound. There is a tantalizing 'obviousness' about what needs to be done to nurture children correctly. Surely it is only a matter of common sense. As McCandless (1969) observes;

> On the basis of our actual contact as parents, teachers, and professional workers both with individual children and groups of children, we 'know

> in our hearts' ... that children's lives and adjustments do vary according to their families' treatment of them. These variations may be temporary—a function of some family crisis or improvement of family condition—or they may be long enduring.

And we can point to the fact that societies are remarkably successful (within broad limits) at inculcating in their members—a majority of them anyway—the approved codes of conduct, the pro-social norms, values, and personal attributes. Granted that the cultures in which children are reared do not completely control their dispositions to behave in a pro-social or adaptive manner, it should nevertheless be possible to tease out the essence of what works. There must surely be significant variables which account for the individual differences in pro-social *vs.* anti-social, adaptive *vs.* maladaptive behaviour patterns.

SOCIALIZATION: AN OVERVIEW

So say the optimists, and they have engaged in detailed investigations of variations in socialization practices within cultures. This meant examining precisely what the chief agents of socialization (especially parents, but also peers, teachers, religious groups, the mass media) actually do to enhance or restrict the development of adaptive and maladaptive behaviour (see: Caldwell, 1964; Eysenck and Nias, 1978; Frank, 1965; Herbert, 1974; Hoffman, 1970; Orford, 1976; Rutter and Madge, 1976; Sears *et al.*, 1957; Yarrow *et al.*, 1968 for literature reviews).

The findings of research studies, most of which are retrospective or cross-sectional, have done nothing to undermine this utopian dream. They typically generate correlational evidence telling us (for example) that there are links between the experience of an unhappy, disharmonious and disrupted family life in childhood and teenage pregnancy, extramarital conception, marriage breakdown, less satisfactory neonatal care, delinquency, and other factors (Rutter, 1977). However, in spite of important and statistically significant associations, most individuals from unhappy homes do not manifest these characteristics in adulthood. The ambiguity of meaning, and complexity, of such evidence does not disabuse us of that compelling sense of continuity and causal connectedness which we feel when we consider our past lives and reflect on the experiences of our childhood. Freud observed that:

> So long as we trace the development [of a mental process] backwards, the connection appears continuous, and we feel we have obtained an insight which is completely satisfactory and even exhaustive. But if we proceed the reverse way, if we start from the premise inferred from the analysis and try to follow up the final result, then we no longer get the impression of an inevitable sequence of events, which could not have been otherwise determined. We notice at once that there might be another result, and that we might have been just as well able to understand and explain the latter. (Freud, 1956, p. 226.)

We also have our theories and prejudices about the related theme of the critical-period concept. Were the Jesuits right about the irreversibility of those first seven formative years of life, or Freud about the first five? Much has been made (because of the respectable-looking conceptual links between psychoanalysis, embryology, and ethology in this instance) of the critical-period hypothesis. An attitude of therapeutic nihilism was created in the minds of many workers because of this concept of fixed and irreversible attributes. One wonders how many youngsters have been written off as psychopathic because of the postulated link between early maternal deprivation and the so-called affectionless personality (see Morgan, 1975). An intolerable burden of anxiety and guilt is placed on parents. The idea of a critical period implies that parents are all-powerful, all-responsible 'and must assume the role of playing preventive Fate for their children' (Bruch, 1954). It would be impossible to count the number of mothers who have asked the 'expert' whether they have done the wrong thing, made an awful mistake by doing X or Y with the child, as if a one-off allegedly 'traumatic' event would leave its indelible mark on the child.

Our knowledge of causality in behaviour development is elementary, and therefore our conjectures about the outcome of conditions—combinations of parental attitudes, home and school circumstances, reinforcement contingencies, genetic influences, etc., must be modest. There is (for example) no hard evidence (see Caldwell, 1964; Lee and Herbert, 1970) of a relationship between specific early child-rearing practices and the child's adjustment and personality development. For example, we have no conclusive evidence about whether breast-feeding, for a long or short time, has more favourable consequences than bottle-feeding; whether early weaning is disadvantageous compared with later weaning; whether feeding from a cup is better than the sucking-type of feeding; or whether unscheduled feeding is superior to scheduled feeding. In fact it is the conclusion from many research reports that no clear adjustment or maladjustment patterns have been demonstrated to result from any aspect of the infant's feeding experience, nor are personality traits shown to be related to such matters as type of infant feeding.

Elimination training—the method and age of initiating toilet training—because it is assumed to be frustrating, has been linked to the development of problem behaviours such as aggression. While there may be short-term differences in a child's reactions to different types of bowel and bladder training, so that coercive and punitive attempts may result in bowel and bladder malfunctioning, there is no apparent relationship to different personality characteristics, either favourable or unfavourable.

Clarke and Clarke (1976) conclude a review of the evidence by proposing that early experience is no more than a link in the development chain, shaping behaviour less and less powerfully as age increases. What is probably crucial in the case (say) of the conduct disorders, with their poor prognosis, is that early (maladaptive) learning is continually reinforced and it is in this way that long-term effects appear. There is also the possibility that later deviance is the result of later reinforcement as well as original learning experiences. At whatever point in the child's development a therapeutic intervention is made, it is important that maladaptive learning processes are disrupted and prosocial actions encouraged in a manner that will persist over long periods of time. The therapeutic perspective is a long one; and herein lies the possibility of doing genuine preventive work (Herbert, 1978). New adaptive behaviours need to become part of a child's life-style. This means that they must be functional, having 'survival' value, and receiving environmental support. Simplistic 'either–or' schemes aimed at changing the child (e.g. at the intra-psychic level) or his environment, are likely to have limited success. A consistent theoretical framework is necessary in order to make reasonable predictions about a child's behaviour. For all its inadequacies, social learning theory (see Bandura, 1977) seems best to fit the bill. This bill requires an amalgam, not only of the social and learning psychologies, but also developmental principles (Herbert, 1974).

The complex interactions of person and social context make a nonsense of the simple classical linear causality which is so pervasive in the literature on parent education and preventive work. The high hopes of preventive education have been dashed because of its focus on content rather than on process, on finding techniques and formulae designed to satisfy an abstract principle of good adjustment in the child, rather than providing parents with a broad theoretical framework within which to analyse, and act upon, unique personal and familial dispositions. Parent education has too often been a passive didactic exercise in which the objective is to mould the child in such a manner that he will become a well-adjusted adult, well-adjusted in terms of the theoretical value system of the educator or therapist. Sometimes this leads to contradictions, especially in the American literature, where it seems to be considered desirable to be both well-adjusted to society and self-actualizing. The important fact that parent education is an active process, involving the interdependence and interaction of various forces, has been almost completely overlooked. It can fruitfully be conceived as a partnership with a family, requiring debate and negotiation over goals (Herbert, 1978), rather than the unilateral provision of 'ex cathedra' doctrines about child-care.

These critical comments on parent education are not meant to challenge the assumption that to a significant extent human behaviour is a product of life experiences. The empirical findings have a use, but as yet a limited one, when formulating general principles about optimal conditions of child-care.

Available evidence suggests that what is important in child-rearing is the general social climate in the home—the attitudes and feelings of the parents which form a background to the application of specific methods and interactions of child-rearing. For example, the mother does best who does what she and the community to which she belongs believe is right for the child (Behrens, 1954). Feeding and toileting are important elements of the child's daily activities; but it is the social interactions they mediate—the manner in which parents undertake these tasks—that give them significance (Ainsworth, 1973). Rutter (1975, 1977) concludes, on the basis of an extensive review, that is how the baby is looked after that is crucial; it is the social and psychological context of the care which matters, rather than its chronology and mechanics.

This raises a further child-rearing issue of note. The child's response to his world is thought to be more than a simple reaction to his environment. He is thought to be actively engaged in attempts to organize and structure his world. Any truly transactional model (Sameroff and Chandler, 1975) must stress the changing character of the environment and of the organism as an active participant in its own development. Learning occurs within a social nexus; rewards, punishments, and other events are mediated by human agents and within attachment systems, and are not simply the impersonal consequences of behaviour. Unfortunately—and it is the case with all forms of learning—the very processes which help the child adjust to life can, under certain circumstances, contribute to his maladjustment. An immature child who learns by imitating an adult is not necessarily to know when it is deviant behaviour that is being modelled. If it is accepted that many deviant behaviours of childhood and adulthood are acquired as a function of faulty learning processes, then there is a case for arguing that problems can most effectively be modified (and indeed, prevented) when and where they occur, by changing the 'social lessons' he receives and the reinforcing contingencies supplied by social agents.

Interpretations of socialization in terms of social reinforcement have shared (in the past) a common view of the infant as an essentially passive organism whose character is moulded solely by the impact of environment upon genetic predispositions. This vertical model presupposes a child who is part of a one-way traffic in which he is under the control of a socializing agent who dispenses rewards and punishments (Zigler and Child, 1969). There is evidence (Harper, 1975; Schaffer, 1977) that the direction of effects of socialization is not always downward—from parent to child—and parents are not the sole possessors of power and influence within the family. What is obvious from recent studies is that important individual differences are manifested in early infancy, among them being autonomic response patterns, social responsiveness (cuddliness), regularity of sleeping, feeding and other biological patterns, and perceptual responses (Thomas *et al.*, 1968; Thomas and Chess, 1977; Graham *et al.*, 1973). There are other factors including maturational processes which predetermine the sequence and structure of developmental stages, as well as hereditary and congenital conditions. It is clear that these early differences set the stage for varying patterns of interaction with the environment, leading to the shaping of personality along lines which are not predictable from knowledge of the environment alone.

Of particular interest are the 'temperamental' factors related to the child's general level of activity, sensory threshold, intensity of response and the general affective tone of his transactions with the environment (Thomas *et al.*, 1968; Thomas and Chess, 1977). These temperamental attributes (e.g. overactivity) are the ones on which we at the Child Treatment Research Unit (University of Leicester, School of Social Work) have focused attention. Given the various caretaking and socializing tasks a mother has to undertake, and which demand a degree of stillness, attention and cooperation from her offspring, overactivity is particularly tiring and sometimes disturbing. The potential stress resulting from a mismatch between the mother's temperament (including her threshold of tolerance) and the child's behavioural style, may well set the stage for discord, conflict, and nervous exhaustion.

CHILD-REARING METHODS

Children labelled 'at risk' have often been regarded in the clinical and social-work literature as passive victims of external forces. The victims have been deliberately excluded from study because their roles have been presumed to be irrelevant. Because much of the research on child neglect and abuse has been prompted by concerns with prevention and remediation, attention has been focused on those aspects of the problem which have been thought to be more easily changed. The parents and their child-rearing practices (again), rather than the children themselves, have been most frequently nominated for this role.

One still hears occasionally what used to be a popular catch-phrase: 'there are no problem children, only problem parents'. This statement refers, in part, to an explanation of why children fail to adapt to society's norms. Indeed, our matricentric culture has provided a refinement in the inculpation of parents as causes of their children's difficulties, pointing the finger mainly in the direction of the mother. Stella Chess felt constrained to write, in an editorial for the *American Journal of Orthopsychiatry* (1964), that this sort of formulation represented the most prevalent approach to the analysis of the causes of children's behaviour problems in child-guidance centres throughout the United States.

> The standard procedure is to assume that the child's problem is reactive to maternal handling in a one-to-one relationship. Having come to this conclusion, the diagnostician turns his further investigations unidirectionally toward negative maternal attitudes and the conflicts presumed to underlie these. Investigation in other directions is done in a most cursory fashion or not at all. At the diagnostic conference, speculations are made concerning the mother's relationship with her own parents, her degree of immaturity, her presumed rejection of this child and her over-compensations for this rejection. Single bits of data fitting in with these speculations are quoted as typical of the child's feelings and the mother's attitudes and are taken as proof of the thesis of noxious maternal attitudes as universal causation.

Chess refers to this phenomenon as 'mal de mere'. The clinical and social-work literature over many years was replete with 'bad mothers': schizophrenogenic mothers, asthmagenic mothers, mothers accused of suffocating their offspring with 'smother' love, or in some other way overprotecting, rejecting, or double-binding them into abnormality. Parents are pulled in two directions; if they are too permissive, the child will become (it is said) a self-centred, unpopular, and wilful tyrant. But if they are too restrictive, authoritarian, and punitive, their discipline will produce slavish conformity in a neurotic, submissive, and obsequious nonentity. Indeed, the breakdown in discipline is blamed for many modern-day problems: drug abuse, the dropout, the rising number of delinquents, and sexual promiscuity. Folklore, although imprecise and exaggerated (it also tends to ignore structural social problems), has a point about discipline—as we shall see later. It is not reactionary to be concerned about the consequences of indiscipline; they are serious (Rutter, 1977). In terms of formal studies of childhood psychopathology, it was in the 1930s that it became explicit that problem children frequently had parents with problems. It was inferred from this that they had become problematic mainly because of this fact. There followed a plethora of studies of parental attitudes and actions, and many simplistic schemata were devised to demonstrate the relationship between parental attitudes and childhood behaviour disorders. For example, Levy (1943) described a relationship between maternal overprotection (of an indulgent type) and the development of a feckless, spoilt child whose behaviour is characterized by disobedience, impudence, tantrums, excessive demands, and varying degrees of tyrannical behaviour.

It is not surprising, given the modern predilection for labelling (the Rumpelstiltskin fixation, as Ross (1968) calls it), that there are two pseudo-diagnostic terms available to accommodate this sort of behaviour: 'the brat syndrome' or 'the hyperactive syndrome'. What is questionable is the aetiological sequence inferred by Levy. Based on research at the Child Treatment Research Unit, we would tell a somewhat different kind of story about the evolution of serious conduct disorders, in most of the children we see (Herbert, 1978). It is these very words, 'the children we see', that explain one of the major sources of error and misunderstanding in the literature. Biased sampling, the generalization of findings from clinic-attending children, has led to many erroneous conclusions. It is not surprising that when special-risk groups of children are examined, relationships between specific parental patterns and subsequent behaviour disturbances in the offspring are found which then disappear when they are looked for in the more general childhood population. What we do not know from aetiological studies of restricted clinical samples is how many run-of-the-mill children have suffered the allegedly 'pathogenic' influence without any particular ill-effect. What we can affirm, on the basis of more broadly based surveys, is that in all the risk categories invoked in the literature on psychopathology (be they prenatal or perinatal pathology, parental characteristics, family problems, etc.), it is possible to identify significant numbers of children who, although subjected to these influences, nevertheless developed normally (Chess, 1971).

Provided the enthusiasm to prescribe is tempered by these cautionary considerations, there are hints for problem-resistance in the findings from more recent studies of parent–child relations. Factor analytic and computer techniques have been used in order to reduce the rich variety of childhood and parental behaviours to a few main dimensions (see chapters by Argyle and Orford in this volume). For example, Schaefer (1959) describes parental attitudes in terms of the interactions of only two main orthogonal attributes. One dimension involves attitudes which are 'warm' (or loving) at one extreme, and 'rejecting' (or hostile) at the other; while the other dimension is made up of attitudes which are restrictive (controlling) at one extreme, and permissive (encouraging autonomy) at the other.

Reviews of research (Becker, 1964) into child-rearing techniques suggest an empirical basis for the notion that there is a 'happy medium', that the extremes of permissiveness and restrictiveness both entail risks. A blend of permissiveness and a warm, encouraging, and accepting attitude fits the recommendations of child-rearing specialists who are concerned with fostering the sort of children who are socially responsible and outgoing, friendly, competent, creative, and reasonably independent and self-assertive (admittedly Western values). Baumrind (1971, 1972) has conducted an important series of studies on the effects of different socialization practices. She, however, denies that attributes such as these are facilitated by a happy compromise between authoritarian and permissive parental practices. For her the evidence points to 'a synthesis and balancing of strongly opposing forces of tradition and innovation, divergence and convergence, accommodation and assimilation, cooperation and autonomous expression, tolerance and principled intractability'. We return to her findings shortly.

There are many inconsistencies, even contradictions, in the literature on parent–child attitudes and relationships and parental child-rearing practices. The isomorphism between parental attitudes as measured and specific behaviours is limited. Global assessments of such independent variables as parental warmth, hostility, rejection, and the like, are too abstract to accommodate many of the subtle nuances of parental behaviour. They lack contextual anchorage; that is to say, they do not specify the variations in behavioural interactions between parents and children which occur in particular situations and which are necessary to define precise relationships between independent and dependent variables. To quote Danziger:

> Extremely hostile and rejecting parents are more likely to have delinquent children, but within the normal range the value of a given reward or punishment depends on its relation to the overall level of nurturance. The same effective reward and punishment can, therefore, occur under quite different overall conditions of nurturance. Behavioural conformity to specific norms in particular situations is more likely to depend on situation-specific sanctions than on the general pattern of parent-child relationships. (Danziger, 1971.)

PROBLEMS OF CHILDHOOD

The issue of situation-specificity makes it difficult to draw precise conclusions about global constructs like normality. Terms like 'normal' and 'abnormal' are commonly applied to children as if they are mutually exclusive concepts like black and white. They are also used in the manner of trait-attributes; thus the label 'abnormal' attached to a particular child seems to suggest that he is deviant in some absolute and generalized sense. This is misleading; the most that can be said of any child is that certain of his actions or attributes are more or less abnormal. The issues of generalized traits and situational specificity have been critically examined by Bowers (1973). He reached the conclusion, from his review of the published studies, that both trait theorists and situationists have overstated their cases. If the total variance in behaviour is 100 per cent then an average of about 13 per cent of this variance is due to the person (personality traits), 10 per cent due to the situation, and 21 per cent to the interaction between persons and situations. A major component of variation remains unaccounted for, and herein lies a massive obstacle for those concerned with predictions.

Sabshin (1968) makes the point that one of the simplest ways to uncover a therapist's implicit or latent definition of mental health is to ask him about his criteria for successful termination of a therapeutic case. As healthy adjustment, in the opinion of this author, cannot be discussed meaningfully as an abstract quality of abstract children, we shall be concerned with the particular strategies and competencies developed by individual children to meet the specific needs and problems of their life situations. In the review that follows, problems are so-called because they have a variety of unfavourable consequences (see Herbert, 1974); when they are not deficit problems (a failure to learn adaptive responses) they are conceptualized as strategies of adjustment which the child has learned to his own disadvantage (and often to the disadvantage of others) in the attempt to cope with the demands of life. They are therefore referred to as maladaptive strategies; they are inappropriate for dealing with the stresses and strains of growing up. The areas of concern (and this has to be a highly selective choice) involve the development in the child (or the failure to develop) of the attitudes and behaviours defining what we call trust, confidence, initiative, industry, social identity, altruism, compliance, self-restraint, helpfulness, self-esteem, and the ability to make friends.

It is obviously very useful to know about the social norms and the norms of development when making a diagnosis. It would be a sizeable step forward if we could identify the periods when a child is most vulnerable to emotional problems, and concentrate our efforts and resources so as to help him (and his parents) through such crises. The term 'crisis intervention' has been used to describe the expert assistance needed at certain times in a person's life when he not only experiences a heightened desire for help, but is more susceptible than usual to the influence of others. Children also experience such periods of crisis when, for example, they go to hospital; endure parental illness, separation, or death; cope with the birth of a sibling; learn to live with a handicapped brother; and so on. A feature of much problem behaviour in childhood is its transitoriness. So mercurial are some of the changes of behaviour in response to the rapid growth and the successive challenges of childhood, that it is difficult to pinpoint the beginning of serious problems. A long-term study (MacFarlane *et al.*, 1954) of the development of 126 American infants provides us with information about the incidence and shifts in their problem behaviours as manifested at different ages between 21 months and 14 years.

For most children, problems manifested themselves briefly at certain periods and then became minimal or disappeared completely. Problems such as moodiness, overdependence, sombreness, and irritability showed the greatest persistence. Among the problems which declined in frequency with age were elimination (toilet training) problems, speech problems, fears, and thumb-sucking. Difficulties which declined at a rather later stage, and at a slower rate, were overactivity, destructiveness, and tempers. In fact, one-third of the boys were still having temper explosions at 13. Problems such as insufficient appetite and lying reached a peak early, and then subsided. Many personality problems showed high frequencies round about or just before school-starting age, then declined in prevalence, and later rose again at puberty. Among these were restless sleep, disturbing dreams, physical timidity, irritability, attention-demanding, overdependence, sombreness, jealousy, and, in boys, food-finickiness. Only one problem increased systematically with age: nail-biting; this reached a peak and began to subside only near the end of adolescence. Among the problems which showed little or no relationship to age was oversensitiveness.

Studies by Rutter *et al.* (1970) and Shepherd *et al.* (1971) provide normative data for British children. The counselling of parents as to the normality of their children can produce a sense of relief and the detached handling which allows them to remain transitory problems that they are when given sensible management (see Herbert, 1975). We know as a result of longitudinal studies that, for the most part, neurotic children become reasonably well-adjusted adults; they are almost as likely to grow up 'normal' as children drawn at random from the general population (Robins, 1966; Shepherd *et al.*, 1971).

THE SEQUENCE OF DEVELOPMENT

Knowledge of 'sensitive periods' in the child's development—as a matter of parent education—could alert the child's care-takers to the developmental tasks which put a heavy burden on his adjustive capacities. Ausubel and Sullivan (1970, p. 115) state that:

> ... one of the chief types of developmental discontinuity is brought about by significant and relatively rapid shifts in the individual's biosocial status. The periods in which qualitatively new and discontinuous (inter-stage) changes in personality organization are being formulated are designated as transitional phases or developmental crises. During these transitional periods the individual is in the marginal position of having lost an established and accustomed status and of not yet having acquired the new

status toward which the factors impelling developmental change are driving him.

Each stage of development is thought to correspond to a particular form of social demand; the child must deal with, and master, a central problem. Erikson (1965) is a major proponent of such a developmental timetable. At each stage a conflict between opposite poles in a pattern of reciprocity between the self and others has to be resolved. The crises are related to trust *vs.* mistrust; autonomy *vs.* shame; initiative *vs.* guilt; industry *vs.* inferiority; identity *vs.* identity diffusion; and so on. Failure to master previous developmental tasks is thought to hinder the individual in the next social endeavour. These formulations are difficult to prove of disprove, although they have compelling face-validity and are articles of faith for many psychologists.

There is insufficient space here to apply a critical analysis to the issues raised by Erikson's work; however it has heuristic value. In the view of the present author, Erikson's developmental outline provides a comprehensive framework within which to formulate clinical hypotheses and to link the theories (see Herbert, 1974; Lowe, 1972) of several important thinkers in developmental psychology—ideas which have a particular bearing on the theme of this chapter. For example, Danziger (1971) sees a connection between the bi-polar pairs (e.g. trust *vs.* mistrust) described by Erikson, and Piaget's ideas concerning assimilation and accommodation. The Piagetian description of cognitive development in terms of the interplay of accommodatory and assimilatory processes is analogous (according to Danziger) to the interplay of 'ego' and 'alter' in personality development—namely, the achievement of a balance between the poles of recognizing and adapting to the needs of others and imposing self-centred demands on the social environment. An extreme lack of balance in reciprocity between self and others in either direction gives rise to unsatisfactory social relationships.

From birth to about four years of age, to illustrate only two of the developmental tasks described by Erikson (1965), the child needs to develop a sense of trust and later, a growing autonomy. A lasting sense of trust, security, confidence, or optimism (as opposed to distrust, insecurity, inadequacy, or pessimism) is thought to be based upon affection, a degree of continuity of care-giving and the reasonably prompt satisfaction of the infant's needs (see Bowlby, 1969; Freud, 1939; Seligman, 1975; and Sullivan, 1953). The major hazards to the development of a perception of a benign, trustworthy, and predictable world—in which the child initiates his independence-seeking—are neglect, abuse, indifference, extreme inconsistency, and other conditions—social and physical—which interfere with the child's sense of personal adequacy or which hinder his acquisition of skills. White (1959), among others, has marshalled data from various sources to demonstrate that even very young babies exhibit a need to be competent, to master or deal effectively with their own environment. He calls this need 'effectance motivation' and considers it to be related to such motives as mastery, curiosity, and achievement.

Some children, because of tragic and depriving life experiences, lack crucial skills required to cope with life in a satisfactory manner. Consequently, they behave dysfunctionally in response to a variety of stresses, frustrations, and humiliations (physically handicapped children are massively over-represented in the population of youngsters with behaviour problems). If such children can be helped to become more competent, then they may have less recourse to problem behaviour. Seligman says:

> The infant begins a dance with his environment that will last throughout childhood. I believe it is the outcome of this dance that determines his helplessness or mastery. When he makes some response, it can either produce a change in the environment or be independent of what changes occur. At some primitive level, the infant calculates the correlation between response and outcome. If the correlation is zero, helplessness develops. If the correlation is highly positive or highly negative, this means the response is working, and the infant learns either to perform that response more frequently or to refrain from performing it, depending on whether the correlated outcome is good or bad. But over and above this, he learns that responding works, that in general there is synchrony between responses and outcomes. When there is asynchrony and he is helpless, he stops performing the response, and further, he learns that in general responding doesn't matter. Such learning has the same consequences that helplessness has in adults: lack of response initiation, negative cognitive set, and anxiety and depression. But this may be more disastrous for the infant since it is foundational: it is at the base of his pyramid of emotional and motivational structures. (Seligman, 1975, p. 139.)

In the same study Seligman suggests that what produces self-esteem and a sense of competence in a child and thus immunizes him against depression and helplessness, is not only the absolute quality of experience, but the perception that his own actions controlled the experience. He states that:

> To the degree that uncontrollable events occur, either traumatic or positive, depression will be predisposed and ego strength undermined. To the degree that controllable events occur, a sense of mastery and resistance to depression will result.

A child's incompetence may lie in the areas of motor activity (Browning and Stover, 1971), academic performance (Cohen and Filipczak, 1971), or interpersonal skills. Socially skilled children will be able to deal with provocative situations by compromise actions, persuasion, humour, and other appropriate verbal responses, which not only reduce the provocation but also preserve self-esteem without resort to extremes. In learning competencies and self-control the child achieves a lasting sense of autonomy. By contrast, children who lack social and verbal skills have few choices when it comes to dealing with (say) aggravations and are likely to become aggressive more easily. Failure leads to a loss of self-esteem and a pervasive sense of doubt and shame. Such children may profit greatly from training in various skills, such as non-aggressive ways of coping with interpersonal conflicts (see Kaufmann and Wagner, 1972). There is a programmatic text available which is designed to develop problem-solving skills in children (Spivack and Shure, 1974).

At each of the stages described by Erikson children demand parental support, and they try to limit the restraints parents put upon their impulses and pleasures. There seems to be a balance in child development which has to do with a compromise between sometimes incompatible mutual demands, and about a style of life which maximizes the mutually rewarding possibilities of the parent–child relationship. This balance, if it is achieved, is effected over a long period of time.

The process begins with the development of compliance in infancy. Stayton *et al.* (1971) distinguish between the process of learning the values and prescriptions of society and the disposition to comply with them. They observe that it is plausible to postulate that the most important step in the process of socialization occurs when a child develops a willingness to behave as his elders wish him to. This is a natural emergent under normal conditions; not having to be forced.

The specific timing and content of parental demands will depend on many factors, including family structure, ethnic heritage, social class, and cultural milieu. The development of an initial unspecified disposition towards compliance may be critical for the effectiveness of all further socialization practices. If a child lacks this tendency he may remain in many ways a stranger to his culture, regarding its rules and values from 'an external point of view'. For example, most parents are prepared to nurture and indulge an infant with a massive commitment for as long as he is palpably helpless and vulnerable. The age deemed appropriate for terminating what Ausubel and Sullivan (1970) call 'the stage of volitional independence and executive dependence' varies between two and four years in age in different cultures—it is nearer to two years in Western society. During this so-called transitional phase, they withdraw much of the attentive and uncritical deference they previously allowed the child because of his helpless status as a baby; furthermore, they begin to make fairly exacting demands of the child's self-restraint. Not surprisingly, this transitional phase is marked by 'problematic' behaviour in the child—a period referred to by these theoreticians as the stage of ego devaluation, but by the general public as the 'terrible two's' or 'three's'. Displays of oppositional and aggressive behaviour are common (see MacFarlane *et al.*, 1954). In the setting of a reasonably robust family, most parents cope with such outbursts. Parents differ in the degree to which they encourage a transition of a baby from a totally 'demanding' to a partly 'demand-obeying' status.

Many of the conduct-disordered children seen at the Child Treatment Research Unit (Herbert, 1978) seemed to be arrested at the demanding (egocentric) stage of development whatever their age. It is, in the opinion of the author, a 'sensitive period' with regard to the development (and therefore prevention) of many conduct disorders. They take root because of the inability of parents (for a variety of reasons: emotional or social) to confront their child's coercive behaviour (in some youngsters of an extreme nature) in a manner that will launch him into the vital later stages of moral development and into those processes of socialization which have to do with empathy and impulse control.

Patterson (1975) lists the following possibilities for the child's failure to substitute more adaptive, more mature behaviours for his primitive coercive repertoire: (1) the parents might neglect to condition prosocial skills (e.g., they seldom reinforce the use of language or other self-help skills); (2) they might provide rich schedules of positive reinforcement for coercive behaviours; (3) they might allow siblings to increase the frequency of aversive stimuli which are terminated when the target child uses coercive behaviours; (4) they may use punishment inconsistently for coercive behaviours; and/or (5) they may use weak conditioned punishers as consequences for coercion. He believes that the average three-year-old in American society has learned all of 14 noxious behaviours. Usually, such coercive behaviours display a steady decline in performance rates from a high point in infancy down to more moderate levels at the age of school entrance. The identified 'aggressive' youngster, according to Patterson, displays coercive behaviours at a level commensurate with a three- to four-year-old child, and, in this sense, is an exemplar of arrested socialization.

CONDUCT DISORDER AND INTERNALIZATION

There is an impressive consensus among studies of childhood problem behaviour using multivariate statistical methods (Hewitt and Jenkins, 1946; Pimm *et al.*, 1967; Quay and Quay, 1965) about the reality of a constellation of problems involving physical and verbal aggressiveness, disruptiveness, irresponsibility, non-compliance, and poor personal relationships. This behaviour pattern has been referred to as conduct disorder. Youngsters with conduct and delinquent disorders demonstrate a fundamental inability or unwillingness to adhere to the rules and codes of conduct, prescribed by society at its various levels. Such failures may be related to the temporary lapse of poorly established learned controls, to the failure to learn these controls in the first place, or to the fact that the behavioural standards a child has absorbed do not coincide with the norms of that section of society which enacts and enforces the rules.

Social learning theorists suggest that children with such serious problems are maladjusted because their early social conditioning has been ineffective. As a consequence they have failed to negotiate adequately the first stage in the internalization of an adequate conscience. There is an absence of a strong emotional aversion to anti-social acts, a diminished capacity to resist temptation, and a lack of feeling of remorse when harm has been inflicted (Herbert, 1978). The long-term implications of persistent and intense non-compliant, and therefore anti-social, behaviour in children are serious (Robins, 1966; West, 1967; West and Farrington, 1973). One of the child's major acquisitions on the road to becoming a social being is the development of internal controls over behaviour—the 'internalization' of standards of conduct and morality implied by the terms conscience or superego. Put in behavioural terms, a series of actions might be considered to be internalized to the extent that their maintenance has become independent of external outcomes—that is, to the extent that their reinforcing consequences are internally mediated, without the support of external events such as rewards and punishments (Aronfreed, 1968). Norm-abiding behaviour ultimately depends not merely on avoidance of externally imposed consequences but, more importantly, on the avoidance of noxious stimulation (anxiety/guilt) which has its source within the individual. The commonly held view (see Wright, 1971) is that anxiety about threatened withdrawal of parental love and approval is the major contributing factor to the child's internalization of parental values and to making the child more susceptible to adult influence. There is evidence that love withdrawal may contribute to the inhibition of anger (Hoffman and Saltzstein, 1967). The suggestion is that any action which threatens the withdrawal of the mother's approval provokes intense anxiety in the child, as distinct from aggression. To be effective (it is hypothesized) any disciplinary technique must enlist already existing emotional and motivational tendencies within the child. In other words, a basis of affection must fuel the child's need for approval and hence his readiness to attend to, and heed, what is being conveyed to him. Because of this identification with his mother, he will join in her criticism of his behaviour.

There is substantial agreement (see Wright, 1971) about further conditions conducive to the acquisition of internalized rule formation—or to put it more colloquially, standards of morality: firm moral demands made by parents upon their youngsters; the consistent use of sanctions; techniques of punishment that are psychological rather than physical (i.e., methods which signify or threaten withdrawal of approval and love); and an intensive use of reasoning and explanations (induction). There seems to be a subtle interaction between the child's cognitive structuring of situations, his ability to represent to himself punishment contingencies, and the extent of emotional arousal which is associated with his cognitions, during the socialization process (Aronfreed, 1968). The child's intellectual level, his verbal ability, and his ability to make a cognitive structure of the learning situation, are important sources of control. They facilitate control by representing the potential outcomes of his behaviour and by enhancing the internalization of the social rules. It is postulated that the moral labels (or concepts) that the child is learning become capable through the processes of generalization and discrimination of evoking the anxiety that was previously conditioned to misdeeds that were externally sanctioned. As the child matures, the way in which he cognitively structures a situation will determine whether or not anxiety is elicited. This has a bearing on whether he inhibits the 'immoral' act or not. What happens then is that disapproved behaviours and the cues associated with the immediate antecedents of such behaviours ('impulses') come to elicit anxiety. Parents may have, in a sense, a choice of whether they bring out, to a lesser or greater degree, one or other of the attributes of guilt and resistance to temptation in their children. This will depend primarily on two things: the timing of the sanctions they administer for misconduct, and the nature of the explanation they provide when they do so. There is evidence suggesting that punishment which immediately precedes a forbidden act (i.e., as the intention to transgress is forming and becoming explicit) maximizes resistance to temptation (Aronfreed, 1968; Aronfreed and Reber, 1965). Punishment has to be modulated. Above a certain optimal level of intensity it produces a state of emotionality in the child which appears to interfere with learning. If discrimination of the punished choice is difficult, intense punishment is actually more likely to lead to transgression. If he is to be able to exercise control over the consequences of his actions a child must be able to distinguish which aspect of his behaviour is being punished.

Socialization is particularly effective when training is presented in terms of a few well-defined principles. The use of inductive methods—explanations and reasons—especially when they elucidate a few clearly defined principles, seem to enhance moral awareness and resistance to temptation. Conformity of behaviour to specific norms in particular situations is more likely to depend on sanctions attached to those particular situations than on the general parent–child relationships. Love alone is not enough in moral training; precise teaching has to be provided in seemingly endless moral learning situations—with great attention paid to the detailed consequences of transgressions on the part of the child.

When the family fails in providing appropriate and consistent socialization experiences, the child seems to be particularly vulnerable to the development of conduct and delinquent disorders. This is reflected in empirical studies (see Bandura and Walters, 1963; Glueck and Glueck, 1950; McCord and McCord, 1959; West and Farrington, 1973). Typically the children with persistent disorders come from families where there is discord and quarrelling; where affection is lacking; where discipline is inconsistent, ineffective and either extremely severe or lax; where the family has broken up through divorce or separation; or where the children have had periods of being placed 'in care' at times of family crisis. Parents, especially fathers, have high rates of psychological problems themselves especially excessive aggression; they show an unusual amount of rejecting, hostile, and critical behaviour towards their offspring. In these cases, the prescriptions for problem resistance have eluded the best-intentioned social engineers and social workers. How does one legislate for the warm, loving, and consistent discipline (in which reasons are given) which appears to produce the rational kind of obedience rather than the blind and emotionally dependent following of orders? This, indeed, assumes that this is what we want!

If the preceding pages seem to imply a return to puritanical ideologies of the Victorian era, it should be emphasized that firmness (strictness)—laxness is a dimension of parenting independent of restrictive control—allowing autonomy.

Goldin's review (1969) of children's reports of their parents' behaviour suggests three rather than the conventional two orthogonal factors; the additional one being a dimension of firm versus lax control. It is possible for children to perceive their parents as firm but allowing autonomy at one and the same time; or indeed, lax but still controlling. Baumrind (1972) provides evidence for the assertion that firm control is associated with independence in the child, provided that the control is not restrictive of the child's opportunities to experiment and to make decisions within the limits defined. She finds support for the claim that parental values which stress individuality, self-expression, initiative, divergent thinking, and aggressiveness facilitate the development of independence in the child, provided that these qualities in the parent are not accompanied by lax and inconsistent discipline and unwillingness to make demands upon the child.

The achievement of such a synthesis is perhaps best illustrated in the philosophy of what Baumrind (1971) calls the 'authoritative parent'. This kind of mother attempts to direct her child's activities in a rational manner determined by the issues involved in particular disciplinary situations. She encourages verbal give-and-take, and shares with the child the reasoning behind her policy. She values both the child's self-expression and his so-called 'instrumental attributes' (respect for authority, work, and the like); she appreciates both independent self-will and disciplined conformity. Therefore, she exerts firm control at points where she and the child diverge in viewpoint, but does not hem in the child with restrictions. She recognizes her own special rights as an adult, but also the child's individual interests and special ways. The 'authoritative parent' affirms the child's present qualities, but also sets standards for future conduct. She uses reason as well as power to achieve her objectives. She does not base her decisions solely on the consensus of the group or the individual child's desires, but she also does not regard herself as infallible or divinely inspired. Such a parent may sound too good to be true; a paragon of the textbook virtues. Nevertheless, Baumrind found that 'authoritative parents' are most likely to facilitate the development of competence and self-reliance in young children by enhancing responsible, purposive, and independent behaviour.

Morgan (1975) paints a sombre picture of growing numbers of poorly socialized individuals who have scarcely acquired the rudiments of human culture. As she puts it:

> The most alarming aspect is probably the sharp increase in crime, violence and aimless destruction of all kinds, with larger proportionate increases as one goes down the age scale. Also much crime, often of a highly dangerous and serious nature, is committed by those well under the age of criminal responsibility. ... Actually, to use the expression 'crime' for much modern and anti-social behaviour is rather misleading, since it has no end beyond the most transitory titillation. The delinquent is frequently far too unsocialized to control his pursuit of instant excitement for rational gain.

Morgan is highly critical of the role of the present-day nuclear family and the vogue for child-centred Rousseauesque schemes of child-rearing. In her opinion they have proved unequal to the task of producing in children such socially desirable qualities as competence, cooperation, responsibility, and moral understanding. These methods represent an idealized or romanticized notion (Stone and Church, 1968) of the child as the 'noble savage'. This view sees original virtue all around and within the developmental forces of the child. Any interference with 'natural', 'instinctive' or 'spontaneous' developmental processes is wrong. 'Nature knows best; freedom is all', summarizes the essence of this simplistic but optimistic view. Tizard (1976) points out the emphasis on learning in pre-school children through self-initiated play, which has dominated the philosophy of ideas injected into education by Susan Isaacs in the 1930s. Tizard believes that these ideas led to the development in children of greater egocentricity and competitiveness, and less pro-social cooperative behaviour than would otherwise have been the case. Bronfenbrenner (1971) offers a critique of our educational philosophy with regard to older children. He regards the emphasis on cooperation in Soviet schools as conducive to more pro-social and less anti-social behaviour in contrast to the stress on individual achievement to be found in most North American and British classrooms. Other commentators (see Morgan, 1978; Wolfenstern, 1953) are scathing about the West's increasingly frivolous attitude to the socialization and acculturation of children with its preoccupation with self-direction and discovery, play, and a kind of 'fun-morality'. These matters are subjects of passionate debate, but are difficult to evaluate coolly or objectively.

Parental supervision relates to this theme and is another important variable (Kallarackal and Herbert, 1976). Several studies have shown that delinquents tend to be poorly supervised by their parents who neither know where they go nor attempt to regulate their activities (Glueck and Glueck, 1950; Craig and Glick, 1964; West and Farrington, 1973). Poor supervision tends to be closely associated with family disadvantage and disorganization. In urban environments, pre-adolescent, as well as adolescent, children tend to acquire their values more and more from outside the family; to some extent, their peers replace the parents as interpreters and enforcers of the moral code. Changes in attitudes and values are so quick to take place these days, that we get a hiatus between one generation and the next—the so-called generation gap. Such alienation between parent and child generations adds to the role of the peer group in the socialization process.

It has been found that the climate or atmosphere of his group can have an important influence on a child's personality (Campbell, 1964). One type of group—for example, a delinquent gang—can foster hostile, disobedient, uncreative individuals; another can develop confused, purposeless drifters; and still another produces cooperative, flexible, purposeful, altruistic children. In turn, the atmosphere of the group is determined by the qualities of its leaders and those of the other group members. When the peer group takes over some of the functions of parents (see Hewitt and Jenkins, 1946; Bronfenbrenner, 1971) the child's attachment to it tends to be extreme and biased toward being problematic (Wright, 1971).

Newson repudiates the arguments—which arise from class differences in rates of delinquency—that parents lower down the social scale are not interested in instilling moral values. As he puts it (Newson, 1972, p. 1):

> In our class-conscious society, one of the wilder stereotypes which must be rejected is what might be called the Fagin Fallacy—i.e. the notion that there exist substantial numbers of parents who deliberately encourage their children towards immoral behaviour. If such parents exist, we have yet to encounter them, despite having interviewed more than 700 mothers covering the entire social spectrum of an urban community, and notwithstanding the fact that our sample certainly includes a few families where the fathers or brothers of the child in question are well known to the police and have criminal records.

The truth, as usual, is more complex. One of the most obvious things which seems to happen to some working-class children is that they simply move out of normal adult control and supervision at an earlier age than their middle-class peers.

PRO-SOCIAL BEHAVIOURS AND SELF-CONTROL

In the public debates about discipline, the term is used as if it refers mainly to the punishment of 'bad behaviour'. In fact, the fostering of pro-social behaviour is at least as important as the suppression of undesirable actions. In the words of the old cliché: 'punishment tells you what you can't do; it doesn't tell you what you should do'. Praise and encouragement are vital for shaping up pro-social behaviour. There is evidence (see Graham, 1976) that from about the age of 7 years anti-social and pro-social behaviours are negatively correlated. Graham states, in an excellent review of the concept of helpfulness, that pro-social behaviour by itself is of little appropriate concern to the clinician. However, if its development is to some degree interrelated with aggressive problems and inability to form rewarding and enduring social relationships, it may become very relevant indeed.

Empathy is one facet of pro-social behaviour which should be of concern to social and clinical psychologists. It involves the child's capacity to control his behaviour by considering its effect on the experiences of others, particularly the potential victims of proscribed behaviour. Little is known about the development of this attribute, although presumably it has some of its antecedents in parental statements involving explanations of the effects of one's behaviour on others. The capacity for empathy requires object permanence, considerable abstract ability, and represents a rather advanced state in the development of moral behaviour. The relationship between the development of aggressive behaviour and empathy has been investigated (see Feshbach, 1973; Feshbach and Feshbach, 1972; Graham, 1976). The findings indicate that up to about the age of 6 years there is a positive correlation between the two: that is, the more aggressive the child the more empathic he is. As time goes by, however, the relationship between the two becomes more and more strongly negatively correlated. The theory postulated is that the early positive correlation arises because of the fact that in very young children both aggressive and pro-social behaviour are seen to a rather limited degree because of the general social immaturity of the child. As children mature the major variation between them is their general level of social maturity rather than the specific ways in which social behaviour is shown. By the age of six or seven, however, variation is greater between types of social behaviour and this differentiation becomes more marked throughout childhood and into adolescence and at least early adulthood.

The pursuit of altruism, idealism, and other moral virtues is explained by learning theorists in terms of instrumental learning. Because honesty and helpfulness have in the past been rewarded by parents, they become established habits; and since the concepts which structure such behaviour have also been associated with positively reinforcing experiences, the individual's recognition of his own honesty becomes rewarding. And, of course, strong habits of 'good' behaviour themselves have an inhibitory effect upon the corresponding but incompatible wrongdoing. Hoffman (1975) provides support for the relevance of parental modelling in helping behaviour. The importance of early learning experiences has also been shown in a controlled laboratory setting using the cooperative avoidance situation of Miller and colleagues (1963). Hartshorne and May (1928/30) found that altruistic behaviour on one test tended to be associated with similar behaviour on other tests and a small, positive association ($r = 0.33$) was found between overall measures of helpfulness and of honesty. Reviews of the concept of helpfulness can be found in Feldman (1977) and Mussen and Eisenberg-Berg (1977).

Bergin (1969) observes that many clinicians are keenly aware of the fact that increasing numbers of clients are seeking treatment for problems of impulse control such as excessive drinking, over-eating or drug-dependence.

Here, then, are further reasons for the growing interest in the self-directed aspects of behaviour modification, especially as it applies to adults. A person displays self-control when, in the relative absence of immediate external constraints, he engages in behaviour whose previous probability has been less than that of alternatively available behaviour. In other words, the person displaying self-control engages in behaviour that has been relatively unlikely in previous situations. So when an individual manipulates his own environment to produce changes in his own behaviour according to some standard we call it self-control. In terms of applications to preventive work, self-control can be a useful skill to develop in parents who are trying to bring about a change in their children (Brown *et al.*, 1976).

Some of the broader social antecedents of self-control have already been discussed above. Of more immediate impact there has been a rapid growth of interest and research into methods of treatment based on self-control training (Mahoney and Thoreson, 1974; Kanfer and Goldstein, 1975). It is now apparent that self-control can be viewed in terms of the systematic manipulation of antecedent stimulus events and response consequences. Another influence comes from cognitive psychology with methods like cognitive self-instruction (Meichenbaum, 1977).

SELF-PERCEPTION

Psychological problems are very much bound up with the child's favourable or unfavourable perception of himself—his self-image—and his perception of, and relationship with, other people. So many of the difficulties which a youngster has to cope with are social ones—the problems of getting on with other children of the same age, with teachers, with his own parents, and, by no means least, getting on with himself. He needs to like himself, to rely on himself, and to know himself. Positive self-attitudes are the basic ingredients of positive mental health, and negative self-concepts among the critical predispositions to maladjustment (Coopersmith, 1967).

There is clear evidence (Herbert, 1966) that all human beings old enough to have acquired even a rudimentary self-image need to perceive themselves in at least a moderately favourable light. A reasonable agreement between the self-concept ('myself as I am') and the concept of the ideal self ('myself as I would like to be') is one of the most important conditions for personal happiness and for satisfaction in life. Marked discrepancies arouse anxiety, and are associated with psychological problems (Marcia, 1967; Miskimins *et al.*, 1971; Rogers, 1959). Such discrepancies are a feature of neurotic personalities.

From a very tender age, people discover and make use of complex defensive reactions (Herbert, 1975; Lee and Herbert, 1970) designed to protect and enhance the gradually evolving self-image. Because the self is the central integrating aspect of the person any threat to its valuation is a vital threat to the very being of the individual. The strategies and tactics soften anxieties and failures and guard the integrity of the ego by increasing the feeling of personal worth. They also serve to fulfil the needs of the individual. When used to excess, involving as they do, a degree of self-deception, they may be labelled neurotic.

Coopersmith (1967) conducted a series of studies of self-esteem, applying the techniques of clinical, laboratory, and field investigation. The subjects consisted of a representative sample of normal boys aged 10–12, who were followed from this pre-adolescent stage to early adulthood. Various indices of self-esteem were used. Coopersmith provides evidence that the optimum conditions required for the achievement of high self-esteem in children are a combination of firm enforcement of limits on the child's behaviour, together with a marked degree of freedom (autonomy) within these limits. As long as the parentally imposed constraints are backed up by social norms outside the home, this provides the youngster with a clear idea of an orderly and trustworthy social reality which, in turn, gives him a solid basis for his own actions. Coopersmith found that children with a high degree of self-esteem are active, expressive individuals who tend to be successful both academically and socially. They initiate, rather than merely listen passively in discussions, are eager to express opinions, do not evade disagreement, are not particularly sensitive to criticism, are very interested in public affairs, showed little destructiveness in early childhood, and are little troubled by feelings of anxiety. They seem to trust their own perceptions and reactions, and are confident in the likelihood of success in their endeavours. Their approach to other persons is based upon the expectation that they will be well received. Their general optimism is not misplaced, but founded upon accurate assessments of their own abilities, social skills, and personal qualities. They are not self-conscious or obsessively preoccupied with personal problems. They are much less frequently affected with psychosomatic disorders (insomnia, headaches, fatigue, intestinal upset) than are youngsters of low self-esteem, who present a picture of discouragement and depression and in general the opposite features of those defining high self-esteem children.

SOCIAL SKILLS AND FRIENDSHIP

These findings have a bearing on the question of friendship and social skills. People who are lacking in social skills, who are clumsy or shy, may lead very miserable and lonely lives. Being friendless can lead to an intense sense of deprivation, alienation, and loneliness. Social isolation, in general, and friendlessness, in particular, have just such consequences for many children. According to the psychoanalyst, Karen Horney (1945) the basic situation of the neurotic is one of being isolated and helpless in what he regards as a hostile world. Horney sees much of the neurotic condition as being due to failures in the sorts of personal relationships that many people are fortunate enough to be able to take for granted. Objective studies (see Herbert, 1975) of well-liked persons showed that they were cooperative, even-tempered, showed initiative, and were willing at times to accept subordinate roles. Those not chosen as friends were characterized as quarrelsome, irritable, nagging, nervous, aggressive, inclined to interrupt group activity, resentful of being criticized, attention-demanding, and praise-seeking. There are obviously lessons to be acquired by increased self-awareness of those traits that are off-putting to people. Many books have been sold on the promise that they will provide the magical formula for friendship, but these usually neglect the vital skills of forming accurate impressions of other people—the foundations upon which personal liking, leading to friendship, is built. There is evidence (Herbert, 1975) that those who are the most popular or influential members of groups, and the most effective leaders, have more accurate perceptions, and discriminate between people more sharply, than other group-members. The most socially competent individuals are particularly sensitive, as can be gauged from the rich, complex and highly organized descriptions they give of other children.

There are important social skills which facilitate the making of friends; some individuals are fortunate to learn them easily, while others have to work at them. These include sensitivity to the needs and feelings of others, the ability to communicate warmth and affection, and the capacity to share goals and activities with others. These and other important social skills are products of childhood experiences, some of which have already been mentioned. There seem to be two basic attitudes which should be enhanced if friendships are going to come with reasonable ease:

(a) other people are perceived primarily as sources of satisfaction rather than deprivation;
(b) the child has opportunities for social interactions that reward and make enjoyable the giving, as well as the receiving, of affection.

There are several manuals and programmes available (e.g. Cotler and Guerra, 1976; Lange and Jakubowski, 1976; Zimbardo, 1977) which offer training in social skills. The topics covered typically include: improving powers of observation and accurate judgement; basic conversation skills such as listening, asking questions and talking; expressive skills such as the use of body language, social techniques for special situations; assertive training, etc. Behavioural methods also offer immediate remediation of, or 'inoculation' against, those destroyers of spontaneous social life: the helplessness associated with depression (Beck, 1970; Lefcourt, 1976; Seligman, 1975), and the avoidance behaviour associated with fear (Krumboltz and Krumboltz, 1972).

Immature, self-centred children are not always able to manage the give-and-take of friendship. Exchange theory (Herbert, 1975) gives us pointers to why this should be so; it provides one method of evaluating friendships and of helping children to improve their social attractiveness. A notable feature of friendship is the balance in the relationship that exists between the partners, often called 'status symmetry'. It concerns the mutual respect and lack of dominance and exploitation which characterize intimate and lasting relationships, involving an overall balance in the influence of each of the participants in friendly relationships.

Those theorists who employ 'exchange theory' in analysing aspects of social behaviour and friendship, view social interactions as a social exchange somewhat analogous to economic exchange; people are influenced (consciously and unconsciously) by the ratio of 'rewards' and the 'costs' incurred in the interaction. In the assessment of those who are friendless, it is useful to draw up a balance sheet. On the debit side, the term 'cost' is applied to deterrents that may be incurred in contacts with another person—such as hostility, anxiety, embarrassment, and the like. For attraction to a potential friend to occur the reward–cost outcome must be above the 'comparison level', a standard against which satisfaction is judged (see Thibaut and Kelley, 1959).

HELPING PARENTS

The approach of the Child Treatment Research Unit (based on the triadic model) has provided encouraging evidence (Herbert, 1978) of the ability of parents to help themselves and their problematic children. The triadic model:

> recognizes the profound influence that parents have on their children's

> development and mental health, an influence far greater than that which any professional could exert even with intensive intervention. It presupposes a cooperative working alliance between the parent and the helping professional, both of whom are interested in the welfare of the child. (Arnold, 1978, p. vii.)

What stands out in the work at the Unit with children who have been described as hyperactive, and with their mothers, is how many of the former have the attributes of what Thomas *et al.* (1968) called 'difficult' children or 'mother-killers'. (These were the infants in their sample who had adverse temperamental attributes and were problematic from birth; 70 per cent of them went on to develop quite serious behaviour problems.) Not surprisingly, many of the mothers (especially if they have borne the main brunt of rearing the child) were depressed, demoralized, and socially isolated. In a partnership between ourselves (acting as consultants) and parents (acting as 'therapists' of their own children) the latter were trained in general developmental principles and theories of behaviour change (Herbert, 1978). The idea was to teach parents to assess how problems are elicited and maintained within family and other social settings, so as to be able to generalize their knowledge and respond to situations in which the psychologist is not working directly with them, be it in the present or future.

O'Dell (1974) suggests that several lines of reasoning converge to reinforce the logic of the triadic model—involving parents (and others in the natural environment) in the psychological problems of childhood. Prevention is better than cure. As parents and teachers exert a significant influence during the formative years of early childhood (Douglas *et al.*, 1968) they are usually in a strong position to enhance satisfactory adjustment and moderate the genesis of behaviour problems. It would seem logical to introduce behaviour modification into parent and teacher education and training in preventive mental health programmes (Liberman *et al.*, 1976).

The triadic model gets around the problem of generalizing change from clinic-based sessions to the child's real world, and is geared to the only people—parents—who can intervene often enough and long enough to produce the long-term changes in what are often (in the case of the more serious problems of childhood) matters of faulty socialization. After all the parents are 'on the spot' most of the time to initiate and consolidate social learning experiences; they are likely to facilitate therapy (or what is better called an educative exercise) because of their emotional significance to the child. Help is therefore most logically directed to the modification of that environment rather than withdrawing the child from it. The common goal of these procedures is to develop in the parents an awareness of their own importance in producing and maintaining desirable and undesirable behaviours in their children. Because the intervention involves the active application of social learning principles, it tends to have 'face validity' for parents; they are all in the business of behavioural change, utilizing informal 'principles' of learning (modelling and operant ones, in particular) to attain the objectives they set for their offspring.

As behaviour is currently viewed as a function of the total environment, behaviour modification is not only about changing the undesirable behaviour of 'problem children'. It is also about altering the behaviour of the persons—parents, teachers and others—who form a significant part of the child's social world. Such assumptions about behaviour change lead inexorably (Tharp and Wetzel, 1969) to the proposition that maladaptive behaviour can most effectively be changed by the therapeutic application of principles of learning to the natural environment in which it has developed. Parents should themselves be provided with what knowledge we have, in order to cope better with their child. This is not the prescriptive, detailed 'do this ... do that ...' formulae of the past; rather it is the application of principles of learning (firmly anchored in Social and Developmental Psychology) to the treatment and, increasingly, the prevention, of personal problems. The fact that this approach has been taught to parents more often than other more traditional approaches may be due to certain advantages that behaviour modification is assumed to have:

(a) persons without a considerable amount of psychological knowledge can grasp the concepts;
(b) many persons can be taught at one time;
(c) a relatively short training period is needed;
(d) parents often prefer a model of problem development and resolution that does not assume 'sick' behaviour based on a medical model;
(e) many childhood problems consist of well-defined behaviours that are conducive to behavioural treatment;
(f) behaviour modification is particularly applicable to the natural environment (O'Dell, 1974).

There have been numerous attempts to train parents to modify their child's behaviour, and there are several reviews which evaluate these studies (Gelfand and Hartmann, 1975; Berkowitz and Graziano, 1972; Repucci and Saunders, 1974; Cone and Sloop, 1974; O'Dell, 1974; Johnson and Katz, 1973; Pawlicki, 1970; MacDonough and McNamara, 1973). These reviews are critical of many of the published accounts of parent training on a number of factors, particularly in terms of poor experimental designs. Tavormina (1975) and Heifetz (1977) have assessed the effects of behaviour modification training with parents of mentally handicapped children using pre- and post-training measures of change.

All these developments have extended the scope of the therapeutic task. It still requires rigorous training and safeguards, but it need not remain so elitist (or esoteric) in the sense of requiring an expensive analytic training on the part of a member of only one or two privileged professions. The practitioners of behaviour modification increasingly include members of professional groups other than psychologists and psychiatrists. Social workers, general medical practitioners, nurses, teachers, and residential child-care staff have been trained to carry out effective programmes. There is more flexibility in what is increasingly becoming a community-based therapeutic approach; there needs to be, given the conjunction of high rates of childhood disorder and scarce mental health resources (Miller *et al.*, 1971). There are far more children in need of help for their psychological problems than there are psychiatrists, psychologists, or specialist social workers working in the traditional dyadic mould, to meet the demand.

Depending upon the requirements of the particular case, a behaviour modification programme may involve work in the consulting room, classroom or institution, the parental home, or even on the neighbourhood street, and the use of specific techniques by a professional, the parents, friends, or the child himself. There are wide variations, in terms of type and extent of parental involvement, in work in the natural environment; these range from carrying out simple instructions in contingency management to a full involvement as co-therapists in all aspects of observation, recording, programme planning, and implementation. The didactic element might range from basic behavioural analysis and practice to the mastery of general learning principles. In some cases the wider family and community are engaged in the programme. For example, siblings have been enlisted to give a helping hand; as have peers and parent groups. Children are also trained to be their own behaviour therapists. The triadic model is also being applied with some success in classroom settings using teachers as mediators of change (O'Leary and O'Leary, 1972).

Thomas *et al.* (1968) are at pains to point out that a given combination of behavioural styles in a specific child does not in and of itself lead to behaviour problems, but that it is the interaction between these stylistic characteristics and the child's environment which can eventuate in clinical referral. They regard individual behavioural style not as an inevitability that must be fatalistically accepted, but as a condition which, once recognized, gives both parent and child logical means of coping with individual differences.

This theme of 'person-in-situation' is a persistent one in the literature on socialization. Minuchin *et al.* (1969) studied modern *v.* traditional school methods and their influence on such attributes as self-acceptance, perception of sex-role, maturity, the sense of stability, uncertainty, and direction. Both educational approaches were found to have their strengths and weaknesses, and clearly neither school environment was good or bad for *all* children. It is an intriguing question whether the incidence of behaviour disorders among 'difficult children' can be reduced by educating parents and teachers to accept a child's individuality and helping them to adapt to his behavioural style so that the child in turn can adapt to the successive demands of socialization. Some children, for example, respond to a structured environment at home (Herbert, 1978) and at school (Minuchin *et al.*, 1969): several bright children in the Minuchin study were floundering, unable to study or perform effectively because their personality style ill-fitted the more open-ended environment. Danziger (1971) makes the interactional point that:

> there is overwhelming evidence that children learn complex acts through cognitive processes based on observation rather than through being

trained by external reinforcements administered by the parent. This does not mean that the reward and punishment of specific components of behaviour plays *no* role in social learning; it does mean that that role is defined in a context provided by the very special reactions that people have to people.

OVERVIEW

The dictates of space (and, admittedly, the author's special interests) have made this a highly selective chapter. Many important issues—such as impaired communication within the family (Waxler and Mishler, 1970); parental deviance (Robins and Lewis, 1966; Rutter, 1966; West & Farrington, 1973); social structure of the family (Clausen, 1966; Rutter and Madge, 1976); socialization by the school (Morrison and McIntyre, 1971); the child's position in the social structure of the classroom (Glidewell *et al.*, 1966)—have been glossed over or omitted. The scope of the subject is limitless (see Lazarus, 1966; Sechrest and Wallace, 1967; Rutter and Hersov, 1977). It is bound to be if one accepts the terms of reference set by Fromm, who asserts that:

> in order that any society may function well, its members must acquire the kind of character which makes them want to act in the way they have to act as members of the society or a special class within it. They have to desire what objectively is necessary for them to do. (Fromm, 1953.)

This statement begs innumerable questions, especially ones concerning the culture-bound methodology and value judgements so pervasive in developmental research and theory (see Danziger, 1971). The literature tells us that the best-adjusted children (nursery children) have parents who are warm, nurturant, supportive, and controlling with high expectations (Baumrind, 1967). Then again, the development of conscience has been shown to be related to such factors as parental warmth and parental use of reasoning (induction) as a technique of discipline; indeed reasoning is also related to the inhibition of aggression (Bandura & Walters, 1963; Baumrind, 1967). But what do such findings really mean? How far can they be generalized across time, culture, and situations outside the scope of the original studies? We require more cross-cultural studies if we are to obtain deeper insights into the absolutes and relativities of socialization processes and problem development; and we need a more refined level of analysis than our present correlations between fairly coarse-grained variables and indices of maladaptive functioning.

We know, for example, that the children of parents with a chronic or recurrent mental disorder are themselves at risk of manifesting psychiatric disturbance; several forms of separation, loss, and disturbed family relationships also contribute significantly to the genesis of different forms of childhood psychopathology. However, it seems that it is family discord and disharmony (rather than the separation of death, divorce, or some other break-up of the home) which are pathognomonic in the development of delinquent patterns. Different causal mechanisms and principles are probably at work, but understanding of them is limited. This is most true of the 'exceptional cases'—the children who are the exception to the empirical 'rule' that says 'by all accounts that child, in those circumstances, *should* be a problem!' Our knowledge is made up of a modestly comprehensive but disparate set of research generalizations which is helpful up to a point; but it lets us down because we cannot spell out precisely the individual factors which make one child highly susceptible (and another resistant) to similar distressing life-circumstances. Nevertheless there are probably enough broad hints concerning the factors which promote or hinder problem development to help families function better in these times of changing social conditions (Herbert and O'Driscoll, 1978). The greatest need for caution is in the neglect of a transactional model of child development. Neither general patterns of parent–child relationships, nor specific methods of child-rearing and discipline—considered *in vacuo*—prove crucial in the development of problems. Nor do intrinsic temperamental or personality attributes of the child. Significance is to be found in a particular care-giver's interaction with a particular child and the social–psychological background to the use of particular child-rearing methods. The affectional background to the behaviours modelled by the parent is important, as is the consistency of the cognitive structuring and sanctioning of specific moral (and other social) 'lessons' the child receives.

REFERENCES

Ainsworth, M. D. (1973). The development of infant–mother attachment. In: B. M. Caldwell and H. N. Ricciuti (Eds.), *Review of Child Development Research*. (Chicago: University of Chicago Press.)

Arnold, L. E. (Ed.) (1978). *Helping Parents Help Their Children*. (New York: Brunner/Mazel.)

Aronfreed, J. (1968). *Conduct and Conscience*. (New York: Academic Press.)

Aronfreed, J. and Reber, A. (1965). Internalized behavioral suppression and the timing of social punishment. *Journal of Personality and Social Psychology*, **1,** 3–16.

Ausubel, D. P. and Sullivan, E. V. (1970). *Theory and Problems of Child Development*, 2nd edn. (London: Grune & Stratton.)

Bandura, A. (1977). *Social Learning Theory*. (Englewood Cliffs: Prentice-Hall.)

Bandura, A. and Walters, R. H. (1963). *Social Learning and Personality Development*. (New York: Holt, Rinehart & Winston.)

Baumrind, D. (1967). Child care practices anteceding three patterns of preschool behaviour. *Genetic Psychology Monographs*, **75,** 43–88.

Baumrind, D. (1971). Current patterns of parental authority. *Developmental Psychology Monograph*, **4**(1), Pt. 2, pp. 1–103.

Baumrind, D. (1972). Socialization and instrumental competence in young children. In: W. W. Hartup (Ed.), *The Young Child: Reviews of Research*, Vol. 2. (Washington DC: National Association for the Education of Young Children.)

Beck, A. T. (1970). Cognitive therapy: nature and relation to behavior therapy. *Behavior Therapy*, **1,** 184–200.

Becker, W. C. (1964). Consequences of different kinds of parental discipline. In: Hoffman, M. L. and Hoffman, L. W. (Eds.), *Review of Child Development Research*, Vol. 1, pp. 169–208. (New York: Russell Sage Foundation.)
Behrens, M. L. (1954). Child rearing and the character structure of the mother. *Child Development*, **25,** 225–238.
Bergin, A. E. (1969). Self-regulation technique for impulse control disorders. *Psychotherapy: Theory, Research and Practice*, **6,** 113–118.
Berkowitz, B. P. and Graziano, A. M. (1972). Training parents as behavior therapists: a review. *Behaviour Research and Therapy*, **10,** 297–318.
Bowers, K. S. (1973). Situationism in psychology: an analysis and a critique. *Psychological Review*, **80,** 307–336.
Bowlby, J. (1969). *Attachment and Loss*, Vol. 1: *Attachment*. (London: Hogarth Press.)
Bronfenbrenner, U. (1971). *Two Worlds of Childhood: U.S.A. and U.S.S.R.* (London: Allen & Unwin.)
Brown, J. H., Gamboa, A. M., Birkimer, J. and Brown, R. (1976). Some possible effects of parent-self-control training on parent–child interactions. In: E. J. Mash, L. C. Handy and L. A. Hamerlynck (Eds.), *Behaviour Modification Approaches to Parenting*, pp. 180–192. (New York: Brunner/Mazel.)
Browning, R. M. and Stover, D. O. (1971). *Behavior Modification in Child Treatment: An Experimental and Clinical Approach*. (Chicago: Aldine-Atherton.)
Bruch, H. (1954). Parent education and the illusion of omnipotence. *American Journal of Orthopsychiatry*, **24,** 723.
Caldwell, B. M. (1964). The effects of infant care. In: M. L. Hoffman and L. W. Hoffman (Eds.), *Review of Child Development Research*, Vol. 1. (New York: Russell Sage Foundation.)
Campbell, J. D. (1964). Peer relations in early childhood. In: M. L. Hoffman and L. W. Hoffman (Eds.), *Review of Child Development Research*, Vol. 1. (New York: Russell Sage Foundation.)
Chess, S. (1964). Editorial: mal-de-mer. *American Journal of Orthopsychiatry*, **34,** 613.
Chess, S. (1971). Genesis of behaviour disorder. In: J. G. Howells (Ed.), *Modern Perspectives in International Child Psychiatry*. (New York: Brunner/Mazel.)
Clarke, A. and Clarke, A. D. B. (1976). *Early Experience: Myth and Reality*. (London: Open Books.)
Clausen, J. A. (1966). Family structure, socialization and personality. In: L. W. Hoffman and M. L. Hoffman (Eds.), *Review of Child Development Research*, Vol. 2. (New York: Russell Sage Foundation.)
Cohen, H. L. and Filipczak, J. (1971). *A New Learning Environment*. (San Francisco: Jossey-Bass.)
Cone, J. D. and Sloop, E. W. (1974). Parents as agents of change. In: A. Jacobs and W. Spradlin (Eds.), *The Group as Agent of Change*. (New York: Behavior Publications.)
Coopersmith, S. (1967). *The Antecedents of Self-Esteem*. (London: W. H. Freeman.)
Cotler, S. B. and Guerra, J. J. (1976). *Assertion Training: A Humanistic–Behavioural Guide to Self-Dignity*. (Champaign, Illinois: Research Press.)
Craig, M. M. and Glick, S. J. (1964). *A Manual of Procedures for Application of the Glueck Prediction Tables*. (New York: City Youth Board.)
Danziger, K. (1971). *Socialization*. (Harmondsworth: Penguin Books.)
Douglas, J. W. B., Ross, J. M. and Simpson, H. R. (1968). *All Our Future*. (London: Peter Davies.)
Erikson, E. (1965). *Childhood and Society* (rev. edn.). (Harmondsworth: Penguin Books.)
Eysenck, H. J. and Nias, D. K. B. (1978). *Sex, Violence and the Media*. (London: Temple Smith.)

Feldman, M. P. (1977). *Criminal Behaviour: A Psychological Analysis.* (London: Wiley.)

Feshbach, N. (1973). 'The relationship of child rearing factors to children's aggression, empathy, and related positive and negative social behaviours'. (Paper presented to NATO Conference on Determinants and Origins of Aggressive Behaviour: Monte Carlo, Monaco, July 1973.)

Feshbach, N. and Feshbach, S. (1972). Children's aggression. In: P. H. Mussen, J. J. Conger, and J. Kagan (Eds.), *Basic and Contemporary Issues in Developmental Psychology.* (London: Harper & Row.)

Frank, G. H. (1965). The role of the family in the development of psychopathology. *Psychological Bulletin*, **64,** 191–203.

Freud, S. (1956). The psychogenesis of a case of homosexuality in a woman. *Collected Papers* Vol. 2. (London: The Hogarth Press, 1956.)

Fromm, E. (1953). Individual and social origins of neurosis. In: C. Kluckhohn and H. A. Murray (Eds.), *Personality in Nature, Society and Culture* (New York: Alfred A. Knopf.)

Gelfand, D. M. and Hartmann, D. P. (1975). *Child Behaviour: Analysis and Therapy.* (Oxford: Pergamon Press.)

Glidewell, J. C., Kantor, M. B., Smith, L. M., and Stringer, L. A. (1966). Socialization and social structure in the classroom. In: L. W. Hoffman and M. L. Hoffman (Eds.), *Review of Child Development Research*, Vol. 2, pp. 221–256. (New York: Russell Sage Foundation.)

Glueck, S. and Glueck, E. (1950). *Unravelling Juvenile Delinquency.* (Cambridge, Mass: Harvard University Press.)

Goldin, T. C. (1969). A review of children's reports of parent behaviours. *Psychological Bulletin*, **71,** 222–236.

Graham, P. (1976). 'The Roots of Helpfulness'. Chairman's address delivered to the Child Psychiatry Section of the Royal College of Psychiatrists on Thursday 23rd September 1976 at St. Catherine's College, Oxford.

Graham, P., Rutter, M., and George, S. (1973). Temperamental characteristics as predictors of behaviour disorders in children. *American Journal of Orthopsychiatry*, **43,** 328–339.

Harper, L. V. (1975). The scope of offspring effects: from caregiver to culture. *Psychological Bulletin*, **82**(5), 784–801.

Hartshorne, H. and May, M. A. (1928/29/30). *Studies in the Nature of Character.* (New York: Macmillan Co.)

Heifetz, L. J. (1977). Behavioral training for parents of retarded children: alternative formats based on instructional manuals. *American Journal of Mental Deficiency*, **82,** 194–203.

Herbert, M. (1966). The development of the self-image and ego-identity. *Common Factor Monographs*, **4,** 61–68.

Herbert, M. (1974). *Emotional Problems of Development in Children.* (London: Academic Press.)

Herbert, M. (1975). *Problems of Childhood: A Guide for All Concerned.* (London: Pan Books.)

Herbert, M. (1978). *Conduct Disorders of Childhood and Adolescence: A Behavioural Approach to Assessment and Treatment* (Chichester: Wiley.)

Herbert, M. and O'Driscoll, B. (1978). Behavioural Casework: A Social Work Method for Family Settings. *Australian Child and Family Welfare Journal*, **3**(2), 14–25.

Hewitt, L. E. and Jenkins, R. L. (1946). *Fundamental Patterns of Maladjustment: The Dynamics of their Origin.* (Springfield, Illinois: Thomas.)

Hoffman, M. L. (1970). Moral development. In: P. H. Mussen, (Ed.), *Carmichael's Manual of Child Psychology*, pp. 261–359. (London: Wiley.)

Hoffman, M. L. (1975). Altruistic behaviour and the parent–child relationship. *Journal of Personality and Social Psychology*, **31,** 937–943.

Hoffman, M. L. and Saltzstein, H. D. (1967). Parent discipline and the child's moral development. *Journal of Personal and Social Psychology*, **5,** 45–57.

Horney, K. (1945). *Our Inner Conflicts*. (New York: Norton.)
Johnson, C. A. and Katz, C. (1973). Using parents as change agents for their children: a review. *Journal of Child Psychology and Psychiatry*, **14,** 181–200.
Kallarackal, A. M. and Herbert, M. (1976). The adjustment of Indian immigrant children. *Growing Up: A New Society Social Studies Reader*, pp. 6–9. (IPC: London.)
Kanfer, F. H. & Goldstein, A. P. (1975). *Helping People Change*. (Oxford: Pergamon Press.)
Kaufmann, L. M. and Wagner, B. R. (1972). Barb: A systematic treatment technology for temper control disorders. *Behaviour Therapy*, **3,** 84–90.
Krumboltz, J. D. and Krumboltz, H. B. (1972.) *Changing Children's Behaviour*. (Englewood Cliffs: Prentice-Hall.)
Lange, A. J. and Jakubowski, P. (1976). *Responsible Assertive Behaviour*. (Champaign, Illinois: Research Press.)
Lazarus, R. S. (1966). *Psychological Stress and the Coping Process* (New York: McGraw-Hill.)
Lee, S. G. M. and Herbert, M. (Eds.), (1970). *Freud and Psychology*. (Harmondsworth: Penguin Books.)
Lefcourt, H. M. (1976). *Locus of Control*. (London: Wiley.)
Levy, D. M. (1943). *Maternal Overprotection*. (New York: Columbia University Press.)
Liberman, R. P., King, L. W., and DeRisi, W. J. (1976). Behaviour analysis and therapy in community mental health. In: H. Leitenberg (Ed.), *Handbook of Behaviour Modification and Behaviour Therapy*. (Englewood Cliffs: Prentice-Hall.)
Lowe, G. R. (1972). *The Growth of Personality: from Infancy to Old Age*. (Harmondsworth: Penguin Books.)
McCandless, B. (1969). *Children: Behaviour and Development* (2nd edn.). (London: Holt, Rinehart & Winston.)
McCord, W. and McCord, J. (1959). *The Origins of Crime: A New Evaluation of the Cambridge–Somerville Youth Study*. (Columbia: Columbia University Press.)
MacDonough, T. S. and McNamara, J. R. (1973). Design criteria relationships in behaviour therapy research with children. *Journal of Child Psychology and Psychiatry*, **14,** 271–282.
MacFarlane, J. W., Allen, L., and Honzik, M. (1954). *A Developmental Study of the Behaviour Problems of Normal Children*. (Berkeley: University of California Press.)
Mahoney, M. J. and Thoreson, C. E. (1974). *Self-Control: Power to the Person*. (Monterey, Cal.: Brooks, Cole.)
Marcia, J. E. (1967). Ego-identity status: relationship to change in self-esteem, general maladjustment and authoritarianism. *Journal of Personality*, **35,** 118–33.
Meichenbaum, D. (1977). *Cognitive Behaviour Modification*. (New York: Plenum Press.)
Miller, R. E., Banks, J. H., and Ogawa, N. (1963). Role of social expression in cooperative–avoidance conditioning in monkeys. *Journal of Abnormal and Social Psychology*, **67,** 24–30.
Miller, L. C., Hampe, E., Barrett, C. L. and Noble, H. (1971). Children's deviant behaviour within the general population. *Journal of Consulting and Clinical Psychology*, **37,** 16–22.
Minuchin, P., Biber, B., Shapiro, E., and Zimiles, H. (1969). *The Psychological Impact of School Experience*. (New York: Basic Books.)
Miskimins, R. W., Wilson, L. T., Braucht, G. N. and Berry, K. L. (1971). Self-concept and psychiatric symptomatology. *Journal of Clinical Psychology*, **27,** 185–187.
Morgan, P. (1975). *Child Care: Sense and Fable*. (London: Temple Smith.)
Morgan, P. (1978). *Delinquent Fantasies*. (London: Temple Smith.)
Morrison, A. and McIntyre, D. (1971). *Schools and Socialization*. (Harmondsworth: Penguin Books.)
Mussen, P. and Eisenberg-Berg, N. (1977). *Roots of Caring, Sharing, and Helping*. (San Francisco: Freeman.)

Newson, J. (1972). 'Some Observations on the Subject of the Development of Conscience in Ordinary Young Children'. Paper read at the symposium 'Aspects of Moral Development'; British Association for the Advancement of Science, University of Leicester, September 1972.

O'Dell, S. (1974). Training parents in behavior modification: a review. *Psychological Bulletin*, **81**(7), 418–433.

O'Leary, K. D. and O'Leary, S. G. (1972). *Classroom Management: The Successful Use of Behavior Modification*. (New York: Pergamon Press.)

Orford, J. (1976). *The Social Psychology of Mental Disorder*. (Harmondsworth: Penguin Books.)

Patterson, G. R. (1975). The coercive child: architect or victim of a coercive system? In: L. Hamerlynck, L. C. Handy, and E. J. Mash (Eds.), *Behavior Modification and Families: I. Theory and Research; II. Applications and Developments*. (New York: Brunner/Mazel.)

Pawlicki, R. (1970). Behavior therapy research with children: a critical review. *Canadian Journal of Behavioral Science*, **2,** 281–291.

Pimm, J. B., Quay, H. C., and Werry, J. S. (1967). Dimensions of problem behavior in first grade children. *Psychology in the Schools*, **4,** 155–157.

Quay, H. C. and Quay, L. C. (1965). Behavior problems in early adolescence. *Child Development*, **36,** 215–220.

Repucci, N. D. and Saunders, J. T. (1974). Social psychology of behavior modification: problems of implementation in natural settings. *American Psychologist*, **29,** 649–660.

Robins, L. N. (1966). *Deviant Children Grown Up*. (Baltimore: Williams & Wilkins.)

Robins, L. N. and Lewis, R. G. (1966). The role of the antisocial family in school completion and delinquency: a three-generation study. *Sociological Quarterly*, **7,** 500–514.

Rogers, C. R. (1959). A theory of therapy, personality and inter-personal relationships, as developed in the client-centred framework. In: S. Koch (Ed.), *Psychology: The Study of a Science*, Vol. 3. (New York: McGraw-Hill.)

Ross, A. O. (1968). Conceptual issues in the evaluation of brain damage. In: J. L. Khanna (Ed.), *Brain Damage and Mental Retardation: A Psychological Evaluation*. (Springfield, Illinois: Thomas.)

Rutter, M. (1966). *Children of Sick Parents*. (London: Oxford University Press.)

Rutter, M. (1975). *Helping Troubled Children*. (Harmondsworth: Penguin Education.)

Rutter, M. (1977). Other family influences. In: M. Rutter and L. Hersov (1977).

Rutter, M. and Hersov, L. (1977). *Child Psychiatry: Modern Approaches*. (Oxford: Blackwell.)

Rutter, M. and Madge, N. (1976). *Cycles of Disadvantage*. (London: Heinemann.)

Rutter, M., Tizard, J., and Whitmore, K. (Eds.) (1970). *Education, Health and Behaviour*. (London: Longmans Green.)

Sabshin, M. (1968). Toward more rigorous definitions of mental health. In: L. M. Roberts, N. S. Greenfield and M. H. Miller (Eds.), *Comprehensive Mental Health*. (Madison: University of Wisconsin Press.)

Sameroff, A. J. and Chandler, M. J. (1975). Reproductive risk and the continuum of caretaking casualty. In: S. Scarr-Salapatek and G. Siegel (Eds.), *Review of Child Development Research*. (Chicago: University of Chicago Press.)

Schaefer, E. S. (1959). A circumplex model for maternal behaviour. *Journal of Abnormal Social Psychology*, **59,** 226–235.

Schaffer, H. R. (Ed.) (1977). *Studies in Mother–Infant Interaction*. (London: Academic Press.)

Sears, R. R. (1975). You ancients revisited: a history of child development. In: E. Mavis Hetherington (Ed.), *Review of Child Developmental Research*, pp. 1–74. (Chicago: University of Chicago Press.)

Sears, R. R., Maccoby, E. E., and Levin, H. (1957). *Patterns of Child Rearing*. (Evanston, Illinois: Row, Peterson.)

Sechrest, L. and Wallace, J. (1967). *Psychology and Human Problems.* (Columbus: Charles Merrill.)

Seligman, M. E. P. (1975). *Helplessness.* (San Francisco: Freeman.)

Shepherd, M., Oppenheim, B., and Mitchell, S. (1971). *Childhood Behaviour and Mental Health.* (London: University of London Press.)

Spivack, G. and Shure, M. B. (1974). *Social Adjustment of Young Children: Cognitive Approach to Solving Real Life Problems.* (San Francisco: Jossey-Bass.)

Stayton, D. J., Hogan, R. and Ainsworth, M. (1971). Infant obedience and maternal behaviour: the origin of socialization reconsidered. *Child Development*, **42,** 1057–1069.

Stone, J. and Church, J. (1968). *Childhood and Adolescence*, 2nd edn. (New York: Random House.)

Sullivan, H. S. (1953). *The Interpersonal Theory of Psychiatry.* (New York: Norton.)

Tavormina, J. B. (1975). Relative effectiveness of behavioural and reflective group counselling with parents of mentally retarded children. *Journal of Consulting and Clinical Psychology*, **43,** 22–31.

Tharp, R. G. and Wetzel, R. J. (1969). *Behaviour Modification in the Natural Environment.* (London: Academic Press.)

Thibaut, J. W. and Kelley, H. H. (1959). *The Social Psychology of Groups.* (New York: Wiley.)

Thomas, A. and Chess, S. (1977). *Temperament and Development.* (New York: Brunner/Mazel.)

Thomas, A., Chess, S., and Birch, H. G. (1968). *Temperament and Behaviour Disorders in Children.* (London: University of London Press.)

Tizard, B. Paper reported in Graham (1976).

Vincent, C. E. (1951). Trends in infant care ideas. *Child Development*, **22,** 199–209.

Waxler, N. and Mishler, E. G. (1970). Experimental studies of families. In: L. Berkowitz, (Ed.), *Advances in Experimental Social Psychology*, Vol. 5. (London: Academic Press.)

West, D. J. (1967). *The Young Offender.* (Duckworth and Penguin Books.)

West, D. J. and Farrington, D. P. (1973). *Who Becomes Delinquent?* (London: Heinemann.)

White, R. W. (1959). Motivation reconsidered—the concept of competence. *Psychological Review*, **66,** 297–333.

Wolfenstern, M. (1953). Trends in infant care. *American Journal of Orthopsychiatry*, **23,** 120–130.

Wright, D. S. (1971). *The Psychology of Moral Behaviour.* (Harmondsworth: Penguin Books.)

Yarrow, M. R., Campbell, J. D. and Burton, R. V. (1968). *Child Rearing: An Inquiry into Research and Methods.* (San Francisco: Jossey-Bass.)

Zigler, E. and Child, I. L. (1969). Socialization. In: G. Lindzey and E. Aronson (Eds.), *Handbook of Social Psychology*, Vol. 3, (New York: Addison-Wesley.)

Zimbardo, P. G. (1977). *Shyness: What It Is; What To Do About It.* (London: Addison-Wesley.)

The Social Psychology of Psychological Problems
Edited by P. Feldman and J. Orford

3

The Personal Context: Intimate Relationships

STEVE DUCK

INTERPERSONAL RELATIONS AND PSYCHOLOGICAL PROBLEMS

Introduction

Whilst the likelihood of a link between social relationships and psychological problems has been apparent for centuries (Euripides, *c.* 442 B.C.), constructive dialogue between those social psychologists who research personal relationships and those clinical psychologists who deal with consequent psychological problems is a relatively recent phenomenon. Henderson (1977) is one recent author to have stimulated such a dialogue. His argument is that inability to satisfy a need for affectively positive interaction with others leads to psychiatric and even medical morbidity, and it is also clear from the work of Perlman and Peplav (in press) that, for some people, loneliness can produce severe psychological traumata and abnormalities (e.g. severe hallucinations, usually about interacting with other people). It is also probable that many psychological problems in adolescence, such as hyperaggressiveness, severe withdrawal or personality disorder, stem from relationship difficulties (La Gaipa and Wood in press).

Yet there is something strangely unsatisfying about the general assertion that psychological problems and social relationships may be linked. What is now needed is a rigorous examination of the *nature* of such links in the light of recent empirical evidence. It is a notion (owing its theoretical origin largely to Caplan, 1974) which is relatively untried and unexplored, except in a general way, and the voluminous experimental research on Interpersonal Attraction (IPA) is rarely a feature of those analyses that do exist. First among several important distinctions that must be made in embarking on this task is the following: we must throughout distinguish (i) the possibility that people with certain types of problem (e.g. those labelled 'personality disorders', seek out or happen to establish strange and destructive sorts of relationship; from (ii) the possiblity that a lack of satisfactory relationships somehow produces the clinical problem (naturally, this is the more interesting and less researched of the two possible directions of causality—Dewhurst and Duck, 1978).

I am extremely grateful to John La Gaipa, University of Windsor, Canada for his generous help with redrafting parts of this chapter.

Second, we need to note that many workers have observed a peculiar similarity between the process of treating problems in the clinic and the process of forming social relationships (Nelson-Jones and Strong, 1976). Some authors (e.g. Henderson, 1974) have suggested that some socially deficient people seek clinical assistance simply to elicit from a therapist the care-giving behaviour that is normally supplied by a close network of social relationships, whilst others (e.g. Goldstein, 1971) have wanted to argue that the proper treatment for clinical problems is likely to be speeded up if the therapist consciously acts in the role of friend for his client.

What then, in general terms, is the nature of the relationship between psychological problems and personal social experience? It will be the thesis of this chapter that the links between psychological problems and social relationships take many forms but derive essentially from the functions that relationships normally serve. In advancing this case the chapter will inevitably run into the obstacle that the study by Brown *et al.* (1975) is just about the only piece of research that has been done directly on the issues from this point of view. Thus the chapter draws mostly on indirect evidence and argument in an attempt to provide a useful theoretical framework for future work. It is important to note, however, that it is *not* part of the present argument that disrupted personal relationships *invariably* cause extreme clinical symptoms (although some such cases are discussed). Rather, it will be suggested that disruption of relationships can often compound clinical disturbances, or can play some part in their aetiology, or may simply lead the individual to explore deviant or abnormal ways of satisfying those functions that personal relationships normally fulfil. Accordingly, this chapter considers general causal links between social relationships and clinical factors, as well as looking at specific examples. A proper understanding of these causal connections is ultimately dependent on a comprehension of the nature and functions of normal relationships.

Do relationships have a function?

Weiss (1969, 1974) proposes six categories of function for relationships (intimacy, social integration through shared concerns, the opportunity for nurturant behaviour, reassurance of worth, a sense of reliable alliance, and guidance). The level of analysis in this chapter is, however, quite different and concerns the notion of 'personality support' derivable from much psychological literature—particularly in the literature that reports empirical research into IPA. 'Personality support' is used in this literature in a special sense that will become clearer through an examination first of what it is not. It is not, as Rogers (1959) suggested, mere 'human warmth' characterized by an absence of threat to the self concept and an assistance in focusing on the perception and reorganization of self. Nor is it in the traditions of Sullivan (1953) or Maslow (1953), equivalent to an opportunity for personal growth provided by the influence of significant others on an individual's conception of himself or his needs. Nor, again, is it personality support based on the role-centred complementarity which Winch (1958) describes. Winch argues that personality needs may be the basis of marital choice; specifically, that partners may complement one another, seeking in each other some characteristic which is lacking in, or complementary to, themselves. There are two sorts of complementarity: Type 1 where the needs are of the same type but different in intensity (e.g. a highly dominant person complements a lowly dominant person who can be controlled); Type 2 where the needs are of a different type but equal in intensity (e.g. a highly Nurturant person, who needs to look after people, complements a highly Succorant person, who needs to be looked after by others). Later work on this hypothesis (Wagner, 1975) has argued that complementarity of role-based activity is also an important factor in this context. It is therefore interesting to note in the context of this chapter that La Gaipa (1977) demonstrates that a group diagnosed as neurotic shows role confusion (especially with respect to sexual identity) in ways that lead to intrapersonal conflict at the behavioural level (see below).

Whilst the above ideas do contribute something to the notion of 'personality support' as it relates to the issues before us, the sense in which this chapter uses the term derives from a large amount of IPA research founded on the belief that relationships happen because of a need for personal validation: that is, for validation of one's way of ordering, structuring, perceiving, dealing with the world. Byrne (1971), for example, argues that attitudinal similarity between two people will provide consensual validation for the attitude concerned (i.e. validation through agreement: at least someone else thinks it is a sensible attitude, too!). He goes on to argue that similarity of attitudes will often (but not always) be reinforcing and thus that attitudinal similarity will, as a general rule, promote attraction and liking. This form of the argument has been extended by Duck and Spencer (1972) to include the attitude-like personality components that are the building blocks of Kelly's (1955) theory of personal constructs. For Kelly, an individual's personality is made up from the beliefs (constructs) that he holds about how the future should be anticipated and about how consistency or order in the environment can be predicted. An individual's personal system of constructs is, in many ways, similar to a system of attitudes and as such (so Duck and Spencer, 1972, argued) will need to be validated similarly. Thus, a person will like those other people who provide support (consensual validation) for his personal construct system. Close personal relationships are viewed from this theoretical position as based on personality support, and their absence would have very serious effects on psychological integrity.

'Different causes, different problems, different solutions'

Against this general background it should now be clear that a variety of clinical problems may derive from dysfunctional or incompetent attempts to achieve or maintain effective social relationships. Examples include paranoia, delusions, and acute anxiety, as well as disturbed sexual relationships and depression of mood. Problems in personal relating may both generate and maintain clinical problems. However, there are many facets to research into 'personal relating' and it is unfortunately the case that because of the paucity of research we have a clearer map of the extreme cases than of the milder ones; it should be borne in mind during the rest of the chapter that the effects of relationship disorder are not always extreme. Lemert (1962), for example, postulated that some forms of psychotic behaviour are the result (or manifestation) of a disorder of communication between the individual and society. In a theoretical article with particular pertinence to the present argument, Lemert extended the view that paranoid individuals were those whose inadequate social learning led them, in situations of unusual stress, to exhibit incompetent social reactions. He proposed that this view focused too narrowly on the individual and left out the *relationship* and how it becomes attenuated as communication is disrupted. From the point of view of others in a relationship, the paranoid person shows a disregard for the norms and values of the primary group coupled with a disregard for the implicit structure of the group (e.g. by presuming to privileges not accorded him). This leads to him being seen as a 'difficult person' and hence to his being treated in a spurious way (e.g. by patronizing, humouring, underreacting). So, from the deviant's point of view now, it begins to become apparent that others interact with him in attenuated fashion, that they avoid him overtly and that they begin to structure their interactions to exclude him both physically and psychologically. In fact, then (rather than in his imagination alone), the deviant's unacceptable social behaviour leads to a structure in his personal relationships which deprives him of personality support of the types considered earlier; creates a discrepancy between the ideas and the affect expressed by those with whom he interacts; and makes the situation troublesomely ambiguous for him. Faced with such a critical and cataclysmic set of circumstances the individual (so Lemert and the present argument would both conclude) will react to the lack of support available from others and would restructure his personality in ways consistent with the responses that others make to him (i.e. would restructure it into a supportable form).

Consistent with such an approach is work by Brown (1976), La Gaipa (1977), and Drewery and Rae (1969). These authors have argued theoretically, or have offered practical demonstration, that failing personal relationships may induce psychological distresses that can lead a person to the final common pathways of traditional psychiatric classifications: depression, anxiety, alcoholism, phobias, and sexual dysfunction. For example, Drewery and Rae (1969) employed an Interpersonal Perception method to analyse how each of two marriage partners expected to be perceived by the other along 15 personality variables, using the Edwards Personal Preference Schedule. Using this technique, a group comparison was made between 22 'alcoholic' marriages and 26 'non-alcoholic' ones, and inferences were drawn about the relationships. The evidence suggested that relationships in the 'alcoholic' marriages were characterized by sociosexual role confusion and by conflicting dependence–independence needs (similar confusions are reported by La Gaipa, 1977). The authors concluded that the patients' difficulties in personal relationships were the substantive cause of the alcoholism.

Thus two existing explanations of two clinical problems (paranoia, alcoholism) are consistent with the general theoretical stance that is being propounded here. However, the examples are extreme ones and the argument so far very general. Consequently, it would be easy to overplay the relationship between social relationships and clinical problems on the basis of this work alone. The remainder of this chapter will therefore consider some more specific aspects of the IPA literature and the more specific consequences that may follow for the aetiology of less extreme psychological problems.

THE EXPLANATION OF ACQUAINTANCE

Broadly speaking, the literature on IPA falls into three loose areas of concern—areas which occasionally overlap and are intermingled. These three areas are: initial attraction; the development of acquaintanceship; the conduct and maintenance of relationships. These different aspects of IPA can make different contributions to an understanding of socially provoked psychological problems. (For example, a repulsive person may never experience personal relationships at all; a closed person may be able to engage in only superficial relationships; a person ignorant of the requirements of the role of friend, lover, workmate will be continually surprising and disappointing his associates and may suffer disruptive or—to him—inexplicably curtailed relationships.) Therefore an examination of the basic concerns, methods, and implications of the three areas is essential in order to clarify their several implications for the themes of this book, given that the aim of this chapter is to develop a theoretical model for acquaintance which can account for the influence (upon psychological problems) of these three separate areas of interest.

Attraction to strangers

The bulk of work on IPA concerns initial attraction responses to strangers. Typical research examines first impressions and the effects of such things as physical attractiveness (Berscheid and Walster, 1974), socioeconomic status (Byrne *et al.* 1966), and many other factors (Duck, 1977; Berscheid and Walster, 1978). At first sight such studies seem to examine superficial aspects of IPA, but there is more to it than that, since the explanation of *why* such things as these are attractive is a difficult question to answer and one which ultimately holds the key to the relevance of such cues to the present discussion. Various suggestions have been made, ranging from claims of genetic preprogramming to proposals that association with physically attractive others will raise one's self-esteem and is thus attractive. It has also been shown, however, that some of the above cues carry strong implications in observers' minds about personality (Dion *et al.* 1972). Thus such cues prompt individuals to speculate about their 'owner's' personality and its likely degree of support for their own personality (Duck, 1977). This may explain why people often assume that the physically disfigured are also psychologically disfigured (Goffman, 1963) and, while there is probably no simple explanation for such an occurrence, may go part of the way towards explaining why ugly, maimed, and physically unattractive individuals are disliked (Perrin, 1921). To the extent, however, that such stereotypes exist, some individuals will clearly find them repercussing on their (satisfaction with) personal relationships.

The implications of such work for the clinic are unclear. Whilst observers do use these superficial cues in forming first impressions, it is not established that they use no other cues, nor that their first feelings may not be modified. It is likely that such factors make little contribution to the disruption of personal relationships therefore, although care over appearance, self-presentation, and so on have a traditionally important place in advice about making a good first impression. Sadly, it is likely that this is all that they do directly, although it is impossible to assess their indirect influence on self-esteem, and consequent behavioural style in personal relationships.

Of more direct use in the present context, therefore, is work on the effects of attitude similarity upon attraction to strangers. This work has been carried out by Byrne and his associates for nearly 20 years (Byrne, 1961, 1971; Clore & Byrne, 1974; Clore, 1977). Essentially, it is concerned with the circumstances in which attitude similarity is reinforcing and the implications that this has for attraction to strangers (see Duck, 1977, for a review). Byrne's interest originally lay in determining the predictions that could be made about liking, given a known degree of similarity and reinforcement. Once the principle of a positive linear relationship between reinforcement and attraction had been established, further work examined the basis of the relationship, the circumstances under which it was modified, and its practical applications (Byrne, 1971; Clore, 1977; Duck, 1977). Despite the fact that the bulk of the original work was almost exclusively laboratory-based, a vast number of 'real-life' studies have also been completed in support of the original theoretical position (Byrne, 1971; Duck, 1977). Among these is a study by Byrne *et al.* (1969) which used samples of many different sorts in terms of age, education and socioeconomic level (ranging from people with drinking problems to surgical patients). However, included in this study was a group diagnosed schizophrenic which yielded a pattern of responses differing in some crucial respects from that usually observed. This group was primarily noteworthy for the unusual slope of the linear relationship that they manifested between similarity and attraction levels. They made less differentiation between similar and dissimilar strangers and, indeed, responded to totally dissimilar strangers with a level of attraction response deemed appropriate only for those showing extremely high similarity (50–70 per cent) by undergraduates, surgical patients and people with drinking problems. Equally, their attraction towards strangers who were totally similar was lower than was the case for the undergraduate comparison group. Clearly, for whatever reason, the schizophrenic group failed to respond to stranger similarity in a way which either reflected the normal pattern or could convince an acquaintance partner that a normal fruitful relationship could be anticipated.

Again, however, it could be objected that this population is an extreme example, so it is important to be clear that, from the present theoretical argument, there is a general significance of Byrne's work: namely, Byrne's work matters in the theoretical framework here because it both indicates the importance of attitudes (and their disclosure) in initial attraction and also shows their possible place in the development of acquaintance. It has been postulated that there will, in real-life contexts, be individual differences in the ability to detect complex levels of attitude similarity, to evoke attitudinal discussions in normal interaction, and to reveal one's own attitudes to partners (Duck, 1977). McCarthy (1978) has shown that subjects who rate themselves as poor relaters are actually deficient in some of these respects, although work extending this to clinical patients remains to be undertaken.

In has already been suggested that the functions of relationships are to be found in the notion of personality support, in the special sense in which that term is used here. It is clear that attitudes, because of their 'personalness' and their privacy, are extremely informative about an individual's personality, and in the moment of expressing an attitudinal position the individual not only tells an observer how he feels about some attitude object but also, in a small way, reveals something of himself. An array of such attitudes, such as may be available in Byrne's experiments or after a short interaction with a stranger, gives an observer information about the person who holds the attitudes—sometimes enough information for him to be able to form in his mind's eye a sketchy picture of the person's personality. Even a sketchy view of someone else's personality permits an observer to assess—sketchily—the extent to which the person and the observer have mutually supportive personalities. The sketch may need changing when more information is collected, but it suffices to start with. Attitudes are thus important in attraction (as are other cues) *to the extent that they inform observers about the holder's personality and its likely support for the observer.* They thus relate to the *functions* of relationships.

In developing such a view, Duck (1977) has referred to a process of prediction and reformulation of predictions during the initial stages of relationships. Predictions about a partner's personality are continually re-evaluated during early encounters, and the decision to continue the relationship is constantly being re-assessed as the model of partner's personality emerges in a more stable form. In other words, the suggestion rests squarely on the proposal that the partners (need to) transmit various sorts of information about themselves in continuing interactions, and so each person is better able to assess the other's personality and construct a model of it. However, the information transmission is not, trivially, simply increased *amounts* of information as the relationship proceeds, but, importantly, different *sorts* of information that must be appropriate to the relevant point of development that the relationship has achieved (Duck, 1976, 1977). As the information is translated into a model of the partner's personality so, progressively, it provides a better basis for judgements about the degree of personality support that the observer can expect from the relationship. Since this proposal is based on prediction and refers to a continual sifting of potential acquaintances to establish their suitability as friends, the proposal has been called the predictive filtering model of acquaintance (Duck, 1977).

It can be seen to have many levels of implication for the present context. Broadly, a person's success in, and satisfaction with, personal relationships will be largely dependent on his ability to encode and transmit the right sorts of information about his own personality at appropriate points of friendship development. He will also need to decode information from his partner, to the same end.

This has two consequences here. First it is relevant that some clinical populations (notably, those diagnosed as schizophrenic) have been shown to be deficient in these respects, lacking the interpretative framework that is most important in such circumstances: namely, description of other people's 'psychology' or character (McPherson, Buckley & Draffan, 1971). Second, and less specifically, it is clear that the experimental work on self-disclosure is informative at this point. In examining the phenomenon of self-disclosure (i.e. verbal presentation to other people of one's more or less private thoughts, feelings, hopes, fears ...) Jourard (1959) suggested that individuals will be regarded by others as mentally healthy to the extent to which they are willing to self-disclose. Individuals who are unwilling to self-disclose will, Jourard suggested, be seen as closed, fearful, defensive people with something to hide, whilst self-disclosers would be seen as healthy, robust persons. One important refinement of this basic view concerns the place of sex norms in self-disclosure in normal relationships (Miell, Duck and La Gaipa, 1979). Females who disclose early in an encounter, and males who disclose later, are regarded as more stable and mentally healthy than disclosers who adopt the reverse pattern. An important feature of self-disclosure, then, is not just that it occurs at all but that it occurs appropriately: presumably inappropriate disclosure will lead to rejection or dislike of the discloser. The skills of self-disclosure are thus important not only to individual interactions (where, say, the degree of reciprocity or intimacy or amount of disclosure may be significant) but also to the longitudinal development of relationships (where, say, the timing and nature of disclosure may define the speed of development of the relationship and the degree of satisfaction or discomfort that it provides to its participants). It is particularly instructive in the present context, therefore, to note that many patients described as neurotic show abnormal emphases on self-disclosure as compared with a normal population (La Gaipa, 1977), and hence presumably fail to derive normal sorts of personality support from social relationships. Moreover, Nelson-Jones and Strong (1976) note that an essential feature of satisfactory therapy is a willingness on the client's part to self-disclose and, one might add, to do it appropriately. Clearly the learning of this skill could of itself constitute a cure in so far as it generalizes outside the clinic and helps the client to form satisfying relationships.

Whilst self-disclosure is important for these reasons it is also important to the present argument through its relevence to *developing* relationships, since it is a primary cause of the translation of a relationship between two strangers into a deeper developing relationship.

The development of relationships (acquaintance)

The second area of research concerns developed and developing relationships and is broadly described by the label 'acquaintance research'. Here the emphasis falls on continuity rather than first reaction, and various types of relationships have been studied (e.g. dating, courtship progress, same-sex friendship). Clearly such work is dealing with a central issue, so far as it concerns the relationship between social psychology and psychological problems. To the extent that prediction of successful relationships becomes possible through such research, social psychological theory and research could advise those who deal with crippled relationships on their likely future; could advise individuals against entering doomed relationships; and could point out propitious ones to predictably successful partners.

One productive area concerns sexual relationships (from dating, courtship, and wedlock to extramarital affairs; Hatfield and Traupmann, in press). Most work has attempted to establish an understanding of the sequential development of courtship from start to marriage, the factors which promote and accelerate it and, beyond that, the antecedents of satisfaction with courtship progress (Murstein, 1977). It is therefore central to certain limited aspects of this chapter since relationship establishment, maintenance, and satisfaction are more important *psychologically* than are simple first impressions of another person. It is an important area also because of the implication that it contains for *sequential* satisfaction of criteria for relationship continuance. This in turn requires that the partners have a working knowledge of the sequence and the ability to perform and execute it (e.g. by recognizing the correct occasion to increase intimacy levels, the changes in behaviour that are called for at each stage and so on; Duck, in press).

The above points are general ones that are pointed up by work on specifically sexual relationships. It remains to be seen (Przybyla and Byrne, in press) whether explanations of the development of such specifically sexual relationships can inform us of any general principles that apply to other forms of human interaction. Whilst a certain number of familiar psychological problems derive especially from disrupted or unsatisfactory sexual relationships, the content of such interactions is peculiar and characteristic only of itself. Sexual relations are recognized, and to some extent governed, by social convention, norms of behaviour, and so on, in a way that is not true of other forms of relationship. Ignorance or incompetent observance of these conventions may not generalize to other ones, therefore.

A further point is that the disruptive effects of poor sexual relating may be more influential at certain ages (e.g. adolescence). It is likely that the solution of several psychological difficulties will be assisted by a detailed analysis of the ways in which adolescents learn to relate to one another in an adult fashion (Duck, 1975; 1978). During adolescence the complexities of adult relating need to be learned, practised, and perfected; reliance on personality judgements about others supersedes the childish cues that have previously been the basis of relationships (Duck, Miell &

Gaebler, 1980) and the sexual aspects of relationships appear for the first time in any significant form.

Work on the *general* nature of acquaintance has been done by Levinger and co-workers (Levinger and Snoek, 1972; Levinger, 1974; Huesmann and Levenger, 1976). In describing growth, Levinger (1974) distinguished between three levels of relationships, each with its characteristic style of interaction of which both praticipants must be aware if the interaction is to be successful. (There is also a level of 'unrelationship': zero contact, where the two persons concerned have never met in any sense.) The three levels are:

(i) *Awareness* (where no interaction occurs and where one person is aware of the other but not vice versa);
(ii) *surface contact* (where some interaction occurs and some basic attitudes about each other exist);
(iii) *mutuality* (a continuum from 'minor intersection' to 'major intersection'—these terms describing the amount of overlap, shared experiences, etc.).

For Huesmann and Levinger (1976) the progression from one level of intimacy to another is promoted, along the lines suggested by various exchange theories, by expectations of good payoffs at the next level of intimacy. Confirmation of the expectation is adequate to sustain the relationship at that new level and lead on to expectations about the next.

The above formulation has some similarities and differences with the proposals of the present author, outlined earlier and in Duck (1977). Both stress that the growth of intimacy is provoked by prediction and expectation but the nature of the groundwork for the expectation is different in the two cases. Equally, one suggestion is based on exchange theory whilst the other is based on information transmission about personality as a 'pure' congnitive process. Such work does offer the prospect of identifying the paths that relationships *usually* follow if they are successful, and this itself may suggest that research psychology may be able to provide a set of guiding principles for those who are unable to achieve satisfactory social relationships (cf. Chapter 5).

It is, however, important not to be too simplistic about this. Individuals differ from one another in the extent and amount of interaction that they seek (Peplau and Perlman, 1977)—to such a degree that norms of 'relationship amount' would be hard to prescribe. In addition the skills of acquainting are multidimensional, complex, and multitudinous. It would therefore be naive at this stage of research development for any claims to be made that an acquaintance phlogiston has been discovered. At this stage in the analysis we have covered only two aspects of successful acquainting, and the third is at once one of the most complex and under-researched, as well as one of the most important to satisfactory relationship continuance.

CONDUCT AND MAINTENANCE OF RELATIONSHIPS

This third and most recent concern of the work on IPA focuses upon conduct and maintenance of relationships. Thus Kerckhoff (1974) and Rosenblatt (1974) have pointed out the cultural limitations and requirements of certain types of friendly interaction (e.g. arranged marriages), and Murstein (1971) has noted the limitations that are imposed by roles upon opportunities for interaction.

However, for the present purposes this level of analysis is relatively uninformative. What is more important is an analysis of the content and nature of irnteractions themselves and an attempt at explanation at that level has been based on Adams' (1965) Equity Theory. Essentially this proposes that individuals follow certain rules in deciding whether they, their partners, other people ... are getting their fair shares out of (and putting their fair shares into) social interactions. Equity theorists thus examine, in general, two related questions (Berscheid and Walster, 1978, p. 125): '(1) How people go about deciding who deserves what ... when; and (2) how people react when they feel that they are getting more ... or less ... than they deserve out of life.' The approach thus concentrates not only on what is exchanged but also on how it is perceived. In the present context this approach clearly has some general relevance, although it will be of interest to us to learn whether: (a) people with clinical problems habitually give too little (or too much) in exchanges; (b) people with clinical problems habitually *perceive* that they are getting (or giving) inequitable amounts from interactions; (c) people who are perceived as giving (or getting) inequitable amounts are the sorts of people who *develop* psychological problems.

Although a considerable amount of work in Equity Theory is reported by Walster *et al.* (1978) they do not point to any with specific clinical relevance. However a number of studies are reported in the context of intimate personal relationships, and the authors are prepared to speculate about the consequences of inequity in such cases. For instance, Berscheid *et al.* (1973) examined relationships where one partner had clearly ended up with a partner that he/she did not 'deserve'. Predictions were that both the superior and the inferior partner in an inequitable relationship would feel uneasy and so the relationship would be (perceived to be) unstable. However, the study was simply a questionnaire survey conducted amongst readers of *Psychology Today*, and although the results confirm the hypotheses, one is not convinced that demands in the experimental methodology do not alone account for the findings.

Other studies within an Equity Theory framework have considered how (in)equity in a dating or marital relationship affects the likelihood of premarital or extramarital sexual activity. Walster, *et al.* (In press) examined the extent to which a person feeling inequitably treated would risk illicit extramarital sex. Using data from the above study by Berscheid *et al.* (1973) they showed that underbenefited persons indulged in extramarital sexual activity earlier than equitable or overbenefited persons.

It is to be regretted that work on Equity in intimate relationships is sparse and limited. Most work examines casual relationships (benefactor–recipient;

victim–harmdoer) or business relationships, and there is, as yet, little other work on intimate ones—particularly from the point of view of Equity Theory's relevance to psychological problems. Most work concerns the psychological distress associated with inequity rather than the consequent behavioural or clinical problems. This lack of work is to be regretted, since it is clear that the theory may have some value in this area.

It will be clear that this latter level of analysis and its consequent research in IPA constitutes and concerns an entirely different level of analysis of relationships, and identifies a significant aspect of relationships that requires different skills from those outlined earlier. Nevertheless whilst the development of acquaintance will indeed be influenced by equity considerations, amongst other things, the equity theorists themselves acknowledge (Walster *et al.*, 1978, p. 147) that considerations of pure equity are more likely to concern relationships at the earlier stages of development. As relationships proceed so partners will be prepared to offset inequities in one exchange against gains in others. Also, deepening relationships are characterized by changes in both the pattern and content of exchange, such that the computation of equity becomes difficult and inexact. However, it is this very feature which accounts for the difficulty of explaining (or, for some interactors, of comprehending) how progress in relationships occurs. It is nonetheless clear that equity is important for maintaining relationships at a given level of intimacy as well as helping them to grow in intimacy. Clearly, therefore, successful maintenance of relationships will depend on the partners' ability to satisfy each other equitably.

Thus whilst it is clear that the psychodynamics of inequitable relationships are of interest to psychologists and may have some value in the field of IPA (e.g. in accounting for relationship collapse) it is too early to judge its value to the field as a whole. Clearly such an appraoch has *something* to contribute to an understanding of a wide variety of human interactions and will have some guidance to offer on why a person should be attracted to one particular relationship as against another. It also leads to some predictions concerning the ways in which individuals will perceive a need to restore equity or maintain equity in established and continuous relationships (e.g. by compensating the victims of one's actions). At present, however, it is impossible to assess the extent to which Equity Theory is a useful predictor of relationship growth or tells us anything that can be generalized from special types of relationships, like benefactor–recipient, harmdoer–victim, which, in a general sense, are not the same *kinds* of interpersonal relationship as are being discussed in this chapter. Indeed in the cases where Equity Theory predictions have been tested in deep personal relationships (as opposed to the more casual ones outlined above) these predictions have failed as often as they have been successful (Walster *et al.*, 1977, 1978).

Behaviour in developing and collapsing relationships

The above three areas of concern in IPA are identified from only one view of the literature, but they do help to illustrate the different aspects of research that may, in different ways, be relevant to the explanation of psychological problems. For one thing their distinction helps to illustrate the multidimensionality and complexity of the 'skills' and knowledge that are necessary for successful acquainting—from the lowest level (appearance and self-presentation) to the intricate complexities of information-transmission, self-disclosure, equitable exchange and personality support. It is therefore important to recognize that attraction, acquaintance, friendship, and all the rest (especially in the context of psychological problems) are not simply affective and attitudinal responses, as the literature so often likes to propose (Berscheid and Walster, 1978). They are all complex and fully fledged social *behaviours*, such that individuals have to know not only how they feel or what they think, but how to translate these cognitive and affective states into practice and do so in agreed and accepted ways.

Research on IPA can thus be construed as relevant to psychological problems in so far as these are caused by inadequacy, inability, or incompleteness of performance of the principles that the above theoretical thinking has identified. For example, they may be improperly learned in childhood (Duck, Miell and Gaebler, 1980) or may be performed correctly but in inappropriate contexts (Duck, 1979). It is not, however, possible to be more than conjectural at this stage, given that there is almost no empirical work on the central question of how and why *friendships* collapse. Indeed it is only recently that social psychological researchers have begun to call for such work (Huston and Levinger, 1978).

In the present theoretical framework, collapse and deterioration of relationships can, however, be explained parsimoniously by reference to the predictions that partners make about one another and the consequences of these predictions' failure. Duck and Allison (1978) built upon this framework with the following arguments. Predictions about one's partner's personality (and its similarity to one's own) have to be based on incomplete evidence at first, but as one becomes more acquainted with the partner, so the nature and extent of available evidence becomes more valuable and reliable. Thus, one can begin to evaluate both whether one's original predictions were accurate and whether they can be extended to future probability of personality support. Where one's predictions are found to have yielded overestimates of personality support the relationship is likely to be terminated. In testing this proposal, Duck and Allison (1978) investigated a population of students who had all been friends during their first year, split up into smaller groups, and moved off campus. Such is life that many of these choices were subsequently regretted—luckily for the investigators, who thus had access to a group of people who had been close friends but whose relationships had collapsed when promoted to closer cohabitation. In support of the general argument here, Duck and Allison (1978) found that members of the small subgroups (friends) were, overall, significantly more similar in personal constructs than other pairs in the population. However, those relationships that subsequently collapsed did manifest characteristically different patterns of the types of similarity involved. This result was supportive of the view that the type of similarity, as well as the amount, is critical to the continuance and development (or alternatively, the collapse and failure) of relationships. At any point in acquaintance where partners suspect that an inadequate or unsatisfactory sort of similarity exists between them, the relationship will be ossified or abandoned.

We therefore reach the point in a complex theoretical argument where it is plausible to argue that individuals who give off false impressions about their personality structure or whose presented (ideal) personality is discrepant from their true personality or who do not reveal enough of their true personality through self-disclosure, will be likely to surprise and disappoint their partners at subsequent points in the relationship—and will often be rejected for that reason.

Is there any evidence that individuals with psychological problems fall into these categories?

RELATIONSHIPS IN DISORDER

It should be clear from the above discussion that the interplay between personal relationships and psychological problems is an extremely complex one. In so far as such problems stem from an inability to satisfy (for oneself or for one's partner) the functions which relationships normally fulfil, the problems are likely to be generated in part by a whole host of factors which relate to an individual's ability to conduct relationships satisfactorily. Thus we have considered above some of the probable necessary skills that this requires (ranging from low-level non-verbal abilities to complex skills of attribution and assessment). Also relevant, however, is an individual's degree of affiliative need, since low affiliators are likely to include a class of people who not only cannot affiliate satisfactorily, but also some who do not desire to do so, whether through 'fear' of other people's responses to them, ready achievement of deep satisfaction with a small number of relationships or a low desire for interaction (e.g. hermits). Furthermore, since there are two free agents in any relationship it is possible that psychological problems may be generated not simply by one's own inabilities or inherent need structure but also by that of one's partner and his or her consequent actions. Even beyond these three points is the fourth, that psychological problems may only appear to be related to personal relationships even when they manifest themselves there. Thus, for example, the anecdotally observed frequency of collapse of personal (cross-sex) relationships in final-year students is as likely to be due to the stresses of final-year degree work as it is to factors more intimately and directly connected with the relationship itself.

All this is a basic framework for a discussion of the direct interconnections between personal relationships and psychological problems. It is intended to underline the fact that throughout the discussion no single interconnection is referred to, and the complexity of the causal links is surpassed only by the complexity of dissolving them in treatment. There are, however, a number of issues that have been studied in this connection in the IPA literature; these are discussed below. As the ambiguity of this section heading is intended to indicate, this work concerns both the nature of personal relationships in disordered, or disturbed, or 'abnormal' individuals and the effects of relationship disorder or destruction upon psychological functioning.

Relationships in the disordered

Studies of the relationships of 'disordered' or 'abnormal' persons are remarkably few (as was indicated in the introductory remarks of this chapter) and much that can be said on the question is merely derived indirectly. However, a corpus of direct research has recently been started in Canada by La Gaipa and his associates, facilitated by the construction of friendship scales tapping friendship values and expectations. Research on children has been concerned mainly with the problems of rejected children, in particular those who are unusually socially withdrawn or aggressive, using an essentially developmental orientation. Research on adults has included a wide range of psychiatric disorders, but much of this work concerns the concept of friendship that is possessed by people with psychological problems. A basic premise is that atypical expectations have implications for satisfactory interpersonal adjustments.

Rejected children La Gaipa and Wood (1973) observed distortions and abnormal patterns of friendship perception in disturbed children: finding, particularly, that withdrawn children had views of friendship that were underdeveloped (i.e. views that were normally found in children of lower ages than those tested). For example, children identified (by a 'guess who' sociometric test) as withdrawn were found to assign less importance in friendship to loyalty and commitment and to empathic disclosure than children described as aggressive or socially accepted. Somewhat surprisingly, aggressive children had views of friendship much like those of popular children, although this finding was not supported in a later study using a different sample. La Gaipa and Irwin (1976) administered the children friendship scales to emotionally disturbed girls who were delinquent, aggressive, and under residential treatment. As compared to a normative sample, they were found to place more value on empathic disclosure and mutual activities. As would be expected, these disturbed, delinquent girls seek friends that are understanding, and with whom they can discuss their personal problems.

Aggressive, maladjusted and socially withdrawn children were also examined in terms of the resolution of specific developmental problems (Wood and La Gaipa, 1978). A projective test employing TAT-type pictures and instructions was used to assess the resolution of psychosocial conflicts (Erikson, 1959). Discriminant analyses revealed that the aggressive children differed from the withdrawn ones on friendship dimensions, whereas the popular children differed from them on both developmental stages and friendship dimensions. In particular, while the aggressive and popular children responded alike in their view of friendship, the withdrawn children placed less importance on empathy and more importance on loyalty. Withdrawn and aggressive children did not differ in stages but only in conceptions of friendship (with the withdrawn ones placing less value on empathy and on conventional morality than did the aggressive children). Essentially, rejected children displayed inadequate conflict resolution and later psychosocial stages were predicted by earler stages, with Stage I (trust *v*. mistrust) being the best predictor of conflict resolution at later stages. In particular, the degree to which withdrawn girls view other persons as friendly and sociable, and the extent to which expressions of warmth and closeness towards others are expressed, were related to the successful resolution of the trust–mistrust conflict.

Klein and La Gaipa (1978) reasoned that some of the problems of withdrawn children might stem from their interpretation of interpersonal events. Brief stories were presented, varying in the type of social interaction and the type of role relationships. Withdrawn girls were found to differ from normal girls in explanatory categories and in affective tone. The withdrawn girls relied more on physical qualities and made fewer explanations in terms of psychological qualities. This suggests that withdrawn girls tend to focus upon the more superficial aspects of social interaction (and so might conceivably hinder the formation of deeper relationships). They do not recognize (and/or do not respond to) the 'deeper', more psychological, aspects of social interaction. This tendency to play down psychological qualities suggests that withdrawn girls are developmentally behind normal girls in social cognition.

Most of the differences between withdrawn and normal girls were elicited by stories which depicted negative interaction between classmates. Withdrawn girls provided fewer explanations with a positive affective tone to them, suggesting that withdrawn girls have a more pessimistic orientation towards others. Withdrawn girls also make more use of causal explanations than normal girls in interpreting negative interactions. Perhaps, in experiencing rejection more frequently, withdrawn girls have become more sensitized to causal motives: withdrawn girls may have a greater need to make sense out of the motives underlying negative social encounters.

Psychiatric disorders A study by Engelhart *et al.* (1975) compared the performance of groups of patients diagnosed as schizophrenic, neurotic, or personality disordered (mainly 'passive–aggressive' or with drinking problems) and a large sample of normal adults. Each subject was given a battery of friendship scales (La Gaipa, 1977) as a means of assessing the characteristics which they perceived to be important in best friends of the same sex as themselves. The most interesting differences were found between the 'neurotic' and the 'normal' groups—particularly in the extent to which they saw self-disclosure of intimate material as a characteristic of friendship. Neurotic males overemphasized it (as compared with normals), whilst neurotic females did the opposite—a result that led La Gaipa (1977) to speculate that confusion over role definition and sexual identity was a possible factor in the symptomatology of these patients.

There were, however, some possible problems in this study regarding the reliability of the psychiatric diagnoses, and there was also a question regarding the homogeneity of the sample. A more standardized approach was therefore subsequently sought using the Eysenck Personality Inventory which provides measures of both neuroticism and extraversion–introversion (La Gaipa and Engelhart, 1977). A sample of 300 male and female undergraduate university students were identified as extraverts or introverts and then further divided into a 'neurotic' (high N) and a stable group (low N). The 'neurotic' females expected to engage in more self-disclosure than did the introverted stable females, but for extraverts no such difference was found. The data for males are the opposite to that found for the females: for introverted males neuroticism had no significant effect on self-disclosure. However the extraverted, 'neurotic', males expected to give more disclosure than the extraverted stable males. It appears, then, that high N scorers who are not under treatment also differ from low N scorers in what they expect from friendship: sex differences are again apparent but are mediated by extraversion–introversion.

An important related point for the thesis of this chapter is that the prognosis for the treatment of disorders, as well as their diagnosis, may be facilitated by information regarding interpersonal relationships during the course of treatment. La Gaipa and Uriel (1974) found that the prediction of success from group therapy could be improved by information on psychosocial satisfaction. This study was conducted on a group of working-class people with drinking problems undergoing a three-week clinical treatment programme. Those who returned to drinking in a one-year follow-up were those who did not get as much out of the treatment. The satisfaction with helping and support, as well as with the intimacy of disclosure as measured upon completion of therapy, was predictive of sobriety ($r = 0.58$). This is consistent with the often-made observation that people with drinking problems are passive-dependent in personality; relying heavily on others for support.

General considerations

The above examples concern some clinical implications of personal relationship failure or distortion, but there is also another side to this question. Whilst much clinical psychological work is *about* personal relationships, the clinical psychologist himself is also involved in personal relationships with his clients. In some cases it can be argued (Dewhurst and Duck, 1978) that his function as a clinical psychologist can be largely accounted for by his ability to provide for; or fulfil, those functions which the client cannot fulfil through normal relationships. Thus he encourages self-disclosure, probes private areas of personality, offers encouragement, warmth, guidance, help, and so on. In a strictly limited sense the clinical psychologist becomes 'the friend' of the client (Dewhurst and Duck, 1978). It should therefore be found that, irrespective of his preferred mode of treatment, the therapist will be regarded as competent, useful, and helpful by his client to the extent that he is able to perform the role of 'friend' for his client and to provide the kinds of personality support that friends do provide (Goldstein, 1971). The parallels between psychotherapy and friendship formation as processes have often been observed (Kelly, 1969; Duck, 1977) but in the context of the present arguments, this parallelism concerns the nature of the interaction that occurs and relates to the function of friendship itself. Such parallelism may account for the occasional observations that patients report being in love with their analysts; or the problems of transference and dependence during the course of therapeutic treatments. It reflects the fact that, in so far as relationship difficulties have provoked the appearance of an individual in the clinic, the person will need to seek out in therapeutic interactions those components of friendship that have, until then, been missing.

This work on clinical problems and personal relationships, both direct and indirect, illustrates the contribution that an understanding of the mechanisms of successful relating can make to the full comprehension of clinical aetiology. It is, however, only part of the story, as has been continually re-emphasized. The effect on personal relationships of clinical symptoms and vice versa is complex and efficient only to the extent that the functions of relationships cannot otherwise be satisfied (e.g. by devaluing social relationships; by coming to perceive oneself as a self-sufficient, independent person). To the extent that persons are led, pushed, or provoked into supporting their personality by bizarre and abnormal means in the absence of 'proper' intimate relations, to that extent the clinical and social psychological interests correspond.

Such abnormal means of personality support may involve distorted perceptions of the intentions of others (e.g. paranoia) where treatment of oneself is perceived as unfair, conspiratorial, unjustified, etc., rather than recognizing that one's own personality structure may be bizarre, unacceptable or invalid (Lemert, 1962). Equally, Kelly (1969) has considered a defintion of hostility which rests on a hostile person's inclination towards misperception of events: for Kelly, hostility is the continued effort to extort validational evidence from events in order to support a prediction which has already been recognized as a failure. These essentially 'interpersonal distortions' (i.e. they result in distortion of perceptions of other people) are as often matched by 'intrapersonal distortions', where the person comes to see himself as worthless (Lowe, 1969). In a general way this self-devaluation involves personality support, in the sense that the person alters his impressions of himself to make them consistent with the impressions that other people apparently hold. However they are also punishing impressions to sustain and further interaction with other people will, in so far as it continues to support them, become unattractive (Byrne, McDonald and Mikawa, 1963).

It is evident from the above that part of the complex connection between personal relationships and clinical problems is to be found in disordered perception of self, other people, and such concepts as the nature and consequences of friendship and intimate relations (La Gaipa, 1977). Not only are disordered persons likely to possess strange concepts of 'friendship', but also their ability to differentiate degrees of relationship is distorted, their expectancies of others' role performance are unusual, and their actual behaviour in those roles themselves may be odd. Much more research is needed in this area before one can make confident general statements about the direction of causality between clinical and social deficiencies.

Disorder in relationships

One can be more certain of the causal connection in those cases where sudden, or unexpected, or broad disruption of intimate relationships precedes psychological collapse; as, for example, in some cases of bereavement, divorce, 'disengagement', or change of home or job. Here, however, whilst depression often is the expression of the effects of loneliness, many of the results of loneliness are physical as well as psychological. Weiss's (1973) book on loneliness considers both those cases where loneliness is the result of a continuous and developing history of events (e.g. loneliness after the death of a spouse from cancer) and those cases where the loneliness follows a bereavement that is sudden and unpredictable. Many bereaved or separated persons experience panic, anger, frustration, unwarranted suspicion of interaction with other people, and a tendency to become obsessed about routine. The contemplation of suicide is a frequent occurrence in both types of loneliness and indeed suicide, heart disease, and psychosomatic illnesses are about twice as likely to kill divorced, bereaved, lonely, or socially isolated individuals (Lynch, 1977).

Other more foreseeable disorders of relationships occur in old age (Chown, in press)—although the general influence and attractiveness of specific cues remains, so far as we know, about the same (Griffitt, Nelson and Littlepage, 1972). In old age and pre-retirement years it is the pattern of relating which alters, and the frequency of interaction. Disengagement theory (Burgess, 1961), for example, notes a tendency for large increases to occur in the social network of an individual, in the years immediately preceding retirement. When retirement itself is reached, however, the network begins to contract and, coupled with other factors in retirement, this can have some deleterious effects on relationships between husband and wife, (grand)parents and (grand)children and so on. Here also the effects of loneliness are often associated with a change in the perception of oneself and one's role in the family, especially now that the traditional roles of the aged as heads of extended families have disappeared in Western society. An increased suicide rate is one of the consequences of loneliness in the elderly. Peplau & Perlman (1977) note that elderly people report feeling less lonely, however, if they are given control of the times at which visitors call. In an experimental study elderly people were visited for a fixed amount of time in one of two conditions: in one they could control the arrival time of the visitor and in the other they could not. Although the lengths of visit were the same, the first group reported feeling less lonely. However, as with other cases of loneliness one consequence of the feeling is an altered perception of oneself: lonely people come, over a period of time, to see themselves as needing fewer social contacts than other individuals. Other coping strategies involve denial that there exists a discrepancy between achieved and desired levels of social interaction, gratification of social needs by non-social means (e.g. keeping a pet) or doing things which alleviate the negative effects of loneliness (e.g. taking to drink, or drugs). Clearly these strategies represent whole classes, and the psychological or clinical problems are created only in those cases where the coping strategies are extreme (see above on alcoholism, for example). What is particularly interesting in Peplau & Perlman's (1977) work is the explication of the connection between the feeling of loneliness and the perception of oneself or others that is embodied in attribution processes. There is a tendency in Western culture to regard the number of one's friends as an indicator of 'success', so that loneliness often has direct implications for an individual's self-esteem and perceptions of himself. Thus the disruption of social relationships is likely to have both physical (psychosomatic) and direct psychological consequences that range from the trivial to the very powerful, but are never entirely absent.

CONCLUDING REMARKS

Several areas for further work have been suggested in the course of the above analysis, and several ways in which the social and clinical psychological work might be mutually instructive, including the treatments, preventive and curative, that may be relevant and useful in special cases. There is, above all, the important point that the choice of (analytical) level of treatment will be relevant and significant—whether to treat at the level of social skills and social performance (cf. Chapters 5 and 8) or at the level of strategic planning of interactions (e.g. from the point of view of Equity Theory) and training or instruction about the essential elements of the roles of friend or lover, etc. In a general sense the 'education' of many clinical patients may be deficient in respect of the social requirements of relating and the conduct or maintenance of relationships. This point therefore raises some more general issues that lurk beneath the surface of the above discussion: these concern the implications of the above model for educational policy, social policy, and general 'preparation for life' in childhood and adolescence.

It should be clear here that, without contradicting or gainsaying anything that is contained in Chapter 5, one can view the general implications of this discussion as stemming from a different, but not mutually exclusive, level of analysing the nature of social performance in intimate relationships. We are more concerned here to consider, for example, the nature of early learning about relationships than the social skills that children develop in Argyle's sense. Thus, for example, Manning and Herrman (in press) reports differences in hostility in children which relate to home background factors, learning about the nature of relationships and general 'role-learning'. La Gaipa (in press) has reported work on the learning about relationships which adolescents undergo, and has discussed the influence of parents, teachers, and, above all, peer groups which defines the adolescent's concepts not only of himself but also of others and his relationship to them. The above analysis suggests that a variety of complex skills, both cognitive and behavioural, are necessary to successful acquainting and satisfactory intimate relationships. It also points to their psychological importance.

In view of this evidence, both empirical and theoretical, it is strange and unsatisfactory that learning about such things is transmitted in a casual and unsystematic way (Duck, Miell and Gaebler, 1980). Children are left to learn these important things for themselves in the context of their interactions with age-peers, who may or may not be at the same stage of cognitive development as themselves (Hartup, 1979). It is not yet established precisely how cognitive development interacts with social relationships, nor whether cognitive growth affects social interaction in ways that may programme the individual for his future adult relationships (Duck, Miell and Gaebler, 1980). There is, however, one clear case where social competence may relate to opportunites for the learning that social interaction provides: individuals just entering adolescence are provided with different amounts of opportunity to learn personality constructs and hence acquire different degrees of understanding of 'personality'. Since relationships at this age are increasingly formed on the basis of personality similarities it is important that adolescents understand (the significance of) the concepts involved (La Gaipa, in press). It therefore seems important that educators should not ignore the social patterns that exist in the classroom and that researchers, in their turn, should pay closer attention to the relationship between social interaction and educational achievement.

Over and above this, given the wide range of relationships that exist and the different skills implied in, and necessary for, each of them, it would seem to be useful if greater attention were paid in research to these aspects of relationships, and especially if a greater amount of work were to be done on the conduct, continuance, and maintenance of relationships. It is of inestimable importance that we understand the processes involved in view of the fact that relationships are functionally related to personality development and individual growth—which is where social psychology and clinical psychology come together.

REFERENCES

Adams, J. S. (1965). Inequity in social exchange. In: L. Berkowitz (Ed.), *Advances in Experimental Social Psychology*, Vol. 2. (New York: Academic Press.)

Berscheid, E. and Walster, E. H. (1974). A little bit about love. In: T. L. Huston (Ed.), *Foundations of Interpersonal Attraction*. (New York: Academic Press.)

Berscheid, E. and Walster, E. H. (1978). *Interpersonal Attraction*, 2nd edn. (Reading, Mass.: Addison Wesley.)

Berscheid, E., Walster, E. H., and Bohrnstedt, G. (1973). The body image report. *Psychology Today*, **7**, 119–131.

Brown, G. W. (1976). Social causes of disease. In: D. Tuckett (Ed.), *An Introduction to Medical Sociology*. (London: Tavistock.)

Brown, G. W., Bhrolcháin, M. N., and Harris, T. (1975). Social class and psychiatric disturbance among women in an urban population. *Sociology*, **9**, 225–254.

Burgess, E. W. (1961). Family structure and relationships. In: E. W. Burgess (Ed.), *Aging in Western Societies*. (Chicago: University of Chicago Press.)

Byrne, D. (1961). Interpersonal attraction and attitude similarity. *Journal of Abnormal and Social Psychology*, **62,** 713–715.

Byrne, D. (1971). *The Attraction Paradigm*. (New York: Academic Press.)

Byrne, D., Clore, G., and Worchel, P. (1966). Effects of economic similarity–dissimilarity on interpersonal attraction. *Journal of Personality and Social Psychology*, **4,** 220–224.

Byrne, C., Griffitt, W., Hudgins, W., and Reeves, K. (1969). Attitude similarity–dissimilarity and attraction: generality beyond the college sophomore. *Journal of Social Psychology*, **79,** 155–161.

Byrne, D., McDonald, R. D., and Mikawa, J. (1963). Approach and avoidance affiliation motives. *Journal of Personality*, **31,** 21–37.

Caplan, G. (1974). *Support Systems and Community Mental Health*. (New York: Behavioural Publication.)

Chown, S. (In press). Relationships in old age. In: S. W. Duck and R. Gilmour (Eds.), *Developing Personal Relationships*. (London: Academic Press.)

Clore, G. (1977). Reinforcement and affect in attraction. In: S. W. Duck (Ed)., *Theory and Practice in Interpersonal Attraction*. (London: Academic Press.)

Clore, G. and Byrne, D. (1974). A reinforcement-affect model of attraction. In: T. L. Huston (Ed.), *Foundations of Interpersonal Attraction*. (London: Academic Press.)

Dewhurst, F. D. and Duck, S. W. (1978). Personal relationships and clinical practice. Paper presented to Conference on Social Psychology and Clinical Practice, Loughborough, March 1978.

Dion, K., Berscheid, E. and Walster, E. H. (1972). What is beautiful is good. *Journal of Personality and Social Psychology*, **24,** 285–290.

Drewery, J. and Rae, J. (1969). A group comparison of psychiatric and non-psychiatric marriages using the interpersonal perception technique. *British Journal of Psychiatry*, **115,** 287–300.

Duck, S. W. (1975). Personality similarity and friendship choices by adolescents. *European Journal of Social Psychology*, **5,** 70–83.

Duck, S. W. (1976). Interpersonal communication in developing acquaintance. In G. Miller (Ed.), *Explorations in Interpersonal Communication*. (New York: Sage.)

Duck, S. W. (1977). *The Study of Acquaintance*. (London: Teakfield Saxon House.)

Duck, S. W. (1978). Order and structure in social relationships. Paper to the meeting of European Association of Experimental Social Psychology, Weimar, DDR, March 1978.

Duck, S.W. (1979). The personal and the interpersonal in construct theory. In: D. Bannister and P. Stringer (Eds.), *Personal Constructs and Social Psychology*. (London: Academic Press.)

Duck, S. W. (In press). Collapsing personal relationships. In: R. Gilmour and S. W. Duck (Eds.), *Personal Relationships in Disorder*. (London: Academic Press.)

Duck, S. W. and Allison, D. (1978). I liked you but I can't live with you: a study of lapsed friendships. *Social Behaviour and Personality*, **6**(1), 43–47.

Duck, S. W., Miell, D., and Gaebler, H. C. (1979). Attraction and communication in children's interactions. In: H. C. Foot, A. Chapman and J. Smith (Eds.), *Friendship and Social Interactions in Children*. (London: Wiley.)

Duck, S. W. and Spencer, C. P. (1972). Personal constructs and friendship formation. *Journal of Personality and Social Psychology*, **23,** 40–45.

Engelhart, R. S., Lockhart, L. M., and La Gaipa, J. (1975). Friendship expectations of psychiatric patients. Paper read at the meeting of Southeastern Psychological Association, Atlanta.

Erikson, E. H. (1959). Identity and the life cycle. *Psychological Issues*, Monograph 1 (no. 1), 1–171.

Euripides (*c*. 442 BC) *Medea*.

Goffman, E. (1963). *Stigma: Notes on the Management of Spoiled Identity*. Prentice Hall: Englewood Cliffs.

Goldstein, A. (1971). *Attraction in Psychotherapy*. (New York: Pergamon.)
Griffitt, W., Nelson, J., and Littlepage, G. (1972). Old age and responses to agreement–disagreement. *Jounal of Gerontology*, **27,** 269–274.
Hartup, W. W. (1979). Children and their friends. In: H. McGurk (Ed.), *Childhood Social Development*. (London: Methuen.)
Hatfield, E. and Traupmann, J. (In press). Intimate relationships: a perspective from Equity Theory. In: S. W. Duck and R. Gilmour (Eds.), *Personal Relationships*. (London: Academic Press.)
Henderson, S. (1974). Care-eliciting behaviour in man. *Journal of Nervous and Mental Disease*, **159,** 172–181.
Henderson, S. (1977). The social network, support and neurosis: the function of attachment in adult life. *British Journal of Psychiatry*, **131,** 185–191.
Huesmann, L. R. and Levinger, G. (1976). Incremental exchange theory: a formal model for progression in dyadic social interactions. In: L. Berkowitz and E. H. Walster (Eds.), *Advances in Experimental Social Psychology*, Vol. 9. (New York: Academic Press.)
Huston, T. L. and Levinger, G. (1978). Interpersonal attraction and relationships. *Annual Review of Psychology*, **21,** 115–156.
Jourard, S. (1959). Healthy personality and self-disclosure. *Mental Hygiene*, **43,** 449–507.
Kelly, G. A. (1955). *The Psychology of Personal Constructs*. (New York: Norton.)
Kelly, G. A. (1969). Hostility. In: B. Maher (Ed.), *Clinical Psychology and Personality: The Collected Papers of George Kelly*. (New York: Wiley.)
Kerckhoff, A. C. (1974). The social context of interpersonal attraction. In: T. L. Huston (Ed.), *Foundations of Interpersonal Attraction*. (New York: Academic Press.)
Klein, H. and La Gaipa, J. J. (1978). Causal explanations of interpersonal behaviour given by socially withdrawn children. Unpublished manuscript, Department of Psychology, University of Windsor, Canada.
La Gaipa, J. J. (1977). Testing a multidimensional approach to friendship. In: S. W. Duck (Ed.), *Theory and Practice in Interpersonal Attraction*. (London: Academic Press.)
La Gaipa, J. J. and Engelhart, R. S. (1977). Extraversion–introversion, neuroticism and self disclosure in friendship. Paper presented at meeting of Southeastern Psychological Association, Hollywood, Florida.
La Gaipa, J. J. and Irwin, K. (1976). The administration of the children's friendship expectancy inventory to emotionally disturbed adolescent females. Unpublished manuscript, Department of Psychology, University of Windsor, Canada.
La Gaipa, J. J. and Uriel, M. (1974). Psychosocial satisfaction and the effectiveness of group therapy for alcoholics. Paper presented at meeting of Canadian Psychological Association, Windsor, Canada.
La Gaipa, J. J. and Wood, D. (In press). Relationships in disturbed adolescents. In: R. Gilmour and S. W. Duck (Eds.), *Personal Relationships in Disorder*. (London: Academic Press.)
La Gaipa, J. J. and Wood, H. D. (1973). The perception of friendship by socially accepted and rejected children. Paper delivered to Eastern Psychological Association, Washington, D.C.
Lemert, E. M. (1962). Paranoia and the dynamics of exclusion. *Sociometry*, **25,** 2–20.
Levinger, G. (1974). A three-level approach to attraction: toward an understanding of pair relatedness. In: T. L. Huston (Ed.), *Foundations of Interpersonal Attraction*. (New York: Academic Press.)
Levinger, G. and Snoek, D. (1972). *Attraction in Relationship: A New Look at Interpersonal Attraction*. (Morristown, NJ: General Learning Press.)
Lowe, G. R. (1969). *Personal Relationships in Psychological Disorders*. (Harmondsworth: Penguin.)
Lynch, J. J. (1977). *The Broken Heart: The Medical Consequences of Loneliness*. (London: Harper & Row.)
McCarthy, B. (1978). Interpersonal behaviour of successful and unsuccessful acquainters: an

exploratory study. Paper presented to Annual Conference of British Psychological Society, Social Psychology Section, Cardiff.

McPherson, F. M., Buckley, F., and Draffan, J. (1971). 'Psychological' constructs, thought-process disorder and flattening of affect. *British Journal of Social and Clinical Psychology*, **10,** 267–270.

Manning, M. and Herrman, J. (In press). The relationships of problem children in nursery schools. In: R. Gilmour and S. W. Duck (Eds.), *Personal Relationships in Disorder*. (London: Academic Press.)

Maslow, A. (1953). Love in healthy people. In: A. Montagu (Ed.), *The Meaning of Love*. (New York: Julian Press.)

Miell, D. E., Duck, S. W. and La Gaipa (1979). Interactive effects of sex and timing in self-disclosure. *British Journal of Social and Clinical Psychology*, **18,** 355–362.

Murstein, B. I. (1971). A theory of marital choice and its applicability to marriage adjustment. In: B. I. Murstein (Ed.), *Theories of Attraction and Love*. (New York: Springer.)

Murstein, B. I. (1977). The stimulus–value–role (SVR) theory of dyadic relationships. In: S. W. Duck (Ed.), *Theory and Practice in Interpersonal Attraction*. (London: Academic Press.)

Nelson-Jones, R. and Strong, S. R. (1976). Rules, risk and self-disclosure. *British Journal of Guidance and Counselling*, **4,** 202–211.

Peplau, L. A. and Perlman, D. (1977). Blueprint for a social psychological theory of loneliness. Paper presented to International Conference on Love and Attraction, Swansea, Wales, September.

Perlman, D. and Peplau, L. A. (In press). Loneliness. In: R. Gilmour and S. W. Duck (Eds.), *Personal Relationships in Disorder*. (London: Academic Press.)

Perrin, F. A. C. (1921). Physical attractiveness and repulsiveness. *Journal of Experimental Psychology*, **4,** 203–217.

Przybyla, D. and Byrne, D. (In press). Human sexual relationships. In: S. W. Duck and R. Gilmour (Eds.), *Personal Relationships*. (London: Academic Press.)

Rogers, C. R. (1959). A theory of therapy, personality and interpersonal relationships as developed in the Client-Centred framework. In: S. Koch (Ed.) *Psychology: A Study of a Science*. (New York: McGraw Hill.)

Rosenblatt, P. C. (1974). Cross-cultural perspective on attraction. In: T. L. Huston (Ed.), *Foundations of Interpersonal Attraction*. (New York: Academic Press.)

Sullivan, H. S. (1953). *The Interpersonal Theory of Psychiatry*. (New York: Norton.)

Wagner, R. V. (1975). Complementary needs, role expectations, interpersonal attraction and the stability of working relationships. *Journal of Personal and Social Psychology*, **32,** 116–124.

Walster, E., Traupmann, J., and Walster, G. W. (In press). Equity and extramarital sexuality. *Archives of Sexual Behaviour*,

Walster, E., Walster, G. W. and Berscheid, E. (1978). *Equity: Theory and Research*. (Boston: Allyn & Bacon.)

Walster, E., Walster, G. W., and Traupmann, J. (1978). Equity and premarital sex. *Journal of Personality and Social Psychology*, **38,** 89–92.

Weiss, R. S. (1969). The fund of sociability. *Trans-Action*, **6,** 36–43.

Weiss, R. S. (1973). *Loneliness: The Experience of Emotional and Social Isolation*. (Cambridge, Mass.: MIT Press.)

Weiss, R. S. (1974). The provisions of social relationships. In: Z. Rubin (Ed.), *Doing Unto Others*. (New York: Prentice Hall.)

Winch, R. F. (1958). *Mate Selection: A Study in Complementary Needs*. (New York: Harper & Row.)

Wood, H. D. and La Gaipa, J. J. (1978). Predicting behavioural types in preadolescent girls from psychosocial development and friendship values. Paper presented at meeting of Canadian Psychological Association, Toronto, June, 1978.

The Social Psychology of Psychological Problems
Edited by P. Feldman and J. Orford

4

Self-Perception, Perception of Others, and Social Personality

MARK COOK

INTRODUCTION

Approaches to explaining how people see themselves and other people are various, involving as they do not just various schools and disciplines of psychology, but also sociology, psychiatry, philosophy, and literature. Several general approaches to psychology argue that the way people perceive things is the most important part of psychology, or even the sum total of psychology, for how people see things determines how they behave. Most of what people perceive that has much consequence is other people, which implies that the study of social perception, or person perception, is *the* most important topic in psychology. Lewin's (1936) theory of 'life space' is one example of this 'phenomenological' approach; another is the theory of Snygg and Coombs (1949). More recently personal construct theory (Kelly, 1955), based on Kelly's fundamental postulate 'A person's processes are psychological, channelised by the ways in which he anticipates events', has provided what phenomenological theories often lack, a measure: the Role Repertory Grid Test.

Roger's theory of the self also has a measure, the Q sort, and like Kelly's construct theory has a clinical background. Rogers defined the self or self-concept as an 'organised, consistent conceptual gestalt composed of perceptions of the characteristics of the "I" or "me" and the perceptions of the "I" and "me", to others and to various aspects of life, together with the values attached to these perceptions'. (Rogers, 1951.)

More narrowly based approaches to self and person perception liken it to perception of the material world, so as to provide a logical framework of explanation. The gestalt school considered that people were seen in the same sort of way as objects, that is as 'gestalts' or meaningful wholes; some gestalt theorists postulated special perceptual mechanisms, such as 'physiognomic perception' (Werner, 1948) or 'isomorphism' (Arnheim, 1949). Later approaches place less emphasis on the perceptual aspects of 'person perception' and more on the cognitive aspects, recognizing that reaching decisions about people and the self is less a matter of sensory input, and more one of organizing and evaluating information. The clinical inference model of Sarbin *et al.* (1960) is an example of this and bases its explanation on an analogy with the Aristotelian syllogism.

The most recent approach finally drops the word 'perception'. 'Attribution theory' recognizes that while seeing a hammer fall and strike someone's foot is a perception, calling on one's knowledge of the present circumstances and past events and saying 'he is clumsy' is an 'attribution'. Attribution theory concerns itself with the conditions under which behaviour is seen as evidence of personality dispositions and not as the result of random outside forces.

Given the amount and importance of research into self and other-perception, and the argument that it is the core topic of psychology, it is not surprising that its practical applications are extensive and significant. Psychiatric diagnosis is essentially a person perception task, as is much of personnel selection. Furthermore the problems of patients, when diagnosed, often involve either poor social skill and inability to sum up others, or an unrealistic self-perception.

The way people see themselves, or other people, forms the basis of most systems of measuring personality. Personality as seen by other people can be studied by rating methods, by behaviour checklists, or by systematic observations. Personality as seen by the person himself is studied by ratings too, but principally by the questionnaire. Fiske (1974) has questioned whether the study of personality can ever progress more rapidly than it has so far until it breaks free from its dependence on people's perceptions. Many would argue that the break is not possible and that the topics of personality and person perception are inextricably linked together.

PERCEIVING OTHER PEOPLE

Conan Doyle's Dr Watson described one of Sherlock Holmes's clients as 'an average common-place British tradesman, obese, pompous, and slow ... there was nothing remarkable about the man save his blazing red hair and the expression of extreme chagrin and discontent upon his features', which gives some idea of the range of things covered by person perception. People form impressions of each other because they need to do so. As Vernon (1964) observed, 'Social intercourse would become chaotic if we did not straightaway react differently to a 60-year-old and a six-year-old, to a society hostess and a prostitute'. They form impressions because they like doing so, as evidenced by the time most people spend gossiping about each other. Finally they form impressions because they are employed to do so. Psychiatrists, social workers, and psychologists in particular, have to reach opinions about people's thoughts, feelings, motives, past and future behaviour, often with little or no 'hard' evidence to work on, and then have to bear the responsibility if their opinion is proved wrong. Instances like that of the patient judged 'safe' and released from a special hospital who then commits further crimes—like the multiple poisoner

Graham Young released from Broadmoor in 1971—occasions bitter criticism of the staff responsible.

Opinions about other people are expressed in words, and the words most commonly used are 'trait' words: 'withdrawn', 'dangerous', 'intelligent' etc. As Mischel (1968) has argued, it is not always clear that there is something being referred to by all trait words. Most people feel happy describing others as 'honest' or 'dishonest', but Hartshorn and May long ago (1928) demonstrated that honesty on one occasion hardly generalizes at all to another, so that the word 'honest', unqualified by reference to the circumstances, is largely meaningless. The research of Zigler and Phillips (1961) shows that most common psychiatric symptoms—anxiety, sleeplessness, depression, etc.—occur frequently in patients in all conventional diagnostic categories, suggesting that calling someone 'schizophrenic' or 'neurotic' is, like saying he is honest, a vague and unhelpful description of him.

The interpretations people make of each others' behaviour vary in depth. In Secord's study (Secord and Backman, 1964), some college students described friends in simple terms like 'good at dancing; fun to be with', whereas others went 'deeper', saying things like 'she can't seem to go toward one boy and when she does like one boy she sort of falls hard and then if the boy doesn't like her as much as she likes him, she has a real rough time ... she's sort of insecure'. Pseudo-profundity is of course the stock in trade of fortune-tellers, astrologers, and of some psychologists. An experiment by Snyder and Larson (1972) has shown how easily most people are taken in by a seemingly deep analysis of an individual's character. The same set of platitudes, e.g. 'disciplined and controlled on the outside, you tend to be worrisome and insecure on the inside', was given to every student in a class, and most accepted it as a genuine and profound interpretation of their own personality. The experimenters dubbed this the 'Barnum Effect', Adinolfi (1971) points out how easy it is for the clinician to fall for the 'siren call of the Barnum effect' and make correct but all-purpose and uninformative statements about his patients.

The way impressions are formed

Given that people form a great number and variety of judgements about others, how do they do it? There have traditionally been two types of explanation: intuition approaches and inference models. Intuition theories are often obscure. Some versions simply say that perception relies on innate mechanisms. Ekman (1972) showed that New Guinea tribesmen could recognize Westerners' facial expressions, and expressed their emotions in a way Westerners could recognize. Other versions of the intuition explanation say that perception of emotions, personality, etc. is direct or immediate. This is a very obscure notion; it may mean that people are not aware of the processes involved when they make the judgement, or it could mean that there are no processes involved, or else that they cannot be investigated. Both the latter propositions are obviously false.

The alternative view (Sarbin *et al.*, 1960) says that perception of emotion, personality, etc. depends on a process of conscious or unconscious inference, somewhat on these lines:

> Teenage girls who smoke cigarettes regularly are not virgins,
> This teenage girl smokes,
> Therefore she is not a virgin.

People reason from general principles and from the evidence before them to a particular conclusion. The usual objection to this explanation is that people are not aware of making any inference, but this is not a valid criticism, since 'unconscious inferences' have been convincingly demonstrated in other types of perception.

Meehl (1961) criticizes the inference model on the grounds that it imposes categories or types on people—aggressive or non-aggressive, nice or nasty—when it would be better to think in terms of dimensions that may be correlated to a greater or lesser extent—the *more* extravert someone is, the *more likely* he is to develop an hysterical type of neurosis. Meehl's correlation model is particularly suited to describing judgements based on a number of cues, not just one. In formal judgements like psychiatric diagnosis, the focus of Meehl's interest, the judge always has more than one cue and often has dozens. To express a syllogistic inference from ten not necessarily consistent cues would be very clumsy.

However, experiments on the way people use information about correlated variables suggest that Meehl is describing the way they ought to think, not the way they actually think. Chapman and Chapman (1967) gave their subjects randomly paired symptom statements and 'Draw-A-Person' productions, and asked them to report any characteristics in the drawings that seemed to go with particular symptoms. The subjects 'discovered' only relationships that corresponded to the ones expert psycho-diagnosticians claimed to find in their clinical practice, e.g. that atypical rendering of the eyes in the drawing indicated a suspicious personality in the drawer. This particular relationship, like many other items of clinical lore, does not stand up to empirical test. Chapman and Chapman's subjects imposed upon correlational data a false categorical notion of their own. Other experiments on the same lines, reported by Kahneman & Tversky (1973), all show that man does not shine as an intuitive statistician.

Opinions based on more than one fact

When people have more than one piece of information about someone, and when the information points in different ways, they have essentially four strategies for reaching a decision.

Favourite cue or cues The story of the personnel man who left selection of staff to his dog—who liked some people and growled at others—is probably apocryphal, but anyone who has had any experience in the personnel field will have come across 'experts' who 'swear by' a particular cue, and think so highly of it they largely ignore the rest of the information.

Adding and averaging, weighted or unweighted Adding and averaging amount to the same thing when the number of cues is constant. The individual items might be treated as equivalent, so that, when selecting an army officer, physical fitness, smartness of appearance, verbal intelligence, spatial intelligence, and motivation would count equally; more usually, some items carry more weight than others. The weighting may reflect the known validity of the cue, or the judge's hunches, experience and biasses.

Configural judgements The questions of configural cues is an important issue in the dispute between 'statistical' or 'actuarial' prediction, and clinical judgement.

In clinical judgements the judge reaches a conclusion about someone from some or all of the available information, but isn't necessarily able to say what cues he uses or how much weight he attaches to each. The clinical method has great appeal, both to its practitioners and to the public, because an effort is seen to be made to study the individual as a unique configuration of abilities, traits, and experiences; an actuarial table by contrast seems crude, inhuman, and bureaucratic. An experienced psychologist or psychiatrist is surely able to predict whether a prisoner will commit further offences, if released, more accurately and sensitively than a clerk filling in a form like a car-insurance proposal?

However, Meehl was unable to find any evidence that the clinical method led to more accurate assessment, and since Meehl's (1954) review little has emerged to challenge his conclusion that the actuarial method—the 'cookbook' as he puts it—is better; Lindzey (1965) reported a study showing that clinical prediction of male homosexuality from TAT protocols was slightly better than a formula based on 20 TAT signs, but the difference was nowhere near statistically significant.

Sawyer (1966) makes the point that the 'cookbook' does not have to be as simple as a weighted average or linear regression, but can be as complicated as the data demand. In fact research shows that it need usually be no more elaborate than a weighted average. Meehl (1959) did find that 'neurotic' and 'psychotic' MMPI profiles could be best distinguished by the 'highly configural' Meehl–Dahlstrom rules, which were superior to simple models, but his result seems exceptional and several studies since, using the MMPI (Goldberg, 1965), or predicting parole violations (Babst *et al.*, 1968; Pritchard, 1977), have found that weighted averages give the best predictions.

The work of Goldberg, Pritchard and Gottfredson suggested that elaborate configural strategies are not usually needed to get the right answer; other research at the Oregon Research Institute makes it doubtful whether expert judges actually make configural judgements very often. In the study of Rorer *et al.* (1967) their judges—nurses, doctors, psychologists, and social workers—assessed psychiatric inpatients' suitability for a weekend pass from six systematically varied cues. Some interactions were found, indicating configural judgement, but overall only 2 per cent of the variance was accounted for by interactions. Judges varied a lot in their strategies; quite a few restricted themselves to a simple linear combination of three out of six cues, while others used up to 22 interactions, including interactions of up to five items. Hoffman *et al.* (1968) showed that consultant radiologists diagnosing ulcers from X-ray photographs of the stomach didn't make nearly as much use of configurations of signs as they claimed. They also disagreed with each others' diagnosis very frequently. The only type of expert so far found who does regularly use information configurally is the stockbroker predicting share prices (Slovic, 1969).

So far it appears: (a) that the human judge is no better than a formula; (b) that he makes little use of configural cues; and (c) that he has little cause to, because valid cues to the things he is predicting are rarely configural.

The 'attribution' of traits to explain behaviour

When someone sees a child kick a dog, he can either say the child did it because he doesn't like dogs or he can say something tending to excuse the action, such as 'he had to do it to protect himself' or 'he was tricked into doing it' or 'he didn't mean to do it'. 'Attribution theory' calls the former—dislike of dogs—a 'dispositional attribution', while the latter reasons are termed 'situational attributions'. Very many experiments have been carried out to determine how and under what circumstances one or other inference is made. Thibaut and Riecken (1955) found that high-status people were seen as making a choice when asked to do something—a 'dispositional inference'—whereas low-status people were seen as having been persuaded—a 'situational inference'. Jones *et al.* (1961) showed that 'out-of-role' behaviour leads to dispositional inferences; when a candidate for the post of sub-marine explorer, or of astronaut, behaved in a way inconsistent with 'the ideal personality type for the job' (as described by the experimenter), observers were more likely to think that that was the real him. If he conformed to the job description, he could just be putting on a front, trying to ingratiate himself—a 'situational inference'. It has been said that the selection interview is essentially a 'search for negative information'.

Jones and Davis (1965) developed a 'theory of correspondent inferences', which contains two stages—the inference from an action to an intention, and the inference from an intention to a disposition. To infer that someone meant to do something because he's like that, is to make a 'correspondent inference'—the disposition corresponds to the intention and the intention corresponds to the action. Factors which tend to make people produce correspondent inferences include whether their own well-being is affected by the behaviour in question, whether it is socially acceptable, whether it is the usual thing to do in the circumstances, and whether they think the person actually capable of controlling the effects of his actions.

Attribution theory in its various forms is not really a theory in the strict sense of the word; its authors say as much, describing it as 'an amorphous collection of observations about naive causal inference' (Jones *et al.*, 1971). Much of it can be criticized as vague, tautologous, or only tenuously related to experimental data (Cook, 1979), but it has had a great influence on theory and research in person perception. Some of the results that have emerged from attribution experiments have been quite surprising.

For example, Nisbett and Caputo, cited by Jones *et al.* (1971), gave the subject in their experiment a very simple task and discovered an 'actor–observer effect'. Each subject was asked to write a paragraph explaining why he had chosen his degree course, and another explaining why he had chosen his girl friend, and was then asked to explain the same choices as made by his best friend. Subjects tended to make 'stimulus attributions'—'chemistry is a high-paying field' or 'she's a very warm person'—to explain their own choices, but 'person attributions'—'he wants to earn a lot of money' or 'he likes warm girls'—when explaining their friends' choices. Jones and Harris (1967) found that observers thought someone believed what he was saying, even when told he was reading from a script provided by the experimenter; they preferred to explain someone else's behaviour in terms of the person's character and outlook, not in terms of his responding to outside pressures.

Accuracy of opinions about other people

The most striking finding to emerge from the extensive, jumbled literature on 'accuracy of person perception' is how very inaccurate most people are most of the time. Archer and Akert (1977) have devised a Social Interpretations task in which short sequences of filmed encounter are followed by simple, relevant questions, which have definite answers—which man won the tennis match?; which of the women is the mother of the child? Pure guesswork would give an average score of six out of sixteen, which compares with an average of 8.85 right for subjects who saw the films, and a dismal 5.50 for subjects who merely read the script. Fancher (1969) used the 'programmed case' method, where judges 'post-dict' key choices a person made at important moments in his life. Twelve 'post-dictions', each from three possibilities, implies a guesswork score of 4; judges actually achieved a score at 5–5½.

Too much person-perception research has studied opinions formed by people, who have no pressing need to form them, about people they have little contact with and will never meet again outside the laboratory. A courting couple are in a much better position to get to know each other, besides having much stronger reasons for needing to. Kirkpatrick and Hobart (1954) found that the ability of couples to predict each others' answers to a 'Family Opinion Survey' was higher if they were married, as opposed to engaged, and higher in engaged couples than in couples merely dating. This finding might be dismissed as a 'glimpse of the blindingly obvious', if it were not for two facts: firstly the tendency Kirkpatrick and Hobart found was very modest; and secondly, subsequent research has not always been able to find even modest correlations between length of relationship and accuracy of perception. Udry (1963) found that most of the variance in couples' predictions of each others' 16PF inventories was accounted for by random error, with tendency to assume similarity, and accurate prediction each accounting for around 10–15 per cent. Murstein (1972) found a modest but reliable tendency for inaccurate perception of each other on the Marital Expectation Test to predict 'poor courtship progress'; Udry (1967), employing the possibly less relevant 16PF, was unable to relate the outcome of a liaison—breakup/marriage—to accuracy of perception.

Attempts to prove that happy marriages are characterized by the partners seeing each other's point of view clearly—a very plausible and widely held assumption—have not been generally successful either. Corsini (1956), using Q sorts, and Clements (1967), using rank orders of marital grievances, found no differences between stable, happy marriages and unstable, unhappy ones. Dymond (1954) found a very modest advantage—38 against 33 out of 55 predictions—for happy couples, while Murstein and Beck's (1972) best result, out of 48 correlations, between adjustment and accuracy of perception, was only 0.37.

Udry (1963) points to one of the reasons for this initially puzzling finding—assumed similarity; married couples seem to get by much of the time in ignorance of what the other really thinks, comfortably assuming the other shares their views. Byrne and Blaylock (1963) found very limited similarity of opinion—on Rokeach's Dogmatism Scale—but much greater perceived similarity, with correlations of 0.69 and 0.89 against 0.30 and 0.44. Some schools of thought use words like 'pseudo-mutuality' to describe families whose members allow their differences to go unrecognized, behind a public front of agreement and solidarity; using such disparaging terms implies that it is a bad practice. If it is a bad habit, it's a very common one. Steiner (1955) questions the assumption that a person who sees clearly what other people think about him is always benefited by his insight, and points out that it would often merely undermine self-confidence and paralyse social interaction.

Personality, psychiatric problems and perception of others

Personality and perception Scodel's work (Scodel and Mussen, 1953) found ample evidence that highly authoritarian people assumed others were as authoritarian as them, but did not show that authoritarians were poorer judges of others, as their supposed possession of rigid and closed minds would seem to imply. However, Gabennesch and Hunt (1971) did find that authoritarians were worse at perceiving the rank order of authoritarians within their groups than were people with a more liberal outlook. Sechrest and Jackson (1961) found no correlation between differential accuracy and a variety of measures: MMPI scales, sociometric ratings, repertory grid, and Rorschach scores, etc. They did find correlations between stereotype accuracy and sociometric ratings of pleasantness and predictability, and absence of psychopathic deviance on the MMPI. Chance and Meaders (1960) found that judges with good differential accuracy showed a pattern of self-ratings of independence, strong-mindedness, participation in social relations and absence of introspection.

Taft (1956) confirmed the results of earlier studies, finding a low positive correlation between intelligence and tasks of rating traits like 'social assertiveness' or deciding which person had produced which mosaic design; a correlation of 0.37 with 'best performance' (from five intelligence tests) is quite impressive, bearing in mind that the judges were all graduate students, representing a very restricted range of ability. Sechrest and Jackson (1961), on the other hand, also using student subjects, found no correlation at all between intelligence and either stereotype or differential accuracy measures in a behaviour prediction task. Wolfe (1974) used adolescents as subjects, to predict how two teachers would complete Cattell's 16PF questionnaire, and found that their ability to do so correlated with their intelligence and with their 'conceptual level'—a measure of the abstractness of responses to a task involving completing paragraphs. On balance there does seem to be a link between intelligence and ability to perceive other people accurately, but more research is needed to give a fuller account of it.

Perceptions by Psychiatric Patients

Research on all aspects of person perception, in psychiatric patients, has been sparse and unsystematic, with the exception of studies of 'schizophrenic' personal construct systems. Of persons diagnosed schizophrenic, it is also known that they are poor at emotion recognition tasks (Davitz, 1964), at predicting word associations (Milgram, 1960), and at synchronizing their speech with that of the person they are conversing with (Matarazzo and Saslow, 1961). On the other hand the work of Braginsky and Braginsky (1967) implies that many 'schizophrenics' can converse normally, and even make a good job of deceiving others. Helfland (1956) showed that partly recovered schizophrenics were just as good as control subjects at predicting responses to a self-rating task. Chronic schizophrenic patients were not, however; the distribution of their accuracy scores centred exactly on chance level. Research findings so far leave it uncertain whether schizophrenics' social perceptions are poor through lack of ability or lack of interest in the task, and whether the lack of interest is caused by 'institutionalization' or something else. An interesting early lead by Lyons (1956) had not been followed up. Lyons found a tendency for schizophrenics, when describing a sequence of behaviour, and telling the experimenter 'all the different things' the other person did, to identify smaller sequences of behaviour. If this finding could be confirmed, it would fit in with theory and research, which identifies limited powers of attention as a fundamental feature of some types of schizophrenia (McGhie and Chapman, 1961).

Bannister (1962) first applied personal construct theory and the Role Repertory Grid Test to person perception in schizophrenics, and argued that a central feature of the illness is 'serial invalidation'. The schizophrenic—as a child—starts forming ideas about other people—'constructs'—in the normal way, but the irrational and inconsistent behaviour of his family consistently 'invalidate' them for him. He never knows what to expect next. The schizophrenic adult therefore is unable to form any stable impression of other people, hence presumably he retreats socially and develops other symptoms because of his social isolation. Bannister and Fransella (1966) developed a psychometric test of this inability to perceive or 'construe' other people, and showed that the schizophrenic does not apply personality trait terms to other people consistently on successive occasions and, in effect, does not show *any* halo effect, using a dozen trait terms in completely different ways. Critics of the theory and test (Frith & Lillie, 1972) point out that these results would be achieved if the schizophrenic simply makes no effort to cooperate with the test procedure; however, McPherson and Buckley (1970) did find schizophrenics showed a greater deficit when 'construing' personality features, as opposed to physical aspects of people and objects.

The paranoid individual, in sharp contrast, has a very well organized set of ideas about other people, so well organized that reality cannot readily change them. McPherson *et al.* (1971) showed that paranoid schizophrenics had as many 'psychological constructs' as normal subjects, unlike schizophrenics with other types of delusion.

Paranoid misperceptions take many and bizarre forms. Weston and Whitlock (1971) described a case of a rare and striking delusion called the 'Capgras Syndrome' in which the patient is convinced that his nearest and dearest are not themselves any more, but that their place has been taken by imposters disguised as them. Colby (1977) reviews several theories of paranoia, and dismisses among others the Freudian theory of repressed homosexuality—'I love him—I mustn't love him—I hate him—he hates me.' Colby considers that the 'shame-humiliation' theory of paranoid ideas fits the data better. According to this the paranoid person checks everything he hears, for anything implying he is inadequate. Acknowledging his inadequacy would be humiliating, so the blame for the inadequacy is attributed to others.

Cameron (1943) argues that paranoia develops over a period of years and that its origins go back to childhood.

> Habits of reticence and concealment imposed earlier in life mean a real inability in adulthood to share experiences and attitudes. Lone thinking, preoccupation and puzzling are apt under these circumstances to take their place. Things seen and heard are thought about, interpreted and brooded over, but not shared with other persons. ... Under the directive influence of some personal stress, this watching and listening and brooding can develop cumulative misunderstandings.

Cameron sees paranoia develop when a solitary introspective person, poor at 'taking the role of the other', is faced with a stressful event.

While the precipitating factor in paranoia is usually something like losing one's job or being divorced, there is evidence—necessarily only in case-history—that paranoia can be caused, or at least triggered off, by physical causes. Weston and

Whitlock's case of 'Capgras Syndrome', mentioned above, first showed symptoms after a head injury. Wharton (1970) describes the case of a man who developed paranoia after taking too many nasal decongestion pills, whose chemical composition closely resembled amphetamine. Oswald (1966) deprived a volunteer subject of sleep for several nights and later discovered the man had placed paranoid interpretations on a trip to a television studio made during his period of sleep-deprivation. Wharton's subject is specifically described as 'of good previous personality' which suggests that a drastic change in the way people think about events and motives may be easily produced by purely physical causes.

Recently the concepts of attribution theory have been used to devise new forms of psychotherapy for paranoia. Paranoia is a difficult problem, because of the ease with which the patient incorporates all new ideas, including the therapist's efforts, into a system of delusions. Johnson *et al.* (1977) describe a case-study in which a man was cured of the paranoid delusion that he had been attacked by a succubus, by encouraging him to re-attribute his sexual arousal to its actual causes—sexual abstinence and pressure from leg movements.

The concept of psychopathy is a very unsatisfactory one, but a theme running through all the various accounts of psychopathic behaviour is the inability to understand disapproval. Gough and Petersen (1952) constructed a test for detecting psychopathic patients, based on the assumption that they do not perceive other people's feelings and do not predict their behaviour accurately; Gough (1948) argues that as a consequence of the psychopath's inability to understand other people's reactions, he does not understand punishment and disapproval.

Howells (1978) discusses 'aggressive offenders', many of whom would be labelled psychopathic, and argues that they characteristically fail to see the causes of events correctly. Whenever anything goes wrong, they make 'other-attributions', they blame someone else, and never see themselves at fault. In this way they develop the suspiciousness, resentment, and hostility so apparent to others; Howells sees aggressive offenders as having much in common with paranoid individuals and points out that the two diagnoses are often hard to distinguish. If Howells's analysis in attribution theory terms is correct, it follows that 'reattribution therapy', like that used by Johnson *et al.* (1977) for paranoia, might be successful, where other forms of treatment are notoriously ineffective.

Attribution theory has also been applied to depression. According to Seligman's (1975) 'learned helplessness' model, the depressed individual has learned that his actions have no effect on what happens to him, and so attributes external causes to everything, and by extension makes no effort to achieve anything himself. Beck (1967) argues that the depressed individual does see himself responsible for things that happen, but only when they are bad. He allows himself no credit when good things happen. Rizley's (1978) experiment found qualified support for Beck's theory, but it remains to be seen whether either theory can give a really informative account of depression, as opposed to merely re-describing depression in attribution theory terms.

Various early studies, reviewed by Taft (1955), found that unstable people are poorer at trait-rating tasks rather than, as is sometimes suggested, more sensitive to others, as a consequence of being more sensitive to themselves. Otherwise there is a curious dearth of research on all aspects of person perception in neurotic individuals.

SELF-PERCEPTION

Behaviourist psychologists are often wary of talking about the 'self', as it often seems a way of re-introducing the notion of the 'ghost in the machine', or of falling into 'homunculus' fallacies. When one has explored the role of the visual cortex in visual perception, it is tempting to leave the burden of explanation of what remains to the 'self', the 'ego', or the like. Fortunately better-thought-out accounts of what is meant by 'the self' are available which avoid the infinite regress of 'explaining' behaviour by the invoking of a 'little man inside the head' who makes all the decisions.

Vernon (1964) distinguished a number of levels of the self, in order of 'depth'. The first level is the *social self*, or rather selves—the various fronts, or self-presentations (Goffman, 1961) the person has for different occasions. Mischel (1973) has recently introduced the cumbersome phrase 'self-regulatory systems and plans' to refer to much the same idea. The concept of 'role' also covers some of what Vernon means by social self. A person who has a limited repertoire of self-presentations will obviously find many encounters or social occasions too difficult for him. Social skill training schemes (see Curran, 1978 and the chapters by Argyle and Shepherd—Chapters 5 and 9—in this volume), exist to help shy or socially awkward people increase the number of roles they can play.

At present there are no very good ways of assessing how extensive and how useful is a person's social repertoire. Paper and pencil 'social intelligence' tests are well known to be little more than disguised measures of general and verbal intelligence, and it has been pointed out recently (Rich and Schroeder, 1976) that knowing what to do in social encounters is not the same as actually being able to produce the right words and actions. The conclusion seems unavoidable that social selves can only be studied and measured behaviourally; Arkowitz *et al.* (1975) has made a start with behavioural tests of the male's ability to ask for a date.

Vernon's second level is the *conscious private self*. This, according to Vernon, is generally but not always revealed to one's close friends. Vernon suggests very plausibly that even the person himself may not see it that clearly. His hypothesis is that some people tend to see themselves only at the level of the social self, believing that the part they are playing is really them.

Vernon's third level is the *insightful self*—the person as he might realize he really is, after Rogerian therapy has helped him break down his defence mechanisms, or friends have pointed out serious inconsistencies in the way he thinks and acts. By definition a person will not generally see himself clearly at this level. At this level too, methodological and conceptual problems arise. Who is to say what the person is 'really' like? An expert perhaps, such as a Rogerian therapist, but experts, especially experts in psychology, are very fallible. 'Reaching a new understanding of oneself' might actually be just a process of verbal conditioning, in which the person learns to say the sort of thing about himself that pleases the therapist.

The fourth level of the self is the *repressed, depth self*, unknowable save through psychoanalysis. Freud and his followers argued that most of the personality functioned at the unconscious level, so that one is never aware of one's drives, or sexual desires for opposite sex parents.

The development of self-awareness

The very young child has not yet learned that his body is part of himself, and may bite his own toe and wonder why it hurts. Experiences of this sort, and proprioceptive feedback from movements the infant makes, teach the child a body image. Occasionally adults lose awareness of the bodily self. A few schizophrenic patients have the delusion that other people are controlling their movements or thinking their thoughts, and certain sorts of brain lesions render the person unable to make simple movements like a military salute, and also unaware that his hand hasn't moved to the right place. In fact all adults, with the possible exception of yoga experts, have limits to their awareness of their physical selves, as recent experiments on 'false feedback' (see below) about bodily symptoms has shown.

The child becomes aware of himself, as a conscious person with continuity of memory and experience, largely through hearing his name applied to himself, his actions, and his possessions (Allport, 1961). Children sometimes confuse reality and fantasy and may expect adults to see them as the bear they imagine themselves to be. Very occasionally cases have been reported of adults who do not have a sense of continuous self-identity, but who rather exhibit the 'multiple personality' of popular fancy, in which separate memories exist with no connection between them. Thigpen and Cleckley's (1957) case of 'Eve', who had three separate unrelated identities, is one example.

The child comes to realize that certain behaviour wins approval, while other sorts do not. Cooley and Mead argued that the way others react to the child is vitally important to the child's development. Cooley (1902) coined the phrase 'the looking-glass self' and said 'we always imagine, and in imagining share, the judgements of the other mind'. Mead (1934) developed the theme and said that a person always 'takes the role of the other' when deciding what to do, and so comes to judge himself and his actions as others—parents, teachers, friends, people in general—have judged him. By anticipating the reaction of others to an action before performing it, the child is able to choose one of several courses of action. According to Mead, no sense of self could develop in a person who never mixed with others, because he would never learn to react to his own behaviour as others do.

Measures of self-perceptions

Those working in the Rogerian tradition favour the 'Q sort technique', devised by Stephenson (1953). The subject is given 100 self-descriptive statements, such as 'I usually like people' or 'I am an interesting person', and is required to sort them into a crude approximation of a normal distribution, along a dimension of 'most like me' to 'least like me'. He does this once to describe himself, and once to describe himself as he would like to be, and the correlation between the two is taken as a measure of self-esteem. Other measures, using adjective checklist or questionnaire formats, are described by Wylie (1974). The Role Repertory Grid Test is readily adapted to measure self concepts (Bannister and Fransella, 1966). Vernon (1964) recommends the use of short written replies to open-ended questions, such as 'what I most like about the world in which I live', for determining the way people see themselves.

The self-ideal discrepancy measure, based on Q sorts, has been quite widely used. Rogers and Dymond (1954) showed that those diagnosed neurotic initially showed near zero correlations between their actual and ideal selves, but after 'client-centred therapy' shifted to a modest average correlation of 0.34. This compares with values of around 0.60 for people with no psychiatric problems. A near-perfect match between real self and ideal self would be as bad a sign as a very poor match, and would indicate a rigid over-defensive personality, according to Byrne (1966). Block and Thomas (1955) went some way to prove this, by comparing the MMPI profiles of subjects with very high 'self-ideal-congruence' and with very low 'self-ideal-congruence'. The latter showed tendencies to depression, hypochondria, introversion, and psychopathic deviance, where the former emerged as overcontrolled, and tending to deny their problems. Byrne went on to develop, from the MMPI, a scale of 'repression-sensitization'; repressors deny and ignore their problems so have an unrealistically favourable self-image, whereas sensitizers are too conscious of their problems and so have an unduly poor self-image.

Self-attribution

It is generally assumed each person has a unique insight into himself. No one would deny that the person himself probably is better qualified than the observer to answer questions like 'Where were you at 2.30 yesterday?', but it has been argued that people do not have access to any superior information when answering questions like 'Why did you do that?' or 'Do you like jam sandwiches?' 'Self-attribution' theory argues that people perceive their own behaviour in much the same way as they perceive other people's. If external causes seem sufficient to explain one's behaviour, then one will see it as caused by them, but if they do not seem sufficient, one will conclude that one's behaviour is internally caused—which is a clumsy way of saying that one will see it as intentional or deliberate.

Bem (1972) explains the results of Festinger and Carlsmith's (1959) well-known 'insufficient reward' experiment in self-attribution terms. The subjects of this study performed a very boring task for a while, before being persuaded by the experimenter to tell the next subject that the task was really very interesting. They were given $1 or $20 to tell this lie, and were then asked again for their own opinion of the task. The heavily bribed $20 subjects still thought it was very boring, but the $1 group now thought it was more interesting. Festinger invoked the motivational state of 'cognitive dissonance'—the awareness of an inconsistency between thought and thought or between thought and action which creates a pressure, most easily relieved for the $1 subjects by changing their opinion of the task. Bem argues that it is unnecessary to bring in subjective pressures and states, and asks what outside observers would make of the $1 and $20 subjects? A person who tells someone something is likely to be telling the truth, *unless* there is some obvious reason for him to lie, such as a $20 bribe. Perhaps the subject sees himself as others see him; he usually means what he says unless he knows that he has a good reason—such as $20—not to.

This interesting theme has been elaborated in a number of ways. Bem (1972) has demonstrated that observers, given the scripts of experiments like that of Festinger and Carlsmith, made the same choices as the subjects in the original experiments, which is consistent with the hypothesis that the person sees his own behaviour as others see it. A series of experiments on motivation (Deci, 1971; Lepper *et al.*, 1973) showed that people who have been offered money, an 'extrinsic' reward, to do something they find interesting, or 'intrinsically' rewarding, tend to 'discount' dispositional factors as explaining their own behaviour. In plain English, paying someone to do something they like doing makes it less interesting and enjoyable. Mark Twain's *Huckleberry Finn* suggests the argument could be taken a step farther; something you pay for the privilege of doing, like whitewashing a fence, stops being a chore and becomes fun. As Staw (1976) notes, the findings of research like Deci's have obvious implications for industry.

Attribution therapy by 're-attribution'?

Self-attribution theory has possible practical implications. An early study by Valins (1966) showed that it is possible to lead men to prefer certain pin-ups, by causing a tape-recorded heart beat to speed up or slow down, when they were presented. The subjects thought the sound was of their own heart, and inferred from its change of rate that the accompanying pin-up was more exciting. Later research (Hirshman, 1975) has extended the effect to unpleasant pictures of people who had died violent deaths, and showed that falsely telling the subject that his heart was beating faster produced a real increase in electro-dermal activity. However Taylor (1975) argues that the 'Valins Effect' only works where the subject's preferences are fairly unimportant to him, so it would not be possible to convince someone that they did not like a close friend, or did like an enemy. In Taylor's experiment subjects' preferences could only be manipulated by 'false feedback' about heart rate, when the subject didn't expect ever to meet the people depicted; if they thought they were selecting partners for the next phase of the experiment, changes in their supposed heart rate did not influence their choice.

If Taylor's argument is correct, 're-attribution' caused by false feedback can never have much practical application, because it could never affect behaviour that mattered to the person. Valins and Ray (1967) had earlier succeeded in changing behaviour, but not attitudes, by false feedback; people previously afraid of snakes were willing to approach them more closely after being given false feedback that their heart rate did not change at the sight of a snake. They still said they were frightened of snakes. Storms and Nisbett (1970) took the possibilities of 'attribution therapy' a stage further. Instead of telling the subject he was excited, when he was not, or that he was not excited when he was, they told their subjects they were indeed excited, but not for the reason they thought. Their subjects were people who had difficulty in sleeping at night, and the treatment took the seemingly paradoxical form of giving them a pill to take before going to bed, which it was said would increase their heart rate, raise their temperature, and send thoughts racing through their minds. In fact the pill was inert and had no physical effect at all. Storms and Nisbett argued that the sleepless subjects would attribute their usual bedtime symptoms of high temperature, racing thoughts, etc. to the pill, not to insomnia, would not worry about not being able to sleep, and would consequently fall asleep sooner. In Storms and Nisbett's experiment, insomniacs given the bogus pill that was supposed to cause tension did fall asleep on average 12 minutes sooner than control subjects.

A similarly ingenious experiment has been reported by Dienstbier and Munter (1971), in which students 'failed' a particularly important test, after being given an inert pill that was supposed to increase heart rate, make the palms sweat, and give a sinking feeling in the pit of stomach. It was made very easy for the students to cheat, after they had 'failed', and to raise their score past the pass mark. Of the males who had the allegedly tension-producing pill, 56 did cheat, as opposed to only 17 of the control group, whose pill was supposed to make them sleepy. Dienstbier's explanation was that all subjects felt tense at the idea of cheating after their 'failure', but the ones who received the supposed tension-producing pill attributed their feelings to the pill, and not to anxiety. Not feeling anxiety at the thought of cheating made it easy for them to do just that—cheat.

Some of these 're-attribution' effects are not easy to obtain, however. Dienstbier's female subjects did not cheat more under the influence of the supposed drug, and Stone and Nisbett's insomnia cure has not always worked (Kellogg and Baron, 1975). Many people have doubts about giving their subjects bogus pills or false information about their heart rate, and it is arguable that a form of treatment based on deliberately lying to the patient could never have much of a future. Fortunately, it is possible to use methods derived from attribution theory, to change people's behaviour without telling them lies. Valins and Nisbett (1971) report several case-studies in which people were helped to 're-attribute' disturbing ideas or experiences.

Men joining combat units in Vietnam and encountering hostility from seasoned soldiers were 'equipped with the attribution "they hate the f—— new guy" instead of the far more distressing attribution "they hate me" '. A schizophrenic patient was helped to understand that 'pressure points' and twitches over his right eye were a normal reaction to tension, and not evidence of spirit possession. Valins and Nisbett make the interesting point that the permeation of psychodynamic ideas, such as 'he's a flirt because he's very insecure about his masculinity', into popular consciousness may be causing some mild psychiatric symptoms of a type readily treated by attribution therapy, or with what one might suggest amounts to much the same thing, a good dose of common sense.

SOCIAL PERSONALITY

The traditional view tended to see personality as something 'inside' the person, which produced or directed behaviour. The something inside the person might be a personality trait, which Allport (1966) defined as a 'neuropsychic system with the capacity to render many stimuli functionally equivalent and to initiate and guide consistent (equivalent) forms of adaptive and expressive behaviour', or it might be a motive, of particular direction and strength, or it might be a defence mechanism that had arisen to cope with a motive whose expression had to be controlled. The discovery that very often no pattern of consistent behaviour could be identified, that verified the existence of the postulated trait, motive or mechanism, led to attempts to state personality theories more precisely and to measure a wider range of behaviour more carefully—developments outlined by Alker (1977). It led also to the argument, first stated in recent times by Mischel (1968), that many aspects of personality exist in the eye of the beholder, rather than in the behaviour or nervous system of the person perceived. This is obviously true of personality concepts that primarily express approval or disapproval, such as 'polite' or 'nasty', but turns out also to be true of at least some trait concepts with a more specific meaning, such as 'curious' (Coie, 1974) or 'has a good sense of humour' (Babad, 1974).

Mischel (1968) argues that people use words like 'honest' or 'friendly' to describe how they feel about other people, as much as to describe what other people are actually like, while Cook and McHenry (1978) argue that people use broad general trait descriptions more to impose order on the incoming mass of information about others, than to detect or describe an order which is actually present. Some backing for this view comes from the study of Dornbusch *et al.* (1965) which showed that choice of adjective to describe a person was much more a characteristic of the person making the description than of the person being described. Rodin (1972) found that trait descriptions were much less useful as aids to identifying someone than were descriptions of the person's typical behaviour, on the lines of 'apt to keep you talking for hours'.

Self-fulfilling prophecy

It appears that trait descriptions are often uninformative and oversimplified, yet they are constantly used. Various theories and lines of research suggest that if someone is given a particular label often enough, it sticks; an initially incorrect description becomes true—the 'self-fulfilling prophecy'. One's personality becomes, at least partly, something constructed by other people, whose expectations shape one's behaviour, rather than the forces of motivation and learning traditionally regarded as important.

This effect can be demonstrated, over a short time-scale, by laboratory experiments; various studies, reviewed by Archibald (1974), show that a history of 'failing' tasks like solving anagrams predicts failure on a further set of items, whereas subjects who have 'succeeded' before succeed again. Archibald distinguishes a number of ways in which the 'self-fulfilling prophecy' might work. It might be that worrying about failing takes up so much of the person's time that he has none left to attend to the task (anxiety distraction), that he finds worrying about failure so much more unpleasant than actually failing that he fails as quickly as possible to put a stop to the anxiety (anxiety reduction), or finally that he justifies anticipated failure, in advance, by not trying as hard as he might (defensive effort). Educational psychologists argue, plausibly enough, that the same effect might be found in some children, who will experience a repeated cycle of failure, leading to the expectation of failure, leading to further failure. The existence of this expectation can be verified by studying the child's self-esteem, and the teacher's opinion of him; Jensen (1973) reviews the evidence on both as determinants of intelligence and academic achievement. The child's opinion of himself does not seem to affect his performance on intelligence tests, which Jensen describes as 'highly resistant to experimental manipulations of incentives and motivational sets'. Teachers' expectations do have some influence, however, on academic work. (The often cited research of Rosenthal and Jacobson (1968) which purported to show that pupils' IQs increased, if the teacher was led to expect that they would, was methodologically unsound (Thorndike, 1968) and has not been replicated (Elsahoff and Snow, 1971)). The test examiner's expectations have been shown capable of biassing certain intelligence tests, however; Babad *et al.* (1975) found that examiners scored parts of the Wechsler Intelligence Scale for Children (WISC) more generously when the child was described as high-achieving and middle-class.

Other aspects of behaviour besides problem-solving can become the subject of self-fulfilling prophecies. Kraut (1975) found that telling people, who had made a donation to one good cause, that they were 'charitable' made them more likely to make a donation to another a week later, while telling people who had not donated that they were 'uncharitable' made them even less generous next time. Miller *et al.* (1975) obtained similar results; telling classes of schoolchildren that they *did not* leave litter in the school grounds—which in fact they did—reduced the amount of litter left (whereas telling them that they *should not* drop litter had no such effect).

The often-cited study of Kelley (1950) showed that students who had been told—incorrectly—that a lecturer was cold, asked fewer questions than students who'd been told he was warm.

Stereotypes

In the studies by Kraut, Miller, and Kelley, behaviour was changed over the short term by information supplied by the experimenter. The research on stereotypes and stereotyping shows that similar effects can be observed over the long term, and that the starting point is often something beyond anyone's control. It is well known that stereotypes can be based on race, nationality, class, age, or sex and that stereotypes which might have only 'a grain of truth' to start with, if that, can achieve truth through the mechanism of the 'self-fulfilling prophecy'. Examples of this abound; several reported recently include the stereotype of the 'drunken (American) Indian' held by American psychiatrists (Westermeyer, 1974), the harmful stereotype of the older woman as sick, sexless, uninvolved except in church work, and alone (Payne and Whittington, 1976), or the incorrect stereotype of the older employee as a physically feebler, less reliable worker (Meier and Kerr, 1976). Goffman (1963) has described how people at the receiving end of the stereotyping process react by playing up to the role expected from them when with normal people—being the happy-go-lucky Negro or the helpless dependent cripple—and reserving their real selves for meetings and clubs of 'their own kind'.

The moulding of behaviour by stereotyped expectation can begin at birth, in several different ways. Jahoda (1954) describes the custom of the Ashanti in Africa of naming children after the day of the week on which they are born, and then expecting them to behave accordingly; 'Monday's child' is expected to be quiet, peaceful and retiring and, as Jahoda found, lives up to this expectation to the extent of featuring less in the delinquency statistics.

Another stereotyping process also has its starting point early in life; its influence can be traced through childhood, adolescence, university, and employment, and the marks it leaves on adult personality can be measured. At nursery school the physically attractive child has more friends (although not at first, in the case of girls) and is seen by other children as less likely to be frightened, to be more likely to enjoy doing things on his own, and to be less in need of help from others (Dion and Berscheid, 1972). The attractive child's teachers are more likely to excuse bad behaviour as a momentary lapse, although the same behaviour in an unattractive child is seen as a sign of an unpleasant nature (Dion, 1972). Teachers also expect the more attractive child to do better in his school work and even on an IQ test (Clifford and Walster, 1973), but do not actually succeed in making this latter prophecy come true (Clifford, 1975).

The attractive child's popularity is maintained through school years (Kleck *et al.*, 1974) and into college, although in college the most attractive members of each sex have become unpopular again with their own sex (Krebs and Adinolfi, 1975), perhaps on account of their marked popularity with the opposite sex. (But although the most attractive students were not popular with their own sex, the students who were thus popular were better looking than the ones who had neither enemies nor friends.) A study by Walster *et al.* (1966) showed that appearance alone predicted whether either party on a first date wanted a second date, and that intelligence and social skill played no measurable part in the decision. Mathes (1975) failed to find any evidence that the influence of appearance wore off after the first five encounters.

As an adult the attractive person is favoured in all sorts of ways: he or she has a better chance of getting a job (Dipboye *et al.*, 1975), is more likely to escape conviction or at least get a lighter sentence in a mock jury experiment (Efran, 1974), and is more likely to win an election (Efran and Patterson, 1974). His or her appearance is likely to affect ratings of personality characteristics like altruism, sensitivity, warmth, and outgoingness (Dion *et al.*, 1972) and its effects 'radiate', so that the attractive person's companion is rated as more self-confident, likeable and friendly (Sigall and Landy, 1973).

Being attractive makes a big difference to a person's social life right from childhood. Does a lifetime—or half a lifetime, allowing for looks fading—of getting one's way more easily, leave its mark on measurable aspects of personality? Mathes and Kahn (1975) found that attractive girls were happier, less neurotic and had a higher opinion of themselves, but failed to demonstrate similar effects for men. Jackson and Huston (1975) showed that attractive girls are more assertive and far quicker to correct a piece of rudeness contrived by the experimenter.

While people have little or no control over many of the factors that lead to stereotyping and self-fulfilling prophecies, they also make choices, with varying degrees of sonscious awareness, that affect other aspects of the way other people see them. People can choose deliberately to play a role, to make a 'self-presentation', as Goffman (1961) puts it. Roles adopted for particular occasions often become habitual, so that the man who initially consciously plays the part of the absent-minded professor eventually does it without realizing it. Often the occupation one chooses shapes how others see one, and many occupations have stereotypes attached to them, which can become self-fulfilling. Skipper and Nass (1966) describe how men expect nurses to be freer than average with sexual favours, partly on the argument that they must in any case be familiar with the male body from their work, and how this expectation then gets fulfilled, because if the nurses do not live up to it, they do not get asked out. Friendship and enmity can be the subject of self-fulfilling prophecies too, particularly enmity, one might argue, because the sequence 'I think he doesn't like me—I'll be unfriendly to him—there, he's being unfriendly to me'—blocks any chance of correcting the mistake.

To conclude, there seems to be a number of mechanisms by which, at various levels, the ways others see someone can determine the way he sees himself, and can over a period of time shape many aspects of his behaviour and personality, producing a 'social personality' alongside his 'inner personality'.

REFERENCES

Adinolfi, A. A. (1971). Relevance of person perception research to clinical psychology. *Journal of Consulting and Clinical Psychology*, **37,** 167–176.

Alker, H. A. (1977). Beyond ANOVA psychology in the study of person–situation interactions. In: D. Magnusson and N. S. Endler (Eds.), *Personality at the Crossroads.* (Hillsdale, N. J.: Erlbaum.)

Allport, G. W. (1961). *Pattern and Growth in Personality.* (New York: Holt.)

Allport, G. W. (1966). Traits revisited. *American Psychologist*, **21,** 1–10.

Archer, D. and Akert, R. M. (1977). Words and everything else: verbal and non-verbal cues in social interpretation. *Journal of Personality and Social Psychology*, **35,** 443–449.

Archibald, W. P. (1974). Alternative explanations for self-fulfilling prophecy. *Psychological Bulletin*, **81,** 74–84.

Arkowitz, H., Lichtenstein, E., McGovern, K., and Hines, P. (1975). The behavioural assessment of social competence in males. *Behavior Therapy*, **6,** 3–13.

Arnheim, R. (1949). The Gestalt theory of expression. *Psychological Review*, **56,** 156–171.

Babad, E. Y. (1974). A multi-method approach to the assessment of humor: A critical look at humor tests. *Journal of Personality*, **42,** 618–631.

Babad, D. Y., Mann, M., and Marheyim, M. (1975). Bias in scoring the WISC subtests. *Journal of Consulting and Clinical Psychology*, **43,** 284.

Babst, D., Gottfredson, D., and Ballard, K. (1968). Comparison of multiple regression and configural analysis techniques for developing base expectancy tables. *Journal of Research in Crime and Delinquency*, **5,** 72–80.

Bannister, D. (1962). The nature and measurement of schizophrenic thought disorder. *Journal of Mental Science*, **168,** 824–842.

Bannister, D. and Fransella, F. (1966). *Inquiring Man.* (Harmondsworth: Penguin.)

Beck, A. T. (1967). *Depression.* (New York: Hoeber.)

Bem, D. J. (1972). Self-perception theory. In: L. Berkowitz (Ed.), *Advances in Experimental Social Psychology*, Vol. 6 (New York: Academic Press.)

Block, J. and Thomas, H. (1955). Is satisfaction with self a measure of adjustment? *Journal of Abnormal and Social Psychology*, **51,** 254–259.

Braginsky, B. M. and Braginsky, D. D. (1967). Schizophrenic patients in the psychiatric interview: an experimental study of their effectiveness of manipulation. *Journal of Consulting Psychology*, **31,** 543–547.

Byrne, D. (1966). *An Introduction to Personality: A Research Approach.* (Englewood Cliffs, NJ: Prentice-Hall.)

Byrne, D. and Blaylock, B. (1963). Similarity and assumed similarity of attitudes between husbands and wives. *Journal of Abnormal and Social Psychology*, **67,** 636–640.

Cameron, N. (1943). The development of paranoiac thinking. *Psychological Review*, **50,** 219–233.

Chance, S. E. and Meaders, W. (1960). Needs and interpersonal perception. *Journal of Personality*, **28,** 200–209.

Chapman, L. G. and Chapman, S. P. (1967). Genesis of popular but erroneous psychodiagnostic observations. *Journal of Abnormal Psychology*, **73,** 193–204.

Clements, W. H. (1967). Mental interaction and mental stability: a comparison of stable and unstable marriages. *Journal of Marriage and the Family*, **29,** 697–702.

Clifford, M. M. (1975). Physical attractiveness and academic performance. *Child Study Journal*, **5,** 201–209.

Clifford, lf. M. and Walster, E. (1973). The effect of physical attractiveness on teacher expectations. *Sociology of Education*, **46,** 248–258.

Coie, J. D. (1974). An evaluation of the cross-situational stability of children's curiosity. *Journal of Personality*, **42,** 93–116.

Colby, K. M. (1977). Appraisal of four psychological theories of paranoid phenomena. *Journal of Applied Psychology*, **86,** 54–59.

Cook, M. (1979). *Perceiving Others: the Psychology of Interpersonal Perception.* (London: Methuen.)

Cook, M. and McHenry, R. (1978). *Sexual Attraction.* (Oxford: Pergamon.)

Cooley, C. H. (1902). *Human Nature and the Social Order.* (New York: Scribner.)

Corsini, R. J. (1956). Understanding and similarity in marriage. *Journal of Abnormal and Social Psychology*, **52,** 327–332.

Curran, J. P. (1978). Social skills training as an approach to the treatment of heterosexual-social anxiety: A review. *Psychological Bulletin*, **85,** 140–157.

Davitz, J. R. (1964). *The Communication of Emotional Meaning.* (New York: McGraw-Hill.)

Deci, E. L. (1971). Effects of externally mediated rewards on intrinsic motivation. *Journal of Personality and Social Psychology*, **18,** 105–115.

Dienstbier, R. A. and Munter, P. O. (1971). Cheating as a function of the labelling of natural arousal. *Journal of Personality and Social Psychology*, **17,** 218–231.

Dion, K. K. (1972). Physical attractiveness and evaluations of children's transgressions. *Journal of Personality and Social Psychology*, **24,** 207–213.

Dion, K. K. and Berscheid, E. (1972). Physical attraction and peer perception among children. *Sociometry*, **37,** 1–12.

Dion, K., Berscheid, E., and Walster, E. (1972). What is beautiful is good. *Journal of Personality and Social Psychology*, **24,** 285–290.

Dipboye, R. L., Fromkin, H. L., and Wiback, K. (1975). Relative importance of applicant sex, attractiveness and scholastic standing in evaluation as job applicant résumés. *Journal of Applied Psychology*, **60,** 39–43.

Dornbusch, S. M., Hastorf, A. H., Richardson, S. A., Muzzy, R. E., and Vreeland, R. S. (1965). The perceiver and perceived: their relative influence on categories of interpersonal perception. *Journal of Personality and Social Psychology*, **1,** 434–440.

Dymond, R. (1954). Interpersonal perception and mental happiness. *Canadian Journal of Psychology*, **8,** 164–171.

Efran, M. G. (1974). The effect of physical appearance on the judgement of guilt, interpersonal attraction, and severity of recommended punishment in a simulated jury task. *Journal of Research in Personality*, **8,** 45–54.

Efran, M. S. and Patterson, E. W. J. (1974). Voters vote beautiful: the effect of physical appearance on a national election. *Canadian Journal of Behavioral Science*, **6,** 352–356.

Elsahoff, J. D. and Snow, R. E. (1971). *'Pygmalion' reconsidered.* (Worthington, Ohio: Charles A. Jones Publ. Co.)

Ekman, P. (1972). Universals and cultural differences in facial expressions of emotion. In: J. Cole (Ed.), *Nebraska Symposium on Motivation.* (Lincoln, Neb.: University of Nebraska Press.)

Fancher, R. E. (1969). Group and individual accuracy in person perception. *Journal of Consulting Psychology*, **33,** 127.

Festinger, L. and Carlsmith, J. M. (1959). Cognitive consequences of forced compliance. *Journal of Abnormal and Social Psychology*, **58,** 203–210.

Fiske, D. W. (1974). The limits for the conventional science of personality. *Journal of Personality*, **42,** 1–11.

Frith, C. D. and Lillie, F. J. (1972). Why does the Repertory Grid indicate thought disorder? *British Journal of Social and Clinical Psychology*, **11,** 73–78.

Gabennesch, H. and Hunt, L. L. (1971). The relative accuracy of interpersonal perception of high and low authoritarians. *Journal of Experimental Research in Personality*, **5,** 43–48.

Goffman, E. (1961). *The presentation of self in everyday life.* (New York: Doubleday.)
Goffman, E. (1963). *Stigma: Notes on the Management of Spoiled Identity.* (Englewood Cliffs, NJ: Prentice Hall.)
Goldberg, L. R. (1965). Diagnosticians *vs* diagnostic signs: the diagnosis of psychosis *vs* neurosis from the MMPI. *Psychological Monographs*, **79,** 9 (Whole no. 602).
Gough, H. G. (1948). A sociological theory of psychopathy. *American Journal of Sociology*, **53,** 359–366.
Gough, H. G. and Petersen, D. R. (1952). The identification and measurement of predispositional factors in crime and delinquency. *Journal of Consulting Psychology*, **16,** 207–212.
Hartshorne H. and May, M. A. (1928). *Studies in Deceit.* (New York: Macmillan.)
Hirshman, R. (1975). Cross-modal effects of anticipatory bogus heart rate feedback in a negative emotional context. *Journal of Personality and Social Psychology*, **31,** 13–19.
Hoffman, P. J., Slovic, P., and Rorer, L. G. (1968). An analysis of variance model for the assessment of configural cue utilisation in clinical judgement. *Psychological Bulletin*, **69,** 338–349.
Howells, K. (1978). The perception of social causality in 'mentally abnormal' aggressive offenders. Unpublished manuscript. University of Leicester, England.
Jackson, J. J. and Huston, T. L. (1975). Physical attractiveness and assertiveness. *Journal of Social Psychology*, **96,** 79–84.
Jahoda, G. (1954). A note on Ashanti names and their relation to personality. *British Journal of Psychology*, **45,** 192–199.
Jensen, R. (1973). *Educability and Group Differences.* (London: Methuen.)
Johnson, W. G., Ross, J. M., and Mastria, M. A. (1977). Delusional behavior: an attributional analysis of development and modification. *Journal of Abnormal Psychology*, **86,** 421–426.
Jones, E. E. and Davis, K. E. (1965). From acts to dispositions: the attribution process in person perception. In: L. Berkowitz (Ed.), *Advances in Experimental Social Psychology*, Vol. 2 (New York: Academic Press.)
Jones, E. E. and Harris, V. A. (1967). The attribution of attitudes. *Journal of Experimental Social Psychology*, **3,** 1–24.
Jones, E. E., Davis, K. E., and Gergen, K. J. (1961). Role playing variations and their informational value for person perception. *Journal of Abnormal and Social Psychology*, **63,** 302–310.
Jones, E. E., Kanouse, D. E., Kelley, H. H., Nisbett, R. E., Valins, S., and Weiner, B. (1971). *Attribution: Perceiving the Causes of Behavior.* (Morristown, NJ: General Learning Press.)
Kahneman, D. and Tversky, A. (1973). On the psychology of prediction. *Psychological Review*, **80,** 237–251.
Kelley, H. H. (1950). The warm–cold variable in first impressions. *Journal of Personality*, **18,** 431–439.
Kellogg, R. and Baron, R. S. (1975). Attribution theory, insomnia and the reverse placebo effect: a reversal of Storms and Nisbett's findings. *Journal of Personality and Social Psychology*, **32,** 231–236.
Kelly, G. A. (1955). *The Psychology of Personal Constructs.* (New York: Norton.)
Kirkpatrick, C. and Hobart, C. (1954). Disagreement, disagreement estimate and non-empathic imputation for intimacy groups varying from favorite date to married. *American Sociological Review*, **19,** 10–19.
Kleck, R. E., Richardson, S. A., and Ronald, L. (1974). Physical appearance cues and interpersonal attraction in children. *Child Development*, **45,** 305–310.
Kline, P. (1972). *Fact and Fantasy in Freudian theory.* (London: Methuen.)
Kraut, A. I. (1975). Prediction of managerial success by peer and training staff ratings. *Journal of Applied Psychology*, **60,** 14–19.

Krebs, D. and Adinolfi, A. A. (1975). Physical attractiveness, social relations and personality stereotype. *Journal of Personality and Social Psychology*, **31,** 245–253.

Lepper, M. R., Greene, D., and Nisbett, R. E. (1973). Undermining children's intrinsic interest with extrinsic rewards: a test of the overjustification hypothesis. *Journal of Personality and Social Psychology*, **28,** 129–137.

Lewin, K. (1936) *Principles of topographical psychology.* (New York: McGraw-Hill.)

Lindzey, G. (1965). Seer versus sign. *Journal of Experimental Research in Personality*, **1,** 17–26.

Lyons, J. (1956). The perception of human action. *Journal of Genetic Psychology*, **54,** 45–55.

McGhie, A. and Chapman, J. S. (1961). Disorders of attention and perception in early schizophrenia. *British Journal of Medical Psychology*, **34,** 103–116.

McPherson, F. M. and Buckley, F. (1970). Thought-process disorder and personal construct subsystems. *British Journal of Social and Clinical Psychology*, **19,** 380–381.

McPherson, F. M., Buckley, F., and Draffan, J. (1971). 'Psychological' constructs and delusions of persecution and 'non-integration' in schizophrenia. *British Journal of Medical Psychology*, **44,** 277–280.

Matarazzo, J. D. and Saslow, G. (1961). Differences in interview interaction behaviour among normal and deviant groups. In: C. A. Berg and C. M. Bass (Eds.), *Conformity and Deviation.* (New York: Harper & Row.)

Mathes, E. W. (1975). The effects of physical attractiveness and anxiety on heterosexual attraction over a series of five encounters. *Journal of Marriage and the Family*, **37,** 769–774.

Mathes, E. W. and Kahn, A. (1975). Physical attractiveness, happiness, neuroticism and self esteem. *Journal of Psychology*, **90,** 27–30.

Mead, G. H. (1934). *Mind, Self, and Society.* (Chicago: University of Chicago Press.)

Meehl, P. E. (1954). *Clinical versus Statistical Prediction.* (Minneapolis: University of Minnesota Press.)

Meehl, P. E. (1959). A comparison of clinicians with five statistical methods of identifying psychotic MMPI profiles. *Journal of Counselling Psychology* , **6,** 102–109.

Meehl, P. (1961). Logic for the clinician. Review of T. Sarbin, R. Taft and D. Bailey, 'Clinical inference and cognitive theory'. *Contemporary Psychology*, **7,** 389–391.

Meier, E. L. and Kerr, E. A. (1976). Capabilities of middle-aged and older workers: a survey of the literature. *Industrial Gerontology*, **3,** 147–156.

Milgram, N. A. (1960). Cognitive and empathetic factors in role taking by schizophrenics and brain-damaged patients. *Journal of Abnormal and Social Psychology*, **60,** 219–224.

Miller, R. L., Brickman, P., and Bolen, D. (1975). Attribution versus persuasion as a means for modifying behaviour. *Journal of Personality and Social Psychology*, **31,** 430–441.

Mischel, W. (1968). *Personality and Assessment.* (New York: Wiley.)

Mischel, W. (1973). Toward a cognitive social learning reconceptualisation of personality. *Psychological Review*, **80,** 252–283.

Murstein, B. I. (1972). Person perception and courtship progress among premarital couples. *Journal of Marriage and the Family*, **34,** 621–622.

Murstein, B. I. and Beck, G. D. (1972). Person perception, marriage adjustment and social desirability. *Journal of Consulting and Clinical Psychology*, **39,** 396–403.

Oswald, I. (1966). *Sleep.* (Harmondsworth: Penguin.)

Payne, B. and Whittington, F. (1976). Older women: an examination of popular stereotyping and research evidence. *Social Problems*, **23,** 488–504.

Pritchard, D. A. (1977). Linear versus configural statistical prediction. *Journal of Consulting and Clinical Psychology*, **45,** 559–563.

Rich, A. R. and Schroeder, H. E. (1976). Research issues in assertiveness training. *Psychological Bulletin*, **83,** 1084–1096.

Rizley, R. (1978). Depression and distortion in the attribution of causality. *Journal of Abnormal Psychology*, **87,** 32–48.
Rodin, M. J. (1972). The informativeness of trait descriptions. *Journal of Personality and Social Psychology*, **21,** 341–344.
Rogers, C. A. (1951). *Client-centred Therapy*. (Boston, Mass.: Houghton Mifflin.)
Rogers, C. R. and Dymond, R. F. (Eds.) (1954). *Psychotherapy and Personality Change*. (Chicago: University of Chicago Press.)
Rorer, L. G., Hoffman, P. J., Dickman, H. R., and Slovic, P. (1967). Configural judgements revealed. *Proceedings of the 75th Annual Convention of the American Psychological Association*.
Rosenthal, R. and Jacobson, L. (1968). *Pygmalion in the Classroom*. (New York: Holt.)
Sarbin, T. R., Taft, R., and Bailey, D. E. (1960). *Clinical Inference and Cognitive Theory*. (New York: Holt.)
Sawyer, J. (1966). Measurement *and* prediction, clinical *and* statistical. *Psychological Bulletin*, **66,** 178–200.
Scodel, A. and Mussen, P. (1953). Social perceptions of authoritarians and nonauthoritarians. *Journal of Abnormal and Social Psychology*, **48,** 181–184.
Sechrest, L. and Jackson, D. N. (1961). Social intelligence and accuracy of interpersonal predictions. *Journal of Personality*, **29,** 167–187.
Secord, P. F. and Backman, C. W. (1964). *Social Psychology*. (New York: McGraw-Hill.)
Seligman, M. (1975). *Helplessness*. (San Francisco: Freeman.)
Sigall, H. and Landy, D. (1973). Radiating beauty: effects of having a physically desirable partner on person perception. *Journal of Personality and Social Psychology*, **28,** 218–224.
Skipper, J. K. and Nass, G. (1966). Dating behaviour: a framework for analysis and an illustration. *Journal of Marriage and the Family*, **28,** 412–420.
Slovic, P. (1969). Analysing the expert judge: a descriptive study of a stockbroker's decision processes. *Journal of Applied Psychology*, **53,** 255–263.
Snyder, C. R. and Larson, G. R. (1972). A further look at student acceptance of general personality interpretations. *Journal of Consulting and Clinical Psychology*, **38,** 384–388.
Snygg, D. and Coombs, A. W. (1949). *Individual Behavior*. (New York: Harper.)
Staw, B. M. (1976). *Intrinsic and extrinsic motivation*. (Morristown, NJ: General Learning Press.)
Steiner, I. D. (1955). Interpersonal perception as influenced by accuracy of social perception. *Psychological Review*, **62,** 268–274.
Stephenson, W. (1953). *The Study of Behavior: Q-Technique and its Methodology* (Chicago: University of Chicago Press.)
Storms, M. D. and Nisbett, T. E. (1970). Insomnia and the attribution process. *Journal of Personality and Social Psychology*, **16,** 319–328.
Taft, R. (1956). The ability to judge people. *Psychological Bulletin*, **52,** 1–23.
Taylor, S. E. (1975). On inferring one's attitudes from one's behavior. Some delimiting conditions. *Journal of Personality and Social Psychology*, **31,** 126–131.
Thibaut, J. W. and Riecken, H. W. (1955). Some determinants and consequences of the perception of social causality. *Journal of Personality*, **24,** 113–133.
Thigpen, C. H. and Cleckley, H. M. (1957). *Three Faces of Eve*. (Kingsport, Tenn.: Kingsport Press.)
Thorndike, R. L. (1968). Review of R. Rosenthal and L. Jacobson, 'Pygmalion in the classroom'. *American Educational Research Journal*, **5,** 708–711.
Udry, J. R. (1963). Complementarity in mate selection: a perceptual approach. *Marriage and Family Living*, **25,** 281–289.
Udry, J. R. (1967). Personality match and interpersonal perception as predictors of marriage. *Journal of Marriage and the Family*, **29,** 722–725.

Valins, S. (1966). Cognitive effects of false heart rate feedback. *Journal of Personality and Social Psychology*, **4,** 400–408.

Valins, S. and Nisbett, R. E. (1971). Attribution processes in the development and treatment of emotional disorders. In: E. E. Jones *et al.* (Eds.), *Attribution: Perceiving the Causes of Behavior.* (Morristown, NJ: General Learning Press.)

Valins, S. and Ray, A. A. (1967). Effects of cognitive desensitisation of avoidance behaviour. *Journal of Personality and Social Psychology*, **7,** 345–350.

Vernon, P. E. (1964). *Personality Assessment.* (London: Methuen.)

Walster, E., Aronson, P. V., Abrahams, D., and Rottmann, L. (1966). Importance of physical attractiveness in dating behavior. *Journal of Personality and Social Psychology*, **5,** 508–516.

Werner, H. (1948). *Comparative Psychology of Mental Development.* (New York: International Universities Press.)

Westermeyer, J. (1974). The drunken Indian: myths and realities. *Psychiatric Annals*, **4,** 29–36.

Weston, M. J. and Whitlock, F. A. (1971). The Capgras syndrome following head injury. *British Journal of Psychiatry*, **199,** 25–31.

Wharton, B. K. (1970). Nasal decongestants and paranoid psychosis. *British Journal of Psychology*, **117,** 439–440.

Wolfe, R. (1974). Conceptual level and accuracy of person perception. *Canadian Journal of Behavioural Science*, **6,** 309–317.

Wylie, R. C. (1974). *The Self-Concept.* (Lincoln, Neb.: University of Nebraska Press.)

Zigler, E. and Phillips, L. (1961). Psychiatric diagnosis and symptomatology. *Journal of Abnormal and Social Psychology*, **63,** 69–75.

The Social Psychology of Psychological Problems
Edited by P. Feldman and J. Orford

5

Interaction Skills and Social Competence

MICHAEL ARGYLE

1. MEANING AND ASSESSMENT OF SOCIAL COMPETENCE

By social competence I mean the ability, the possession of the necessary skills, to produce the desired effects on other people in social situations. These desired effects may be to persuade the others to buy, to learn, to recover from a psychological problem, to like or admire the actor, and so on. These results are not necessarily in the public interest—skills may be used for social or anti-social purposes. And there is no evidence that social competence is a general factor: a person may be better at one task than another, e.g. interviewing *vs.* lecturing, or in one situation than another, e.g. parties *vs.* committees. In this chapter I shall discuss a variety of social competences. Professional social skills are mainly about performances in set-piece situations, like teaching, interviewing, and public speaking. Social skills training (SST) for students and other more or less normal populations has been directed to the skills of dating, making friends, and being assertive. SST for psychiatric patients has been aimed at correcting failures of social competence, and also at relieving subjective distress, such as social anxiety.

For professional selection purposes, and for the validation of professional SST, a single index of competence, e.g. at teaching, would be useful; but to find out who needs training, and in what areas, a detailed descriptive assessment is more useful. We want to know for example which situations a trainee finds difficult—formal situations, conflicts, meeting strangers, etc., and which situations he is inadequate in, even though he does not report them as difficult. And we want to find out what he is doing wrong—failure to produce the right non-verbal signals, low rewardingness, lack of certain social skills, etc.

Social competence is easier to define and agree upon in the case of professional social skills: an effective therapist cures more patients, an effective teacher teaches better, an effective salesgirl sells more. When we look more closely, it is not quite so simple: examination marks may be one index of a teacher's effectiveness, but usually more is meant than just this. A salesgirl should not simply sell a lot of goods, she should make the customer feel she would like to go to that shop again. The general idea is clear however: an effective performer of a professional skill is one who gets better results of the kinds relevant to the task. So a combination of different skills is required and the overall assessment of effectiveness may involve the combination of a number of different measures or ratings. The range of competence is quite large: the best salesmen and salesgirls regularly sell four times as much as some others behind the same counter; some supervisors of working groups produce twice as much output as others, or have 20–25 per cent the labour turnover and absenteeism rates (Argyle, 1972).

For everyday social skills it is more difficult to give the criteria of success; lack of competence is easier to spot—failure to make friends, or opposite-sex friends, quarrelling, and failing to sustain cooperative relationships, finding a number of situations difficult or a source of anxiety, and so on.

Self-report methods of assessment

The assessment of social competence is usually based at least in part on some kind of interview or questionnaire.

(a) Interview Clients for SST are usually assessed by a kind of clinical interview. A person with interpersonal problems will probably speak first about his own depression or anxiety, or about the difficult behaviour of others. He can be asked to describe in detail the behaviour which occurs in his main social encounters and relationships, especially the ones he finds difficult, and focusing on his own behaviour to the extent that he is able to describe it. This can be supplemented by the use of rating scales, on which he reports which situations are most difficult.

(b) Rating scales and questionnaires There are several questionnaires which assess general assertiveness, e.g. The Rathus Assertive Schedule (Rathus, 1973). However, since the discovery that individual assertiveness varies greatly between situations, scales have been devised which ask about assertiveness in specific situations. Such scales have been found to correlate 0.6–0.8 with ratings of assertive behaviour. Other scales have been constructed for measuring social anxiety, and a number of separate factors have been found, as will be described below. Trower *et al.* (1978) devised a list of 30 situations, on which subjects rate five levels of difficulty, the fifth point being 'avoidance if possible'. Argyle and Furnham (in press) have devised a set of scales showing which kinds of difficulty people have, in different kinds of situation.

(c) Self-monitoring Self-monitoring has been developed in connection with behavioural self-control techniques of therapy. The trainee reports systematically on selected aspects of his behaviour and keeps a record of some kind; the behaviour recorded is itself the target of therapy, and this method leads to direct attempts to change the behaviour; in addition the very act of recording is 'reactive', i.e. it changes the level of smoking, eating, or whatever is being recorded. Social behaviour

has rarely been recorded in this way, apart from frequency of dating, and may be more difficult to record accurately. Eisler (in press) suggests that trainees be trained during role-playing to record the required aspects of their behaviour. Synder and Monson (1975) have devised a scale which distinguishes between those who normally do and do not monitor their own behaviour.

However self-reports do not always correlate highly with behavioural measures, or with physiological measures of anxiety. It has been found that self-reports correlated better with behavioural measures if the self-report inventory described in detail the situation in which behaviour was observed (Rich and Schroeder, 1976).

Observation of social performance

Samples of an individual's performance may be obtained and analysed from role-playing, or from real life.

(a) Role played The subject may be presented with a number of assertiveness situations (e.g. laundry loses shirt), dating situations, or situations like those in his real environment. In view of the extent of situational variability, it is desirable to sample a number of different kinds of assertiveness situation, or whatever dimension of behaviour is being assessed. We have used a social interaction test based on different phases of a getting-acquainted encounter, with two partners—one male, one female; there are periods of interruption, of non-response, and of assertive behaviour. The role-playing is videotaped and scored, in terms of the use of elements of verbal behaviour (use of questions, etc.), and non-verbal behaviour (use of facial expression, etc.) and also in terms of general dimensions of behaviour (e.g. assertiveness, warmth, etc.). Raters are found to have a high degree of agreement on such ratings of behaviour, and indeed on overall judgements of social competence (Trower *et al.*, 1978).

While some of these ratings are based on carefully defined criteria, others are deliberately 'subjective', leaving the observer to decide how far the trainee's behaviour is 'warm', 'rewarding', 'socially competent', etc. (Eisler, 1976).

(b) Staged events If a person knows that his assertiveness, for example, is being assessed, his behaviour changes a lot, thereby making the measure invalid. To avoid this happening, in some follow-up studies of assertiveness training staged events have been created in which, for example, a trainee encounters a person in a waiting room, who look like another trainee, and who makes a series of unreasonable demands for loan of books, notes, etc., the whole encounter being recorded (Rich and Shroeder 1976). This is possibly an unethical procedure, but does provide a valid measure of assertiveness.

(c) Observation in real-life settings Several investigators have made use of ratings by colleagues, relations, or friends. For example in some studies of marital therapy

each partner has recorded the other's rewarding and unrewarding behaviour for a two-week period (Wills *et al.*, 1974).

(d) Tests of social competence It would be very useful to have such a test. One such test, the George Washington test, consisted of items of social knowledge and judgement, but correlated more with IQ than with social competence. A number of investigators have confronted *S*s with descriptions of a series of difficult situations, asked them what they would say or do, and rated the adequacy of the replies. However this probably fails to measure the ability to actually perform the skills described, and gives too much weight to armchair judgemental competence. It is possible to measure some of the components of social competence, to be described later, such as ability to recognize emotions from tones of voice and facial expression, and the Pons test, devised by Rosenthal, *et al.* (1974) does this by presenting non-verbal stimuli with brief exposures. However it is not yet agreed what the main components of social competence are, or how general such competences are across situations.

Physiological measures

These have been used, for example, in training to reduce public-speaking anxiety (Paul, 1966). However physiological measures of anxiety have not been found to correlate at all well with self-reported discomfort, or behavioural measures. This is probably because the same state of physiological arousal may sometimes be labelled as euphoria or excitement, and sometimes as anxiety. Some people can perform very effectively while in a state of high physiological arousal, as in the case of many entertainers (Eisler, op citi).

Conclusions

In the present state of research on social competence, competence at professional social skills is easiest to measure. Everyday skills can be assessed from self-reports and observed behaviour in real-life or role-played situations; preferably self-report and observed behaviour should both be used since they are partly independent. Tests and physiological measures have so far been found to be less successful. Any method should discover competence over a range of situations, and describe the patterns of social behaviour involved.

2. COMPONENTS OF SKILLED PERFORMANCE

(1) Perception of other people

It does not need to be demonstrated that to respond effectively to a stimulus it is first necessary to perceive that stimulus, and to perceive it accurately. If we are going to respond effectively to another person, he or she must be perceived accurately. By perception of a person is meant forming an impression, in terms of categories or dimensions like *intelligent*, *honest*, etc. These judgements are partly based on stereotypes—about the usual characteristics of psychology students for example; it is important that such stereotypes should be accurate, and easily abandoned if the other person turns out to be an exception. Research in personal construct theory shows that individuals use different dimensions, and also vary in complexity by using a larger or smaller number of them. They should also be able to use categories or dimensions which are relevant to the situation. Research on social skills shows the importance of attending to particular events at certain points in the sequence, for example attending to other's reactions at the ends of one's own utterances (cf. p. 131). This involves gaze at the other's face, and listening carefully to what he says: both require paying close attention and taking a keen interest in the other. Non-verbal communication research has shown that there are great individual differences in decoding non-verbal signals, like tone of voice (Davitz, 1964). Attribution theory research has shown that certain common errors of attribution of the causes of behaviour are made—attributing too much to the personality of a person observed and too little to the situation he is in, overlooking the impact the presence of the observer is having on another's behaviour, and attaching too much responsibility to the victims of accidents or attacks.

Psychiatric patients and people with inadequate social skills are often deficient in person perception. We have found that socially unskilled patients often do not attend to or show much interest in other people, and may not look very much (Trower *et al.*, 1978). Patients suffering from schizophrenia have been found to be poor at decoding non-verbal signals, and appear to make less use of personal constructs for persons or emotions (Bannister and Salmon, 1966). A major feature of manic and paranoid behaviour is inaccuracy in the perception of events, and in one study delinquents were found to be very insensitive—failing to recognize either approval or annoyance in others (McDavid and Schroder, 1957).

The most accurate social perceivers are people who are well adjusted, intelligent, cognitively complex, not authoritarian, and somewhat introverted and detached (Argyle, 1969).

(2) Taking the role of the other

As well as perceiving others' reactions accurately, it is also important to perceive the others' perceptions; this is sometimes called 'meta-perception'. An interviewer studies the candidate, but the candidate is more interested in the interviewer's perception of him than in the interviewer himself. This is one way in which social performance is different from a motor skill. Meta-perception is activated in situations like interviews, where the other is evaluating, and in front of audiences.

There are many situations where people may regard others as audiences. Duval and Wicklund (1972) called this state 'objective self-awareness'—i.e. being aware of oneself as an object for others. People are also made self-conscious if they are in some way different from everyone else present, such as being the only female present. Some people feel more self-conscious than others, and suffer more from audience anxiety. They tend to be people who are shy, have rather low self-esteem, and have failed to form an integrated identity.

There are individual differences in the ability to see another person's point of view, as measured by tests in which subjects are asked to describe situations as perceived by others. Those who are good at it have been found to do better at a number of social tasks (Feffer and Suchotliffe, 1966), and to be more altruistic.

Socially competent performance calls both for the ability to take the role of the other, and the motivation to do it appropriately. It a person performing in front of an audience thought all the time about audience reactions his performance would deteriorate; if an interviewer empathized fully with each candidate, he would want to give them all the job. Meldman (1967) found that psychiatric patients are more egocentric, i.e. talked about themselves more than controls, and it has been our experience that socially unskilled patients have great difficulty in taking the role of the other.

(3) Non-verbal communication (NVC) of interpersonal attitudes and emotions

Non-verbal signals are often 'unconscious', i.e. are outside the focus of attention. A few signals are unconsciously sent and received, but there are a number of other possibilities, as shown in Table 5.1, which apply to the majority of signals. One of the main messages conveyed by NVC is attitude to another person. The main attitudes fall along two dimensions (as shown in Figure 5.1). In addition there is love, which is a variant of like. These attitudes can be conveyed clearly by non-verbal signals, as facial expression, tone of voice, and posture. Liking is conveyed by smiling, a friendly tone of voice, and so on.

Table 5.1 Different combinations of sender and receiver awareness during communication

Sender	*Receiver*	
Aware	Aware	Verbal communication, some gestures, e.g. pointing
Mostly unaware	Mostly aware	Most NVC
Unaware	Unaware, but has an effect	Pupil dilation, gaze shifts and other small non-verbal signals
Aware	Unaware	Sender is trained in the use of e.g. spatial behaviour
Unaware	Aware	Receiver is trained in the interpretation of e.g. bodily posture

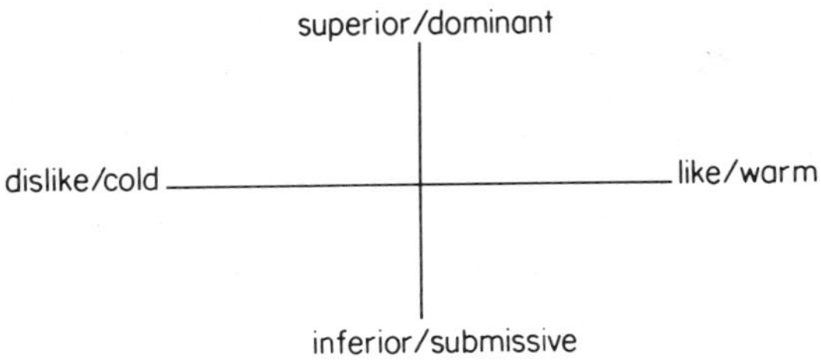

Figure 5.1

The author and his colleagues compared the effects of verbal and non-verbal signals for communicating interpersonal attitudes. It was found that non-verbal signals had a far greater effect than verbal ones on judgements of whether the performer was friendly or hostile, dominant or submissive (Argyle *et al.*, 1970; Argyle *et al.*, 1971).

The attitudes of others are perceived, then, mainly from their non-verbal behaviour. It is found that people can judge with some accuracy when others like them, but are much less accurate in perceiving dislike (Tagiuri, 1958). The reason for this is probably that expressions of dislike are concealed to a large extent, and only the more subtle ones remain, such as bodily orientation.

Non-verbal signals also communicate the emotional state of the sender. The common emotions are anger, depression, anxiety, joy, surprise, fear, and disgust/contempt (Ekman *et al.*, 1972). An anxious state, for example, can be shown by (a) *tone of voice*; (b) *facial expression*—tense, perspiring, expanded pupils; (c) *posture*—tense and rigid; (d) *gestures*—tense clasping of objects, or general bodily activity; (e) *smell*—of perspiration; and (f) *gaze*— short glances, aversion of gaze. Interactors may try to conceal their true emotional state, or to convey that they are in some different emotional condition, but it is difficult to control all of these cues, and impossible to control more autonomic ones. Emotional states can be conveyed by speech—'I am feeling very happy'—but probably statements will not be believed unless supported by appropriate NVC, and the NVC can convey the message without the speech.

This is a sphere in which social performance often fails: if interactors do not send clear facial and vocal signals, others simply do not know what the performer's attitudes or feelings are. Some people do send such signals, but they are all negative—sarcastic, superior, hostile, etc.

(4) Non-verbal accompaniments of speech

Most social behaviour involves speech, but this is accompanied and supported by a number of non-verbal signals. To begin with, two (or more) people must be able to hear and preferably see one another, which has clear implications for proximity and orientation. There are three main ways in which NVC supports speech.

(a) Completing and elaborating on verbal utterances Some utterances are meaningless or ambiguous unless the non-verbal accompaniments are taken into account. A lecturer may point at part of a diagram: a tape-recording of this part of the lecture would be meaningless. Some sentences are ambiguous if printed—'They are hunting dogs', but not if spoken—'they are hunting *dogs*'. Gestural illustrations are used to amplify the meanings of utterances, and succeed in doing so, as will be shown below. The way in which an utterance is delivered 'frames' it; i.e. the intonation and facial expression indicate whether it is intended to be serious, funny, sarcastic (implying the opposite), rhetorical or requiring an answer, and so on; the non-verbal accompaniment is a message about the message, which is needed by the recipient in order to know what to do with it. There are finer comments and elaborations too: particular words can be given emphasis, pronounced in a special accent, or in a way suggesting a particular attitude. The most important non-verbal signals here are the 'prosodic' aspects of vocalization—the timing, pitch, and loudness of speech. The gestural accompaniments of speech are also important, particularly illustrators. Facial expression and glances accompany speech in a similar way.

(b) Managing synchronizing When two or more people are talking they have to take turns to speak. This is achieved mainly by means of non-verbal signals. For example if a speaker wants to avoid being interrupted, he will be more successful if he does not look up at the ends of sentences, keeps a hand in mid-gesture at these points, and if, when interrupted, he immediately increases the loudness of his speech. The actual contents of speech, e.g. asking a question, are also important. Not only is synchronizing usually successful, but interactors may help each other, by finishing their utterances for them. Some interruptions are mistaken anticipations of the other's ending, rather than attempts to break in.

(c) Sending feedback signals When someone is speaking he needs intermittent, but regular, feedback on how others are responding, so that he can modify his utterances accordingly. He needs to know whether the listeners understand, believe or disbelieve, are surprised or bored, agree or disagree, are pleased or annoyed. This information could be provided by *sotto voce* verbal mutterings, but is in fact obtained by careful study of the other's face: the eyebrows signal surprise, puzzlement, etc., while the mouth indicates pleasure and displeasure. When the other is invisible, as in telephone conversation, these visual signals are unavailable, and more verbalized 'listening behaviour' is used—'I see', 'really?', 'how interesting', etc.

In addition there is one non-verbal signal which is of particular importance: gaze acts as a channel for the person looking, but as a signal for the person looked at. The social-skills model suggests that the monitoring of another's reactions is an essential part of social performance. The other's verbal signals are mainly heard, but his non-verbal signals are mainly seen—the exceptions being the non-verbal aspects of speech, and touch. It was this implication of the social-skill model which directed us towards the study of gaze in social interaction. In dyadic interaction each person looks about 50 per cent of the time, mutual gaze occupies about 25 per cent of the time, looking while listening is about twice the level of looking while talking, glances are about 5 seconds, and mutual glances about $2\frac{1}{2}$ seconds, with wide variations due to distance, sex combinations, and personality (Argyle and Cook, 1976). Kendon (1967) found that long glances are given by speakers at the ends of utterances, and it is likely that one function of these is to collect feedback on reactions to the utterance.

Social performance may fail in this area if a person (a) has a very low level of gaze, as with some people with psychological problems; (b) fails to manage the synchronizing system, so that there are interruptions or long pauses; or (c) fails to add sufficient facial, gestural or vocal signals to his speech.

(5) Rewardingness

Many experiments have shown that if A reinforces B's behaviour, that is if he follows some kind of behaviour of B's with smiles, head-nods, gazes, or approving noises, B rapidly increases his production of the behaviour in question. If A frowns or gives other negative reactions, B reduces the amount of this behaviour. Almost any aspect of B's behaviour can be influenced in this way. The effect is markedly greater if B is aware which behaviour is approved or disapproved of, but a number of studies show that the effect can occur outside B's awareness. The effect is usually very rapid, and occurs in under a minute. People do not often produce systematic reinforcement deliberately, though they can do so; for instance, an ingratiator smiles and flatters preparatory to asking a favour. In ordinary conversation, participants are simply reacting positively or negatively to what pleases or displeases them in the other's behaviour. The effect works in both directions: while A is influencing B, B is also influencing A. This is one of the main processes whereby people are able to modify each other's behaviour in the desired direction. Clearly, if people do not give clear, immediate and consistent reinforcements, positive and negative, they will not be able to influence others in this way, and social encounters will be correspondingly more frustrating and difficult for them. This appears to be a common problem with many psychiatric patients, who characteristically fail to control or try to over-control others.

If an individual provides rewards, interaction with him is enjoyable and he is liked. If he fails to provide sufficient rewards, others will leave. In a celebrated study of girls at a reformatory, Jennings (1950) found that the popular girls helped and protected others, encouraged and cheered them, made them feel accepted and wanted, controlled their own moods so as not to inflict anxiety or depression on others, and were concerned with the needs and feelings of others. In other words, the popular girls were rewarding in a variety of ways. The unpopular girls did just the opposite—they were boastful, demanded attention, and tried to get others to do things for them—they were trying to extract rewards, at a cost to others. There are a number of different sources of popularity and unpopularity but there is little doubt that being a source of rewards is one of the most important (Rubin, 1973). One of the most common characteristics of socially unskilled patients is their low rewardingness; this is particularly the case with people who have suffered from schizophrenia for many years, who have been described as 'socially bankrupt' (Longabaugh *et al*,. 1966).

A person may be rewarding because the interaction with him is enjoyable, e.g. making love, playing squash; it may be rewarding because he is kind, helpful, interesting, etc; and people are rewarding just by being attractive or of high status.

(6) Plans and feedback in skilled performance

Competent social performance is similar to performance of a motor skill (Argyle and Kendon, 1967). In each case the performer is pursuing certain goals, makes continuous response to feedback, and emits hierarchically organized motor responses (fig 5.2). This analogy emphasizes the motivation, goals and plans of interactors. It is postulated that every interactor is trying to achieve some goal, whether he is aware of it or not. These goals may be for example to get another person to like him, to obtain or convey information, to modify the other's emotional state, and so on. Such goals may be linked to more basic motivational systems. Goals have sub-goals: for example a doctor must diagnose the patient before he can treat him.

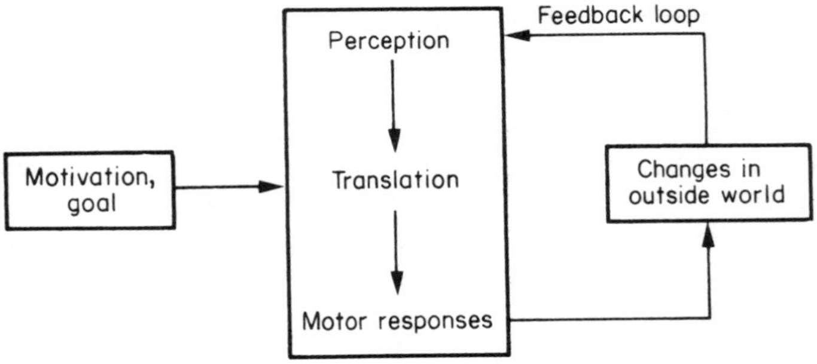

Figure 5.2 Motor skill model

Patterns of response are directed towards goals and sub-goals, and have a hierarchical structure—large units of behaviour are composed of smaller ones, and at the lowest levels these are habitual and automatic.

Harré and Secord (1972) have argued persuasively that much human social behaviour is the result of conscious planning, often in words, with full regard for the complex meanings of behaviour and the rules of situations. This is an important correction to earlier social psychological views, which often failed to recognize the complexity of individual planning and the different meanings which may be given to stimuli, for example in laboratory experiments. However it must be recognized that much social behaviour is *not* planned in this way: the smaller elements of behaviour and longer automatic sequences are outside conscious awareness, though it is possible to attend for example to patterns of gaze, shifts of orientation, or the latent meanings of utterances. The social-skill model, in emphasizing the hierarchical structure of social performance, can incorporate both kinds of behaviour.

The social-skill model also emphasizes feedback processes. A person driving a car sees at once when it is going in the wrong direction, and takes corrective action with the steering wheel. Social interactors do likewise—if another person is talking too much they interrupt, ask closed questions or no questions, and look less interested in what he has to say. Feedback requires perception, looking at and listening to the other person's reactions to one's behaviour. It requires the ability to take the appropriate corrective action, referred to as 'translation' in the model—not everyone knows that open-ended questions make people talk more and closed questions make them talk less. It depends on a number of two-step sequences of social behaviour whereby certain social acts have reliable effects on another.

This analysis of social performance is most applicable to asymmetrical social situations (see Figure 5.3), like interviewing and teaching, where the performer is in charge. The plans of someone interviewing a candidate for a job would be something like those shown in Figure 5.3 under 'asymmetrical contingency'.

The skill system may go wrong in a number of ways:

(a) The plans may be inappropriate—as in the case of Berne's patients who wanted to make other people feel uncomfortable or look foolish (Berne, 1966).
(b) An interactor may have no persistent plans; some socially inadequate neurotic patients take the subordinate side of encounters and leave other people to take all the initiative.
(c) Some individuals are very unresponsive to feedback, either because they don't notice the effect their behaviour has on others, or because they don't know what corrective action to take.

(7) Self-presentation

This refers to the signals which are sent to indicate a person's role, status, or other aspects of his identity. This is a normal and important component of social performance. From these signals others know what to expect, including what rewards are likely to be forthcoming, and how to deal with him. Self-presentation is also needed for professional roles—teachers teach more effectively if their pupils think they are well-informed, for example. If people tell others how good they are in words, this is regarded as a joke and disbelieved, in Western cultures at least. Jones (1964) found that verbal ingratiation is done with subtlety—drawing attention to assets in unimportant areas for example. Most self-presentation is done non-verbally—by clothes, hair-style, accent, badges, and general style of behaviour. Social class is very clearly signalled in these ways, as is membership of rebellious social groups (Argyle, 1975).

Goffman (1956) maintained that social behaviour involves a great deal of deceptive self-presentation, by individuals and groups, often in the interest of observers, as in the work of undertakers and doctors. In everyday life deception is probably less common than concealment. Most people keep quiet about discreditable events in their past, and others do not remind them. Stigmatized individuals, like homosexuals, drug addicts and members of certain professions, also keep it dark, though they are usually recognized by other members. Goffman's theory gives an explanation of embarrassment—this occurs when false self-presentation is unmasked. Later research has shown that this is the case, but that embarrassment also occurs when other people break social rules, and when social accidents are committed—unintentional *gaffes*, and forgetting names, for example (Argyle, 1969).

Self-presentation can go wrong in a number of ways: (a) bogus claims which are unmasked; (b) being too 'grey', i.e. sending too little information; (c) sending too much, overdramatizing, as hysterical personalities sometimes do; (d) inappropriate self-presentation, e.g. a bank manager who dresses like a criminal, a female research student who looks and sounds like a retired professor.

(8) Situations and their rules

The traditional trait model supposed that individuals possess a fixed degree of introversion, neuroticism, etc., and that it is displayed consistently in different situations. This model has been abandoned by most psychologists, following an increasing awareness of the great effect of the situation on behaviour (e.g. people are more anxious when exposed to physical danger than when asleep in bed), and the amount of personality–situation interaction (e.g. A is more frightened by heights, B by cows), resulting in low inter-situational consistency (Mischel, 1968).

But how do interactors know what to do in different situations? In fact people classify situations, using dimensions like formal–informal, friendly–hostile, equal–unequal, task–social, etc. (Wish, 1976). This is a good start, but doesn't tell us much about the behaviour required in, for example, a selection interview, a confessional, a visit to a psychoanalyst, or a judo lesson—all of which are task, friendly, and unequal. To do this we have to study the fundamental features of situations (Argyle, 1976).

(1) Rules One important feature of situations is their rules. Two people can't play a game of squash, or anything else, unless they agree to follow the same rules. Such rules are not empirical laws, but rather shared conventions, which enable sufficient coordination of behaviour for pursuing certain goals, and engaging in a desired form of interaction. Experiments on rule-breaking can be designed to discover detailed principles of sequence. We found for example that interruption is allowed at main grammatical breaks, and that it makes no difference how long the other has been speaking. We also found that some rules are 'intrinsic', in the sense that interaction is totally disrupted if they are broken: examples are an interview candidate asking all the questions, or telling obvious lies. Of course rules are only part of the story; there

is also play within the rules. A study of cricket behaviour would need to find the rules first: the next step would be to find out how the goals, strategies, and skills of different players interact *within* the rules.

(2) Repertoire of elements Every situation defines certain moves as relevant. For example at a seminar it is relevant to show slides, make long speeches, draw on the blackboard, etc. If the moves appropriate to a cricket match or a Scottish ball were made they would be ignored or regarded as totally bizarre. We have found the 50 or so main elements used in several situations, like going to the doctor (Graham *et al.*, in press); we have also found that the semiotic structure varies between situations, i.e., the way in which different elements are grouped and contrasted (Argyle, *et al.*, in press).

(3) Motivational themes All parties to social encounters are motivated in some way. Sometimes they have different motives (buying and selling, teaching and learning), sometimes the same (affiliative, sexual).

(4) Roles Every situation has a limited number of roles, e.g. a classroom has the roles of teacher, pupil, janitor, and school inspector. These roles carry different degrees of power, and the occupant has goals peculiar to that role.

(5) Cognitive structure We found that the members of a group of people classified each other in terms of the concepts *extraverted* and *enjoyable companion* for social occasions, but in terms of *dominant*, *creative* and *supportive* for seminars. There are also concepts related to the task, e.g. 'amendment', 'straw vote', 'agenda item', for committee meetings.

(6) Environmental setting and pieces Most situations involve special environmental settings or props. Cricket needs bat, ball, stumps, etc.; a seminar requires blackboard, slides, projector, and lecture notes.

(7) Skills In order to participate in many situations it is necessary to possess certain skills, social or otherwise. This is obviously true of games like polo and water-polo, and is also true of many social situations like dances, debates, and seminars.

It is found that psychiatric patients, and especially those with a psychosis, are more consistent across situations than other people—they do not accommodate to the special requirements of situations (Moos, 1968).

People with social-skills problems often have difficulty with particular social situations—parties, dates, interviews, etc. This is often because they have failed to understand the situation, for example thinking that an interview is an occasion for vocational guidance, that a date is a kind of philosophy tutorial, or bidding less than the last person at an auction sale. In some cases they lack the special skills needed for the situation.

(9) Sequences of interaction

Social behaviour consists of sequences of utterances and non-verbal signals. For such a sequence to constitute an acceptable piece of social behaviour, the moves must fit together in order.

Utterances follow each other in a conversation in special ways. The meaning of an utterance may depend on other utterances (e.g. 'I disagree'), or on the social setting ('forty–love'), and it may not be what it seems: 'Could you pass the salt' is not a question, 'Come in' is not an order but a welcome. A speaker usually produces utterances that he thinks the hearer can understand, and he adjusts its technicality, and the use of local references. Encoding involves anticipatory decoding. Rommetveit (1974) has shown how each utterance takes account of the shared information and objects of attention of speaker and hearer, and adds to them. The new is nested in the old.

The sequence of events in an encounter is somewhat like the sequence of words in a sentence. In both cases, there appear to be rules of sequence, elements take their meaning in part from their position in a larger whole, sequences can be interrupted by embedding, and whole structures can be transformed, as in jokes and satire. Rules of sequence link categories of words, like nouns and verbs; are there similar categories of social act, which can replace each other at points in a sequence? Duncan and Fiske (1977) found that turn-taking depended on certain categories of act; for example the 'back-channel signal' from listener to speaker gives the latter permission to carry on talking; it consists of five equivalent acts, head-nods, uh-huh noises, etc. We have tried to find the repertoire of social acts for different social situations, and have found rather large repertoires of about 50 acts in each situation studied so far. The same acts are grouped and contrasted differently in different situations; for example touching another's body is grouped with different equivalent acts when done on a date and during a visit to the doctor. Clarke (1975) has found that people have tacit knowledge of rules of sequence, and can put scrambled conversations back nearly in the right order. He found that artificial dialogues constructed by asking subjects to add a second, third, or fourth utterance, were rated as being as good as real dialogue if three previous utterances had been taken into account at each point. However the linguistic model overlooks a crucial difference between the production of sentences and the generation of conversations. When a speaker produces a sentence, he can do so unhindered by others; in most social encounters on the other hand, at least two people can exercise some initiative (Figure 5.3). In 'asymmetrical contingency' one person is in charge and takes most of the initiative, as in the case of a doctor or interviewer. The social-skills model fits the behaviour of the dominant performer—he can make plans and control the other's behaviour. The linguistic model also fits his behaviour, in that he can run off a complex sequence whose beginning, middle, and end can be planned, and will not be upset by the behaviour of the other.

Sequences of interaction consist partly of a number of two-step linkages. Some of

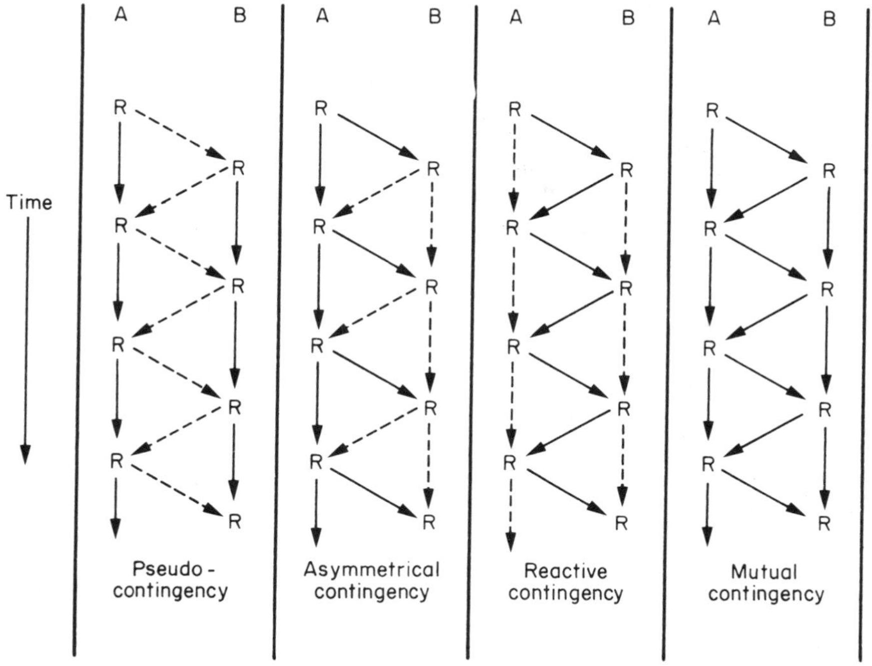

Figure 5.3 Classes of social interaction in terms of contingancy. (Reprinted, with permission, from Jones and Gerard, 1976)

these are based on rules of the situation, like the order of bidding at an auction sale; others are cases of more universal rules, like question leads to answer, and question leads to relevant answer. Some are based on psychological principles, e.g. the effects of reinforcement, response-matching, basic non-verbal signals for friendly and hostile attitudes, and so on. Three-step sequences are a bit different, as shown in Figure 5.4. This consists of two two-step sequences, A_1–B_1 and B_1–A_2. It also involves a linkage between A_1 and A_2, often due to continuity of plans on the part of A. For example:

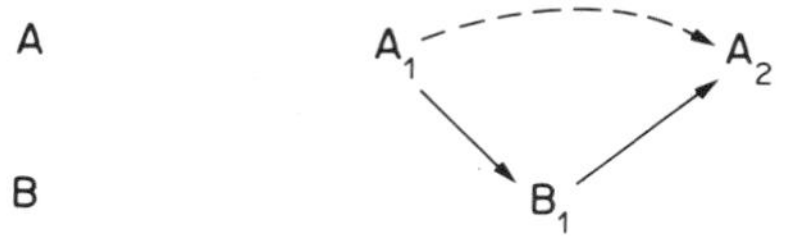

Figure 5.4

Doctor:	asks patient to take off clothes
Patient:	takes off clothes
Doctor:	examines patient

Much longer sequences can be generated if A's plans require things to be done in a certain order. Longer sequences sometimes consist of repeated cycles (see Figure 5.5). In this example several alternative cycles of teacher–pupil interaction can be seen. Flanders believes that teaching skills consist partly of the ability to control these cycles. This example illustrates another point—the importance of 'pro-active' sequences, i.e. of more than one move at a time by one interactor.

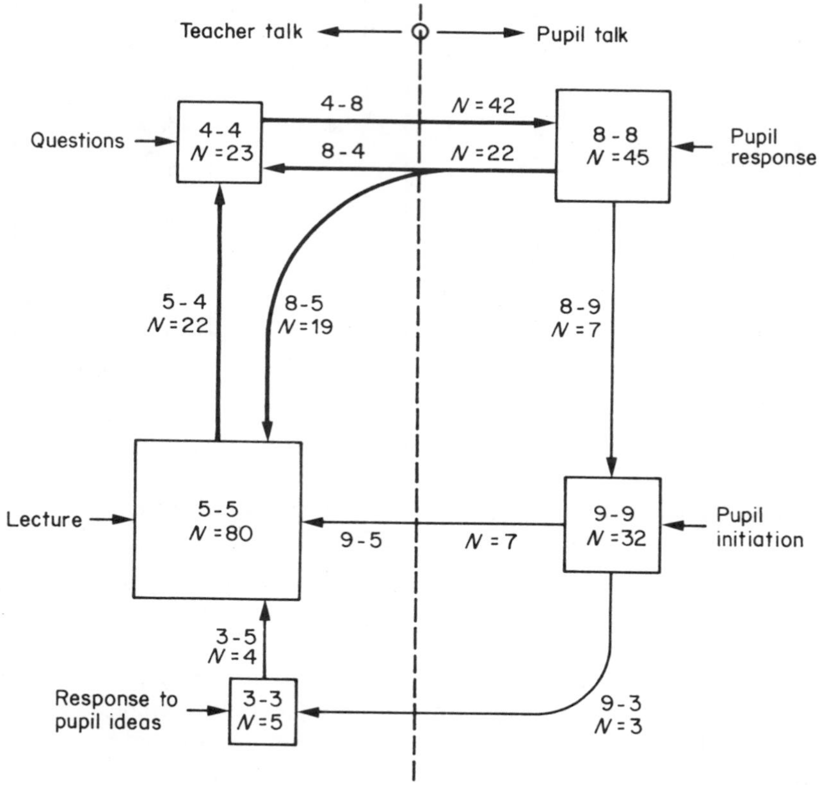

Figure 5.5 Some of the cycles of behaviour which can occur in the classroom. For example: teacher lectures—teacher asks question—pupil responds. This sequence includes a pro-active sequence consisting of the two moves of the teacher. (Reprinted, with permission, from Flanders, 1970)

Interaction sequences can be divided into episodes or phases; there may be shifts of topic, or other aspects of interaction. Committee meetings, meals, and formal occasions have clearer episodes than less formal ones. Episodes of different sizes can be located by asking observers to indicate the break-points while watching video-tapes. Episodes may consist of repeated cycles, as in classroom interaction, or run through once, as in greetings. An episode involves temporary agreement to collaborate in a familiar sequence, and is started by episode-negotiating signals, which may be verbal or non-verbal, e.g.:

Interviewer: I'd like to ask you a few questions about what you did at University.
Candidate: O.K.

An episode may go through repeated cycles until one or more interactors consider that their goals have been reached; another episode is then negotiated.

Some unskilled people are incapable of conducting a conversation; probably they have not mastered these rules of sequence. Some of these principles of sequence however are more applicable at higher levels of skill, like teaching and doctor–patient skills.

3. TYPES OF SOCIAL INADEQUACY AND DISTRESS

1. Social Anxiety

Anxiety consists of the perception of a situation as dangerous or threatening, a physiological emotional state of arousal, subjective feelings of fear etc., and behavioural responses such as avoidance and shaking. Some people tend to be anxious in many situations—they have *trait* anxiety; this interacts with perception of situations as dangerous or threatening to produce a *state* of anxiety (Spielberger, 1972). Social anxiety as a trait is the tendency to be made anxious by social situations. Anxiety is produced when people perceive the situation as threatening, there is a state of autonomic arousal, and people label their state of arousal as anxiety, rather than for example excitement or eager anticipation (Schachter, 1964). A state of social anxiety if produced when people high in interpersonal anxiety are confronted by threatening social situations but not by physical danger (Endler and Magnusson, 1975).

Social anxiety can be divided up into smaller factors corresponding to different kinds of social threat. The factors most commonly obtained are:

1. fear of performing in public, being the focus of attention;
2. fear of conflict, rejection or disapproval;
3. fear of intimacy, heterosexual or otherwise.

Other factors which have been obtained are:

4. fear of meeting strangers;
5. anxiety about assertiveness.

(Stratton and Moore, 1977; Richardson and Tasto, 1976; Hodges and Felling, 1970).

Different sets of factors have been obtained by different investigators, using different populations and samples of situations. Some individuals are anxious in specific situations, or a group of similar situations, such as performing in public, or conflict with others.

Anxiety can take more than one form. Endler and Okada (1975) found four main types: fear of interpersonal threat, of physical danger, of new and strange situations, and of ambiguous situations. There are other kinds of distress, discomfort or annoyance, in addition to anxiety. Furnham and Argyle (in press) carried out three-way factor analyses for several different populations. The factors of situations were much the same as in previous studies, though the main factor varied between different populations. For students, for example, the main dimension of difficulty consisted of formal situations. For all groups studied, however, the main response factor consisted of being anxious and upset.

Social anxiety can be assessed by self-rating scales of trait or state anxiety, ratings of behaviour, and physiological measures. As noted earlier, physiological measures do not correlate well with the other measures. One important behaviour manifestation of social anxiety is avoidance of situations. Bryant and Trower (1974) found that a considerable proportion of a sample of students simply did not go to parties, pubs, or other situations they couldn't cope with. Paul (1966) in his study of public-speaking anxiety, obtained ratings on 20 items, such as 'knees tremble', 'moistens lips', 'perspires', etc. The behaviour which is now known to reflect social anxiety includes: breathy voice, rapid speech with speech errors, low level of gaze, tense, flushed and perspiring face, tense and defensive posture, self-touching gestures (Argyle, 1975).

Social anxiety does correlate (negatively) with assertiveness, but the correlation is only of the order of -0.2 to -0.4, so these two forms of failure (social anxiety and lack of assertiveness) are fairly independent of one another (Hollandsworth, 1976). Social anxiety probably results from negative experiences in the past, in certain social situations—leading to anticipation of rejection, etc., in the future. This in turn may be due to lack of social skills in these situations. If so it would be expected that social skills training (SST) would first lead to improved performance, and, a little later, to improved self-reports. Marshall *et al.* (1977) found that SST improved rated behaviour more than systematic desensitization (SD) did, but that SD had more effect on self-reports of anxiety. Since the self-reports were made immediately after the training, this would be expected, on our hypothesis.

2. Lack of assertiveness

Assertiveness training is one of the most widely practised forms of SST. Assertiveness is taken to include a number of somewhat different, but it is believed related, patterns of social behaviour. In the early days of behaviour therapy this treatment was devised for people who were too passive and submissive. Assertiveness is now taken to include: (a) the ability to say No, (b) the ability to ask for favours or to make requests, (c) the ability to express positive and negative feelings, and (d) the ability to initiate, continue and terminate general conversations

(Lazarus, 1973). It is also often taken to include an individual's ability to stand up for his rights, and to act in his own best interests. Typical instances of assertiveness are dealing with laundries who lose shirts and with other students who borrow notes and fail to return them.

It was originally believed that assertiveness was a general trait; however, a number of studies have shown that assertiveness consists of a number of different factors, corresponding to different situations, and different modes of response (e.g. Eisler *et al.*, 1975). The most valid measures of assertiveness ask for self-reports for a number of specific assertiveness situations (p. 125).

It is believed in some quarters that assertiveness is the whole of social skills. However research in social psychology has repeatedly shown that there are two main dimensions of social performance: control (or assertiveness) and warmth (or concern with social relationships). Making friends, of either sex, is not a matter of bullying others to be friendly, but requires quite different skills, which are described later. Assertiveness includes those social skills which are intended to obtain rewards for the performer, but at the risk of losing social rewards, hence the fear of rejection and the link with social anxiety. Controlling skills use verbal behaviour: directing, ordering, persuading; and non-verbal behaviour: loud and firm tone of voice, unsmiling face, erect but relaxed posture, breaking gaze last (Argyle, 1975). However assertiveness alone is not likely to be successful unless accompanied by sufficient rewards. Control is more successful when it is not authoritarian—when the controller advises, persuades, coordinates, explains, and suggests rather than orders or criticizes; and assertive behaviour should be distinguished from aggressive behaviour (Rich and Schroeder, 1976.)

3. Social isolates

These are people who have no friends and are upset about it. This is one of the commonest complaints from people who present themselves for SST. We should probably not include those very introverted people who simply prefer their own company. There are important situational effects here—the same person is often very popular in one group but rejected by another, where perhaps his attitudes are deviant, his skills not needed, or he is of the wrong race, class, or age. There is, however, a definite percentage of the population who are not very popular in any group, and who have not managed to form a close relationship with anyone.

Social isolates can be identified in sociometric surveys of who chooses whom, for various joint activities—a number of individuals are not chosen by anyone (Lindzey and Byrne, 1968).

Some assertiveness trainers see making friends as a form of assertiveness, and indeed some assertiveness is required. Research on interpersonal attraction, however, shows that a number of specific skills are required which have little to do with assertiveness. At the early stages of acquaintance, physical proximity and frequency of interaction are important. So is physical attractiveness, for men as well as women, and most aspects of this can be manipulated. At the next stage it is important for individuals to signal non-verbally that they like the other person (Argyle *et al.*, 1970), to provide rewards for the other, and to discover joint interests and similar attitudes. There will be gradually increasing and reciprocated self-disclosure, and the relationship is sustained by certain rituals such as invitations to drinks, meals and outings, and presents (Duck, 1977).

4. Heterosexual social problems

There are two broad groups of heterosexual social problems: lack of contact with the opposite sex ('minimal dating'), and anxiety in the presence of the opposite sex ('heterosexual anxiety'); these are alternate targets for SST. It can be assessed by self-rating scales on, for example, the level of anxiety, discomfort, or difficulty experienced when asking someone for a date, or going on a first date with someone. The origins of these problems have been suggested to be lack of social skills, conditioned anxiety, or inaccurate perception of own performance together with anticipation of aversive consequences (Curran, 1977). Twentyman and McFall (1975) found that after SST a number of shy males showed lower physiologically measured anxiety in dating situations.

The extent of social difficulty in the population

Non-clinical groups There is no doubt, from common experience and various social surveys, that all of the kinds of social difficulty which we have described are very common—anxiety in various situations, assertiveness problems, difficulty in making friends and in forming relationships with the opposite sex. It is, however, difficult to decide on a cut-off point, beyond which a person is said to suffer from social behaviour problems. Possible criteria are:

(a) seeking help, or accepting it when it is available—though this will depend on how readily available it is and how attractively presented;
(b) reporting avoidance of everyday situations, or 'great difficulty' etc. or reporting that loneliness, social anxiety, etc. is one of their greatest problems;
(c) behavioural evidence of social inadequacy, such as not having any friends, being very unsuccessful as a salesman, teacher, etc., or the object of complaints from others.

Bryant and Trower (1974) surveyed a 10 per cent sample of Oxford undergraduates and found that a high proportion reported moderate or severe difficulty with common social situations, especially 'approaching others' (36 per cent), 'going to dances/discotheques' (35 per cent), 'going to parties' (26 per cent). These were the figures for second-year students; first-year students reported much higher levels of difficulty. Nine per cent of the sample reported 'great difficulty' or avoidance of six common situations out of thirty, and were regarded as suffering from serious social problems. From this, and various other surveys, it seems likely that at least 7 per cent of the normal adult population have fairly serious difficulties with social behaviour.

Clinical groups: neurosis Bryant *et al.* (1976) found that 28 per cent of a sample of out-patients in this category were regarded by clinical psychologists and psychiatrists as socially unskilled. They were low in components of both control (assertiveness) and rewardingness, and were deficient in basic skills like conducting conversations. A distinction can be drawn between those who have social phobias and those who have inadequate social skills, though the two groups overlap. Patients suffer from each of the main components of social inadequacy described above. Their behaviour can also be described in terms of mechanisms described earlier—deficient production of NVC, disruption of skilled behaviour by anxiety, inappropriate goals as in the case of Berne's socially destructive patients, low rewardingness, and inability to take the role of the other. Henderson *et al.* (1978) found that a sample of patients with neurosis had far fewer friends than a matched control group, and that the friends they did have did not form a social network.

Delinquents have been found to be very deficient in social skills, and are often given SST, for example, to train them in how to get and keep a job (Sarason and Ganzer, 1971). Disturbed adolescents are similarly found to need training, both in how to get on with each other and with adults. Some conditions may be mainly due to lack of social skills: social inadequacy leads to rejection and isolation, which in turn leads to anxiety, depression, and other symptoms. There is some evidence that SST can result in the remission of such symptoms as anorexia and amenorrhoea. However for many people, social behaviour difficulties are neither the only symptom, nor the sole factor in the aetiology.

Psychosis

Patients suffering a psychosis are frequently deficient in certain areas of social competence. Schizophrenia is often associated with social withdrawal, poor social relationships, and difficulty in conducting conversations. These deficiencies can be described in terms of the processes reviewed earlier, e.g. inappropriate use of NVC (especially face, gesture, and posture), failure in the production of verbal messages and poor synchronizing, low rewardingness, poor perception of others, etc. (Argyle, 1969). Some depressed individuals have difficulty in eliciting positive responses from others, since their level of social activity and initiation of behaviour is frequently so low (Lewinsohn, 1975). However, the social inadequacy associated with psychosis is probably not a cause of the other symptoms and is more likely to be caused by deeper cognitive, affective, or other disturbances; but the lack of social skills results in rejection and isolation, this adding to the overall stress and resulting in further deterioration.

4. SOCIAL SKILLS TRAINING (SST)

This section will include a brief account of the main techniques of SST, together with evidence of their effectiveness and of the use of these methods for different populations.

The main methods of SST

(1) Training on the job This is the most widely used method, for teachers, interviewers, managers, and others. It can be surprisingly unsuccessful, and performers may actually become worse (Argyle, 1969, p. 397 f). It is essential to have a trainer who is expert on the skill in question, who sees the trainee in action, and holds feedback sessions at which he draws attention to faults and suggests new skills. When feedback is given, the behaviour of trainees is greatly improved (Gage *et al.*, 1960). This method has the great advantage that there is no problem of transfer of newly learnt skills from the training lab. to the real situation.

(2) T-groups were widely used at one time as a form of professional SST. There was a certain measure of success in that 30–40 per cent of trainees were found to be improved in general social sensitivity and awareness of the effect of their own behaviour on others. On the other hand a proportion of trainees (estimates differ) seem to have been harmed by the experience, and in many cases needed psychiatric help. Furthermore there was little gain in specific social skills unless role-playing exercises were included—as they were in the original T-groups at Bethel, Maine. This has led to a modification of T-groups so that there is more task content, or to the abandonment of this method in favour of others (Argyle, 1969; Lieberman *et al.*, 1973).

(3) Lectures, discussion and other educational methods Lectures and discussion have been found to have almost no effect on social competence. However the study of programmed texts, like the Culture Assimilator (Fiedler *et al.*, 1971) has been found to improve intercultural skills. It seems likely that reading materials containing instructions for exercises would be useful. Instructional films are successful for teaching motor skills, and it seems probable that they can be useful for SST also.

(4) Role-playing is now the most widely used method of SST. There are four stages:

(a) instruction and modelling—by demonstration or film;
(b) role-playing with other trainees or other role partners, for 5–8 minutes;
(c) feedback—verbal comments from the trainer, and playback of video-tape recordings;
(d) repeated role-playing.

A typical laboratory set-up is shown in Figure 5.6 here. This also shows the use of an ear-microphone, for instruction while role-playing is taking place. Role-playing has been found to be effective for training teachers and other professional social skill performers, for psychiatric patients, and for training students on dating, assertiveness, or to reduce public speaking phobia. There is some doubt over whether the video-tape recording really adds to the effectiveness. Research is required to find out what are the main problems, and the best skills to be taught. Trainers have difficulty advising trainees who come from a different social background, to induce the right attitude to the role-playing, and to give the feedback comments gently and tactfully, yet clearly enough to have some impact. There is the problem of transferring skills to real-life situations; this can be achieved by 'homework'—practice in real settings between training sessions.

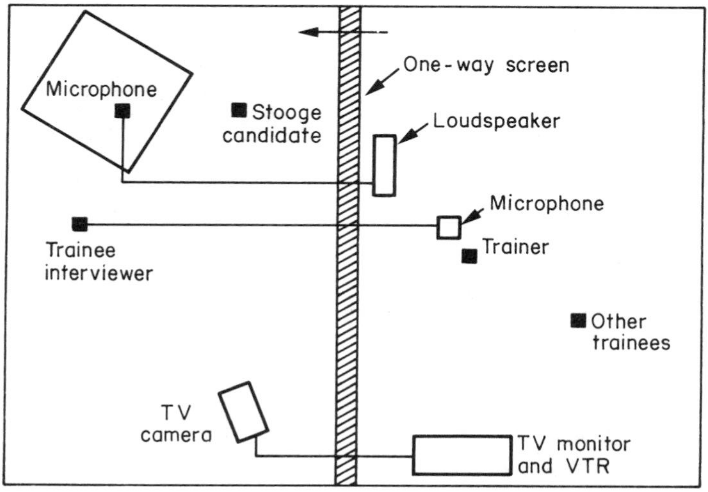

Figure 5.6 Laboratory for social skills training

(5) Specialized methods of SST In our work with psychiatric patients at Oxford we have developed a series of methods related to the specific forms of social skill deficit mentioned in section (3) above. These include (a) training in the perception of facial expression and tone of voice; (b) training in the use of NVC; (c) role reversal; (d) training in planning; (e) self-presentation, by modification of appearance and voice; (f) instruction on the repertoire, rules, goals, etc. of particular situations. In addition desensitization is given where there is strong anxiety in particular situations.

Areas of application of SST

(1) Clinical groups Role-playing and the more specialized methods described above

have been found to be slightly more effective than psychotherapy, desensitization, or other alternative treatments (Trower *et al.*, 1978). Only one study so far has found really substantial differences—Maxwell (1976) in a New Zealand study of adults reporting social difficulties and seeking treatment for them. It is noteworthy that she insisted on homework between training sessions. A few patients can be helped by SST alone, but most have other problems as well, and may require other forms of treatment in addition.

Psychotic patients have been treated in the USA by varieties of assertiveness training. Follow-up studies have shown greater improvement in social behaviour than from alternative treatments, but the gains have usually been small, and insufficient for the patients to be discharged from hospital (Hersen and Bellack, 1976). It has been argued by one practitioner that SST is more suitable than psychotherapy for working-class patients in view of their poor verbal skills (Goldstein, 1973).

Alcoholics have been given SST to improve their assertiveness, for example in refusing drinks, and to enable them to deal better with situations which they find stressful and make them drink. Similar treatment has been given to drug addicts. In both cases treatment has been fairly successful, though the effects have not always been long-lasting; SST is often included in more comprehensive packages.

Delinquents and prisoners have often been given SST with some success, especially in the case of aggressive and sex offenders. SST can also increase their degree of internal control. It has been given to disturbed children, especially those who are aggressive or withdrawn and unpopular. Modelling and coaching are the main methods used, and it is common to obtain the collaboration of teachers and parents.

(2) Non-clinical groups SST is increasingly being included in the training of those whose work involves dealing with people. The most extensive application so far has been in the training of teachers by 'microteaching'. The pupil teacher is instructed in one of the component skills of teaching, e.g. the use of different kinds of question, explanation and the use of examples; he then teaches five or six children for 10–15 minutes, followed by a feedback session and 're-teaching'. Follow-up studies show that this is far more effective than a similar amount of teaching practice, and it is much more effective in eradicating bad habits (Brown, 1975). In addition to role-playing, more elaborate forms of simulation are used, for example to train people for administrative positions. Training on the job is a valuable addition or alternative, provided that the trainer really does his job.

Students have received a certain amount of SST, especially in North American universities, and follow-up studies have shown that they can be successfully trained in assertiveness (Rich and Schroeder, 1976), dating behaviour (Curran, 1977), and to reduce anxiety at performing in public (Paul, 1966). Although many normal adults apart from students have social behaviour difficulties, very little training is available unless they seek psychiatric help. It would be very desirable for SST to be more widely available, for example in community centres.

A number of attempts have been made to introduce SST into schools, though there are no follow-up studies on its effectiveness. There are certain problems here—few teachers will be experts on social behaviour, and elaborate equipment will often not be available. McPhail *et al.* (1978) devised extensive curriculum materials emphasizing taking the role of the other, using cards and case-studies for discussion, and episodes to be role-played.

OVERVIEW

I have defined social competence as the ability to produce the desired effects on other people in social situations. It can be measured most easily for professional social-skills performers like salesmen and teachers, where there is a clear index of success. Social competence in everyday life can be assessed from self-reports or ratings of observed behaviour in real-life situations or role-played situations; competence is found to vary greatly between different situations.

Skilled social performance is produced by a number of social psychological processes—perception of other people, production of non-verbal signals, rewardingness, and so on. Some of these have become known through quite recent research, for example into the analysis of situations and into sequences of social interaction. Each of these processes can go wrong in various ways, producing a number of different kinds of inadequate social performance. The main forms of social inadequacy and distress, however, are social anxiety, lack of assertiveness, social isolation, and heterosexual social problems. Studies of the extent of these problems suggest that at least 7 per cent of normal adults (more than this for young people), 25 per cent or more of neurotics, and most psychotics are seriously handicapped by lack of social skills.

Social-skills training can be carried out in a number of ways, but role-playing with video-tape feedback is now the main method. This can be supplemented by more specialized exercises, like training in NVC, and by 'homework', and training on the job. It is being widely used for neurotic patients with social behaviour difficulties, teachers, and other professionals, and is being introduced for normal adults and in schools.

REFERENCES

Argyle, M. (1969). *Social Interaction*. (London: Methuen.)

Argyle, M. (1972). *The Social Psychology of Work*. (London: Allen Lane, The Penguin Press.)

Argyle, M. (1975). *Bodily Communication*. (London: Methuen.)

Argyle, M. (1976). Personality and social behaviour. In: R. Harré (Ed.), *Personality*, pp. 145–188. (Oxford: Blackwell.)

Argyle, M. and Cook, M. (1976). *Gaze and Mutual Gaze*. (Cambridge: Cambridge University Press.)

Argyle, M., Alkema, F., and Gilmour, R. (1971). The communication of friendly and hostile attitudes by verbal and non-verbal signals. *European Journal of Social Psychology*, **1,** 385–402.

Argyle, M., Furnham, A., and Graham, J. A. (In press). *Social Situations*. (Cambridge: Cambridge University Press.)

Argyle, M. and Kendon, A. (1967). The experimental analysis of social performance. In: L. Berkowitz (Ed.), *Advances in Experimental Social Psychology*, Vol. 3. (New York: Academic Press.)

Argyle, M., Salter, V., Nicholson, H., Williams, M., and Burgess, P. (1970). The communication of inferior and superior attitudes by verbal and non-verbal signals. *British Journal of Social and Clinical Psychology*. **9,** 221–231.

Bannister, D. and Salmon, P. (1966). Schizophrenic thought disorder: specific or diffuse? *British Journal of Medical Psychology*, **39,** 215–219.

Berne, E. (1966). *Games People Play*. (London: Deutsch.)

Brown, G. A. (1975). Microteaching: research and developments. In: G. Channon and S. Delamont (Eds.), *Frontiers of Classroom Research*. (Slough: NFER.)

Bryant, B. and Trower, P. (1974). Social difficulty in a student population. *British Journal of Educational Psychology*, **44,** 13–21.

Bryant, B., Trower, P., Yardley, K., Urbieta, H., and Letemendia, F. J. J. (1976). A survey of social inadequacy among psychiatric out-patients. *Psychological Medicine*, **6,** 101–112.

Clarke, D. (1975). The use and recognition of sequential structure in dialogue. *British Journal of Social and Clinical Psychology*, **14,** 333–339.

Curran, J. P. (1977). Skills training as an approach to the treatment of heterosexual–social anxiety. *Psychological Bulletin*, **84,** 140–157.

Davitz, J. R. (1964). *The Communication of Emotional Meaning*, (New York: McGraw-Hill.)

Duck, S. (1977) (Ed.). *Theory and Practice in Interpersonal Attraction*. (London: Academic Press.)

Duncan, S. and Fiske, D. W. (1977). *Face-to-Face Interaction*. (Hillsdale, NJ: Erlbaum.)

Duval, S. and Wicklund, R. A. (1972). *A Theory of Objective Self Awareness*. (New York: Academic Press.)

Eisler, R. M. (1976). The behavioral assessment of social skills. In: M. Hersen and A. S. Bellack (Eds.), *Behavioral Assessment: A Practical Handbook*. (New York: Pergamon.)

Eisler, R. M., Hersen, M., Miller, P. M., and Blanchard, E. B. (1975). Situational determinants of assertive behaviour. *J. Consult. Clin. Psychol.*, **43,** 330–340.

Ekman, P., Friesen, W. V., and Ellsworth, P. (1972). *Emotion in the Human Face*. (Elmsford, NY: Pergamon.)

Endler, N. S. and Magnusson, D. (1976). *Interactional Psychology and Personality*. (Washington: Hemisphere.)

Endler, N. S. and Okada, M. (1975). A multidimensional measure of trait anxiety: the S–R inventory of General Trait Anxiousness. *Journal of Consulting and Clinical Psychology*, **43,** 319–329.

Feffer, M. and Suchotliffe, L. (1966). Decentering implications of social interaction. *Journal of Personal and Social Psychology*, **4,** 415–442.

Fiedler, F. E., Mitchell, T., and Triandis, H. C. (1971). The culture assimilator: an approach to cross-cultural training. *Journal of Applied Psychology*, **55,** 95–102.

Flanders, N. A. (1970). *Analyzing Teaching Behavior*. (Reading, Mass.: Addison-Wesley.)

Flavell, J. H. (1968). *The Development of Role-taking and Communication Skills in Children*. (New York: Wiley.)

Furnham, A. and Argyle, M. (In press) Responses to social situations in four groups. In: M. Argyle, A. Furnham and J. A. Graham, *Social Situations*. (Cambridge: Cambridge University Press.)

Gage, N. L., Runkel, P. J., and Chatterjee, B. B. (1960). *Equilibrium Theory and Behavior Change: An Experiment in Feedback from Pupils to Teachers*. (Urbana, Illinois: *Bureau of Educational Research.)*

Goffman, E. (1956). The Presentation of Self in Everyday Life. (Edinburgh: Edinburgh University Press.)

Goldstein, A. J. (1973). *Structured Learning Therapy: Toward a Psychotherapy for the Poor*. (New York: Academic Press.)

Graham, J. A., Argyle, M., Clarke, D. D., and Maxwell, G. (In press). The salience, equivalence and sequential structure of behavioural elements in different situations. *Semiotica*.

Harré, R. and Secord, P. (1972). *The Explanation of Social Behaviour*. (Oxford: Blackwell.)

Henderson, S., Duncan-Jones, P., McAuley, H., and Ritchie, K. (1978). The patient's primary group. *British Journal of Psychiatry*, **132,** 74–86.

Hersen, M. and Bellack, A. S. (1976). Social skills training for chronic psychiatric patients: rationale, research findings and future directions. *Comprehensive Psychiatry*, **17,** 559–580.

Hodges, W. F. and Felling, J. P. (1970). Types of stressful situations and their relation to trait anxiety and sex. *Journal of Consulting and Clinical Psychology*, **34,** 333–337.

Hollandsworth, J. G. (1976). Further investigation of the relationship between expressed social fear and assertiveness. *Behaviour Research and Therapy*, **14,** 85–87.

Jennings, H. H. (1950). *Leadership and Isolation*. (New York: Longmans, Green.)

Jones, E. E. (1964). *Ingratiation: A Social Psychological Analysis*. (New York: Appleton-Century-Crofts.)

Jones, E. E. and Gerard, H. B. (1967). *Foundations of Social Psychology*. (New York: Wiley.)

Kendon, A. (1967). Some functions of gaze direction in social interaction. *Acta Psychologica*, **28**(1), 1–47.

Lazarus, A. A. (1973). On assertive behavior: a brief note. *Behavior Therapy*, **4,** 697–699.

Lieberman, M. A., Yalom, I. D., and Miles, M. B. (1973). *Encounter Groups: First Facts*. (New York: Basic Books.)

Lewinsohn, P. M. (1975). The behavioral study and treatment of depression. In: M. Herson *et al.* (Eds.), *Progress in Behavior Modification*, Vol. 1. (New York: Academic Press.)

Lindzey, G. and Byrne, D. (1968). Measurement of social choice and interpersonal attractiveness. In G. Lindzey and E. Aronson (Eds.), *Handbook of Social Psychology*, Vol. 2, pp. 452–525. (Reading, Mass.: Addison-Wesley.) **2,** 452–525.

Longabaugh, R., Eldred, S. H., Bell, N. W. and Sherman, L. J. (1966). The interactional world of the chronic schizophrenic patient. *Psychiatry*, **29,** 319–344.

McDavid, J. and Schroder, H. M. (1957). The interpretation of approval and disapproval by delinquent and non-delinquent adolescents. *Journal of Personality*, **25,** 539–549.

McPhail, P., Middleton, D., and Ingram, D. (1978). *Moral Education in the Middle Years*. (London: Longman.)

Marshall, W. C., Stoian, M., and Andrews, W. R. (1977). Skills training and self-administered desensitization in the reduction cf public speaking anxiety. *Behaviour Research and Therapy*, **15,** 115–117.

Maxwell, G. M. (1976). An evaluation of social skills training (unpublished). University of Otago, Dunedin, New Zealand.

Meldman, M. J. (1967). Verbal behavior analysis of self-hyperattentionism. *Diseases of the Nervous System*, **28,** 469–473.

Mischel, W. (1968). *Personality and Assessment*. (New York: Wiley.)

Moos, R. H. (1968). Situational analysis of a therapeutic community milieu. *Journal of Abnormal Psychology*, **73,** 49–61.

Paul, G. L. (1966). *Insight vs. Desensitization in Psychotherapy*. (Stanford: Stanford University Press.)

Rathus, S. A. (1973). A 30-item schedule for assessing assertive behavior. *Behavior Therapy*, **4,** 398–406.

Rich, A. R. and Schroeder, H. E. (1976). Research issues in assertiveness training. *Psychological Bulletin*, **83,** 1081–1096.

Richardson, F. C. and Tasto, D. L. (1976). Developments and factor analysis of a social anxiety inventory. *Behavior Therapy*, **7,** 453–462.

Rommetveit, R. (1974). *On Message Structure*. (London: Wiley.)

Rosenthal, R., Archer, D., Koivumaki, J. H., DiMatteo, M. R., and Rogers, P. L. (1974). Assessing sensitivity to nonverbal communication: The PONS test. *Division 8 Newsletter*. (Division of Personality and Social Psychology.)

Rubin, Z. (1973). *Liking and Loving*. (New York: Holt, Rinehart, & Winston.)

Sarason, I. G. and Ganzer, V. J. (1971). *Modeling: an approach to the rehabilitation of juvenile offenders*. (U.S. Department of Health, Education and Welfare.)

Schachter, S. (1964). The interaction of cognition and physiological determinants of emotional state. *Advances in Experimental Social Psychology*, **1,** 49–80.

Spielberger, C. D. (1972). Conceptual and methodological issues in research on anxiety. In: C. D. Spielberger (Ed.), *Anxiety: Current Trends in Theory and Research*, **1,** 481–493. (New York: Academic Press.) **1,** 481–493.

Stratton, T. T. and Moore, C. L. (1977). Application of the robust factor concept to the fear survey schedule. *Journal of Behavior Therapy and Experimental Psychiatry*, **8,** 229–235.

Synder, M. and Monson, T. C. (1975). Persons, situations, and the control of social behavior. *Journal of Personal and Social Psychology*, **4,** 637–644.

Tagiuri, R. (1958). Social preference and its perception. In: R. Tagiuri and L. Petrullo (Eds.), *Person Perception and Interpersonal Behavior*. (Stanford: Stanford University Press.)

Trower, P., Bryant, B., and Argyle, M. (1978). *Social Skills and Mental Health*. (London: Methuen.)

Twentyman, G. T. and McFall, R. M. (1975). Behavioural training in shy males. *Journal of Consulting and Clinical Psychology*, **43,** 384–395.

Weitz, S. (1972). Attitude, voice and behavior. *Journal of Personal and Social Psychology*, **24,** 14–21.

Wills, T. A., Weiss, R. L. and Patterson, G. R. (1974). A behavioural analysis of the determination of marital satisfaction. *Journal of Consulting and Clinical Psychology*, **42,** 802–811.

Wish, M. (1976). Comparisons among multidimensional structure of interpersonal relations. *Multivariate Behavioural Research*, **11,** 297–324.

The Social Psychology of Psychological Problems
Edited by P. Feldman and J. Orford

6

Life Stresses and Psychological Consequences

RAYMOND COCHRANE AND MICHAEL SOBOL

Our plan in this chapter is to review briefly systematic studies of life events and psychological disturbance, to consider the extent to which the methodology of the research to date makes it possible to draw inferences about the existence of a causal relationship and finally, and at somewhat greater length, to look at possible intervening variables and explanations of the link between life stresses and psychological disturbance. Questions of definition will largely be avoided. Life events, social stress, social readjustment and personal distress will all be used synonymously to refer to the kind of events contained in Table 6.1. Psychological disturbance will be used as a very broad term to cover any psychopathology however mild, but specific disorders such as schizophrenia will be discussed where appropriate.

It has long been accepted as obvious that social stress, however defined, can play an important aetiological role in the genesis of many forms of psychological disturbance ranging from the psychoses to mild anxiety. It is, however, only recently that well-controlled, systematic studies of the possible causal relationship between stress and psychopathology have been conducted.

Several factors may have contributed to this upsurge of interest in the topic. First, the observation that rates of admission to mental hospitals, outpatient contacts and GP contacts for psychological problems have all be increasing. The tendency has been to account for at least some of this increase in recorded psychopathology by the supposed increased stresses and strains of modern life.

Second, several large epidemiological studies conducted during the 1950s and 1960s revealed both that some forms of psychological disturbance were very widespread and that an important correlate of subclinical psychological disturbance was life stress. The Midtown study of Langner and Michael (1963) is a clear example. Of the 1660 people they interviewed in New York fully 80 per cent showed some forms of psychopathology and 20 per cent were sufficiently disturbed to warrant comparison with psychiatric cases in treatment. A linear relationship was found between the number of childhood and adult stresses the person had encountered and his mental health score (Langner and Michael, 1963, p. 376).

The third and most important factor has been the recent availability of economical and reliable methods of assessing psychosocial stress. The Social Readjustment Rating Scale (SRRS) developed by Holmes and Rahe (1967) and its successors made possible the very rapid, apparently objective and quantifiable assessment of life stresses. Since the advent of this technique the study of the effects of psychosocial stress has burgeoned.

MEASUREMENT OF LIFE EVENTS

The psychometrics involved in the method are extraordinarily simple—consisting usually of assembling a list of possible stressful events. The definition of stressful event typically involves the idea that someone encountering such an event would need to adjust his life to some degree to cope with it. Events with positive connotations, such as getting married, are included along with definitely negative events because they too require some readjustments to be made. The list of events is then submitted for judging by some expert or lay group who is required to assign a weighting to each event to reflect the amount of readjustment each would require of an average person compared to some arbitrary standard event. The average of the scores assigned by the judges to each item is then used to weight that item in subsequent studies. An individual score on the whole scale is the sum of the weightings of all the events that have happened to him within a fixed time period—for example one year. There have been several attempts to improve upon the original SRRS but most have remained with the same basic method of construction. One example is given in Table 6.1.

Table 6.1 Examples of items from the Life Events Inventory (Cochrane and Robertson, 1973)

Event	*Weight*
Unemployment	68
Retirement	54
Moving house	42
Getting into debt beyond means of repayment	66
Death of a close friend	55
Miscarriage	65
Marriage	50
Son or daughter leaves home	44
Infidelity of spouse	68
Break-up with steady boy-friend or girl-friend	51

Although instruments such as the SRRS, the Life Events Inventory (LEI) and the Schedule of Recent Experiences (SRE) have the obvious advantages of simplicity, a standardized format, and wide applicability, they also have disadvantages. The fact that a fixed weight is applied to an event does not allow for the very real possibility that the circumstances surrounding an incident may dramatically alter its impact.

The fixed but arbitrary length of the list is also a limitation as it does not allow for the inclusion of the rarer but quite probably important types of items that may befall people. Some researchers, notably George Brown and his colleagues in London, have opted for an alternative way of ascertaining stress based upon a structured interview method. This technique, fully described in Brown and Birley (1968) and Brown, *et al.* (1973a), offers some advantages over the inventory format but considerably increases the time and costs involved in obtaining life event information.

LIFE EVENTS AND PSYCHOLOGICAL DISTURBANCE

Life events inventories of one type or another have been used in a wide variety of contexts and links sought to many disorders both physical and psychological. The strengths and weaknesses of this kind of approach are illustrated by the study of Jacobs and Myers (1976) which is quite representative of endeavours in this area. In this study 62 first-admission schizophrenics in Connecticut hospitals were carefully matched on the basis of age, marital status, sex, race, and social class with 62 people randomly selected from the catchment area of the hospitals. Along with other questionnaire material each of the patients and controls was administered a modified version of the Schedule of Recent Experiences (Holmes and Rahe, 1967). One year prior to illness onset for patients, and one year prior to time of interview for controls, was covered for the occurrence of events, but all life events measurements were, of course, done retrospectively.

A comparison of the number of events reported by each group showed that the schizophrenics averaged 3.2 and the normal comparison group 2.1 per person. The difference between the groups was statistically significant ($t = 2.67$; $p < 0.01$). Jacobs and Myers went on to compare their groups on the occurrence of events which were almost certainly independent of the respondent's influence, such as 'death of a spouse' or 'reorganization at work'. The schizophrenics did report more of these events but the difference was small and non-significant, so it seems that events which may have been at least partially caused by the persons themselves accounted for the difference between schizophrenics and normals. Some other studies which have used this division of controlled and uncontrolled events have not found that the relationship between psychopathology and life events has been confined to events possibly influenced by the persons themselves (Cochrane and Robertson, 1975; Dohrenwend, 1973a) although neither of these studies included schizophrenic patients. Jacobs and Myers also found that the schizophrenics reported significantly more undesirable events (e.g. divorce) while the normals reported more desirable events (e.g. promotion) although here the difference was not significant. Other studies have tended to support the conclusion that it is the occurrence of undesirable life events which correlates with psychological disturbance, but this has not been a universal finding (e.g., Cochrane and Robertson, 1975; Gersten *et al.* 1974; Vinokur and Selzer, 1975; but see also Dohrenwend, 1973a for an exception).

Using a variety of methodologies and definitions, several studies have produced quite similar results to those mentioned above. These studies are summarized in Table 6.2. Only studies for which we were able to estimate the strength of the relationship between life events and psychological disturbance are included in this table. There are a number of other studies which produced results very similar in nature to those contained in Table 6.2, but which could not so easily be quantified (Brown *et al.* 1975; Cadoret *et al.* 1972; Langner and Michael, 1963; Leighton *et al.* 1963; Myers *et al.* 1971, 1975; Payne, 1975; Rahe, 1974; Thomson and Hendrie, 1972; Wyler *et al.* 1971).

Relationships of a similar magnitude have also been found between life events and physical disorders such as tuberculosis, glaucoma, rheumatoid arthritis, and cardiac failure among others (see Dohrenwend and Dohrenwend, 1974; and Gunderson and Rahe, 1974 for reviews).

For completeness it should be recorded that there are a few studies which have failed to find a relationship between life events and psychological disturbance but they are, at present, in a distinct minority and may not constitute complete contradictions of the results of the supporting studies. Murphy *et al.* (1962) found no differences in the stressful life experiences of pregnant women who consulted a physician for reasons unconnected with their pregnancy and those women who did not. However, when all the women were interviewed by a psychiatrist those judged to be psychiatrically disturbed had experienced significantly more stressful events in the preceding year than those judged free of psychiatric symptoms. Forrest *et al.* (1965); Hudgens, (1974); Hudgens *et al.* (1967); and Morrison *et al.* (1968) found no difference in the extent of stress experiences of psychiatric patients and matched controls, but in each study the control group consisted of hospitalized medical or surgical patients. Given that there is a link of similar magnitude between life events and physical disorder, as has been found between life events and psychological disorder, then the failure to find a difference between two groups of patients is not unexpected.

An examination of Table 6.2 reveals a very consistent moderate positive relationship between personal distress and psychological disorder, however these variables are measured. The correlations tend to cluster quite tightly around an average value of +0.35. The fact that 10 per cent or more of the variance in psychological states ranging from psychotic through mild disturbance to normal is consistently accounted for by a variable as vaguely defined and measured as life stresses is quite remarkable. Of course, a correlation does not indicate causality in any particular direction and this has posed considerable difficulties for the interpretation of these findings.

One other set of findings also needs to be articulated with the pattern of results that has emerged from the life events tradition. Studies of situations which might reasonably be assumed to be stressful, but which are not specifically personal in nature, often do not appear to produce anticipated stress reactions. Ecological level analyses of mental illness as measured by mental hospitalization rates sometimes do not show any elevation in populations exposed to such stress as bombing and rioting and international migration (Burbury, 1941; Cochrane, 1977; Fraser, 1971; Lewis, 1941). Indeed, occasionally a decline in mental illness rates has been noted to accompany such stress. Where adverse psychological reactions are recorded these are very often described as transient and with excellent prognosis. Many of the people surviving the extreme stresses of being in combat, being taken prisoner of war, and even being exposed to the horrors of concentration camp life rapidly lost most of the symptoms that were apparent in the stressful situation once they were out of the threatening situation (Antonovsky *et al.* 1971; Coleman, 1976; Eitinger, 1959; Sanua, 1970). Borus (1974) in a carefully controlled study found that the incidence of emotional maladjustment in a group of 577 soldiers returning to the US from the stresses of combat in Vietnam was no greater than that found in a matched group of soldiers who had never been to Vietnam or seen combat elsewhere. This does, however, conflict with reports of less well controlled studies which suggest that Vietnam stress reactions often go unnoticed because of the ex-soldiers' hostility towards the military establishment, including its medical services (DeFazio *et al.* 1975; Putten and Emory, 1973).

A community survey of psychiatric symptomatology being carried out by Greenley *et al.* (1975) in New Haven, Connecticut, was interrupted by a serious race riot. The researchers took advantage of this natural experiment to contrast symptom levels recorded before, during, and after the riots. They found that the whites in their samples, who might be considered to be under threat, actually showed a *decline* in symptom levels during and after the riots compared to pre-riot levels. Similarly in Belfast, Lyons (1972) noted a considerable decline in depressive illness during rioting periods compared to the same city prior to the troubles and compared to a neighbouring peaceful rural area. Even within the city the decline in depression was most marked in the areas most affected by rioting. Suicide in Belfast also declined dramatically during the riots. Fraser (1971), studying the same city, also found no change in psychiatric hospital admission or referral rates in areas directly exposed to riot conditions but detected an increase in some disorders in areas only slightly exposed to disorder. However, general practitioners in the riot-affected areas did prescribe significantly more tranquillizers for their patients than they did in the year before rioting began.

Coser (1956) has suggested several means whereby *shared* stressful experiences might have beneficial effects leading to an improvement in community mental health. The feeling of confronting a common threat might lead to increased group cohesiveness, increased social interaction, provide a distraction from strictly personal worries, offer new roles and perhaps status to people who previously were isolated, and finally offer to the person experiencing some degree of personal distress an external reason for their state of mind which means they do not have to resort to an explanation based on personal inadequacy or illness. The experience of a strictly personal tragedy such as a bereavement or a divorce will not have such beneficial side-effects.

Table 6.2 Correlations between life events and psychological disturbance in several studies

Authors	*Year*	*Groups*	*Illness measure*	*Stress measure*	*Correlation*
Brown, Harris, and Peto	1973	50 Schizophrenics 325 GP	Patient status	Interview	0.40*
Brown, Harris, and Peto	1973	114 Depressives 152 GP	Patient status	Interview	0.40*
Cochrane and Robertson	1975	100 Parasuicides 100 GP	Suicide attempt	LEI	0.55*
Cochrane and Stopes-Roe	1977	100 GP	Langner scale	LEI	0.52*
Cooper and Sylph	1973	100 Neurotics 58 GP	Neurotic diagnosis	PES	0.30*
Dohrenwend	1973b	124 GP	Langner scale	SRE	0.35
Garrity, Somes, and Marx	1977	250 Students	Composite index	SRE	0.35
Gersten, Langner, Eisenberg, and Orzeck	1974	674 GP	Child's symptoms	Mothers' life events	0.24
Jacobs and Myers	1976	62 Schizophrenics 62 GP	Patient status	SRE	0.25*
Markush and Favero	1974	2129 GP	CES-D Langner scale	LES LES	0.22 0.21
Miller, Ingham, and Davidson	1976	68 GP	Psychological symptoms	Interview	0.61
Murphy, Kuhn, Christensen, and Robins	1962	101 Mothers	Psychiatric diagnosis	Interview	0.40*

Phillips	1968	598 GP	Langner scale	Adult stress factors	0.45*
Schless, Teichman, Mendals, and DiGiacomo	1977	56 Psychiatric 56 Medical/surgical	Patient status	SRE	0.30*
Serban	1975	125 Acute schizophrenics 95 GP	Patient status	SSFIPD	0.20*
Uhlenhuth, Lipman, Balter, and Stern	1974	721 GP	HSCL	Inventory	0.30
Vinokur and Selzer	1975	774 GP	Depression index	SRE	0.26
			Paranoia index	SRE	0.34
			Suicidal proclivity	SRE	0.23
			Anxiety index	SRE	0.23

* Recalculated from data presented in original paper (Friedman, 1968).
CES-D Center for Epidemiologic Studies—Depression Scale (Markush and Favero, 1974).
GP General population.
HSCI Hopkins Symptoms Checklist (Derogatis, Lipman, and Rickels, 1974).
LEI Life Events Inventory (Cochrane and Robertson, 1973).
LES Life Events Scale (Markush and Favero, 1974).
Langner Scale (Langner, 1962).
PES Precipitating Events Schedule (Cooper and Sylph, 1973).
SRE Schedule of Recent Experiences (Holmes and Rahe, 1967).
SSFIPD Social Stress and Functionability Inventory for Psychotic Disorders (Serban, 1975).

The division of stresses into personal and shared is by no means clear-cut, however. Brenner (1973) in his correlational study of economic indicators and mental hospitalization rates found that economic downturns were clearly associated with increases in recorded mental illness. However, he was not able to demonstrate conclusively whether this increase was accounted for by those individuals who suffered directly, for example through unemployment, or by a general increase in psychopathology in society as a whole or even by tolerance levels for odd behaviour fluctuating along with economic indicators.

The tendency for the results of studies focusing on large-scale stressful situations to be at variance with the results of those studies looking at specific individual stresses needs to be resolved in any explanation of the relationship between personal distress and psychological disorder.

IS THERE A CAUSAL LINK?

The consistency of the direction and magnitude of the relationship between personal distress and psychological disturbance does not definitely establish that such a link is genuine or give any indication of the direction of causation. There are, in fact, telling criticisms of many of the studies relating life events, measured by an inventory, to pathology that have led some to suggest that the area be abandoned as fruitless (e.g., Antonovsky, 1974; Hudgens, 1974; Wershaw and Reinhart, 1974). These criticisms can be divided into a group concerning psychometric and methodological problems, and a set of conceptual issues.

The first of the methodological problems revolves around the reliability and validity of the life event inventories themselves. While there is little dispute about the reliability of the weights assigned to the items on these scales (Cochrane and Robertson, 1973; Komaroff *et al.* 1968; Rahe, 1969), there is evidence that there is something less than a perfect correspondence between the reporting of an event and the actual occurrence of that event. Hudgens *et al.* (1970) found that only 57 per cent of events reported by one of a pair of informants (patients and relatives) were confirmed by the other member of the pair, and there was no consistent tendency for either the patient or his relative to under- or over-report events. What is more, there was a significant inverse relationship between the amount of stress reported and the reliability of the report as judged by intra-pair agreement. Other investigations, notably Brown and Birley (1968, 1971), have however found much higher levels of intra-pair agreement ranging up to 80 per cent.

This leads to the very difficult question of the relationship between mental state and the recall and reporting of recent stressful experiences. It does not appear too far-fetched to suggest that individuals who have been hospitalized are both more motivated to recall life events which might be possible antecedents of their present state, and are more likely to report such events when recalled than those in a control group. This would be especially true if the controls are from the general population and interviewed in their own home. While a hospital ward may be conducive to frank revelations, the home environment with the possibility of relatives overhearing may inhibit revelations to a stranger concerning the sexual, financial, and interpersonal problems which make up the typical life events schedule. The patient may not only be more honest about recent experiences but the events may also be more salient if he too is looking for an explanation for his illness. Therefore the patient status may be an important variable. This is borne out by the fact that three studies (Forrest *et al.*, 1965, Hudgens *et al.*, 1967; Morrison *et al.*, 1968) where medical patients served as controls for psychiatric patients found no differences in reported life experiences.

The main argument that stands out against this problem being a total explanation of the correlation between life events and psychological disturbance is that correlations of the same magnitude are recorded in studies based entirely on community surveys. That is, when the context variable is controlled and everyone is interviewed at home the relationship still exists. Even this could be accounted for by a 'Yea-Saying' bias affecting the reporting of psychological symptoms and life events were it not for the fact that several studies have used more detailed multidirectional probes (e.g. Brown *et al.*, 1975; Miller *et al.*, 1976) or have found that reporting the occurrence of positive and negative events are not correlated (e.g. Phillips, 1968; Cochrane and Robertson, 1975; Vinokur and Selzer, 1975; Ruch, 1977).

The final methodological problem, which is perhaps not so easy to dismiss, questions not the existence of a relationship but the direction of a *causal* link if any such there be. It is equally plausible to explain a high rate of disruptive life events in terms of them being brought about by a disturbed personality as it is to explain the psychological disturbance resulting from the life events. Indeed sometimes the two variables are operationally inseparable. Several of the events on a typical schedule could be regarded as psychiatric symptoms (e.g. change in sleeping habits, change in social activities, sex difficulties) and many others could be the direct result of psychiatric impairments (e.g. fired from work, marital separation, quarrels with neighbours). A variant of this argument is that even if it were not the case that psychological disturbance brings about a higher rate of life events it may be that some individuals are predisposed, for whatever reason, to lead a disrupted social and personal life. Thus, the same people who are prone to divorce, trouble at work, debts, jail sentences, and frequent moves might also be more likely to become psychologically disturbed. Both aspects of disruption might be caused by some third, unspecified, variable.

These related hypotheses have received considerable attention from those who suspect a causal relationship exists between life events and psychopathology. Brown (1972) and Brown *et al.* (1973a and b) in particular have given this question a lot of thought. Although it is not possible to go into the details of all the arguments brought forward to support the causal-link hypothesis two pieces of evidence will be mentioned. First, several studies have attempted to classify events into those which may have been caused in whole or in part by the person to whom they happened and those which were almost certainly independent of his actions.

The second attack on at least a part of this problem has been made by plotting the frequency of the occurrence of events accurately in relation to the onset, rather than the reporting, of symptoms. Brown *et al.* (1973a) showed quite clearly that those who become depressed patients experienced a very high rate of distressing events before the appearance of any symptoms but that this elevated rate was peculiar to the three weeks immediately prior to onset. In the 45 weeks before the three-week period prior to onset they had experienced no more events than those individuals who never became ill. The hypothesis that the illness produces the events rather than vice-versa is made untenable by these findings. Brown *et al.* (1973a) also found a similar relationship between life events and the onset of reactions diagnosed schizophrenic.

INTERVENING VARIABLES

Although by and large most investigations of life events and illness have not been overly concerned with explaining the link between the two variables, several attempts have been made to look for those factors which intervene between the occurrence of events and the formation of symptoms. Commonly the point has been seen as how to uncover differences between those people who do become upset following stressful life experiences and those others, probably a majority, who do not. In this way it is hoped that the nature of the causal link might be explicated. Attempts to consolidate and integrate the diverse findings will be dealt with in the subsequent section.

An early impetus to this research was given by one of the major findings of the Midtown study to which reference has already been made. Lower social status was found to be associated with a higher incidence of stress, analogous to life events, and a higher rate of psychopathology. Controlling for stress levels, however, still left more psychological disturbance in the lowest social class groups. There was also an interaction with level of stress experienced. Basically, those individuals who experienced very little or no stress had few symptoms whatever their social class. For those with a high level of stress, on the other hand, psychological disturbance was much more common in the lowest social class than in the middle or highest classes. Phillips (1968) followed up this intriguing finding in a community survey of 600 New England adults. Phillips added the variables of positive- and negative-feeling states to those of stress and psychopathology. His hypothesis was that positive or pleasant feelings might counteract the influence of stressful experiences. This in turn led to the notion of an 'affect balance score' (ABS) which is the difference between an individual's scores on measures of positive and negative feelings. After having confirmed the relationship between social class, stress, and psychological disturbance, Phillips went on to look at the distribution of positive and negative affect. There was very little difference between the proportions of each social class reporting many negative feelings (such things as being bored, lonely, and upset), but proportionately more than twice as many individuals from the highest social class reported positive experiences (feeling pleased, proud, excited, or interested) as did individuals from the lowest social class. This was reflected in the ABSs of the classes. Over 72 per cent of the highest social class reported positive affect balance (a predominance of positive over negative affect) compared to only 43 per cent in the lowest social class. A more detailed analysis of these data showed that when psychological disturbance was taken as the dependent variable, and stress, social class, and ABS as the independent variables, it became evident that affect balance was having the greatest influence on mental health. Next came the amount of stress experienced while social class *per se* had the least influence. It was because low social status was associated with *both* higher stress levels and the absence of positive experiences, which together lead to psychological disturbance, that social class and poorer mental health appeared to be related. A more efficient and perhaps less expensive way of alleviating stress-related psychological disturbance might be to increase the positive factors that aid mental health rather than attempt to eliminate the inevitable stresses and strains of life.

A whole series of studies have investigated the social context of those who do not become ill following stressful experiences. Myers *et al.* (1971) looked at those respondents to a community survey who did not fit the modal patterns of either having high stress and high symptom levels or low stress and low symptom levels. Those who were more psychologically disturbed but who had experienced relatively few stresses in the previous two years were more likely to be unemployed, never married and dissatisfied with their lot than those with less stress and low symptoms. Exactly the opposite was true for those who had experienced a lot of stress but who had not developed correspondingly high levels of symptomatology—they tended to have intact marriages, be of higher social class, and be satisfied with their roles. The differences found between the groups are explained in terms of social integration at the societal, family, and instrumental role level. 'People who have ready and meaningful access to others, feel integrated into the system, and are satisfied with their roles seem better able to cope with the impact of life events' (Myers, *et al.*, 1971, p. 426).

Theorell (1976) also found that life changes alone were not sufficient to produce symptoms of stress reaction—in this case general illness, hypertension, and signs of neurosis. He added a 'discord index' to life events to obtain a better prediction of psychosomatic illness. Theorell identified life events as acute stressors, and discord as more chronic psychosocial situations such as dissatisfaction with work or home life, death of a parent before age 15, and tendency to react to frustrations with hostility. These types of stress might be missed by a life events inventory. Among the low discord group those with many life changes had no excess of illness but those subjects who had high discord and high acute stress were more prone to cardiovascular disorders and neurotic symptoms than any other group. There are several similarities between Theorell's notion of discord and what Myers *et al.* (1971) call social integration.

Antonovsky (1974), in a preliminary report, has also suggested that this same variable—called by him 'ties to others'—is related to the ability to resist the negative effects of stress. This variable was operationally defined as a combination of frequency of interaction with significant others and a feeling of alienation from other people in general. Antonovsky also considered two other important intervening variables to be: 'homeostatic flexibility' or the ability to perceive and accept alternative social roles and behaviours in the face of life-changing events, and 'ties to the total community'—in this case equated with commitment to a kibbutz in Israel.

The most detailed and systematic study of the social context variable has been undertaken by Brown *et al.* (1975), and more recently by Miller and Ingham (1976). Brown and his co-workers began at much the same place as Phillips (1968). They found that the social class differences in rates of depression in women could not be entirely accounted for by the greater frequency of severe life events and major long-term difficulties experienced by working-class women. These women were, in addition, much more likely to break down once one of the events had occurred than were middle-class women. Working-class women were, in fact, five times more likely to become depressed following a severe life stress than were middle-class women. Brown identified four factors which accounted for the greater vulnerability of some women: (1) loss of their mother in childhood; (2) lack of an intimate confiding relationship with husband or boy-friend; (3) three or more children aged 14 or younger living at home; (4) no job. The first three of these accounted for the social class differences in response to stress. These vulnerability factors were found to be additive in their impact but did not in themselves produce depression. Thirteen out of nineteen of the women with at least two of the vulnerability factors *and* a stressful experience became depressed, compared to none of the fourteen women with the same level of vulnerability but no stress. On the other hand, among those women who were not vulnerable as defined here only two out of 34 became depressed following a severe stress. Of those with low vulnerability and low stress only one out of 59 became depressed. With the notable exception of having young children, the remaining three vulnerability factors all appear similar to the variable previously called social integration. Losing a mother by death or desertion, lack of employment, and lack of an intimate friend all mean that the person is relatively socially isolated. Even having young children to look after may mean that only a very restricted range of social contact is possible. Brown speculates that the psychological effect of these variables is to produce low self-esteem which in turn lowers resistance to stress, but what this means precisely remains to be spelled out.

The relationship between having an intimate confiding relationship with at least one other person and vulnerability to stress was confirmed by Miller and Ingham (1976). They found that among patients of a general practice in Scotland, the fact of not having a confidant and having few acquaintances was related to a high level of psychiatric symptomatology.

Attempts to find personality differences between those who are vulnerable to the effects of stress and those who are not have been less successful. Hendrie *et al.* (1975) using the MMPI, found no evidence that some personalities are more vulnerable than others. All they could suggest was that among women only those who were impulsive, insecure, and distrustful generated more stresses in their own lives. Garrity *et al.* (1977), found that 12.9 per cent of the variance in Langner symptom scale scores was predictable from life events and that this increased to only 17.9 per cent when the various scales of the Omnibus Personality Inventory (OPI) were added to the regression equation. It was not clear, either, whether those who were more conforming, less intellectual, and less emotionally sensitive on the OPI were in fact at less risk after a stressful experience or just reported fewer symptoms. Finally, Robertson and Cochrane (1976a) reported that a hypothesized relationship between life stress, personality, and attempted suicide was only marginally true for some groups and not at all true for others.

EXPLAINING THE RELATIONSHIP

This might be an appropriate place to take stock of what consistencies have been found in the life events and psychological disturbance literature. First, it is clear that there is a relationship between personal distress and psychological disturbance to the tune of explaining 10 per cent of the variance. Second, it is unlikely that his is in any major part due to an artifact of methodology producing a spurious relationship. Third, by far the most likely relationship is that life stresses cause, or at least contribute to, the aetiology of psychological disturbance. Fourth, of the intervening variables examined to date those relating to social integration and having the possibility of rewarding social encounters seem to be the ones which contribute most to the variation in vulnerability between individuals. We will now turn to a consideration of the theories or models which may be able to integrate these strands of evidence.

We will first examine three conceptual schema that can be used to relate a wide range of types of psychological disturbances to life-changing events and then turn to two more specific models which deal uniquely with schizophrenia and depression respectively.

1. Rahe's Optical Analogy

Perhaps pride of place should go to the model suggested by Richard H. Rahe, who has been one of those most directly involved in opening up this area for research. In a recent paper Rahe *et al.* (1974) have suggested a detailed model for the relationship between recent life changes and subsequent illness reports based on several longitudinal studies of men in the US and Norwegian navies. Using an optical analogy Rahe posits that a series of filters and lenses are interposed between exposure to stress and reporting of symptoms. The first modifying factor built into this model is a filter representing past experiences, which may alter the perception of the significance of the life-changing events. Second, stress has to pass through a negative lens representing defence mechanisms which may successfully divert some of the events and so prevent them from becoming translated into stress. Those events which do pass this stage then encounter a 'black box' which stands for physiological responses to external stimuli. The rays, in this analogy rays of light, coming out of the other side of this box no longer represent stressors but bodily and mental reaction to stress. Step four is another filter which may absorb some of the psychophysiological reactions emerging from the black box. In other words the filter represents the coping process in its broadest sense. Prolonged failure to cope with the psychophysiological reactions eventually leads them to be manifested in specific symptoms of pathology. The final step is the reporting of these symptoms to appropriate others, so that they can become recorded as a measure of illness. This tendency to complain, or not complain, about subjective distress is represented by a positive, focusing lens.

Although this model may act as an indicator of where research effort might be directed in the future, it is not very satisfactory as an explanatory system. In fact it hardly says more than that there are probably intervening variables between life events and illness. No hints are given as to how the various lenses and filters came to be there, or of how it can be known in advance whether they serve to magnify or reduce the level of stress produced by a life event. Neither is it possible to predict which of the many varieties of symptoms will actually manifest themselves in any particular instance with the model as it stands. Each of the elements needs considerable fleshing out before any practical or theoretical use can be made of the model. The inclusion of a 'black box' which translates psychosocial stress into psychophysiological reactions is really an evasion of the central issue. Certainly there are psychophysiological changes following immediate situational stressors but whether these transient responses are the precursors of long-lasting pathology is very much an open question. Ever since Lacey *et al.* (1953) advanced their notion of response specificity as the mechanism accounting for individual differences in susceptibility to psychosomatic illnesses these ideas have been current, but there is very little evidence to back them up (Hassett, 1978). Similarly, to say that people vary in the extent to which they can cope with stress reactions is little more than stating the obvious and certainly goes no further than Selye's general adaptation syndrome.

2. A value change model

A second explanatory model which attempts to encompass a variety of psychological disorders as well as other forms of deviant behaviour was developed by Robertson and Cochrane (1976a and b) who were particularly impressed by consistent trends in rates of mental hospitalization, attempted suicide, drug abuse, alcoholism, and crime. All of these aspects of deviance have been apparently increasing markedly during a period when they might have been expected to decline. The 1950s and 1960s saw real and continuing increases in the standard of living in most Western industrial countries including Britain, the diffusion of increased wealth throughout society, and enormous expansion of welfare provisions. At the same time, however, deviant behaviour and evidence of psychological disturbance were also increasing; in the case of crime and drug addiction the increases were dramatic. What is more, the increase in deviant behaviour was by no means equally distributed through the whole population. While it is probable that all subsections of the population have been affected to some extent, it appears to be the young, the working-class and males who have shown the largest increase in rates of deviant behaviour. The group with all three of these characteristics—young, working-class and male—may show not only the highest absolute rate of deviant behaviour but also the fastest rate of increase in deviance. Yet this group, perhaps more than most others, is one section of the population that has benefited enormously by increases in material standards of living. Faced with this apparent paradox Robertson and Cochrane suggested that stress might be one of the explanatory variables. Given that it is probable that the absolute level of stress encountered has typically declined it could be that heightened sensitivity to remaining stresses was producing problems. This heightened sensitivity to stress has, it is argued, been brought about by significant changes in value systems that have led people to adopt a particular view of the relationship between themselves and their environment, and accordingly to perceive and react to external circumstances, particularly those of a stressful or unpleasant nature, in a different way from that characteristic of individuals socialized a decade or two earlier.

Robertson and Cochrane contend that since about the end of World War II there has taken place a change in popular consciousness, or values, that has had a particular impact on the attitudes and perceptions of everyone in society, but the young in particular; this change has made people much less tolerant of the distressing events which befall most of us. The emergent value system is organized around two core assumptions. First there has arisen a belief that all human beings are endowed with a set of innate potentials which it is the purpose of life to express or fulfil. Thus every individual has an intrinsic and equal value to every other, no matter what their station in life, because they have within them great possibilities. This idea is given some support by the contemporary emphasis on psychological growth, self-actualization, subjective experience and self-exploration.

The second belief is that the extent to which a person is able to develop and fulfil these potentials is contingent upon the social and physical environment within which he finds himself. To invoke a partial analogy the 'potentials' can be seen as a flower which will flourish in a congenial environment but become stunted in an impoverished environment. Further the responsibility for providing the environmental means for satisfying the need to express potentials is held to lie in society, not in the individual himself. That is, the state or the government is responsible for making it possible for the person to grow and develop. One of the effects of the interaction between these two beliefs has been to extend the concept of welfare beyond providing minimal material needs to providing for psychological needs. Educational institutions in particular have responded by transforming those elements of schooling held to be inhibiting or constricting personality growth into opportunities for creativity and self-expression.

Implicit in this description of a new value system is a contrast with an older system which puts personal achievement, accomplishment, and reputation in the place of self-development, and locates responsibility for success or failure in these endeavours firmly within the individual, or perhaps luck is allowed to play some part for good or ill.

While everyone, both old and young, will have been affected by this change in prevailing social definition it is suggested that the young, who were socialized into the new system of values, will have been influenced to a much greater extent than those socialized before this era. There is in fact evidence that value systems once formed remain stable and are relatively unaffected by changes in personal circumstances (Inglehart, 1977).

Any attempt to explain this change in values will clearly require to take account of factors that are as complex as they are diffuse. The decline in influence of religious belief, and the search for an alternative secular basis for morality, has undoubtedly played a part in this, as perhaps too has the advent of the welfare state. The content of the new value system has possibly been shaped also by an antithetical reaction to the tenets of self-reliance and personal responsibility mentioned above. It is, however, suggested that a particularly important element in this trend has been the post-Keynesian transition from an economy based on low average wages and fluctuating high levels of unemployment, to one in which (until the late 1970s) employment is maintained at relatively high and constant levels, and wages have correspondingly increased. One result has been a shift in emphasis in the economic life of Britain from the production to the consumption of goods. In turn, it is suggested this has fostered the development of new attitudes and assumptions, which are appropriate to the notion of consumption, rather than production, as a dominant goal in life.

Of course, it is realized that the elements of these value systems will not necessarily be explicit in the thinking of most people who subscribe to them. This does not, however, reduce their power as motivating forces or guides to action.

Turner (1969) gives voice to a similar idea when he detects an emphasis in contemporary social thought on the importance of experiencing a sense of 'identity' or personal 'worth'. He also argues that central to contemporary social movements:

> is the view that men have the right to demand assurance of a sense of personal worth from society. ... The novel idea ... that a lack of a sense of personal worth is not private misfortune, but public injustice, is carried by youth, who are the main constituency for the new movements in the same manner that a rising industrial class and later a rising working class were constituencies in the earlier era. (p. 394.)

The link with stressful events is fairly straightforward. It is predicted that an individual with the 'new value system' will react differently to life stresses than will individuals with the traditional value system who encounter the same stresses. He will be more aware of, or more sensitive to, such pressures because he views them both as unjust because they stem from social rather than personal causes, and as intolerable because they tend to obstruct progress towards (and direct attention and energy away from) self-expression and the fulfilment of individual potentials—which is seen as the purpose of life. There is no room in the new value system for the equivalent of stoicism or fulfilment through suffering which may moderate the responses to stress of those guided by the precepts of self-help, individual initiative, and self-denial which are fostered by the old value system. The prediction is that those imbued with the new world-view will have a diminished threshold of tolerance for stress. They will feel that they should not be called upon to undergo frustrations to any degree because these constitute an affront to expectations about freedom to develop and a betrayal by the society seen as responsible for guaranteeing these freedoms. Upon encountering life stresses such an individual is more likely to resort to one or more forms of deviance and to experience more psychological problems. It is suggested that possessors of the new value system will tend to interpret relatively minor feelings of tension, anxiety, or depression, brought about by life stresses, as evidence of mental disturbance, whereas individuals whose perceptions are governed by the old value system will define these same feelings as a morbid preoccupation or as indicating that they need to 'get a grip' on themselves. Individuals in the former group are therefore predicted to report more symptoms and to be more likely to seek professional help when stressed than are the possessors of the old ethos.

It is worth repeating here that this model was developed primarily as an explanation of the rapidly escalating rates of recorded mental illness as well as other forms of deviance among the young in a material environmental context that was also rapidly improving. As such it is not an attempt at a total elucidation of the link between stress and psychological disorder in general. Neither can the model as it stands offer any help with the difficult problem of explaining the different deviant responses of different individuals in similar circumstances. In addition there have been few attempts to apply the model and even these have met with only limited success (Robertson and Cochrane, 1976a). It is, however, an attempt to go beyond establishing just an empirical causal link between life stresses and psychological disturbance, and provides hypotheses relating the apparently selective impact of similar stresses on different people that remain to be tested.

3. Adaptation and coping

The final general model to be considered is based upon the notion of adaptation hierarchies. In this approach psychological disturbance is not considered as a pathological response to unbearable stress but is to be seen as a valuable adaptive reaction that is resorted to when other forms of adaptation are not available or have been tried and been seen to fail. Before discussing this theory it is worth considering one extreme version of it which includes as modes of adaptation not only psychological disturbance but life events themselves. Fontana *et al.* (1972 and 1976) found that their psychiatric patients had experienced significantly more life events in the year preceding their hospitalization than had non-patient controls, but that this disproportionate number of events was entirely due to events which were contingent upon the patient's own behaviour and to events involved in a chronic conflict between the patient and others in his primary group. (It has already been noted that other investigations have not always found that these types of events account completely for the differences in stress levels between patients and non-patients.) The model of Fontana, *et al.* begins with the assumption that stable social relationships involve mutual expectations. When this pattern is disrupted for any reason and a readjustment of expectations is required this may be achieved by negotiation or by a manipulative act on the part of one individual which is aimed at creating a change in the expectation of others indirectly. Life events may be deliberately brought about by a participant to induce such a change unilaterally, or naturally occurring events may be exploited for the same end-purpose. In either case Fontana *et al.* suggest that a 'majority of life events can be seen to be instrumentally involved in this coping process' (1976, p. 89). Whenever this strategy does not work and the extra tension resulting from this failure is overlaid on top of that created by the original conflict then the person involved may try an alternative strategy of becoming ill and/or hospitalized. The authors supplement evidence from a multiple regression study which supports their basic hypothesis with some very illuminating case histories. Applying their analytic model to what otherwise appear as straightforward cases of stress-induced breakdown it becomes apparent that such events as losing jobs, illness among relatives, and distancing from family contacts can be created or manipulated in an attempt to achieve a desired effect—such as improving marital relationships or reducing conflict with siblings. Where these attempts are not successful then a period of illness and hospitalization may be resorted to, and this may have the desired result.

It is possible to work with a model of the relationship between life stresses and psychological disturbance which does not go quite this far. The model to be presented below represents a composite of ideas and evidence found in the writings of, among others, Averill (1973), Borgman and Monroe (1975), Brown *et al.* (1975), Carveth and Gottlieb (1977), Cobb (1974), Davis (1970), Davis, *et al.* (1974), Lazarus (1966), Phillips (1968) and Rahe *et al.* (1974). Broadly speaking, the theory suggests that people have a more or less extended hierarchy of coping mechanisms available to them which is used sequentially in dealing with life stresses. All of the responses are aimed at neutralizing the stress experienced and so none is pathological in the true sense. The personally and socially preferred kinds of adaptation to stress obviously will be more likely to occur earlier in the hierarchy and will only be supplanted by a less preferred option should they fail to deal with the stress. Psychological disturbance may be close to the bottom of the hierarchy for most people, but there are still more desperate behaviours available to the individual whose stressful circumstances defeat all attempts to neutralize them. Extreme escape behaviours such as vagrancy and suicide come to mind.

A complete hierarchy of coping mechanisms will include the following in a speculative order of the likelihood of the mechanisms being used. Table 6.3 contains a summary of this model and examples of evidence which supports it.

First, there may be *intrapsychic defence mechanisms* which allow potentially threatening events to be misperceived or reinterpreted in such a way as to reduce or entirely neutralize their impact. An objective loss may come to be seen as an opportunity for improvement, or the loss may be minimized by devaluing the object concerned. A stressful experience may be fitted into a religious or philosophical framework and seen as a challenge or an opportunity to prove oneself. The normal use of defence mechanisms in dealing with threat is well documented by Lazarus (1966), for example. We would also point to the work of Kaplan (1976) on the very great importance of positive self-esteem in enabling people to cope with unpleasant situations.

Pearlin and Schooler (1978) in their detailed empirical analysis of the structure of coping mechanisms found that several intrapsychic defence mechanisms were effective in reducing stress. Although the precise order varied with the context of the stresses (marriage, parenting, household economics, and occupation were studied) absence of self-denigrating attitudes was found to be the most important psychological variable in enabling people to manage stress, followed by a sense of mastery and positive self-esteem.

Second, the existence of *stress-opposing experiences*, which although they do not directly prevent stresses from befalling the individual, may make them more tolerable. If sufficient positive experiences are encountered along with life's negative experiences then the latter will do less harm. Someone who receives compliments, makes achievements, and is successful in some spheres of life will be more successful in coping with stress in other spheres. As previously discussed Phillips (1968) found that it was necessary to include the concept of 'affect balance', which encompasses positive as well as negative experiences, in order to improve the correlation between stress and illness. He found also that the occurrence of positive experiences was much more frequent in higher than in lower social classes.

The third resource available to some individuals is *intimate personal relationships* which can be deployed in one or both of two ways. They may be used as a source of help in dealing with the actual stresses, as when a wife seeks work to help maintain an unemployed husband, or as a refuge or source of solace if the stresses must be borne. The sharing of misery and the provision of alternative sources of reinforcement and satisfaction may also prevent extreme stresses from producing physical or psychological breakdowns. Here, obviously, it is only necessary to mention the work of Brown and Miller and their respective colleagues, to which reference has already been made, to get some idea of the tremendous importance of this variable in buffering the effects of life events.

In various studies Brown has found that, of the factors which make people more or less vulnerable to the impact of life stresses, the presence of an intimate confiding relationship was the most salient protecting factor (Brown and Harris, 1978). In the study of depression in women in the community by Brown *et al.* (1975) it was found that only a very close intimate and confiding relationship with a husband or boy-friend gave any protection—confiding but less close relationships seemed to be no more protective than entirely non-intimate relationships. However the degree of protection afforded by an intimate relationship was remarkable. Brown *et al.* suggest that life stresses are causal agents in depression only for those women without a close relationship—a highly intimate relationship gave almost complete protection against the ravages of life's stresses and strains.

Less intense *social support* or helping networks have been considered by other researchers to be effective moderators of life stress. Cobb conceived social support to be information belonging to one of three categories:

1. information leading the subject to believe that he is cared for and loved;
2. information leading the subject to believe that he is esteemed and valued;
3. information leading the subject to believe that he belongs to a network of communication and mutual obligation. (Cobb, 1976, p. 300).

People such as relatives, friends, neighbours, and workmates would form the helping networks which provide social support. Again this resource may be used to deal with the stress directly by finding jobs or housing or by lending money for example. Social support may also be provided through relating shared experiences, sympathy, and advice if the stress is in fact intractable such as the loss of a loved one. The studies which show that shared and inpersonal stressful experiences, such as being the victim of bombings and riotings, may have fewer health implications than individually experienced stress support the model here.

There are also those studies which have directly demonstrated the significance of social integration at a lower level of intimacy than suggested by Brown as a variable mediating the effects of stress. The work of Myers *et al.* (1971) has been referred to above. Myers *et al.* (1975) looked at those respondents to a community survey who did not fit the expected patterns of high stress/high symptom levels or low stress/low symptom levels. The crucial variable was integration as measured by marital status, employment, and role involvement. Those who had more psychological symptoms than would be predicted from their stress levels were less integrated, whereas those with few symptoms but high stress were well integrated. These results have been confirmed by a re-analysis of the source of the same data by Eaton (1978).

In reviewing a large and very diverse literature Cobb (1976) found that social support not only afforded, to people who experienced life stresses, some protection from a wide variety of physical illnesses, psychological disorders, and behavioural deviations to which they may otherwise have been susceptible, but also accelerated recovery and release from hospital should illness ensue from life events.

Further down the hierarchy from this point the modes of coping come more and more to resemble what is externally recognizable as illness. However, this is illness behaviour which may itself have adaptive consequences. The *development of symptoms* of one type or another may enable the person to reduce stresses by manipulating the source of the stress, by relieving him of feelings of responsibilities for dealing with it, or both. There have been several analyses of psychological distubance—particularly depression—as attempts at affecting environmental changes rather than as passive pathological responses.

If these behaviours are not successful then professional advice on how to deal with symptoms may be sought, and this in turn can offer relief through a *formal recognition and legitimation of illness status*. This may work in a number of ways:

1. by providing an alternative focus of concern which distracts from the original stress;
2. by providing a legitimate reason for not actively coping with or even addressing the stressful situation;
3. by temporarily removing pressure being exerted by others which may have arisen as a consequence of, or source of, stress;
4. by legitimating pharmacological relief from the tension aroused by stress.

Somewhere between this and the next response lies deliberate self-injury or *parasuicide*, as a coping mechanism. Deliberate self-injury is a dramatic demonstration of despair or frustration which may produce a variety of responses in observers. Overdosing will temporarily at least make the person 'ill' and may even produce hospitalization. Depending upon circumstances surrounding the act, significant others may be made to feel guilty, may be made to ease pressure, and to take action on behalf of the parasuicide. At the least the act may effectively communicate the subject's extreme distress. In fact Kreitman *et al.* (1970) have suggested that suicide attempts might be best regarded as an act of communication.

Even further along this road lies *removal from the stressful environment by hospitalization*. In this case the person may not only be removed somewhat from the stress, but will not be expected to deal with it personally. Indeed hospitalization may very well provoke others into dealing with it on behalf of the unfortunate individual. Family members, other relatives, friends, social workers, housing departments, or creditors might respond differently and perhaps more helpfully if a person is so ill that he must be hospitalized.

The final level in the hierarchy which is reached when all other strategies have been abandoned or are unavailable to the individual is *detachment from reality*. This may occur through alcoholism, drug addiction, vagrancy, psychosis and ultimately suicide. While existing in any of these states the individual is not consciously enduring stress at all. Obviously the individual is precluded from any attempt actually to deal with the stress in a practical or material way for so long as he is in one of the detached states.

The extent to which these resources are available to different people will vary with their personal and social circumstances. A restricted hierarchy will lead to illness-related behaviours emerging more rapidly as they are the one resource which is equally available to all. The person with low self-esteem, inadequate defence mechanisms, an environment that provides few positive experiences, who has no

Table 6.3 A hierarchy of coping responses following life stress (From Cochrane, 1978)

Hierarchy level	*Example*	*Empirical support for possible success of coping response*
1. Intrapsychic defence mechanisms	Self-esteem, perceptual distortion	Kaplan, 1976; Pearlin and Schooler, 1978
2. Stress-opposing experiences	Positive affect, success, achievements	Phillips, 1968
3. Intimate personal relationships	Spouse, mother	Brown *et al.*, 1976; Miller and Ingham, 1976
4. Social support (informal helping networks)	Friends, neighbours, relatives	Myers *et al.*, 1975; Eaton, 1978; Antonovsky, 1974; Cobb, 1976
5. Symptom development	Psychophysiological symptoms	Uhlenhuth *et al.*, 1974
6. Illness status	Depression	Davis, 1970
7. Parasuicide	Overdosing	Bostock and Williams, 1973; Kreitman *et al.*, 1970
8. Hospitalization	Admission to hospital	Fontana *et al.*, 1976
9. Detachment from reality	Psychoses, vagrancy, alcoholism	Borgman and Monroe, 1975; Davis *et al.*, 1974; Pearlin and Radabaugh, 1976; Sadava, Thistle, and Forsyth, 1978.

intimate confidant and a very restricted informal social support network may very quickly resort to illness or parasuicide in the face of stress. This expectation is matched quite well by the empirical findings on mediating variables between life stresses and psychological disturbance. Pearlin and Radabaugh (1976), for example, found increased drinking of alcohol to cope with the effects of stress was much more likely to occur in those individuals with poorer intrapsychic defence mechanisms (in this case lower self-esteem and having little sense of mastery). Elsewhere Pearlin and Schooler (1978) have shown that coping mechanisms which we have placed higher in the hierarchy (and which are perhaps more desirable or efficacious) are more readily available to the male, the educated, and the affluent; this may go some way to explaining why these groups tend to be under-represented in official estimates of those with psychological and physical health problems.

A related prediction is that the behaviour from the hierarchy which is ultimately found to be most successful in neutralizing the stress will then rise in the hierarchy. Other things being equal, this behaviour will be more likely to occur subsequently when stress is encountered. If the model is extended in this way it may even be possible to account for the differential resort to the wide variety of illness behaviours that occur in response to stress.

We are in no way suggesting that all illness, all depression, all alcoholism or even all suicide attempts may be explained by this model. It is only applicable to those cases where life stresses are important in the aetiology of these behaviours. We are attempting to explain correlations of 0.20 and 0.30, so it is clear that there are likely to be other major causes of these disorders. Although this model exists only in a bare outline form, it does go further than the other general formulations considered in encompassing what factors are known to intervene between stress and psychological disturbance, and in providing the framework for specific directional hypotheses.

4. Theories specific to particular problems

A number of attempts have been made to explain the relationship between life events on the one hand and specific psychological disorders on the other. Space precludes a comprehensive review of these models but two have been selected as illustrations: Kohn's thesis concerning the origins of schizophrenia, and the concept of learned helplessness as a possible link between life events and depression. It may indeed be quite reasonable to expect there to be different kinds of relationship between life events and different psychological problems. In some disorders such as anxiety, psychosomatic symptoms, and, perhaps, depression, life events may have a direct causative effect. For other conditions such as schizophrenia, where there are likely to be other overriding aetiological factors, or genetic predisposition, life events may produce something more akin to a 'triggering effect' rather than constituting a prime cause of the disorder.

Kohn (1968, 1972) offers a tripartite explanation for the development of schizophrenia in which life stress is one cornerstone, the others being genetic transmission of susceptibility and socialization experiences. Although Kohn was especially interested in explaining the higher incidence of schizophrenia in the lower classes than in the middle classes, he is basically asking why some people who encounter stress become schizophrenic while others do not. Kohn's answer, although related specifically to lower social class individuals, is equally applicable to the much smaller proportion of middle-class individuals who became psychotic.

For the first part of the answer Kohn looks to familial transmission of 'conceptions of social reality' which render the offspring incapable of dealing with life stresses if they are encountered. In a nutshell Kohn speculates that the experiences of many lower-class parents (and of some, but relatively fewer, middle-class parents) leads them to develop and inculcate in their children a limited and rigid outlook which cannot cope with complex stressful situations.

> To be lower class is to be insufficiently educated, to work at a job of little substantive complexity, under conditions of close supervision, and with little leeway to vary a routine of flow of work. These are precisely the conditions that narrow one's conceptions of social reality and reduce one's sense of personal efficacy. (Kohn, 1972, p. 301.)

A lifetime of exposure to such situations leaves a person with a fatalistic attitude to life and a belief that one's own destiny is beyond personal control or even understanding. This outlook is accompanied by a distrust of the motives of others and a conservative view of social institutions. These values are passed on to the subsequent generation by stressing to children the importance of conformity to external authority because 'such conformity is all that his own capacities and the exigencies of the world allow'.

Even so, all individuals who grow up with this rigid, fatalistic, inadequate orientation to life do not develop schizophrenia when exposed to stress. The final piece of the jigsaw is provided by genetic predisposition to schizophrenia. Only when all three elements converge in one individual is a schizophrenic breakdown predicted. The inclusion of the necessary condition of a genetic predisposition helps account for the fact that even among lower-class individuals who encounter stress the rate of schizophrenia is very low. However, Kohn does allow that not only is the impaired ability to deal resourcefully with stress conspicuously more common in lower social classes, but so also may be life stresses and the genetic predisposition to schizophrenia.

Some people, particularly Mechanic (1972), have found this model unconvincing, but it does appear to encompass a great deal of what is known of the social correlates of schizophrenia and to articulate them in a way which is plausible and amenable to verification. From the point of immediate concern here, Kohn's formulation does provide some kind of answer to questions which have not been dealt with successfully by the other models considered so far.

Finally, the notion of 'learned helplessness' has been invoked to explicate the relationship between life events and depression. The concept of learned helplessness has been derived from a series of experimental studies on laboratory animals from which extrapolations have been made to clinical depression in humans (Seligman, 1975). Neither the debate concerning the adequacy of the original experimental work nor the advisability of inter-species generalization will be considered here. It is assumed that the theory is well enough known to make any detailed account of it redundant. Rather the applicability of the model as it stands to the explanation of empirical evidence of the life events approach will be reviewed.

The possible link between learned helplessness and life events is fairly straightforward and has been summed up by Seligman as follows:

> Learned helplessness is caused by learning that responding is independent of reinforcements; so the model suggests that the cause of depression is the belief that action is futile. What kind of events set off reactive depressions? Failure at work and school, death of a loved one, rejection or separation from friends and loved ones, physical disease, financial difficulty, being faced with insoluble problems, and growing old. There are many others, but this list captures the flavour.
>
> I believe that what links these experiences and lies at the heart of depression is unitary: the depressed patient believes or has learned that he cannot control those elements of his life that relieve suffering, bring gratification, or provide nurture—in short, he believes that he is helpless. Consider a few of the precipitating events: What is the meaning of job failure or incompetence at school? Often it means that all of a person's efforts have been in vain, that his responses have failed to achieve his desires. When an individual is rejected by someone he loves, he can no longer control this significant source of gratification and support. When a parent or lover dies, the bereaved is powerless to elicit love from the dead person. (Seligman, 1975, pp. 93–4.)

The events mentioned by Seligman are indeed the same kind of events that commonly appear on life events inventories and which have in turn been shown to be causally related to the onset of depression. However, a strict application of Seligman's model suggests that it is only those events that follow from the failure of the person's behaviour to have the desired consequences, or those events over which he has no control at all, that should precipitate depression. It is not clear to what extent this conflicts with the results of those studies discussed previously which show that both uncontrolled and possibly controlled events are more common in the lives of those destined to experience psychological disturbance. The studies which examined these relationships were not specifically or uniquely dealing with depression; neither did they establish that the events possibly caused by the subject were in fact the intended consequences of his action. It is quite likely that someone who creates the circumstances of his own dismissal from work and the consequent unemployment may not have intended this to happen. It is only those events deliberately engineered by the victim himself which fail to fit into Seligman's framework. A hypothesis about these latter kind of events is central to the explanation proposed by Fontana *et al.* (1976).

The motivational deficit described as learned helplessness is accompanied by changes in the cognitive and emotional state of the person too. The cognitive effects of learned helplessness are such that after a series of uncontrollable experiences a person has trouble in perceiving as successful a piece of behaviour that was in fact successful. Strangely, an isolated, accidental, but instrumentally effective piece of behaviour does not convince the person (or the animal) that he can have an effect upon his environment. The *emotional disturbance* produced by the experience of helplessness is described by Seligman as depression. As the person comes to realize that he cannot control the circumstances which are adversely affecting him the fear which is the dominant emotional state initially gives way to feelings of helplessness and depression.

There is, in fact, an impressive degree of similarity between the symptoms accompanying learned helplessness produced in animal and human subjects in the laboratory and what are generally accepted as some of the defining features of clinical depression. We have already seen that subjects with experimentally induced learned helplessness show only a low level of voluntary responses, apparently preferring instead to act passively; and this reduced activity level is indeed characteristic of depressed patients. The negative cognitive set found in the laboratory which makes the person believe that all his responses are ineffectual is also common in depression. So too is the occasional apparent absence of hostility and aggression directed towards *other* people, the loss of libido and appetite and the feeling that life has no interest any more. All of these symptoms have been observed not only in depressed patients but also in helpless animals. Although these similarities are far from conclusive evidence that learned helplessness is causally related to clinical depression they are nonetheless sufficiently intriguing for a hypothesis such as this to be entertained.

There remain, however, several areas where the learned helplessness model may conflict with some of the less central generalizations drawn from life events research. First Seligman extends his model to apply to positive as well as negative uncontrolled events. So long as the occurrence of the positive event is not contingent upon the behaviour of the individual concerned, then these too should lead to helplessness and depression (Seligman, 1975, p. 98). The evidence for this contention is virtually non-existent outside of some anecdotal material about depression following conspicuous success. This is seen as the result of the person continuing to be rewarded for his past achievements *whatever* his present behaviour may be. It has already been pointed out that the empirical evidence so far as it is relevant favours exactly the opposite hypothesis. Positive events have been shown either to be unrelated to psychological disturbance or even to promote psychological well-being by mitigating the impact of negative experiences. However, the extent to which these positive outcomes are contingent upon the person's own behaviour has not been examined.

The second aspect of the life events research evidence, with which this model does not appear able to cope, concerns the effects of the vast, traumatic, but shared experiences produced by impersonal events such as wars, riots, bombings, and internment in concentration camps. Although these events are often very definitely not under the control of those who suffer their impact, their actual consequences have frequently been shown to be less severe than the helplessness model might lead one to anticipate. Although these experiences do create lasting psychological damage to many individuals it is by no means the most common outcome, at least among the survivors. Difficulty in handling this aspect of the data is not confined to the learned helplessness model by any means, but it does perhaps detract from its overall comprehensiveness.

Certainly the extent to which the learned helplessness model can accommodate what is known about the impact of life events far exceeds in importance the few and perhaps marginal areas where such an integration is more difficult. To this extent the model must be considered as worthy of consideration as a possible explanation of the relationship between life events and depression.

CONCLUDING COMMENTS

On the basis of this brief overview of a large and quite disjointed body of literature it is perhaps not unexpected that few if any definitive conclusions can be drawn. Equally, however, there is a surprising degree of coherence about the material reviewed if something less than absolute consistency is tolerated.

There is a whole series of studies using a wide variety of definitions and methodology which have shown a link between life stresses, on the one hand, and psychological problems on the other. The evidence for there being a causal link between the two variables, while not overwhelming, is also reasonably convincing. The exact nature of the process whereby life events cause pathology and how some people avoid succumbing to their effects remains more problematic, but even here a promising start on the development of an adequate theory has been made.

If the idea of a hierarchy of coping responses is accepted as a model of the way in which people deal with social stress then a large portion of the work reviewed in this chapter falls into a rather neat framework. This model is not necessarily inconsistent with the other general and specific models which have also been outlined. Brown's vulnerability factors, Kohn's conceptions of social reality, learned helplessness, value systems and Rahe's filters and lenses can all be easily translated and adapted to fit in quite conveniently with the hierarchical model. Moreover this model, and also some of those it encompasses, has certain fairly definite implications for dealing with psychological problems which may result from stressful experiences. Obviously, if psychological symptoms are seen both as an attempt to cope with stress rather than as a passive reaction, and at the same time as being undesirable, then a prevention approach rather than a treatment approach is indicated. Only if those who are potentially at risk have, or can be provided with, other effective coping responses which are personally and socially preferable to psychological disorder can the ravages of stress be mitigated.

As is often the case the obvious intervention strategies suggested by a theoretical model may be exceedingly difficult to implement in practice. Equally it also holds that if some types of psychological symptom are in fact coping attempts, then symptomatic treatment or treatment based on a disease model may be not only ineffective but potentially harmful. Unless alternative methods of dealing with personal distress can be offered, psychological symptoms may be a way of making the best of a bad situation. The clear implication is that some of the attention of those in the helping professions should be directed at attempts to create suitable intrapsychic and social environments which will make the experience of life's inevitable stresses less disruptive.

REFERENCES

Antonovsky, A. (1974). Conceptual and methodological problems in the study of resistance resources and stressful life events. In: B. S. Dohrenwend and B. P. Dohrenwend (Eds.), *Stressful Life Events: Their Nature and Effects.* (New York: John Wiley & Sons.)

Antonovsky, A., Maoz, B., Dowty, N. and Wijsenbeck, H. (1971). Twenty-five years later: a limited study of the sequelae of the concentration camp experience. *Social Psychiatry*, **6,** 186–193.

Averill, J. R. (1973). Personal control over aversive stimuli and its relationship to stress. *Psychological Bulletin*, **80,** 286–303.

Borgman, R. D. and Monroe, N. R. (1975). Life experiences and the decision to become a mental patient. *Journal of Nervous and Mental Disease*, **160,** 428–434.

Borus, J. F. (1974). Incidence of maladjustment in Vietnam returnees. *Archives of General Psychiatry*, **30,** 554–557.

Bostock, T. and Williams, C. L. (1973). Attempted suicide as an operant behavior. *Archives of General Psychiatry*, **31,** 482–486.

Brenner, M. H. (1973). *Mental Illness and the Economy.* (Cambridge, Mass.: Harvard University Press.)

Brown, G. W. (1972). Life events and psychiatric illness: some thoughts on methodology and causality. *Journal of Psychosomatic Research*, **16,** 311–320.

Brown, G. W. (1974). Meaning, measurement and stress of life events. In: B. S. Dohrenwend and B. P. Dohrenwend (Eds.), *Stressful Life Events: Their Nature and Effects.* (New York: John Wiley & Sons.)

Brown, G. W., Bhrolchain, M. N. and Harris, T. (1975). Social class and psychiatric disturbance among women in an urban population. *Sociology*, **9,** 225–254.

Brown, G. W. and Birley, J. L. T. (1968). Crises and life change and the onset of schizophrenia. *Journal of Health and Social Behavior*, **9,** 203–214.

Brown, G. W. and Birley, J. L. T. (1971). Letter to the Editor. *British Journal of Psychiatry*, **118,** 378–379.

Brown, G. W. and Harris, T. O. (1978). *Social Origins of Depression: A Study of Psychiatric Disorder in Women.* (London: Tavistock.)

Brown, G. W., Harris, T. O. and Peto, J. (1973a). Life events and psychiatric disorder. Part 2. Nature of the causal link. *Psychological Medicine*, **3,** 159–176.

Brown, G. W., Sklair, F., Harris, T. O. and Birley, J. L. T. (1973b). Life events and psychiatric disorder. Part 1. Some methodological issues. *Psychological Medicine*, **3,** 74–87.
Burbury, W. M. (1941). Effects of evacuation and of air-raids on city children. *British Medical Journal*, **ii,** 660–662.
Cadoret, R. J., Vinokur, G., Dorzab, J. and Baker, M. (1972). Depressive disease: life events and onset of illness. *Archives of General Psychiatry*, **26,** 133–136.
Carveth, W. B. and Gottlieb, B. H. (1977). The role of social support in mediating stress among new mothers. Paper read at Convention of Canadian Psychological Association, Vancouver, BC, Canada.
Cobb, S. (1974). A model for life events and their consequences. In: B. S. Dohrenwend and B. P. Dohrenwend (Eds.), *Stressful Life Events: Their Nature and Effects*. (New York: John Wiley & Sons.)
Cobb, S. (1976). Social support as a moderator of life stress. *Psychosomatic Medicine*, **38,** 300–314.
Cochrane, R. (1977). Mental illness in immigrants to England and Wales: an analysis of mental hospital admissions, 1971. *Social Psychiatry*, **12,** 25–35.
Cochrane, R. (1978). Psychological aspects of life events: a tentative model. Paper read at British Psychological Society, Clinical Division Meeting, University of Sheffield.
Cochrane, R. and Robertson, A. (1973). The life events inventory: a measure of the relative severity of psychosocial stressors. *Journal of Psychosomatic Research*, **17,** 215–218.
Cochrane, R. and Robertson, A. (1975). Stress in the lives of parasuicide. *Social Psychiatry*, **10,** 161–171.
Cochrane, R. and Stopes-Roe, M. (1977). Psychological and social adjustment of Asian immigrants to Britain: a community survey. *Social Psychiatry*, **12,** 195–207.
Coleman, J. C. (1976). *Abnormal Psychology and Modern Life*. (Glenview, Ill.: Scott Foresman.)
Cooper, B. and Sylph, J. (1973). Life events and the onset of neurotic illness: an investigation in general practice. *Psychological Medicine*, **3,** 421–435.
Coser, L. A. (1956). *The Functions of Conflict*. (Glencoe, Ill.: The Free Press.)
Davis, D. R. (1970). Depression as adaptation to crisis. *British Journal of Medical Psychology*, **43,** 109–116.
Davis, D. I., Berenson, D., Steinglass, P. and Davis, S. (1974). The adaptive consequences of drinking. *Psychiatry*, **37,** 209–215.
DeFazio, V. J., Rustin, S. and Diamond, A. (1975). Symptom development in Vietnam era veterans. *American Journal of Orthopsychiatry*, **45,** 158–163.
Derogatis, L. R., Lipman, R. S. and Rickels, K. The Hopkins Symptom Check List (HSCL): a measure of primary symptom dimensions. In: P. Pichot (Ed.), *Psychological Measurements in Psychopharmacology*. (Basel, Switzerland: Karger.)
Dohrenwend, B. S. (1973a). Life events as stressors: a methodological inquiry. *Journal of Health and Social Behaviour*, **14,** 167–175.
Dohrenwend, B. S. (1973b). Social status and stressful life events. *Journal of Personality and Social Psychology*, **28,** 225–235.
Dohrenwend, B. S. and Dohrenwend, B. P. (1974). *Stressful Life Events: Their Nature and Effects*. (New York: John Wiley & Sons.)
Eaton, W. W. (1978). Life events, social support and psychiatric symptoms: a re-analysis of the New Haven data. *Journal of Health and Social Behaviour*, **19,** 230–234.
Eitinger, L. (1959). The incidence of mental disease among refugees in Norway. *Journal of Mental Science*, **105,** 326–338.
Fontana, A. F., Davids, B. N., Marcus, J. L. and Rakusin, J. M. (1976). Coping with interpersonal conflicts through life events and hospitalisation. *Journal of Nervous and Mental Disease*, **162,** 88–98.

Fontana, A. F., Marcus, J. L. and Rakusin, J. M. (1972). Pre-hospitalisation coping styles of psychiatric patients: the goal-directedness of life events. *Journal of Nervous and Mental Disease*, **155,** 311–321.

Forrest, A. D., Fraser, R. H. and Priest, R. G. (1965). Environmental factors in depressive illness. *British Journal of Psychiatry*, **111,** 243–253.

Fraser, R. M. (1971). The cost of commotion: an analysis of the psychiatric sequelae of the 1969 Belfast riots. *British Journal of Psychiatry*, **119,** 287–296.

Friedman, H. (1968). Magnitude of experimental effect and a table for its rapid estimation. *Psychological Bulletin*, **70,** 245–251.

Garrity, T. F., Somes, G. W. and Marx, M. B. (1977). Personality factors in resistance to illness after recent life changes. *Journal of Psychosomatic Research*, **21,** 23–32.

Gersten, J. C., Langner, T. S., Eisenberg, J. G., and Orzeck, L. (1974). Child behavior and life events. In: B. S. Dohrenwend and B. P. Dohrenwend (Eds.), *Stressful Life Events: Their Nature and Effects*. (New York: John Wiley & Sons.)

Greenley, J. R., Gillespie, D. P. and Lindenthal, J. J. (1975). A race riot's effects on psychological symptoms. *Archives of General Psychiatry*, **32,** 1189–1195.

Gunderson, E. K. E. and Rahe, R. H. (Eds.). (1974). *Life Stress and Illness*, (Springfield, Ill.: Charles C. Thomas.)

Hassett, J. (1978). *A Primer of Psychophysiology*. (San Francisco: W. H. Freeman & Co.)

Hendrie, J. C., Lachar, D. and Lennox, K. (1975). Personality trait and symptom correlates of life change in a psychiatric population. *Journal of Psychosomatic Research*, **19,** 203–208.

Holmes, T. H. and Rahe, R. H. (1967). The social readjustment rating scale. *Journal of Psychosomatic Research*, **11,** 213–218.

Hudgens, R. W. (1974). Personal catastrophe and depression. In: B. S. Dohrenwend and B. P. Dohrenwend (Eds.), *Stressful Life Events: Their Nature and Effects*. (New York: John Wiley & Sons.)

Hudgens, R. W., Morrison, J. R. and Barchha, R. G. (1967). Life events and the onset of primary affective disorders: a study of 40 hospitalized patients and 40 controls. *Archives of General Psychiatry*, **16,** 134–145.

Hudgens, R. W., Robins, E. and Delong, W. B. (1970). The reporting of recent stress in the lives of psychiatric patients. *British Journal of Psychiatry*, **117,** 635–643.

Inglehart, R. (1977). *The Silent Revolution: Changing Values and Political Styles Among Western Publics*. (Princeton, New Jersey: Princeton University Press.)

Jacobs, S. and Myers, J. (1976). Recent life events and acute schizophrenic psychosis: a controlled study. *Journal of Nervous and Mental Disease*, **162,** 74–87.

Kaplan, H. B. (1976). Self-attitudes and deviant response. *Social Forces*, **54,** 788–799.

Kohn, M. L. (1968). Social class and schizophrenia: a critical review. In: D. Rosenthal and S. S. Kety (Eds.), *The Transmission of Schizophrenia*. (Oxford: Pergamon Press.)

Kohn, M. L. (1972). Class, family and schizophrenia: a reformulation. *Social Forces*, **50,** 295–304.

Komaroff, A. L., Masuda, M. and Holmes, T. H. (1968). The social readjustment rating scale: a comparative study of Negro, Mexican and White Americans. *Journal of Psychosomatic Research*, **12,** 121–128.

Kreitman, N., Smith, P. and Tan, E. S. (1970). Attempted suicide as language: an empirical study. *British Journal of Psychiatry*, **116,** 465–473.

Lacey, J. I., Bateman, D. E. and Van Lehn, R. (1953). Autonomic response specificity. *Psychosomatic Medicine*, **15,** 8–21.

Langner, T. S. (1962). A twenty-two item screening scale of psychiatric symptoms indicating impairment. *Journal of Health and Social Behavior*, **11,** 219–225.

Langner, T. S. and Michael, S. T. (1963). *Life Stresses and Mental Health: The Midtown Study*. (Glencoe, Ill.: Free Press.)

Lazarus, R. S. (1966). *Psychological Stress and the Coping Process.* (New York: McGraw-Hill.)
Leighton, D. C., Harding, J. S., Macklin, D. B., MacMillan, A. M. and Leighton, A. H. (1963). *The Character of Danger.* (New York: Basic Books.)
Lewis, A. (1941). Incidence of neuroses in England under war conditions. *Lancet*, **ii,** 175–183.
Lyons, H. A. (1972). Depressive illness and aggression in Belfast. *British Medical Journal*, **1,** 342–345.
Markush, R. E. and Favero, R. V. (1974). Epidemiologic assessment of stressful life events, depressed mood and psychophysiological symptoms—a preliminary report. In: B. S. Dohrenwend and B. P. Dohrenwend (Eds.), *Stressful Life Events: Their Nature and Effects.* (New York: John Wiley & Sons.)
Mechanic, D. (1972). Social class and schizophrenia: some requirements for a plausible theory of social influence. *Social Forces*, **50,** 305–309.
Miller, P. McC. and Ingham, J. G. (1976). Friends, confidants and symptoms. *Social Psychiatry*, **11,** 51–61.
Miller, P. McC., Ingham, J. G., and Davidson, S. (1976). Life events, symptoms and social support. *Journal of Psychosomatic Research*, **20,** 515–522.
Morrison, J. R., Hudgens, R. W. and Barchha, R. G. (1968). Life events and psychiatric illness. *British Journal of Psychiatry*, **114,** 423–432.
Murphy, G. E., Kuhn, N. O., Christensen, R. F., and Robins, E. (1962). Life stress in a normal population: a study of 101 women hospitalized for normal delivery. *Journal of Nervous and Mental Disease*, **134,** 150–161.
Myers, J. K., Lindenthal, J. L. and Pepper, M. P. (1971). Life events and psychiatric impairment. *Journal of Nervous and Mental Disease*, **152,** 149–157.
Myers, J. K., Lindenthal, J. L. and Pepper, M. P. (1975). Life events, social integration and psychiatric symptomatology. *Journal of Health and Social Behavior*, **16,** 421–427.
Payne, R. L. (1975). Recent life changes and the reporting of psychological states. *Journal of Psychosomatic Research*, **19,** 99–103.
Pearlin, L. I. and Radabaugh, C. W. (1976). Economic strains and the coping functions of alcohol. *American Journal of Sociology*, **82,** 652–663.
Pearlin, L. I. and Schooler, C. (1978). The structure of coping. *Journal of Health and Social Behaviour*, **19,** 2–21.
Phillips, D. L. (1968). Social class and psychological disturbance: the influence of positive and negative experiences. *Social Psychiatry*, **3,** 41–46.
Putten, T. V. and Emory, W. H. (1973). Traumatic neurosses in Vietnam returnees. *Archives of General Psychiatry*, **29,** 695–698.
Rahe, R. H. (1969). Multicultural correlations of life change scaling: America, Japan, Denmark and Sweden. *Journal of Psychosomatic Research*, **13,** 191–195.
Rahe, R. H. (1974). Life change and subsequent illness reports. In: E. K. E. Gunderson and R. H. Rahe (Eds.), *Life Stress and Illness*, (Springfield, Ill.: Charles C. Thomas.)
Rahe, R. H., Fløistad, I., Bergan, T., Ringdal, R., Gerhardt, R., Gunderson, E. K. E., and Arthur, R. J. (1974). A model of life changes and illness research. *Archives of General Psychiatry*, **31,** 172–177.
Robertson, A. and Cochrane, R. (1976a). Attempted suicide and cultural change: an empirical investigation. *Human Relations*, **9,** 863–883.
Robertson, A. and Cochrane, R. (1976b). Deviance and cultural change: attempted suicide as a case study. *International Journal of Social Psychiatry*, **22,** 1–6.
Ruch, L. O. (1977). A multidimensional analysis of the concept of life change. *Journal of Health and Social Behavior*, **18,** 71–83.
Sadava, S. W., Thistle, R., and Forsyth, R. (1978). Stress, escapism and patterns of alcohol

and drug use. *Journal of Studies on Alcohol*, **39,** 725–736.

Sanua, V. D. (1970). Immigration, migration and mental illness: a review of the literature with special emphasis on schizophrenia. In: E. B. Brody (Ed.), *Behavior in New Environments*. (Beverley Hills: Sage Publications.)

Schless, A. P., Teichman, A., Mendels, J., and DiGiacomo, J. N. (1977). The role of stress as a precipitating factor of psychiatric illness. *British Journal of Psychiatry*, **130,** 19–22.

Seligman, M. E. P. (1975). *Helplessness*. (San Francisco: W. H. Freeman & Co.)

Serban, G. (1975). Stress in schizophrenics and normals. *British Journal of Psychiatry*, **126,** 397–407.

Theorell, T. (1976). Selected illness and somatic factors in relation to two psychosocial stress indices. *Journal of Psychosomatic Research*, **20,** 7–20.

Thomson, K. C. and Hendrie, H. C. (1972). Environmental stress in primary depressive illness. *Archives of General Psychiatry*, **26,** 130–132.

Turner, R. (1969). The theme of contemporary social movements. *British Journal of Sociology*, **20,** 390–405.

Uhlenhuth, E. H., Lipman, R. S., Balter, M. B., and Stern, M. (1974). Symptom intensity and life stress in the city. *Archives of General Psychiatry*, **31,** 759–764.

Vinokur, A. and Selzer, M. L. (1975). Desirable versus undesirable life events: their relationship to stress and mental distress. *Journal of Personality and Social Psychology*, **32,** 329–337.

Wershaw, H. J. and Reinhart, G. (1974). Life change and hospitalization—a heretical view. *Journal of Psychosomatic Research*, **18,** 393–402.

Wyler, A. R., Masuda, M., and Holmes, T. H. (1971). Magnitude of life events and seriousness of illness. *Psychosomatic Medicine*, **33,** 115–122.

PART II

Social problems and community intervention

The Social Psychology of Psychological Problems
Edited by P. Feldman and J. Orford

7

The Making and Control of Offenders

PHILIP FELDMAN

INTRODUCTION

The scope of the chapter

This chapter falls into four major sections, preceded by an introduction to definitions and to the pitfalls of the official figures of offences and offenders. The first deals with social influences and experiences which increase the likelihood that individuals will acquire and carry out various criminal behaviours. The second concerns the possibility that social responses to offending, from surveillance to imprisonment, may actually increase the possibility of re-offending by some of those singled out for response. The next two sections counterpoint the two earlier ones: section three reviews social factors which might be developed so as to counteract those which increase the possibility of becoming an offender; similarly, section four is concerned with reducing the extent to which social responses to convicted offenders often achieve the opposite of the intended effect.

Definitions

'Crime' is used interchangeably with 'offences' and 'delinquency'. It has been defined as 'an act capable of being followed by criminal proceedings, having one of the types of outcome known to follow these proceedings' (Williams, 1955, p. 221). An offender/delinquent/criminal is a person 'known' (either because of the formal finding of guilt, or from his self-report) to have carried out a crime. The most simple method of classifying crimes is to divide them into crimes against property (theft, fraud, etc.) and crimes against the person (assault, rape, etc.). The former comprise the great majority of recorded offences of the more serious kind (i.e. excluding motoring offences such as parking violations). Increasingly the law is being 'decriminalized'; that is, offences in which there is no victim, to do with drink, drugs, sex and gambling, are being removed from the statute book. Although their explanation is unlikely to differ from that for offences in general their status is shifting and controversial, and it is appropriate to confine this chapter to offences likely to remain as crimes.

The problem of the dark figure—the unknown percentage of the events under study—is common to all the social sciences. Criminologists are in agreement that very large numbers of crimes go unreported; some categories more so than others. The reason why crimes go unreported include ignorance that an event witnessed constitutes a crime; connivance by the victim (e.g. abortion or homosexual behaviours); and ignorance on the part of the victim that he has been injured in some way (e.g. goods pilfered by an employee); there may be no immediate 'victim'—so that the likelihood of a 'complaint' is reduced (e.g. a tax offence). Finally, the victim may be both aware and unwilling, but either fears retaliation by the offender, doubts the ability of the police or would be the loser were he to report the offence (stolen money might have been undeclared for tax purposes and employees are often unwilling to call the police because of the unpleasant atmosphere of resulting suspicion—Robin, 1970).

Even when offences are reported to the police they may not be recorded by them, possibly due to the sheer volume of reports and the need to select those judged soluble or so serious as to require investigation even though an arrest seems unlikely. Hood and Sparks (1970, p. 34) cite American evidence that one-third of the more serious crimes victims claim to have reported were unrecorded by the police. Two types of attempt have been made to fill in the dark figure: self-reports by offenders (Hood and Sparks, 1970) and reports by victims (Ennis, 1967). The former indicate the very widespread nature of offending. Essentially, respondents are provided with a list of offences and are asked to indicate, usually anonymously, which ones they have carried out. There are various technical problems associated with the method and the samples reported have often been unrepresentative (Feldman, 1977) but a number of satisfactory studies have now appeared. A careful British study by Belson (1975) found that 70 per cent of a large sample of London teenage boys had stolen from a shop; 17 per cent had broken into a house or shop. Such findings abolish the comforting view of a world divided into offenders and the law-abiding. According to Hood and Sparks (1970) self-report studies indicate that only about a quarter of those who have committed offences are actually convicted—and so figure in the official statistics concerning offenders.

Victim studies indicate the reasons for under-reporting. For example, the most important reason for failing to report a crime against a person was that the offence was a private matter, to be accepted, or to be settled personally.

This brief survey indicates that a great deal of social behaviour concerned with perception, attention, and selection lies behind the official figures for offences. We shall return later to the important part played by social response when we consider the effects of the agents of the legal system in the second phase of the social construction of convicted offenders. The first phase takes place in the social settings and experiences to which potential offenders are exposed.

SOCIAL INFLUENCES ON POTENTIAL OFFENDERS

Economic factors

In a characteristically striking phrase George Bernard Shaw asserted that 'poverty is a crime' and went on to argue that if only poverty were abolished crime would also disappear. The evidence is against him. Over 50 years ago, Burt (1923) was not much impressed by poverty as a cause of crime: 'nearly half the offenders [he studied] come from homes that are far from destitute'. Moreover, '[there are] spectacular long-term trends of both economic conditions and crime in which a steep and steady rise in the standard of living of practically all social classes in Western Europe and the Americas has been accompanied by a steep and steady rise in the rates of crime including property crime' (Walker, 1965, p. 91). Walker speculates that affluence and the media combine to increase both the existence and the awareness of material possessions as well as the opportunities for illegal gains—for example, theft from unattended vehicles increases as vehicle ownership increases, and shoplifting is more possible in the supermarket than in the corner shop. Such broad trends overshadow the specific evidence that the frequency of breaking and entering tends to increase in the lean years of the economic cycle (Thomas, 1925).

There are positive correlations between unemployment and police arrests (Glaser and Rice, 1959) but this should not lead to the conclusion that unemployment causes offending. Below we discuss in some detail the possibility that the official statistics of offenders exaggerates the actual differences in offending between the young, the male, the working-class, and the black; and their older, female, middle-class, and white counterparts. The same may be true of the apparent disparity in crime between the unemployed and those in work. Firstly, the unemployed lack the opportunity for the relatively 'safe' pilfering provided by the work-place. Secondly, it is likely to be the less skilled, on average, who lose their jobs; they may also be less skilled at the less 'safe' crimes and hence more likely to be caught.

However, Chapman (1976) has developed and tested a complex statistical model which suggests that both economic and environmental variables contribute to the explanation of crime. For example, economic factors relevant to property crime include the disparity between legally and illegally accessible money and possessions and the chances of obtaining employment, as well as those of being arrested. Chapman's study suffers, as do most in this field, from being concerned with officially recorded offenders—that is those who have been arrested and convicted—among whom the poor, and particularly the unemployed, may figure out of proportion to their numbers among the total population of actual offenders, as we shall see later. Self-report studies of economic factors and offending would be preferable. So far as unemployment is concerned the blanket term is in any event too simple. It may be that, once well established, offending will be performed for an expected reward where an alternative response (paid employment) is either totally unavailable or requires more effort than a criminally attained reward perceived as carrying little risk of detection. Conversely, when further employment seems likely—providing the person is seen as law-abiding—and the risk of the offence is great, the individual concerned may be even more law-abiding than when he is in secure employment.

Social failure and 'alienation'

Alienation, as a term in sociology, is descended from and related to the Durkheimian concept 'anomie', which Merton (e.g. 1969) conceives of as:

> a disjuncture between the cultural goal of success and the opportunity structure by which the goal might be achieved, and since the lower strata were discriminated against in educational and occupational market places, this was the group least likely to realise the American dream ... no wonder that from these strata so many pursued deviant activities; only such activities offered an available route to success (cited by Box, 1971, p. 105).

Several other sociologists (e.g. Cloward and Ohlin, 1960) have joined Merton in developing theories of a similar kind in order to explain the apparent heavy concentration of crime among the young, the working-class (and by implication) the black. The combination of all three (and in males much more than females) produces the heaviest concentration of all. Essentially the 'social failure' theories assert that working-class children initially accept middle-class values, then reject them when they fail to lead to educational success and instead acquire and carry out criminal behaviours to achieve the commonly held goal of material advancement. A British study by Hargreaves (1967) provides some apparent supporting evidence. He found the percentage in each 'stream' of a British secondary school admitting recent involvement in stealing to be as follows: A stream, 7 per cent; B, 43 per cent, and C 64 per cent. The upper-stream boys had similar values to the middle-class teachers; those in the lower streams did not. Hargreaves suggests that the boys responded to the 'social label' assigned by their teachers: educationally bright or dull. Those labelled bright retained middle-class values, and refrained from offending; those labelled dull rejected the values, and turned to offending. However, Hargreaves failed to show that the dull boys initially held the same middle-class values as the teachers; that the process of labelling and 'rejection' by teachers occurred; and, if it did occur, that the rejected boys were aware of the process. Moreover, he should have demonstrated that an awareness of rejection by teachers was followed by the boys' rejection of middle-class values contrary to offending, and culminated in an actual increase in offending. Instead of a sequential, longitudinal study, which would enable the direct testing of the hypothesized causal relationship, Hargreaves carried out a correlational study, at one point in time, making further untested inferences from the results obtained. Finally, Belson's British data (1975, see below) call into question the great disparity obtained by Hargreaves in self-reported offending between upper- and lower-stream boys.

Empirical data on self-reported offending raise serious doubts about the picture given by the official statistics of young offenders as being heavily working-class in membership and hence, it is inferred, less successful educationally. A very comprehensive study in Philadelphia by Wolfgang *et al.* (1972) did indeed find great differences between the police records of juveniles according to ethnic group and social class, the differences becoming more marked as the offences became more serious in nature. A similarly comprehensive British study by Wadsworth (1975) found similar results: the relative proportions of upper middle-, lower middle-, upper working- and lower working-class boys were in the ratio 1:3:3:6.

However, the self-report method reveals rather different results. An American study by Gold (1966) found a ratio of 1.5 to 1 between lower and higher status boys for self-reported offences; the official figures indicated a ratio of 4.5 to 1. Belson's British self-report study (1975) is in broad agreement: class differences in crime exist but are markedly exaggerated by the official statistics. For all types of theft the proportion admitting to at least one offence rose from 32 per cent to 36 per cent as the social scale declined (compare the disparity of 1 to 6 at the extremes found by Wadsworth for British official figures).

Nor is the official bias confined to social class membership. For all offences combined males figure about five times as often as females, although the gap has been declining recently. Two sources of data give a rather different picture: the disparity may remain but it is much less sharp than the official figures suggest. An observational study of American shoppers (*New York Times*) found that of the women observed 7.4 per cent stole something; for the men the figure was 5 per cent. British self-report studies, both of schoolchildren (e.g. Jamison, 1978) and of adults (Canning, 1977) have found that at least for the less serious varieties of theft (shoplifting as opposed to housebreaking) the male–female disparity is 2–1 or less.

What conclusions can we draw? First, we have to account for the considerable discrepancy between the official version of offenders—as consisting largely of young working-class males—and the reality, which is that offending is widely distributed among the population, although *tending* to be more frequent among certain groups. Later in this chapter we trace the process whereby the distortion occurs. Secondly, if it is untrue that crime is confined largely to certain special groups we do not need special explanatory theories peculiar to those groups—for example the social failure and alienation theories briefly discussed above. Instead, we can contemplate theories to account for criminal behaviours acquired and performed by all sections of the population.

Childhood experiences

Maternal deprivation This approach is associated with the name of John Bowlby (e.g. Bowlby and Salter-Ainsworth, 1965). The child is said to require a warm and continuous relationship with the mother or mother-substitute; the absence or disruption of this is said to lead to certain ill-effects including delinquent behaviour. Bowlby's own study (1946) provided apparent support, in the form of a close relationship between separation, 'affectionlessness', and thieving found in a child-guidance group. This study and Bowlby's work in general has been subjected to a most powerful critique by Morgan (1975); this indicates so many methodological inadequacies as to leave the basic assertion in much doubt. Moreover, many studies (e.g. Naess, 1959; Rutter, 1971; Little, 1965) have found very little support for the theory.

Offending is very widespread, as we have seen; so is separation—about one-third of children are separated from their mother before the age of 4½ for at least a week (Douglas and Bromfield, 1958). A *special* association between the two seems unlikely.

Home background The general finding (exemplified by Douglas and Ross, 1968) is that the home background (e.g. housing conditions and general child care) of convicted offenders is significantly worse than that of control groups. Other studies have focused on the method of child-training used. Both punitiveness and inconsistency have been said to mark the parents of offenders as opposed to controls (e.g. McCord *et al.*, 1959).

Studies such as these suffer from many faults. First, the description of the child-training technique is typically vague, so that it is difficult for other studies to replicate the observations made. Some progress is being made (e.g. Hoffmann and Saltzstein, 1967) but a completely satisfactory study is inevitably extremely expensive—it requires a very lengthy period of observation and a long-term follow-up of the offending behaviour of children exposed to the different methods. Second, it cannot be assumed that the only important variation is that between parents and their methods of training; Bell (1968) and Harper (1975) have cited much evidence that individual differences between children are important in determining parental behaviour. Some differences appear congenital, such as person-orientation and assertiveness. In very simple terms, some children are harder to train than others (see chapter 2, by Herbert, for a full account). Thus, in addition to information about training techniques and later offending, data concerning the child are also relevant—and should be obtained from as early an age as possible.

Third, proponents of the key role of childhood experiences tend to ignore the effects of social influences on the child outside the home. In contrast, Belson (1975) reported that training in 'not stealing' significantly reduced the level of theft only when such training was consistently received from school and church as well as from home. Fourth, the reference to 'other influences' reminds us that social learning occurs in a variety of settings, not only within the home, as well as throughout the full lifespan; childhood is important, but not so important as to reduce into insignificance subsequent experiences in both work and leisure settings.

In common with most studies of offending, those concerning parental techniques tend to use official records of offending rather than self-reports. But both police surveillance and penal response may be greater for homes considered inadequate in some way than for those regarded as more satisfactory. The result is the kind of self-confirming prophecy which is common in the field of crime. Finally, and most important of all, the childhood experience approach focuses on learning *not* to offend. In sharp contrast is the view that criminal behaviours are acquired, performed, and maintained in response to positive rather than negative events; people *'learn to offend'*, as well as 'fail to learn not to offend'. Such positive learning takes place throughout the life-span and in a variety of social settings.

Observational learning: an overview

Social learning theory has been developed by Bandura and his associates, (see Bandura, 1977, for a full account). It has been applied in detail to the field of crime by Feldman (1977). The following is a brief summary of this complex approach.

Learning occurs both through the individual's own direct experiences and his observation of those of significant others, termed models. The effects of observational learning include the acquisition of new patterns of behaviour, the strengthening or weakening of previously learned inhibitions and the facilitation or suppression of previously learned responses—in fact all the features of learning by direct experience. For observational learning to occur requires exposure to a model, and the accurate perception and selection of certain behaviours. The model's behaviour may then be practised either publicly or privately, overtly or covertly. Finally, the new responses are performed and lead to consequences, both positive and negative.

As well as being exposed to actual models of criminal or law-abiding behaviour, people are also exposed to verbal attempts to persuade them to keep or to break the law. McGuire (1969, and in Chapter 12 of this book) has reviewed the literature on persuasive communications. Such communications, for example in favour of criminal activity, are most effective when they are transmitted, face to face, to a potential offender by an existing offender with whom he is in frequent contact—the latter being known by the former to be successful at crime and considered by him to be likeable as well as able to deliver or withhold valued reinforcements. Such social transmissions of criminal attitudes and behaviours may occur both in two-person situations and in larger groups. In the latter case the referent and coercive power of the group may be of great importance for the rapid acquisition of criminal behaviour. Other members of the group both supply standards of approved behaviour and punish departures from those standards. Examples include price-fixing by a closely associated network of dealers, and theft from work by a group of shop-floor operatives.

Much attention has been paid by social psychologists to self persuasion—the process whereby people bring their attitudes and thinking into line with their external behaviour. A great deal of the relevant research has been concerned with behaviours analogous to crime, particularly in laboratory studies of aggression.

Essentially, by various perceptual and cognitive distortions, individuals have been found able to derogate the victim, deny the severity of his pain or loss, and even to attribute to him the blame for his own distress (e.g. Glass and Wood, 1964). The process of self-persuasion and justification is assisted by lack of contact with the victim (Milgram, 1974).

Once criminal behaviours have been acquired, the acts concerned—thefts, assaults, etc.—will be performed when relevant situational cues occur. For example an offence against property is most probable when detection is unlikely, punishment minimal, incentives high, legitimate alternatives are absent, transgressing models are present, little or no skill is required, the victim is both a stranger and unlikely to report the offence, and self-esteem is temporarily low (Feldman, 1977). Some of the same determinants apply to offences against the person, particularly the presence of an aggressing model. In addition, prior emotional arousal, aversive physical or verbal experiences, and the withdrawal of valued reinforcements, are all relevant, as is whether or not an aggressive act in the particular situation has led previously to an outcome judged favourable by the person concerned.

Finally, the long-term schedule of reinforcement for the criminal behaviour concerned will help to determine whether it will be maintained or diminished. In this connection it is crucial to note that for most offences, particularly the more minor ones, the odds are heavily on the side of the offender—on average crimes *do* pay, particularly those of shoplifting and stealing from unattended vehicles. Moreover, the returns of crime are social as well as material, and include attention and friendship from fellow offenders, as well as the access to socially approved settings allowed by significant illegal gains—as witness the move of organized criminals into legitimate business and social circles in the USA.

Social settings in which crime is learned

The great majority of research into observational learning has consisted of laboratory studies of young children modelled by other children or by adults, and not of real-life studies of adolescents or adults modelled by their peers. Yet the latter idea was abroad many years ago: 'the depredator who has escaped punishment due to his offences is constantly present; an encouraging example of sucess to all his class' (Chadwick, 1829). It is assumed that parents will attempt to train their children in socially acceptable behaviours, but while we may comfort ourselves by discounting the possibility that parents will *intentionally* model crime to their offspring, at least a proportion of parents will, from time to time, carry out successful criminal acts and some of these will become known to their children. In other instances children will hear conversations between parents or others about the criminal acts of other adults. There is also evidence (Wootton, 1959) that the presence of one offender in the family is associated with the increased probability of another.

There is no particular onus on peer-groups to train socially acceptable behaviours before, during, or after adolescence; some will do so—others will model crime to their members, often repeatedly over long periods of time. Evidence comes from Belson's (1975) British study: he found that the onset of offending was strongly related to associating with boys already stealing. Another British study (Knight and West, 1975) which is part of the large-scale longitudinal study of a London working-class area (West and Farrington, 1977) also reported the importance of exposure to social models of offending in the development of persistent offending.

Clinard (1952) gives an example from a more respectable part of the social scale. He describes how businessmen learned black-market practices during World War Two by association with existing black-market operators. Examples of 'white-collar crime' (or 'occupational offending', a more inclusive term) are not confined to the unusual circumstances of wartime. They occur, at all times and places, from the shop floor to the executive suite, whenever there is the combination of successful offending models, easily available rewards, a low probability of detection, and minimal punishment. Such conditions seem likely throughout both industry and the professions (indeed illegal gains at low risk may be less possible for a school-child than his parent). Clinard (1968) includes under the heading of occupational offenders large and small businessmen, politicians, government employees, doctors, pharmacists, and others. Investigations, particularly in the USA, have shown widespread violation of the criminal law by businesses, up to the largest size and in all areas of industry and commerce. The illegal activities included acts in restraint of trade, such as monopoly practices, patent infringement, financial manipulations, and (particularly in wartime) black-marketeering. Convictions of American public and elected officials occur with some frequency. *Time* (1972) noted in an article headed 'Busting Public Servants' that in New Jersey alone 67 officials had been indicated and 35 convicted over the past three years, including mayors, legislators, judges, highway officials, postmasters, and a congressman. Trade-union officials (again the evidence is largely American) have engaged in such criminal activities as misappropriation of union funds and the use of fraudulent means to maintain control of their unions.

All of this is not to argue that the average adult spends his entire working life in pursuit of illegal self-advantage; simply that such activities are not totally confined to the 'criminal classes', but are found in varying degrees of frequency, in different forms according to the nature of the occupation, throughout the majority of the population, and that their occurrence depends in large part on the presence of existing models of successful offending. Clarke (1978) has discussed how occupational offending is often deeply embedded in the organization concerned, including the availability of social models for the systematic avoidance of detection, rather than mere escape after the event.

Finally, some settings provide *planned* models of criminal behaviours. Cressey (1971) has described organized specialist groups of criminals as having existed for centuries. Their areas of activity today include burglary, shoplifting, robbery, confidence games, pickpocketing, and car theft, all of which need experience and training both for carrying out the criminal act itself and for coping with the situation if detected. Skills are developed like any other occupational expertise, by both example and practice.

The importance of models carrying out illegal behaviours in a particular social setting is at least as great for offences against the person as for those against property. The acceptance of violence as a means of resolving personal disputes (in fact, of course, illegal) varies from country to country, region to region, and even by neighbourhood within a single city (Clinard, 1968). Nearly 90 per cent of all cases of murder in Houston, Texas, were found to occur in a small number of areas in the centre of the city. In the most careful study to date, of the crime of rape, Amir (1972) found the rates for forcible rape to be highest for young, single, poor, non-whites; the victim tended to come from the same background. Amir emphasizes a particular subculture as supplying a social learning setting for the crime of rape. (However, he was careful to point out that his study inevitably excluded the 'unknown rapist' whose inclusion might change the ethnic and class picture of the known rapist.)

Observational learning: television

The controversy about the effects of television viewing on aggression has continued for many years and has led to many research studies, some of them extremely large-scale. They have recently been reviewed by Eysenck and Nias (1978) who tend to agree with Bandura's view:

> Given the evidence for observational learning, there is no longer any justification for equivocating about whether children or adults learn techniques of aggression from televised models. People who watch commercial television for any length of time will learn a number of tactics of violence and murder. Television is a superb tutor. It teaches how to aggress and by the way it portrays the functional value of aggressive behaviour (Bandura, 1973, p. 271).

A detailed questionnaire study by Belson (1978) is again in agreement with the view that exposure to at least certain kinds of televised violence, occurring in certain settings, increases the probability of violent behaviour by at least some of the observers. Yet experimental, as opposed to correlational, data are still rare. One of the very few examples is provided by Leyens *et al.* (1975) who carried out a study of a Belgian private institution for boys lacking adequate home care or who were referred as behaviour problems. The boys, who lived in four cottages, divided on the basis of careful observation into two groups, each of two cottages, one relatively high in aggression, the other relatively low. Every evening for a week aggressive films were shown to one cottage of each group, and neutral films to the other. Observations of behaviour were carried out during the viewing week, and again in the post-movie week. As compared to the pre-movie week, there was a sharp increase in physical aggression both in high- and low-aggression cottages immediately after exposure to violent films. This was in spite of the presence of the observers. In the post-movie week the aggression persisted only in the originally high-aggression cottage. Conversely (though unexpectedly) physical aggression decreased in the cottages exposed to neutral films, an effect which persisted in the post-movie week.

Concluding comment

In this section we have found rather little need for special theories of social failure to account for criminal behaviour: it is far from confined to certain social groups. Nor are failures in learning not to offend during childhood nearly as exclusively important as claimed by earlier research. Instead it has been emphasized that much learning is acquired from other people, and that certain social settings favour the positive acquisition of criminal behaviours by exposure to relevant persuasive communications and social models, as well as by direct experience. The first two are peculiarly 'social' in nature, hence the emphasis they have received.

In our story of the making of offenders we have reached the point at which the individual has learned and executed a criminal act. Some of these individuals then come into contact with the legal agencies set up to control offending. Whether or not they become part of the official statistics of offending, as well as their subsequent career as offenders or law-abiding citizens, depends only in part on their actual past and continued criminal behaviour; much is determined by the social response of the legal agencies. This comprises the next section of the story.

SOCIAL RESPONSE

We have seen that the official statistics of both offences and offenders represent only a sample of the total number of both; is the sample representative or is it biased in some particular direction or directions? My main concern in this chapter is with persons (offenders) rather than with events (offences), but before going on to offenders a brief look at offences is of interest.

Because of the opportunities provided by 'middle-class' work situations it is plausible to regard as 'middle-class' offences, fraud, forgery, embezzlement, and corporation crime, in contrast to theft, robbery, and car theft. The latter group, according to official statistics of offenders, are working-class offences and Box (1971) has argued that they are more likely to be reported than are those in the 'middle-class' group. Unfortunately, there appear to be no studies, comparing the reporting of the two groups of offences, which have used acceptable sampling procedures. An inferential argument suggests that reporting requires first that the victim is aware of his loss. Householders are likely to be aware of burglary, both because of the missing possessions and of signs of entry. In contrast, a business organization may lack adequate inventory control, and robbery by an employee obviates the need for access. The argument is a plausible one but unequivocal supportive research remains to be carried out.

In contrast, much effort has been expended to test the assertion that officially denoted offenders represent a biased sample. Chambliss (1969) has stated that the 'lower-class' person is (i) more likely to be scrutinized and therefore to be observed in any violation of the law; (ii) more likely to be arrested if discovered under suspicious circumstances; (iii) more likely to spend the time between arrest and trial in jail; (iv) more likely to come to trial; (v) more likely to be found guilty; and (vi) if found guilty more likely to receive harsh punishment than his middle- or upper-class counterpart.

In considering Chambliss' general claims we have already seen that the official statistics of offending, compared to self-reports, overstate quite markedly the disparities between working-class and middle-class young men and that this is particularly true for the less serious offences. There are several stages at which the process of exaggeration might occur.

Offenders: who is caught

Belson's British self-report study (1975) found that the better-educated sons of better-off fathers were markedly less likely to be apprehended for theft than their less well-educated and less well-off counterparts. Why should this be so? There are at last two possibilities. The first is that 'middle-class' boys are more skilled, either in selecting those thefts with a lower probability of detection, or in carrying out thefts of all levels of difficulty and of probability of detection. There are no data concerning this explanation. The second is a bias both in surveillance and police reporting. Cameron (1964) reported that store detectives were not only more likely to observe and follow adolescents and blacks, rather than white adults, particularly those perceived as middle-class, but were also selective in prosecuting those arrested. Whereas only 6.5 per cent of all adults arrested were blacks, they made up 24 per cent of those prosecuted, the bias extending to both male and female blacks. May (1978) has given a detailed account of how store detectives seek to select for further action those, from the total population of observed shoplifters, judged least likely to make difficulties for the store or for the security officer. (Difficulties include an ability to put up a successful defence against the accusation; perhaps even to sue for damages or for defamation of character.)

A similar bias has been found for the police, who have rather wide powers of discretion, which include deciding not to proceed against an arrested person but instead to issue him or her with a verbal or written caution—in which case there is no court appearance and no possibility of a finding of guilt followed by an appearance in the official statistics. Cautioning rather than prosecution is more likely with younger suspects (Hood and Sparks, 1970), females (Walker, 1965), middle-class as opposed to working-class boys (Gold, 1966) and whites as compared to blacks (Wilson, 1968).

Several studies have looked at the possibility that over and above actual class membership both the appearance of the suspect and his general demeanour contribute, together with the seriousness of the offence and the (police-perceived) likelihood of effective parental control, to the decision to arrest or to caution. Piliavin and Briar (1964) reported that the most important cue used by the police is the way the suspect responds; for example, a quick confession as opposed to a denial increased the chances of an informal response by the police. Very similar results have been reported by Werner *et al.* (1975), the key behaviours being politeness, cooperation, presenting prompt evidence of identity, and answering questions. Box (1971) suggests, although he cites no actual data, that middle-class persons are better than their working-class counterparts at creating the desired impression on the police. Garrett and Short (1975) suggest that the presentation of a 'cooperative' demeanour may be hindered for some boys, questioned in the presence of their peers, by a contrary requirement (modelled and reinforced by the same peer group) to appear tough and hostile even at the cost of a more severe response by the police.

Offenders in court; lawyers

A further opportunity to escape an appearance in the official statistics occurs when the person, having been arrested, appears in court, where he may plead guilty as charged, not guilty, or guilty though to a lesser charge. The last-named is associated with what is termed plea bargaining. It is rewarding to all concerned: the offence joins those 'cleared up by the police'; the overloaded court machinery proceeds more swiftly; the accused receives a lesser sentence than he might have done otherwise. The last point is particularly relevant to the present discussion; the result of a plea bargain may be a non-custodial sentence, thus avoiding the criminogenic social training experience associated with penal settings (see below). Plea bargaining is widely acknowledged in the USA. Officially, it does not exist in Britain. A study by Baldwin and McConville (1977) indicates that it occurs in Britain more than occasionally, a conclusion bitterly denied by the Bar Council and criticized on technical grounds by Sealy and Gaskell (1978). American evidence on plea bargaining indicates that those legally represented *at all* were much more likely to plead guilty to a lesser charge (Newman, 1956) as were those employing private counsel as opposed to being represented by a publicly funded defender (Oaks and Lehman, 1970). It is a reasonable assumption that the better-off are more likely to be legally represented, and if represented to employ private rather than public counsel. Moreover, the latter are likely to be less competent than the former (the contrary assumption, that the most able lawyers prefer to work for the smallest fees, seems unlikely). The granting of bail, enabling a greater length of time for the preparation of the defence—and hence a more successful defence—is related to the economic level of the person seeking bail (Nagel, 1970). The results of all of the above factors is that a further potential contribution is made to the social construction of official statistics. This is the situation in the USA, the British Legal Aid system equalizes the possibility of access to high-calibre counsel.

Offenders in court; jurors and judges

In a very broad sense decisions as to guilt are made in the lower courts by magistrates (roughly they are concerned with less serious offences, but nevertheless are able to pass short prison sentences) and by jurors under the direction of judges in the higher courts (concerned with more serious offences). A great deal of work has been carried out on the variables influencing jury decisions as to guilt; very much less on the magistracy where the research concentration has been on sentencing practice—that is on the type and severity of sentence.

A comprehensive review by Mitchell and Byrne (1973) found that three major classes of variables influenced jury decisions; the procedural characteristic of the trial, the personal characteristics of the defendant and those of the juror. Unfortunately, there is an absolute ban on research on real trials with real juries; research has used either simulated situations and volunteer (typically undergraduate) juries or (much more rarely) there has been a questionnaire study of how judges sitting alone would have decided a trial actually tried by jury. Much the best-known example of the latter is that by Kalven and Zeisel (1966). They found agreement between judge and jury in 78 per cent of nearly 4000 cases; of the remainder the jury was more lenient in 19 per cent of cases, the judge in 3 per cent. Both 'doubt' (i.e. the need to be certain beyond reasonable doubt) and 'sentiment' were major influences on the greater average leniency of the juries. The latter influence is of particular interest. It includes the following: the defendant has had a hard time in his daily life (loss of close relatives, illness, etc.); an accomplice has escaped punishment; the victim is held partly to blame (e.g. in rape cases); the defendant has certain personal attributes (old age, widowhood) or follows certain occupations (e.g. clergyman); he makes a good courtroom impression (attractiveness, or repentance). The converse of these sentiment factors, of course, holds good (unpleasant personal attributes, a poor courtroom impression, and so on).

The question of personal presentation is of particular interest and has attracted much research of the simulated type. Unfortunately, as pointed out by Elwork and Sales (1978) this work is largely unsatisfactory in that in the real world juries decide only guilt—whereas most of the simulated work is concerned with severity of sentence—and the importance of 'sentiment' is in those cases in which the legal issues do not point clearly one way or the other. In contrast the simulated studies tend to associate the more attractive defendent with a less-than-strong prosecution case. Elwork and Sales criticize severely most of the psychological research on juries as indicating marked ignorance of courtroom realities. Nevertheless, something remains. In general, the more attractive a person, both psychologically (good citizen, kind, etc.) and physically, the more he is liked; and the more he is liked the more leniently he is judged (e.g. Efran, 1974; Dion, 1972). A limitation has been shown by Sigall and Ostrove (1975): in a simulated situation somewhat harsher 'sentences' were given to an attractive than to an unattractive swindler—swindling being considered an 'attractiveness-related' crime. The attractive–leniency relationship held strongly for burglary, an unattractive burglar being given a much more severe 'sentence' than an attractive one. It should be noted that real-life juries do not give sentences, but it is not unreasonable to expect some sentencing agents to be influenced by attractiveness.

There seems to be no simulated jury work on general demeanour (e.g. answering fully and immediately, a polite and respectful yet dignified manner, etc.) yet it is likely to be the total impression—appearance, and personal attributes, plus behaviour, perhaps maintained over several days, which exerts its effect on the jury—rather than immediate physical appearance only. The inclusions of a range of such cues would allow this research to parallel work on police—juvenile encounters (see above). The results might indicate a greater skill in self-presentation by middle-class persons—in the courtroom as well as in the street.

Offenders in court: sentencing agents

There is ample evidence of wide differences between magistrates' courts in the sentences given for the same range of offences. For example, in the courts of two neighbouring Northern England towns, Rotherham and Halifax, the proportions of young persons put on probation in the early 1950s were 12 per cent and 79 per cent respectively (Grünhut, 1956). One possibility is that the two benches had developed different philosophies, concerning sentencing, which influenced their responses to a wide range of offences, partly irrespective of the details of the individual case. A major study of Canadian full-time magistrates by Hogarth (1971) demonstrated this very well. He asked a large sample to assign a sentence to 150 cases described in detail in writing. Only 7 per cent of the variation between the magistrates was related to objective facts about the case and the offender; 50 per cent was accounted for by the general attitude of judges (separately surveyed) to 'justice', 'deviance', and 'punishment'. The last point is of great interest; those who believed 'punishment corrects' were much more likely to use an institutional sentence than a fine.

Although the generalized attitudes of the judges in this study had a marked effect on their sentencing practices they seemed much less affected than lay magistrates by the personal attributes of the offender. A study by Hood (1962) of sentencing in magistrates' courts in Britain concluded: 'There is some evidence in favour of the hypothesis that middle-class magistrates dealing with working-class offenders, in relatively small and stable middle-class communities, are likely to be relatively severe.' American evidence of sentencing bias is rather more clear but mostly concerns bias between the races. For example, a study of shoplifting by Cameron (1964) found that while 22 per cent of black women found guilty were sent to jail, only 4 per cent of white women found guilty were so sentenced. Further, only 10 per cent of the white women sentenced to imprisonment were sent to jail for more than 30 days, as compared to 26 per cent of the black women.

What can we conclude from our survey of the evidence on the part played by the legal process, from surveillance to sentence, in the making of offenders? It is clear that at each stage a degree of selection occurs; only a proportion will go forward successively and finally to the stage at which they enter a custodial institution. But is the selection biassed? There seems some evidence for the view that the working-class, the black and the male are more likely to enter penal institutions, particularly when they have behaved 'inappropriately' (in crucial encounters with police, juries, or lay magistrates) than their middle-class, white and female equivalents following the same offence. Exactly how powerful is the selection effect is still far from clear, but it does seem likely that it exists to more than a trivial extent.

Schools for crime

Penal institutions contain informal social systems with well-defined codes of behaviour to which new inmates are exposed and which they learn. Many of the behaviours approved of 'outside'—and by the prison officers—may be punished by other prisoners, and vice-versa. The process is termed *criminalization*. According to Erikson,

> such institutions gather marginal people into tightly segregated groups, give them an opportunity to teach each other the skills and attitudes of a deviant career, and often provoke them into employing these skills by reinforcing their sense of alienation from the rest of society (Erikson, 1964, p. 15).

Acceptance of the inmate code of behaviour eases the adjustment to life in the institution (Tittle and Tittle, 1964). Institutions for juveniles follow the same pattern of aggregating offenders together and ensuring that the greater part of their social contract with peers is with other offenders, rather than with non-offending social models. As such juvenile institutions are usually several times as expensive as the most prestigious boarding school and the failure rates (measured by reconviction within three years) are well in excess of 50 per cent, their cost-effectiveness must be in some doubt.

Unfortunately, although the view that penal institutions have a criminalizing effect is a persuasive one, empirical studies are still few in number and provide data which are largely indirect. For example, Thomas (1973) found that scores on scales of prisonization (acceptance of a code of loyalty to other inmates and manipulation of prison officers) and of post-release expectations ('I will stay out of trouble', etc.) were negatively correlated with the number of letters and visits. (The more letters and visits, the less prisonization and the more optimism about staying out of trouble.) He reported no data on the relationship between letters and visits and actual reconviction rate. Such a study would be the obvious next step. Similarly, Zingraff (1975) reported a link between acceptance of inmate norms and adaptation to a social role in the institution acceptable to the inmate culture.

Other studies have provided clear evidence of *counter-control by the peer group.*

Buehler *et al.* (1966) have shown how an institutional group of female adolescent offenders positively reinforced anti-social behaviour (i.e. those behaviours disapproved by the staff) such as rule-breaking, criticism of adults, and aggression; and punished behaviours approved by the staff. They also found that the staff were less consistent in their use of positive and negative reinforcers than were the girls, and applied them less frequently. In other words, the girls not only had a contrary set of goals to the staff; they also pursued them more effectively. Detailed observations of small units for male offenders were made by Polsky (1962) who showed that the peer subculture developed social hierarchies based on status, the highest esteem going to the boys who most exemplified the very opposite of the values and behaviours approved of by the staff. Newcomers to the unit were shaped into the behaviours valued by the boys. Because the staff were outnumbered by the boys, they needed the cooperation of the high-status boys to maintain order. Thus they confirmed the status of such boys and hence that of the behaviours they exemplified, so that pursuing the short-term goal of maintaining order made more difficult the long-term goal of changing undesirable behaviour. Finally, Polsky points out, many of the boys would spend further periods in other institutions to which they would transfer the value systems acquired in their first institution.

However, the formal inmate structure may also pursue goals which are similar to those of staff. Fry (1976) reported an institution-based drug control programme largely run by inmates. There was high inmate cohesion, much hostility to the rather remote administrative staff, and good results in terms of reduced relapse. The crucial difference to the studies demonstrating counter-control may be that the goal concerned (the control of drug abuse) was shared by inmates and staff. This theme of shared goals will be returned to in the section on social factors which might reduce re-offending.

Social labelling theory

The large-scale study by Wolfgang *et al.* (1972) referred to earlier provides interesting evidence that the apparent disparity in crime, according to colour and class, revealed by the official statistics, only partially survives a closer examination. The authors found that whereas 13 per cent of white 'one-time' offenders were arrested—as opposed to some unofficial action—the figure was 30 per cent for non-white. A similar disparity was found for recidivists. The authors comment; 'However we split and splice the material at hand, non-whites received more severe dispositions' (Wolfgang *et al.*, 1972 p. 220). They traced the impact of disposition for a particular offence on the probability of subsequent offences. This showed a greater probability of a second offence if the first offence had led to an arrest than if it had led to a remedial disposition. The same was true of subsequent offences. In sum: 'two factors—seriousness of the offence and severe disposition—are associated with a substantial proportion of recidivism' (*ibid.*, p. 237). Thus, the suggestion is that the heavy representation of non-white lower socioeconomic boys in the recidivist category may have been due partially to the severity of police action—arrest rather than remedial disposition. The implication follows that if, for example, white higher-SES boys carrying out the same initial offence as non-whites had been dealt with as severely as the latter, they would have been more strongly represented in the recidivist group than actually was the case.

It is this kind of effect which is the heart of what is termed social labelling theory. Lemert (1951) argued for transferring attention from the behaviour itself to the reactive pattern it elicited. There are many acts to which reactions are possible, a pool from which control organizations select only some which are thus labelled 'deviant', as 'criminal', or 'mentally ill', etc. The aim of 'explanation' should be to uncover the process by which labels are acquired and accepted, and the focus thus shifts from those who receive labels to the activities of those given the power to label. Thus, the central theme of social labelling theories is that deviant behaviour arises from attempts at control—it is a response to activity on the part of those officially designated as 'labellers and controllers'.

From a very different theoretical prospective, that of behaviourist psychology, Ullmann and Krasner (1969) have used the insights of labelling theory to account for the maintenance, possibly even the development, of bizarre behaviours such as those assigned the label 'schizophrenia'. They argued that it is only bizarre responses which are attended to by the hospital staff and so are reinforced; everyday behaviours are ignored as not conforming to the label, and so are extinguished. The well-known study by Rosenhan (1973), in which 'pseudo-patients', simulating bizarre symptoms, found discharge difficult once the diagnosis had been made, provides further evidence for the social labelling view. In the field of crime, labelling theory has three key hypotheses (Welford, 1975):

1. No act is intrinsically criminal. In the sense that human societies have to decide to label a behaviour as criminal, and they may equally decide not to do so, this is correct; but in practice most societies at most times regard the taking of property as punishable and many societies have the same response to violent acts against persons.
2. The sequence of events from surveillance to sentence is a function of offender rather than offence characteristics. We have reviewed a good deal of evidence concerning this view and concluded that it is too powerful to be ignored although the hypothesis as set out above rather overstates the case—the police and jurors do take *some* account of offence characteristics; professional magistrates and judges take a good deal of account as well as being influenced by general attitudes about crime and punishment; the more serious the offence the less is the part played by the characteristics of the offender.

As well as the Wolfgang *et al.* (1972) study other reports (by Hirschi, 1970 and Gold, 1970) support the view that arrest increases future offending by officially designated offenders. However, neither of these studies controlled for the possibility of a greater surveillance of known offenders and hence a greater possibility of detection and conviction. Self-report studies largely overcome this problem. Using a large representative sample of American teenagers, Gold and Williams (1969) found that those previously not labelled increased their self-reported and unpunished delinquency *after* arrest. Similar results were obtained in Britain by Farrington (1977) and Farrington *et al.* (1978). However, the last-named study also found a subsequent decrease—by age 21—in self-reported offending in those first convicted before the age of 14, whether or not further convictions occurred and whether or not institutional sentences were received. The decrease did not occur in those first convicted between 14 and 18.

These studies did not record the actual gains, material and social, from the full sequence of self-reported offences. While labelling theory expects an increase in offending due to official labelling, reinforcement theory expects an increase according to the total balance of gains and losses and the schedule of reinforcements on which they are received, as well as the total complex of alternative non-criminal behaviours in the individual's repertoire, and the opportunities for carrying these out (Feldman, 1977). Future studies should record data on returns, alternatives, and opportunities, in addition to the official labelling which is only one type of consequence experienced by convicted offenders. The offence for which the offender has been convicted is hardly likely to be the only one he had actually carried out.

Another implication of the second hypothesis is that it is not only the agents of the legal system who impose labels; the families and friends of offenders, as well as employers, may also do so. Their reaction to the labelled individual may help to maintain his deviant behaviour, perhaps even enhance it, either by reducing the possibility of alternative, legal, behaviours or by their social reinforcement of the deviant behaviours, or both. A number of studies support the first possibility. For example, Christiansen (1969) studied the recidivism rates of wartime Danish collaborators sent to prison for a minimum of two years following the end of the war. The rate of recidivism was markedly lower for those who returned to South Jutland, an area of strong Nazi sympathies, than for those returning to other areas where such sympathies were less marked. This result may be interpreted as indicating that post-prison social rejection was less severe for the South Jutland group than the rest; thus they were less likely to turn to other crimes. Such studies would be improved by the use of direct measures of social rejection rather than reliance on an indirect inference from recidivism rates.

There is good evidence of a correlation between recidivism and unemployment (Reitzes, 1955), but the relationship could be due to those with a worse record either being less likely to seek employment, or failing to obtain it despite earnest efforts. A study which controlled for the variable of employment-seeking was carried out by Schwartz and Skolnick (1964). They found that the potential employers of unskilled workers, when presented with the files of imaginary applicants, were markedly less likely to offer employment when the file mentioned a police record than when it did not. Even when an acquittal, confirmed by an exonerating letter, followed a recorded charge, the probability of an offer of employment was reduced as compared to a file free of any police involvement.

Examples of the possibility of enhancement of crime by social support are largely anecdotal. The literature on organized crime (for example Messick, 1971; Teresa, 1973) indicates that the 'organization' frequently 'looks after' a professional criminal's family during his time in prison, assisting the stability of the marriage; in return, the organization retains the 'loyalty' (i.e. the silence) and the continued services of the criminal concerned. Fordham (1968), writing about the participants in the 'Great Train Robbery' stresses the compatibility of the roles of good husband and father and major criminal.

3. The process of labelling eventually produces identification with a deviant image and a deviant subculture (that is the labelled person finally accepts the label originally applied by the agents of social control). This section of labelling theory has attracted much theoretical interest (e.g. Matza, 1969) but little empirical study.

It can be seen that labelling theory helps to provide a framework for understanding the contribution of the agents of the legal system to the making of offenders. So far we have remained at a descriptive level. What explanations can be suggested for the activity of labelling?

Anything more than a cursory description is outside the scope of this chapter but even a brief account implicates two broad approaches: the political and the psychological. The political view has two variants; the Marxist and the 'latent social function'. Briefly, the Marxist view (e.g. Quinney, 1974) asserts that capitalism both generates and must control excess labour; control is exerted by the criminal justice system which helps to remove excess labour. The alternative political view (e.g. Box, 1971) suggests that some deviant behaviours are encouraged by the controlling group (capitalist and non-capitalist equally) because deviance clarifies the rules and provides constant reminders of their existence and also that of the controlling group's power.

For one political approach, crime has an economic function; for the other an instructive function. Neither approach has generated much in the way of empirical data but both carry sufficient plausibility not to be dismissed out of hand. Certainly they provide accounts of the functions served by social stereotyping of offenders and hence of how the stereotype comes into being in the first instance.

The psychological approach does not necessarily contradict the political one: it provides a detailed account of what happens *once* the stereotype is in existence (that the typical offender against persons and property is a young, working-class male, and in the USA and increasingly in Britain is also black). As indicated earlier, Garrett and Short's (1975) study showed that American police accept this stereotyped view. There appear no data, as yet, either on British police or on the magistracy in general, but it would be surprising if the stereotype was not held by those groups. Once held the stereotype perpetuates itself: by greater surveillance and hence greater detection, by arrest rather than caution, and by more severe rather than lighter sentencing, particularly of a custodial kind. It is reinforced sufficiently frequently to be strengthened further—everyone meets plenty of examples of the 'typical' offender, particularly at the custodial stage. The process of selection by legal agents is assisted by the different responses of the detected offender to those agents: middle-class humble contrition increases the likelihood of a caution; working-class surly aggression increases the likelihood of arrest. There appear to be no data on differential *police* demeanour in response to apprehended offenders who are perceived by the police as fitting, or differing from, the stereotype. There is a clear possibility that a relatively restrained police reaction to an appropriate demeanour assists the suspect to behave appropriately, and vice-versa. The theme of social responses which might reduce rather than enhance the development of offenders is set out in the next section of this chapter.

IMPROVING PREVENTION

Predicting future offenders

After several decades of work, Sheldon and Eleanor Glueck (1964) claimed a high rate of success in predicting offending by those who had not yet begun. Having reviewed many studies, including those of the Gluecks, Rose (1967) found that all predicted poorly in the most numerous 'middle-risk' range. Moreover, the high level of successful predictions for the 'high-risk' group may have reflected the greater surveillance, and hence greater detection rate, of those in the poorer sections of society. Rose raised a particularly crucial question: even if high-risk children can be identified accurately, what can be done about preventing future offending? It may be desirable to focus attention on people in general rather then those assessed as being particularly at risk of offending.

Training parents

There are several examples of attempts, usually by behaviour-modification techniques, to help the parents of young offenders to cope with them more effectively. Results vary from considerable success (e.g. Hall *et al.* (1972)) to a lack of effect (Weathers and Liberman, 1975) depending on such factors as cooperation by parents and the extent of counter-control by peers. More certain success might be achieved by helping parents to acquire effective methods of child management and directing them to the development in their children of pro-social behaviours and relevant associated skills before offending begins. Such possibilities are discussed in more detail by Herbert, in chapter 2.

A variant of this approach is to replace the biological parents by carefully selected foster-parents with whom convicted young offenders are placed for lengthy periods. The foster-parents are provided with some training, and are paid at a level markedly greater than the cost to them of keeping the child. They thus receive recompense for their skill and efforts in much the same way as do the professionals employed in residential institutions. Nevertheless, the costs per child are very much less than those in institutions, and because only one or two children are placed with each family the problems of criminalization and of group opposition to staff norms are avoided. In addition, the children have an opportunity both to learn by observation and to practise relevant social skills in real, as opposed to artificial, environments. Systematic data on the long-term effects of such schemes (major examples are those in the State of Massachusetts in the USA and the County of Kent in Britain) are still to be published.

Exposure to models of pro-social behaviours

A great deal of attention has been focused on the potentially harmful effects of televised violence; little is known of the possible use of television as a *beneficial* influence and empirical research provides only a few scattered clues, one of which comes from the study by Leyens *et al.* (1975; see above). It will be recalled that there was a decrease in physical aggression in the cottages exposed to neutral films. The explanation may have been a modelling effect by the heroes of the 'neutral' films—in fact they were 'good, naive and altruistic' (Leyens *et al.*, 1975, p. 57). If so, this is a finding of some importance.

There is ample experimental and field evidence that just as anti-social behaviours can be modelled, so can their pro-social counterparts (see Bar-Tal, 1976 and Feldman, 1977 for reviews). In the present context pro-social behaviours will include assisting victims, or potential victims, and not taking advantage of the latter when the opportunity arises.

Effective schools programmes

Just as parents can learn to help to become more effective in developing pro-social behaviours in children, so may teachers. In both cases exhortation to morality is ineffective unless the child has already acquired the relevant behaviours and has been reinforced systematically for carrying them out in the situation concerned. There seems little planned attempt to train teachers either in child management in general or in the development in children of pro-social behaviours in particular. The literature on behaviour modification now includes many examples of the training of teachers in the more effective classroom management of difficult children. It should not be a major extrapolation to help teachers develop pro-social behaviours in children before they become difficult. It is likely that many children begin offending when truanting from school (Belson, 1975), the initial reinforcement being 'fun' rather than material return. More effective teachers (and more positively reinforcing school activities) might be expected to cut down truanting and so reduce the exposure of some children to social models of offending and of opportunities for imitation. Improved leisure-time facilities (of the kind sought by children; not assumed by adults) are also relevant to the provision of behaviours alternative to criminal activities.

A report by Azrin *et al.* (1975) suggests that job-finding consists of a set of skills which can be systematized, taught, and applied to job-seeking in general rather than to particular jobs. They note that job-seekers are usually left to their own devices. If they do receive vocational guidance this is confined to advice on what job to seek, not how to get it. They set up a Job Finding Club in a small American college town with an above-average level of unemployment. Clients, mainly white, referred by social workers and other sources, were divided into 60 matched pairs. One member of each pair was trained in job-finding skills; the other served as a control. Training was carried out in small groups, each successive group assisting in the training of the next one. Daily sessions were held until a job was found. The participants were trained in interview skills, how to prepare a job resumé, and to improve their appearance. Flexibility in job requirements was emphasized, and families and friends were involved as sources of job leads and of encouragement to persevere. Participants kept a record of their attempts and a car pool was set up to give widespread access to jobs at a distance. On average, the trainees took two weeks to find a job, the control group eight weeks. Three weeks after the experiment started 92 per cent of the trainees had obtained a job, compared with 60 per cent of the controls. The successful trainees had obtained higher-paid jobs than the successful controls. Regularity of attendance speeded up job-finding, suggesting that special incentives might be necessary to ensure initial attendance—after which the knowledge of success obtained by others should help to maintain participation. Finally, special training may be necessary to help previously unemployed youngsters in appropriate work habits—arriving on time, carrying out assignments accurately, not leaving early, etc.

Police behaviour

There are a number of ways in which appropriate training might modify police behaviour so as to reduce the extent to which police—juvenile encounters initiate the lengthy sequence which culminates in an institutional sentence. Toch (1969) found that those policeman who were most prone to use violence in the course of their duties used strong as opposed to mild, verbal threats very early in a confrontation with a suspect. If these proved ineffective, possibly because they aroused more hostility than would have been provoked by mild threats, overt physical violence was the only step remaining—the alternative, backing down, would lose too much 'face'. The appropriate training of such policeman, as well as of police recruits, is indicated.

Second, a question raised by Wolfgang *et al.* (1972) is of interest. They asked: 'at what point in a delinquent boy's career an intervention programme should act'? They concluded that because (in their Philadelphia study) '46 per cent of young offenders stopped after the first offence, a major and expensive treatment programme at this point would appear to be wasteful'. They went so far as to suggest that intervention be delayed until the third offence, because an additional 35 per cent of second-time offenders have desisted by that point. 'Thus one could reduce the number of boys requiring attention in this cohort from 3475 after the first offence to 1862 after the second offence, to 1212 after the third offence, rather than concentrating on all 9945' (all quotations from Wolfgang *et al.*, 1972, p. 254). The strictures concerning the ineffectiveness of conventional intervention programmes noted earlier in this chapter would still, of course, apply, but if the resulting improvement were only in terms of a lower financial outlay and reduced criminalization it would still be well worthwhile to follow the Wolfgang *et al.* suggestion, providing that the deterrent effects of earlier intervention were not lost by postponing formal programmes until after the third offence. In support of this recommendation, Klein (1974) found that juvenile first offenders were less likely to be re-arrested in police departments with a 'high diversion' policy—not taking juvenile offenders to court—than those with the contrary 'low diversion' policy. The opposite was true for recidivists.

A third possibility concerns the juvenile side of the police—juvenile interaction. A study by Werner *et al.* (1975) indicates that juveniles may be trained to display behaviours acceptable to the police. Three juveniles with a police record, but still living in the community, were trained to behave appropriately—in terms of facial and other non-verbal expressions, general cooperativeness and mode of answering questions. Police officers shown films of the boys before and after training judged that they would have been less likely to take the boys into custody after than before training. Such training might, of course, reduce the deterrent effect of prospective police contact; a controlled study is indicated.

Community persuasion and planning

In chapter 12 of this book, McGuire describes some large-scale community persuasion programmes. Such a programme might well be developed in the interest of crime prevention and would include the following elements: reducing the opportunities provided by open doors and windows and poorly lighted and isolated public places; avoiding danger spots completely or entering them only in groups rather than singly; the desirability of helping the police, victims, and potential victims. Crime-prevention exercises should extend to the design of buildings and public places—those which are open and well-lit provide less opportunity for crime. In addition Clarke (1977) has pointed out that the Post Office has virtually eliminated theft from telephone kiosks through the fitting of steel coin boxes (vandalism is still a problem); the West Germans have dramatically reduced car theft by compulsory steering locks on all vehicles, and opportunistic theft of motor vehicles was unintentionally cut in this country by the law requiring motor cyclists to wear crash helmets.

REDUCING OFFENDING

Even the most effective social policies aimed at prevention will succeed, at best, only in reducing the number of new offenders; the very real returns of crime will continue to act as effective recruiting and maintaining agents, and social responses to convicted offenders will continue to be required. In this section I consider possibilities for increasing their effectiveness in preventing re-offending while reducing criminalization by exposure to inmate norms.

Sentencing practices

In view of the evidence that non-custodial sentences may well be more effective than imprisonment in preventing re-offending (Hood and Sparks, 1970; see above) it would be helpful to communicate to magistrates and others the desirability of using such sentences to the maximum extent possible. The seminars held periodically for all sentencing agents are now a common feature of the British penal system and provide an opportunity for conveying this type of information. (On the other hand, from time to time popular sentiment virtually demands 'exemplary' prison sentences for particularly unpopular kinds of offences, such as football hooliganism.)

A recently developed British alternative to the conventional roster of fines, probation, and confinement, is provided by the Community Service Order (Pease *et al.*, 1975). This represents an attempt to apply the principle of reparation to the control of crime. Offenders are 'sentenced' to a fixed number of hours of work on such worthy projects as working with the handicapped, repairing churches, and clearing canals. But the reparation is to the community at large and not to the particular victim. A study of direct reparation, or rather 'over-reparation', to the victim himself has been carried out by Azrin and Wesolowski (1974). They applied to a group of intellectually handicapped inmates of an institution Azrin's 'over-correction' principle, already shown to be effective with aggressive acts, toilet-training and enuresis. Briefly, the principle asserts that disruptive activity is discouraged if the offender both corrects and over-corrects, and that the restored situation is better than the original one. The extension of the principle to the control of thefts was tested with this group because thefts, typically of food items during mealtimes, were easily detected; it followed that theft-prevention measures could be evaluated accurately. A group of 34 patients who stole were required to 'correct'—to return what was stolen—for five days and to 'over-correct'—to return the stolen items *plus* an additional one—for the next 20 days. During the correction phase there were 20 episodes of theft per day, and as many on the last as on the first day. There was an immediate sharp fall in the over-correction period, with no further thefts past the third day.

Training in the natural environment

The major premise of this approach is stated by Tharp and Wetzel (1969, p. 7) as follows: 'The environment in which the individual is embedded is principally responsible for the organisation, or disorganisation, the maintenance or change, the appearance or disappearance, of any behaviour.' It follows, according to the authors, who go on to give many illustrative and well-analysed examples, that intervention and prevention should occur in the individual's 'natural environment' (family, school, friendship group, etc.) and not in the artificial environment of an institution.

Tharp's general approach lays much emphasis on the 'triad': the psychologist trains a care professional (probation officer, teacher, etc.) who then trains those such as parents or peers who are the most important people in the natural environment of the offender—who continues to live in his own home. Constant monitoring, both of care professionals and of parents and peers, and feedback to them, is essential, as is accurate assessment both of the impact of training and its effects on the behaviour of the offenders concerned. Examples of this community-based approach include several reported from Hawaii. Fo and O'Donnell (1975) reported on the outcome of a 'buddy system' whereby boys received the friendship of an adult in their own community (Hawaii consists of a number of relatively separate ethnic groups) in return for the performance of certain approved behaviours. The results of a controlled comparison were somewhat mixed: whereas those with a previous offence record improved as compared with untreated controls, those with no previous record did. The authors suggest that their participation in the study enabled social contacts with offenders who taught them criminal behaviours to which they were previously not exposed. Clearly, the exact numerical mix between youngsters of differing previous-offence histories must be carefully planned. The selection of the 'buddy' might also be of great importance: there is much evidence that social learning by imitation is more effective the more similar are the model and the learner (e.g. Bandura, 1973); hence the greater power of the inmate culture as compared to the examples set by institution staff.

What the buddy has to offer or withhold might also be of great importance. O'Donnell *et al.* (1973) set up an athletics programme for which any youngster from an economically poor community was eligible. The opportunity to play football and other games was offered as a reward for academic work. During the four years of the project *not a single one* of the 200 youngsters who participated in the project had an official arrest record. Although no comparison group was set up which did not have access to coaching, the complete absence of arrests is obviously much better than could have been expected in almost any group of disadvantaged youths. However, it is possible that the fact that parents of the boys had themselves to apply for their sons' participation may have resulted in a group from concerned homes which provided a good degree of social control which supplemented that provided by the project. Moreover, there are no data on the pretreatment arrest records of the youths. Nevertheless, it is obvious that the opportunity to play games and be coached by experts is a very potent reinforcer for approved behaviours by young people, and the converse—the prospect of losing the opportunity to do so—is likely to be an effective cue to avoid forbidden behaviour. In general, it is important to match reinforcers to their order of preference in the group under study.

Wilner *et al.* (1977), in the context of the Achievement Place programme (see below), have shown the importance of first ascertaining which are the social behaviours of child-care personnel preferred by young people and then ensuring, by careful training, that such behaviours are carried out.

Training in special settings

Achievement Place (AP) provides the best known example of a systematic behavioural programme for young people on the edge of an offending career. It was originally developed by Phillips and his associates at the University of Kansas (Phillips, 1968) and is now copied in many parts of the USA. Essentially, boys between 12 and 14, who have carried out minor offences or are regarded by the County Court as being at risk of committing more serious ones, live in small groups 'as in a family' with a pair of experienced 'house parents'. The boys undergo a complex programme of behavioural management based on token economy principles, but also a degree of self-government; much attention is given to skills and achievements, both social and educational, in the outside world. It seems clear that a stay in AP achieves substantial benefits in educational attainment and social skills (Braukmann *et al.*, 1975) but what of legally related indices? Outcome data are scarce as yet, and we still await a fully controlled trial, but some early results are available (Fixsen *et al.*, 1972). Two years after release, the re-conviction rate of a group of AP boys was only 19 per cent as against over 50 per cent for those either placed on probation or committed to a conventional institution. The authors point out that the boys were not randomly assigned to each group, so that the results may have been due either to 'a population effect or to a treatment effect'.

A British approach is provided by the Shape programme (Reid *et al.*, 1980) which is engaged in setting up and running behavioural training programmes for male adolescents who have identifiable social, behavioural, and occupational deficits, and are at risk in the community. The clients are aged 16–24, and all participate on a volunteer basis, nearly all of them after at least one period in an institution for juvenile offenders. The first stage (on group-living lines) identifies and remedies deficits in social and work-related skills. The second stage (two-person units) practises and maintains the gains of the first stage and increases community contact, and the third (single-person units) completes the return to the community. The evaluation of this programme is now under way.

Problems of social training programmes

The major obstacle of counter-control by the peer group mentioned in connection with conventional institutions for offenders must be assumed also to affect programmes designed on psychological lines. It may be mitigated by placing considerable emphasis, as at AP, on the group control of rule-making and rule-keeping and other examples of self-government, care being taken by staff—who need much prior training and practice—to move the programme participants gradually to a set of preferred behaviours in line with staff preferences. In addition, once a 'nuclear group' (Buehler, 1973) is established, it models and shapes newcomers to the group. The problem is how to begin the process—how to establish the nuclear group in the first instance.

It is striking that those working with young offenders tend to assume that their charges inevitably have *problems*: psychotherapists expect emotional disturbance and treat by setting up 'caring relationships'; behaviourists assume deficits in the personal repertoire and treat by training in educational and social skills. There is rarely a specific attempt to identify the instigating stimuli for the criminal behaviours which led to a court appearance, and then to train in ways of avoiding temptation and in carrying out alternative behaviours. Yet neither the ability to maintain an emotional relationship nor to read fluently is a bar against criminal activities, and all approaches have as a major criterion of treatment effectiveness that of re-conviction. It is going to be very difficult to devise training methods directly related to criminal behaviours in addition to emotional or educational difficulties, but the effort is likely to be worthwhile. Even then, a further problem will remain: whereas those suffering from psychological problems typically benefit little from their problems, often seek help without prompting, and usually welcome any improvement, none of these is equally true for offenders. Instead, they often 'benefit', both materially and socially, they typically do not seek help and may well not welcome a reduction in criminal behaviours. The achievement of the last depends partially on whether alternative behaviours have been made available, so as to provide access to the valued reinforcers previously consequent on criminal activities. It is to achieve this alternative access that social, educational, and job training become relevant. But the impact of training is likely to be diminished unless the legally received punishments have proved so aversive as to outweigh the rewards of crime and/or a direct attempt is made to train the offender—with his consent—to avoid the situations in which criminal opportunities occur and the associates who suggest and model such activities are met.

CONCLUDING COMMENT

In this chapter I have reviewed some of the social factors relevant to the process of becoming and remaining an offender. These factors include the unintended negative effects of the persons and institutions delegated to control criminal behaviour, as well as the more obvious social influences favourable to its acquisition, such as association with existing offenders and ineffective parental and school training in pro-social behaviour. I have reviewed some current work aimed at mitigating such unfavourable social factors, interspersed with a number of speculations not yet tested empirically.

It would be incorrect to assume that it is only social factors which are relevant to the development and control of crime, and little or no mention has been made either of personality variables or of direct experience. There is increasing evidence that extreme scores on the major Eysenckian personality dimensions of psychoticism and extraversion are associated with high levels of self-reported offending by schoolchildren (e.g. Allsopp and Feldman, 1975, 1976; Jamison, 1978). It may be that the extreme personality scores are a consequence of criminal experience and not a cause of that experience: longitudinal studies remain to be carried out, but the strength of the association is considerable and requires investigation.

Direct experiences are at least as important a source of learning as the observation of the experiences of others. The two are not in opposition. The sequence may be: exposure to a persuasive communication favourable to offending; the observation of an offence; and finally carrying it out for oneself. Once this has occurred it may well be positively reinforced, by materially beneficial consequences as well as by social attention and approval. Indeed there is some evidence that offending is first learned in group settings, the returns being social, and is then carried out, increasingly by individuals, solely for material rewards (Belson, 1975; May, 1978).

Nor has this chapter touched upon the overriding questions of personal responsibility for actions, including criminal actions, and the civil rights, sometimes competing, of offenders and victims. Yet both are as socially determined and trasmitted as are any other rules and beliefs, and they are crucial in controlling the behaviours of legislators, sentencing agents, and workers in the penal and care systems (Feldman, 1977). Developments in scientific knowledge and professional practice are only just beginning to influence social policy in the field of crime; the next few decades will see a considerable expansion of the mutual influence of law and the social sciences.

REFERENCES

Allsopp, J. F. and Feldman, M. P. (1975). Extraversion, neuroticism and psychoticism and anti-social behaviour in school girls. *Social Behaviour and Personality*, **2,** 184–190.

Allsopp, J. F. and Feldman, M. P. (1976). Item analyses of questionnaire measures of personality and anti-social behaviour in school. *British Journal of Criminology*, **16,** 337–351.

Amir, M. (1972). *Patterns in Forcible Rape*. (Chicago: University of Chicago Press.)

Azrin, N. H., Flores, T., and Kaplan, S. J. (1975). Job finding club: a group assisted programme for obtaining employment. *Behaviour Research and Therapy*, **13,** 17–28.

Azrin, N. H. and Wesolowski, M. D. (1974). Theft reversal: an overcorrection procedure for eliminating stealing by retarded persons. *Journal of Applied Behaviour Analysis*, **7,** 577–582.

Baldwin, J. and McConville, M. (1977). *Negotiated Justice: Pressures on Defendants to Plead Guilty*. (London: Martin Robertson.)

Bandura, A. (1973). *Aggression: A Social Learning Analysis*. (New York: Prentice-Hall.)

Bandura, A. (1977). *Social Learning Theory*. (Englewood Cliffs, N.J.: Prentice Hall.)

Bar-Tal, D. (1976). *Prosocial Behaviour*, (Washington: Hemisphere.)
Bartlett, F. C. (1932). *Remembering*, (Cambridge: Cambridge University Press.)
Bell, R. Q. (1968). A reinterpretation of the direction of effects in studies of socialization. *Psychological Review*, **75,** 81–95.
Belson, W. (1975). *Juvenile Theft: The Causal Factors.* (New York: Harper & Row.)
Belson, W. A. (1978). *Television Violence and the Adolescent Boy.* (Farnborough: Teakfield.)
Bowlby, J. (1946). *Forty-Four Juvenile Thieves.* (London: Baillière, Tindall & Cox.)
Bowlby, J. and Salter-Ainsworth, M. D. (1965). *Child Care and the Growth of Love.* (2nd edn., abridged and edited by Margery Fry). (Harmondsworth: Penguin Books.)
Box, S. (1971). *Deviance, Reality and Society.* (London: Holt, Rinehart & Winston.)
Braukmann, C. J., Fixsen, D. L., Phillips, E. L., and Wolf, M. M. (1975). Behavioural approaches to treatment in the crime and delinquency field. *Criminology*, **13,** 299–331.
Buehler, R. E. (1973). Social reinforcement experimentation in open social systems. In: J. S. Stumphauzer (Ed.), *Behaviour Therapy with Delinquents*, pp. 250–262. (Springfield, Illinois, C. C. Thomas.)
Buehler, R. E., Patterson, G. R., and Furniss, J. M. (1966). The reinforcement of behaviour in institutional settings. *Behaviour Research and Therapy*, **4,** 157–167.
Burt, C. (1923). *The Young Delinquent.* (London: University of London Press.)
Cameron, M. I. (1964). *The Booster and the Snitch.* (New York: Free Press.)
Canning, L. (1977). Sexual and social class differences in adult criminality. Undergraduate research project. University of Birmingham.
Chadwick, E. (1829). Preventive Police. *London Review*, **1,** 301–302.
Chambliss, W. J. (1969). *Crime and the Legal Process.* (New York: McGraw-Hill.)
Chapman, J. I. (1976). An economic model of crime and police: some empirical results. *Journal of Research in Crime and Delinquency*, **13,** 48–63.
Christiansen, K. O. (1969). Recidivism among collaborators. In: M. E. Wolfgang (Ed). *Crime and Culture: Essays on Honour of Thorsten Sellin*, pp. 254–283. (New York: Wiley.)
Clarke, M. J. (1978). White collar crime, occupational crime and legitimacy. *International Journal of Criminology and Penology*, 6, 121–136.
Clarke, R. G. V. (1977). Psychology and crime. *Bulletin of the British Psychological Society*, **30,** 280–283.
Clinard, M. B. (1952). *The Black Market.* (New York: Holt, Rinehart & Winston.)
Clinard, M. B. (1968). *Sociology of Deviant Behaviour*, 3rd edn. (New York: Holt, Rinehart & Winston.)
Cloward, R. A. and Ohlin, L. E. (1960). *Delinquency and Opportunity.* (New York: Free Press.)
Cressey, D. R. (1971). Delinquent and criminal structures. In R. K. Merton and R. Nisbett (Eds.), *Contemporary Social Problems*, 3rd edn., pp. 147–185. (New York: Harcourt Brace Jovanovich.)
Dion, K. (1972). Physical attractiveness and evaluation of children's transgressions. *Journal of Personality and Social Psychology*, **24,** 207–213.
Douglas, J. M. B. and Bromfield, J. M. (1958). *Children Under Five.* (London: Allen and Unwin.)
Douglas, J. W. B. and Ross, J. M. (1968). Characteristics of delinquent boys and their homes. In J. M. Thoday and A. S. Parkes (Eds.), *Genetic and Environmental Influences on Behaviour*, pp. 114–127. (Edinburgh: Oliver & Boyd.)
Efran, M. G. (1974). The effect of physical aggression on the judgement of guilt; interpersonal attraction, and severity of recommended punishment in a simulated jury task. *Journal of Research in Personality*, **8,** 45–54.
Elwork, A. and Sales, B. D. (1978). Psychological research on the jury and trial processes. In: C. Petty, W. Curran, and L. McGarry, (Eds.), *Modern Legal Medicine and Forensic*

Science. (Philadelphia, Pa.: F. A. Davis.)
Ennis, P. H. (1967). *Criminal Victimisation in the United States: A report of a National Survey*. (Washington, DC: US Government Printing Office.)
Erikson, K. T. (1964). Notes on the sociology of deviance. In H. S. Becker (Ed.), *The Other Side: Perceptives on Deviance*, pp. 9–21. (New York: Free Press.)
Eysenck, H. J. and Nias, D. K. B. (1978). *Sex, Violence and the Media*. (London: Temple-Smith.)
Farrington, D. P. (1977). The effects of public labelling. *British Journal of Criminology*, **17,** 112–125.
Farrington, D. P., Osborne, S. G., and West, D. J. (1978). The persistence of labelling effects. *The British Journal of Criminology*, **18,** 277–284.
Feldman, M. P. (1977). *Criminal Behaviour*. (London: Wiley.)
Fixsen, D. L., Phillips, E. L., Harper, D. S., Mesigh, J. A., Timbers, G. D., and Wolf, M. M. (1972). The teaching-family model of group home treatment. Presented at the American Psychological Association Annual Convention, Honolulu, Hawaii.
Fo, W. S. D. and O'Donnell, C. R. (1975). The buddy system: effect of community intervention of delinquent offenders. *Behaviour Therapy*, **6,** 522–524.
Fordham, P. (1968). *The Robbers Tale*. (London: Penguin.)
Fry, L. M. (1976). The impact of formal inmate structure on opposition to staff and treatment goals. *British Journal of Criminology*, **16,** 126–141.
Garrett, M. and Short, J. F. Jr. (1975). Social class and delinquency: predictions and outcomes of police juvenile encounters. *Social Problems*, **22,** 368–382.
Glaser, D., and Rice, K. (1959). Crime, age and employment. *The American Sociological Review*, **24,** 679–686.
Glass, D. C. and Wood, J. D. (1964). Changes in liking as a means of reducing cognitive discrepancies between self-esteem and aggression. *Journal of Personality*, **32,** 531–550.
Glueck, S. and Glueck, E. (1964). Potential juvenile delinquents can be identified. What next?. *The British Journal of Criminology*, **4,** 215–226.
Gold, M. (1966). Undetected delinquent behaviour. *Journal of Research in Crime and Delinquency*, **3,** 27–46.
Gold, M. (1970). *Delinquency in an American City*. (California: Brooks Cole.)
Gold, M. and Williams, J. R. (1969). National study of the aftermath of apprehension. *Prospectus: a Journal of Law Reform*, **3,** 3–12.
Grünhut, M. (1956). *Juvenile Offenders Before the Courts*, pp. 53–84. (Oxford: The Clarendon Press.)
Hall, R. V., Axelrod, S., Tyler, L. G. E., Jones, F. C., and Robertson, R. (1972). Modification of behaviour problems in the home with a parent as observer and experimenter. *Journal of Applied Behaviour Analysis*, **5,** 53–64.
Hargreaves, D. H. (1967). *Social Relations in a Secondary School*. (London: Routledge & Kegan Paul.)
Harper, L. V. (1975). The scope of offspring effects: from caregiver to culture. *Psychological Bulletin*, **82,** 784–801.
Hirschi, T. (1970). *Causes of Delinquency*. (California: University of California Press.)
Hoffman, M. L. and Saltzstein, H. P. (1967). Parent discipline and the child's moral development. *Journal of Personality and Social Psychology*, **5,** 45–57.
Hogarth, J. (1971). *Sentencing as a Human Process*. (Toronto: Toronto University Press.)
Hood, R. (1962). *Sentencing in Magistrates Courts*. (London: Stevens.)
Hood, R. and Sparks, R. (1970). *Key Issues in Criminology*. (London: Weidenfeld & Nicolson.)
Jamison, R. N. (1978). Personality, antisocial behaviour and risk perceptions in adolescents. Unpublished PhD thesis, University of London.

Kalven, H. Jr. and Zeisel, H. (1966). *The American Jury*. (Boston: Little, Brown.)
Klein, M. W. (1974). Labeling, deterrence and recidivism: a study of police dispositions of juvenile offenders. *Social Problems*, **22,** 292–303.
Knight, B. J. and West, D. J. (1975). Temporary and continuing delinquency. *British Journal of Criminology*, **15,** 43–50.
Lemert, E. M. (1951). *Social Pathology*. (New York: McGraw-Hill.)
Leyens, J. P., Camino, L., Parke, R. D., and Berkowitz, L. (1975). Effects of movie violence on aggression in a field setting as a function of group dominance and cohesion. *Journal of Personality and Social Psychology*, **32,** 346–360.
Little, A. (1965). The increase in crime 1952–1962: an empirical analysis of adolescent offenders. *British Journal of Criminology*, **5,** 77–82.
McCord, W., McCord, J., and Zola, I. K. (1959). *Origins of crime: A new Evaluation of the Cambridge-Somerville Youth Study*. (New York: Columbia University Press.)
McGuire, W. J. (1969). The nature of attitudes and attitude change. In: C. Lindzey and E. Aronson (Eds.), *Handbook of Social Psychology*, Vol. 3. (2nd ed.), pp. 136–314. (Reading, Mass.: Addison-Wesley.)
Matza, D. (1969). *Becoming Deviant*. (Englewood Cliffs, NJ: Prentice-Hall.)
May, D. (1978). Juvenile shoplifters and the organisations of store security: a case study in the social construction of delinquency. *International Journal of Criminology and Penology*, **6,** 137–160.
Merton, R. (1969). Social structures and anomie. In: D. R. Cressey and D. A. Wood (Eds.), *Delinquency, Crime and Social Process*, pp. 254–284. (New York: Harper & Row.)
Messick, H. (1971). *Lansky*. (New York: Berkly Publishing Co. Ltd.)
Milgram, S. (1974). *Obedience to Authority*. (London: Tavistock.)
Mischel, W. (1968). *Personality and Assessment*. (New York, Wiley.)
Mitchell, H. E. and Byrne, D. (1973). Minimizing the influence of irrelevant factors in the courtroom: the defendant's character, judge's instructions, and authoritarianism. Unpublished manuscript, Purdue University.
Morgan, P. (1975). *Child Care: Sense and Fable*. (London: Temple-Smith.)
Naess, J. (1959). Mother–child separations and delinquency. *British Journal of Delinquency*, **10,** 22–35.
Nagel, S. S. (1970). The tipped scales of American justice. In: A. S. Blumberg (Ed.), *The Scales of Justice*. (Chicago: Aldine.)
Newman, D. J. (1956). Pleading guilty for considerations: a study of bargain justice. *Journal of Criminal Law, Criminology and Police Science*, **46,** 780–790.
Oaks, D. H. and Lehman, W. (1970). Lawyers for the poor. In: A. S. Blumberg (Ed.),*The Scales of Justice*. (Chicago: Aldine.)
O'Donnell, C., Chambers, E., and Ling, K. (1973). Athletics as reinforcement in a community programmefor academic achievement. Unpublished manuscript, University of Hawaii.
Pease, K., Durkin, P., Earnshaw, I., Payne, D., and Thorpe, J. (1975). *Community Service Orders*. (London: HMSO.)
Phillips, E. L. (1968). Achievement place: token reinforcement procedures in a home style rehabilitation setting for 'pre-delinquent' boys. *Journal of Applied Behaviour Analysis*, **1,** 213–223.
Piliavin, I. and Briar, S. (1964). Police encounters with juveniles. *American Journal of Sociology*, **70,** 206–214.
Polsky, H. W. (1962). *Cottage Six: The Social Systems of Delinquent Boys in Residential Treatment*. (New York: Russell Sage Foundation.)
Quinney, R. (1974). *Critique of Legal Order: Crime Control in Capitalist Society*. (Boston: Little, Brown.)
Reid, I. D., Feldman, M. P., and Ostapiuk, E. B. (1980). The Shape Project for young

offenders: Introduction and overview. Journal of Offender Counselling, 4. (In Press).

Reitzes, D. C. (1955). The effect of social environment upon former felons. *Journal of Criminal Law, Crimonology and Police Science*, **46,** 226–231.

Robin, G. D. (1970). The corporate and judicial dispositions of employee thieves. In E. O. Smigel and H. L. Ross (Eds.), *Crimes Against Bureaucracy*, pp. 124, 146. (New York: Van Nostrand Reinhold.)

Rose, G. (1967). Early identification of delinquents. *British Journal of Criminology*, **7,** 6–35.

Rosenhan, D. L. (1973). On being sane in insane places. *Science*, **179,** 250–258.

Rutter, M. (1971). Parent–child separation: psychological effects on the children. *Journal of Child Psychology and Psychiatry*, **12,** 233–260.

Schwartz, R. D. and Skolnick, J. H. (1964). Two studies of legal stigma. In: H. S. Becker (Ed.), *The Other Side*, pp. 103–118. (New York: Free Press.)

Sealy, A. P. and Gaskell, G. (1978). Negotiated justice. The dynamics of credibility. *Bulletin of the British Psychological Soceity*, **31,** 261–264.

Sigall, H. and Ostrove, N. (1975). Beautiful but dangerous: effects of offender attractiveness and nature of the crime on juridic judgements. *Journal of Personality and Social Psychology*, **31,** 410–414.

Teresa, V. (with Renner, T.) (1973). *My Life in the Mafia*. (New York: Doubleday.)

Tharp, R. G. and Wetzel, R. J. (1969). *Behaviour Modification in the National Environment*. (New York: Academic Press.)

Thomas, C. W. (1973). Prisonization or resocialization? A study of external factors associate with the impact of imprisonment. *Journal of Research in Crime and Delinquency*, **13,** 13–21.

Thomas, D. S. (1925). *Social Aspects of the Business Cycle*. (London: Routledge.)

New York Times (1970). One of fifteen shoplifts, study discloses. December 2nd, C. 45.

Time (1972). Busting Public Servants. April 23rd, p. 26.

Tittle, C. R. and Tittle, D. P. (1964). Social organisation of prisoners: an empirical test. *Social Forces*, **43,** 216.

Toch, H. (1969). *Violent Men*. (Chicago: Aldine.)

Ullmann, L. P. and Kraser, L. (1969). *A Psychological Approach to Abnormal Behaviour*. (New York: Prentice-Hall.)

Wadsworth, M. E. J. (1975). Delinquency in a national sample of children. *British Journal of Criminology*, **15,** 167–174.

Walker, N. (1965). *Crime and Punishment in Great Britain*. (Edinburgh: Edinburgh University Press.)

Weathers, L. and Liberman, R. P. (1975). Contingency contracting with families of delinquent adolescents. *Behaviour Therapy*, **6,** 356–366.

Welford, C. (1975). Labelling theory and criminology: an assessment. *Social Problems*, **22,** 232–345.

Werner, J. S., Minkin, N., Minkin, B., Fixsen, D. L., Phillips. E. L., and Wolf, M. M. (1975). 'Intervention package': an analysis to prepare juvenile delinquents for encounters with police officers. *Criminal Justice and Behaviour*, **2,** 22–36.

West, O. J. and Farrington, D. P. (1977). *The Delinquent Way of Life*. (London: Heinemann.)

Williams, G. (1955). *Current Legal Problems*, **8,** 107–123.

Wilner, A. G., Braukmann, C. J., Kirigin, K. A. M., Fixsen, D. L., Phillips, E. L., and Wolf, M. M. (1977). The training and validation of youth preferred social behaviour of child-care personnel. *Journal of Applied Behaviour Analysis*, **10,** 219–230.

Wilson, J. Q. (1968). The police and the delinquent in two cities. In: S. Wheeler (Ed.), *Controlling Delinquents*, pp. 9–30. (New York: Wiley.)

Wolfgang, M. E. (1958). *Patterns in Criminal Homicide*. (Philadelphia: University of Philadelphia Press.)

Wolfgang, M. E., Figio, R. M., and Sellin, T. (1972). *Delinquency in a Birth Cohort*. (Chicago: University of Chicago Press.)

Wootton, Barbara (1959). *Social Science and Social Pathology*. (London: Allen and Unwin.)

Zingraff, M. T. (1975). Prisonization as an inhibitor of effective socialization. *Criminology*, **13,** 366–388.

The Social Psychology of Psychological Problems
Edited by P. Feldman and J. Orford

8

Handicap

WILLIAM YULE

INTRODUCTION

One of the most important points to remember when considering handicap is that, like all psychosocial phenomena, the quality, extent, and severity of handicap can only be understood in relation to the particular set of social circumstances in which the handicapped person finds himself. This being so, applied psychologists have potentially a great deal to offer in understanding, alleviating, and even preventing handicap.

This chapter examines the concept of handicap and discusses the problems involved in estimating the prevalence of handicapping conditions within a community. To understand some of these difficulties, as well as to prepare the way for a discussion of the role of psycho-social factors in preventing handicap, it is necessary to examine epidemiological methods and concepts of prevention in social medicine.

The prevalence of handicapping conditions in childhood is then examined. Whilst certain relatively common clinical conditions will be described in some detail, a major focus of concern is the extent to which there are common problems across handicapping conditions. In particular, the impact of a handicapped child on family life will be examined, and the needs of both the child and the family considered.

Historically, society has often dealt with handicapped people by segregating them. Currently, the concept of 'community care' holds sway. Some of the issues in the segregation–integration debate will be highlighted by considering the question of integrated education of handicapped children. Finally, the chapter will consider the potential contribution of psychologists at all levels of prevention. These latter considerations, in particular, have implications for the training of applied psychologists. Whilst the bulk of the material is concerned with handicap in childhood, extensions into adult problems are also made.

THE CONCEPT OF HANDICAP

To most people, the concept 'handicap' conjures up a picture of a severely crippled child or adult; someone who has difficulty in moving around independently. Some people will recognize that anyone suffering from a chronic illness is likely to be handicapped, in the sense that their daily living is likely to be somewhat restricted. Increasingly, the term 'mental handicap' is being used instead of such earlier terms as 'mentally subnormal', 'mentally retarded', 'educationally subnormal'. Whatever term is used to describe the problem, it is obvious that people suffering from it are indeed severely handicapped in everyday living.

Less clearly, perhaps, it can be argued that many people suffering from chronic mental illness or behavioural disorders are handicapped. The schizophrenic adult who has to spend considerable periods of life in institutions, and may have to live and work within a sheltered environment, is to a large degree socially handicapped. The child of fourteen who cannot read independently is severely handicapped within the school setting. He may be less handicapped once he leaves school if he gets a job which requires little reading, but even then his private life may be restricted by his failure to learn to read.

Like so many concepts in applied fields, handicap is difficult to define. Indeed a recent government report concluded: 'It is thus impossible to establish precise criteria for what constitutes handicap' (DES, 1978). Nevertheless, the examples given above have sufficient communality to warrant retaining the concept.

In the field of medical and physical problems, the issues are somewhat clearer than in the field of behavioural, psychiatric, educational, and social problems. There, it has been found helpful to distinguish between 'defect', 'disability' and 'handicap'.

> A *defect* is some imperfection, impairment or disorder of the body, intellect or personality. It can, when viewed from an objective standpoint, be minor, even trivial, or it may be gross. But in itself, the word carries no necessary implication of malfunctioning or of an adverse effect upon the individual. A *disability* is a defect which does result in some malfunctioning but which does not necessarily affect the individual's normal life. A *handicap* is a disability which for a substantial period or permanently retards, distorts or otherwise adversely affects normal growth, development or adjustment to life. (Younghusband *et al.*, 1970.)

Pless and Pinkerton (1975) make the same point by noting that the defect or impairment operates at the *biological* level; disability is the direct behavioural manifestation of impairment and operates at a *personal* level; and handicap is the net effect of disability on the performance of specific activities. Handicap therefore operates at the *social* level. As they say, 'Handicap is a term that should be reserved for the consequences of disablement *in relation to the performance of specific goal directed activities*. ... It refers ... to the extent to which patients are disadvantaged in the performance of some action' (Pless and Pinkerton, 1975; italics added). Thus, if handicap is defined in terms of thwarting goal-directed activities, then it can be more easily measured. The goals can be set personally, or are those set normally by the rest of society. In this way, the concept of handicap is easily extended to deal with the effects of mental illness and behavioural dysfunction even though the biological defect is either unknown or irrelevant.

It follows from the above analysis that the severity of a handicap can only be assessed in relation to a specified social setting. For example, a person who is born blind will have a recognizable disability and will also be handicapped to some extent. The severity of the handicap will depend on whether or not they can learn braille, whether they can work with a guide-dog, whether they can use one of the new print-reading devices, and so on. In other words, the impact of the disability will be affected by the environmental demands. Difficulty in reading will constitute a handicap in a society which aims at universal literacy, but not in a society where reading is restricted to a privileged few. At a more personal level, a musician who loses his hearing is more likely to be handicapped by that acquired disability than are others.

Handicap is not, then, an inevitable consequence of being born with a defect or of developing a disability. It depends on factors within the person and within his social environment. More importantly, handicap should not be thought of as a generalized consequence. It is misleading to categorize people as either normal or handicapped, as if the latter group were handicapped in the same ways and to the same extent. Such loose and prejudicial reasoning leads to the sort of situation where people suffering from, say, epilepsy get regarded as 'epileptics' and are soon seen as having 'typical epileptic personalities'. As will be seen later, the same attitudes of society led to mentally handicapped people being regarded as totally disabled. By focusing on their identifying disabilities, the presence of abilities, and how to capitalize on these, was ignored. Nevertheless, it is useful to define handicap in terms of the specific goals which the person is prevented from attaining normally. This helps underline the point that we are discussing people who are handicapped in attaining goals, rather than talking about 'handicapped people' as if the label helped us to understand their predicament.

SOME EPIDEMIOLOGICAL CONSIDERATIONS

Having formulated a rough but functional definition of handicap, the next question is to consider how to plan and deliver services in such a way that the impact of a disability is lessened, and the handicap is reduced. To do this, one needs reliable information on the nature and severity of handicap facing individuals within a given community. Planners need to have some idea of the numbers of individuals who are faced with particular problems. Such information is best obtained from *epidemiological* studies.

It is not enough to know how many people are already receiving services. To some extent, people come forward to utilize the services available. For example, in 1946 some 10,000 children awaited admission to ESN schools. Twenty years later, following the provision of 34,000 places, the number awaiting admission was still

10,000 (Rigley, 1968). Even allowing for increases in population, it is clear that the earlier waiting list seriously underestimated the need for places. Administrative prevalence rates (i.e. the number of cases already known to the responsible authorities) are only rough approximations to the true prevalence rates—the numbers actually requiring services. Epidemiology is the technology developed within a social medicine framework to help investigate questions on the prevalence, distribution, and characteristics of particular problems within a community.

As Gruenberg (1964) puts it:

> ... epidemiology makes a contribution to what can be called 'community diagnosis'. The purpose of such studies of the cases of disorder in a community is to provide quantitative information to (i) estimate the size, nature and location of the community's problems, (ii) identify the component parts of the problem, (iii) locate populations at special risk of being affected, and (iv) identify opportunities for preventive work and needs for treatment and special services. Thus, epidemiology serves as the diagnostician for the official or community leader who is practising community medicine, social medicine, public health or public welfare. The nature of the community's health problems is approached diagnostically with epidemiological methods.

These far-sighted views have echoes in the recent DHSS Report of the Committee on Child Health Services (The Court Report; DHSS, 1976). They propose the setting up of interdisciplinary district handicap teams who, in addition to a clinical function, would have a duty to be '... involved with others at district and area level in epidemiological surveys of need; to monitor the effectiveness of the district service for handicapped children; to present data and suggestions for the development of the service; and to maintain the quality of its institutions' (DHSS, 1976, para. 14.24). Thus, the psychologist member of the district handicap team will need skills not only in advising others on the treatment of handicapped children but also in epidemiological and other social intervention techniques.

Epidemiology is much more than mere head-counting. To be useful, surveys must have clear objectives. For some purposes, large surveys using simple questionnaires may give useful information; for other purposes, surveys of small, clearly defined populations using intensive interviewing techniques will be more appropriate. In both instances the investigators will have to define as objectively as possible the variables in which they are interested.

Rare conditions, such as early infantile autism, are more difficult to study than commoner conditions such as reading disorders. In the latter case it is theoretically feasible to study a large group of children over many years so as to investigate the natural history of the disorder and its impact on the individual. In the case of autism, this occurs in about 4 to 5 cases per 10,000 births, so it is not economically feasible to study tens of thousands of children in order to identify a large enough group of autistic children. This means that groups of autistic children will be formed from already identified cases and this strategy introduces all sorts of referral and case-identification biases.

The point that is being made is that epidemiology is a sophisticated methodology. To use it to the benefit of handicapped people, professionals need to understand its strengths and limitations. There is no space to elaborate on these further in this chapter and readers are referred elsewhere for a consideration of some of the issues (Rutter *et al.*, 1970b; Rutter, 1977).

Some conditions are easier to define than others. It is probably easier to define most medical disorders and their associated disabilities than it is to define educational and psychiatric disabilities. For example, it is relatively easy to agree criteria on what constitutes a squint or German measles. It is more difficult to get agreement on what constitutes a disabling psychiatric condition or, say, a severe spelling disorder. In large part, this emphasizes the fact that the latter type of disorders are defined in terms of criteria which are relative to social expectations rather than any absolute criteria. Perhaps this is why the pioneering work of Burt (1925, 1937) into estimating service needs from epidemiological studies was not followed up until 40 years later.

It is difficult enough to get agreement on what constitutes disorder and disability. It is more difficult to get agreement on what constitutes handicap. For example, it is clear that the presence of a mentally handicapped child in a family imposes many stresses on family life. How can these best be measured? Without good measures of the quality of ordinary family life in all its diversities, the problem is difficult. Nonetheless, Tizard and Grad (1961) made an important contribution by setting up a relatively simple index of problems facing families of the mentally handicapped. They considered aspects as diverse as income, overcrowding, housing problems, social contacts outside the home, and the health of the family members. Simply getting objective data on areas of family life indicated that two-thirds of the families with their mentally handicapped child living at home faced three or more severe problems. More sophisticated measures may be desirable, but even the simple measures underlined the plight of the families of mentally handicapped children.

CONCEPTS OF PREVENTION

Historically, applied psychologists have made more of a contribution to the treatment of individuals with already developed conditions—particularly psychiatric, educational, and mental handicap—and much less to the prevention of the problems. This situation is changing and there is currently a great deal of interest in the potential of psychological and particularly behavioural methods for preventing disability and handicap (Albee and Joffe, 1977; Yule, 1977; Gelfand and Hartmann, 1977; Poser and Hartman, 1979). Caplan (1964) distinguishes between three temporal stages in prevention. Within social medicine these stages—primary, secondary, and tertiary—are usually considered in relation to the development of disease processes. As Cooper and Morgan (1973) define them:

Primary prevention: Here one is concerned with preventing the disease occurring in the first place. To do this effectively, one requires considerable information on the cause of the disease.

Secondary prevention: Here one is concerned with the early detection or diagnosis and the early and effective treatment of established disease. If this is successful, one should prevent the affected individual from developing further undesirable effects.

Tertiary prevention: When one has been unable to prevent individuals contracting diseases and has also been unsuccessful in coping with them early on, at least one can try to prevent the development of further chronic handicap. For example, where a physical disability leads to institutionalization, one can at least try to prevent the development of typical institutional dependency and lack of self-respect.

This conceptualization of preventive measures has been helpful in social medicine, especially when considering the disabilities and handicaps associated with disease processes. The three levels of prevention are less easily applied to psychiatric, behavioural, emotional, and educational problems. All these psychosocial conditions have multifactorial causes. For example, the connection between reading failure and anti-social disorder is probably as well documented as is the recognition of the great difficulty in treating children who have anti-social problems. In so far as there is a *causal* connection between the two disorders (Yule, 1974; Rutter and Yule, 1970), in most cases the reading failure has preceded the appearance of the anti-social disorder. It follows that better teaching of reading will prevent a proportion of anti-social disorders from appearing. Such intervention would consist of better teaching of reading so that fewer children develop difficulties (primary prevention for reading failure), or remedial reading help (secondary prevention for reading failure). This latter would also consist of primary prevention for the expected anti-social disorder. Despite these obvious difficulties in applying Caplan's conceptual model to other than physical disease categories (Butollo, 1977; Gelfand and Hartmann, 1977), no wider alternative conceptual models within the behavioural sciences exist at present.

The World Health Organization (WHO, 1976) recently demonstrated that it can be a useful exercise to apply concepts of prevention across the whole range of disabling conditions in an effort to identify potential areas for intervention and priorities for such intervention. As the WHO report states:

> Disease oriented medicine needs to be complemented by disability oriented medicine, and it should be realized in every country that the objectives of medicine are not only the prevention and care of disease but also the restoration of the individual as far as possible to normal social function.

Thus, as the major killer diseases are brought under control, society needs to be more concerned with the prevention of residual handicap.

THE NATURE AND PREVALENCE OF HANDICAPPING CONDITIONS

It is widely recognized that the incidence and prevalence of disorders and disability varies from one part of the country to another. Nevertheless, it is still of some value to consider national prevalence estimates in order to gain a perspective on the relative frequency of occurrence of different conditions. To do this, handicapping conditions of childhood and of adulthood are considered separately in the next few pages. Having considered a broad spectrum of disorders, some will be examined in greater detail to explore further the impact the disability may have on the lives of the afflicted.

1. Disorders of childhood

The average health district will contain about 60,000 children under 16 years of age. Of these, prevalence studies suggest that:

> about 1,125 children aged 0–4 years will be moderately or severely handicapped by either physical (somatic), motor, visual, hearing and communication, or learning disorders which require special health care: 140 of them might need to attend a special school, full-time or part-time according to their age. 4,125 children of compulsory school age will be similarly handicapped. Of these 700 might need to attend special schools. (DHSS, 1976, para. 14.4.)

These estimates *exclude* estimates of psychiatric disorders in childhood. As the Report later states:

> Well-based epidemiological studies demonstrate that, at a conservative estimate, over the course of one year between 5 and 10% of children have [psychiatric] disorders of sufficient severity significantly to handicap them in their every day life ... [of these] ... at least a third to a half require some kind of therapeutic intervention. (para. 15.7.)

Clearly, there is an enormous challenge to any civilized society to alleviate and prevent problems which affect so many of its children.

Another way of looking at the total problem is to consider the type of handicapping conditions in more clinical terms. Table 8.1 is adapted from Appendix Q of the Seebohm Report (DHSS, 1968), and Table 1 of the Younghusband Report (1970), and shows the estimated rate per 1000 for a variety of conditions. Overall, the two sets of figures show remarkable agreement. Many readers may be surprised to discover how common asthma is in childhood, affecting some 2–2½ per cent of children. However, the largest single group of handicaps in school-age children involve the mildly and severely mentally retarded. Speech defects are very common at age five, but rapidly diminish in numbers and severity thereafter.

Table 8.1 Prevalence Estimates of Handicapping Conditions in Childhood

Condition	*Rate per 1000 (aged 5–15 years)*	*National Child Development Study (1958 Cohort) (aged 7 years)*
Blind and partially sighted	1.2	1.9
Deaf and partially hearing	1.2	1.1
Epileptic	7.2	6.2
Speech defects	27.0 (at age 5 only)	23.3
Cerebral palsy	3.0	2.2
Heart disease	2.4	3.6
Orthopaedic condition	3.4	4.6
Asthma	23.2	27.4
Eczema	10.4	24.7
Diabetes	1.2	0.2
Other physical handicaps	6.7	6.7
Severely subnormal	3.5	2.7
(NB mildly subnormal	25.0)	—

The apparently slight disagreements in prevalence rates have enormous implications for planning services. Take for example the differing estimates of 7.2 per 1000 and 6.2 per 1000 for the prevalence of epilepsy. In the average health district this means the difference between 432 and 372 children with epilepsy—a considerable difference if special resources are needed to alleviate the disabilities concerned.

Let us look more closely at one set of epidemiological studies of childhood disorders which examined not only the prevalence of a variety of conditions but also their interrelationship and nature. The Isle of Wight surveys (Rutter *et al.*, 1970b) studied in detail two complete age-groups of children aged 10 and 11 years—some 2334 children in all. The investigators were interested in four broad groups of handicaps—intellectual retardation, educational disorders, psychiatric disorders, and physical disorders.

(a) Mental handicap A total of 2.53 per cent of the population were found to have IQs below 70. Of the children in the 50–70 IQ range, as many were functioning well in ordinary junior schools as were placed in the ESN special school. This again illustrates the point that whereas an IQ in this range may be termed a disability, it is not necessarily handicapping. Kushlick (1961, 1966) has argued that IQ tests alone are not helpful in establishing prevalence rates since, by 15–19 years, many people regarded as mildly subnormal survive in the community without extra help. Since

they are deficient in precisely those skills that are at a premium in school, they can meet the other demands of society once the demands of school are over.

Severe mental handicap, roughly equivalent to IQs of 50 and below, has been estimated at about 3.7 per 1000 by a number of different studies in many countries (Rutter *et al.*, 1970a; Kushlick, 1966; New York State, 1955; Lemkau *et al.*, 1943). Severe mental handicap occurs evenly across all social classes, and evidence of brain damage is present in the majority (Crome, 1960). The aetiology is unknown in most cases, but the largest known cause is the chromosomal abnormality, Down's syndrome, which occurs in about 1 in 600 births.

In terms of handicap, severely mentally retarded children are prevented from reaching many of the goals of independent living. The lower the child's intelligence, the more likely he is to have multiple defects and disabilities. However, as the Wessex survey showed (Kushlick and Blunden, 1974), two-thirds of severely mentally handicapped children are continent, can walk, and have no severe behaviour problems. The problems facing their families are immense (Carr, 1974, 1975), but with suitable help, many more could be kept in the community.

(b) Educational disorders Two types of reading disorder were studied. 6.6 per cent of children were found to be backward readers, scoring at least 2 years 4 months below their age level; 3.7 per cent were found to be severely under-achieving and said to have specific reading retardation (Rutter and Yule, 1975; Yule, 1967). When these children were followed up at the end of their secondary schooling, it was found that neither group had made much progress in reading in four years (Yule, 1973). Even though, as a group, the retarded readers were of average intelligence, at age 14½ they rarely read any newspapers or books, and over two-thirds of them intended leaving school at the earliest opportunity. Only 15 per cent of them (compared with 60 per cent of a random control group) aimed to take any examination (Yule and Rutter, 1976).

Clearly, poor readers emerge from the school system handicapped both educationally and socially in the sense that their vocational opportunities have been significantly reduced. When it is realized that the rates of reading problems are three times higher in an inner city area (Berger *et al.*, 1975), then prevention of reading failure must be seen as a priority in education.

(c) Psychiatric disorders In the Isle of Wight studies, a psychiatric disorder was:

> judged to be present when there was an abnormality of behaviour, emotions, or relationships which was continuing up to the time of assessment and was sufficiently marked and sufficiently prolonged to cause handicap to the child himself and/or distress or disturbance in the family or community. (Rutter *et al.*, 1970b, p. 148.)

Overall, it was estimated that some 6.8 per cent of the 10–11-year-old children had such a psychiatric disorder; 2.5 per cent had neurotic problems; and those with anti-social or mixed conduct/neurotic disorders accounted for 4.0 per cent.

One of the notable findings of the study was that there was very little overlap between those children who manifested disorder at home and those who manifested it at school. Neurotic or anti-social disorder was found in both settings, but the degree of situation specificity was remarkable. This has implications for both intervention and prevention. Any comprehensive service for child mental health must work with both the parent and the school system.

(d) Physical disorders In the Isle of Wight study, notice was taken of:

> physical disorders which (a) were of a type which in childhood usually lasted at least one year (i.e. were chronic), (b) were associated with persisting or recurrent handicap of some kind and (c) were known to have been present during the twelve months preceding the survey (i.e. was currently present). (Rutter *et al.*, 1970b, p. 275.)

Of the children studied, 5.7 per cent were identified as having a chronic severe physical disorder.

Asthma was the commonest disorder, being found in 2.3 per cent. Although these children were brighter than average, they still had double the expected rate of specific reading retardation. Epilepsy occurred in 8.9 per 1000 children, and these children, too, were disabled in their reading. Cerebral palsy was found in 2.6 per 1000 children, and other brain disorders were found in 1.7 per 1000. In general, whenever the brain and central nervous systems are involved, the child is likely to have more than one handicap. Most severely subnormal children have at least one additional physical defect.

(e) Overall prevalence Looking at the overlap amongst the four broad groups of handicap studied in the Isle of Wight, the following picture emerged:

one handicap only	120.8 per 1000
two handicaps	30.5 per 1000
three handicaps	7.8 per 1000
four handicaps	2.3 per 1000

This means that 161.4 per 1000 children at the end of their junior schooling have at least one major handicap of educational concern. In other words, 16 per cent, or *one child in six* in the total population at these ages is handicapped to a significant extent. Nationally, these figures are likely to prove underestimates. Certainly we now know that the rate of specific reading retardation is higher in inner city areas.

Before looking more closely at some examples of handicapping conditions and at what they mean to the children and their families, let us briefly consider some data on the prevalence of handicap in adulthood.

2. Disorders in adulthood

It is difficult to obtain comprehensive data on the prevalence of handicaps in adulthood. Too often, medical and functional criteria alone have been used in establishing prevalence rates and too little attention has been paid to the social and emotional aspects of disability.

A recent working party on the training for social work with handicapped people (CCETSW, 1974) looked at the social work needs of adults suffering from one or more chronic disabling conditions. It concerned itself primarily with potential clients who, as a result of some chronic impairment, were disadvantaged by one or more of the following:

> Inability to come up to overall expectations within their social group, or indeed to meet their own.
>
> In need of assistance in looking after themselves and/or running their homes.
>
> Inability wholly to support themselves and their families by their employment.
>
> Ability to cope independently in the home or in employment but only at considerable emotional and personal cost to themselves and/or others.

After considering data from many surveys, they concluded that 2.8 per cent of all those living at home and aged over 16 years suffer some kind of marked impairment. Of these, 4 per 1000 require special care, 9 per 1000 are severely handicapped and 15 per 1000 are appreciably handicapped. However, handicap is not evenly spread across all age-groups. The incidence rises sharply in the over 65s. For every 1000 old

Table 8.2 Approximate numbers of adults at home with handicaps (Great Britain)

	CCETSW Estimates		Harris Estimates
	Number	Percentage of population	Number
Physically handicapped	1,288,000	2.4	1,750,000
Blind and partially sighted	132,118	0.2	215,000
Totally deaf	58,000	0.1	46,000
Hard of hearing	1,500,000	2.9	—
Chronically mentally ill	500,000	0.9	72,000
Mentally retarded*	150,000	0.3	27,000
Chronic alcoholics	365,000	0.7	—
Epilepsy	290,000	0.5	21,000
Other	—	—	940,748
TOTAL	4,333,118	8.0	3,071,748

* This figure excludes those in residential institutions.
Adapted from CCETSW, 1974, Paper 5.

folk who survive beyond this age and remain in the community, 18 require special care, 34 are severely handicapped and 58 are appreciably handicapped.

Estimates of the numbers suffering specific problems vary, as Table 8.2 shows. The table also shows some measure of agreement in terms of rank ordering the groups of handicapping condition, but amazing disagreement in terms of actual numbers. In large part, this is due to the Harris *et al.* (1971) study's definitions which were primarily concerned with impairment of locomotor function. However, these workers attempted to estimate the severity of the handicaps they did study. They rated them on a three-point scale, viz.:

special care—constant care or supervision every day and practically every night;
severely handicapped—difficulty in doing everything, or most things difficult and some impossible;
appreciably handicapped—able to do a fair amount for themselves but may need help with certain things.

When the handicaps listed in Table 8.2 are subdivided both into finer clinical subgroups and by severity of handicap, it becomes clear that simple headcounts are not a sufficient guide to estimating need for services. For example, the commonest impairment in adults is arthritis, yet less than half of these people require assistance from others, and only 5 per cent need 'special care'. In contrast multiple sclerosis, which affects 8 per 1000, and Parkinson's disease, which affects 7 per 1000, both result in severe degrees of handicap. Between 70 and 80 per cent of people afflicted by their conditions require assistance from others. The deaf, the blind, the mentally ill, and the mentally retarded all need more continuity of care than other groups.

In summary, handicap clearly continues into adulthood. New handicapping conditions arise, and the over-65s experience a particularly high level of handicapping conditions: Different sorts of clinical conditions give rise to varying degrees of need for outside assistance. Unfortunately, data are inadequate to allow one to present more than a sketchy picture of the total situation.

3. Some clinical conditions

Statistics of the sort quoted above often appear dry and boring. One can easily forget that one is discussing the needs of real people—in fact people who have more unmet needs than most. To remedy this, and to give a feel for the impact which a chronic disability can have on a child and his family, let us examine some specific clinical conditions in greater detail.

(a) Spina bifida After cerebral palsy, spina bifida is the second major physically handicapping condition in childhood. Its incidence is relatively high in Britain, occurring in about 2.4 per 1000 livebirths, and there are marked regional variations. For reasons that are not yet clear, but which may be linked to causal factors, the incidence is higher in the north and the west of the islands.

Spina bifida is 'a developmental defect of the spinal column in which the arches of one or more of the spinal vertebrae have failed to fuse together so that the spine is ... split in two' (Anderson and Spain, 1977). The spinal cord or its membranes protrude through this gap. Where the spinal cord protrudes (the condition is then called myelomeningocele), the child will usually be unable to move those muscles which are served by nerves lower down the spinal cord than the point of the lesion. Equally, the child receives no sensations from below that point, so that pressure sores can be a common problem. Incontinence of bladder and bowel occurs in most children with myelomeningocele. About half the children can learn to cope with their incontinence problems, but it all adds to the strain on the family. It also adds to the interpersonal problems of the young child. Many have to wear special urinary incontinence appliances, and this can cause embarrassment in school and in more intimate circumstances.

Hydrocephalus is an associated condition in four out of five babies with myelomeningocele. The more the head expands, the greater the probability of brain damage. Until the mid-1950s, most children born with spina bifida died within weeks of birth, either as a result of infection or as a result of the hydrocephalus. Then the engineer father of a hydrocephalic child, in association with a surgeon, developed a valve which allowed the fluid on the brain to recirculate and so prevented the further cerebral complications. The effect of these developments has been dramatic: now nearly 50 per cent of those born will survive the first year of life, and 9 in 10 of these will stay alive at least until six years. Overall, there are about 4000 children with spina bifida in England and Wales.

The most obvious restriction on the life of the child with spina bifida is that on mobility. The extent of his motor handicap will depend on the position of the lesion. Between one-third and one-half of those with myelomeningocele have no effective use of their lower limbs and most of the others have significant locomotor problems. These can be alleviated, to differing extents, by the use of aids varying from crutches to specially built motor vehicles.

Clearly, spina bifida is associated with more than simple motor handicap. The problems of incontinence have already been mentioned. In some cases there are also associated intellectual handicaps. Even those children who have been treated since birth have, on average, an intelligence level in the dull normal to ESN (mild) range. As Anderson and Spain (1977) demonstrate, there is an association between the presence of hydrocephalus and intellectual impairment, with verbal skills being especially affected.

It seems almost inevitable that children with such severe physical handicaps become more dependent on their parents than most. This becomes a difficulty in later years when the adolescent want to develop personal independence. According to Dorner (1975, 1976), most of the spina bifida teenagers he interviewed had a good relationship with their parents but complained that parents did too much for them. Two-thirds complained of real feelings of misery—a rate significantly greater than in the normal population of $14\frac{1}{2}$-year-olds where 41 per cent had such recurring feelings (Rutter *et al.*, 1976). More girls than boys admitted to suicidal feelings, and in girls the feelings of misery were related to social isolation. Outside school, many teenagers had no social contacts, and this was particularly true of those who had attended special schools. Nearly all the teenagers expressed interest in the opposite sex, but only a small minority had ever had a heterosexual friendship. The issue of sex and the handicapped will be discussed briefly later.

One of the strains that having a child with spina bifida places on the family is the large number of hospitalizations for complex surgery. It is estimated that by four years of age the children have experienced an average of six hospital placements (Anderson and Spain, 1977). The potential effects of frequent hospital admissions below five years is now well documented (Douglas, 1975; Quinton and Rutter, 1976), but the immediate impact is that of increased worry and concern for survival. As with other handicapping conditions, parents complained that breaking the news of their child's disability was handled very badly (see later). Later, the children's locomotor problems have a very disrupting effect on family life. Families often have to restrict the number of occasions they go out, particularly if only one adult is available to lift the child. Dealing with incontinence and visiting hospitals both bring their own toll on the parents. The mothers of spina bifida children show a higher rate of stress symptoms than do the mothers of non-handicapped children (Tew and Laurence, 1975; Spain, 1973; Dorner, 1975). However, there is no good evidence that marital problems and divorce rates are higher among the parents of children with spina bifida (Stevenson *et al.*, 1978).

In spina bifida, then, one can see the complex relationship between a defect, a disability and the extent of the resulting handicap. The incidence varies across the country, but presumably not greatly across time. The invention of the shunt to alleviate hydrocephalus, the use of improved antibiotics to combat infection, and the earlier and improved surgical intervention, all resulted in a significantly higher proportion of children surviving to adulthood—but at what cost? Despite developments in prosthetic devices, no one can doubt that children with spina bifida remain severely handicapped in many areas of everyday living. Their families have had to shoulder an enormous burden throughout their childhood. With the advent of amniocentesis (see later under 'prevention') this picture will dramatically alter yet again, illustrating that 'handicap' is not a static phenomenon, but is intimately related to complex changes in society.

(b) Cerebral palsy 'Cerebral palsy is a disorder of movement and posture resulting from a permanent, non-progressive defect or lesion of the immature brain' (Bax, 1964). Cerebral palsy is the result of a number of problems arising during pregnancy and the perinatal period. Some, such as rhesus incompatibility with associated jaundice, can be prevented by better obstetric monitoring and care. Overall, cerebral palsy occurs in about 2.0–2.5 per 1000 (Rutter *et al.*, 1970a). About 60 per cent of the cerebral palsied population have spasticity—a pyramidal lesion resulting in

increased muscle tone. In turn, this produces the characteristic stiff and jumpy movements of the limbs. The other two subgroups of cerebral palsy are: athetosis—increased involuntary, uncoordinated movements; and, less commonly, ataxia—gross clumsiness associated with damage to the cerebellum.

In the Isle of Wight study (Rutter *et al.*, 1970a), children with cerebral palsy were found to be somewhat more handicapped than children with other brain disorders. A total of 37 per cent were found to have a severe handicap, defined as: 'Substantial help needed with daily activities such as dressing, undressing, washing, bath, and feeding. The rating was also applicable where the child required special transport or was unable to go out unaccompanied.' Only one-third of the children with cerebral palsy attended ordinary day-schools. Nearly half of the children were in schools or institutions for the mentally handicapped. Although 24 per cent of the children had IQs above 100, 54 per cent had IQs below 70. This is similar to the findings of other studies. Of those testable, 41 per cent of the cerebral palsied children were more than two years retarded in their reading. Thus not only are they, as a group, intellectually retarded, they are also significantly underachieving.

In the Isle of Wight study, the impact of the handicapped child on the family was assessed by interviewing the parents about the extent to which the family's routine had had to be altered to meet the child's special needs; the extent to which the child's handicap was thought to be responsible for impaired social relations among members of the family; and the extent of the family's dissatisfaction with services. It was found that, not surprisingly, the more severe the child's handicap, the more areas of family life were disrupted. Over half the families with cerebral palsied children reported difficulties in going out with the child; nearly as many had problems going out without their child; one-third complained about the length of time taken to visit the clinic. Of the parents of cerebral palsied children 28 per cent reported some increase in parental quarrelling, compared with only 8 per cent of the parents of asthmatic children. A majority of parents were dissatisfied with existing services. Even so, the mothers of cerebral palsied children did not report any increase in their own symptoms of ill-health.

These findings are closely parallel to those of Hewett's (1970) study of young cerebral palsied children in Nottingham. She reports that half the parents whose children had special equipment found difficulty in using it. Even though twice as many cerebral palsied as normal children had daily temper tantrums, a third of the parents (compared with 3 per cent of the controls) never smacked their child. Twice as many of the physically handicapped children shared their parents' bedroom. Thus it can be concluded that the presence of a cerebral palsied child does substantially interfere with normal family living. Both the child and other family members may have their social outings curtailed. Some of the particular issues relating to the education of cerebral palsied children are discussed by Haskell *et al.* (1977) and by Anderson (1973), and will not be repeated here. Suffice it to say that the special physiotherapy and the skills needed to deal with associated perceptual handicaps will rarely be available in ordinary day-schools.

(c) Juvenile rheumatoid arthritis—(Still's disease) Juvenile rheumatoid arthritis (sometimes known as Still's disease) is a very painful disorder. Pain can be controlled by drugs, but with the risk of side-effects. It is a chronic disorder which affects about 1 child in 1500, and girls are affected more than boys. The disease has a variable onset, a capricious course and about two-thirds of the children eventually recover. However, the extent of the recovery depends on the amount of damage to the joints in the intervening years. The children's growth is affected and their bones may become deformed. The intermittent 'flare-ups', characteristic of the disease, interfere with school attendance (Haskell *et al.*, 1977; Travis, 1976).

This disease, out of the many others affecting children and causing handicap, is mentioned here for a number of reasons. Firstly, it is a chronic handicapping condition, affecting substantial numbers of children, and yet its educational and social consequences have been little studied. Secondly, the burden of treatment placed on the families raises some real challenges to applied psychologists.

The problem of treatment is this: the disease has a variable painful course; if the child's joints are kept mobile, then, when the disease burns itself out, the child retains that degree of mobility. Once joints seize up, the handicap is magnified. To maintain mobility, each affected joint has to be exercised daily for a number of hours. Such exercise is both monotonous and painful. For the young child, the certainty of immediate pain is hardly compensated for by the uncertain promise of future mobility. The harassed parent is placed in the unenviable position of insisting that the exercises are done despite the child's protests. For the applied psychologist, the challenge is to devise ways of motivating the child to carry out the exercises so that the least pain is experienced in the pursuit of maximum exercise of each joint. Since the condition is chronic, a simple set of games is insufficient, as novelty will wear off, but a series of alternative, pleasurable routines might be developed. In any case, placing the parents in the dilemma of giving them the responsibility for ensuring that their child carries out the exercises without simultaneously providing them with the means to do so makes a mockery of the concept of parents as partners in treatment.

(d) Other handicapping conditions There are many other medical conditions associated with handicap in children and adults. Anyone working in the area needs to be familiar with the specific attributes of each condition and the demands these make on the affected individual and his family. The three examples given above highlight some of the problems posed.

One aspect that is not directly touched upon in these conditions is the experience of death. This is a common occurrence in many children with major chronic diseases, such as chronic kidney disease, cystic fibrosis, and leukaemia. There are problems both in helping the family and the child face impending death (Travis, 1976), and it seems to be only relatively recently that the taboo on discussing these issues has been raised. In leukaemia, for example, Travis (1976) reports that the dying child usually wants someone to remain with him, but this is very difficult for parents to cope with. If anything, parents and staff ignore the child as much as possible. Clearly this is an area where applied psychologists have a great deal to offer. Developmental psychology contains a small literature relating to the child's understanding of death (Childers and Wimmer, 1971; Koocher, 1974 ⟷), and this, together with a better understanding of bereavement and mourning, should form the basis for developing helpful techniques for comforting families in this sad situation. Unfortunately, at present, there appear to be only crude models based on simplistic psychodynamic theories, and it is time that parents were offered more realistic help.

SOME GENERAL ASPECTS AND CONSIDERATIONS

So far, in this chapter, the size of the problem of handicap facing any community has been estimated. Some of the major handicapping conditions have been described in detail so as to give a feel of the impact the disability may have on the individual. Different disabilities have unique personal impacts. In this section, some of the more general aspects of handicap which cut across many conditions will be considered.

(a) Impact on the family Various studies already cited (Rutter *et al.*, 1970a, 1970b; Hewett, 1970; Carr, 1975) testify to the impact that the birth of a handicapped child can have on family life. Ordinary routines of everyday living can be disrupted; physical strain is placed on parents who have to lift immobile children; the child's special needs may make babysitting arrangements difficult, and so the parents' social life is curtailed; alterations to the home may cause extra expense; and so on. Families can bear a heavy burden, and yet, despite complaints about lack of resources, most families survive the strains.

However, almost universally, there is criticism about the manner in which the parents were told of their child's disability. Both the Court Committee and the Warnock Committee received harrowing evidence from parents testifying to how badly this had been managed by professionals of all disciplines. Both Hannam (1975) and Carr (1975) quote verbatim records of parents of mentally handicapped children who were told of their child's handicap in the brusquest, cruellest of ways.

Parents prefer to be told earlier rather than late (Carr, 1975). In fact, many parents suspect something is wrong before they are told 'officially'. Even so, the news still comes as a shock. In the case of deafness, it is often parents who suspect a problem first and spend many crucial months trying to persuade professionals that something is wrong. In Freeman's (1977) epidemiological studies, there was a delay of 9.7 months in the case of the profoundly deaf and of 16.4 months in the severely deaf between the parents' first suspecting something was wrong and the deafness being diagnosed. These parents were not shocked by having their suspicions confirmed. By contrast, there was a much shorter delay in diagnosing blindness, and parents were shocked to have the diagnosis made.

A number of issues need clarification. Who should break the news to parents? How soon should this be done? How should the news be broken? At present it is no one person's or profession's duty. Clearly it is wrong for any professional to brush aside a parents' worry with 'It's not my job to discuss that with you.' Moreover, the telling should not be a once-and-for-all affair. Parents need time to adjust to the information; they need opportunities to discuss the information and its implications for their child's future. It is not at all clear how best parents can be helped at this time. Some workers draw parallels with grief reactions and say that a mourning process should be facilitated. Others concentrate on helping parents to face the future by encouraging skills of coping with practical problems. From the reported dissatisfaction of parents with the way the solution is handled at present, there is an urgent need for different approaches to be evaluated experimentally.

A second set of shared family needs has to do with information—information about the disability, its course and prognosis, the sort of help available, advice on schooling, advice on residential services where appropriate. In the future, parents can look to the district handicap team as a source of such information. There are many voluntary societies which act as information clearing houses as well as pressure groups. Parents need to be pointed in their direction. Booklets such as *Help Starts Here* (Voluntary Council for the Handicapped, 1976) are invaluable in alerting parents to their rights. Finally, many parents will require sensitive genetic counselling when thinking of adding to their family.

A third set of needs is related to advice on everyday management. Most first-time parents face this task with a certain lack of confidence. This is greatly magnified in parents of handicapped children. Many such parents complain that they get insufficient advice on what actually to do with their child. They want not only to help their children develop as normally as possible, but also to avoid secondary behaviour problems developing. They want concrete suggestions on what they should actually do.

Recently, it has become much more accepted for professionals to regard parents as co-therapists. This egalitarian move which respects the rights of parents is closely associated with the application of behavioural techniques to the children's problems. The new technology has been well described and reviewed elsewhere (O'Dell, 1974; Yule, 1975; Tavormina, 1975). To date, the parents of mentally handicapped children have been offered most help and guidance in this way (e.g. Shearer and Shearer, 1972) but there are texts appearing which are aimed at parents of asthmatic and other physically handicapped children (Creer and Christian, 1976). There is an urgent need for these welcome approaches to be more rigorously evaluated so that parents do not have their hopes raised too highly.

(b) 'Community care' Society's attitudes to the handicapped are changing. There is still a great deal of wrong information in society about the needs and capabilities of its handicapped members. At times, there is frank rejection and prejudice. People with physical handicap are slightly less rejected than people with mental handicap (Shakespeare, 1975), but too often lay people assume that any handicapped person must be incapable of answering for himself.

In the past, handicapped people were even more segregated than they are today.

This was clearly seen in the practice of institutionalizing the mentally handicapped in asylums at long distances from their homes. Today, the fashion is for 'normalization' and 'community care'. Bayley (1973) makes the important distinction between care IN the community and care BY the community. It is not enough to have a mentally handicapped person living at home rather than in an institution if no real support is given to the family unit BY the community. The sorts of experimental community services being evaluated by Kushlick (1972) in Wessex and beginning to be copied elsewhere represent an important step towards providing community services on a rational basis.

(c) The 'integration' debate One specific aspect of the debate on keeping handicapped people in the community is that concerned with whether or not handicapped children should receive education in ordinary day-schools. Since it is less than a decade since all children irrespective of degree of mental handicap were offered full-time education in Britain, it may seem to some to be early days to be arguing for complete integration.

Many people looked to the Warnock Report (DES, 1978) to examine the issue in some detail. The report distinguished three overlapping forms of integration which they term locational, social, and functional. 'LOCATIONAL integration exists where special units or classes are set up in ordinary schools' (7.7). The mixing of handicapped and non-handicapped children may be minimal, but it is regarded as valuable for all. 'The second form of integration ... relates to its SOCIAL aspects, where children attending a special class or unit eat, play and consort with other children, and possibly share organized out-of-classroom activities with them' (7.8). Here, there is a positive effort to have handicapped and non-handicapped children meet on school premises for everything other than teaching activities. '... FUNCTIONAL integration ... is achieved where the locational and social association of children with special needs with their fellows leads to joint participation in educational programmes' (7.9).

Whilst the Warnock Committee were deliberating on their distinctions, Parliament decreed a modification to the 1944 Education Act. Under the 1976 Education Act, Section 10 requires local education authorities to arrange for the special education of all handicapped pupils to be given in ordinary day-schools except where this is impracticable, incompatible with efficient teaching, or too costly. Thus, functional integration is the ideal to be aimed for. In fact, if a broad definition of educational handicap is taken, then it is clear that most handicapped children are already being educated in ordinary day-schools. The real problem is in deciding which small groups of children *need* to be educated outside the ordinary system. The Warnock Committee seem to be suggesting that blind (but not necessarily partially sighted), deaf (but not necessarily partially hearing), some physically handicapped, and most severely mentally handicapped children will continue to require some degree of segregated education for the foreseeable future.

Anderson (1973) examined some of the issues in relation to the education of physically handicapped children. Her findings suggest that while children with purely physical disorders can cope well with the social and intellectual demands of ordinary school, many children with neurological and sensory abnormalities need much more help from specialist advisory services. To date, there has been little in the way of empirical investigation of all of these issues, and so the debate is likely to rage on in the absence of data for some considerable time.

(d) Mobility The Snowdon Working Party (National Fund for Research into Crippling Diseases, 1976) recognize the right of all handicapped people to participate in everyday activities. As they say:

> Integration for the disabled means a thousand things. It means the absence of segregation. It means social acceptance. It means being able to be treated like everybody else. It means the right to work, to go to cinemas, to enjoy outdoor sport, to have a family life and a social life and a love life, to contribute materially to the community, to have the usual choices of association, movement and activity, to go on holiday to the usual places, to be educated up to university level with one's unhandicapped peers, to travel without fuss on public transport ...

One of the keys to achieving these goals is independent mobility.

It is clear from the studies of the impact of a handicapped child on family life (see earlier), that physical, mental, and psychiatric handicap can restrict the mobility of the child and his family. This is most obvious when a physical disability reduces the ability to walk independently, but, less obviously, where children cannot cope with the dangers of traffic or where their behaviour interferes with others, then both the child's and his care-takers' movements will be curtailed.

The Warnock Report (DES, 1978) notes that 'Mobility is the passport today to a full and independent life for the young.' The government has recognized this by introducing mobility allowances for handicapped people. However, not all handicapped people benefit from such allowances. It is still the case that most of the physical environment is not adapted appropriately for wheelchairs, for example. While the introduction of electronically controlled wheelchairs potentially expands the independent mobility of some of the most severely physically handicapped, the value of this transport is reduced where cinemas, theatres, and other places of public entertainment are not properly adapted. While it might reasonably be argued that psychologists have little *specific* contribution to make to general environmental design, it can also be argued that their expertise in training and motivation should be made available to all those involved in training and re-training the handicapped to use special wheelchairs and other forms of transport.

(e) Prosthetic devices and prosthetic environments A great deal of ingenuity has gone in to providing various prosthetic devices which can reduce the severity of a handicap. Artificial limbs are becoming increasingly sophisticated as micro-

electronic technology is used to translate residual movements into fine motor movements. Wheelchairs exist which are controlled by mini-computers operated by slight muscle movements. Electronic scanners can translate the printed page either into pulses which can be 'read' on to a finger, or into electromechanical voices.

The impact of these prosthetic devices on the life of the handicapped person is almost incalculable. Take the blind adult, for example. One of the less obvious consequences of blindness (until pointed out) is that the blind person can never enjoy the privacy of a personal or otherwise confidential letter. He is dependent on some sighted person reading out the letter at a convenient time. The advent of cheap audio-tape-recorders overcomes this problem to some extent, but the development of the visual scanner means that the letter-writer need use no special equipment and the blind recipient can read it at his leisure, in private.

As Jay (1974) comments, aids can help people cope with disablement. The problem is getting the correct aids and then learning how to use them. Advice on aids comes from three main sources—local authority social services, the National Health Service, and voluntary organizations. One of the functions of the proposed district handicap teams will be to give advice to disabled people on what help is available. However, even when skilled assessment of needs is made by occupational therapists and other professionals, it appears that there is less expertise available to teach the disabled person to make most use of the device. Here again, the skills of applied psychologists should be readily available to other professionals involved in teaching handicapped people to use prosthetic appliances.

Many handicapped people will spend part of their lives in an institutional setting. Going into hospital can be a disturbing event, especially for young children. These effects can be minimized by appropriate preparation of the children and their care-takers (Malamed, 1977). With respect to longer-term residential care, a great deal is now known about the effects of institutions on development. For the most part, small, autonomous living units closely integrated with community services have less deleterious effects on their inmates than do large, isolated institutions (King *et al.*, 1971; Tizard *et al.*, 1975).

In the last decade, psychologists have increasingly investigated the application of token economy techniques to help motivate both chronic psychiatric and mentally handicapped patients. In terms of producing change *within the institutions*, token economies seem to be very promising (Kazdin, 1977). However, it is not yet clear to what extent the gains made within institutions really do help inmates towards independent living in the community, nor is it clear to what extent they are merely counteracting the undesirable effects of institutionalization *per se*.

(f) Transition to adult life Despite their many shortcomings, the educational and health services for handicapped children are reasonably well developed in Britain. However, recent reports have drawn attention to one major set of weaknesses. When children leave school, the arrangements to transfer responsibility for their continued treatment are patchy or non-existent.

The National Development Group for the Mentally Handicapped (1977) draws attention to some of the inadequacies in relation to services for mentally handicapped school-leavers. Two thousand children leave special schools for the mentally handicapped each year. Many go straight to adult training centres (ATCs), but many others remain at home, without outside support. The net result is that these children and their families suffer unnecessary hardship, and there is a peak of admissions into long-term care. Too often, leaving school is treated as an unexpected crisis, even though the event is readily predictable.

Apart from the argument that many mentally handicapped children are only just beginning to benefit from full-time schooling at the end of compulsory school-days, it is a surprising finding that most leave school without the benefit of any assessment geared to their future needs in an adult environment. In a recent survey of 300 ATCs Whelan and Speake (1977) found that although 50 per cent of new clients entered straight from special schools, the staff of the ATC were rarely provided with information relevant to the clients' needs. The National Development Group for the Mentally Handicapped (1977) strongly recommend that all mentally handicapped children should have their needs properly reassessed no later than six months before they reach statutory school-leaving age. The child and his parents should be fully involved in this process which should define specific teaching objectives for the immediate future.

Whelan and Speake's (1977) survey also brought to light the fact that where adult mentally handicapped trainees were placed in open or sheltered employment by the ATC, only about one-third of them had experienced similar work whilst attending the ATC. Apart from the very real difficulties in finding employment for any handicapped person during times of high unemployment, it is nevertheless clear that the training within ATCs is not, as presently constituted, geared to smooth transition to sheltered employment.

The Warnock Report (DES, 1978) documents many other disadvantages faced by handicapped school-leavers. Careers guidance falls far short of what is required. Three times more handicapped children than non-handicapped attend schools without a careers teacher. Five times as many non-handicapped 18-year-olds stay on to further education than do handicapped. Of the sample studied by the National Children's Bureau on behalf of the Warnock Committee, 27 per cent of the handicapped, compared with only 4 per cent of the non-handicapped, were either unemployed or not seeking work. Nearly one-third of the handicapped had been out of work for at least six months since leaving school, compared to only 3 per cent of the non-handicapped. When in work, the handicapped were more likely to be in industrial jobs such as those of packer and labourer. Their non-handicapped peers were less likely to have industrial jobs, and when they did these were three times as likely to be in engineering trades.

It is clear, then, that the services for all handicapped school-leavers need to be streamlined. There needs to be much closer liaison between schools and further training agencies, employers, careers guidance bodies and so on. One of the keys to this better integration of services is more goal-oriented assessment during the final year of schooling. Not only should clear and realistic goals be set, but it should be clearly spelled out how these goals should be reached and who, within which service, is responsible for reviewing progress.

(g) Sexual needs and problems One consequence of the relative social isolation of handicapped people is an even greater need, particularly during adolescence, for counselling on sexual matters. Until recently society as a whole, and even professionals working with handicapped clients, failed to recognize the normal sexual needs of the handicapped (Shearer, 1972). The situation is now rapidly changing as pressure groups such as the Committee on Sexual Problems of the Disabled (SPOD) (Stewart, 1975) and research groups draw attention to the problems.

Dorner's (1976) study of adolescents with spina bifida showed that boys had worries about their potency while girls had concerns about whether they could bear children. A few had discussed their worries with professionals, but the counselling had left them with unduly optimistic expectation of their ability to cope as parents. A Swedish study of adolescents with various physical handicaps revealed a need for discussions on both the norms and ethics of sexual relationships, as well as for technical information on sexual aids and contraception (Bergstrom-Walan, 1972).

This latter study advocates the need for some form of expert counselling on sexual matters to be provided at school. This is a view endorsed by the Warnock Report (DES, 1978), although they call for more research into how sexual counselling can best be provided for adolescents with special needs.

COMMENTS ON TREATMENT AND PREVENTION

From what has been discussed earlier, it is already clear that psychologists are making considerable contributions to the care and the treatment of handicapped clients. It is also clear that there is considerable potential for increasing the application of psychological skills and knowledge. Rather than finish this chapter with a chauvinistic plea for an increase in the number of psychologists working and researching in their areas, let us instead consider what contributions might be made at various points in the natural history of chronic disabilities.

1. Certain mothers—either because of age or by virtue of having already given birth to a child with a particular disability—are at high risk for having more handicapped children. Modern obstetric techniques such as amniocentesis and ultra-sound scanning can identify such conditions as Down's syndrome, anencephaly and spina bifida sufficiently early in pregnancy for termination to be offered. Whilst the technical advances are remarkable, one wonders to what extent the mothers are sufficiently prepared psychologically for these events, and indeed, what the emotional consequences are. Thus, both in terms of genetic

counselling and advice on appropriate contraception, as well as in terms of the effects of abortion, there is a need for improved counselling.

2. As soon after the birth of a handicapped child as is possible, there is a need for someone to break the news to both parents. This must be done expertly and sympathetically, giving time for the information to be assimilated and to allow the parents to deal with their emotional reactions. There must be recognition that this is an ongoing, time-consuming process. Parents must have the opportunity to come back to someone to ask for clarification. Personnel in the district handicap team have a vital role in educating other professionals in these tasks.
3. With the increased awareness of the importance of early days in facilitating emotional attachment between mother and children (Klaus and Kennell, 1970; Klaus *et al.*, 1972), it is important that even where babies are placed in special care units, the mothers are encouraged to handle them. Although not yet demonstrated beyond doubt, it is safest on present knowledge to avoid the old practice of keeping a handicapped baby away from the mother 'until she is ready to see it'.
4. It is still not clear how best to help parents 'come to terms' with having a handicapped child. That parents have strong, mixed, emotional reactions is not in doubt. What is in doubt is whether they really mourn the passing of the normal child they had expected, and therefore need to be helped through some mourning process. This is an interesting hypothesis, but surely cannot yet be used as the basis for informed professional practice. What is clearer is that many parents of handicapped children express the view that the best way to help them is to give advice on helping their own children.
5. Parents need practical advice in how best to help their children. As noted earlier, the various techniques of parent-training using methods derived from the behaviour-modification literature are now being widely applied. Just what the limitations of these approaches are is not yet clear. The concept of treating the parent as a partner in a therapeutic endeavour has received warm support from parents' organizations.
6. Parents are often given advice by various clinics. Advice given in rushed circumstances is often misunderstood and treatment regimes are not properly followed (Ley, 1977). The handicapped children would benefit greatly if clinic personnel improved their methods of giving advice on treatment.
7. Handicapped children have special educational needs. Whether these can best be met within ordinary schools or in special units depends in part on the type of disability and in part on the availability of scarce resources, both teaching and other professional help. The Warnock Report (DES, 1978) spells out the issues in relation to education. Here, the need for better coordination of services between school and adult services must be emphasized. It is both wasteful and harmful not to build on the progress made during compulsory school years.
8. Many handicapped people have to go into hospitals, often for painful

procedures. The worry associated with such admissions, and even some of the experience of pain, can be lessened be better preparation for hospitalization.

9. Handicapped people have the same needs as everyone else, but they have greater problems in getting their needs met. This applies to social/recreational areas of living as much as to employment. The problem is especially acute in the area of sexual relations. As society recognizes these needs, so will there be a need for more expert counselling. This should be made available from adolescence onwards.
10. Finally, one of the harsh realities of many handicapping conditions is that the life-span of the sufferer is shortened. Neither the child, the parents, nor the professionals are particularly well equipped to deal with death. Yet it must be the professional duty of the helping professions to investigate better ways of preparing both the child and the parents.

Intervention at any of these points may involve the child, the parents, care-takers, teachers, or any combination thereof. Psychologist involved in treatment will, as always, pay attention both to factors involved in the aetiology of particular episodes of illness or dysfunction, and to factors involved in the maintenance. In addition, it must be remembered that many treatment procedures designed to attain long-term benefits may be extremely painful in the short term. This is seen as a major challenge in improving treatment procedures, but one that is within the professional competence of applied psychologists to solve.

With improvements in treatment and earlier intervention, psychologists can be said to be contributing to secondary and tertiary prevention of handicap. This is being done both directly and indirectly by such develpments as parent-training and medical education. However, at present, there is little evidence that psychologists are playing any major role in primary prevention, at least of physical handicaps.

There is one major exception of note in the field of mental handicap which can reasonably be classified as a primary prevention programme. In the Milwaukee Project (Heber and Garber, 1974; Falender and Heber, 1975; see also Cowen in this volume), mildly mentally retarded mothers are enrolled in a long-term project to improve their child-care and employment skills. Previous research has shown that this group of mothers produce mildly retarded children. Children in the project not only failed to show the progressive drop-off in measured IQ, they actually showed an advantage of 20–30 IQ points over the control group, a difference which persisted several years after treatment terminated (Trotter, 1976). It has long been recognized that social factors are important determinants of mild mental retardation, and the Milwaukee Project is the most exciting primary prevention programme yet to appear. It is doubtful if psychosocial approaches have as great a role in the primary prevention of severe mental handicap.

The concept of primary prevention is less relevant to educational and psychiatric handicap where causes are multifactorial. To date, programmes of prevention in the field of mental health have not been dramatically successful. Within education, ill-conceived compensatory education programmes, particularly those of short duration, like Head Start, did not result in many gains. However, it may have taken such dramatic failure to make people realize that years of social disadvantage cannot be alleviated in a few weeks of enjoyable schooling. Instead, comprehensive and long-term programmes of intervention in schools, such as Project Follow-Through (Bushell, 1977), show much more promise in bringing real and lasting academic gains to children who would previously have failed.

These tentative moves towards larger-scale preventive work represent a recognition on the part of applied psychologists of the social factors involved both in the aetiology and maintenance of many handicapping conditions. This chapter has indicated the extent of the problem facing any community and the nature of some of the social forces which determine the severity of any handicap. One may hope that a better understanding of these forces will result in more effective methods both for treating and preventing so much human suffering.

REFERENCES

Albee, G. W. and Joffe, J. M. (Eds.) (1977). *Primary Prevention of Psychopathology.* Vol. 1. *The Issues.* (Hanover, New Hampshire: University Press of New England.)

Anderson, E. M. (1973). *The Disabled School Child.* (London: Methuen.)

Anderson, E. and Spain, B (1977). *The Child with Spina Bifida.* (London: Methuen.)

Bax, M. C. (1964). Terminology and classification of cerebral palsy. *Devolopmental Medicine and Child Neurology*, **6,** 295–297.

Bayley, M. (1973). *Mental Handicap and Community Care: A Study of Mentally Handicapped People in Sheffield.* (London: Routledge & Kegan Paul.)

Berger, M., Yule, W., and Rutter, M. (1975). Attainment and adjustment in two geographical areas. II: The prevalence of specific reading retardation. *British Journal of Psychiatry*, **126,** 510–519.

Bergstrom-Walan, M. B. (1972). The problems of sex and handicap in Sweden: and investigation. In: D. Lancaster-Gaye (Ed.), *Personal Relationships, the Handicapped and the Community.* (London: Routledge & Kegan Paul.)

Burt, C. (1925). *The Young Delinquent.* (London: University of London Press.)

Burt, C. (1937). *The Backward Child.* (London: University of London Press.)

Bushell, D. (1977). The behavioral analysis follow-through project: an engineering approach to the elementary classroom. In: T. Brigham and A. Catania (Eds.), *Analysis and Modification of Social and Educational Behavior.* (New York: Wiley.)

Butollo, W. H. L. (1977). Comment on W. Yule: the potential of behavioural treatment in preventing later childhood difficulties. *Behavioural Analysis and Modification*, **2,** 33–38.

Caplan, G. (1964). *Principles of Preventive Psychiatry.* (New York: Basic Books.)

Carr, J. (1974). The effects of the severely subnormal on their families. In: A. M. Clarke and A. D. B. Clarke (Eds.), *Mental Deficiency: The Changing Outlook* (3rd edn.). (London: Methuen.)

Carr, J. (1975). *Young Children with Down's Syndrome.* (London: Butterworths.)

CCETSW (Central Council for Education and Training in Social Work) (1974). *Social Work: People with Handicaps Need Better Trained Workers.* Paper No. 5. (London: CCETSW.)

Childers, P. and Wimmer, M. (1971). The concept of death in early childhood. *Child Development*, **42,** 1299–1301.

Cooper, B and Morgan, H. G. (1973). *Epidemiological Psychiatry*. (Springfield, Ill.:, Charles C. Thomas.)
Creer, T. L. and Christian, W. P. (1976). *Chronically Ill and Handicapped Children: Their Management and Rehabilitation*. (Champaign, Ill.: Research Press.)
Crome, L. (1960). The brain and mental retardation. *British Medical Journal*, **1,** 897–904.
DES (Department of Education and Science) (1978). *Special Educational Needs*: Report of the Committee of Enquiry into the Education of Handicapped Children and Young People (Chairman: Mrs Warnock). (London: HMSO)
DHSS (Department of Health and Social Security) (1968). Report of the Committee on Local Authority and Allied Personal Social Services (Chairman: Baron Seebohm). (London: HMSO)
DHSS (Department of Health and Social Security) (1976). *Fit for the Future*. The Report of the Committee on Child Health Services (Chairman: Professor Court). (London: HMSO.)
Dorner, S. (1975). The relationship of physical handicap to stress in families with an adolescent with spina bifida. *Developmental Medicine and Child Neurology*, **17,** 765–776.
Dorner, S. (1976). Adolescents with spina bifida—how they see their situation. *Archives of Disease in Childhood*, **51,** 439–444.
Douglas, J. W. B. (1975). Early hospital admissions and later disturbances of behaviour and learning. *Developmental Medicine and Child Neurology*, **17,** 456–480.
Falender, C. A. and Heber, R. (1975). Mother–child interaction and participation in a longitudinal intervention program. *Developmental Psychology*, **11,** 830–836.
Freeman, R. (1977). Psychiatric aspects of sensory disorders and intervention. In: P. J. Graham (Ed.), *Epidemiological Approaches in Child Psychiatry*. (London: Academic Press.)
Gelfand, D. M. and Hartmannn, D. P. (1977). The prevention of childhood behavior disorders. In: B. B. Lahey and A. E. Kazdin (Eds.), *Advances in Clinical Child Psychology*, Vol. 1. (New York: Plenum.)
Gruenberg, E. M. (1964). Epidemiology. In: H. A. Stevens and R. Heber, (Eds.), *Mental Retardation: A Review of Research*. (Chicago: University of Chicago Press.)
Hannam, C. (1975). *Parents and Mentally Handicapped Children*. (Harmondsworth: Penguin.)
Harris, A. *et al.* (1971). *Handicapped and Impaired in Great Britain*. Part I. (London: HMSO.)
Haskell, S. H., Barrett, E. K., and Taylor, H. (1977). *The Education of Motor and Neurologically Handicapped Children*. (London: Croom Helm.)
Heber, R. and Garber, H. (1974). An experiment in prevention of cultural–familial mental retardation. In: D. A. Primrose (Ed.), *Proceedings of the Third Congress of the International Association for the Scientific Study of Mental Deficiency*. (Warsaw: Ars Polona.)
Hewett, S. (1970). *The Family and the Handicapped Child*. (London: George Allen & Unwin.)
Jay, P. (1974). *Coping with Disablement*. (London: Consumers Association.)
Kazdin, A. E. (1977). *The Token Economy*. (New York: Plenum Press.)
King, R., Raynes, N., and Tizard, J. (1971). *Patterns of Residential Care*. (London: Routledge & Kegan Paul.)
Klaus, M. H., Jerauld, R., Kreger, N. C., McAlpine, W., Steffa, M., and Kennell, J. H. (1972). Maternal attachment: importance of the first post-partum days. *New England Journal of Medicine*, **286,** 460–463.
Klaus, M. H. and Kennell, J. H. (1970). Human maternal behaviour at first contact with her young. *Pediatrics*, **46,** 187–192.
Koocher, G. P. (1974). Talking with children about death. *American Journal of Orthopsychiatry*, **44,** 404–411.
Kushlick, A. (1971). Subnormality in Salford. In: M. W. Susser and A. Kushlick (Eds.), *A Report on the Mental Health Services of the City of Salford for the Year 1960*. (Salford Health Department.)

Kushlick, A. (1966). A community service for the mentally subnormal. *Social Psychiatry*, **1,** 73–82.

Kushlick, A. (1972). Evaluating residential services for mentally handicapped children. Paper presented to Second Symposium on Psychiatric Epidemiology, Mannheim, July 1972.

Kushlick, A. and Blunden, R. (1974). The epidemiology of mental subnormality. In: A. M. Clarke and A. D. B. Clarke (Eds.), *Mental Deficiency: The Changing Outlook* (3rd edn.). (London: Methuen.)

Lemkau, P., Tietze, C., and Cooper, M. (1943). lfental hygiene problems in an urban district. Fourth paper. *Mental Hygiene*, **27,** 279–295.

Ley, P. (1977). Psychological studies of doctor–patient communication. In: S. Rachman (Ed.), *Contributions to Medical Psychology*, Vol. I. (Oxford: Pergamon.)

Melamed, B. G. (1977). Psychological preparation for hospitalization. In: S. Rachman (Ed.) *Contributions to Medical Psychology*, Vol. I. (Oxford: Pergamon.)

National Development Group for the Mentally Handicapped (1977). *Helping Mentally Handicapped School Leavers.* (Pamphlet No. 3). (London: DHSS.)

National Fund for Research into Crippling Diseases (1976). *Integrating the Disabled.* Report of the Snowdon Working Party. (London: NFRCD.)

New York State Mental Health Research Unit (1955). *A Special Census of Suspected Referred Mental Retardation, Onondaga County, New York.* Technical Report (cited in Kushlick, 1966).

O'Dell, S. (1974). Training parents in behavior modification: a review. *Psychological Bulletin*, **81,** 418–433.

Pless, I. B. and Pinkerton, P. (1975). *Chronic Childhood Disorder; Promoting Patterns of Adjustment.* (London: Henry Kimpton.)

Poser, E. G. and Hartman, L. M. (1979). Issues in behavioural prevention: preliminary empirical findings. *Advances in Behaviour Research and Therapy*, **2,** 1–26.

Quinton, D. and Rutter, M. (1976). Early hospital admissions and later disturbances of behaviour: an attempted replication of Douglas' findings. *Developmental Medicine and Child Neurology*, **18,** 447–459.

Rigley, L. V. (1968). The relevance of the Isle of Wight Study, In *Research Relevant to the Education of Children with Learning Handicaps.* (London: The College of Special Education.)

Rutter, M. (1977). Surveys to answer questions: some methodological considerations. In: P. J. Graham (Ed.), *Epidemiological Approaches in Child Psychiatry.* (London: Academic Press.)

Rutter, M., Graham, P., Chadwick, O. F. D., and Yule, W. (1976). Adolescent turmoil, fact or fiction? *Journal of Child Psychology and Psychiatry*, **17,** 35–56.

Rutter, M., Graham, P., and Yule, W. (1970). *A Neuropsychiatric Study in Childhood* (Clinics in Developmental Medicine Nos. 35, 36). (London: Heinemann Medical.)

Rutter, M., Tizard, J., and Whitmore, K. (Eds.) (1970b). *Education, Health and Behaviour.* (London: Longmans.)

Rutter, M. and Yule, W. (1970). Reading retardation and antisocial behaviour—the nature of the association. In: M. Rutter, J. Tizard, and K. Whitmore (Eds.), *Education, Health and Behaviour.* (London: Longmans.)

Rutter, M. and Yule, W. (1975). The concept of specific reading retardation. *Journal of Child Psychology and Psychiatry*, **16,** 181–197.

Shakespeare, R. (1975). *The Psychology of Handicap.* (London: Methuen.)

Shearer, A. (1972). *A Right to Love?* (London: Spastics Society/National Association for Mental Health.)

Shearer, M. S. and Shearer, D. E. (1972). The Portage Project: A model for early childhood education. *Exceptional Children*, **39,** 210–217.

Spain, B. (1973). Spina bifida: the need for community support. *GLC Intelligence Unit Quarterly Bulletin*, **23,** 66–71.
Stewart, W. F. R. (1975). *Sexand the Physically Handicapped.* (Horsham: National Fund for Research into Crippling Diseases.)
Stevenson, J., Graham, P. and Dorner, S. (1978). Parental reactions to birth of a handicapped child. *British Journal of Psychiatry*, **132,** 105.
Tavormina, J. B. (1975). Relative effectiveness of behavioural and reflective group counselling with parents of mentally handicapped children. *Journal of Consultative and Clinical Psychology*, **43,** 22–31.
Tew, B. and Laurence, K. (1975). Some sources of stress found in mothers of spina bifida children. *British Journal of Preventive and Social Medicine*, **29,** 27–30.
Tizard, J. and Grad, J. C. (1961). *The Mentally Handicapped and their Families: A Social Survey.* Maudsley Monograph No. 7. (London: Oxford University Press.)
Tizard, J., Sinclair, J., and Clarke, R. V. G. (Eds.) (1975). *Varieties of Residential Experience.* (London: Routledge & Kegan Paul.)
Travis, G. (1976). *Chronic Illness in Children: Its Impact on Child and Family.* (Stanford: Stanford University Press.)
Trotter, R. (1976). Environment and behavior: intensive intervention program prevents retardation. *American Psychological Association Monitor*, Sept./Oct. 1976, 4–5, 19, 46.
Voluntary Council for the Handicapped (1976). *Help Starts Here.* (London: National Children's Bureau.)
Whelan, E. and Speake, B. (1977). *Adult Training Centres in England and Wales: Report of the First National Survey.* (Manchester: Hester Adrian Research Centre.)
WHO (World Health Organization) (1976). Disability prevention and rehabilitation. *World Health Organization Chronicle*, **30,** 324–328.
Younghusband, E., Birchall, D., Davie, R., and Pringle, M. L. K. (Eds.) (1970). *Living with Handicap.* (London: National Bureau for Cooperation in Child Care.)
Yule, W. (1967). Predicting reading ages on Neale's analysis of reading ability. *British Journal of Educational Psychology*, **37,** 252–255.
Yule, W. (1973). Differential prognosis of reading backwardness and specific reading retardation. *British Journal of Educational Psychology*, **43,** 244–248.
Yule, W. (1974). Educational retardation and maladjustment. *Theraputic Education*, Autumn issue, 5–13.
Yule, W. (1975). Teaching psychological principles to non-psychologists: training parents in child management. *Journal of the Association of Educational Psychologists*, **10**(3), 5–16.
Yule, W. (1977). The potential of behavioural treatment in preventing later childhood difficulties. *Behavioural Analysis and Modification*, **2,** 19–32.
Yule, W. and Rutter, M. (1976). Epidemiology and social implications of specific reading retardation. In: R. M. Knights and D. J. Bakker (Eds.), *The Neuropsychology of Learning Disorders.* (Baltimore: University Park Press.)

The Social Psychology of Psychological Problems
Edited by P. Feldman and J. Orford

9

The Treatment of Social Difficulties in Special Environments

GEOFF SHEPHERD

INTRODUCTION

This chapter will be concerned with the issue of how best to help those individuals who have difficulties with various aspects of social functioning. My own interest stems from a practical and research involvement with adult psychiatric patients whose social difficulties are of a chronic and pervasive nature. This interest will be reflected in the content of the research reviewed. The chapter does not pretend to be an exhaustive survey of the literature. However, I do wish to make a fair representation of the evidence while placing emphasis on specific areas so as to make certain points more clearly. It is also my intention to draw on relevant areas of psychological research outside the clinical field, particularly in the field of social psychology, personality and learning theory, and some aspects of cognitive psychology.

The phrase 'difficulties in social functioning' will be used to refer to problems both at the level of social integration, i.e. the maintenance of key social roles, such as worker, friend, spouse and parent; and also at the level of social interaction, i.e. difficulties with interpersonal performance. Evidence will be cited later to suggest that a relationship exists between social difficulties at these two levels. Consideration of the problem will involve examining why adequate social functioning is so important for general psychological well-being, and how effectively social difficulties can be treated by various means both in hospital and in the community. The limitations in our ability to treat social difficulties effectively are highlighted in the problems of generalizing and maintaining treatment effects; these will be discussed at some length with reference to social skills training. In the light of all the problems some alternative solutions outside the traditional 'treatment' model will be considered. The chapter ends with a brief discussion of some of the ethical issues involved.

The chapter begins by looking at the possible relationship between various indices of social functioning and aspects of general psychological distress, (involvement with professional services, changes in symptom levels, etc.)

WHY IS SOCIAL FUNCTIONING IMPORTANT?

Psychological problems and social integration

Many psychological problems occur in the context of poor or unstable social integration. For example, there is epidemiological evidence to suggest that high rates of admission to psychiatric services are correlated with high rates of social isolation (Bloom, 1968). It has also been shown from community surveys that poor social functioning, particularly within the family, results in a vulnerability to various psychological symptoms (Brown *et al.*, 1975; Miller and Ingham, 1975). The onset or exacerbation of symptoms can also be said to be 'triggered' by the occurrence of certain life-events (Brown *et al.*, 1973), and these can often take the form of loss or disruption of key social relationships (Paykel *et al.*, 1969). There are methodological problems with these studies; for example, the definition of what constitutes a 'case' and the provision of reliable and valid assessment of changes in functioning often present major difficulties. We must also be cautious in how far conclusions can be generalized from one study to another since there is evidence that the pattern of social isolation and instability may be different for different problems or diagnostic groups. Furthermore the results are correlational and so it is not possible to tell if the association between social integration and psychological symptoms reflects a direct causal link, or is only a spurious result of their joint association with some third variable, e.g. socioeconomic status (Dohrenwend and Dohrenwend, 1974; Dunham, 1976). Even if a direct causal connection does exist, the precise nature and direction of this connection remains unclear.

We may consider next the relationship between previous social adaptation, current social functioning, and outcome in terms of symptoms. The work of Zigler and his colleagues has demonstrated a strong relationship between early problems in social integration and the capacity to adjust following an episode of psychological disturbances (Zigler and Phillips, 1960; 1961; 1962; Levine and Zigler, 1973). Those individuals who seem to have been well adapted socially and who have not had great difficulties in making relationships early in life are the ones least likely to be rehospitalized or frequently in contact with services in the future. In a similar vein, it has been repeatedly shown that being married is a reliable indicator of relatively good prognosis and that this holds up over a range of diagnostic groups (Rawls, 1971; Rifkin *et al.*, 1972; Sims, 1975; Copas and Whitely, 1976). (It will be interesting to see if this finding is modified with changing cultural attitudes towards marriage and the family.) Current social integration is also related to the subsequent course of psychological problems. Both in hospitalized and community samples it has been shown that the better the current social integration the more favourable the likely outcome (Pokorny *et al.*, 1976; Beiser, 1976). With inpatients the attitude of the family and other key relatives is of particular importance (Freeman and Simmons, 1963; Brown *et al.*, 1972; Vaughn and Leff, 1976). Family and other community attitudes very largely determine how long a person is likely to remain in hospital and how much support he will receve once discharged. As the time in hospital increases so the likelihood of discharge decreases, as does the amount of contact and support from family and friends outside (Gore and Jones, 1961; Hassall and Hellon, 1964). (See chapter 1 for a fuller discussion of the domestic context.)

As with the previous studies there are methodological problems which should be borne in mind when considering this evidence. Firstly, there is the problem of obtaining accurate information about early functioning. This is often done retrospectively and the possible unreliability of such data is well know. Related to this is the fact that it is sometimes difficult to distinguish between different phases of disturbed behaviour. Many disorders—schizophrenia for example—have an insidious onset and it may be difficult to say precisely when the problems start. It is then unclear whether the social difficulties do actually predate the other psychological problems and therefore are more likely to be causal. Secondly, causal interpretations are again complicated by the possibility of there being other hidden variables which account for the observed association. For example, Rosen *et al.* (1971) have suggested that the relationship between marital status and outcome is accounted for by their joint association with age. Thirdly, it is apparent that outcome itself is not a unitary variable. There are a number of separate outcome 'systems': employment, hospitalization, social funtioning, and so on (Strauss and Carpenter, 1972; 1974). Each has unique properties, and can show quite different patterns of change over time (Fontana and Dowds, 1975). The patterns of outcome can also be different for different diagnostic groups. Despite all these qualifications there is evidence from the prospective studies, such as those by Brown using reliable and specific measures of functioning and outcome, and controlling for hidden associations, which still suggests a relationship between difficulties in social functioning and outcome in terms of symptoms.

The linking role of social difficulties

The concept proposed by Strauss and Carpenter (1972; 1974), that outcome be thought of in terms of a number of systems, seems an important one. It implies that aspects of a patient's history in a particular area of functioning can be used to predict subsequent functioning in that area, i.e. history of hospitalizations predicts future hospitalization; social history predicts future social functioning; work history predicts future employment prospects; and so on (see Watts and Bennett, 1977). However, each outcome system also shares some common variance. Strauss and Carpenter refer to the systems being linked in the sense of having 'definite but incomplete interdependence'. The question then arises, what is the possible source of such linking?

If we consider employment, it is apparent that employability depends on a number of characteristics (Griffiths, 1973), of which the ability actually to do the job may be of minor importance. Watts (1978) found that for psychiatric rehabilitees attending a vocational workshop, it was their social functioning—relationships with peers and supervisors in work—that was much more important in predicting their future employment than was their performance on the actual work tasks involved. Thus, social functioning plays an important role in determining outcome with regard to employment. With regard to hospitalization the importance of social functioning in terms of community and family attitudes has already been discussed. Thus, it seems possible that social difficulties represent a common factor linking the relationship between different aspects of history and outcome. This idea of the central and underlying importance of social functioning to successful adjustment has been raised and discussed by several writers, notably Phillips (1968).

To summarize, it would seem that there is evidence to support the general proposition that those who experience psychological problems of various kinds do so in the context of poor or unstable social functioning. Furthermore the outcome of psychological problems seems to be related to the individual's history of social adaptation and to factors in his current social environment. There is also some reason to suppose that social functioning represents a general factor linking outcome systems. Thus far the association between psychological problems and social difficulties is correlational and it has been emphasized that we must be careful about making causal interpretations. If there are true causal connections they are most likely to be complex and interactional. Nevertheless it does seem worth considering the possibility that by improving social functioning we might be able to improve outcome. We might even be able to influence the course of other psychological symptoms. To achieve this demands that we can treat social difficulties effectively.

APPROACHES TO THE TREATMENT OF SOCIAL DIFFICULTIES

Hospital-based approaches

The idea that disturbed individuals could be helped to function more adequately in their social interactions given the right kind of environment is an old idea which has only been rediscovered fairly recently (Bockhoven, 1956). Current approaches to this problem vary along a dimension of the degree of structure the environment is given. This can vary from, on the one hand, using the social milieu in a rather unsystematic fashion based on rather loose theoretical principles (the 'therapeutic community', e.g. Jones, 1968); to, on the other hand, using the environment in a highly systematic fashion according to strict operant principles (the 'token economy', e.g. Ayllon and Azrin, 1968). The evidence for the effectiveness of the different approaches also varies, but in general the advocates of token economy systems can claim rather better empirical support than their rivals (Kazdin and Bootzin, 1972; Gripp and Magaro, 1974). The therapeutic community approach has provided some evidence in its support, but on the whole the amount and quality of the evaluative research is rather less (Clark, 1974; Moline, 1976). At the moment there are relatively few comparative trials of the two approaches and those which are available seem to find relatively few clear-cut differences (Erickson, 1975).

Both approaches are therefore plausible, but they share some common problems. Firstly, there is a danger with social treatments that the new environment will be overstimulating and will produce a relapse in symptoms, particularly for schizophrenic patients. This danger is present both with token economy and therapeutic community approaches (Van Putten, 1973; Hemsley, 1978). Secondly, there are methodological difficulties resulting from the use of inadequate and non-comparable outcome criteria. Gross measures of functioning are often used, e.g. discharge from hospital, time in the community, and time spent working, although such measures give very little useful information about the effects of treatments on specific aspects of functioning. One individual may be discharged from hospital although functioning very badly (Lamb and Goertzel, 1971, 1972); conversely another may be in hospital but functioning relatively well. Similarly, a person may be surviving in open employment but experiencing great difficulty or, conversely, managing a sheltered work setting very well. The fact that an idividual is out of hospital or in work may reflect prevailing attitudes to hospital admission or local employment opportunities, but not necessarily very much about their actual functioning. As outcome criteria such measures give very little information about the specific effects of any treatment programme. Thus, reviews like that of Anthony *et al.* (1972) which conclude that there is little evidence for the effectiveness of various in-hospital programmes on the basis of re-admission and re-employment rates are not particularly convincing.

The Anthony *et al.* paper also illustrates another problem for reviewers, namely the attempt to estimate 'base-rates' for re-admission and employment against which the effects of treatment programmes can then be evaluated. This is similar procedure to that adopted by Eysenck (1960) to estimate the 'spontaneous remission' rate in order to evaluate psychotherapy. It means taking a number of studies with different samples, under different conditions, and different outcome measures, and manufacturing a single figure to represent the 'base-rate'. We have already seen that outcome is influenced by many variables, including the characteristics of the sample, the intervening conditions, and the methods used to evaluate it, and hence a single figure purporting to summarize a number of different and essentially non-comparable studies can only be a statistical artefact. (A similar argument can be made with regard to 'spontaneous remission' rates; see Lambert, 1976.) To evaluate psychological interventions, whether they are psychotherapy or social treatments, requires prospective controlled trials with clearly defined populations and replicable, specific, outcome criteria. In short, it requires 'specificity': which treatments? for which patients? according to which measures? (see Kiesler, 1966; Paul, 1967). There is not a great deal of specific evidence of this kind available. However we may conclude that social treatments in hospital do seem capable of producing changes, albeit sometimes according to rather dubious outcome criteria and across a range of often rather poorly defined samples.

The mechanisms by which they effect this change is another question. An environmental treatment, whether token economy or therapeutic community, constitutes an exceedingly complex independent variable and precisely which aspects of the total package are therapeutic is by no means clear. Thus, it has not been shown convincingly that any of the principles underlying the therapeutic community are actually crucial to mediating change, the appropriate control groups to answer the question have simply not been employed. Similarly, it is unclear which aspects of the token economy are actually critical. The contingent application of tokens may not be a necessary element (Baker *et al.*, 1974, 1977; Hall *et al.*, 1977). Given the uncertainty over mechanisms and the relative similarity of outcomes, perhaps it is useful to consider what these treatments have in common, rather than their theoretical differences.

They all involve the setting up of a new treatment regime, often with new facilities, and creating new expectancies and enthusiasm on the part of the staff involved. It is well known that these 'non-specific' variables in themselves can produce quite major changes in patients' functioning (Higgs, 1970). All the programmes also involve setting targets or goals for new behaviour, with or without demonstration by modelling. They also involve an opportunity to practise, and some kind of feedback from staff or peers regarding success or failure in achieving these targets. These common elements can be subsumed under a general 'social learning' rationale and perhaps represent common mechanisms mediating change. They are reflected in the 'hybrid' programmes which combine, with some success, certain features of both therapeutic community and token economy (Sanders *et al.*, 1962; Marks *et al.*, 1968; Heap *et al.*, 1970; Jacobs and Trick, 1974). For the moment we may agree with Erickson (1975) that practically any reasonable innovation will lead to some kind of improvement. As we shall see, obtaining an improvement is only the first step.

Community-based approaches

There are now a number of convincing demonstrations that many individuals with psychiatric disturbances can be cared for in the community, while avoiding the necessity of long admissions to a mental hospital (Herz *et al.*, 1975, 1977; Glick *et al.*, 1977; Hargreaves *et al.*, 1977). The research suggests that community and day care as opposed to traditional hospital admissions lead to a better outcome in terms of various aspects of social functioning (e.g. employment, community, and family adjustment) and that this can be achieved without there being a cost in terms of untreated symptoms and without an unacceptable burden being placed on the families of the patients involved (Stein and Test, 1978; Michaux *et al.*, 1973; Washburn *et al.*, 1976). Similar results have been reported with more behavioural approaches (Samuels and Henderson, 1971; Hunt and Azrin, 1973; Azrin, 1976), and as with in-hospital programmes the similarities between different programmes seem to be more important than any theoretical differences (Austin *et al.*, 1976).

The same methodological issues discussed in relation to evaluating hospital-based programmes are relevant again in this connection. There are the problems with outcome criteria, and uncertainties as to the mechanisms of change. There are also some special problems encountered in community-based approaches, e.g. difficulties in getting chronic and marginally motivated patients sufficiently involved in community services. It is much easier to treat patients, whether by psychological or physical means, when they are relatively 'captive' in hospitals, as opposed to 'free' in the community. These difficulties are sometimes reflected in rather poorer results obtained when social treatments are applied in the community. For example, Griffiths (1974) reported an evaluation of a vocational resettlement workshop for patients organized on a day-treatment basis and the results compared rather unfavourably with earlier work using similar facilities and patients on an inpatient basis (Bennett *et al.*, 1961; Wing *et al.*, 1964). The practical implications of such findings have led people to emphasize the necessity of an 'aggressive' delivery of services (Davis *et al.*, 1972) and one which attempts to involve much more closely the families of those patients receiving treatment (Herz *et al.*, 1976). This can raise further problems as one tries to work with uncooperative and unmotivated families (Stevens, 1972, 1973). An alternative to working with families and expecting them to provide the social support is to create special sheltered social environments in the community by extending the hospital facilities. For example, the classic work of Fairweather and his colleagues (Fairweather, 1964; Fairweather *et al.*, 1969), which showed that patients organized in small problem-solving groups in hospital could be successfully transferred to 'lodges' in the community and could eventually achieve a high degree of autonomy and mutual support sufficient to keep their members functioning adequately outside hospital for significantly longer than controls who received traditional after-care. The effects lasted for as long as the members remained resident in the lodge.

The problems of generalization and durability

The most important limitations of both hospital- and community-based approaches have been the difficulties in demonstrating any transfer of improvements outside the immediate treatment setting (the problem of stimulus generalization); and the problem of maintaining treatment gains over long periods of time (the problem of durability). Whether one looks at token economies or therapeutic communities, there is little evidence of successful stimulus generalization or of great durability of treatment gains (Hollingsworth and Foreyt, 1975; Shedletsky and Voineskos, 1976; Whiteley, 1970). A similar conclusion also applies to community-based approaches (Davis *et al.*, 1972) and even to the lodge experiment of Fairweather *et al.* (see Sanders, 1972). Working directly in the community and being directly concerned with criterion functioning to some extent circumvent the problem of generalization, but there are still problems with maintaining treatment effects. There are many possible reasons for this state of affairs. For example, what patients learn in token economies or therapeutic communities may bear little relationship to events as they occur in the outside world. Gagnon and Davison (1976) have commented on this.

They note that token economies embody a predictability, a relationship between effort and reward, that simply does not reflect reality outside the token ward, hence, the likelihood of generalization is reduced. Most writers have recognized the problems of generalization and durability, and some suggestions have been made as to how they could be tackled (e.g. Kazdin and Bootzin, 1972; Liberman *et al.*, 1976). However at the moment there is very little evidence that 'programming for generalization' has been successful. Since these problems seem to be central, I will now look at them in rather more detail in relation to the attempt to treat social difficulties directly through the creation of a special therapeutic social environment, the social skills training group.

SOCIAL SKILLS TRAINING

Generalization and reactivity of measurement

Social skills training represents an attempt to apply a theory of social behaviour (the social skills model, Argyle, 1969), to the analysis and treatment of social difficulties. We will also include assertive-training procedures in the discussion although they have developed from a slightly different theoretical background (Rich and Schroeder, 1976). The research on this topic has been considerable and there are a number of reviews which support the growing promise of the approach (Hersen and Bellack, 1976; Lange and Jakubowski, 1976; Trower *et al.*, 1978). However, the effectiveness of social skills training is limited by the problems of generalization and durability encountered with other social treatments (Marzillier, 1978).

Again, there are many possible explanations, but certainly one reason why so little generalization has been found is that so little energy has been spent looking for it. Much of the research relies almost entirely on outcome measures which are tied very closely to the treatment setting, e.g. 'stooge' interviews, taped 'scenes', etc. Where measures of generalization are attempted in the 'real world' these are usually methodologically weak, e.g. simple self-reports, or highly restricted, e.g. a single telephone call follow-up. Measuring outcome in the natural environment is a difficult methodological problem, but unless interventions can be shown to affect functioning *outside* the immediate treatment context they lose much of their appeal. The problem of dependent measures which are closely tied to the treatment context and have high 'demand characteristics' (reactivity) is one that has received some attention with regard to other psychological treatments (Meltzoff and Kornreich, 1970). Indeed it has been suggested recently that if reactivity of measurement is taken into account then many of the differences found between psychological treatments largely disappear (Smith and Glass, 1977). Measures which are non-reactive, and which directly assess generalization, are difficult to obtain but not impossible (see Webb *et al.*, 1966). This kind of measurement needs to involve relatives, care-staff, and other independent observers not directly involved in the treatment. In our own research we have developed a method of rating clients' social functioning by independent observers in a setting completely separate from the treatment groups, and this method could be extended to other settings. Using this very stringent outcome criterion we were initially unable to find any evidence of social skills training having improved the interaction skills of chronic patients in a psychiatric day-hospital (Shepherd, 1977). In the light of these results we gave some close thought to the problems involved.

From a learning theory viewpoint stimulus generalization must be regarded as a strictly empirical phenomenon. 'As a consequence of prior training with one stimulus, some other stimulus, never itself associated with reinforcement, may be able to elicit a response from the subject' (Mackintosh, 1974, p. 484). Thus, the first condition for generalization is that a response be established to the original training stimulus. In social skills training there are a number of problems to be overcome before this initial aim can be achieved.

Technical and procedural problems

As indicated, social skills training packages usually involve three major techniques: (a) modelling, (b) practice, and (c) feedback. The most common type of modelling employed in the research has used videotape or audio-tape. From a research point of video taped models provide a convenient standard stimulus although they may limit the external validity of the conclusions drawn. Covert modelling (imagination) has also been used (Kazdin, 1974). Practice usually takes the form of behavioural rehearsal (role-playing), and once again this may be overt or covert (McFall and Lilliesand, 1971). The feedback consists of verbal instructions and 'coaching' in alternative responses, and reinforcement for successful performance (Liberman *et al.*, 1975). Once again it is difficult to summarize the research because so few of the studies are really comparable—there being major differences in subjects, measures, etc. (see Hersen and Bellack, 1976). However, it does seem that these techniques, whether used alone or in combination, are usually superior to no-treatment controls, although there are some notable exceptions even to this conclusion (e.g. Marzillier *et al.*, 1976). It should also be noted that there have been relatively few adequate comparisons with alternative treatments or credible placebos, and when comparisons have been made the differences are often small (McFall and Marston, 1970; Rathus, 1972; Argyle *et al.*, 1974). This is an important qualification and is consistent with the evidence concerning the outcomes of other kinds of psychological treatments; they do seem better than no treatment at all, but the differences between treatments are not great (Luborsky *et al.*, 1975). The evidence on the relative importance of the different techniques suggests, again tentatively, that if the techniques were used in isolation, practice is probably the weakest single component and modelling is probably the strongest. However, this conclusion may not apply to student populations where modelling has been shown to add very little to the total treatment package (McFall and Twentyman, 1973). It may not even apply to some clinical samples. For example, in at least one study simple instructions were just as effective as watching the model (Goldstein *et al.*, 1973). On the question of which technique for which problems, the evidence is again rather sparse, although there are some reports of specific techniques, e.g. modelling to improve verbal content and instructions to improve loudness (see Hersen *et al.*, 1973).

The research does not therefore, suggest strongly that any one technique, applied in isolation, will yield the maximum therapeutic benefit. It seems necessary to use multiple techniques according to the needs of the clients and their problems. The more components that are included in the treatment package in general the greater the changes obtained (Hersen *et al.*, 1974). A 'multiple-technique approach' thus seems necessary despite any possible disadvantages with regard to cost-effectiveness and the special difficulties it poses for replication (Shepherd and Durham, 1977). It will be seen that this conclusion places considerable responsibility on the therapist to select and combine suitable techniques, and at the moment this process must be largely intuitive rather than empirical. The central importance of therapist skills will be further discussed later.

The question then arises, given that we have decided which technique to use, how should it be applied? Again, there is little consensus in the research with regard to such basic parameters as the number of sessions, and this can vary from one to more than twenty. This variability undoubtedly reflects different populations and different aims. A single session may be sufficient to investigate how college students learn a socially skilled reply to a taped stimulus, but if the aim is to help chronically disabled patients learn highly complex sequences of social behaviour then rather more sessions will be required. If the aim is long-term management and maintenance then no limit can be set in advance on the number of sessions. Other procedural details also have to be decided, for example the spacing of sessions and how best to present new material. Again, this will be influenced by the characteristics of the populations involved. Clinical groups may be characterized by relatively low levels of intelligence, or high levels of anxiety (or both). It follows that they are likely to have particular difficulties in acquiring new material, especially complex skills, and that there is likely to be a rapid decay of newly learned material between sessions. Spacing sessions fairly close together, and overlearning new responses beyond a first correct performance may help reduce these difficulties. The research with clinical groups confirms the importance of intensive, highly repetitive practice (Bellack *et al.*, 1976; Goldsmith and McFall, 1975; Gutride *et al.*, 1974). It can similarly be argued that a slow rate of presentation and some kind of pure-part or progressive-part learning method may reduce other information-processing problems (Hemsley, 1977; Nettlebeck and Kirby, 1976). As in the case of teaching schizophrenic patients new work skills it is necessary to break down the task into small units each one of which must be thoroughly mastered before proceeding to the next and before attempting to chain the units into a complete sequence (Wing, 1967). Thus, characteristics of the individual clients will affect the way in which the treatment is carried out and the ease with which new learning will take place. There are some other important individual differences that also need to be considered; these are discussed below.

Anxiety, cognitions, and motivation

The prominence of anxiety symptoms in patients with social difficulties has been noted by several writers (e.g. Hall and Goldberg, 1977). There is some debate over whether the physical symptoms of anxiety should be seen as primary (hence a social 'phobia', Marks, 1969), or secondary to a skills deficit (the 'skills' model, Argyle, 1969), or simply as a mediating variable (somewhere 'in-between', Hall and Goldberg, 1977). Social anxiety, like other fears, is a complex construct (Lang, 1966), and the different components (self-report, behaviour, physiological changes) interact in a complex way (Rachman and Hodgson, 1974). The important question is whether treating the subjective symptoms of anxiety as the primary component will produce better results than treating the behavioural problems? Studies which have compared anxiety-reducing techniques (desensitization) and skills training treatments have usually found very few differences, although there may be some slight superiority of skills training for improving actual behaviour (Marzillier *et al.*, 1976; Trower *et al.*, 1976; Curran and Gilbert, 1975; Wright, 1976). Hall and Goldberg (1977) found an opposite effect in their study: desensitization actually produced the greatest improvement in self-reported social participation, but the results are difficult to compare with the other studies because of the sample differences and because of the dependent measures used (mainly self-reports). If patients were carefully screened with anxiety particularly in mind, and then the treatments evaluated specifically with regard to their effectiveness in reducing anxiety, perhaps a clearer conclusion might be reached, e.g. Shaw (1976).

A similar situation holds with regard to the role of cognitive factors. There is little doubt that they are often prominent (Nichols, 1974) and 'cause'—in some sense—behavioural and other responses, but precisely how important they are, and how effectively they can be changed, is another matter. Lange and Jakubowski (1976) suggest the use of self-talk procedures (after Meichenbaum, 1973) and 'rational restructuring' (after Ellis, 1962). Both these approaches hold promise but the available empirical evidence for their effectiveness is weak (Margolis and Shemberg, 1976; Thorpe *et al.*, 1976). It will be recognized that this question of whether changes in behaviour follow from changes in cognitions is one of the central issues in the current controversy over the effectiveness of traditional psychotherapies. Perhaps approaches based on learning theories will provide more unequivocal evidence, but this is not yet the case.

There is one other individual difference that needs to be considered, and this is perhaps the most important one: motivation. It is a difficult, some would argue even an unnecessary, concept but the fact is that some patients do not seem particularly interested in improving their social functioning and this factor in itself can make any treatment impossible. It therefore seems important to have some way of conceptualizing motivational problems. Irwin (1971) has suggested that motivation depends on the expectations held with regard to the consequences of our actions. We have goals which we seek to approach or avoid according to whether we expect that such approaches or avoidances will be associated with positive or negative consequences. It also seems important that we feel some kind of direct, instrumental relationship between our actions and these consequences (De Charms, 1968). It has been suggested that not feeling 'in control' in this sense contributes to the state of 'learned helplessness' which is supposed to be associated with depressed mood and inactivity (Seligman, 1975). Thus, if a client does seek a particular goal but seems poorly motivated to acquire the relevant new responses then we must either enhance the positive consequences of new learning and/or decrease the negative consequences. Furthermore we should attempt to give him some feeling of being in control of his behaviour and environment. This analysis implies that the extensive use of contingent, positive reinforcement and clear feedback on performance, will be particularly important in treatment, a point which is stressed in most of the training manuals (Liberman *et al.*, 1976; Trower *et al.*, 1978). It also implies that if the possible negative consequences of learning new social behaviour can be reduced, either in terms of cognitions or anxiety symptoms, then this will also be valuable.

In conclusion, although important individual differences have been identified which do seem to affect the treatment process, and we do seem to have a pragmatic understanding of how to change behaviour, our knowledge of the mechanisms through which treatment effects are mediated is slight. In the absence of the empirical data, a considerable responsibility thus falls on therapists to decide which techniques are to be used, how they are to be applied, and how to tailor them to the individual differences of the clients involved. It is therefore important that in the future some research is directed towards identifying the characteristics of effective therapists. This will undoubtedly mean going beyond the therapist variables identified by the research into non-directive techniques (Truax and Carkhuff, 1967), and attempting to observe more directly what it is that effective therapists actually do (Alexander *et al.*, 1976). In the long term we need to produce individual-centred treatment routines so that the decision-making processes of effective therapists can be successfully replicated. Strategies which take account of individual differences and suggest the more effective methods of instruction are beginning to appear in the work skills field (Dallos and Winfield, 1975), and there is an obvious need for similar devices in the area of psychological treatment. The problem of reconciling individual differences in an experimental science is one that has concerned psychologists for some time (Cronbach, 1957, 1975; Shapiro, 1961, 1971). For the moment, the most scientific solution seems to be for each individual therapist to investigate the effects of individual differences and their relationship to treatment outcome for the clients he/she is currently working with.

Having considered the problems of establishing new responses we need now to look at the problem of how to promote generalization proper, i.e. how to get a response established during training to generalize to a new and independent context.

In simple terms this means transferring the improvements to the patient's everyday life, their family, friends and day-to-day social encounters, can the treatment be arranged such that generalization is 'programmed-in'?

Programming for generalization

As indicated earlier a good deal has been written about the problem of generalization but there seems to be a gap between the academic recognition of the problem and its practical solution; certainly there was in our own work. The results of the first trial (Shepherd, 1977) had shown no evidence of generalized improvements and although we recognized the importance of practice outside the group we had not analysed the problem in theoretical terms. We did not therefore appreciate the importance of trying to maximize the similarity between the conditions obtaining in treatment and those in other settings. To quote Mackintosh again:

> Subjects respond in the test situation to the extent that it contains stimulus elements identical to those associated with reinforcement during training; they fail to respond in a test situation to the extent that it contains no elements that were originally associated with reinforcement (Mackintosh, 1974, p. 540.)

The crucial determinant is the number of common elements present. This degree of similarity between training and generalization (test) conditions defines the familiar 'gradient' of generalization. The problem of programming for generalization is therefore a problem of designing treatment programmes which contain conditions as similar as possible to those in real life.

Replicating stimulus and response conditions

From the point of view of stimulus conditions it follows that the training stimuli should be as relevant as possible to the problems likely to be encountered outside treatment. This point is well illustrated by Goldsmith and McFall (1975) who spent some time compiling a set of problem situations that were most closely relevant to the patients' real-life difficulties. In our own training programmes we have also built up a list of those situations most commonly reported by patients as presenting the greatest difficulty, and used these in treatment. There are other ways in which treatment can be made more like the problems in a real-life situation. For example, if a client's difficulties lie in meeting new people then in treatment he should actually have the opportunity to practise meeting new people. This argues for the use of a 'stooge' in treatment who is unfamiliar to the patient, rather than a group member trying to role-play a 'stranger' who is well-known and 'safe' as far as the patient is concerned. In a similar way, it is useful to do as much of the treatment as possible '*in vivo*'; i.e. in the natural environment, such as shops, cafés, or in the street. This does require careful prior planning but it is possible to accomplish this with the minimum of artificiality (Shepherd, 1978). There is an extra complication here in that the training stimuli should not only be actually similar to the generalization stimuli but they must also be *perceived* as similar. It follows from current personality theory that it is the interaction component between stimulus and person that is the major determinant of the response (Wiggins, 1973; Endler and Magnusson, 1976). Recognition of the role of perceived stimulus meaning underlines the necessity of looking very carefully at clients' cognitive processes during treatment. When patients complain that treatment seems to them 'artificial' they are saying something of real psychological importance.

Response conditions and reponse consequences (reinforcement) must also be replicated as far as possible between the training and the generalization context. It is worth emphasizing that, from a strictly operant point of view, unless the reinforcement conditions are replicated in the generalization context then in treatment we have done nothing more than performed a simple reversal design (A–B–A). If the reinforcement conditions are not altered from pre-treatment (baseline) levels, then there is little reason to suppose that new responses will generalize, or will be maintained over time. It is therefore crucial that the new responses should have a maximum probability of being reinforced in the natural situation. This argues again for training those responses which are most relevant to day-to-day life, and which are most likely to be socially 'effective', and which thus have the highest probability of natural reinforcement. Some recent research which has aimed at defining more clearly what constitute effective, skilled responses in particular social situations is therefore relevant in this connection.

These studies usually proceed by taking two criterion groups, defined as skilled or unskilled by independent criteria, and then comparing their social behaviour in detail. Eisler and his colleagues (Eisler *et al.*, 1973, 1975) compared assertive and non-assertive psychiatric inpatients and found a number of behavioural differences: the high assertive subjects tended to talk longer, with greater affect and speech volume, and made clearer requests for new behaviour. Eisler *et al.* note the importance of situational determinants of the assertive response, e.g. the content and the nature of the interaction. Arkowitz *et al.* (1975) found that only one clear behavioural difference—number of conversational silences—discriminated between high- and low-frequency dating college men. Glasgow and Arkowitz (1975) report similar results. In their study, cognitions (negative self-evaluations) and ratings of physical appearance were more important in discriminating high-frequency dating men than were behavioural differences. For women there did seem to be some kind of skills deficit, although its precise nature was not clear. Bryant *et al.* (1976) also found that only some of the total range of verbal and non-verbal behaviours discriminated their socially adequate and inadequate groups (outpatients), and there was considerable overlap between the groups. They also note the importance of interaction skills, e.g. inviting others to respond, showing an interest, etc. Similarly Libet and Lewinsohn (1973) compared depressed and non-depressed individuals, and their results suggested that the skills deficit in depression was primarily one of failure to emit behaviours that are positively reinforced, rather than the emission of behaviours that are punished by others.

This research points to the subtle complexities of skilled social behaviour and also raises some questions with regard to aspects of the social skills model. For example, is it true that socially skilled individuals do differ from the unskilled in terms of verbal and non-verbal behaviours; or are other variables, e.g. cognitive, interactional, even physical ones, just as important? The answer to this question has obvious implications for the choice of suitable targets for treatment. The research implies that theories of socially 'skilled' interaction must be sufficiently flexible to allow for the influence of individuals, problems, and situations. Social interactions may be rule-governed as Harré and Secord (1972) suggest, but these rules are not precise, and they allow a certain latitude within which acceptable or 'skilled' social behaviour is defined. A skills model cannot therefore be expected to provide a kind of 'blueprint' defining effective social behaviour. The responsibility for choosing exactly which pattern of responses are likely to be most effective for each individual once again falls largely on the therapist.

In addition to training those responses that are most likely to be reinforced, what other measures can we take to maximize the reinforcement given to newly acquired responses when they are produced in real-life situations? During treatment, reinforcement is under the control of the therapist, whereas in the real world this control is very limited. However, the therapist can sometimes influence social contexts outside the immediate treatment setting—for example, by alerting and 'programming' other staff members to generalize gains from a treatment group to social performance in other places around a hospital ward, hostel, or day-centre. Similarly, it may be possible to persuade the family to cooperate in reinforcing new responses, and some preliminary work on this approach has been reported (Hudson, 1975; Atkinson, 1978). However, the problems are still formidable and it is often not possible to enlist the help of 'natural therapists' in this way. In these circumstances the professional therapist may want to accompany the patient into the new situations, at least initially. This arrangement is similar to the 'buddy' system described by Fo and O'Donnel (1975), and the work using volunteers to support psychiatric outpatients reported by Katkin *et al.* (1971). If all else fails, the clients can at least be encouraged to reinforce theselves for progress and new learning (for a description of the 'self-reinforcement' technique, see Rehm and Marston, 1968).

The importance of contingent and continuous reinforcement for the acquisition of new responses is widely accepted, and it should be appreciated that the same parameters apply to the problem of generalizing and maintaining improvements. For most of us our social behaviour may be adequately maintained on partial and non-contingent reinforcement schedules, but for clients struggling to transfer new responses or maintain ones which are only weakly established, such schedules make transfer or maintenance difficult, if not impossible. So, there are problems in establishing new responses, and problems in generalizing them, but there may be an even more fundamental problem: there may be virtually no 'independent social context' into which new responses can generalize.

Providing a context for generalization

In the Introduction to this chapter it was suggested that there might be a relationship between social difficulties at the level of interaction and social difficulties at the level of integration. This relationship has been confirmed in several surveys; those individuals who have interpersonal problems also tend to be socially isolated, to be single, to be unemployed, to have few contacts with friends or family (Bryant *et al.*, 1976; Hall and Goldberg, 1977). It may therefore be more sensible to try and find a client employment—hence some kind of independent social context—before training him in socially skilled responses which he will have no real opportunity to use. Similarly, it may be necessary to introduce him to some new social club or activity before starting on treatment. It may even be necessary to consider the use of artificial social environments, for example, an ongoing group, even a hostel, to give long-term support and to provide a controlled context where the new responses can generalize through practice and reinforcement. From all that has been said so far it is apparent that the gains obtained within such artificial systems should still not be expected to generalize outside them. In our own research, although we were able to find some evidence of generalized improvements after modifying our procedures the improvements were still limited to within the day-hospital and we have yet to demonstrate any significant benefits in terms of general social adjustment (Shepherd, 1978).

It can be seen that the problems of establishing and maintaining generalized improvements in social functioning are considerable. Where does this leave us? Firstly, we could discard our rather strict learning-theory model and aim at producing changes in underlying cognitions in the hope that they would exert a determining influence on behaviour which would then generalize. There is some evidence to support such an approach (Glass *et al.*, 1976), but in general our ability to produce such changes, and their relation to subsequent behaviours, remains doubtful. Alternatively, but in the same vein, we might argue that an approach which aims at teaching the 'rules' of appropriate social interaction, rather than specific responses, might be more effective in promoting generalization. This is a sensible suggestion, but again it awaits empirical validation. Thirdly, we might hope that a better understanding of individual differences would contribute to a better match between problems and techniques and hence to more strongly established responses during the training phase (and so, presumably, to more generalization). Given the complexity of the relationship between individual differences and outcome, this is a solution which again seems plausible, but also technically and empirically rather remote. There are probably other improvements in technique that might help, but we will now consider some alternatives which differ more radically in their conceptualization.

ALTERNATIVE SOLUTIONS

Prevention

Caplan (1964) distinguishes between three different types of preventive model:

(a) primary—a reduction in incidence by the direct prevention of new cases occurring;
(b) secondary—a reduction in prevalence by reducing a number of cases present in a population at any one time, usually achieved through early identification and rapid and effective treatment;
(c) tertiary—a reduction in the handicaps consequent upon illness by the application of effective treatment techniques.

Primary prevention obviously has the most appeal if it is feasible and practical. To achieve successful primary prevention requires precise and detailed information about aetiological factors, and the availability of an effective intervention to influence them. In the case of social difficulties we lack both the information and the means. Unfortunately, social difficulties are not like physical conditions where the factors responsible for causing the conditions may be limited and identifiable; it is then often a relatively straightforward matter to intervene and eliminate the causal agent, e.g. a virus or bacillus, thereby preventing new cases from occurring. Social difficulties, however, have a number of 'causes', and different causes can lead to similar outcomes. The causal pathways are complex and interactional and there is therefore doubt that even if potential causal relationships could be found, and effective interventions mounted, that this would actually affect the incidence of new cases.

In physical conditions epidemiological evidence often provides important clues to possible causal factors, and it has been suggested that such evidence might be similarly useful with regard to social problems (Cowen, 1973). However, the epidemiological evidence in relation to social and psychological difficulties is basically inconclusive (Dohrenwend and Dohrenwend, 1974; Dunham, 1976); and if broad social or cultural factors are implicated (e.g. Sartorius *et al.*, 1977; Cooper and Sartorius, 1977), then it is difficult to see both ethically and empirically how such processes could be influenced. The theories of social difficulty couched at a more psychological level—emphasizing the importance of modelling and other learning experiences, e.g. Trower *et al.*, 1978—are also very much speculative ones and do not provide clear justification for where, how (and whether) to intervene. Primary prevention of social difficulties must therefore remain a worthy objective, but with little empirical basis as yet. (But see Chapter 5 in this volume for a different view.)

Secondary prevention aims at reducing prevalence by the early identification of new cases and hence the provision of more rapid and effective treatment. Once again, this is a concept which is more easily applicable to physical conditions where the assumption that early identification will necessarily lead to more rapid and effective treatment is perhaps more easily defended. In the case of social difficulties there is evidence that valid early identification of problems is possible. Zax and Specter (1974) review a number of studies indicating that children with social and other difficulties can be identified quite early in their school careers. The classic study by Robins (1966) also illustrates how behavioural problems in childhood can be valid indicators of adjustment difficulties in the future. Similarly, the research on these children at high risk for schizophrenia (children of schizophrenic parents) has shown that they can be discriminated from normal controls on the basis of their physiological responsiveness (Mednick and Schulsinger, 1968), and disturbances in classroom behaviour (Weintraub *et al.*, 1975). So, in several areas early identification of 'high-risk' groups seems possible, but whether this will necessarily lead to more rapid and effective treatment is a more open question. It is evident that early intervention programmes tend to produce dramatic improvements at first, but there have been few convincing demonstrations that these improvements are maintained after long follow-up periods (Yule, 1976). There is thus a potential for secondary prevention, but as with other treatment interventions the problem seems to be maintaining the effects of the intervention over long periods of time. (Since tertiary prevention refers to treatment of the kind already covered it will not be further discussed.)

Long-term Management

All that I have said so far suggests a general conclusion that the social difficulties of psychiatric patients are often pervasive and long-standing, and that this applies whether or not they receive available treatments. There are some important implications for the nature and organization of services which follow from this conclusion. Firstly, it seems that the effective management of social difficulties will depend on providing services which are concerned as directly as possible with the problems as they arise in the patient's ordinary life, i.e. in the community, in his family, with his friends, etc. Only in this way, by working directly on 'criterion' behaviour, can the problem of generalization be, at least partially, circumvented. This would argue in favour of partial hospitalization and community-based services and for minimizing the use of inpatient admissions. These services need to use the natural networks of social supports (family, friends, etc.), or where these are not available to provide artificial systems through day-hospitals, day-centres, hostels, group homes, etc. A range of interventions is required to suit the needs of different individuals, and there is a need to accept a rather longer-term supportive role than perhaps is usually envisaged.

The aims and organization of these services, however they differ in terms of setting, will have much in common. We have seen how difficult it is to 'treat' social difficulties effectively in the sense of producing significant and generalized improvements; a more realistic aim is simply to maintain functioning at the highest possible level. This aim may be characterized as 'management' rather than 'treatment'. It needs to be emphasized that to aim at maintaining social functioning and adaptation over long periods of time is by no means a modest goal. If the experience of institutional care has taught us anything, it is that some systems of long-term care in fact allow deterioration to occur. Given the other evidence presented in this chapter concerning the untreated, or post-treatment, course of social difficulties, it is apparent that in many cases to be 'standing still' is a considerable achievement. Of course, if significant improvements can be achieved and these can be maintained, this is to be welcomed.

In order to design systems of care which will be effective we need to understand very clearly what features of traditional long-term care contributed to deterioration. By now it is clear that the functional deterioration of chronic patients is not something that occurs only in institutions; studies of community-based care have already highlighted the fact that patients can become 'institutionalized' while living in the community (Wing and Hailey, 1972). 'Institutionalization' is the product of an interaction between features of the patients' condition and features of the environment (Paul, 1969). These environmental features can be present in various non-hospital settings, e.g. day-centres, hostels, even families. Can we define them more clearly?

The 'total institution' was first described by Goffman (1961), but it was not until more recently that King *et al.* (1971) reported an attempt to operationalize Goffman's concepts and to examine empirically how aspects of the management and organization of institutional settings related to staff–client interactions. They developed a questionnaire measure of management practices along four dimensions (rigidity of routine, block treatment, depersonalization, and social distance) and scored the items on each dimension according to whether they seemed to be 'institutionally oriented' or 'client-oriented'. Institutionally oriented practices were those which seemed to exist mainly to serve the needs of a smooth-running organization; 'client-oriented' practices were those which seemed to attempt to meet the needs of individual clients more directly. They found striking differences between the institutions (residential homes for mentally handicapped children) in terms of the orientation of their management practices as defined above. These differences were mirrored in the staff–child interactions. In 'client-oriented' institutions staff were observed to interact with the children to a much greater degree than in the institutionally oriented homes. They did so in a way that was more personalized, and they were seen by observers as 'warmer', more accepting, and less rejecting. These differences did not seem attributable to differences in the nature of the handicaps of the children, to size of institution, or to staff ratios. The study has recently been replicated on a smaller scale, using psychiatric day-centres for the adult chronically metally ill (Shepherd and Richardson, 1978).

These workers found evidence of differences in management practices which were associated with particular day-centres and with aspects of the staff–client, but not staff–staff, interactions. Current management practices were assessed by pooling staffs' responses to questionnaire items which could be scored in either a 'client-oriented' or 'institutionally oriented' direction. The interactions between staff and clients were assessed by direct observation and coded according to their content and quality. These instruments resembled very closely those used by King *et al.* (1971). The centres which were found to be organized in the most 'client-oriented' directions showed the highest rates of staff–client interactions. These interactions showed a greater recognition of each individual's problems and were rated as affectively 'warmer' in quality. In the more 'institutionally oriented' centres lower rates of staff–client interactions were observed and they were rated as more 'functional' (i.e. less personal), and less 'warm'. The findings were supported by correlations within staff between their individual attitudes towards management practices ('client-oriented' or 'institutionally oriented') and their observed interactions. The results did not seem attributable to other differences between the centres; for example, different kinds of clients, facilities, etc. Thus, background variables such as age, sex, diagnosis, and chronicity did not differentiate between the clients from different centres.

This was a relatively small-scale project and the results obviously require wider replication. It is possible that more detailed measures of client characteristics might reveal differences which are associated with particular centres. Nevertheless, the findings do raise interesting questions, particularly about possible causal relationships. For example, is it possible to influence staff–client interactions by changing management practices? Would high levels of staff–client interaction ('personalized' and 'warm') lead to improvements in functioning? Conversely, do low levels of interaction ('functional', relatively 'cold') lead to deterioration? In the context of day-care we do not yet have direct answers to these questions and they require experimental investigation.

However, there is some evidence from related areas to suggest that changes in organization and staff behaviour can directly influence functioning. For example, Jenkins *et al.* (1977) working in residential homes for the elderly showed that changes in organization to provide suitable materials increased the number of clients who were actively engaged in their environment. Similarly, Powell *et al.* (1978) showed that the provision of materials, with clear instructions to staff on how to organize the activity, resulted in marked increases in the levels of engagement of elderly clients. This finding has been replicated in a day-centre for profoundly mentally handicapped adults (Porterfield *et al.*, 1978). We also saw earlier how the opportunity for individuals to observe and practise new behaviour relevant to their problems and to receive clear informational feedback from staff probaby accounts for the effectiveness of token economy systems (Baker *et al.*, 1977). Thus, there are reasons to suppose that environments which are organized in such a way as to provide opportunities to engage in adaptive behaviour, are tailored to individual needs, with relatively high levels of reinforcing and informative interaction from staff, do seem effective in improving or maintaining functioning.

Success in establishing and maintaining such environments will rest very critically on the attitudes of the staff involved. Raynes *et al.* (1977) has shown that one of the most important factors influencing the degree to which institutional practices are likely to arise is the extent to which staff perceive themselves as genuinely involved in the decision-making and running of the unit. It may be, then, that just as cognition and motivation are crucial for the generalization and maintenance of new social skills in clients' behaviour, so they are equally crucial in the generalization and maintenance of new therapeutic skills in the behaviour of staff (or family, or friends, or any other 'direct-carers'). This raises a new direction for future research. It shifts the emphasis away from the refinement of techniques and their short-term implementation in research settings and towards the problems of involving and motivating staff in long-term practice settings.

It also represents a reconceptualization of the problem of treating social difficulties which is more radically environmental and more completely rejects medical and neo-medical models. While there remains an idea that social difficulties can be 'cured' then medical models are still operating, for they are most clearly reflected in concepts of 'treatment' and 'cure'. Treatments are applied to cure internal disease states; they can be evaluated before and after their application; it is assumed that their effects will be evident across different settings, and that a follow-up may be performed to discover how long the 'cure' has lasted. This kind of model locates pathology, whether formulated in physical or psychological terms, very firmly inside the organism. It is something that the patient carries around with him. This view can be contrasted with one which sees the problem as a genuine interaction between the individual's internal difficulties and the environment—particularly the social environment—in which he finds himself. Given that there are limitations in the extent to which it is possible to intervene effectively and to alter internal psychological states (attitudes, feelings, etc.) we are led towards a strategy which emphasizes the importance of creating and maintaining therapeutic (social) environments. With this emphasis on the environmental component, it becomes less surprising that changes to a no-treatment condition, such as when assessing generalization or follow-up, cause the treatment effects to disappear. With regard to the long-term care of social difficulties the evidence seems compelling in making the shift from medical models to more purely psychological and environmental ones.

ETHICAL CONSIDERATIONS

It would be a pity to leave this area without at least a brief consideration of some of the ethical issues involved. The ethical position of many treatments in psychiatry has come under close scrutiny in recent years (Shepherd, 1975; Braun, 1975; Halleck, 1974). In general the recommendation has been made that treatments should not be applied without the informed consent of the patient or responsible guardian. This principle rests on the idea that if the patient is supplied with all the available information concerning the potential benefits and the personal 'costs' involved, then the decision as to whether to proceed with treatment must be left with him. This seems like a sound principle but its application in practice may still give rise to controversy.

With many social treatments it is often difficult to specify with any degree of accuracy the likely outcome, or to convey fully what treatment will entail. For example, the dangers of overstimulating some chronic patients have been mentioned but at the moment it is not possible to predict accurately who is most at risk. The therapist can therefore only be cautious and honest about the uncertainties and lack of information, and try to minimize the amount of verbal coercion employed. Most importantly, he should be very much aware of the poorly motivated patient who by his own behaviour, or lack of it, indicates at least a partial withholding of consent. If, after careful counselling, motivation cannot be improved then there is little that the therapist could, or should, wish to do about it. The final safeguard must be that the whole system of treatment and management is sufficiently open to outside inspection, so that if ethically doubtful practices do occur then they can be given adequate scrutiny.

SUMMARY

In this chapter I have tried to show that difficulties in social functioning and adaptation lie at the heart of psychological and psychiatric difficulties. We have seen how they are implicated in the aetiology and onset of problems and how they provide some guide as to the likely outcome. We have also seen how difficult it is to 'treat' social difficulties effectively—in any usual sense of that word—and how in order to overcome the problems of transferring and maintaining treatment effects we need to consider how to organize and maintain special therapeutic environments which will manage the problems successfully over long periods of time. This view of the treatment of social difficulties demands a revision of our traditional outlook; we need to think not only more in environmental and organizational terms but also in terms of the attitudes as well as the behaviour of those concerned with long-term care. It would be a change for researchers to shift from their usual focus on technique and technical improvements to looking at organization and staff practice and attitudes, but the latter do constitute perfectly respectable dependent variables. For the moment, perhaps, our problems lie not so much in a lack of knowledge about how to change behaviour, but in a failure to be able to implement efficiently what we already know.

REFERENCES

Alexander, J. F., Barton, C., Schiavo, R. S., and Parsons, B. V. (1976). Systems-behavioural intervention with families of delinquents: Therapist characteristics, family behaviour, and outcome. *Journal of Consultative and Clinical Psychology*, **44,** 656–664.

Anthony, W. A., Buell, G. J., Sharratt, S., and Althoff, M. E. (1972). Efficacy of psychiatric rehabilitation. *Psychological Bulletin*, **78,** 447–456.

Argyle, M. (1969). *Social Interaction*. (London: Methuen.)

Argyle, M., Bryant, B., and Trower, P. (1974). Social skills training and psychotherapy: a comparative study. *Psychological Medicine*, **4,** 435–443.

Arkowitz, H., Lichtenstein, E., McGovern, K., and Hines, P. (1975). The behavioural

assessment of social competence in males. *Behavior Therapy*, **6,** 3–13.
Atkinson, J. M. (1978). Community care of chronic schizophrenic patients using behavioural methods. Part II. Paper presented at British Association for Behaviour Psychotherapy Annual Conference, Stirling, Scotland.
Austin, N. K., Liberman, R. P., King, L. W., and DeRisi, W. J. (1976). A comparative evaluation of two day-hospitals. *Journal of Nervous and Mental Disease*, **163,** 253–262.
Ayllon, T. and Azrin, N. (1968). *The Token Economy: A Motivational System for Therapy and Rehabilitation*. (New York: Appleton-Century-Crofts.)
Azrin, N. H. (1976). Improvements in the community reinforcement approach to alcoholism. *Behaviour Research and Therapy*, **14,** 339–348.
Baker, R., Hall, J. N. and Hutchinson, K. (1974). A token economy project with chronic schizophrenic patients. *British Journal of Psychiatry*, **124,** 367–384.
Baker, R., Hall, N. J., Hutchinson, K., and Bridge, G. (1977). Symptom changes in chronic schizophrenic patients on a token economy: a controlled experiment. *British Journal of Psychiatry*, **131,** 381–393.
Beiser, M. (1976). Personal and social factors associated with the remission of psychiatric symptoms. *Archives of General Psychiatry*, **33,** 941–945.
Bellack, A. S., Hersen, M., and Turner, S. M. (1976). Generalisation effects of social skills training in chronic schizophrenics: an experimental analysis. *Behaviour Research and Therapy*, **14,** 391–398.
Bennett, D., Folkard, S., and Nicholson, A. J. (1961). Resettlement unit in a mental hospital. *Lancet*, **2,** 593–541.
Bloom, B. L. (1968). An ecological analysis of psychiatric hospitalization. *Multivariate Behavioral Research*, **3,** 423–463.
Bockhoven, J. S. (1956). Moral treatment in American psychiatry. *Journal of Nervous and Mental Disease*, **124,** 167–94, 292–321.
Braun, S. H. (1975). Ethical issues in behaviour modification. *Behavior Therapy*, **6,** 51–62.
Brown, G. W., Birley, J. L. T., and Wing, J. K. (1972). Influence of family life on the course of schizophrenic disorders: A replication. *British Journal of Psychiatry*, **121,** 241–258.
Brown, G. W., Harris, T. O., and Peto, J. (1973). Life events and psychiatric disorders. Part 2: Nature of causal link. *Psychological Medicine*, **3,** 159–176.
Brown, G. W., Bhrolchain, M. N., and Harris, T. (1975). Social class and psychiatric disturbance among women in an urban population. *Sociology*, **9,** 225–254.
Bryant, B., Trower, P., Yardley, K., Urbieta, H., and Letemendia, F. J. J. (1976). A survey of social inadequacy among psychiatric outpatients. *Psychological Medicine*, **6,** 101–112.
Caplan, G. (1964). *Principles of Preventive Psychiatry*. (New York: Basic Books.)
Clark, D. H. (1974). *Social Therapy in Psychiatry*. (London: Penguin.)
Cooper, J. and Sartorius, N. (1977). Cultural and temporal variations in schizophrenia: a speculation on the importance of industrialization. *British Journal of Psychiatry*, **130,** 50–55.
Copas, J. B. and Whiteley, J. S. (1976). Predicting success in the treatment of psychopaths. *British Journal Psychiatry*, **129,** 388–392.
Cowen, E. L. (1973). Social and community interventions. *Annual Review of Psychology*, **24,** 423–472.
Cronbach, L. J. (1957). The two disciplines of scientific psychology. *American Psychologist*, **12,** 671–684.
Cronbach, L. J. (1975). Beyond the two disciplines of scientific psychology. *American Psychology*, **30,** 116–127.
Curran, J. P. and Gilbert, F. S. (1975). A test of the relative effectiveness of a systematic desensitization program and an interpersonal skills training program with date anxious subjects. *Behavior Therapy*, **6,** 510–521.

Dallos, R and Winfield, I. (1975). Instructional strategies in industrial training and rehabilitation. *Journal of Occupational Psychology*, **48,** 241–252.

Davis, A. E., Dinitz, S., and Pasamanick, B. (1972). The prevention of hospitalization in schizophrenia: five years after an experimental program. *American Journal of Orthopsychiatry*, **42,** 375–388.

De Charms, R. (1968). *Personal Causation: the Internal Affective Determinants of Behaviour*. (New York: Academic Press.)

Dohrenwend, B. P. and Dohrenwend, B. S. (1974). Social and cultural influences on psychopathology. *Annual Review of Psychiatry*, **25,** 417–452.

Dunham, H. W. (1976). Society, culture, and mental disorder. *Archives of General Psychiatry*, **33,** 147–156.

Eisler, R. M., Miller, P. M., and Hersen, M. (1973). Components of assertive behaviour. *Journal of Clinical Psychology*, **29,** 295–299.

Eisler, R. M., Hersen, M., Miller, P. M., and Blanchard, E. B. (1975). Situational determinants of assertive behaviour. *Journal of Consultative and Clinical Psychology*, **43,**, 330–340.

Ellis, A. (1962). *Reason and Emotion in Psychotherapy*. (New York: Lyle Stuart.)

Endler, N and Magnusson, D. (1976). Toward an interactional psychology of personality. *Psychological Bulletin*, **83,** 956–974.

Erickson, R. C. (1975). Outcome studies in mental hospitals: A review. *Psychological Bulletin*, **82,** 519–540.

Eysenck, H. J. (1960). The Effects of Psychotherapy. In: H. J. Eysenck (Ed.), *Handbook of Abnormal Psychology*. (London: Pitman.)

Fairweather, G. W. (Ed.) (1964). *Social Psychology in Treating Mental Illness*. (New York: Wiley.)

Fairweather, G. W., Sanders, D. H., Maynard, H., and Cressler, D. L. (1969). *Community Life for the Mentally Ill*. (Chicago: Aldine.)

Fo, W. S. and O'Donnell, C. R. (1975). The buddy system: effect of community intervention on delinquent offenses. *Behavior Therapy*, **6,** 522–524.

Fontana, A. F. and Dows, B. N. (1975). Assessing treatment outcome. I. Adjustment in the community. *Journal of Nervous and Mental Disease*, **161,** 221–230.

Freeman, H. E. and Simmons, O. G. (1963). *The Mental Patient Comes Home*. (New York: Wiley.)

Gagnon, J. H. and Davison, G. C. (1976). Asylums, the token economy, and the metrics of mental life. *Behavior Therapy*, **7,** 528–534.

Glasgow, R. E. and Arkowitz, H. (1975). The behavioural assessment of male and female social competence in dyadic heterosexual interactions. *Behavior Therapy*, **6,** 488–498.

Glass, C. R., Gottman, J. M., and Shmurak, S. H. (1976). Response acquisition and cognitive self-statement modification apprroaches to dating-skills training. *Journal of Counselling Psychology*, **23,** 520–526.

Glick, I. D., Hargreaves, W. A., Drues, J., Showstack, J. A., and Katzow, J. J. (1977). Short *vs.* long hospitalization: a prospective controlled study. VII. Two year follow-up results for non-schizophrenics. *Archives of General Psychiatry,* **34,** 314–317.

Goffman, E. (1961). *Asylums: Essays on the Social Situation of Mental Patients and Other Inmates*. (New York: Anchor Books, Doubleday.)

Goldsmith, J. B. and McFall, R. M. (1975). Development and evaluation of an interpersonal skill-training program for psychiatric in-patients. *Journal of Abnormal Psychology*, **84,** 51–58.

Goldstein, A.P., Martens, J., Hubben, J., van Belle, H. A., Schaaf, W., Wiersma, H., and Goedhart, A. (1973). The use of modelling to increase independent behaviour. *Behaviour Research and Therapy*, **11,** 31–42.

Gore, C. P. and Jones, K. (1961). Survey of a long-stay mental hospital population. *Lancet*, **2**, 544–546.
Griffiths, R. D. P. (1973). A standardised assessment of the work behaviour of psychiatric patients. *British Journal of Psychiatry*, **123**, 403–408.
Griffiths, R. D. P. (1974). Rehabilitation of chronic psychotic patients. *Psychological Medicine*, **4**, 316–325.
Gripp, R. F. and Magaro, P. A. (1974). The token economy program in the psychiatric hospital: A review and analysis. *Behaviour Research and Therapy*, **12**, 205–228.
Gutride, M. E., Goldstein, A. P., Hunter, G. F., Carol, S., Clark, L., Furia, R., and Lower, W. (1974). Structured learning therapy with transfer training for chronic inpatients. *Journal of Clinical Psychology*, **30**, 277–279.
Hall, J. N., Baker, R. D. and Hutchinson, K. (1977). A controlled evaluation of token economy procedures with chronic schizophrenic patients. *Behaviour Research and Therapy*, **15**, 261–283.
Hall, R. and Goldberg, D. (1977). The role of social anxiety in social interaction difficulties. *British Journal of Psychiatry*, **131**, 610–615.
Halleck, S. L. (1974). Legal and ethical aspects of behaviour control. *American Journal of Psychiatry*, **131**, 381–385.
Hargreaves, W. A., Glick, I. D., Drues, J., Showstack, J. A., and Feigenbaum, E (1977). Short *vs*. long hospitalization: a prospective controlled study. VI. Two year follow-up results for schizophrenics. *Archives of General Psychiatry*, **34**, 305–311.
Harré, R. and Secord, P. F. (1972). *The Explanation of Social Behaviour*. (Oxford: Blackwell.)
Hassall, C. and Hellon, C. P. (1964). Survey of long-stay population at a psychiatric hospital. *British Journal of Psychiatry*, **110**, 183–185.
Heap, R. F., Boblitt, W. E., Moore, C. H. and Hord, J. E. (1970). Behaviour-milieu therapy with chronic neuropsychiatric patients. *Journal of Abnormal Psychology*, **76**, 349–354.
Hemsley, D. R. (1977). What have cognitive deficits to do with schizophrenic symptoms? *British Journal of Psychiatry*, **130**, 167–173.
Hemsley, D. R. (1978). Limitations of operant procedures in the modification of schizophrenic functioning: the possible relevance of studies of cognitive disturbance. *Behavioural Analysis and Modification*, **2**, 165–173. (In bress)
Hersen, M., Eisler, R. M., Miller, P. M., Johnson, M. B., and Pinkston, S. G. (1973). Effects of practice, instructions and modeling on components of assertive behaviour. *Behaviour Research and Therapy*, **11**, 443–451.
Hersen, M., Eisler, R. M., and Miller, P. M. (1974). An experimental analysis of generalisation in assertive training. *Behaviour Research and Therapy*, **12**, 295–310.
Hersen, M. and Bellack, A. S. (1976). Social skills training for chronic psychiatric patients: rationale, research findings and future directions. *Comparative Psychiatry*, **17**, 559–580.
Herz, M. I., Endicott, J., and Spitzer, R. L. (1975). Brief hospitalization of patients with families: Initial results. *American Journal of Psychiatry*, **132**, 4.
Herz, M. I., Endicott, J., and Spitzer, R. L. (1976). Brief versus standard hospitalization: the families. *American Journal of Psychiatry*, **133**, 795–780.
Herz, M. I., Endicott, J., and Spitzer, R. L. (1977). Brief hospitalization: A two-year follow-up. *American Journal of Psychiatry*, **134**, 5.
Higgs, W. J. (1970). Effects of gross environmental change upon behaviour of schizophrenics: a cautionary note. *Journal of Abnormal Psychology*, **76**, 421–422.
Hollingsworth, R. and Foreyt, J. P. (1975). Community adjustment of released token economy patients. *Journal of Behavior Therapy and Experimental Psychiatry*, **6**, 271–274.
Hudson, B. L. (1975). A behaviour modification project with chronic schizophrenics in the community. *Behaviour Research and Therapy*, **13**, 239–241.
Hunt, G. M. and Azrin, N. H. (1973). A community reinforcement approach to alcoholism.

Behaviour Research and Therapy, **11,** 91–104.
Irwin, F. W. (1971). *Intentional Behaviour and Motivation*. (Philadelphia: Lippincott Co.)
Jacobs, M. K. and Trick, O. L. (1974). Successful psychiatric rehabilitation using an inpatient teaching laboratory—a one-year follow-up study. *American Jornal of Psychiatry*, **131,** 145–148.
Jenkins, J., Felce, D., Lunt, B. and Powell. L. (1977). Increasing engagement in activity of residents on old people's homes by providing recreational material. *Behaviour Research and Therapy*, **15,** 429–434.
Jones, M. (1968). *Social Psychiatry in Practice*. (Harmondsworth: Penguin.)
Katkin, S., Ginsberg, M., Rifkin, M. J., and Scott, J. T. (1971). Effectiveness of female volunteers in the treatment of outpatients. *Journal of Counselling Psychology*, **18,** 97–100.
Kazdin, A. E. (1974). Effects of covert modeling and model reinforcement on assertive behaviour. *Journal of Abnormal Psychology*, **83,** 240–252.
Kazdin, A. E. and Bootzin, R. R. (1972). The token economy: an evaluative review. *Journal of Applied Behavior Analysis*, **5,** 342–372.
Kiesler, D. (1966). Some myths of psychotherapy. *Psychological Bulletin*, **65,** 110–136.
King, R., Raynes, N., and Tizard, J. (1971). *Patterns of Residential Care*. (London: Routledge & Kegan Paul.)
Lamb, H. R. and Goertzel. V. (1971). Discharged mental patients—are they really in the community? *Archives of General Psychiatry*, **24,** 29–34.
Lamb, H. R. and Goertzel. V. (1972). High expectations of long-term ex-state hospital patients. *American Journal of Psychiatry*, **129,** 471–475.
Lambert, M. J. (1976). Spontaneous remission in adult neurotic disorders: a revision and summary. *Psychological Bulletin*, **83,** 107–119.
Lang, P. J. (1966). Fear Reduction and Fear Behaviour. Proceedings of Third Conference on Research in Psychotherapy. (Chicago, Illinois.)
Lange, A. and Jakubowski, P. (1976). *Responsible Assertive Behaviour*. (Illinois: Research Press.)
Levine, J. and Zigler, E. (1973). The essential–reactive distinction in alcoholism. *Journal of Abnormal Psychology*, **81,** 242.
Liberman, R. P., King, L. W., De Risi, W. J., and McCann, M. (1975). *Personal Effectiveness*. (Champaign, Illinois: Research Press.)
Liberman, R. B., McCann, M. J., and Wallace, C. J. (1976). Generalisation of behaviour therapy with psychotics. *British Journal of Psychiatry.*, **129,** 490–496.
Libet, J. M. and Lewinsohn, P. M. (1973). Concept of social skill with special reference to the behaviour of depressed persons. *Journal of Consultative and Clinical Psychology*, **40,** 304–312.
Luborsky, Y. L., Singer, B., and Luborsky, L. (1975). Comparative studies of psychotherapies. *Archives of General Psychiatry*, **32,** 995–1008.
McFall, R. M. and Lilliesand, D. B. (1971). Behaviour rehearsal with modeling and coaching in assertion training. *Journal of Abnormal Psychology*, **77,** 313–323.
McFall, R. M and Marston, A. R. (1970). An experimental investigation of behaviour rehearsal in assertive training. *Journal of Abnormal Psychology*, **76,** 295–303.
McFall, R. M. and Twentyman, C. T. (1973). Four experiments on the relative contributions of rehearsal, modeling and coaching to assertion training. *Journal of Abnormal Psychology*, **81,** 199–218.
Mackintosh, N. J. (1974). *The Psychology of Animal Learning*. (New York: Academic Press.)
McMiller, P. and Ingham, J. G. (1976). Friends, confidants and symptoms. *Social Psychiatry*, **11,** 51–58.
Margolis, R. B. and Shemberg, K. M. (1976). Cognitive self-instruction in process and reactive schizophrenics: a failure to replicate. *Behavior Therapy*, **7,** 668–671.

Marks, I. M. (1969). *Fears and Phobias*. (London: leinemann.)
Marks, J., Somoda, B., and Schalock, R. (1968). Reinforcement *vs*. relationship therapy for schizophrenics. *Journal of Abnormal Psychology*, **73,** 397–402.
Marzillier, J. (1978). Outcome studies of skill training: a review. In: P. Trower *et al*. (Eds.), *Social Skills and Mental Health*. (London: Methuen.)
Marzillier, J. S., Lambert, J. C., and Kellett, J. (1976). A controlled evaluation of systematic desensitisation and social skills training for chronically inadequate psychiatric patients. *Behaviour Research and Therapy*, **14,** 225–239.
Mednick, S. A. and Schulsinger, F. (1968). Some premorbid characteristics related to breakdown in children with schizophrenic mothers. In: D. Rosenthal and S. S. Kety (Eds.), *The Transmission of Schizophrenia*. (New York: Pergamon Press.)
Meichenbaum, D. H. (1973). Cognitive factors in behaviour modification: modifying what clients say to themselves, In: C. Franks and T. Wilson (Eds.), *Annual Review of Behaviour Therapy: Theory and Practice*. (New York: Brunner/Mazel.)
Meltzoff, J. and Kornreich, M. (1970). *Research in Psychotherapy*. (New York: Atherton Press.)
Michaux, M. H., Chelst, M. R., Foster, S. A., Pruim, R. J., and Dasinger, E. M. (1973). Post-release adjustment of day and full-time psychiatric patients. *Archives of General Psychiatry*, **29,** 647–651.
Miller, P. McC. and Ingham, J. G. (1976). Friends, Confidants and symptoms. *Social Psychiatry*, **11,** 51–58.
Moline, R. A. (1976). Hospital psychiatry in transition. *Archives of General Psychiatry*, **33,** 1234–1238.
Nettlebeck, T. and Kirby, N. H. (1976). A comparison of part and whole training methods with mildly mentally retarded workers. *Journal of Occupational Psychology*, **49,** 115–120.
Nichols, K. A. (1974). Severe social anxiety. *British Journal of Medical Psychology*, **47,** 301–306.
Paul, G. L. (1967). Strategy of outcome research in psychotherapy. *Journal of Consultative Psychology*, **31,** 109–118.
Paul, G. (1969). Chronic mental patient: current status—future directions. *Psychological Bulletin*, **71,** 81–94.
Paykel, E. S., Myers, J. K., Dienelt, M. N., Klerman, G. L., Lindenthal, J. J., and Pepper, M. P. (1969). Life events and depression. *Archives of General Psychiatry*, **21,** 753–760.
Phillips, L. (1968). *Human Adaptation and its Failures*. (New York: Academic Press.)
Pokorny, A. D., Thornby, J., Kaplan, H. B., and Ball, D. (1976). Prediction of chronicity in psychiatric patients. *Archives of General Psychiatry*, **33,** 932–937.
Porterfield, J., Blunden, R., and Blewitt, E. (1978). Improving environments for profoundly handicapped adults: Estabishing staff routines for high client engagement. *Behaviour Modification* (In press.)
Powell, L., Felce, D., Jenkins, J., and De Lunt, B., (1978). Increasing engagement in a home for the elderly by providing an Indoor Gardening activity. Research Report No. 128, Health Care Evaluation Research Team, Wessex Regional Health Authority.
Rachman, S. J. and Hodgson, R. (1974). Synchrony and desynchrony in fear and avoidance. *Behaviour Research and Therapy*, **12,** 311–318.
Rathus, S. A. (1972). An experimental investigation of assertive training in a group setting. *Journal of Behavior Therapy and Experimental Psychiatry*, **3,** 81–86.
Rawls, J. R. (1971). Toward the identification of re-admission and non re-admissions to mental hospitals. *Social Psychiatry*, **6,** 58–61.
Raynes, N. V., Pratt, M. W., and Roses, S. (1977). Aides' involvement in decision-making and the quality of care in institutional settings. *American Journal of Mental Deficiency*, **81,** 570–577.

Rehm, L. P. and Marston, A. R. (1968). Reduction of social anxiety through modification of self-reinforcement: An instigation therapy technique. *Journal of Consultative and Clinical Psychology*, **32,** 565–574.

Rich, A. R. and Schroeder, H. E. (1976). Research issues in assertiveness training. *Psychological Bulletin*, **83,** 1081–1096.

Rifkin, A., Levitan, S. J., Galenski, J., and Klein, D. F. (1972). Emotionally unstable character disorders—a follow-up study. II. Predictors of outcome. *Biological Psychiatry*, **4,** 81–88.

Robbins, L. N. (1966). *Deviant Children Group Up*. (Baltimore: Williams & Wilkins.)

Rosen, B., Klein, D. F., and Gittelman-Klein, R. (1971). The prediction of re-hospitalization: the relationship between age of first psychiatric treatment contact, marital status and premorbid asocial adjustment. *Journal of Nervous and Mental Disease*, **152,** 17–22.

Samuels, J. S. and Henderson, J. D. (1971). A community-based operant learning environment. IV. Some outcome data. In: R. D. Rubin, H. Fensterheim, A. A. Lazarus and C. M. Franks, (Eds.), *Advances in Behaviour Therapy*.(New York: Academic Press.)

Sanders, D. J. (1972). Innovative environments in the community: a life for the chronic patient. *Schizophrenia Bulletin*, **6,** 49–59.

Sanders, R., Weinman, B., Smith, R. S., Smith, A., Kenny, J., and Fitzgerald, B. J. (1962). Social treatment of the male chronic mental patient. *Journal of Nervous and Mental Disease*, **134,** 244–255.

Sartorius, N., Jablensky, A., and Shapiro, R. (1977). Two-year follow-up of the patients included in the WHO International pilot study of schizophrenia. *Psychological Medicine*, **7,** 529–541.

Seligman, M. E. P. (1975). *Helplessness: On Depression, Development, and Death*. (San Francisco: Freeman.)

Shapiro, M. B. (1961). The single case in fundamental clinical psychological research. *British Journal of Medical Psychology*, **34,** 285.

Shapiro, M. B. (1971). Intensive assessment of the single case. In: P. J. Mittler (Ed.), *Psychological Assessment*. (London: Methuen.)

Shaw, P. (1976). A comparison of three behaviour therapies in the treatment of social phobia. *British Association for Behavioural Psychotherapy Bulletin*, **4,** 69–70.

Shedletsky, R. and Voineskos, G. (1976). The rehabilitation of the chronic psychiatric patient: beyond the hospital-based token economy system. *Social Psychiatry*, **11,** 145–150.

Shepherd, G. (1975). The ethical problems of behaviour therapy. *Newsletter* (Clin. Div. Brit. Psychol. Soc.), **16,** 11–17.

Shepherd, G. (1977). Social skills training: the generalisation problem. *Behavior Therapy*, **8,** 1008–1009.

Shepherd, G. (1978). Social skills training: the generalisation problem—some further data. *Behaviour Research and Therapy*, (In press.)

Shepherd, G. and Durham, R. (1977). The multiple techniques approach to behavioural psychotherapy: a retrospective evaluation of effectiveness and an examination of prognostic indicators. *British Journal of Medical Psychology*, **50,** 45–52.

Shepherd, G. and Richardson, A. (1978). Organisation and interaction in psychiatric day centres. *Psychological Medicine*, (In press.)

Sims, A. (1975). Factors predictive of outcome in neurosis. *British Journal of Psychiatry*, **127,** 54–62.

Smith, M. L. and Glass, G. V. (1977). Meta-analysis of psychotherapy outcome studies. *American Psychologist*, **32,** 752–760.

Stein, L. I. and Test, M. A. (1978). *Alternatives to Mental Hospital Treatment*. (New York: Plenum Press.)

Stevens, B. C. (1972). Dependence of schizophrenics on elderly relatives. *Psychological Medicine*, **2,** 17–32.

Stevens, B. C. (1973). Evaluation of rehabilitation for psychiatric patients in the community. *Acta Psychiatrica Scandinavica*, **49,** 169–180.

Strauss, J. and Carpenter, W. (1972). The prediction of outcome in schizophrenia. I. Characteristics of outcome. *Archives of General Psychiatry*, **27,** 739–746.

Strauss, J. and Carpenter, W. (1974). The prediction of outcome in schizophrenia. II. Relationships between predictor and outcome variables. *Archives of General Psychiatry*, **31,** 37–42.

Thorpe, G. L., Amatu, H. I., Blakey, R. S., and Burns, L. E. (1976). Contributions of overt instructional rehearsal and 'specific insight' to the effectiveness of self-instructional training: a preliminary study. *Behavior Therapy*, **7,** 504–511.

Trower, P., Yardley, K. and Bryan, T. B. (1976). The treatment of social failure: SST and SD compared. *British Association for Behavioural Psychotherapy Bulletin*, **4,** 70–71.

Trower, P., Bryant, B. and Argyle, M. (1978). *Social Skills and Mental Health*. (London: Methuen.)

Truax, C. B. and Carkhuff, R. R. (1967). *Toward Effective Counseling and Psychotherapy*. (Chicago: Aldine.)

Van Putten, T. (1973). Mileu therapy: contraindications? *Archives of General Psychiatry*, **29,** 640–643.

Vaughn, C. E. and Leff, J. P. (1976). The influence of family and social factors on the course of psychiatric illness: a comparison of schizophrenic and depressed neurotic patients. *British Journal of Psychiatry*, **129,** 125–137.

Washburn, S., Vannicelli, M., Longabaugh, R., and Scheff, B. J. (1976). A controlled comparison of psychiatric day treatment and inpatient hospitalization. *Journal of Consultative and Clinical Psychology*, **44,** 665–675.

Watts, F. N. (1978). A study of work behaviour in a psychiatric rehabilitation unit. *British Journal of Social and Clinical Psychology*, **17,** 85–92.

Watts, F. N. and Bennett, D. H. (1977). Previous occupational stability as a predictor of employment after psychiatric rehabilitation. *Psychological Medicine*, **7,** 709–712.

Webb, E. J., Campbell, D. J., Schwartz, R. D., and Sechrest, L. (1966). *Unobtrusive Measures: A Survey of Nonreactive Research in the Social Sciences*. (Chicago: Rand McNally.)

Weintraub, S., Neale, J. M., and Liebert, D. E. (1975). Teacher ratings of children vulnerable to psychopathology. *American Journal of Orthopsychiatry*, **39,** 755–759.

Whiteley, J. S. (1970). The response of psychopaths to a therapeutic community. *British Journal of Psychiatry*, **116,** 517–529.

Wiggins, J. S. (1973). *Personality and Prediction: Principles of Personality Assessment*. (Reading, Mass.: Addison Wesley.)

Wing J. K. (1967). Social treatment, rehabilitation and management. In: A. Coppen and A. Walk (Eds.), *Recent Developments in Schizophrenia*. (Royal Medico-Psychological Assn.)

Wing, J. K., Bennett, D. H., and Denham, J. (1964). The industrial rehabilitation of long-stay schizophrenic patients. Medical Research Council Memo., No. 42, (London: HMSO.)

Wing, J. K. and Hailey, A. (1972). *Evaluating a Community Psychiatric Service: The Camberwell Register 1964–71*. (London: Oxford University Press.)

Wright, J. C. (1976). A comparison of systematic desensitization and social skill acquisition in the modification of a social fear. *Behavior Therapy*, **7,** 205–210.

Yule, W. (1976). The potential of behavioural treatment in preventing later childhood difficulties. Paper read to the Sixth Annual Conference of the European Association of Behaviour Therapy, Spetsae, Greece.

Zax, M. and Specter, G. A. (1974). *An Introduction to Community Psychology*. (New York: Wiely.)

Zigler, E. and Phillips, L. (1960). Social effectiveness and symptomatic behaviours. *Journal of*

Abnormal and Social Psychology, **61,** 231.
Zigler, E. and Phillips, L. (1961). Social competence and outcome in psychiatric disorder. *Journal of Abnormal and Social Psychology*, **63,** 264.
Zigler, E. and Phillips, L. (1962). Social competence and the process–reactive distinction in psychopathology. *Journal of Abnormal and Social Psychology*, **65,** 215.

The Social Psychology of Psychological Problems
Edited by P. Feldman and J. Orford

10

Environmental Design and the Prevention of Psychological Problems

CLIFFORD R. O'DONNELL

I. INTRODUCTION

Environmental design is often discussed with respect to the arrangement of physical objects in our environment. However, most of our activities take place in settings with other people, with objects used as resources, i.e., for social purposes. Therefore, in this chapter, environment refers to the presence of people as well as physical resources. The central topic is how the number of people and the use of physical resources influence our behaviour and relate to psychological problems.

The prevention of psychological problems is a potentially useful strategy borrowed from public health and is one of the central goals of community psychology (Rappaport, 1977). Programmes have been designed to prevent problems from beginning (primary prevention) and from developing (secondary prevention). A concept of tertiary prevention has also been used to indicate community-based attempts to reduce the rate of existing problems. Most prevention programmes have involved intervention at the secondary level.

The overall results of these programmes, however, are disappointing. An early identification and intervention programme which provided services to teachers, parents, and children, showed mixed results, with school grades and attendance lower for the participating children than for the controls (Zax and Cowen, 1969, Table 5). The results of family intervention programmes, in which the parents of young boys referred for aggressive behaviour received training and supervision in behaviour modification, indicated that very few families stayed in the programmes, lowered the rate of their children's aggressive behaviour, and maintained this improvement during a 12-month follow-up (O'Donnell, 1977, pp. 81–91).

Delinquency prevention has not fared any better. In a 30-year follow-up of one project, McCord (1978) concluded 'the objective evidence presents a disturbing picture. The program seems not only to have failed to prevent its clients from committing crimes—thus corroborating studies of other projects ... but also to have produced negative side effects' (p. 288). Similarly, when comprehensive social services were provided to boys with a record of school and police offences, their families, teachers, and school counsellors, averaging 342 contacts over 12–24 months, the data showed that the few differences favoured the controls (Berleman *et al.*, 1972). Davidson and Wolfred (1977) reported initial success in lowering disruptive classroom behaviour in a residential behaviour modification programme for pre-delinquents, but nine months after leaving the programme experimentals fared worse than controls on measures of school attendance, police contacts for both juvenile and criminal offences, and institutionalization. Some success did occur in a non-residential behaviour modification programme for youths who had been arrested for a major criminal offence in the prior year. However, the majority of youngsters were not arrested in the prior year and the subsequent arrest rate for them was higher for project than for control youths (O'Donnell *et al.*, 1979).

These results point out that there is much to learn before intervention programmes to prevent psychological problems can be developed with confidence. However, two similar areas of research have recently converged to suggest that efforts to obtain that knowledge should focus on the natural environment. They are the stability of behaviour problems over time and the generalization of intervention effects.

In the first, several studies indicate that the psychological problems of many children improve independently of treatment. Shechtman (1970) reported that data extracted from the files of children seen at a mental health centre indicated that the number of symptoms decreased with age. Children observed in Head Start classrooms showed an increase in both cooperative and appropriate behaviours during the school year without intervention (Melahn and O'Donnell, 1978). In an epidemiological study, Shepherd *et al.* (1971) found that, after three years, three-quarters of the children considered the most deviant reported fewer symptoms, and one-half reported none at all. Other studies noted similar improvements, but also suggested the importance of age (Gersten *et al.*, 1976) and the nature of the problem (Feldhusen, *et al.*, 1970; Gersten *et al.*, 1976; Robins, 1974). In the second area of research, recent reviews have documented that many target behaviours improve during intervention, but fail to generalize to other settings or to be maintained over time (Conway and Bucher, 1976; Kazdin, 1975; O'Donnell, 1977). The results of these studies from both areas of research suggest that variables may exist in natural settings which affect both the alleviation and the maintenance of psychological problems. Identification of these variables might be useful not only in resolving the problem of generalization and maintenance, but also in the development of effective prevention strategies. The purpose of this chapter is to review research which may help to identify some of these variables.

The framework for this review is that environmental design influences the frequency and nature of participation in activities with others, that our attachments and responsibilities to others are based in the social interaction inherent in this participation, and that these relationships contribute to the prevention and alleviation of many psychological problems. The importance of social relationships has been recognized in methods for the assessment of psychological problems (e.g., Goldfried and D'Zurilla, 1969; Kanfer and Saslow, 1969; Linn *et al.*, 1969; Phillips *et al.*, 1966; Sundberg *et al.*, 1978) and has also been noted in discussions of the development of psychological problems. For example, Bernstein *et al.* (1972) stated that:

> human interaction provides the medium through which societies and, indeed, all social systems perform their functions and carry out their purposes. For, unless individuals interact, no social system can exist. Interaction serves purposes such as information exchange, socialization, and the maintenance of physical and emotional well being (p. 444).

Glidewell (1972) stated that:

> although the etiology of most functional psychiatric disorders remains indeterminate, there is one deficiency common to most disorders. From the schizophrenics to the depressions, from the hysterias to the obsessions, the deprivation of simple human acceptance is found in nearly every history. To be regularly—and individually—friendless, discounted, degraded, and humiliated is a psychosocial experience with which few humans can cope for a prolonged time (p. 221).

A variety of research also suggests that a relative lack of social interaction may be associated with a wide range of problems. Fanning (1967) compared families who were non-systematically assigned to different types of military housing, and reported that the rate of illness was higher in women and children who lived in apartments than in those who lived in houses. He attributed it to the likelihood of less social interaction among those living in apartments above the ground floor. This interpretation was supported in that the rate of illness increased with the height of the apartment. Wechsler and Pugh (1967) found that those who were in a demographic minority in their communities (by age, marital status, place of birth, and occupation), and therefore less likely to participate in community activities, had higher rates of psychiatric hospitalization than those in the majority. People without strong social relationships have also been reported to have higher death-rates than those with such relationships (Berkman and Syme, 1979). Other reviewers have noted similar findings. For example, Rowland (1977) showed that the death rate of the elderly increases when they are relocated or when a significant-other dies. Glidewell (1972) cited evidence relating social isolation to susceptibility to 'brainwashing' during the Korean War, anxiety, emotional handicaps in children, and interpersonal tensions and somatic complaints in industrial workers. Moos (1976, pp. 308–312), in a review of the effects of being in a minority where one lives, reported associations with higher rates of schizophrenia, mental illness, delinquency, and crime. He argued that this may be due to social isolation, citing studies showing a higher rate of admission to mental hospitals for those living alone, more social isolation in communities with higher rates of schizophrenia, and less family support for schizophrenics from lower socioeconomic classes. Stress was also cited as an important factor. Possibly, social isolation contributes to these problems by increasing the degree of stress experienced in problem situations and by reducing the likelihood of coping responses which depend on others.

This emphasis on social interaction is not meant to deny the desire or need for privacy. Social interaction and privacy are regarded as complementary. Indeed, a lack of privacy in one's living quarters tends to result in less, not more, social interaction (Baum *et al.*, 1975; Ittelson *et al.*, 1970; Tars and Appleby, 1973; Valins & Baum, 1973; Wolfe, 1975).

Consistent with this emphasis, this chapter is organized around two categories of environmental design which influence participation and social interaction: people and resources. The section on people primarily reviews the effects of numbers of people and organization size. The content of the resources section ranges from the effects of toys to housing and land-use. These are followed by a discussion of general conclusions and implications.

II. PEOPLE

The size of the unit in which people interact may be divided into micro- and macro-settings. Micro-settings refer to those units in which it is at least possible for one to come into personal contact with the majority of people in the setting. Examples include most schools, hospital wards, families, social groups, local chapters of organizations, and departments at work. Macro-settings refer to those units in which it is virtually impossible to have personal contact with most others. Large organizations, cities, states, and nations are all examples. The effects of numbers of people in micro- and macro-settings are presented separately below.

A. Micro-settings

There is some evidence that people prefer small-sized groups. James (1951) observed pedestrians in groups and found that 71 per cent consisted of two people, 21 per cent of three, 6 per cent of four, and only 2 per cent of more than four. In a study of decision making groups, Miller (1952) reported that as group size increased, people started forming smaller cliques. The correlation between the number of group members and the number of cliques was .77.

In addition, people participate more in organizations and settings with fewer people. This effect has been found in studies in a variety of settings. Juniors in smaller high schools performed in an average of over twice as many activities as those in larger high schools. Only 2 per cent of the small-school junior, compared to 28 per cent of those in the larger schools, did not perform in any activity (Gump, 1974). Members of smaller churches participated more, as indicated by the number of different activities, the number of leadership positions, time spent in church activities, church attendance, and financial contributions (Wicker, 1969). Newer members of a smaller church reported greater assimilation and also attended and contributed more (Wicker and Mehler, 1971).

Baird (1969) demonstrated that this effect is due to the number, rather than the characteristics, of people in smaller organizations. His results showed that while students from smaller schools participated more in high school, they did not do so in college. Instead, measures of college participation were negatively associated with the number of students in the college graduating class.

In other research, involving the study of helping behaviour in simulated emergencies, Latane and Darley (1970) found that the 'victim' was more likely to receive help in situations with fewer bystanders. Help was also more likely to be offered if the bystanders had had personal contact with the victim which, of course, is more probable in settings with fewer people. Helping behaviour has also been found to occur more often in college dormitories with fewer students (Bickman *et al.*, 1973). A similar effect has been noted in mental hospitals. Those with fewer patients and a higher staff–patient ratio have had higher discharge rates both historically (Bockover, 1963) and recently (Linn, 1970; Ullmann, 1967). Data presented by Linn (1970) showed that the discharge rates were positively associated with the frequency of patient interactions with others.

Just as these studies consistently show that participation is greater in settings with fewer people, the reverse is also true, i.e., people withdraw more from settings with larger numbers of people. Studies in industry have found a positive relationship between the size of the unit in which people work and absence rates (Indik, 1963, 1965; Ingham, 1970; Porter and Lawler, 1965). Studies of crowding and density have also demonstrated the withdrawal effect. When Hutt and Vaizey (1966) varied the number of normal children playing together in groups, they found that aggression increased and social interaction decreased with more children. Likewise, McGrew (1970) found that children in larger groups engaged in more solitary play and interacted less with other children. College students also interacted less when they were housed in dormitories with a larger number of students, even though the amount of space per person was the same (Baum *et al.*, 1975; Valins and Baum, 1973). In studies of psychiatric facilities, social activity and room occupancy declined as more patients were assigned to a room, and isolated passive activity increased (Ittelson *et al.*, 1970; Wolfe, 1975).

Thus there seems to be a continuum with smaller numbers of people, participation, and social interaction on one end and larger numbers of people and withdrawal on the other. Participation and social interaction seem to lead to greater attachment and responsibility to others in the setting, which inhibits withdrawal. This has been pointed out by Ingham (1970) who noted that there is a greater opportunity for social interaction in smaller work units and suggested that this increases a sense of obligation to fellow-workers. Because of this obligation, people go to work even when they do not feel well, resulting in the exceptionally low absence rates of smaller units. Such an interpretation is in agreement with findings by both Gump (1974) and Willems (1967) that marginal students in smaller schools reported a greater sense of obligation and responsibility to their school and extracurricular activities than did those in larger schools. It is also consistent with studies which show that this effect of numbers of people is more frequently found on social-oriented, rather than task-oriented measures. For example, effects have been reported on perceptions of social climate (Moos, 1974, 1975), job satisfactions (Kornhauser, 1965; Porter and Lawler, 1965), friendship choice, intimacy, and satisfaction with group members (Thomas and Fink, 1963), attraction to others (Griffitt and Veitch, 1971), and numerous moods (Griffitt and Veitch, 1971; Nogami, 1976). In one study, when the amount of communication and attraction to others was statistically removed, the effect of unit size on absence rate and personnel turnover was considerably reduced (Indik, 1965). In contrast, typically there has been no effect on measures of task performance (Freedman *et al.*, 1971; Nogami, 1976), and the reverse finding (i.e., positive effects of more people) on measures of group problem-solving (Nogami, 1976; Thomas and Fink, 1963) and business success (Caplow, 1957). An exception is a study in which performance on a stress-sensitive task was impaired by the presence of a larger number of people (Paulus *et al.*, 1976).

A popular explanation of the effect on social-oriented measures is that increasing numbers of people reduce the amount of space per person and tend to produce an experience of crowding, which leads to withdrawal. Three factors argue against this view. First, a numbers effect occurred even in those studies in which space per person was specifically controlled. Second is the existence of other cultures (e.g., Draper, 1973) in which people live in densely populated areas, but have a low incidence of social problems. They seem to achieve this by limiting their social interaction to a small number of people. Finally, studies which varied the amount of space per person, but held the number of people relatively constant, reported inconsistent results. These depended on sex (Edney and Jordan-Edney, 1974; Ross *et al.*, 1973; Stokols *et al.*, 1973), individual differences (Freedman, 1975), and physical distance among people (Worchel and Teddlie, 1976).

Perhaps the most adequate theoretical explanation is the concept of manning (Barker, 1960, 1968). The degree of manning depends on the number of people available to fulfil the roles of a setting. Settings with relatively few people for the number of roles are said to be undermanned. In these settings demands to participate are greater and standards for participation lower. As a result, those with marginal abilities are more likely to be sought out and accepted. In overmanned settings, of course, the reverse is true. Therefore, the concept of manning helps to explain how the number of people in a setting affects the degree of participation and interaction. Participation is encouraged in undermanned settings and withdrawal is encouraged in overmanned settings. In mental hospitals, for example, a higher number of staff members may well maximize the number of roles for patients (who are needed in staff programmes and duties) and, in combination with a low number of patients, create an undermanned hospital setting for patients. Therefore, those with marginal behaviours are more likely to participate in ward activities and less likely to withdraw. Because of their activity, staff members tend to notice their responsible behaviour and discharge them.

In general, an effect of numbers of people on participation and social interaction has been consistently found. Confidence in this result is increased because of the wide variety of research areas in which the effect has been reported. In contrast, the number of people typically does not seem to affect task-oriented behaviours, although it would be of interest to see if such behaviours are affected in cultures in which productivity is based on cooperation and social interaction (e.g., Hawaiian).

Although manning theory is currently best able to explain these results, greater precision could be achieved by considering a number of variables. The finding of Wicker (1968), that not all of the settings of smaller schools were undermanned, suggests that accuracy is increased when analysis occurs at the setting, rather than the organization, level. Wicker *et al.* (1972) have suggested that consideration of the capacity of the organization, the number of people available for each position, and the minimum number of people required to maintain the organization would also increase precision. The results of Price and Blashfield (1975), that many settings are segregated by age and sex, indicate that the demographic characteristics of people in the setting are important. Finally, Kelly (1967) reported that a greater variety of behaviours were observed in high schools with a higher turnover of students, but how the turnover of people in a setting affects the level of manning is unknown.

B. Macro-settings

Interest in the effects of the geographical concentration of large numbers of people has produced a tradition of urban studies extending throughout this century (Fischer, 1975). A common finding has been the association of density and a higher incidence of social problems, such as crime (Harries, 1974) and mental disorders (Levy and Rowitz, 1973). However, three major problems preclude attributing this to density.

First, density is also related to many other variables (e.g., social class, income, ethnicity, and education) and so interpretation is difficult. Although attempts have been made to remove the effects of other variables statistically (e.g., Galle *et al.*, 1972), when they are strongly associated with the variable of interest, removal of their common variance may distort the results and thus make interpretation difficult (cf. Ward, 1975). An example is the *negative* relationship between the rate of tuberculosis and density reported by Winsborough (1965).

Second, the crime rates in many of the studies were based on the number of offenders living in a specified area. These crime rates were then associated with census data. However, because of possible bias in methods of arrest, plea-bargaining, prosecutor decisions, and the lengthy process leading to conviction, the 'crime rates' may more accurately be described as the distribution of a highly selected group of individuals. Therefore, associations with census data may tell us something about the living conditions of these individuals, but little about the relationship between crime and the density of people within urban areas.

Finally, in other studies the crime rate has been computed by dividing the number of offences reported to the police by some unit of the resident population in each area under study. While this procedure solves the problem of basing the rate on offenders, it may distort data in areas which attract large numbers of people but which have a small resident population, such as business districts, resort areas, and entertainment centres (see O'Donnell and Lydgate (1980) for a discussion of alternative methods). For these reasons, few conclusions can be drawn from the traditional studies of density and social problems.

Others have suggested that density increases the pace of life and thereby affects how people interact. Bornstein and Bornstein (1976) timed the walking speeds of pedestrians in 15 cities and found a correlation of .91 with the population of the city Newman and McCauley (1977) reported that eye contact with strangers decreased with the size of the urban area. Milgram (1970) has articulated the position in some detail. He suggested that density contributes to sensory overload, which is caused either by too many inputs or by too fast a rate of input. People cope by giving less time to each input, disregarding those of low priority, blocking inputs (e.g., having an unlisted telephone number), reducing intensity through non-involvement, and developing an allegiance to a smaller group of people (e.g., an ethnic group). Milgram cited evidence that helping behaviour is greater in small towns than in cities to support the view that people living in cities may be more subject to sensory overload.

The sensory overload theory has received some support in laboratory tests (e.g., Sherrod and Downs, 1974) and may be correct in the sense that coping strategies are more likely to be used in high-input situations. It does not necessarily follow, however, that sensory overload is more prominent among people living in cities. In fact, the reverse may be true. If sensory overload is partly a function of input and demands made on people, then it should be more prominent in undermanned settings. Undermanned settings are more likely where there are fewer people.

The greater potential for overload in areas with fewer people was demonstrated in a study of two small towns, Midwest with 715 people and Yoredale with 1300 (Barker, 1960). Although only about half as many people lived in Midwest, there were more behaviour settings (perhaps reflecting the cultural difference between those towns). The data showed that Midwest's undermanned settings had more responsible people per setting than Yoredale's larger settings. In other words, Midwest had more behaviour settings, more roles for people per setting, and fewer people to fill those roles. Thus Barker noted that 'in a year's time Midwest provides and requires more than three times as many responsibilities of each of its residents as Yoredale' (p. 43). This suggests that helping behaviour may be more a function of manning level than sensory overload. Perhaps people from small towns are more likely to help others (Gelfand *et al.*, 1973; Latane and Darley, 1970; Milgram, 1970) because they come from undermanned settings where people are needed more than they are in the overmanned settings of larger cities. It may also be that the coping strategies cited by Milgram (1970) are the withdrawal behaviours found in overmanned settings, rather than responses to sensory overload.

These data indicate that the study of the relationship between manning levels and social problems in urban areas may be more fruitful than a continued focus on the effects of density. Although the assessment of behaviour settings has continued in small towns (e.g., Barker and Schoggen, 1973; Price and Blashfield, 1975) it is less practical in large cities. What is needed are more easily obtained indicators of manning levels. One possibility is the unemployment rate. By definition the unemployment rate is higher in geographical areas with overmanned work settings, since there are more people available than there are positions.

Consistent with the present framework where overmanning contributes to withdrawal and leads to psychological problems, unemployment has been linked to a variety of problems, including mental illness, alcoholism, more frequent institutionalization, and recorded crime (Nietzel *et al.*, 1977, p. 299). Brenner (1973) has presented a detailed analysis of the relationship between manufacturing employment and admission to mental hospitals. In general an inverse relationship was found, with correlations of −.75 for males and −.60 for females (Brenner, 1973, Appendix II). The association between unemployment and recorded crime, especially property crime, has been consistently documented. Feeney and Weir (1975) reported that 75 per cent of the adults arrested for robbery were unemployed. Kvalseth (1977) concluded in a review that male unemployment increases the robbery rate and total unemployment increases the rate of burglary and larceny. Sjoquist (1973) found a positive relationship between unemployment and property crimes in a cross-sectional sample of 53 municipalities with populations between 25,000 and 200,000. This relationship has also been supported in many other studies (e.g., Phillips and Votey, 1975; Phillips *et al.*, 1972; Votey and Phillips, 1974), with unemployment accounting for as much as 57 per cent of the crime rate variance (Allison, 1972). It should also be noted that the inverse relationship between employment and crime may be restricted to a low to moderate range of unemployment. A much higher rate of unemployment, as during the depression of the 1930s, may not result in a proportionate increase in crime. Perhaps, at least in the short run, the effects of unemployment on criminal behaviour are limited to those who are more likely to engage in these activities depending on their immediate circumstances.

Some investigators have attempted to estimate the crime reduction that might be expected from an increase in employment. Chapman (1976) suggested that on the average each 1 per cent increase in employment might decrease violent crimes by 1.1 per cent and property crimes by 1.8 per cent. Fleisher (1966) calculated that a reduction of unemployment from 10 to 5 per cent could reduce the delinquency rate by 10 per cent. That an increase in employment would lower the crime rate is supported by the association of employment with lower recidivism rates among prison parolees (Rehabilitation Research Foundation, 1974), those released from transitional facilities (Social Welfare Development and Research Center, 1974a, 1974b), probationers (Wood and O'Donnell, in press), and juveniles (Quay and Love, 1977; Schwitzgebel and Kolb, 1964).

Although a review of methods to reduce unemployment is beyond the scope of this chapter (see Nietzel *et al.*, 1977, chapter 10, for an excellent presentation), the importance of social contact in the employment process points out how social relationships may contribute to the prevention and alleviation of psychological problems. Jones and Azrin (1973) presented the employment process as a job information network, in which those who have early knowledge of openings exchange such information with relatives and friends for social rewards. Granovetter (1973) has suggested that job leads are more a function of the number of social contacts than of the strength of those relationships. In other words, because of their access to different information about job openings, a large number of acquaintances may be more helpful than a few close friends. In a procedure designed for those seeking employment, Azrin *et al.* (1975) formed a job-finding club. The club set up a network of social contacts to provide assistance with job leads, resumés, interview skills, transportation, vocational choices, time planning, family understanding, and mutual support. The results showed that club members, in comparison to a randomly assigned control group, found more jobs, in less time, and at higher salaries.

In one study of the job performance and retention of 478 of the hard-core unemployed (Friedlander and Greenberg, 1971), attitudes towards work, demographic characteristics, and job training made no difference. Effects occurred only for the degree of social support received from supervisors and peers. Furthermore, the work performance of the hard-core unemployed did not differ from that of other employees; only absence from work and lateness did. These findings and manning theory suggest that the hard-core unemployed would be more likely to retain their jobs if they were placed in small work units, since absence rates are lower and the potential for social support higher in such units.

In summary, people are sought out and valued in undermanned settings. In overmanned settings the opposite occurs because people simply are not as needed. It was suggested that in larger geographical areas where direct assessments of behaviour settings are not as practical, attempts be made to use more easily obtained indicators of manning levels. The unemployment rate was discussed as one example. The higher the unemployment rate, the greater the indication that work settings are overmanned. Just as withdrawal from other overmanned settings is associated with psychological problems, so too is withdrawal from work settings. In particular, unemployment has been linked to mental hospital admissions and crime. Social contact was found to be important in finding and maintaining employment and thereby avoiding the problems related to withdrawal from work settings. This, of course, is similar to the importance of social interaction in maintaining participation in other settings.

III. RESOURCES

Evidence was presented in the previous section that the number of people can influence participation in activities and social interaction and is thereby related to the alleviation and prevention of some psychological problems. Research in both micro- and macro-settings showing that participation and interaction can also be influenced by the design and availability of physical resources is reviewed in this section.

A. Micro-settings

Studies from the 1930s to the present have documented the importance of early sensory and motor stimulation for the normal development of children (for recent overviews see Ittelson *et al.*, 1974, pp. 176–177; Rappaport, 1977, pp. 237–241). This stimulation has included social contact, participation in activities, and the use of toys.

Assessments of home environments, which include the availability of various play materials, have been positively related to measures of cognitive abilities (Hanson, 1975; Jones, 1972; Marjoribanks, 1971; Wolf, 1966). Elardo *et al.* (1977), for example, reported a correlation of .55 between the provision of appropriate play materials at 24 months of age and language competence at 37 months. The ability of first-graders to make and use maps has also been attributed to toy-play in which children look down at and manipulate objects (Blaut *et al.*, 1970).

It has been recognized for many years that toys can also be useful in the development of interaction with peers (e.g., Buell *et al.*, 1968; Maudry and Nekula, 1939; Shure, 1963). Recently, Mueller and Brenner (1977) found that among 12-month-old toddlers 92 per cent of peer social relations developed during object-focused contact; for 62 per cent, these social interactions were sustained through six months of play and, as a result, interaction skills improved. New skills are learned because the presence of toys alters the type of children's behaviour. This was most clearly demonstrated in an investigation of the interactions of one- and two-year-olds with and without toys (Eckerman and Whatley, 1977). The use of toys reduced several types of peer-related behaviour and provided the opportunity for other behaviours. Without toys, the youngsters smiled and gestured to one another, contacted each other, and duplicated each others' actions more frequently. With toys, they exchanged, showed, simultaneously manipulated, and struggled over toys.

Toys also can be important in the learning of solitary play. In a study of oppositional children, Wahler and Moore (1975) reported that youths who were less social both with teachers and peers, and who played with toys more often, were less likely to be involved in fighting, stealing, and other problem activities. They suggested that juveniles who are involved in these activities may lack skills for productive solitude.

Thus it tentatively appears that different, but equally useful, behaviours are acquired in peer-related activities with and without toys and during solitary toy-play. It may be worthwhile to consider including the opportunity for each type of activity in children's recreation programmes. Assessments of their participation and skills could also be categorized by these types of activities. The development of behavioural norms (cf. Melahn and O'Donnell, 1978) would be particularly helpful in determining which children could benefit from additional participation in each activity and might also indicate other children whose behaviour would complement or model the needed skills.

A recent revival of interest in the relationship between specific types of toys and various behaviours has provided helpful information for the planning and organization of these activities. Studies in the 1930s focused on how different types of play influenced cooperation among nursery-schoolers. For example, Green (1933) reported on several activities, noting that sand play was the most quarrelsome, Updegraff and Herbst (1933) found that more sociable, cooperative behaviour occurred during play with clay than with blocks, and Johnson (1935) showed that the use of playground equipment reduced cooperation and led to more individually oriented play. In the 1970s, DeStefano (1976) reported that more social interaction occurred during play with large objects, while small objects tended to foster conflict. Quilitch and Risley (1973) observed the play of seven-year-olds with toys designed for either social or isolate play. They found that social play occurred far more frequently (78 per cent to 16 per cent of the time) with the social than with the isolate toys. In addition, Quilitch *et al.* (1977) have presented a method for determining the appeal and use of different toys for boys and girls of different ages. This research suggests that the availability and use of specific toys may facilitate the activities in which children learn the behaviours appropriate both for interactions with peers and 'productive solitude'.

The opportunity for activity is also important for the elderly and for hospitalized mental patients. In an analysis of time–activity patterns, Chapin and Logan (1969) reported that while the elderly had the most discretionary time, they spent less time socializing or being out of the house than any other group. A recent review of institutional treatment of geriatric patients cited evidence that participation in various activities improved physical well-being, cognitive abilities, and affect (Nietzel *et al.*, 1977, pp. 293–298). Moreover, the rate of discharge from mental hospitals has been found (Linn, 1970) to be positively correlated with interaction with staff members (.64), other patients (.52), visitors (.51), normal activity (.57), and negatively with underactivity (−.77).

One way to encourage social contact is to provide easy access to group activities. McClannahan and Risley (1975) increased the use of a lounge in a nursing home from 20 to 74 per cent by providing puzzles and games. The constant availability of these materials allowed people to come together spontaneously. When the materials were available only by request—therefore requiring prior social contact—use was reduced to only 25 per cent. Similarly, Holahan and Saegert (1973) found more social activity, less passive behaviour, and more positive attitudes on a remodelled mental hospital ward which included new game equipment, than on a control ward.

The physical elements of a setting can also be arranged to facilitate social contact. People who are more directly oriented towards each other (e.g., sitting opposite and facing each other) are more likely to interact and to engage in more conversation

(Mehrabian and Diamond, 1971a, 1971b; Steinzor, 1950). This finding has been successfully developed in nursing homes to encourage conversation by rearranging small areas so that the chairs are placed around tables (Peterson, *et al.*, 1977; Sommer, 1969, pp. 83–86). The question, of course, is whether these procedures encourage the less socially inclined to interact or simply attract more affiliative people. Holahan (1972) reported a greater amount of social interaction when these seating arrangements were used on a mental hospital ward, but only among socially inclined patients. More direct evidence has been provided by Koneya (1976) who classified students as high, moderate, or low verbalizers, based on the amount of conversation in discussion groups. When these students could select their own seats in the classroom, the high verbalizers preferred centrally located seats, while the moderate and low verbalizers avoided them. When the students were randomly assigned to seats, the high verbalizers assigned to non-central seats talked less, while moderate verbalizers assigned to central seats talked more. Seating location had no effect on low verbalizers. This study suggests that a setting can be designed to facilitate or to discourage social contact among the majority of people, but that some people will tend to avoid interaction regardless of the design of the setting. It is possible, however, that if other means of intervention were to increase the social interaction (verbalization in this study) of these people, settings might be used to maintain the interaction.

The variables which distinguish those who avoid social contact are not known. One possibility, especially for those in institutional living quarters, is a lack of privacy. A lack of privacy has been associated with a withdrawal from social interaction and with signs of stress. For example, there was greater turnover in student room-mates when privacy was reduced by furnishing dormitories with twin rather than bunk beds (Rohner, 1974). Moreover, as noted before, when additional people were assigned to bedrooms in mental institutions, social activity declined and isolated passive behaviour increased (Ittelson *et al.*, 1970; Wolfe, 1975). Stress was indicated in studies which reported that men living in prison dormitories complained of illness more (McCain *et al.*, 1976) and had higher blood pressures (D'Atri, 1975) than did men living in cells, and that people living in multi-household apartments scored higher on an emotional illness index (Mitchell, 1971). Possibilities other than a lack of privacy include, at least for patients, behaviour deficits and the effects of medication.

Overall, the studies in micro-settings indicate that toy-play is important for the cognitive and social development of children. In particular, different behaviours may be acquired in peer-related activities with and without toys and during solitary toy-play. Specific toys are related to various behaviours and can be used to facilitate social or isolate play. The facilitation of social contact is also important for the elderly and for mental patients. Although access to group activities and seating arrangements can be used to encourage interaction, some people tend to avoid interaction regardless of the design of the setting. For some in institutional settings, this may occur because of a lack of privacy in their living quarters.

B. Macro-settings

One of the most important variables for social interaction in macro-settings is proximity. Naturally enough, social contact is more likely where people come together to live, work, and spend their leisure time. For example, where students live influences their choice of room-mate, friends, and activities. Students tend to select their future room-mates from among those who live in the same dormitory unit as they do (Warr, 1964), friendships are based on propinquity, and those who live on campus are more active in campus activities (Heilweil, 1973).

Proximity, of course, can be influenced by the physical design of the setting. When space is partitioned, for example, greater interaction occurs among people within the enclosed area (Blake *et al.*, 1956; Gullahorn, 1952; Wells, 1965). The classic study illustrating the effect of physical design on proximity and social contact is that of Festinger *et al.* (1950). They studied a university housing project for married veterans and found that the closer the physical distance between housing units, the more likely it was that the residents were friends. Friendship patterns were also influenced by functional distance, i.e., the number of doors residents passed as they entered and left their unit. The physical design of the project, particularly the location of stairways, determined functional distance. Moreover, these friendship patterns affected the opinions of the residents on issues they considered important. Friends were much more likely to express similar opinions.

Recent studies support these findings on the importance of proximity. Athanasiou and Yoshioka (1973) reported that, in a town-house development, both the number of friends and the frequency of contact decreased with distance. Half of the friends lived within 100 feet or five dwelling units. Negative social interactions are also related to proximity. Ebbesen *et al.* (1976) found that a higher proportion of both liked and disliked individuals lived closer to each other in a middle-income condominium complex. Proximity seems to be especially important in the formation of friendships between people with different demographic characteristics. This was most clearly demonstrated in a study of a public-housing project in Manhattan (Nahemow and Lawton, 1975). Once again there was a strong proximity effect: 88 per cent of first-chosen friends lived in the same building and almost half on the same floor. Their figures were the same for people of different races and sexes and were only slightly lower for young residents. But, while friendships between people of differing age and race were rare between people in different buildings (16 per cent and 0 per cent of friendships respectively; computed from data presented in Tables 2 and 3, Nahemow and Lawton, 1975), they were quite common for residents living on the same floor (47 per cent and 32 per cent respectively).

The effect of proximity, of course, is not limited to where people live, but occurs wherever people engage in activities. Therefore, more relationships outside of the neighbourhood are formed by families with employed wives (Michelson, 1973) and with greater financial mobility (Bell and Boat, 1957; Smith *et al.*, 1954).

It is also true that people do not interact simply because they live near each other.

As Festinger *et al.* (1950) made clear, interaction also depends on how physical design affects functional distance. One of the major influences of physical design on functional distance is the increasing use of high-rise buildings in late twentieth-century life. Many studies indicate that the influence is a negative one thus far. Residents prefer single-family homes (Onibokun, 1976), stay indoors more (Heilweil, 1973), have a higher rate of illness (Fanning, 1967), and report difficulty in supervising children (Becker, 1976; Yancy, 1971). Becker (1976) observed children's play and found that those who lived in high-rise buildings engaged in more passive activities. These findings suggest that multiple-family housing reduces social contact by decreasing the amount of time spent outside of the apartment and in the supervision of children. This inference was recently confirmed in a study which compared public-housing families residing in single-family homes, duplexes, and multiple units (Mullins and Robb, 1977). The type of dwelling made a difference on contact with neighbours in the last month (single 61 per cent, duplex 47 per cent, multiple 19 per cent), having no best friend (single 4 per cent, duplex 7 per cent, multiple 10 per cent), and planning to relocate (single 23 per cent, duplex 31 per cent, multiple 46 per cent).

A number of suggestions have been made to help prevent some of these problems by increasing social contact through physical design. One way is to provide for a shared area designed for various activities. Sanoff and Coates (1971) observed children's play in a planned residential environment and found this type of area to be a social contact centre in which 54 per cent of the observed activities occurred. It was used for playing basketball, horse-shoe pitching, watching others play, etc. Brower and Williamson (1974) investigated outdoor recreation in an inner-city residential area. They found that home-based recreation accounted for the major portion of recreation time because of the convenience, safety, and quality of social interaction. They made a variety of suggestions to facilitate home-based recreation by designing the public areas around the streets so they are more suitable for recreational use. For example:

> sidewalks should be widened, traffic lanes should be reduced and traffic speed cut down by using such devices as bumps in the roadbed. Suitable spaces should be provided for sitting, playing games, congregating around activity nodes such as bookmobile stops, places for vendors. ... These spaces should be suitably paved, well-lighted, equipped with mailboxes, telephone booths, trash containers (p. 342).

Holahan (1976) showed that similar ideas can be used in high-rise housing. He compared a traditional low-rise neighbourhood with a regular and an innovative high-rise project, designed to encourage outdoor use. The behaviour-mapping data indicated that more socializing occurred in the traditional and the innovative housing areas, primarily because of their outdoor play areas for youngsters. Furthermore, he suggested that outdoor socializing among adults might be encouraged by designing areas for

> mixed functional uses—recreation, leisure, consumer, task-oriented—in order to attract individuals to use available space. Then, innovative design features—nooks, benches, tables—might be added to facilitate and support the informal social contact likely to occur between persons who meet accidently [sic] while pursuing diversified tasks in such multi-functional space (p. 62).

Not only is it important to design ways to bring people together, but it is also important to provide the resources necessary to help make the contacts positive. Ebbesen *et al.* (1976) found that proximity also increases the proportion of disliked individuals. The sources of friction among people living in multiple-family housing can often be pinpointed. Common examples include noise, lack of privacy, proper areas for recreation, parking, etc., supervision of children and pets, and the maintenance of shared areas. Some of these problems can be prevented through the use of physical means such as soundproofing, semi-private areas as a buffer between private and public space, adequate facilities for children's play, adult recreation, parking, etc., and dog runs (cf. Ebbesen *et al.*, 1976). Others require the development of a social network for their prevention or resolution.

Social networks emphasize the structure of interpersonal links and have received much research attention in the last decade (Mitchell, 1969, 1974). They provide needed information and access to resources for their members (Craven and Wellman, 1973). In a review of informal neighbourhood networks, Yancy (1971) concluded that they are particularly important in lower- and working-class neighbourhoods. He described the Pruitt–Igoe housing project, where the design did not facilitate such a network and the friendships of residents bore no relationship to physical proximity. As a result, there were problems in the supervision of children. The conflicts among residents also tended to escalate, since there was no network to help resolve them.

Social networks are also helpful in crime control. Crime rates are higher in transient neighbourhoods where people are less likely to know each other because of the turnover (Harries, 1974). It has also been found that people are more likely to come to the aid of someone with whom they have had contact (Latane and Darley, 1970). Thus, networks help to control crime by the natural surveillance of everyday activities and, as a consequence, low-surveillance areas tend to have higher crime rates. In a study of housing projects, Newman (1973) showed that crime rates were higher in low-surveillance areas (e.g., elevators), and when the number of housing units made it difficult to distinguish between intruders and residents. Ley and Cybriwsky (1974) ascertained that the low-surveillance areas of a neighbourhood (institutions, vacant houses, empty lots) accounted for 26 per cent of the street frontage, but 56 per cent of the neighbourhood's stripped cars. These studies suggest that the crime rates of an area are partly a function of the natural surveillance provided by the everyday activities in the area and the type of people attracted by these activities. The type of people influence crime rates through the likelihood of detection (e.g., the proportion of transients) and the proportion of those more likely to commit crimes (e.g., young males).

The activities of an area are, of course, greatly influenced by zoning and land-use. O'Donnell and Lydgate (1980) found land-use to be related to different crime patterns in Honolulu. They developed a land-use classification code and counted the number and type of physical resources in the city. Examples of categories were retail goods, eating places, alcohol consumption, sex-related businesses, entertainment, recreation, transient and permanent residences, manufacturing, transportation, and a number of service items (financial, medical, education, etc.). The distribution of these resources was then correlated with the distribution of crimes reported to the police during four consecutive years. Only correlations of at least .40 were considered.

Five crime-resource patterns were identified:

(a) vandalism with permanent residence;
(b) burglary with residences, alcohol consumption, and entertainment;
(c) forgery with retail goods, eating places, alcohol consumption, commercial offices, and various services;
(d) property crimes with retail goods, eating places, alcohol consumption, entertainment, and transient residences; and
(e) potentially violent crimes with retail goods, eating places, alcohol consumption, entertainment, and sex-related businesses.

These results suggest that the zoning of physical resources may affect the frequency and the type of crime within the zoned areas. For example, the sex-related businesses category appeared to differentiate property from potentially violent crimes (which were otherwise associated with similar resources). It is therefore worth considering whether the rate of violent crime might be affected by the zoning of sex-related businesses. O'Donnell and Lydgate noted that the violent crime rate was high in areas with the complete resource pattern associated with these crimes, i.e., high in retail goods, eating places, alcohol consumption, entertainment, and sex-related businesses, but only average in the one area with a less complete pattern, i.e., high in sex-related businesses and average in the other resources. Therefore, it may be that a high rate of violent crime is sustained not by the presence of sex-related businesses alone, but by an adult entertainment pattern. Perhaps, as was speculated, the rate might be reduced by zoning ordinances which disrupted this pattern by dispersing these resources, e.g., segregating sex-related businesses into locations low in retail goods, eating places, bars, and entertainments, such as a light manufacturing district.

In general, zoning ordinances might be used to lower crime rates by:

(a) encouraging multiple-use of low-surveillance areas, e.g., school facilities, vacant buildings, and empty lots could be made available for neighbourhood activities such as meetings, garage sales, sports, and fund-raising events;
(b) requiring new housing developments and renewal projects in established neighbourhoods to include shopping, recreational, and entertainment facilities

for residents, these facilities being designed to improve social contact; and
(c) discouraging patterns of resources which are found to be associated with a higher incidence of crime, such as the adult entertainment pattern discussed above.

Such a situationally based approach may be a useful adjunct to our current criminal justice system, which is dominated by a focus on the capture and correction of individuals. The problem is that, all too often, it neither captures nor corrects. Moreover, as Monahan (1976) has pointed out so clearly, our methods of predicting individual violence so vastly overpredict (i.e., yield false positives) that they are virtually useless. In contrast, high crime areas don't have to be captured—they are always there—but only identified. Furthermore, identification is facilitated by the very concentration of crime. For example, Feeney and Weir (1975) reported that in a three-year period in which the robbery rate in Oakland was one of the highest in the country, two-thirds of the city reported no robberies at all, while 25 per cent of the robberies were reported in only 4 per cent of the city. Whether intervention on situations will be any more successful than those on individuals remains to be seen, but efforts to develop such intervention strategies are clearly indicated.

In summary, proximity is important in macro-settings. The physical design of our environment influences proximity by facilitating or inhibiting social contact. In particular, the design of multi-family dwellings tends to inhibit social interaction, but a number of suggested design changes could help to alleviate this problem. One of the desirable outcomes of increased social contact is the development of a social network. Social networks can help to prevent and resolve problems by providing needed information, access to resources, and natural surveillance for crime control. Natural surveillance is partly a function of the everyday activities in an area and the type of people attracted to them. Since these activities are influenced by zoning and land-use, it may be possible to reduce some crimes through the geographical distribution of physical resources.

IV. CONCLUSIONS AND IMPLICATIONS

The relationship between environmental design and psychological problems is the central topic of this chapter. Research on the variables important in this relationship was reviewed in the previous sections. Conclusions and implications for prevention and research are presented below.

A. Conclusions

The influence of environmental design on participation in activities and social interaction with others is strongly supported by this research. Effects have been noted both for number of people and physical resources. The effect of the number of people is especially persuasive because of the wide variety of research areas and settings in which it has been reported. It was suggested that the most adequate explanation of this effect is the concept of manning, with participation encouraged by the pressures of undermanned settings and withdrawal by those of overmanned settings. The key concept in explaining the effect of physical resources, in both micro- and macro-settings, seems to be proximity. Resources which bring people together, assuming privacy in living quarters, quite naturally increase social interaction and participation.

The evidence that psychological problems are affected by such participation and interaction is more circumstantial and, therefore, somewhat less convincing. Although participation and interaction are frequently used in the assessment of psychological problems, the question is the traditional one of correlation or causation. Still, findings from separate areas of research showing that those who were likely to have had less social contact had higher rates of illness, hospitalization, and death are consistent. There is also little doubt that interaction can facilitate the social development of children and enrich the well-being of the elderly. Moreover, social relationships appear to be an important, and often overlooked, factor in obtaining and keeping jobs. Regardless of the effect of social interaction on psychological problems, too little participation and interaction with others can be a problem itself.

In addition, the development of social networks is dependent on social contact. The concept of a network is useful to account for the attachment and responsibility to others reflected in the exceptionally low absence rates of workers in smaller units (Ingham, 1970), the greater sense of obligation reported by marginal students in smaller schools (Gump, 1974; Willems, 1967), and the numerous effects of the number of people on social-oriented measures (see section II-A). In networks, a set of relationships evolve which extend beyond mere contact, engender a system of attachment and responsibility, and provide members with access to information and resources, and better protection against crime. Of course, networks may also support personal and social problems. Associates of the hard-core unemployed also tend to be unemployed (Goodman *et al.*, 1973) and probationers who spend more time in bars and pool halls are more likely to become unemployed (Wood and O'Donnell, in press). This suggests that the bringing together of people with similar problems, as in drug programmes, prisons, and delinquency prevention projects, may result in the development of a social network which provides support for the continuation of these problems. Thus, the influence of networks may be either positive or negative.

The concept of a social network, therefore, may prove to be a better mediator between environmental design and psychological problems than social interaction alone. Since networks develop from social contact, they are sensitive to the key variables of environmental design: manning level and proximity. Moreover, their potential to influence an array of psychological problems is enhanced by the variety of networks which may develop.

This framework suggests that the stability of behaviour may be partly a function of involvement in social networks. The continued shyness of a six-year-old, for example, may well depend on the proximity of neighbourhood children and the manning level of school activities. These variables may help to determine the frequency of social contact with other children and the development of friendship networks. In most cases these variables might function so as to alleviate the problem within a few years. Other problems may be more resistent to change. In some cases, marginal students in large schools may find the settings for school-related activities overmanned and the settings for anti-social activities undermanned. As a consequence they may participate in the anti-social activities, interact with other marginal students in these settings, and become part of a social network which supports the anti-social behaviour.

Therefore, in assessing the potential stability of a behaviour or the likelihood of its generalization to other settings, examination of the following variables may be useful: the manning level of the setting in which the behaviour occurs, the proximity of others who participate in the activities in which the behaviour is a part, the skills necessary to be accepted by others in the setting, and the existence, size, and strength of a supporting social network. In addition, other settings, people, and networks which might support an alternative behaviour should be compared on these variables.

B. Implications for prevention

The research reviewed suggests that the prevention of psychological problems may be linked to participation in activities, social interaction, and involvement in social networks. One of the strategies to facilitate participation and interaction is to lower the manning level of overmanned settings. A possible means to accomplish this is by decentralization. When Ullmann (1967) found that small size was associated with a high early release rate from Veterans Administration hospitals, he suggested that size could be reduced by the unit system, in which hospitals are divided into separate autonomous sections. There is some evidence that this is a viable suggestion. In a study of the unit system in 39 Veterans Administration hospitals, it was reported that decreasing the number of patients per unit increased the turnover of patients (Ellsworth *et al.*, 1972). Therefore, adoption of the unit system might lower institutional manning levels. It is important to note, however, that the unit system insures neither small size nor an undermanned setting. Of the 39 hospitals studied, in 31 the average number of patients per unit was over 100 and the range for all 39 was from 31 to 490. An assessment of the manning level of each unit would be valuable in any evaluation of the effects of a decentralized unit system.

The creation of smaller units in other aspects of life might also lower manning levels. Large housing projects could be designed into units with separate facilities (e.g., recreation, parking, and laundry areas) for a small number of families. A lower absenteeism rate would be an incentive for decentralization in industrial and business settings. An undermanned work setting seems to be particularly important for the hard-core unemployed. Tax incentives for decentralization could be offered to businesses which employ the hard-core unemployed, and employment programmes could attempt to place these people in small work units. With declining birth-rates, it is likely that there will be increasing pressure to consolidate schools. Data showing greater participation and commitment for marginal students in smaller schools (Gump, 1974; Willems, 1967) suggest it may be better to maintain a more decentralized school system. The possibilities extend to recreation areas, shopping malls and, indeed, to all facets of life.

Sometimes settings are overmanned not because of too many people, but because of too few roles. In these cases the manning level could be lowered by increasing the number of activities and roles for people in the setting. The demand for people would thereby be increased. Schools, for example, might increase student participation in plays, concerts, clubs, athletics, etc. by sponsoring these events for students of all ability levels, rather than only for those able to compete for a limited number of openings in these programmes. Likewise, parents might increase their children's responsibility and commitment to the family by providing additional roles for them, as in the care of pets or a garden, in the performance of household tasks, and in family activities.

A second strategy to increase participation and social contact is to increase the proximity of people through physical design. The potential of this approach was demonstrated in studies of the use of toys and games to increase the participation of children and adults, the provision of privacy in living quarters, the use of seating arrangements, and the design of housing projects. Although the adults in most of these studies were either institutionalized or living in housing projects, the basic idea is applicable to everyone. Participation and interaction are more likely to occur if there are activities to attract people and the setting is designed to facilitate contact.

A number of useful suggestions have been made for the design of settings to achieve these purposes. Freedman (1975, chapter 10) suggested that public facilities be designed for a variety of activities to attract people. For example, in housing projects the laundry area could be combined with a children's play and refreshment area. Resources which are open at night (news stands, grocery stores, etc.) would encourage people to use the streets and thereby make them safer. Both Gold (1970) and Sommer (1974) have emphasized the importance of natural surveillance, provided by a setting which attracts people and encourages contact, in the control of crime. O'Donnell and Lydgate (1980) found the distribution of physical resources to be related to crime patterns and offered the possibility that crime may be affected by the zoning of these resources.

Another prevention strategy is to ensure that people have the skills needed to participate in a specified setting. This strategy may be particularly applicable with children. The settings and skills of older children could be assessed and activities organized to help younger children learn the behaviours which they will need in order to participate in these settings. This approach might also be useful with people leaving institutions. Normative data on successful former patients and prisoners would be valuable in determining which skills are needed in which settings for a successful readjustment to community life.

One of the desired goals of increasing participation and social interaction is that the person should become part of a social network which will support the desired behaviours and help prevent psychological problems. However, in cases where such a network is unlikely to develop it may be possible to establish one. An example is the job-finding club formed by Azrin *et al.* (1975) which provided members with assistance in obtaining a job and social support. Hunt and Azrin (1973) organized a similar network for alcoholics, which included a social club for non-alcoholic friendships and activities. The positive results reported in these studies suggest that the strategy may have promise in the prevention of other problems as well.

In other cases a social network might exist which supports undesirable activities, such as anti-social behaviour. Programmes should be examined to see if their procedures encourage the development of such a network. In one delinquency prevention programme, for example, it is possible that the higher arrest rate of project youth with no record of major offences in the preceding year occurred because they formed relationships *while in the programme* with those who had been arrested for major offences (O'Donnell *et al.*, 1979). Given the persistence of anti-social behaviour (Feldhusen *et al.*, 1970; Gersten *et al.*, 1976; Robins, 1974), we should be particularly cautious about implementing programmes which place marginal students, delinquents, etc., in touch with each other. Alternatively, our efforts could be directed towards their participation in activities in which they are likely to interact with others who do not engage in anti-social behaviour.

These prevention strategies may be primary, secondary, or tertiary depending on who they are designed for. Decentralizing a school to underman the school settings, designing housing to increase the proximity of people, and organizing specific skill-learning activities for all third-graders, are examples of primary prevention efforts, since they are directed towards all who participate in the setting. However, if an undermanned school unit is set up only for marginal students, housing designed for proximity is available only to those with special needs such as the elderly, or skill-learning activities are available only to those who have been shown to be deficient in these skills, the strategies would be considered examples of secondary prevention. When used with those who have received treatment for a specified problem, they are clearly tertiary prevention or remedial programmes.

Our social priorities at present favour the development and funding of remedial programmes. Primary and secondary prevention strategies are likely to cost additional money. For example, decentralizing a school or providing more roles for students may well require additional staff and facilities. Initially, primary and secondary prevention programmes will have to compete with remedial programmes for support. It is possible, however, that these programmes will eventually acquire an independent and broader base of support. Prevention programmes are of potential benefit to more people than remedial programmes and therefore might attract more political backing, both from voters and legislators. In primary prevention there is no need to identify people with problems requiring special services. Thus the divisiveness that sometimes occurs when public support is requested for services for a small portion of the population identified as 'problems', is avoided. These advantages could mean greater support and stability for prevention services. It is necessary, however, for effectiveness to be demonstrated before prevention programmes can receive this degree of support. Small-scale pilot projects, carefully designed for evaluation and further research, are needed to test the effectiveness of prevention strategies.

C. Implications for research

The studies reviewed raise many important research questions. Much of the data linking environmental design with the prevention of psychological problems is correlational. Bowers (1973) has pointed out that causality is derived from theory, not methodology, and interpretations can be supported by correlational as well as experimental data. The question, however, is not yet one of causality, but of practice. Experimental data based on interventions would indicate whether these prevention strategies can succeed. In short, more data are needed from intervention studies in which the effects of lowering manning levels, increasing proximity, etc. are evaluated.

Research is also needed to develop additional methods to assess manning levels, proximity, skill-learning activities, and social networks. The need for more easily obtained measures of manning levels in macro-settings was discussed in section II-B. Similarly, a method for coding the functional proximity of a setting would be highly useful. A preliminary code might be constructed from the variables suggested in studies of friendship formation (see section III-B), architectural effects (Kaplan, 1975; Newman, 1973; Sommer, 1974), and personal space (Hayduk, 1978). In addition, there is currently no means readily to determine the skills which are acquired in the various activities of children. The studies of these activities, reviewed in section III-A, are a beginning in this direction. Finally, although the complete assessment of a social network (Mitchell, 1969) might be too laborious for most purposes, behaviour mapping, sociograms, and self-report techniques might be adapted to serve the more limited purpose of indicating the extent of an individual's involvement in various social networks.

Another important area of research is the relationship between the stability and generalization of behaviour and the activities and skills of people. The study of Gersten *et al.* (1976), which related the stability of various behaviour problems to the age of children, focused attention on the importance of variables which may interact with the stability and generalization of behaviour. The fact that there was more stability at some ages than at others may reflect the changes in activities and skills which occur with age. The maintenance of a behaviour problem over time may be affected by changes in the type of settings in which people participate, the skills they have and those that are required for participation, and the resulting changes in social networks. The importance of many behaviours obviously changes with age. For example, driving a car may be irrelevant for a nine-year-old, provide status for a teenager, and serve as a convenience for an adult. Depending on one's setting, the ability to play marbles, dance, get good examination marks, discuss the influence of Bo Diddley or Lawrence Durrell, make mulligatawny soup, or qualify for a desirable job, may affect participation in activities, the learning of new skills, social interaction, the development of social networks, and eventually, the development, prevention, or alleviation of psychological problems.

Finally, there are many questions on the interrelationships of settings, networks, and psychological problems, How does involvement in one setting affect participation in others? In which settings is participation more important and for what purpose? How does the extent of participation in various settings affect the type of social networks that develop and their influence on psychological problems? How are social networks influenced by economic variables (cf. Dooley and Catalano, 1977) and land-use? More specific information is also needed on the means by which networks influence psychological problems and the types of problems likely to be affected. Overall, this research could help to establish a data-base for new intervention approaches and for the design of environments which might more effectively maintain desired behaviours and improve efforts to prevent psychological problems.

REFERENCES

Allison, J. P. (1972). Economic factors and the rate of crime. *Land Economics*, **48,** 193–196.

Athanasiou, R. and Yoshioka, G. A. (1973). The spatial character of friendship formation. *Environment and Behaviour*, **5,** 43–65.

Azrin, N. H., Flores, T., and Kaplan, S. J. (1975). Job-finding club: a group-assisted program for obtaining employment. *Behaviour Research and Therapy*, **13,** 17–27.

Baird, L. L. (1969). Big school, small school: a critical examination of the hypothesis. *Journal of Educational Psychology*, **60,** 253–260.

Barker, R. G. (1960). Ecology and motivation. In: M. R. Jones (Ed.), *Nebraska Symposium on Motivation*, pp. 1–49. (Lincoln: University of Nebraska Press.)

Barker, R. G. (1968). *Ecological Psychology*. (Stanford: Stanford University Press.)

Barker, R. G. and Schoggen, P. (1973). *Qualities of Community Life*. (San Francisco: Jossey-Bass.)

Baum, A., Harpin, R. E., and Valins, S. (1975). The role of group phenomena in the experience of crowding. *Environment and Behavior*, **7,** 185–198.

Becker, F. D. (1976). Children's play in multifamily housing. *Environment and Behavior*, **8,** 545–574.

Bell, W. and Boat, M. D. (1957). Urban neighbrhoods and informal social relations. *American Journal of Sociology*, **62,** 391–398.

Berkman, L. F. and Syme, S. L. (1979). Social networks, host resistance, and mortality: A nine-year follow-up study of Alameda County residents. *American Journal of Epidemiology*, **109,** 186–204.

Berleman, W. C., Seaberg, J. R., and Steinburn, T. W. (1972). The delinquency prevention experiment of the Seattle Atlantic Street Center: a final evaluation. *Social Service Review*, **46,** 323–346.

Bernstein, A., Epstein, L. J., Lennard, H. R., and Ransom, D. C. (1972). The prevention of drug abuse. In: S. E. Golann and C. Eisdorfer (Eds.), *Handbook of Community Mental Health*, pp. 439–447. (Englewood Cliffs, NJ: Prentice-Hall.)

Bickman, L., Teger, A., Gabriele, T., McLaughlin, C., Berger, M., and Sunaday, E. (1973). Dormitory density and helping behavior. *Environment and Behavior*, **5**, 465–490.

Blake, R. R., Rhead, C. C., Wedge, B., and Mouton, J. S. (1956). Housing architecture and social interaction. *Sociometry*, **19**, 133–139.

Blaut, J. M., McCleary, G. S., Jr., and Blaut, A. S. (1970). Environmental mapping in young children. *Environment and Behavior*, **2**, 335–349.

Bockover, J. S. (1963). *Moral Treatment in American Psychiatry*. (New York: Springer.)

Bornstein, M. H. and Bornstein, H. G. (1976). The pace of life. *Nature*, **259**, 557–559.

Bowers, K. S. (1973). Situationism in psychology: an analysis and a critique. *Psychological Review*, **80**, 307–336.

Brenner, M. H. (1973). *Mental Illness and the Economy*. (Cambridge, Mass.: Harvard University Press.)

Brower, S. N. and Williamson, P. (1974). Outdoor recreation as a function of the urban housing environment. *Environment and Behavior*, **6**, 295–345.

Buell, J., Stoddard, P., Harris, F. R., and Baer, D. M. (1968). Collateral social development accompanying reinforcement of outdoor play in a preschool child. *Journal of Applied Behavior Analysis*, **1**, 167–173.

Caplow, T. (1957). Organizational size. *Administrative Science Quarterly*, **1**, 484–505.

Chapin, F. S. and Logan, T. H. (1969). Patterns of time and space use. In: H. S. Perloff (Ed.), *The Quality of Urban Environment: Essays on 'New Resources' in an Urban Age*, pp. 303–332. (Baltimore: Johns Hopkins Press.)

Chapman, J. I. (1976). An economic model of crime and police: some empirical results. *Journal of Research in Crime and Delinquency*, **13**, 48–63.

Conway, J. B. and Bucher, B. D. (1976). Transfer and maintenance of behavior change in children: a review and suggestions. In: E. J. Mash, L. A. Hamerlynck, and L. C. Handy (Eds.), *Behavior Modification and Families*, pp. 119–159. (New York: Brunner/Mazel.)

Craven, P. and Wellman, B. (1973). The network city. *Sociological Inquiry*, **43**, 57–88.

D'Atri, D. A. (1975). Psychophysiological responses to crowding. *Environment and Behavior*, **7**, 237–252.

Davidson, W. S. and Wolfred, T. R. (1977). Evaluation of a community-based behavior modification program for prevention of delinquency: the failure of success. *Community Mental Health Journal*, **13**, 296–306.

DeStefano, C. T. (1976). Environmental determinants of peer social behavior and interaction in a toddler playgroup. *Dissertation Abstracts*, **36**, 5861–5862B.

Dooley, D. and Catalano, R. (1977). Money and mental disorder: toward behavioral cost accounting for primary prevention. *American Journal of Community Psychology*, **5**, 217–227.

Draper, P. (1973). Crowding among hunter-gatherers: the !Kung Bushmen. *Science*, **182**, 301–303.

Ebbesen, E. B., Kjos, G. L., and Konecni, V. J. (1976). Spatial ecology: its effects on the choice of friends and enemies. *Journal of Experimental Social Psychology*, **12**, 505–518.

Eckerman, C. O. and Whatley, J. L. (1977). Toys and social interaction between infant peers. *Child Development*, **48**, 1645–1656.

Edney, J. J. and Jordan-Edney, N. L. (1974). Territorial spacing on a beach. *Sociometry*, **37**, 92–104.

Elardo, R., Bradley, R., and Caldwell, B. M. (1977). A longitudinal study of the relation of infants' home environments to language development at age three. *Child Development*, **48**, 595–603.

Ellsworth, R. B., Dickman, H. R., and Maroney, R. J. (1972). Characteristics of productive and unproductive unit systems in VA psychiatric hospitals. *Hospital and Community Psychiatry*, **23,** 261–268.

Fanning, D. M. (1967). Families in flats. *British Medical Journal*, **4,** 382–386.

Feeney, F. and Weir, A. (1975). The prevention and control of robbery. *Criminology*, **13,** 102–105.

Feldhusen, J. F., Thurston, J. R., and Benning, J. J. (1970). Longitudinal analyses of classroom behavior and school achievement. *The Journal of Experimental Education*, **38,** 4–10.

Festinger, L., Schachter, S., and Back, K. (1950). *Social Pressures in Informal Groups*. (New York: Harper & Row.)

Fischer, C. S. (1975). The study of urban community and personality. In: A. Inkeles, J. Coleman, and N. Smelser (Eds.), *Annual Review of Sociology*, Vol. 1. Annual Reviews, 67–89.

Fleisher, B. M. (1966). The effect of income on delinquency. *American Economic Review*, **56,** 118–137.

Freedman, J. L. (1975). *Crowding and Behavior*. (New York: Freeman.)

Freedman, J. L., Klevansky, S., and Ehrlich, P. R. (1971). The effect of crowding on human task performance. *Journal of Applied Social Psychology*, **1,** 7–25.

Friedlander, F. and Greenberg, S. (1971). Effect of job attitudes, training, and organization climate on performance of the hard-core unemployed. *Journal of Applied Psychology*, **55,** 287–295.

Galle, O. R., Gove, W. R., and McPherson, J. M. (1972). Population density and pathology: what are the relations for man? *Science*, **176,** 23–30.

Gelfand, D. M., Hartmann, D. P., Walder, P., and Page, B. (1973). Who reports shoplifters? A field-experimental study. *Journal of Personality and Social Psychology*, **25,** 276–285.

Gersten, J. C., Langner, T. S., Eisenberg, J. G., Simcha-Fagan, O., and McCarthy, E. D. (1976). Stability and change in types of behavioral disturbance of children and adolescents. *Journal of Abnormal Child Psychology*, **4,** 111–127.

Glidewell, J. C. (1972). A social psychology of mental health. In: S. E. Golann and C. Eisdorfer (Eds.), *Handbook of Community Mental Health*, pp. 211–246. (Englewood Cliffs, NJ: Prentice-Hall.)

Gold, R. (1970). Urban violence and contemporary defensive cities. *Journal of the American Institute of Planners*, **36,** 146–159.

Goldfried, M. R. and D'Zurilla, T. J. (1969). A behavioral–analytic model for assessing competence. In: C. D. Spielberger (Ed.), *Current Topics in Clinical and Community Psychology*, Vol. 1, pp. 151–196. (New York: Academic Press.)

Goodman, P. S., Salipante, P., and Paransky, H. (1973). Hiring, training, and retaining the hard-core unemployed: a selected review. *Journal of Applied Psychology*, **58,** 22–33.

Granovetter, M. S. (1973). The strength of weak ties. *American Journal of Sociology*, **78,** 1360–1380.

Green, E. H. (1933). Group play and quarreling among preschool children. *Child Development*, **4,** 302–307.

Griffitt, W. and Veitch, R. (1971). Hot and crowded: influences of population density and temperature on interpersonal affective behavior. *Journal of Personality and Social Psychology*, **17,** 92–98.

Gullahorn, J. T. (1952). Distance and friendship as factors in the gross interaction matrix. *Sociometry*, **15,** 123–134.

Gump, P. V. (1974). Big schools—small schools. In: R. H. Moos and P. M. Insel (Eds.), *Issues in Social Ecology: Human Milieus*, pp. 276–285. (Palo Alto, Calif.: National Press Books.)

Hanson, R. A. (1975). Consistency and stability of home environmental measures related to I.Q. *Child Development*, **46,** 470–480.
Harries, K. D. (1974). *The Geography of Crime and Justice*. (New York: McGraw-Hill.)
Hayduk, L. A. (1978). Personal space: an evaluative and orienting overview. *Psychological Bulletin*, **85,** 117–134.
Heilweil, M. (1973). The influence of dormitory architecture on resident behavior. *Environment and Behavior*, **5,** 377–412.
Holahan, C. (1972). Seating patterns and patient behavior in an experimental dayroom. *Journal of Abnormal Psychology*, **80,** 115–124.
Holahan, C. and Saegert, S. (1973). Behavioral and attitudinal effects of large-scale variation in the physical environment of psychiatric wards. *Journal of Abnormal Psychology*, **82,** 454–462.
Holahan, C. J. (1976). Environmental effects on outdoor social behavior in a low-income urban neighbrhood: a naturalistic investigation. *Journal of Applied Social Psychology*, **6,** 48–63.
Hutt, C. and Vaizey, M. J. (1966). Differential effects of group density on social behaviour. *Nature*, **209,** 1371–1372.
Hunt, G. M. and Azrin, N. H. (1973). A community-reinforcement approach to alcoholism. *Behaviour Research and Therapy*, **11,** 91–104.
Indik, B. P. (1963). Some effects of organization size on member attitudes and behavior. *Human Relations*, **16,** 369–384.
Indik, B. P. (1965). Organization size and member participation. *Human Relations*, **18,** 339–350.
Ingham, G. K. (1970). *Size of Industrial Organization and Worker Behaviour*. (London: Cambridge University Press.)
Ittelson, W. H., Proshansky, H. M., and Rivlin, L. G. (1970). Bedroom size and social interaction of the psychiatric ward. *Environment and Behavior*, **2,** 255–270.
Ittelson, W. H., Proshansky, H. M., Rivlin, L. G., and Winkel, G. H. (1974). *An Introduction to Environmental Psychology*. (New York: Holt, Rinehart, & Winston.)
James, J. (1951). A preliminary study of the size determinant in small group interaction. *American Sociological Review*, **16,** 474–477.
Johnson, M. W. (1935). The effect on behavior of variation in the amount of play equipment. *Child Development*, **6,** 56–68.
Jones, P. A. (1972). Home environment and the development of verbal ability. *Child Development*, **43,** 1081–1086.
Jones, R. J. and Azrin, N. H. (1973). An experimental application of a social reinforcement approach to the problem of job-finding. *Journal of Applied Behavior Analysis*, **6,** 345–353.
Kanfer, F. H. and Saslow, G. (1969). Behavioral diagnosis. In: C. M. Franks (Ed.), *Behavior Therapy: Appraisal and Status*, pp. 417–444. (New York: McGraw-Hill.)
Kaplan, P. R. (1975). Building design, neighborhoods, and crime: a study of environments in which crimes occur. Unpublished master's thesis; University of Hawaii.
Kazdin, A. E. (1975). Recent advances in token economy research. In M. H. Hersen, R. M. Eisler, and P. M. Miller (Eds.), *Progress in Behavior Modification*, Vol. 1, pp. 233–274. (New York: Academic Press.)
Kelly, J. G. (1967). Naturalistic observations and theory confirmation: an example. *Human Development*, **10,** 212–222.
Koneya, M. (1976). Location and interaction in row-and-column seating arrangements. *Environment and Behavior*, **8,** 265–282.
Kornhauser, A. W. (1965). *Mental Health of the Industrial Worker*. (New York: Wiley.)
Kvalseth, T. O. (1977). A note on the effects of population density and unemployment on urban crime. *Criminology*, **15,** 105–110.

Latane, B. and Darley, J. M. (1970). *The Unresponsive Bystander: Why Doesn't He Help?* (New York: Appleton-Century-Crofts.)

Levy, L. and Rowitz, L. (1973). *The Ecology of Mental Disorder*. (New York: Behavioral Publications.)

Ley, D. and Cybriwsky, R. (1974). The spatial ecology of stripped cars. *Environment and Behavior*, **6,** 53–68.

Linn, L. S. (1970). State hospital environment and rates of patient discharge. *Archives of General Psychiatry*, **23,** 346–351.

Linn, M. W., Sculthorpe, W. B., Evje, M., Slater, P. H., and Goodman, S. P. (1969). *Journal of Psychiatric Review*, **6,** 299–306.

Marjoribanks, K. (1971). Environmental correlates of diverse mental abilities. *Journal of Experimental Education*, **39,** 64–68.

Maudry, M. and Nekula, M. (1939). Social relations between children of the same age during the first two years of life. *The Journal of Genetic Psychology*, **54,** 193–215.

McCain, G., Cox, V. C., and Paulus, P. B. (1976). The relationship between illness complaints and degree of crowding in a prison environment. *Environment and Behavior*, **8,** 283–290.

McClannahan, L. E. and Risley, T. R. (1975). Design of living environments for nursing-home residents: increasing participation in recreation activities. *Journal of Applied Behavior Analysis*, **8,** 261–268.

McCord, J. (1978). A thirty-year follow-up of treatment effects. *American Psychologist*, **33,** 284–289.

McGrew, P. L. (1970). Social and spatial density effects on spacing behavior in preschool children. *Journal of Child Psychology and Psychiatry*, **11,** 197–205.

Mehrabian, A. and Diamond, S. G. (1971a). Effects of furniture arrangement, props, and personality on social interaction. *Journal of Personality and Social Psychology*, **20,** 18–30.

Mehrabian, A. and Diamond, S. G. (1971b). Seating arrangement and conversation. *Sociometry*, **34,** 281–289.

Melahn, C. L. and O'Donnell, C. R. (1978). Norm-based behavioral consulting. *Behavior Modification*, **2,** 309–338.

Michelson, W. (1973). The reconciliation of 'subjective' and 'objective' data on physical environment in the community: the case of social contact in high-rise apartments. *Sociological Inquiry*, **43,** 147–173.

Milgram, S. (1970). The experience of living in cities. *Science*, **167,** 1461–1468.

Miller, N. E. (1952). The effect of group size on decision-making discussions. *Dissertation Abstracts*, **12,** 229.

Mitchell, J. C. (1969). The concept and use of social networks. In: J. C. Mitchell (Ed.), *Social Networks in Urban Situations*, pp. 1–50. (Manchester: Manchester University Press.)

Mitchell, J. C. (1974). Social networks. In: B. J. Siegel, A. R. Beals, and S. A. Tyler (Eds.), *Annual Review of Anthropology*, Vol. 3. Annual reviews, 279–299.

Mitchell, R. E. (1971). Some implications of high density housing. *American Sociological Review*, **36,** 18–29.

Monahan, J. (1976). The prevention of violence. In: J. Monahan (Ed.), *Community Mental Health and the Criminal Justice System*. (New York: Pergamon Press.)

Moos, R. H. (1974). *Evaluating Treatment Environments: A Social Ecological Approach*. (New York: Wiley.)

Moos, R. H. (1975). *Evaluating Correctional and Community Settings*. (New York: Wiley.)

Moos, R. H. (1976). *The Human Context: Environment Determinants of Behavior*. (New York: Wiley.)

Mueller, E. and Brenner, J. (1977). The origins of social skills and interaction among playgroup toddlers. *Child Development*, **48,** 854–861.

Mullins, P. and Robb, J. H. (1977). Residents' assessment of a New Zealand public-housing scheme. *Environment and Behavior*, **9,** 573–624.

Nahemow, L. and Lawton, M. P. (1975). Similarity and propinquity in friendship formation. *Journal of Personality and Social Psychology*, **32,** 205–213.

Newman, J. and McCauley, C. (1977). Eye contact with strangers in city, suburb, and small town. *Environment and Behavior*, **9,** 547–558.

Newman, O. (1973). *Defensible Space: Crime Prevention Through Urban Design.* (New York: Collier.)

Nietzel, M. T., Winett, R. A., MacDonald, M. L., and Davidson, W. S. (1977). *Behavioral Approaches to Community Psychology*. (New York: Pergamon Press.)

Nogami, G. Y. (1976). Crowding: effects of group size, room size, or density? *Journal of Applied Social Psychology*, **6,** 105–125.

O'Donnell, C. R. (1977). Behavior modification in community settings. In: M. Hersen, R. M. Eisler, and P. M. Miller (Eds.), *Progress in Behavior Modification*, Vol. 4, pp. 69–117. (New York: Academic Press.)

O'Donnell, C. R. and Lydgate, T. (1980). The assessment of physical resources and their relationship to crimes. *Environment and Behavior*, in press.

O'Donnell, C. R., Lydgate, T., and Fo, W. S. O. (1979). The buddy system: review and follow-up. *Child Behavior Therapy*, **1,** 161–169.

Onibokun, A. (1976). Social system correlates of residential satisfaction. *Environment and Behavior*, **8,** 323–344.

Paulus, P. B., Annis, A. B., Seta, J. J., Schkade, J. K., and Matthews, R. W. (1976). Density does affect task performance. *Journal of Personality and Social Psychology*, **34,** 248–253.

Peterson, R. F., Knapp, T. J., Rosen, J. C., and Pither, B. F. (1977). The effects of furniture arrangement on the behavior of geriatric patients. *Behavior Therapy*, **8,** 464–467.

Phillips, L., Broverman, I. K., and Ziegler, E. (1966). Social competence and psychiatric diagnosis. *Journal of Abnormal Psychology*, **71,** 209–214.

Phillips, L. and Votey, H. L., Jr. (1975). Crime control in California. *The Journal of Legal Studies*, **4,** 327–349.

Phillips, L., Votey, H. L., Jr., and Maxwell, D. (1972). Crime, youth, and the labor market. *Journal of Political Economy*, **80,** 491–504.

Porter, L. W. and Lawler III, E. E. (1965). Properties of organization structure in relation to job attitudes and job behavior. *Psychological Bulletin*, **64,** 23–51.

Price, R. H. and Blashfield, R. K. (1975). Explorations in the taxonomy of behavior settings: analysis of dimensions and classification of settings. *American Journal of Community Psychology*, **3,** 335–351.

Quay, H. C. and Love, C. T. (1977). The effect of a juvenile diversion program on rearrests. *Criminal Justice and Behavior*, **4,** 377–396.

Quilitch, H. R., Christophersen, E. R., and Risley, T. R. (1977). The evaluation of children's play materials. *Journal of Applied Behavior Analysis*, **10,** 501–502.

Quilitch, H. R. and Risley, T. R. (1973). The effects of play materials on social play. *Journal of Applied Behavior Analysis*, **6,** 573–578.

Rappaport, J. (1977). *Community Psychology: Values, Research, and Action.* (New York: Holt, Rinehart, & Winston.)

Rehabilitation Research Foundation (1974). *The post-prison analysis of criminal behavior and longitudinal follow-up evaluation of institutional treatment.* RRF 910. Rehabilitation Research Foundation.

Robins, L. N. (1974). *Deviant Children Grown Up.* (New York: Robert E. Krieger.)

Rohner, R. P. (1974). Proxemics and stress: an empirical study of the relationship between living space and roommate turnover. *Human Relations*, **27,** 697–702.

Ross, M., Layton, B., Erickson, B., and Schopler, J. (1973). Affect, facial regard and reactions to crowding. *Journal of Personality and Social Psychology*, **28,** 68–76.

Rowland, K. F. (1977). Environmental events predicting death for the elderly. *Psychological Bulletin*, **84,** 349–372.

Sanoff, H. and Coates, G. (1971). Behavioral mapping: an ecological analysis of activities in a residential setting. *International Journal of Environmental Studies*, **2,** 227–235.

Shechtman, A. (1970). Age patterns in children's psychiatric symptoms. *Child Development*, **41,** 683–693.

Shepherd, M., Oppenheim, B., and Mitchell, S. (1971). *Childhood Behaviour and Mental Health*. (New York: Grune & Stratton.)

Sherrod, D. R. and Downs, R. (1974). Environmental determinants of altruism: the effects of stimulus overload and perceived control on helping. *Journal of Experimental Social Psychology*, **10,** 468–479.

Shure, M. B. (1963). Psychological ecology of a nursery school. *Child Development*, **34,** 979–992.

Schwitzgebel, R. and Kolb, D. A. (1964). Inducing behaviour change in adolescent delinquents. *Behaviour Research and Therapy*, **1,** 297–304.

Sjoquist, D. L. (1973). Property crime and economic behavior: some empirical results. *American Economic Review*, **63,** 439–446.

Smith, J., Form, W. H., and Stone, G. P. (1954). Local intimacy in a middle-sized city. *American Journal of Sociology*, **60,** 276–284.

Social Welfare Development and Research Centre (1974a). *The Adult Furlough Center: Variables Related to Successful Parole*. No. 137. University of Hawaii.

Social Welfare Development and Research Center (1974b). *Liliha House: An In-Community Residential Program*. No. 131. University of Hawaii.

Sommer, R. (1969). *Personal Space: The Behavioral Basis of Design*. (Englewood Cliffs, NJ: Prentice-Hall.)

Sommer, R. (1974). *Tight Spaces: Hard Architecture and How to Humanize it*. (Englewood Cliffs, NJ: Prentice-Hall.)

Steinzor, B. (1950). The spatial factor in face to face discussion groups. *Journal of Abnormal and Social Psychology*, **45,** 552–555.

Stokols, D., Rall, M., Pinner, B., and Schopler, J. (1973). Physical, social and personal determinants of the perception of crowding. *Environment and Behavior*, **5,** 87–115.

Sundberg, N. D., Snowden, L. R., and Reynolds, W. M. (1978). Toward assessment of personal competence and incompetence in life situation. In: M. R. Rosenzweig and L. W. Porter (Eds.), *Annual Review of Psychology*, Vol. 29. Annual reviews, 179–221.

Tars, S. E. and Appleby, L. (1973). The same child in home and institution: an observational study. *Environment and Behavior*, **5,** 3–27.

Thomas, E. J. and Fink, C. F. (1963). Effects of group size. *Psychological Bulletin*, **60,** 371–384.

Ullmann, L. P. (1967). *Institution and Outcome: A Comparative Study of Psychiatric Hospitals*. (New York: Pergamon Press.)

Updegraff, R. and Herbst, E. K. (1933). An experimental study of the social behavior stimulated in young children by certain play materials. *Journal of Genetic Psychology*, **42,** 372–391.

Valins, S. and Baum, A. (1973). Residential group size, social interaction, and crowding. *Environment and Behavior*, **5,** 421–439.

Votey, H. L., Jr. and Phillips, L. (1974). The control of criminal activity: an economic analysis. In: D. Glaser (Ed.), *Handbook of Criminology*, pp. 1055–1093. (Chicago: Rand McNally.)

Wahler, R. G. and Moore, D. R. (1975). School–home behavior change procedures in a 'high risk community'. Paper read at the meeting of the Association for Advancement of Behavior Therapy, San Francisco.

Ward, S. K. (1975). Methodological considerations in the study of population density and social pathology. *Human Ecology*, **3,** 275–286.

Warr, P. B. (1964). Proximity as a determinant of positive and negative sociometric choice. *British Journal of Social and Clinical Psychology*, **4,** 104–109.

Wechsler, H. and Pugh, T. F. (1967). Fit of individual and community characteristics and rates of psychiatric hospitalization. *American Journal of Sociology*, **73,** 331–338.

Wells, B. W. P. (1965). The psycho-social influence of building environment: sociometric findings in large and small office spaces. *Building Sciences*, **1,** 153–165.

Wicker, A. W. (1968). Undermanning, performances, and students' subjective experiences in behavior settings of large and small high schools. *Journal of Personality and Social Psychology*, **10,** 255–261.

Wicker, A. W. (1969). Size of church membership and members' support of church behavior settings. *Journal of Personality and Social Psychology*, **13,** 278–288.

Wicker, A. W., McGrath, J. E., and Armstrong, G. E. (1972). Organization size and behavior setting capacity as determinants of member participation. *Behavioral Science*, **17,** 499–513.

Wicker, A. W. and Mehler, A. (1971). Assimilation of new members in a large and a small church. *Journal of Applied Psychology*, **55,** 151–156.

Willems, E. P. (1967). Sense of obligation to high school activities as related to school size and marginality of student. *Child Development*, **38,** 1247–1260.

Winsborough, H. H. (1965). The social consequences of high population density. *Law and Contemporary Problems*, **30,** 120–126.

Wolf, R. (1966). The measure of environments. In: A. Anastasi (Ed.), *Testing Problems in Perspective*, pp. 491–503. (American Council on Education.)

Wolfe, M. (1975). Room size, group size, and density: behavior patterns in a children's psychiatric facility. *Environment and Behavior*, **7,** 199–224.

Wood, Y. R. and O'Donnell, C. R. (in press). Adult probation adjustment: a twelve month follow-up. *Journal of Community Psychology*.

Worchel, S. and Teddlie, C. (1976). The experience of crowding: a two-factor theory. *Journal of Personality and Social Psychology*, **31,** 30–40.

Yancy, W. L. (1971). Architecture, interaction, and social control: the case of a large-scale public housing project. *Environment and Behavior*, **3,** 3–21.

Zax, M. and Cowen, E. L. (1969). Research on early detection and prevention of emotional dysfunction in young school children. In: C. D. Spielberger (Ed.), *Current Topics in Clinical and Community Psychology*, Vol. 1, pp. 67–108. (New York: Academic Press.)

The Social Psychology of Psychological Problems
Edited by P. Feldman and J. Orford

11

The Community Context

EMORY L. COWEN

I: CONCEPTUAL AND HISTORICAL CONSIDERATIONS

Human maladaptation is shaped by and, in turn, leads to social as well as individual problems. Although most mental-health people would pay lip service to that statement, it does not really reflect the field's predominant thinking or practices—past *or* present.

The ultimate goal of this chapter is to consider how the still amorphous entity 'community context' can serve future efforts to understand, and cope more effectively with, psychological dysfunction. That goal may best be reached, however, by considering first: (a) how the mental health field has evolved historically and came to define its turf; and (b) its *current* dilemmas and problems.

The historical context

Early man's first concerns with behaviour focused on aberrance—i.e. florid, indisputable departures from then-prevalent norms of expectancy about human behaviour (Zax and Cowen, 1976). Because such deviance was not understood, it was both threatening and frightening. Significant vestiges of that view, and the isolation and stigmatization it leads to, remain in modern society.

Over the centuries concepts ranging from early demonaic, supernatural interpretations to recent, more 'rational' ones (both biological and environmental) have been advanced in seeking to understand, and treat, disordered behaviour. Yet, notwithstanding centuries of serious thought, effort and research, the mystery of how to cope with profound psychological dysfunction is virtually as great today as it was 2000 years ago. Major mental illness (e.g. schizophrenia) is still identified as mental health's premier problem and challenge (Joint Commission Report, 1961; President's Commission Report, 1978). Some things in mental health have, however, changed; as for example, our views about the *nature* of deviant behaviour. Thus, gradually, many less-than-profound dysfunctions have been admitted to the family of conditions seen as belonging to mental health's proper domain, e.g. symptom neuroses, character neuroses, psychosomatic disorders, and, more recently, philosophical or existential neuroses—conditions that question man's very being or place in life (Zax and Cowen, 1976).

Complex social forces underlie that expansion of mental health's scope. One such force, visible in several ways, is Western civilization's technological evolution. Thus, as problems of survival and physical well-being (e.g. disease, pestilence) have come under society's control, time and energies were freed for concern with man the psychological being. Similarly, as society became more automated, people had more leisure time and opportunities to consider matters of psychological importance. Another force in that same direction is the ascent of a social philosophy that all people should have equal access to education, opportunity, and well-being. Thus, today, many conditions short of profound deviance, e.g. waste of talent, chronic unhappiness, anxiety, lack of purpose, and internal suffering, fall well within mental health's purview. Indeed some of the main tools our field has developed in the past century seek to address (undo) precisely such states. Psychotherapy is an excellent case in point.

Mental health's ever-expanding scope, and growing sensitivity to man the psychological being (Rieff, 1959) have created mounting pressures for: (a) helping services in many new settings and contexts; and (b) identifying effective ways to resolve many new types of problem that the health care system is now called on to address. Dr Burton Brown, former Director of the National Institute of Mental Health, underscores that point:

> the system that serves the largest collection of this diverse, oppressed and needful group is mental health. Mental health services ... increasingly represent the court of last resort for the poor, the ill, the underprivileged, the hungry and the disenfranchised (Brown, 1977, p. 4).

What we have so far pictured as an evolutionary process is seen by some to involve more revolutionary marker-points. Speaking about scientific advance generally, Kuhn (1962, 1970) argues that science develops primarily through major crises, or revolutions, born of the realization that prevalent concepts ('i.e. paradigms') no longer accommodate existing knowledge or solve current problems. 'Paradigm-shift', the term he uses to describe such major changes, has been applied by Rappaport (1977) to an analysis of mental health's current situation.

Historians of mental health (Hobbs, 1964; Zax and Cowen, 1976; Prevention Task Panel Report, 1978) agree that there have, thus far, been three major mental health revolutions. The first, powered by the humanitarian concerns of Phillipe Pinel in France in 1792, 'removed the chains binding the insane in the fetid dungeons of Paris' (Prevention Task Panel Report, 1978). The second, at the turn of this century, was Freud's emphasis on the continuities in human thought and behaviour between the sane and the insane, children and adults, and dream and reality worlds. The third revolution, which began quite recently, is the so-called community mental health revolution. Through it, people in psychological need may find appropriate help within a single setting, for a vast range of psychological problems.

Each revolution addressed issues important to its era. Each found answers to real, pressing questions. Each built on the knowledge and strengths of prior revolutions. Yet time has shown that each was incomplete either because it failed to capture, omnisciently, *all* issues of the time or, more likely, because subsequent change and social evolution brought pressing new issues and problems into focus (Rappaport, 1977).

Thus, mental health revolutions (major paradigm-shifts) occur when the best concepts and tools of the time cannot resolve serious problems being faced. Understanding what our needs for change are, and identifying alternative directions that might be pursued in meeting such needs, depend on candid, searching analysis of the failings of contemporary ways. The section to follow offers such an analysis, which should help to spotlight the potential importance of community contexts for engaging mental health's current, pressing, unresolved problems.

The problem context

Accepting as valid the concept of mental health revolutions, the preceding summary described the thrusts of the three prior revolutions. It did not, however, identify assumptions and practices that have *not* changed through these revolutions. Among such constancies, the most significant have been the assumptions that mental health's prime focus should be on malfunctioning, sick people and that its prime goal should be to minimize, or repair, casualty. Those are key limiting factors to keep in mind as we go on to consider several vexing mental health problems of *our* time.

1. Albee (1959), who carefully reviewed professional manpower resources for the original Joint Commission on Mental Illness and Health (1961), concluded that all major health fields had serious manpower shortages—then, and for the foreseeable future. Such shortages resulted from the expanding definition of mental health's scope, the growing list of human problems seen to have psychological components, and society's growing sensitivity to man's psychological well-being. Though we were not necessarily becoming a sicker society, demands for service on the mental health system had grown more rapidly than society's ability to train qualified people to furnish them. Subsequent statements on this topic (Albee, 1966; Sarason, 1976) are even more extreme, i.e. if we continue to define and engage mental health problems as we have in the past, there will *never* be sufficient professional personnel to meet express demand, much less latent need.
2. The mental health fields have failed to find satisfactory solutions to baffling problems of profound psychic dysfunction (e.g., schizophrenia and the functional psychoses) known to man from time immemorial. Although such conditions—described under the rubric of 'major mental illness'—have long attracted heavily invested, dedicated, clinical, and research efforts from many talented, higly motivated mental health professionals, they have resisted resolution (Scheff,

1966; Kety, 1967). They stand today, both as a blight and challenge to our field. The magnitude of that blight, and its attendant problems, has prompted some observers to urge qualitatively different approaches, based on abandoning mental hospitals, to deal with them (Braginsky *et al.*, 1969).

3. Starting with Freud's pioneering efforts, the mental health fields have developed technologies to address less than extreme dysfunction. The many existing variants of psychotherapy well exemplify those approaches. However difficult the initial struggle to gain solid acceptance for psychotherapy, many people have come over time to see it as *the* mental health intervention of choice. Cowen (1973) makes the same point in stronger form by noting that many mental health professionals accept as an identify: 'Helping people in distress = Psychotherapy' (p. 424). Psychotherapy's early history was anchored in a clinical, rather than a research, tradition. As outcome data began slowly to accumulate, early reviews of findings both with adults (Eysenck, 1952, 1961) and children (Levitt, 1957, 1971) were pessimistic. Current, more searching analyses of a greatly expanded body of psychotherapy outcome data (Strupp and Bergin, 1969; Bergin, 1971; Bergin and Suinn, 1975), though perhaps less harsh, still conclude that the approach is, at best, only moderately effective and inexact. Recently psychotherapy researchers have drifted away from the simple question: 'Does therapy work?' to the more complex one: 'Under what conditions, and with what types of clients, do which therapy approaches work best?' (Kiesler, 1966, 1971; Bergin, 1971; Gomes-Schwartz *et al.*, 1978). The point to emphasize here is that psychotherapy can no longer be seen as an all-embracing, saviour approach in mental health.
4. The preceding concern is that one of mental health's most respected and pivotal technologies, i.e. psychotherapy, has at best limited *clinical* effectiveness with those it reaches. An even more fundamental *social* concern, is *who* psychotherapy, and other mental health services, reach. There is much evidence to suggest that such services have been allocated disproportionately to people who are 'fortunately placed' in society (Hollingshead and Redlich, 1958; Sanua, 1966, 1969; Ryan, 1969; Lorion, 1973, 1974). Schofield (1964) caricatures that reality by using the acronym YAVIS to describe people who have had preferential access to mental health services. YAVIS decoded means Young, Attractive, Verbal, Intelligent and Successful. Schofield's point is that help is least available where it is most needed. Consistent with that view, a powerful recurrent theme of the recent President's Commission on Mental Health (1978) is the urgent need to strengthen services to the 'unserved and underserved'. Whereas those words were once linked specifically to inner-city poor and disadvantaged minority groups, the Commission's current usage is broader, to include children, retired people, rural dwellers, and the chronically sick, all of whom, it is argued, have been short-changed by mental health.
5. Moreover, mental health services, historically, have been packaged in formats governed by white, middle-class folkways and mores: e.g., fixed, prescheduled 50-minute hours, well-appointed, broadloomed offices brightly decorated with

copies of current magazines such as *National Geographic*, *The New Yorker*, *Better Homes and Gardens*, and well managed by cadres of sophisticated secretary/receptionists. For some (sizeable) segments of society such trappings are at least unnatural, and at most alien; both in their inflexibility and symbolic value, they turn people off prospective services before they ever take hold (Bredemeier, 1964; Reiff and Riessman, 1965; Reiff, 1966). Compounding the 'felony' is the fact that some mental health practitioners have been less than eager to take on clients whose characteristic styles of thinking and acting, use of language, and economic status differ so much from what they are used to and comfortable with. The conviction of some clinicians that such differences automatically bespeak poor therapy outcomes can readily lead to self-fulfilling prophesies.

Although there has been much recent effort to find mental health approaches better suited to the needs and styles of other than white middle-class clientele (Lerner, 1972), it can still be said that the 'cream' of mental health's services is both tailored for, and disproportionately allocated to a white, middle-class, well-educated clientele.

6. The mental health fields have generally been unresponsive to a wide range of destructive, irrepressible social problems such as racism, addiction, urban violence, prison riots, delinquency, and other forms of anti-social behaviour. Whether that aloofness results from lack of interest, inadequate technology, or failure to perceive such problems as relevant to mental health's domain, the fact remains that we have contributed little to their solution. Shifting focus away from the context and dynamics of the individual towards the community may help to identify opportunities for mental-health professionals to address the challenges posed by such grave, pressing social problems.

The above summary identifies major failings of our mental health delivery system. It can be added that subcomponents of the larger system, e.g. school mental health services, are affected by similar maladies (Cowen and Lorion, 1976). Although each of the six problems represents a widespread, serious system-failing, two key common denominators should be underscored: (1) existing mental health resources are both insufficient to meet need as defined and inequitably distributed, and (2) mental health, as a system, has always been overwhelmingly fixated on psychological casualty and its repair. Elsewhere (Cowen, 1973, 1977; Zax and Cowen, 1976), the term 'end-state mentality' is used to describe that historic bias. We see ourselves, and are seen by others, as 'doctors of the mind'. When we assess we focus on the assessment of deficit. Our typical interventions start when established, often serious deficit comes forcibly to our attention. We wait to react, rather than reaching out. Thus, unwittingly, we invoke our finest efforts at the poorest possible times, in that the more rooted and crystallized an end-state is the more does it resist change. The lion's share of mental health's scarce energies and resources has gone to conditions that offer the least promise for positive change. In an era of major worldwide concern about energy deficit and fuel conservation, the current mental health dilemma can be put in exactly those terms, i.e. 'To what extent has mental health, planfully or by default, engineered a delivery system that works toward the *fewest* possible miles per gallon?'

The collective weight of the foregoing problems is enormous. In the USA alone, 17 billion dollars, about 12 per cent of the nation's total health costs in 1976, were spent on mental health. Yet the Report of the President's Commission (1978) concluded: 'This [expenditure] is not commensurate with the magnitude of mental health problems.' Awareness of the great unresolved problems facing the mental health fields today, as Kuhn (1962) suggested, creates constructive pressures for yet another major significant paradigm-shift. Viable conceptual alternatives are sorely needed. Some (Prevention Task Panel Report, 1978) have argued that certain of those alternatives (e.g. primary prevention) are sufficiently different and important to hold the seeds of a fourth major mental health revolution.

Alternative frames of reference and approaches

The mental health fields come together through a prime, shared concern with people's adjustment, adaptation, self-image, security, happiness—in other words, with their psychological well-being. Although that statement is sufficiently broad to apply to all the mental health professions, for simplicity's sake we shall focus on psychology in elaborating it. Historically, within psychology, concerns about people's well-being have been the province of clinical psychology. Only as clinical psychology's practices started to be recognized to be insufficient to the problems at hand did other subfields such as community mental health and community psychology begin to evolve. Thus, although those three subspecialties are interested in common problems and share the same ultimate goals, they differ sharply in the nature, timing, and locations of their defining practices (Cowen, 1977).

Traditional clinical psychology's thrust, like those of psychiatry and social work, is to assess and, hopefully, repair deficits. Psychotherapy is one of its most important repair tools. Operating primarily out of hospitals, clinics, and private offices, its fundamental mode has been 'passive–receptive' (Cowen, 1967), rather than 'active–seeking'. Thus, clinical psychologists have characteristically waited for personal problems to find them. When engaged, those problems are often severe and pressing. Although clinical psychologists are not blind to the shortcomings of their delivery system, their way of addressing them is to develop different, more sensitive, assessment methods and more effective treatment approaches.

The wellspring of the community mental health (CMH) movement in the USA is a deeply felt concern about the failings of past mental health repair strategies. The CMH approach does not actually abandon clinical psychology's casualty-repair orientation; rather it seeks to find alternatives that meaningfully address obvious, chronic shortcomings of the existing delivery system. Since some clinical psychologists share the same concerns, and engage in similar quests, demarcation lines between the two fields are sometimes blurred. Practically speaking, CMH's main activities include:

(a) identifying psychological problems earlier, at times when intervention can be more effective;
(b) extending mental health's sphere of operation to more 'natural' settings than just clinics or hospitals, i.e. schools, churches, neighbourhood store fronts, to engage dysfunction sooner; in other words CMH strives to change mental health's classic passive–receptive orientation to a more active–outreach mode;
(c) developing more flexible approaches, better suited to the needs and styles of those in society who cannot, or do not, avail themselves of traditional services;
(d) fostering activities such as consultation that heed the realities of distressed people's help-seeking behaviours and hold promise for geometric expansion of services;
(e) training and using new breeds of direct-help agents, including non-professionals, to provide additional, more flexible and, sometimes, more realistic, person-helping power in an under-resourced system.

Community mental health centres (CMHCs) in the USA represent one, but not the only, recent significant development of this type. Many of the above activities are central to the mandate of CMHCs, though individual settings differ, in the extent to which they pursue them, as opposed to more traditional clinical activities. A key point for this discussion, however, is that the true importance of the word community, in CMH, lies in the fact that it harbours settings and contexts that make it possible to do those new things.

Although the evolving field of community psychology shares with traditional clinical and CMH approaches the ultimate goal of optimizing people's psychological well-being, it departs sharply from them in timing and practices. The assumptions and orienting strategies of primary prevention are central to community psychology. As noted in the Prevention Task Panel Report (1978), primary prevention:

(a) is proactive not reactive, i.e., it seeks to build health in people from the start, not to undo deficit;
(b) is mass-oriented and before-the-fact, rather than targeted to already dysfunctional individuals;
(c) assumes that equipping people with resources to cope effectively from the start, is the best of all ways to forestall maladaptation; and
(d) uses education and social engineering, rather than therapy or rehabilitation, as its prime tools.

Marker characteristics such as building health, being mass oriented, and prime reliance on education and social engineering, highlight the potential importance of community contexts for community psychologists.

The preceding account at least oversimplifies, and at most ignores, several key realities. For one thing, all three approaches are represented simply and unidimensionally, when in fact each includes a broad family of strategies and practices. Bloom (1977), for example, documents CMH's complexity. Another limiting factor is that the account presents distilled essences of 'pure' models which, in nature, are blurred at numerous overlap points. But if, notwithstanding those limitations, broad cross-approach distinctions can be preserved, one can see that community contexts become an ever more central force as one moves from traditional clinical, to CMH, to true community psychology approaches.

The rest of the chapter documents and expands the preceding sentence by providing examples of ongoing efforts to improve psychological well-being by harnessing special aspects of community contexts. Both CMH and community psychology strategies are considered.

II: CMH ALTERNATIVES BASED ON COMMUNITY CONTEXTS

This section overviews a variety of programmes aimed at different substantive areas but linked by the common element of exploring promising, community-anchored solutions to refractory mental health problems.

A. Severely disturbed school-aged children

Hobbs (1966) noted that about 1½ million young American children are so severely disturbed that they cannot progress reasonably in their natural home environments, communities, or schools. Standard treatment is neither available, nor necessarily the approach of choice, for them. Often they mark time or languish, failing to develop in ways commensurate with their potential. Community programmes and resources to meet their unique needs have not been available.

In his work with the original Joint Commission on Mental Illness and Health (1961), Hobbs discovered that several European countries (e.g., France, Britain) with fewer resources than the USA had developed successful community-based programmes for severely disturbed children, predicated on two assumptions, that:

(a) age-appropriate behavioural adaptation to a community setting is more than important than psychodynamics; and
(b) intensive round-the-clock, day-by-day education, rather than individual therapy is the approach of choice, for them.

On that basis he launched Project Re-Ed (Hobbs, 1966, 1967; Lewis, 1967).

Re-Ed is a community educational setting in which children live five days a week. While they are in residence, home and community ties are maintained and abrupt transitions are avoided. Re-Ed's prime service agent is the teacher–counsellor, a new type of help-agent drawn from the ranks of experienced teachers with special talent for this demanding role. Following extensive preparation and training, teacher—counsellors live and work with programme children in a community setting, 24 hours a day. Re-Ed:

(a) capitalizes on its mini-community structure by building a climate of trust and *esprit de corps*, encouraging appropriate expression of feeling and using constructive limit-setting to help children to manage their impulses more effectively; and
(b) counts heavily on education to impart requisite skills and competencies to the children. Behaviour, not dynamics, is the programme's key focus.

Re-Ed effectiveness data (Hobbs, 1966; Weinstein, 1969) indicate an overall 80 per cent success rate. Specific negative symptoms such as tantrums, bed-wetting, and aggressiveness diminished in Re-Ed children and their social and school adjustment, as well as overall competence, improved. One impressive finding, especially given the programme's short-term nature, (children are, on the average, in residence for only five months), is that all Re-Ed graduates were found to be functioning adequately in regular schools at the 18-month post-discharge follow-up point. Per-child costs in Re-Ed are much lower than those of private or residential treatment, or state hospital placement, the major prior alternatives.

Donahue (1967) and Donahue and Nichtern (1965) report a conceptually similar programme in Elmont, LI, also for profoundly disturbed (i.e. schizophrenic) children. Elmont, which unlike Re-Ed is a day-care programme, shares Re-Ed's assumption that education is a more natural vehicle than therapy for child growth. The Elmont programme clearly illustrates how a community context can broaden intervention options. Elmont planners knew *what* they wanted to do—i.e. to provide an enriched, highly individualized educational experience for profoundly disturbed children—but not *how* to do it. Faced with a school district's perennial budgetary and personnel shortages, they eventually pieced together an amalgam of community resources to address the problem: space from a synagogue, equipment, materials and supplies from a local Kiwanis club (a local businessmen's philanthropic group), and a new breed of volunteer help-agent, i.e. the 'teacher–mom'. Such women, selected for their warm, empathic, giving qualities, worked intensively with programme children on individualized study plans, under professional supervision. Although Elmont's evaluation was less rigorous than Re-Ed's, it still reflected substantial programme success. More than 50 per cent of otherwise 'lost' children were able to return to normal classroom settings where they functioned well educationally and interpersonally. Thanks to major community inputs, the programme was very inexpensive, i.e. only $38/year more per child than the district's base-rate, per capita educational cost.

B. Mental handicap*

Mental handicap poses difficult problems for families and communities. Past

* Terminology in this section has been brought into line with that currently in use in the UK (see the chapter in this volume by Yule). The term 'mental deficiency' may be more commonly employed in the USA, along with the adjectives 'defective' and 'retarded'. Similarly in section C, the expression 'chronically jobless and/or delinquent' has been used to replace the American expression 'hard-core youth'.

planning in this area often starts with buildings, based on the assumption that an appropriate building site can *per se* solve the problems at hand. In his role as a consultant to a state planning agency, Sarason, with several co-authors (Sarason *et al.*, 1971), wrote a provocative treatise urging critical re-examination of past assumptions about the care and treatment of the mentally handicapped. He argued, intriguingly, that new buildings, rather than necessarily solving problems, might have several distinct *dis*advantages:

1. geographically isolating children from their natural homes; and
2. inadvertently absolving the community of responsibility for, and involvement in, the problems posed by mental handicap.

His cogent argument led to the articulation of a three-pronged, community-based programme for the mentally handicapped:

1. a day-care centre run by the parents' association;
2. an independent living unit to house handicapped youths while they worked in the community; and
3. a special family-involvement living programme in which handicapped young people with difficult family situations were placed five days a week.

Individual problems that could not be handled by this combination of new community services were referred to other settings. All three new programmes had deep community roots. Collectively they provided a new community-anchored solution to a community problem, based on assumptions and practices that differed from past, traditional ones.

C. Delinquent youth

Virtually all communities are troubled and embarrassed by the problems of chronically jobless and/or delinquent youth. Direct, clinical treatment of such youth has had a poor history; indeed, many clinicians avoid them like the plague. In recent years, however, several community-based programmes, bypassing prior clinical 'givens', have been developed and successfully implemented for such youth. Goldenberg's (1968, 1971) Residential Youth Center (RYC) is an example. Goldenberg's key assumption was that the creation of settings to potentiate positive, situationally realistic change, rather than individual clinical treatment, was the approach of choice for such youths. Specifically, he questioned the following past assumptions that:

1. the problems of disadvantaged youth are best solved on turfs removed from their natural habitats;
2. mental health professionals can provide the best services for them, and
3. settings for them should be based on professionals' values and technologies.

An RYC structure was established in the heart of New Haven's inner-city, staffed by relatively young people raised in that area. *All* staff members—cooks, secretaries, custodians, as well as professionals, had major responsibilities both for *some* residents and for programme, and building, and maintenance. The RYC had a homelike structure, with open access to and from the surrounding community. Its programmes emphasized educational and vocational training as well as personal counselling.

Residency for youths, ages 16–21, was voluntary, the average stay being five months. Residents participated actively in RYC's governance and operation and were assigned daily responsibilities. Programme evaluation showed that residents, compared to controls, had significantly higher employment rates, better on-the-job attendance, more income, and fewer arrests and incarcerations. The average residence cost was about $3000; less, for example, that the cost of processing *one* youth through the juvenile courts (Duggan, 1965).

Fishman *et al.* (1969) describe a conceptually related programme, for inner-city delnquent youths, conducted by the Howard University Institute for Youth Studies (IYS) in Washington, DC. Like RYC, the IYS programme emphasized concrete skill and competence training; it placed participants in jobs in fields such as day-care, welfare, recreation, geriatrics, counselling, and schools. The IYS programme involved more than 100 black inner-city residents, most under age 21 and with chronic histories of delinquency, unemployment, and school drop-out. Comprehensive programme evaluation reflected major gains in employment, job stability, and income, and reductions in anti-social and criminal behaviour.

The documented workability of the RYC and IYS underscores the fact that innovative community-based programmes, bypassing traditional assumptions and settings, can help to identify meaningful solutions to personal and social problems heretofore seen as largely intractable.

D. Mental health approaches for the poor

Mounting social forces such as the social philosophy that all people are entitled to a square deal in life, and black identity, pride and activism have converged to focus attention on the nature and extent of human services, including mental health services, to the poor. Indeed, as noted earlier, that issue was a vital concern of the recent President's Commission Report (1978). Starting with Faris and Dunham's (1939) classic work four decades ago and including many well-known later reports (e.g. Hollingshead and Redlich, 1958; Myers and Roberts, 1959; Sanua, 1966, 1969; Srole *et al.*, 1962; Ryan, 1969; Lorion, 1973, 1974) two key conclusions have been reached repeatedly, that:

1. the incidence and diagnosed severity of psychological disorder increases sharply going from the periphery to the geographic centre of urban communities; and
2. the poor have last call on mental health's most experienced and skilled practitioners and most highly valued services.

Those conclusions need not be accepted uncritically; indeed, as noted elsewhere (Zax and Cowen, 1976), they leave unsettled issues pertaining to how mental illness and psychological problems are defined; the meaning of cultural, linguistic, attitudinal, and stylistic differences between races, social bias, and economic realities. But a fundamental fact is that mental health services have evolved in middle-class traditions and formats that have not effectively reached, or served, the poor. Bredemeier (1964) presents a detailed analysis both of the factors that turn the poor away from traditional mental health services and those that lead mental health professionals, and agencies, to avoid working with them.

The preceding concerns led to much ferment during the 1960s, and to the exploration of new mental health service structures to more effectively meet the needs and realities of the poor. The New Careers movement (Pearl and Riessman, 1965; Riessman and Popper, 1968), an early step in that direction, was designed to address two major problems of the poor: (1) their historically low employment rates, and (2) their lack of access to human services. A further step was the development of the Neighborhood Service Center (NSC) model (Reissman, 1967, Peck and Kaplan, 1969), particularly via programmes pioneered at the Lincoln Hospital, in New York's South Bronx area. At the time the South Bronx, with more than one third of a million people, was one of New York's worst slum-blighted areas, with very high unemployment, poverty, divorce, delinquency, homicide, suicide, and disease rates. Income, education, and housing figures were bleak and virtually no mental health services were available. Speaking of the NSC's overall objective, Riessman (1967) said: 'It is an effort to meet the low-income person on his own "turf" and to utilize [his] style (and strengths) as a basis for working with him' (p. 162). Mental health was one key area in which such a goal was vital. The NSC concept was based on understanding relationships between a community's social organization and the psychological make-up of its constituents, including how they dealt with personal problems.

The NSC emphasized three concrete goals:

1. providing, and expediting, mental health services first by attracting clientele and second by packaging services in modalities consistent with their perceptions, needs and styles;
2. strengthening a neighbourhood's social cohesion by promoting groups and activities to increase peoples involvement and reduce their sense of powerlessness;
3. initiating institutional changes, especially access to, and coordination of, community services.

Two key steps, each addressed to prior classic problems, were taken to improve mental health services to the poor. First, indigenous nonprofessionals (Reiff and Riessman, 1965) were recruited and trained for such work. Selected from the ranks of neighbourhood people, their language, style, and cultural backgrounds matched those of prospective clients. They understood the problems and natural styles of the poor and could operate comfortably, from neighbourhood store-fronts that were not hamstrung by the usual formats and trappings of the middle-class mental health establishment. They were, and could be seen as, trustworthy and as 'one of us'. Second, services including mental health services (e.g. counselling and psychosocial first aid) were provided in concrete, problem-oriented ways that corresponded realistically to the ways in which constituents defined and perceived their problems.

The NSC development, because of its complexity, multi-level involvements and repackaging of service, does not lend itself readily to standard methods for evaluating the effectiveness of mental health services. The centre's services were, indeed, widely used by a population that did not previously have access to such services. Its per-capita service costs were low. Clinically, those associated with the development saw it as a highly effective, down-to-earth approach to a previously inaccessible population vulnerable to serious human and psychological problems. The development illustrates well how community settings, resources, and personnel can be used to frame imaginative new approaches to major social and mental health problems.

E. Chronic patients

Earlier we spoke of the stubborn, unremitting qualities of major mental illness and the problems it poses for individuals and for society. Although we are still far from basic solutions to those problems, work by Fairweather and others (Fairweather, 1964; Fairweather *et al.*, 1969) points toward a community-based alternative to address several of its important dimensions. In earlier work Fairweather found that a hospital-based programme, emphasizing patient autonomy and governance, significantly improved discharge rates for chronic mental patients. Recidivism (i.e. re-admission to the hospital following relapse), a perennial problem, however, remained high; perhaps because the programme did not provide the skills and resources needed by patients to live in the community. Accordingly, an autonomous, communal-living lodge was created that emphasized the acquisition of skills and experiences needed for community living. Key programme elements included training patients to assume administrative responsibilities in the lodge and to develop a patient-conducted business. Otherwise put, the new community structure rested on assumptions and practices that differed from those previously used with such patients. The programme's core aim was to provide an alternative structure that enabled socially 'marginal' ex-patients to develop new adaptive skills, with the help of supporting resources.

Lodge residents spent significantly more time in the community, and had better records of full-time employment, than matched controls in regular after-care programmes. Moreover, per capita costs for the programme were significantly lower than those of traditional care programmes. However, after discharge from the lodge, alumni did not maintain good employment records and their recidivism was comparable to that of controls. Thus, the programme's main accomplishments were to de-stigmatize patients and help them to live more autonomously—rather than to 'cure' them. The latter remains an elusive goal. Even so, the way-station gains of the lodge programme should not be dismissed casually. Although some were less than ideal or enduring, they still point the way towards constructive change in community concepts and structures that carried patients some way down a difficult road. The remaining challenge is to build, from that base, towards even more meaningful and enduring solutions.

Fairweather's efforts are directed to the goal of constructive social change. In full awareness both of the importance and difficulty of bringing such change, Fairweather (1972) argues that social scientists must take active responsibility for furthering social change after they have identified and documented effective new ways. Based on the lodge experiment, later work by Fairweather's group (Fairweather *et al.*, 1974, Fairweather and Tornatzky, 1977) was directed to studying the social change process itself.

One key study of that process began with a telephone contact to many hundreds of mental hospitals about a recently developed programme establishing non-hospital, autonomous living units for chronic patients. Telephone contacts varied systematically on two dimensions: (a) the hierarchical position of the person contacted (e.g. superintendent *vs.* chief nurse); and (b) the mode of programme explanation suggested (i.e. brochure materials, workshop, or having a staff person actually visit the setting to talk about setting up a demonstration unit). Although less obligating entrée steps such as brochures or a workshop were better accepted, in the last analysis, a higher proportion of new programme implementations took place in settings that chose a visit as the entrée step. In other words action-oriented, personally involving entrée steps facilitated the rooting of new programmes.

Although the problems and programmes explored in this section range widely, they share common elements. All programmes speak to complex end-state conditions that have thus far eluded good solutions. All start by reconceptualizing the problem, i.e. by subjecting past assumptions to careful re-examination. From that process, attractive alternatives involving new community structures, resources, and/or personnel uses have been identified. The resulting programmes, all promising, if less than 100 per cent effective, point the way towards exciting options that community contexts can offer, which circumvent chronic shortcomings of past mental health approaches.

III: COMMUNITY PSYCHOLOGY ALTERNATIVES BASED ON THE COMMUNITY CONTEXT

This section presents examples of evolving community psychology (i.e. prevention) approaches to formidable problems in mental health. Such approaches seek to build health and competence, rather than to engage already manifest problems. Although community psychology's long-term goals are similar to those of clinical psychology and CMH, its strategies and practices are qualitatively different from theirs. Because education and systems modification are among its most important tools, community psychologists need different types of skills and training than the types that have classically gone into the making of mental health professionals.

A. Social systems analysis and change

Mental health is slowly relinquishing the once-sacred view that most psychological problems have psychodynamic roots. Clear associations between poverty, hopelessness, lack of opportunity, and psychological problems highlight the important 'relationships between societal systems and mental health behavior' (Smith *et al.*, 1978, p. 12). Social environments, far from being neutral, either facilitate or hamper people's development. Approaches that seek to build health must understand and constructively harness social-system attributes. A first necessary step in that direction is to develop methods for assessing the high-impact dimensions of social environments. Past attempts to do so have ranged from macromolar efforts to describe whole communities (e.g. Barker and Schoggen, 1973; Price and Blashfield, 1975), schools and families (Barker and Gump, 1964; Lennard and Bernstein, 1969) to more micromolar attempts to describe specific environments. Thus, Stallings (1975) developed a complex observational framework, involving 600+ separate rating categories to describe the principal physical dimensions, work activities, child-groupings, locomotion patterns, teacher–pupil, and pupil–pupil interaction patterns, and aspects of the social environment, in primary grade classes.

Among the most significant, persistent efforts to assess social environments is the work of Moos and others (Moos, 1973, 1974a, 1974b; Insel and Moos, 1974; Moos and Insel, 1974; Price and Moos, 1975). Those investigators developed a parallel series of measures to assess nine different types of social environments ranging from therapy groups, to high-school classrooms, to military units, to mental hospital wards. Of particular interest is the fact that certain key dimensions such as how people interact with each other (relational), how they develop personally (personal development), and how the system conducts its business (goal orientation) cut across these diverse environments. Moreover, settings exemplifying any one cluster of environments (hospital wards, therapy groups, or whatever) vary considerably on such dimensions.

Developing frameworks to assess environmental properties facilitates a next critical step, i.e. examining relationships between them and person outcomes. Examples of such work have been reported. Thus, Trickett and Moos (1974) found greater student satisfaction and more positive mood in class environments that scored high in interpersonal relations and rule clarity. Similarly Stallings (1975) found systematic relationships between aspects of class environment and measures of persistence, curiosity, cooperativeness, adjustment and adaptation in young children. At a more macromolar level different personal outcomes have been shown for children educated in modern, *vs*. traditional, class environments (Minuchin, *et al.*, 1969; Zimiles, 1967) and in open *vs*. self-contained class environments (e.g.,

Reiss and Martell, 1974). The key point, however, is that there are systematic relationships between qualities of social environments and relevant variables such as people's happiness, sense of comfort, satisfaction, mood state, or effective functioning.

Lest this account seem oversimplified, let it be stressed that environmental effects are not necessarily linear. Things that suit one person hamper another. In other words, person–environment interactions, or 'fits', must be considered in evaluating environmental effects. That point is well recognized conceptually, within the ecological framework proposed by Kelly and co-workers (Kelly, 1968, 1969; Kelly *et al.*, 1971, 1977) and also has empirical documentation (e.g. Grimes and Allinsmith, 1961; Reiss and Dydhalo, 1975; Kelly *et al.*, 1979). Its practical implication is reflected in Insel and Moos' (1974) observation: 'A source of distress and ill health is the situation in which a person attempts to function within an environment in which he is basically incompatible'. Studies of environmental effects that fail to take into account the complexities of person–environment matches, will be incomplete at best, and misleading at worst.

Knowing a system's qualities and their consequences are preconditions for its constructive modification. A simple case in point: Susskind (1969), starting with the assumption that curiosity behaviour in young children is a universally valued goal, studied it by tracking question-asking behaviours in elementary classrooms. His main finding was eye-opening. Based on 30-minute classroom observation units, teachers asked an average of 50 + questions but entire classes averaged fewer that two questions. That state of affairs was 180° reversed both from the theoretical ideal (i.e. high-curiosity behaviour in children) and people's before-the-fact estimates of the reality of question-asking behaviours in classrooms. Equally striking was the finding that most teacher-posed questions called for answers based on fact and memory, rather than thought. Identifying that *de facto* 'regularity' (Sarason, 1971) led to a system-modification input, i.e., training teachers to pose questions and to lead discussions in ways that encouraged children's curiosity. An unintended system flaw was identified and corrected; as a result teachers were able to change from fact to process-centred leading techniques and children's curiosity (question-asking) behaviour increased.

To sum up, tools for assessing social environments are now available, and variations in environment have been found to relate to adjustive outcomes in people. Although much remains to be learned in this complex area, we may at least have located some useful primary prevention building-blocks. A further intriguing challenge is to apply such knowledge to the engineering of environments—e.g. schools, communities, or whichever—that help people to cope effectively and to develop resources and competencies.

B. Educational approaches

Many observers (Prevention Task Panel Report, 1978) regard education as primary prevention's most powerful tool. Accordingly, community-based educational programmes, both specific and generic, have been widely explored as part of the social effort to optimize people's well-being. Behind that development is the conviction held by some (Cowen, 1977) that acquiring adaptive skills from the very start may be the best possible defence against maladaptation. That point can be illustrated with several examples.

Much evidence has by now been gathered showing that defects in a family of interpersonal cognitive problem-solving (ICPS) skills, e.g. problem-sensing, generating alternative solutions, and evaluating the consequences of solutions, differentiate between adjusted and maladjusted people at various ages (Spivack and Shure, 1974; Spivack *et al.*, 1976). One interpretation of those data is that ICPS skills actively mediate positive adjustment, a view that has nourished the development of complex, formal training programmes to teach ICPS skills to young children and clinically vulnerable groups. Spivack and Shure's basic (1974) programme showed that four-year old inner-city Head-Start children did indeed acquire rudimentary ICPS skills. However, from the standpoint of mental health, several of the study's other findings were even more intriguing: (1) initially maladapted children gained more in ICPS skills than the initially well-adjusted; (2) there were direct linkages between ICPS acquisition and adjustive gain. In other words acquiring a set of cognitive competencies 'radiated' positively to the adjustment sphere. Related findings have been reported by other, independent investigators (Allen *et al.*, 1976; Elardo and Cooper, 1976; Elardo and Caldwell, 1979; Gesten *et al.*, 1979). The significance of such work lies both in its proactive, health-building thrust and its modelling value for other adjustment-related competencies. In other words ICPS skills are not necessarily the only ones that relate significantly to good adjustment. Recent evidence suggests that such concrete skills such as the abilities to set realistic goals, plan ahead, make decisions, be curious, be appropriately assertive, take the role of the other, also differentiate adjusted from maladjusted people. Accordingly, training people in those skills may also radiate positively to adjustment. Early work by Ojemann and others (Ojemann, 1961, 1969; Bruce, 1958; Muuss, 1960; Griggs and Bonney, 1970) on teaching children to think causally is in that tradition. As trained children acquired key programme skills, their overall adjustment and security increased and their anxiety dropped.

Many generic, community-based educational programmes have been undertaken with primary prevention goals in mind (Prevention Task Panel Report, 1978). Examples include prenatal and post-delivery parent-education programmes, those that focus on age-appropriate content as children develop, and direct educational programmes for children and youth emphasizing topics such as interpersonal relationships, sex education, and education for marriage and parenthood. The Stanford Heart Disease Project (Maccoby and Farquhar, 1975, 1976), exemplifies another type of preventive education programme (see McGuire, chapter 12 in this volume.)

C. Stress reduction and crisis involvements

Primary prevention's two main strategies are to build health and to reduce sources of stress. There are intimate relations between environmental or life stresses and psychological maladjustment (Dohrenwend and Dohrenwend, 1974; also the chapter by Cochrane and Sobol, chapter 6, in this volume). Bloom (1977) and Bloom *et al.* (1978) marshal an impressive body of data showing strong associations, for example, between marital disruption and virtually all forms of psychopathology. Based on many studies reviewed, they found that divorced or separated adults were disproportionately represented on all dependent measures of emotional turmoil and profound mental disorder, leading to the conclusion that marital disruption is a major life stress with potentially debilitating, long-term effects. Goldston (1977) has done much the same with regard to the monumental familial problems posed by the Sudden Infant Death Syndrome (SIDS). Epidemiological approaches are prime tools in establishing such relationships based on a model that differs qualitatively from past mental health approaches. First, life experiences that have adverse effects on large numbers of people are identified. Next, people undergoing such experiences are located and their subsequent health/illness histories are compared to those who are not. Those epidemiological/descriptive steps led to the mounting and evaluation of programmes designed to reduce the occurrence of stressful events and/or to help people to cope more effectively with them. Programme success can be measured either as adjustive gain or by short-circuiting what might, otherwise, be colossal loss.

Specific crises such as bereavement, job loss, birth of a child, and hospitalization for surgery are often critical life junctures that lead either to serious adversity or consolidation and gain, depending on their handling. Crises, by definition (Caplan, 1964), are relatively brief periods of acute disturbance. During such periods, individuals feel serious discomfort, preoccupation, emotional upset, confusion about where to turn or what to do, and a subjective sense of vacillation. Their experiences during the crisis have disproportionate impact, for better or worse, on their future well-being. Some observers (Caplan, 1964; Bloom, 1977; Goldston, 1977) see the constructive management of life stress and crisis situations to be at the very nerve centre of primary prevention in mental health.

Although many life crises are both unpredictable and primarily affect individuals or relatively small groups, others are predictable consequences of events (e.g. unemployment, natural disasters) that affect large groups or entire communities. Similarly, concepts of stress reduction apply at levels ranging from the individual to macromolar units such as communities or societies. There has, in fact, been much interest in the challenge of engineering new communities that optimize psychological well-being and reduce stress (Lemkau, 1969; Murrell, 1971; Klein, 1978). But there are important differences in programme feasibility, management, and tactics in trying to reduce stress for individuals *vs.* for a society. At the latter level we have less knowledge, fewer resources, and less control over what can be done. The advantages of engaging concrete stress or crisis situations such as bereavement or marital disruption are that:

1. they are already seen as part of mental health's area of concern;
2. we have relevant knowledge and skills for working with them, to promote well-being;
3. direct programme effects can be observed in finite periods of time.

D. Approaches with low-income groups

Iscoe (1974) wrote about the 'competent community', stressing the need to focus, and build on, a community's strong points. He identified specific strategies such as identifying families of alternatives, and providing knowledge about how to acquire resources that could contribute to those ends. Operating from a University base, Rappaport *et al.* (1975) have implemented such a strategy by creating a setting called the Community Psychology Action Center (CPAC) jointly with inner-city black residents of Champaign, Illinois. CPAC's overarching goal is to identify competencies within the community and to nourish their development (i.e., to take strength where, and as, it is). It avoids efforts to reshape people to conform to existing systems or to modify residents' values or cultural styles (Rappaport, 1977). Far from being an anti-problem programme, CPAC seeks to foster positive, independent behaviours and actions (e.g. a day-care centre, a local press) within the black subcommunity, based on a premise stated earlier, i.e., developing skills and competencies may be the best possible inoculation against adversity.

A qualitatively different building approach, also directed primarily to the inner-city poor, can also be noted. Over many years, a major body of data has been developed testifying to the adverse consequences of certain environmental conditions on young, inner-city children's intellectual and socioemotional development (Deutsch *et al.*, 1968; Hellmuth, 1969; Stendler-Lavatelli, 1968; Hess and Bear, 1968; Miller and Dreger, 1973, Jason, 1975). A key issue in interpreting those data is the extent to which they reflect 'deficits' *vs.* cultural 'differences' (Horowitz and Paden, 1973; Hunt, 1969; Smith *et al.*, 1978). Whatever the answer to that question, the findings have given rise to a variety of broad-gauge compensatory educational (e.g. Bereiter and Englemann, 1966; Bereiter, 1968; Deutsch and Deutsch, 1968; Gottfried, 1973) and infant stimulation (e.g. Caldwell, 1968; Gordon, 1971; Gray and Klaus, 1968) programmes.

Heber's (1978) doggedly persistent effort epitomizes that thrust (see also Yule, chapter 8 of this volume). His saturated, 10-year longitudinal programme was aimed at the offspring of inner-city mothers with IQs of 75 or less—children who, by all known criteria, are at great risk for maldevelopment. This massive project provided training for mothers and a highly enriched programme (i.e. all day, every day for the first five years of life) for children, designed to impart age-appropriate perceptual, motor, language, cognitive, and socioemotional skills. Programme children were tracked closely and evaluated comprehensively. They outperformed non-programme controls dramatically on language, cognitive, and IQ measures—an average of 30 + points on the latter. At age nine they scored in the high-average IQ range—in other words around the 85th to 90th percentile when, on base-rate, one would have predicted the 10th or 15th percentile, i.e., the fate of the controls.

E. Community helping networks and support systems

One major surprise of the recent Report of the President's Commission on Mental Health (1978) was that its very first set of recommendations dealt with 'community supports', an area not previously seen as part of mental health's mainstream. The commission's recommendations emphasize '... the strengths and potential that various support networks bring to communities and neighborhoods and ... the need to develop linkages between those systems and the formal mental health services system' (p. 14). That theme has captured much interest in recent years (Caplan and Killilea, 1976; Collins and Pancoast, 1976; Gershon and Biller, 1977; Sarason *et al.*, 1977).

The Commission defined community support systems broadly to include:

(a) family, friends, and neighbours:
(b) organized community groups such as churches, schools, unions, civic clubs, and voluntary organizations;
(c) self-help groups such as Alcoholics Anonymous and widow-to-widow programmes; and
(d) formal volunteer programmes such as Foster Grandparents.

Beyond that, they also called attention to large systems such as education, justice, and health-care, within which community support systems might be anchored. The Commission believed that most people will seek and accept help from people in those less formal, less stigmatizing systems long before they enter the formal mental health system. The Commission took the strong position that personal and community support systems 'can provide a basic underpinning for mental health in our society' and that the nation 'can ill afford to waste such valuable resources' (p. 15).

How did the Commission reach that view? We have learned from research studies and surveys (Gurin *et al.*, 1960; Roberts *et al.*, 1966; Gottlieb, 1976a) that most people do *not* for many reasons take their personal problems to mental health professionals. Other potential helpers may be better known and trusted, more accessible, less expensive, and/or available when troubles peak. Primary care-givers whose main training is in areas other than mental health (e.g. clergymen, physicians, lawyers) field many psychological problems because their everyday work often brings them close to distressed people who have come to know and trust them. Indeed, the mental health consultation movement (Caplan, 1970; Mannino *et al.*, 1975) developed precisely to address that reality by increasing the knowledge-base and strengthening the hand of caregivers.

But even before personal problems reach such a quasi-formal level, most people have available in their everyday lives spontaneous help outlets (e.g. family members, friends, neighbours, co-workers) to whom they can turn when troubled. Moreover, all communities have people who, because of their compassion and understanding, or the social roles they play (e.g. hairdressers, bartenders), are called upon to deal with interpersonal distress and thus exercise an important potential influence on people's well-being. In some quarters of society, e.g. for the poor, such 'natural neighbours', as Collins and Pancoast (1976) call them, may be the only available sources of help.

Several converging lines of research have recently surfaced to clarify the roles played by support systems and natural care-givers in helping people to deal with personal problems. Gottlieb (1976b), for example, reports a systematic effort to: (a) track down the types of community support systems used by welfare mothers; and (b) understand what those support sources actually do and how helpful they are. Verdone's (1975) Project Outreach trained bartenders as referral agents for patrons who needed mental health services. In a pre-survey about 80 per cent of the bartenders reported feeling a sense of responsibility for patrons with personal problems, and 58 per cent described specific personal efforts (e.g. phone calls to friends) which they had made, to help disturbed patrons. Bissonette (1977) presents a more specific role analysis of bartenders' interpersonal help-giving behaviours. Dumont (1967, 1968), who spent six months observing and listening in a skid-row bar, concluded that for some homeless, anomic men, such settings served a life-sustaining function. The title of his work, '*Taverns as Outposts*', reflects his underlying view that bars should become part of an expanded network of mental health resources.

A recent study by Cowen *et al.* (1979), found that hairdressers, on the average, spend about one-third of their talking-time listening and reacting to moderate-to-serious personal problems raised by clients. Such problems range enormously; in fact, they cover content areas not unlike those brought to mental health professionals. What challenges and opportunities for the mental health fields reside in those facts? How can that reality of the community context be joined in working toward psychological well-being?

Beyond the preceding fact-finding, a variety of programmes designed to harness community support systems have sprung up in recent years. Silverman's (1969, 1976) 'widow-to-widow' programme, addressing the serious and the very special problems involved in the loss of a spouse, is a good example. In that programme women who have adapted successfully to widowhood serve as help-agents to the newly bereaved widows, both for concrete management problems (e.g. legal, social, financial, and readjustment) that often come up during this difficult period, and personal advice-giving and counselling. Widows who have themselves gone through the experience are sometimes better able than professionals to help and to understand. They may also have greater credibility, and be easier to talk to, for the newly bereaved.

At a different level Sarason *et al.* (1977) described the formation of a complex network of people from various walks of life to exchange human services for their mutual benefit, through a type of barter economy. Their work both illustrates how community support systems can furnish a powerful resource for addressing human problems and emphasizes how such networks can promote a 'psychological sense of community' (Sarason, 1974) itself a proactive, health-building force.

Several key points of this discussion bear emphasis:

1. the formal mental health system accounts for only a minor fraction of the real mental health action;
2. our knowledge about how people are helped interpersonally, rests asymmetrically on a very small (biased) group of formal mental health interactions;
3. much human help-giving goes on within community structures, with community people who do not have mental health training or associations serving as help-agents;
4. we are largely uninformed about how such community helping resources work or their effectiveness;
5. all communities harbour potentially large pools of talent and energies, and as yet unformed support systems or networks that can be tapped to support mental health's goals.

SUMMARY

Viewed longitudinally over many centuries, two key qualities characterize mental health's evolution: (a) its ever-expanding, ever-broadening scope; and (b) periodic, major paradigm-shifts that lead to new concepts and approaches for addressing previously refractory problems. Mental health's current problems are numerous and serious. The resulting ferment brings us to the threshold of another significant paradigm-shift. The community—its settings, structures and resources—is critical to that shift, not because it is an end in itself, but because it holds the means to amplify the reach and effectiveness of services and the raw materials to develop new, qualitatively different health-building approaches.

Two evolving new families of approaches, i.e. community mental health and community psychology, were identified and their differences both from past traditional mental health approaches and each other were considered. Community mental health, accepting much of mental health's past casualty orientation, looks for ways to accelerate and improve repair processes, e.g. identifying problems earlier in more natural settings and dealing more flexibly and realistically with them. Systematic screening, early intervention, using non-traditional help-agents, and broadening professional roles to include activities such as consultation, are intrinsic to its ways. Community psychology, by contrast, rests on qualitatively different assumptions and practices. Its overriding goal is to build health rather than fight deficit. Its key tools are social-system analysis and modification and rooting competencies in people—functions that implicate new bodies of knowledge and different skills for mental health personnel.

Because those two areas are still crystallizing, lines of demarcation between them remain somewhat blurred. Within the limits of that constraint, examples of representative programming in 10 sub-areas of the two emergent fields were cited. Although those programmes involve markedly different problem areas, technologies, settings, and timings, they share two common features: (a) they seek to identify useful solutions to past, vexing mental health problems; and (b) they are set in community contexts. There is reason to hope that such approaches, individually and collectively, will provide *bona fide* alternatives to past mental health practices. The obvious weaknesses of the existing delivery system, the commonsensical and conceptual appeal of community approaches and the early availability of programme and research data testifying to their effectiveness, suggest that in the future people's psychological well-being may be better served by reallocating a substantial portion of society's limited mental health resources to those significant evolving alternatives.

REFERENCES

Albee, G. W. (1959). *Mental Health Manpower Trends*. (New York: Basic Books.)

Albee, G. W. (1966). Give us a place to stand and we will move the earth. In: J. C. Harris (Ed.), *Mental Health Manpower Needs in Psychology*, pp. 15–25. (Lexington, KY: University of Kentucky Press.)

Allen, G. J., Chinsky, J. M., Larcen, S. W., Lochman, J. E., and Selinger, H. V. (1976). *Community Psychology and the Schools: A Behaviorally Oriented Multilevel Preventive Approach*. (Hillsdale, NJ: Lawrence Erlbaum Associates.)

Barker, R. G. and Gump, P. (1964). *Big School, Small School*. (Stanford, CA: Stanford University Press.)

Barker, R. G. and Schoggen, P. (1973). *Qualities of Community Life*. (San Francisco: Jossey-Bass.)

Bereiter, C. (1968). A nonpsychological approach to early compensatory education. In: M. Deutsch, I. Katz, and A. R. Jensen (Eds.), *Social Class, Race, and Psychological Development*, pp. 337–346. (New York: Holt, Rinehart & Winston.)

Bereiter, C. and Englemann, S. (1966). *Teaching Disadvantaged Children in the Preschool*. (Englewood Cliffs, NJ: Prentice-Hall.)

Bergin, A. E. (1971). The evaluation of therapeutic outcomes. In: A. E. Bergin and S. L. Garfield (Eds.), *Handbook of Psychotherapy and Behavior Change: An Empirical Analysis*, pp. 217–270. (New York: Wiley.)

Bergin, A. E. and Suinn, R. M. (1975). Individual Psychotherapy and behavior therapy. In: M. R. Rosenzweig and L. C. Porter (Eds.), *Annual Review of Psychology*, **26,** 509–556.

Bissonette, R. (1977). The bartender as a mental health service gatekeeper: a role analysis. *Community Mental Health Journal*, **13,** 92–99.

Bloom, B. L. (1977). *Community Mental Health: A General Introduction*. (Monterey, CA: Brooks-Cole.)

Bloom, B. L., Asher, S. J., and White, S. W. (1978). Marital disruption as a stressor: a review and analysis. *Psychological Bulletin*, **85,** 867–894.

Braginsky, B. M., Braginsky, D. D., and Ring, K. (1969). *Methods of Madness: The Mental Hospital as a Last Resort*. (New York: Holt, Rinehart, & Winston.)

Bredemeier, H. C. (1964). The socially handicapped and the agencies: a market analysis. In: F. Riessman, J. Cohen, and A. Pearl (Eds.), *Mental Health of the Poor*, pp. 98–112. (New York: Free Press.)

Brown, B. S. (1977). Remarks to the World Federation for Mental Health, Vancouver, BC, August 24.

Bruce, P. (1958). Relationship of self-acceptance to other variables with sixth-grade children oriented in self-understanding. *Journal of Educational Psychology*, **49,** 229–238.

Caldwell, B. M. (1968). The fourth dimension in early childhood education. In: R. D. Hess and R. M. Bear (Eds.), *Early Education*. (Chicago: Aldine.)

Caplan, G. (1964). *Principles of Preventive Psychiatry*. (New York: Basic Books.)

Caplan, G. (1970). *Theories of Mental Health Consultation*. (New York: Basic Books.)

Caplan, G. and Killilea, M. (Eds.) (1976). *Support Systems and Mutual Help: Multidisciplinary Explorations*. (New York: Grune & Stratton.)

Collins, A. H. and Pancoast, D. L. (1976). *Natural Helping Networks: A Strategy for Prevention*. (Washington, DC: National Association of Social Workers.)

Cowen, E. L. (1967). Emergent approaches to mental health problems: an overview and directions for future work. In: E. L. Cowen, E. A. Gardner, and M. Zax (Eds.), *Emerent Approaches to Mental Health Problems*, pp. 389–455. (New York: Appleton-Century-Crofts.)

Cowen, E. L. (1973). Social and community interventions. In: P. Mussen and M. Rosenzweig (Eds.), *Annual Review of Psychology*, **24,** 423–472.

Cowen, E. L. (1977). Baby-steps toward primary prevention. *American Journal of Community Psychology*, **5,** 1–22.

Cowen, E. L., Gesten, E. L., Boike, M., Norton, P., Wilson, A. B., and Destefano, M. A. (1979). Hairdressers as caregivers: I: A descriptive profile of interpersonal help-giving involvements. *American Journal of Community Psychology*, **7,** 633–648.

Cowen, E. L. and Lorion, R. P. (1976). Changing roles for the school mental health professional. *Journal of School Psychology*, **14,** 131–132.

Deutsch, C. P. and Deutsch, M. (1968). Brief reflections on the theory of early childhood enrichment programs. In: R. D. Hess and R. M. Bear (Eds.), *Early Education*, pp. 83–90. (Chicago: Aldine.)

Deutsch, M., Katz, I., and Jensen, A. R. (Eds.) (1968). *Social Class, Race, and Psychological Development*. (New York: Holt, Rinehart, & Winston.)

Dohrenwend, B. P. and Dohrenwend, B. S. (1974). Social and cultural influences on psychopathology. *Annual Review of Psychology*, **25,** 417–452.

Donahue, G. T. (1967). A school district program for schizophrenic, organic and seriously disturbed children. In: E. L. Cowen, E. A. Gardner, and M. Zax (Eds.), *Emergent Approaches to Mental Health Problems*, pp. 369–386. (New York: Appleton-Century-Crofts.)

Donahue, G. T. and Nichtern, S. (1965). *Teaching the Troubled Child*. (New York: Free Press.)

Duggan, J. N. (1965). An example of secondary prevention activities in the schools: talent searching in a culturally deprived population. In: N. M. Lambert (Ed.), *The Protection and Promotion of Mental Health in Schools*, pp. 48–52. Bethesda, MD: US Dept. of Health, Education and Welfare, Public Health Service Publication No. 1226.

Dumont, M. P. (1967). Tavern culture: the sustenance of homeless men. *American Journal of Orthopsychiatry*, **36,** 938–945.

Dumont, M. P. (1968). *The Absurd Healer: Perspectives of a Community Psychiatrist*. (New York: Science House, Inc.)

Elardo, P. T. and Caldwell, B. M. (1979). The effects of an experimental social development program on children in the middle childhood period. *Psychology in the Schools*, **16,** 93–100.

Elardo, P. T. and Cooper, M. (1976). *Project AWARE: A Handbook for Teachers*. (Reading, MA: Addison-Wesley.)
Eysenck, H. J. (1952). The effects of psychotherapy: an evaluation. *Journal of Consulting Psychology*, **16,** 319–324.
Eysenck, H. J. (1961). The effects of psychotherapy. In: H. J. Eysenck (Ed.), *Handbook of Abnormal Psychology*, pp. 697–725. (New York: Basic Books.)
Fairweather, G. W. (Ed.) (1964). *Social Psychology in Treating Mental Illness: An Experimental Approach*. (New York: Wiley.)
Fairweather, G. W. (1972). *Social Change: The Challenge to Survival*. (Morristown, NJ: General Learning Press.)
Fairweather, G. W., Sanders, D. H., Maynard, H., and Cressler, D. L. (1969). *Community Life for the Mentally Ill: An Alternative to Institutional Care*. (Chicago: Aldine.)
Fairweather, G. W., Sanders, D. H. and Tornatzky, L. (1974). *Creating Change in Mental Health Organizations*. (New York: Pergamon.)
Fairweather, G. W. and Tornatzky, L. G. (1977). *Experimental Methods for Social Policy Research*. (New York: Pergamon.)
Faris, R. E. L. and Dunham, H. W. (1939). *Mental Disorders in Urban Areas*. (Chicago: University of Chicago Press.)
Fishman, J. R., Denham, W. H. Levine, M., and Shatz, E. O. (1969). *New Careers for the Disadvantaged in Human Services: Report of a Social Experiment*. (Washington, DC: Howard University Institute for Youth Studies.)
Gershon, M. and Biller, H. B. (1977). *The Other Helpers: Paraprofessionals and Nonprofessionals in Mental Health*. (Lexington, MA: Lexington Books.)
Gesten, E. L., Flores de Apodaca, R., Rains, M. H., Weissberg, R. P., and Cowen, E. L. (1979). Promoting peer related social competence in young children. In: M. W. Kent and J. E. Rolf (Eds.), *Primary Prevention of Psychopathology,* Vol. 3: *Promoting Social Competence and Coping in Children*. (Hanover, NH: University Press of New England.)
Goldenberg, I. I. (1968). The Residential Youth Center: the creation of an assumptions-questioning rehabilitative setting. In *Criminal Corrections in Connecticut: Perspectives and Progress*, pp. 40–59. (West Hartford, CT: Connecticut Planning Committee on Criminal Administration.)
Goldenberg, I. I. (1971). *Build Me a Mountain: Youth, Poverty and the Creation of New Settings*. (Cambridge, MA: MIT Press.)
Goldston, S. E. (1977). Primary Prevention: a view from the federal level. In: G. W. Albee and J. M. Joffe (Eds.), *Primary Prevention of Psychopathology*, Vol. 1: *The Issues*, pp. 297–315. (Hanover, NH: University Press of New England.)
Gomes-Schwartz, B., Hadley, S.H., and Strupp, H. H. (1978). Individual psychotherapy and behavior therapy. In: M. R. Rosenzweig and L. W. Porter (Eds.), *Annual Review of Psychology*, **29,** 435–471.
Gordon, I. J. (1971). *A Home Learning Center Approach to Early Stimulation*. (Bethesda, MD: National Institute of Mental Health (DHEW).)
Gottfried, N. W. (1973). Effects of early intervention programs. In: K. S. Miller and R. M. Dreger (Eds.), *Comparative Studies of Blacks and Whites in the United States: Quantitative Studies in Social Relations*, pp. 273–293. (New York: Seminar Press.)
Gottlieb, B. H. (1976a). Lay influences on the utilization and provision of health services: a review. *Canadian Psychological Review*, **17,** 126–136.
Gottlieb, B. H. (1976b). The development of a classification system of primary group influences on the coping process: preliminary findings. Paper presented at the annual meeting of the Canadian Psychological Association, Toronto, Canada. June, 1976.
Gray, S. W. and Klaus, R. (1968). The early training project and its general rationale. In: R. D. Hess and R. M. Bear (Eds.), *Early Education*, pp. 63–70. (Chicago: Aldine.)

Griggs, J. W. and Bonney, M. E. (1970). Relationship between 'causal' orientation and acceptance of others, 'self-ideal self' congruence, and mental health changes for fourth- and fifth-grade children. *Journal of Educational Research*, **63**, 471–477.

Grimes, J. W. and Allinsmith, W. (1961). Compulsivity, anxiety, and school achievement. *Merrill-Palmer Quarterly*, **7**, 247–261.

Gurin, G., Veroff, J., and Feld, S. (1960). *Americans View their Mental Health: A Nationwide Interview Survey*. (New York: Basic Books.)

Heber, F. R. (1978). Research in the prevention of sociocultural mental retardation. In: D. C. Forgays (Ed.), *Primary Prevention of Psychopathology*, Vol. 2, pp. 39–62. (Hanover, NH: University Press of New England.)

Hellmuth, J. (Ed.) (1969). *Disadvantaged Child*, Vols I, II. (New York: Brunner-Mazel.)

Hess, R. D. and Bear, R.M. (Eds.), *Early Education*. (Chicago: Aldine.)

Hobbs, N. (1964). mental health's third revolution. *American Journal of Orthopsychiatry*, **34**, 822–833.

Hobbs, N. (1966). Helping disturbed children: psychological and ecological strategies. *American Psychologist*, **21**, 1105–1115.

Hobbs, N. (1967). The reeducation of emotionally disturbed children. In: E. M. Bower and W. G. Hollister (Eds.), *Behavior Science Frontiers in Education*, pp. 339–354. (New York: Wiley.)

Hollingshead, A. B. and Redlich, F. C. (1958). *Social Class and Mental Illness: A Community Study*. (New York: Wiley.)

Horowitz, F. D. and Paden, L. Y. (1973). The effectiveness of environmental intervention programs. In: B. M. Caldwell and H. Ricciuti (Eds.), *Review of Child Development Research*, Vol. 3. (New York: Russell Sage Foundation.)

Hunt, J. McV. (1969). *The Challenge of Incompetence and Poverty*. (Urbana, Ill.: University of Illinois Press.)

Insel, P. M. and Moos, R. H. (1974). Psychosocial environments: expanding the scope of human ecology. *American Psychologist*, **29**, 179–188.

Iscoe, I. (1974). Community psychology and the competent community. *American Psychologist*, **29**, 607–613.

Jason, L. (1975). Early secondary prevention with disadvantaged preschool children. *American Journal of Community Psychology*, **3**, 33–46.

Joint Commission on Mental Illness and Health. (1961). *Action for Mental Health*. (New York: Basic Books.)

Kelly, J. G. (1968). Towards an ecological conception of preventive interventions. In: J. W. Carter (Ed.), *Research Contributions from Psychology to Community Mental Health*, pp. 75–97. (New York: Behavioral Publications.)

Kelly, J. G. (1969). Naturalistic observations in contrasting social environments. In: E. P. Willems and H. L. Raush (Eds.), *Naturalistic Viewpoints in Psychological Research*, pp. 183–199. (New York: Holt, Rinehart & Winston.)

Kelly, J. G., Edwards, D. W., Fatke, R., Gordon, T. A., McGee, D. P., McClintock, S. K., Newman, B. M., Rice, R. R., Roistacher, R. C., and Todd, D. M. (1971). The coping process in varied high school environments. In: M. J. Feldman (Ed.), *Studies in Psychotherapy and Behavior Change*, No. 2: *Theory and Research in Community Mental Health*, pp. 95–166. (Buffalo, NY: State University of New York.)

Kelly, J. G. *et al.* (1979). *Adolescent Boys in High School: A Psychological Study of Coping and Adaptation*. (Hillside, N.J.: Laurence Erlbaum.)

Kety, S. S. (1967). The relevance of biochemical studies to the etiology of schizophrenia. In: J. R. Romano (Ed.), *The Origins of Schizophrenia*, pp. 35–41. (Amsterdam: Excerpta Medica Foundation.)

Kiesler, D. J. (1966). Some myths of psychotherapy research and the search for a paradigm. *Psychological Bulletin*, **65,** 110–136.

Kiesler, D. J. (1971). Experimental designs in psychotherapy research. In: A. E. Bergin and S. L. Garfield (Eds.), *Handbook of Psychotherapy and Behavior Change: An Empirical Analysis*. (New York: Wiley.)

Klein, D. C. (Ed.) (1978). *Psychology of the Planned Community: The New Town Experience*. (New York: Human Sciences Press.)

Kuhn, T. S. (1962). *The Structure of Scientific Revolutions*. (Chicago: University of Chicago Press.)

Kuhn, T. S. (1970). *The Structure of Scientific Revolutions*, 2nd edn. (Chicago: Univeristy of Chicago Press.)

Lemkau, P. V. (1969). The planning project for Columbia. In: M. F. Shore and F. V. Mannino (Eds.), *Mental Health and the Community: Problems, Programs and Strategies*, pp. 193–204. (New York: Behavioral Publications.)

Lennard, H. L. and Bernstein, A (1969). *Patterns in Human Interaction*. (San Francisco: Jossey-Bass.)

Lerner, B. (1972). *Therapy in the Ghetto: Political Impotence and Personal Disintegration*. (Baltimore: Johns Hopkins University Press.)

Levitt, E. E. (1957). The results of psychotherapy with children: an evaluation. *Journal of Consulting Psychology*, **21,** 189–204.

Levitt, E. E. (1971). Research on psychotherapy with children. In: A. E. Bergin and S. L. Garfield (Eds.), *Handbook of Psychotherapy and Behavior Change: An Empirical Analysis*, pp. 474–494. (New York: Wiley.)

Lewis, W. W. (1967). Project Re-ED: educational intervention in discordant child rearing systems. In: E. L. Cowen, E. A. Gardner, and M. Zax (Eds.), *Emergent Approaches to Mental Health Problems*, pp. 352–368. (New York: Appleton-Century-Crofts.)

Lorion, R. P. (1973). Socioeconomic status and traditional treatment approaches reconsidered. *Psychological Bulletin*, **79,** 263–270.

Lorion, R. P. (1974). Patient and therapist variables in the treatment of low-income patients. *Psychological Bulletin*, **81,** 344–354.

Maccoby, N. and Farquhar, J. W. (1975). Communication for health: unselling heart disease. *Journal of Communications*, **25,** 114–126.

Maccoby, N. and Farquhar, J. W. (1976). Bringing the California health report up to date. *Journal of Communications*, **26,** 56–57.

Mannino, F. V., MacLennan, B. W., and Shore, M. F. (1975). *The Practice of Mental Health Consultation*. (Washington, DC: Department of Health, Education and Welfare, Publication No. (ADM) 74–112.)

Miller, K. S. and Dreger, R. M. (Eds.) (1973). *Comparative Studies of Blacks and Whites in the United States: Quantitative Studies in Social Relations*. (New York: Seminar Press.)

Minuchin, P., Biber, B., Shapiro, E., and Zimiles, H. (1969). *The Psychological Impact of School Experience*. (New York: Basic Books.)

Moos, R. H. (1973). Conceptualizations of human environments. *American Psychologist*, **28,** 652–665.

Moos, R. H. (1974a). *The Social Climate Scales: An Overview*. (Palo Alto, CA: Consulting Psychologists Press, Inc.)

Moos, R. H. (1974b). *Evaluating Treatment Environments: A Social Ecological Approach*. (New York: Wiley.)

Moos, R. H. and Insel, P. M. (1974). *Issues in Social Ecology: Human Milieus*. (Palo Alto, CA: National Press Books.)

Murrell, S. A. (Ed.) (1971). *Newcom: The Psychosocial Environment*, Vol. 2. (Louisville, KY: University of Louisville Urban Studies Center.)

Muuss, R. E. (1960). The effects of a one and two year casual learning program. *Journal of Personality*, **28,** 479–491.

Myers, J. K. and Roberts, B. H. (1959). *Family and Class Dynamics in Mental Illness.* (New York: Wiley.)

Ojemann, R. H. (1961). Investigations on the effects of teacher understanding and appreciation of behavior dynamics. In: G. Caplan (Ed.), *Prevention of Mental Disorders in Children.* (New York: Basic Books.)

Ojemann, R. H. (1969). Incorporating psychological concepts in the school curriculum. In: H. P. Clarizio (Ed.), *Mental Health and the Educative Process.* (Chicago: Rand-McNally.)

Pearl, A. and Riessman, F. (1965). *New Careers for the Poor.* (New York: Free Press.)

Peck, H. B. and Kaplan, S. R. (1969). A mental health program for the urban multi-service center. In: M. F. Shore and F. V. Mannino (Eds.), *Mental Health and the Community: Problems, Programs and Strategies*, pp. 123–142. (New York: Behavioral Publications, 1969.)

President's Commission on Mental Health (1978). *Report to the President*, Vol. I. (Washington, DC: US Government Printing Office, Stock No. 040–000–00390–8.)

Prevention Task Panel Report, *Task Panel Reports Submitted to the President's Commission on Mental Health*, Vol. 4, pp. 1822–1863. (Washington, DC: US Government Printing Office, Stock No. 040–000–00393–2.)

Price, R. H. and Blashfield, R. K. (1975). Explorations in the taxonomy of behavior settings: analysis of dimensions and classification of settings. *American Journal of Community Psychology*, **3,** 335–357.

Price, R. H. and Moos, R. H. (1975). Toward a taxonomy of inpatient treatment environments. *Journal of Abnormal Psychology*, **84,** 181–188.

Rappaport, J. (1977). *Community Psychology: Values, Research, and Action.* (New York: Holt, Rinehart, and Winston.)

Rappaport, J., Davidson, W. S., Wilson, M. N., and Mitchell, A. (1975). Alternatives to blaming the victim or the environment: our places to stand have not moved the earth. *American Psychologist*, **30,** 525–528.

Reiff, R. (1966). Mental health manpower and institutional change. *American Psychologist*, **21,** 540–548.

Reiff, R. and Riessman, F. (1965). The indigenous nonprofessional: a strategy of change in community action and community mental health programs. *Community Mental Health Journal*, Monogr. No. 1.

Reiss, S. and Dydhalo, N. (1975). Persistence, achievement and open-space environments. *Journal of Educational Psychology*, **67,** 506–513.

Reiss, S. and Martell, R. (1974). *Educational and Psychological Effects of Open Space Education in Oak Park, Illinois.* (Final Report to Board of Education, District 97, Oak Park, Illinois.)

Rieff, P. (1959). *Freud: The Mind of the Moralist.* (New York: Viking Press.)

Riessman, F. (1967). A neighborhood-based mental health approach. In: E. L. Cowen, E. A. Gardner, and M. Zax (Eds.), *Emergent Approaches to Mental Health Problems*, pp. 167–184. (New York: Appleton-Century-Crofts.)

Riessman, F. and Popper, H. I. (1968). *Up from Poverty: New Career Ladders for Nonprofessionals.* (New York: Harper and Row.)

Roberts, J., Price, R., Gold, B., and Shiner, E. (1966). *Social and Mental Health Survey: Summary Report.* (Montreal, Quebec: Mental Hygiene Institute.)

Ryan, W. (Ed.) (1969). *Distress in the City: Essays on the Design and Administration of Urban Mental Health Services.* (Cleveland, OH: Case-Western Reserve University Press.)

Sanua, V. D. (1966). Sociocultural aspects of psychotherapy and treatment: a review of the literature. In: L. E Abt and L. Bellak (Eds.), *Progress in Clinical Psychology*, Vol. VIII, pp. 151–190. (New York: Grune & Stratton.)

Sanua, V. D. (1969). Socio-cultural aspects. In: L. Bellak and L. Loeb (Eds.), *The Schizophrenic Syndrome*, pp. 256–310. (New York: Grune & Stratton.)

Sarason, S. B. (1971). *The Culture of the School and the Problem of Change.* (Boston: Allyn-Bacon.)

Sarason, S. B. (1974). *The Psychological Sense of Community: Prospects for a Community Psychology.* (San Fransisco, CA: Jossey-Bass.)

Sarason, S. B. (1976). Community psychology, networks and Mr. Everyman. *American Psychologist*, **31,** 317–328.

Sarason, S. B., Carroll, C., Maton, K., Cohen, S., and Lorentz, E. (1977). *Human Services and Resource Networks.* (San Francisco, CA: Jossey-Bass.)

Sarason, S. B., Zitnay, G., and Grossman, F. K. (1971). *The creation of a community setting.* (Syracuse, NY: Syracuse University Press.)

Scheff, T. J. (1966). *Being Mentally Ill: A Sociological Theory.* (Chicago: Aldine.)

Schofield, W. (1964). *Psychotherapy: The Purchase of Friendship.* (Englewood-Cliffs, NJ: Prentice-Hall.)

Silverman, P. R. (1969). The widow-to-widow program: an experiment in preventive intervention. *Mental Hygiene*, **53,** 333–337.

Silverman, P. R. (1976). The widow as a caregiver in a program of preventive intervention with other widows. In: G. Caplan and M. Killilea (Eds.), *Support Systems and Mutual Help: Multidisciplinary Explorations*, pp. 223–243. (New York: Grune & Stratton.)

Smith, W. D., Burlew, A. K., Mosley, M. H., and Whitney, W. M. (1978). *Minority Issues in Mental Health.* (Reading, Mass: Addison-Wesley.)

Spivack, G. and Shure, M. B. (1974). *Social Adjustment of Young Children.* (San Francisco, CA: Jossey-Bass.)

Spivack, G., Platt, J. J. and Shure, M. B. (1976). *The Problem Solving Approach to Adjustment.* (San Francisco, CA: Jossey-Bass.)

Srole, L., Langner, T. S., Michael, S. T., Opler, M. K., and Rennie, T. A. (1962). *Mental Health in the Metropolis.* (New York: McGraw-Hill.)

Stallings, J. (1975). Implementation and child effects of teaching practices in Follow-Through classrooms. *Monographs of the Society for Research on Child Development*, **40** (Serial No. 163).

Stendler-Lavatelli, C. B. (1968). Environmental intervention in infancy and early childhood. In: M. Deutsch, I. Katz, and A. R. Jensen (Eds.), *Social Class, Race, and Psychological Development*, pp. 347–380. (New York: Holt, Rinehart, & Winston.)

Strupp, H. H. and Bergin, A. E. (1969). Some empirical and conceptual bases for coordinated research in psychotherapy: a critical review of issues, trends, and evidence. *International Journal of Psychiatry*, **7,** 18–90.

Susskind, E. C. (1969). The role of question-asking in the elementary school classroom. In: F. Kaplan and S. B. Sarason (Eds.), *The Psycho-Educational Clinic: Papers and Research Studies.* (Massachusetts Department of Mental Health.)

Trickett, E. J. and Moos, R. H. (1974). Personal correlates of contrasting environments: student satisfaction in high school classrooms. *American Journal of Community Psychology*, **2,** 1–12.

Verdone, P. (1975). Early identification, referral, and treatment of bar patrons in crisis. Symposium presented at the 83rd Annual APA Convention, Chicago, Illinois, September, 1975.

Weinstein, L. (1969). Project Re-ED schools for emotionally disturbed children: Effectiveness as viewed by referring agencies, parents and teachers. *Exceptional Children*, **35,** 703–711.

Zax, M. and Cowen, E. L. (1976). *Abnormal Psychology: Changing conceptions*, 2nd edn. (New York: Holt, Rinehart & Winston.)

Zimiles, H. (1967). Preventive aspects of school experience. In E. L. Cowen, E. A. Gardner and M. Zax (Eds.), *Emergent Approaches to Mental Health Problems*, pp. 239–251. (New York: Appleton-Century-Crofts.)

The Social Psychology of Psychological Problems
Edited by P. Feldman and J. Orford

12

Communication and Social Influence Processes

WILLIAM J. MCGUIRE

Our moment in history has been called by many names: the age of anxiety, of alienation, of absurdity, the automobile age, atomic age, American age, Atlantic age, etc., just to start at the head of the alphabet. An equally apt title, relevant to the present chapter, is the 'age of advertising'. In the United States $25,000,000,000 is spent each year on mass media advertising, urging people to buy certain goods or services, to vote for one or another political candidate, to stop smoking for the sake of their lungs, or to switch brands of cigarettes for the sake of their manufacturers, etc. Through persuasive communication campaigns our material and intangible wants are aroused, our modes of consumption directed, and our life-styles formed. We shall start by considering the historical origins of this peculiar situation where social influence through communication has become so prevalent in our lives. Then we shall describe the basic research on the topic, before devoting the remainder of the chapter to a description of how this persuasive communication research is applied to practical problems.

HISTORICAL BACKGROUND TO AN AGE OF PERSUASION

The clear emergence of a preoccupation with persuasive communication as an art, craft, and science is discernible in early nineteenth-century economic and political developments including the overthrow of the old regimes, the secularization of culture, the upsurge of commercial interests, the increased productivity resulting from the industrial revolution, and the decay of old behavioural guidelines as the merchant interests began to push aside the landed aristocracy. Already in the late 1700s the art of persuasive communication was flourishing in gifted political orators and pamphleteers. As is usual, once the art flourished a craft gradually developed whose professionals supplement or replace artistic inspiration with practical rules of thumb developed through experience. Advertising appeared as early as the late 1600s in the *London Gazette* and other English newspapers, became a full-time speciality practised in large advertising agencies by the mid-nineteenth century (the first large agency, N. W. Ayer, was founded in 1841), but approached its present magnitude only after the electronic media arrived, radio in the 1920s and television in the 1950s. Currently those craftspeople design persuasive communications not only for commercial advertising but also for domestic political proselytizing, international propaganda, public health promotions, etc. More recently, these craftspeople, whose engineering of consent via rules of thumb was itself a step toward formalizing the intuitions of the persuasive artist, have themselves been supplemented by psychologists intent on developing a science of persuasion, which adds empirical testing to the practitioners' rules of thumb and organizes them into broader theories from which additional principles of social influence can be derived.

Earlier ages of persuasion

The art, craft, and science of persuasive communication seems so prevalent now that it takes an effort to realize that such a preoccupation with social influence processes is atypical in human history, occurring in only three other periods of European culture. The first such occurrence was the century of Sophist ascendency and democratic contentiousness in Athens, stretching from the arrival of Gorgias in 427 BCE until Alexander's Macedonian hegemony imposed alternative means of social control, but in its hour producing insights into the persuasion processes that are preserved in the rhetorical treatises of Aristotle, Isocrates, and other Athenians. Another century of flourishing rhetorical theory and practice occurred late in the Roman republican period (Kennedy, 1972) with Cicero as its most famous practitioner and its finest distillation in Quintillian's *Institutio Oratoria* (95 CE) a book that compares favourably with our current textbooks on persuasion (cited below) as regards insights it offers into social influence processes.

The third great flourishing of interest in techniques of persuasion did not occur until the sixteenth-century Italian Renaissance, when humanistic studies culminated in the apotheosis of eloquence. The orator, skilful in the arts of persuasion regardless of topic, conformed to the Renaissance ideal of the generalist *uomo universale*, while his role in inciting his hearers to action resonated with the Renaissance ideal of knowledge for action versus the preoccupation with knowledge for knowledge's sake that had characterized the speculative mediaeval scholastic (Gray, 1963). Our own contemporary society constitutes the fourth period of preoccupation with social influence through persuasive communication.

Social significance of preoccupation with persuasion

Each of these four flourishings occurred at a disturbed time in a society confronted by new problems or opportunities for which traditional guidelines were lacking, due to the irrelevance of the old cultural guidelines and a loss of faith in the old traditional certainties. These were times of social conflict and public contentiousness, characterized by a momentary shift of power from the classes to the masses, a vulgarization of art forms and a decline of liturgy and of social conventions. Into the power vacuum on each of the four occasions plunged demagogues (and even those few of the best who did not quite lack all conviction) speaking with passionate intensity; following in the footsteps of these passionate practitioners came deliberative craftspeople, the rhetorical specialists with their professions, theories, and training institutes for persuasion.

Contemporaneously, there set in an opposition to the rhetorical movement on the part of the cultural elites, the sophisticates from the political, religious, artistic, and intellectual Establishments. In our present situation, as in the previous three, sensitive people of discernment express dismay and distaste over the vulgar prevalence of advertising and other forms of self-promotion through persuasive communication. It may be little consolation for us whom the current hucksterism moves to revulsion, that each of the three previous periods when persuasive communication flourished as a means of social influence was short-lived. Each time the skilful pen and the silver tongue soon gave way to the iron fist and the hobnail boot. But for the moment, the art, craft, and science of persuasive communication flourishes. The next section will describe briefly the basic research on persuasion and then the remainder of the chapter will illustrate its applications to the amelioration of social problems.

BASIC RESEARCH ON PERSUASIVE COMMUNICATION

Our thoughts, feelings, and behaviour are affected by many factors including our genetic endowment, level of maturation, transient physical states, direct experience with objects, etc., as well as by social influence in the form of persuasive communication from other people, but as social psychologists we here focus on this latter determinant. Even limiting our focus to interpresonal communication, we include a wide variety of processes, since others may influence us intentionally or unintentionally, in face-to-face situations or through mediated channels, etc. A friend may influence our voting behaviour through vehement intentional argumentation or may influence our purchasing behaviour quite unintentionally by wearing shoes whose style appeals to us so that we purchase similar ones for ourselves. The mass media may influence us intentionally through advertisements, or unintentionally by modelling, in entertainment shows, styles of behaviour the viewer then imitates.

Types of social influence situations

Basic psychological research on persuasion has focused on a half-dozen types of social influence situations. One of the earliest to receive research attention is 'suggestion' situations involving the repetitive statement that one will act in a certain way without giving reasons or threats. Examples such as hypnotic inductions in which the person is told repetitively that his or her eyes are closing, and repetitive advertising slogans like 'Drink Coca-Cola' show typical 'learning' curves of increased compliance with continuing repetition of the suggestion (Barber, 1969). A second type of social influence involves 'conformity' situations in which a peer or authority model simply speaks or behaves in a given way and the observer, without being urged, imitates the model's opinions or behaviours. These studies show that conformity with a group norm is pervasive, but dissipates if there is even one additional deviant who departs from the group consensus (Allen, 1975). A third type of influence situation involves more coercive methods like brainwashing. For ethical reasons, research on this way of exerting influence has been confined to post-factum observational analyses rather than a manipulational experiment; it is found that the typical brainwashing procedure is more effective in inducing overt compliance than in achieving true ideological conversion (Schein, 1961; Frank, 1973). A fourth type of social influence occurs through elicitation (typically via imitated models) of a desired pattern of behaviour and reinforcement of this pattern when it occurs; applications of this approach in the form of behavioural therapy, vicarious learning, and behavioural modification are common (Bandura, 1969). Interpersonal influence is also studied within small face-to-face groups suggesting, for example, that more deviant, risk-taking members may prevail with groups (Janis, 1972; Moscovici, 1976; Triandis, 1977). A sixth type of widely studied social influence situation is that exercised through mass media, both intentionally via advertising (Lipstein and McGuire, 1978) and unintentionally via entertainment shows (Comstock, 1975).

The communication/persuasion matrix

Over a thousand studies are published each year (McGuire, 1978a) reporting the findings of research on these half-dozen social influence situations. Mastering so vast a literature sufficiently so that one can bring it creatively to bear upon social problems requires a conceptual framework in which to organize it. We find that an input/output matrix provides a useful organizing framework. On the input side, constituting the column headings of the matrix, are the components of the communication that produce the persuasive impact, namely, source, message, channel, receiver, and target variables. That is, the communication is analysed into who says what, via what mode of transmission, to whom, and aiming at what kind of a change. Each of the five classes of variables may be subdivided into narrower groups of variables; for example, source factors may be divided into variables having to do with source credibility, likability, power, and source demographics; and message factors may by analysed into type of appeal used, style, inclusions and organization, quantitative aspects of the message, etc.

The output side of the communication/persuasion matrix involves analysing the process of being influenced into its successive steps which constitute the row headings of the matrix. We analyse the process of being persuaded into the seven successive steps of being exposed to the communication, paying attention to it, comprehending its contents, accepting the claims made in it, retaining this new position until the issue becomes relevant, then acting on the basis of it, and finally doing the post-behavioural cognitive consolidation that maintains the new position.

Each of these steps can be analysed into subclasses of dependent variables, any of which may be used to measure the impact of the persuasive communications up to that stage of the process. A more detailed analysis of this communication/persuasion matrix can be found in McGuire, 1978b. Use of the matrix is easily mastered so that as one reads each new study one checks the column that corresponds to the communication (independent) variable that was manipulated in the study and the row corresponding to the dependent variable in terms of which the effect was measured, so one can fill in the cell where the column and row intersect to show the relationship found between the communication and the effect variables.

Once one has absorbed the psychological research on social influence and stored it in such a communication/persuasion matrix, one can bring the findings of past basic research to bear on the construction of an applied persuasion campaign. For example, in a public health campaign to lessen cardiac risk by reducing salt and other sodium intake in the diet, a question might arise about which kind of a source would have most impact in producing the desirable nutritional changes, whether 'ordinary' people like the recipients or experts, whether women or men, etc. By considering the findings stored in the appropriate cell of the matrix, one can answer questions such as these. Anyone wishing to apply social influence research to the solution of social problems should master the published research, not by passively reading it, but by actively analysing and storing it in a mental matrix of a type with which one feels comfortable and which one is able to use creatively.

Theories of social influence

To develop and apply the basic research on social influence, one needs, besides an organizing framework for past findings such as the communication/persuasion matrix, also a guiding theory about human functioning in communication situations that clarifies the meanings of findings, guides their generalization to new situations, and suggests further relationships to be tested. There is a diversity of alternative theories behind the research on social influence, each stressing (and perhaps overstressing) one aspect of the person which is used creatively to make a prediction about how variables in the communication situation are related to persuasive impact. These partial views should be regarded as supplementary to one another rather than mutually exclusive. Here we can mention briefly only a few of these guiding theories behind social influence research. The interested reader can find a fuller description of the sixteen partial views of human nature which have been most influential in this area in McGuire, 1974.

The three viewpoints that have had the most impact on social influence research in recent years have been the consistency, attribution, and learning theories. Consistency theories (Abelson *et al.*, 1968) typified by Festinger's theory of cognitive dissonance (Wicklund and Brehm, 1976) stress the person's need to maintain a coherence among beliefs, feelings, and actions. For example, adherents of this position have stressed, in opposition to the usual assumption that one first changes attitudes in order to produce behavioural change, that it is at least equally effective first to induce a behavioural change and thereby cause the person to change his or her attitude to justify the new behaviour. More recently, the attribution theories (Jones, 1971) have become more fashionable, stressing that the effectiveness of a persuasive attempt depends in part upon the motives which the recipient attributes to the source in sending the communication. Social learning theories (Bandura, 1976) have also been widely used, calling attention to how models can elicit imitative behaviour (e.g., pro-social helping behaviour or anti-social aggression) which, if it is reinforced when the imitation occurs, tends to become the person's own characteristic way of behaving on subsequent occasions, even when models are not present.

Among other theories that have guided social influence research are the ego-defensive and perceptual formulations. The former, functional theories (Katz, 1960) stress that the person's attitudes are based not only on information about the object but also on one's own subjective needs; for example, one can change hostile attitudes and behaviours towards ethnic groups not only by changing the person's knowledge of, or experience with, members of those ethnic groups, but also by providing the prejudiced person with new modes of coping with unconscious hostility to parents and other authority figures that are unconsciously redirected toward the minorities. Perceptual theories (Asch, 1952) have also provoked attitude change research by postulating that social influence is more a matter of perceptual change than belief change; that is, persuasion involves not so much changing the person's attitude towards a given object but changing the person's perception of what object he or she is expressing an attitude about. More detail on these and eleven other partial views of the person that have guided social influence research can be found in McGuire, 1974.

Those requiring a thorough presentation of the results of basic research on social influence might read a standard textbook in the area (Fishbein and Ajzen, 1975; Oskamp, 1977; Zimbardo *et al.*, 1977) and to keep current one can read the triennial chapter reviewing the area in *Annual Reviews of Psychology* (most recently by Eagly and Himmelfarb, 1978). The rest of this chapter will describe, not the basic research itself, but rather applications of it to the solution of social problems.

APPLICATIONS OF SOCIAL INFLUENCE RESEARCH TO HEALTH CAMPAIGNS

The earliest and still most popular application of social influence research is in designing public health campaigns to induce such behaviours as adopting safety practices (using automobile seat-belts, etc.), taking disease-prevention measures (getting inoculations, ceasing to smoke, etc.), and obtaining early diagnoses (to detect hypertension or cancer symptoms at a treatable stage, etc.). We shall describe here three styles of such applications, the three going progressively further from the basic research designs involving a few experimenter-manipulated independent variables that characterize laboratory situations, towards the multivariate complexities that characterize the natural environment outside the laboratory.

Applications of fear-arousal theorizing

One of the earliest large-scale applications of social influence research was to call into question the use of fear campaigns to promote healthful practices. When one is advocating a health practice such as getting an inoculation against tetanus or measles, having a diagnosis to detect cancer or hypertension at an early stage, brushing one's teeth after every meal, using a seat-belt while in automobiles, etc., one is usually urging these practices to avoid a danger to health and safety; hence, one is tempted to use a threat appeal, reminding the person of the danger involved in failing to adopt the practice being advocated. But learning theory and psychoanalytic theory analyses of anxiety states have both suggested that a fear-arousing communication on so anxiety-laden a topic as physical vulnerability might backfire, causing the person not so much to adopt the practice being advocated but rather to repress the whole topic of cancer or whatever, thus actually decreasing the person's likelihood of obtaining the recommended diagnosis. On the other hand, these theories indicate that some motivation is needed to induce compliance, so that leaving the person too complacent about the danger might also result in neglect of the desirable health practice.

Putting these considerations together, two practical predictions can be derived: first, that positive appeals will be more effective than negative ones; secondly, that if negative fear-arousing appeals must be used, a moderate level of threat will be more effective than a very high or very low threat. As regards the relative efficacy of positive and negative appeals, Evans *et al.* (1970) did an elaborate study in which children in some El Paso city schools received a positive, reassuring appeal about the benefits that would result if they adopted some recommended tooth-brushing practices; while students in other schools received a negative appeal stressing the bad effects of not adopting the practices. The study showed that the negative threat appeal produced more intention to comply and more reported compliance, but that the positive reassuring appeal produced more actual compliance as measured by an objective 'disclosing wafer' test of how thoroughly the children had actually been brushing their teeth in the weeks following the communications.

The second prediction, that if negative threatening appeals are used, intermediate levels of anxiety arousal will be more effective than very high or low arousal, is based on a two-factor theory of social influence (McGuire, 1968) that is so elegant and plausible that it deserves to be true, but its empirical track-record is rather poor. Leventhal's (1970) review of numerous studies on this topic suggests that higher levels of threat tend to be more effective so long as they channel the person's thinking into ways of coping rather than into worry about the problem. This fear-arousal research shows the great importance in public health campaigns of giving the public terribly explicit and detailed instructions on how to cope with the danger. That is, if one is trying to induce people in hazardous occupations to obtain inoculations against tetanus, the communication should be devoted, not so much to worrying the workers about the seriousness of tetanus in order to motivate them to obtain the inoculation, but rather to providing very specific information about how, when, and where the tetanus inoculation can be obtained.

Applications of cognitive behavioural modification theory

While the fear-appeals applications have been primarily in mass media campaigns, the applications of the behaviour-modification theorizing to influencing more healthful life-styles has been applied primarily in more individualized therapist–client face-to-face campaigns. The approach grew out of clinical therapeutic procedures that had been developed to eliminate undesirable habits (e.g. phobias, smoking, etc.) by reinforcement and extinction techniques developed in instrumental conditioning research by learning theorists Hull and Skinner (Bandura, 1969, 1976). More recently the procedures have been elaborated by use of imagery techniques derived from cognitive and clinical psychology (Mahoney, 1974). The cognitive behaviour modification approaches have been used to train people to overcome health-detrimental habits, with some success in providing people with the skills in maintaining reduced body-weight (Mahoney, 1975), though they have been less successful in permanently maintaining smoking cessation (Bernstein and McAlister, 1976). Programmes of still-undetermined efficacy are being developed for hypertension reduction, stress control, dietary modification, etc.

The diverse set of techniques used can be mentioned only briefly here. The person may be taught self-monitoring procedures to identify cues within the self and the environment which evoke the undesired behaviour (smoking, eating, tenseness, etc.). Procedures are taught for managing the environmental press by avoiding evoking cues, by mastering substitute responses, by cognitively restructuring one's perception of the environment to channel behaviour away from the undesirable responses, to act upon the environment to manipulate it so that the evoking cues do not arise, etc. One also monitors one's own food intake, the occasions when one smokes, etc., to get insight into one's needs that the undesired behaviour satisfies so that one can find effective substitute gratifications. The person is taught to cope with the 'withdrawal' symptoms of dieting or stopping smoking via training in relaxation techniques, substitute physical activities, cognitive skills in urge-repression, mutual support by other participants, learning of self-reinforcement techniques, etc. Role-playing techniques are used to induce motivation (for example, by role-playing a smoker being told that he or she has lung cancer or the surgeon giving this information to the smoker) and for increasing skills (for example, role-playing to practise techniques for refusing offers of cigarettes). Individualized instruction may be given in specialized skills (such as nutritional counselling, relaxation training, etc.). The person is trained to set up achievable sub-goals such as manageable weight-loss over a period of time. Aversive conditioning techniques are used such as rapid smoking: the smoker puffs at a rapid pace while concentrating on the unpleasant symptoms, and later revivifies these unpleasant sensations when the smoking urge returns. Self-control skills are also used, as in teaching blood-pressure control under stress by relaxation training such as successive tensing and relaxing of the various major muscle groups (arms, head, neck, etc.) and using meditation techniques such as deep and slow breathing, holding one's breath and then thinking about relaxing and pleasant imagery while one exhales.

Regarding these personalized techniques for inducing health-improving practices, there are still unresolved questions of their effectiveness plus the question of whether, even if they work, would they be cost-effective. An analogous question is asked about psychoanalysis whether, even if it were an effective form of therapy (which is debatable) would it be economically feasible so long as it requires a highly skilled therapist to be in a prolonged relationship with a single client. These behavioural modification treatments are mercifully shorter than psychoanalysis but are still costly in skilled talent. Before they could come into wide-scale use, society would have to decide to invest appreciably more resources in such treatment programmes and to lessen expenditures in other areas (though in the long run some of the costs might be returned through reduced morbidity and morality).

The community wide, packaged-programme approach

In contrast with the manipulational studies done in laboratory or field settings to test the fear-appeal hypotheses or the small-scale control- *vs.* treatment-group approach used in the behavioural modification experiments just discussed, are the large-scale field interventions where a treatment package using a wide variety of techniques derived from social psychological research is used to influence a whole community towards a more healthful life-style. In the 'Stanford three-cities' study (Farquhar *et al.*, 1977; Maccoby *et al.*, 1977), three comparable cities in California were chosen for a demonstration study: one received only the ordinary health care and thus served as a control; a second community received an intensive mass media campaign to induce more healthful life-styles, particularly in the form of reducing cardiac risk factors; and a third received both the intensive mass media campaign plus face-to-face treatments of the behavioural modification type. The lessened risk-factor targets included decreased cigarette smoking, a more nutritious diet (lower sodium, animal fat, cholesterol, sugar, etc., and higher fibre and vegetable protein), weight reduction, increased physical activity, and stress reduction. The campaign extended over several years and its effects were measured in three annual surveys that included testing health knowledge, reported risk behaviour (such as smoking), and physiological measures in a sample of people in the high-risk group (35–59-year-old males) in the three communities.

It was found that the intervention did affect health-related behaviour considerably, resulting in sizeable increases in knowledge of risk factors for heart disease, lowered reported intake of saturated fats, significant decrease in plasma cholesterol, decrease in the reported number of cigarettes per day (validated by blood plasma thiocyanate assay), lower systolic blood-pressure, though less clear evidence of an effect on other targets such as weight-decrease. The effects on most of these measures were almost as great by use of just the relatively economical mass media as by mass media plus expensive face-to-face interventions, raising the issue of the cost-effectiveness of these latter personalized interventions.

SOCIAL INFLUENCE EXERTED BY THE MASS MEDIA

In contrast to one's worry regarding the public health campaigns just considered, that they may not be effective enough, one worries regarding the mass media influence that it might be too effective. People in North America, Britain, and the Continent spend a formidable amount of their time consuming the mass media: the UN time-use study (Szalai, 1972) shows that adults in the larger countries like the USA and the USSR average two hours and ten minutes a day on mass media consumption (primarily television) and in smaller countries such as Belgium, Czechoslovakia, and Poland almost three hours per day. This means that the average person spends before the mass media half of his/her discretionary leisure time and the equivalent of two-thirds of the amount of time spent working for pay. We shall consider first the intended social influence impact of the mass media through advertisements and other contents explicitly designed to persuade, and then we shall discuss the unintended effects of the media through the contents of the programme designed to entertain.

Impact of media content designed to persuade

In the USA and Europe, vast sums are spent each year on advertising, primarily on television. Anecdotal case-histories can be found to illustrate how one or another commercial product greatly increased its sales through advertising; but solid empirical evidence on the persuasive impact of this vast expenditure on advertisements is surprisingly sparse. The better studies suggest that, overall, these considerable advertising expenditures have little effect.

A fair example is the research on non-prescription drug advertising, these being one of the most heavily advertised product groups, with a $400,000,000 annual television budget in the USA. In 1976 a petition was presented by the Attorneys-General of the State of Massachusetts and many other of the American states requesting that the Federal Communicatn Commission and the Federal Trade Commission (the main television-regulating agencies of the US Federal Government) forbid advertising of over-the-counter drugs on television, at least during the hours when large numbers of children are included among the viewers. Behind the petition was the belief that this heavy advertising of pharmaceutical agents, as a mode of coping, was contributing to over-medication, including illegal drug use by children (deemed to be especially susceptible to social influence). A number of careful studies were done, measuring how the amounts of televised drug advertising to which children were exposed related to the amount of their illicit drug use. These studies give little evidence for any substantial positive relationship, and some suggestions even find a slight negative relationship between the two variables (Weigel and Jessor, 1973; Milavsky *et al.*, 1976). More surprisingly, the studies find little evidence of any substantial effect of exposure to televised drug advertisements, even on use of the very drugs advertised (McGuire, 1976). The impact of political advertising seems equally evasive. In a USA presidential election year, about the same number of dollars is spent by the political parties on mass media presentations to influence the voters as is spent annually on the over-the-counter drug advertising just described. Again, ingenious methods of relating exposure to the media campaign and voting choice have failed to show the expected sizeable relationship (Patterson and McClure, 1976).

Despite these failures of research to demonstrate the effectiveness of mass media commercial and political advertising, there is reluctance to accept an outcome that goes so flagrantly against general belief and the financial interests of the communication industry. A number of arguments to explain away the seemingly negative outcomes have been put forward, a few of which will be mentioned here. Perhaps our measures of media exposure and of the target behaviour are too poor to pick up the effect; perhaps opposed advertisements cancel out one another's impact or there may be a two-step process such that the mass media affect the opinion-leaders who then affect the public. Or it may be that television has an impact where attitudes are still fluid, as with new products or new political figures. Or even if they do not change anyone's opinions on issues the media may set the agenda, determining the salience of political issues or product characteristics on the basis of which the public will choose. Note, however, that these are post-factum explanations to salvage the unconfirmed hypothesis that the media have powerful social influence effects.

Unintended effects of the mass media entertainment content

Since the evidence indicates that mass media content intended to persuade has so little effect, it might seem perverse to discuss whether programme content, designed to entertain rather than persuade, might exert appreciable unintended social influence. Yet there has been a great deal of discussion of the possible anti-social, pro-social, and life-style influence of the entertainment content of the mass media, directed in the 1920s against the cinema, in the 1950s against the comic books, and more recently against television's explicit violence and sexuality. It is calculated that, in the USA, television presents an average of eight acts of violence per hour, so that in an average year the viewer witnesses over 5000 acts of violence on television.

It might seem absurd to deny that witnessing so much violence tends to induce imitative aggressiveness in the viewer, even though the violence is presented as undesirable and without the reinforcement postulated by the social learning theorists

(Bandura, 1976) to be necessary. Yet some theorists from the psychoanalytic view have suggested an opposite 'catharsis' relationship such that witnessing so much violence gives the aggressive child an opportunity vicariously to act out anti-social impulses in fantasy, thus relieving him or her of the tendency to initiate violent attacks on people in the actual environment (just as Aristotle proposed that watching tragedy provides us with an opportunity to purge our pity and fear vicariously). The evidence for any such negative-relationship catharsis effect is extremely weak (Geen and Quanty, 1977). There is evidence for a positive effect in laboratory studies in which children are shown mass media contents of different degrees of violence and then are tested for aggressive behaviour (e.g., imitating an adult's kicking of a doll). These studies typically show a positive relationship: more imitative aggression by the child who has seen the more violent audiovisual content, provided that the children have been put in an angry mood prior to the exposure. In field situations there is much less convincing evidence that the amount of violence one sees on actual television programming contributes any appreciable percentage of individual differences in actual aggressiveness: some of the studies have shown effects that reach conventionally accepted levels of statistical significance but account for little enough of the variance in aggressiveness, so that they are only of modest practical significance (Belson, 1979; Parke *et al.*, 1977; Lefkowitz *et al.*, 1972). It has been argued also that even if watching televised violence does not induce aggression directly in the viewer, it contributes indirectly to crime in the street because it frightens viewers into staying at home, leaving the semi-deserted streets to the perpetrators of violence and their unwary victims; but while survey research has demonstrated some positive relationships between these variables the direction of causality is quite ambiguous.

Other anti-social effects, besides the perpetration of interpersonal mayhem, have been attributed to the mass media. It has been argued that the prevalence of frightening material has tended to cause nightmares and other undesirable anxiety symptoms in the viewers, though Bettelheim (1976) has argued that frightening fairy tales teach children to cope. It has also been argued that a great amount of smoking, drinking, risk-taking, undesirable sexual behaviour, etc., have been modelled on television and evoked emulation by the viewers, particularly susceptible children. Television has also been accused of perpetrating unfavourable stereotypes and role attributions of women and some ethnic groups. One must weigh the probability and magnitude of such possible detrimental effects against the values of artistic freedom and freedom of expression. These latter are treasured by many members of society who consequently are reluctant to urge censorship without firmer evidence than there is available at present of substantial negative effects.

Just as media content can have anti-social effects, one might argue that they can and should be designed to have pro-social effects. For example, it has been argued that admired figures on television should be shown refusing cigarettes and intoxicating beverages, engaging in healthy nutrition and exercise, showing group toleration and respect, etc., so that the viewer's imitation might benefit him/herself and society. As with anti-social effects, there are laboratory confirmations of such pro-social effects as when children emulate the generous behaviour they witness (Schwartz, 1977). Here again, even if we accept the questionable conclusion that media could have appreciable pro-social effects, difficult questions would remain regarding whose values should be promulgated and whether freedom of expression should be restricted by prescription any more than by proscription.

DESIGNING COMMUNICATION CAMPAIGNS IN SOCIAL PROBLEM AREAS

The previous section on mass media effects examined how we are being influenced by social forces beyond our direct control. In this section we examine the process from the opposite perspective, describing how we can use social psychological research to influence society in ways that contribute to the solution of social problems. Policy-makers do increasingly call upon social psychologists to help design persuasion campaigns in social problem areas, though typically the ways in which the social psychologist contributes are too narrowly conceptualized both by social psychologists and policy-makers. When the social influence researcher consults with policy-makers, both parties typically think of the psychologist as contributing to the design of communications which maximize information assimilation and/or attitudinal and behavioural change. Yet as one's experience in working with policy-makers grows, one realizes that there are a number of other aspects of the design of a campaign on which the social psychologist can be at least as helpful as in this obvious way. The design of a public service communication campaign is a seven-step process, only the sixth step of which involves the obvious attitude change contribution of constructing effective communications. We shall describe how the social psychologist can contribute to each of the seven steps in designing a public service communication campaign, using for illustration two target areas: energy conservation and reduction of cardiac risk factors.

The need for the attitude-change researcher to contribute to all seven steps of campaign construction, and not just to the obvious sixth step of designing communication copy, can be clarified by an example. People in a government agency dealing with residential energy conservation may approach the attitude change researcher with a question of whether their campaign to lower household thermostat settings to 19°C in daytime and 16°C at night should use expert engineers or home-owners like the audience as the sources of the message on how much one's heating bill can be reduced by the thermostat lowering. We are impressed that these policy-makers are sufficiently aware of the attitude-change controversy (discussed below) about the relative persuasiveness of expert *vs.* peer sources to raise the question in the first place. However, when one incidentally asks the policy-makers why they have chosen to stress the theme of money-saving as the motivation, or why the campaign is aimed at thermostat-lowering rather than at installation of caulking and weather-stripping, one often finds that these themes and targets have emerged rather accidentally without adequate consideration of alternative options. These earlier decisions in campaign design call for various kinds of expertise in addition to psychological expertise, but the psychologists must take the initiative if necessary to assure that all the steps have been adequately carried out, rather than abdicating responsibility and sticking to our own narrow area of expertise in Step Six. Below we describe all seven steps, indicating psychological issues that arise in each step.

Step One: analysing the environmental realities

The first step that must be taken in the design of a public service communication campaign is mastering the actualities of the situation in order to assemble a list of promising targets for behavioural change. Since such mastery often calls for the expertise of an automotive engineer, architect, biomedical scientist, politician, economist, etc. the attitude-change researcher must hope that these others will collaborate on this step. Still, the social psychologist must also participate since psychological considerations have to be taken into account in drawing up the list of targets.

For example, as regards energy conservation, one quickly learns that a campaign aimed at the public should concentrate on residential and personal transportation uses of energy, each of which accounts for about 20 per cent of the total national US energy consumption, primarily in the form of space heating (11 per cent of the national total), water heating (3 per cent), local travel by automobile (10 per cent) and intercity automobile travel (5 per cent). One naturally focuses on big uses for cost-effective conservation targets, searching within them for promising conservation behaviours. As regards space heating, for example, one is attracted towards lowering thermostat settings (which can save 5 per cent of space heating fuel use per degree Celsius, though at a loss of comfort and a demand for constant vigilance if the setting is to be changed at various parts of the day). Increased attic insulation, installation of storm windows, and weather-stripping and caulking can save even more and without loss of comfort, and require only a one-time decision rather than constant vigilance; on the other hand they require initial capital and access to expertise. Replacement of pilot lights on stoves, water-heaters, and furnaces are attractive targets (pilot lights may consume a third of the fuel used by the average household's gas stove) without affecting the person's life style but require investment capital, awareness-raising, etc. As regards transportation, lighter automobiles can save much fuel but this is perhaps more effectively handled by legislation than by a communication campaign directed at the public. It will have its effect only gradually as old cars are replaced. Reducing driving speed from 70 to 55 mph can cut fuel consumption by 20 per cent, so that compliance with the 55 mph speed limit is an attractive target, having extra dividends of lowering accident and injury rates as well as reducing pollution, but at some psychic and economic pain to the drivers and others. Improved engine tuning, switching to radial tyres, etc., could each save 2 or 3 per cent of US petrol consumption, and more efficient driving (smoother acceleration, etc.) could save even more but require investment capital, skills, periodic vigilance, etc., all difficult to transmit in a public communication campaign.

In the cardiac risk area, one must familiarize oneself with the possible gains and costs of alternative targets such as hypertension reduction, increased exercise, reduced smoking, weight control, improved nutrition, stress management, etc. For each of these potential risk-reduction targets one must become aware of the contribution of each to circulatory morbidity and mortality (alone and in combination, to the general population and to identifiable subpopulations). The availability of procedures for reducing these risks, and the extent to which a public communication campaign could influence the adoption of the risk-reduction measures as well as the undesirable side-effects of any such procedure must also be taken into account. Adequate conduct of this first step requires the collaboration of people with complementary expertise; the social influence researcher should involve him or herself because part of the needed expertise is to take into account the feasibility of a communication campaign for affecting the selected target behaviours.

Step Two: examining the values involved

The social influence researcher drawn into applied research to improve social conditions is obligated to give serious attention to the extent to which the nominated targets for the campaign, and the means of their attainment, are indeed acceptable within his or her own value system. To this end, one must make one's own values explicit. One is also required to consider the indirect unintended effects, as well as the direct goal of the behaviour being urged, as regards both its cost and its benefits, not only to people in general but towards special subgroups in the population. Such an axiological analysis may bring to light some unintended side-effect that the social influence researcher might feel imposes costs exceeding the benefits of the campaign, so that he or she should withdraw from the enterprise and urge that it be discontinued or replaced by a different objective. At the least, such a value analysis may bring to light subtle costs which make it advisable to augment the objective by adding a compensatory policy that avoids an undesired side-effect or provides an adequate compensation to those who might be hurt.

For example, in evaluating the desirability of some energy-conservation goals, a value analysis brings up problems with which one must deal: would compliance with the 55 mph speed limit appreciably increase the cost of food, a large part of which is trucked? To what extent will the switch to lighter cars affect wages and profits in the automotive sector of the economy? Does lowering the thermostat cause discomfort to the elderly to an extent unappreciated by the younger policy-maker, and does it have unexpected benefits in preventing upper respiratory infections? Does regular engine tuning for one's automobile, or installing storm windows, require initial cash surpluses so that low-income people would be further disadvantaged and, if so, what kind of loan, tax credit, or other compensatory measure might be taken? Does promoting insulation of already-built homes cause problems like increased fire hazard, shoddy work, air pollution, and wall rot due to a shortage of adequate expertise and materials needed to meet the immediate demand and, if so, could one adopt some alternatives such as the Canadian region-by-region approach rather than a nationwide campaign?

In the cardiac risk area, value problems loom at least as large. The attitude-change researcher must weigh difficult value choices between the immediate undesirable side-effects of drugs for controlling hypertension *vs.* the long-term detrimental effect of the hypertension itself. In urging weight control or cigarette cessation, one must balance the cost in lost self-esteem, anxiety, etc., of the majority who enter such programmes and fail, against the benefits to the minority who succeed. The personal and social costs of increased exercising, such as large amount of time 'lost' daily in jogging, must be taken into account as well as the increased likelihood of shin injuries, automobile accidents, etc., and one must also consider the beneficial side-effects of such exercising even aside from reducing cardiac risk. As a result of this Step Two value analysis, the social influence researcher will usually reorder somewhat the priorities among the list of possible targets and may eliminate some targets as unacceptable under existing conditions. At the least, certain of the targets will be elaborated to include compensatory or cost-ameliorating subcomponents.

Step Three: describing the sociocultural context

This step involves discovering the social context in which the target practice is embedded, the cultural conditions which instigate and maintain the current behaviour or that might bolster the new substitute behaviour that is to be encouraged. For example, one needs to obtain information on family decision-making regarding household thermostat setting (when was the thermostat setting last changed, by whom, why, etc?), the demographic and situational determinants of obeying *vs.* exceeding the 55 mph speed limit (who exceeds, on what kinds of trips, under what circumstances, with what other people present, etc?). What is the decision-making chain regarding family meals which would provide opportunities for lowering sodium intake in the diet? The pressures in the school situation and elsewhere on the child (peer conformity, advertising, parental example, etc.) which instigate him or her to commence smoking and continue smoking should be described, so that the campaign could be designed to provide the child with modes of coping.

Ways of obtaining information on the sociocultural context include informal retrospection, imaginary role-playing, and recall of own experiences. In addition, it should involve new data collection; for example, fieldwork (including highway observation of who exceeds the 55 mph speed limit and under what observable circumstances); and open-ended and structured interviews (via phone, face-to-face, etc.) with different segments of the population.

Step Four: mapping the psychological matrix

The aim in this fourth step is to describe the thoughts, feelings, and behaviours that instigate and sustain the undesirable energy consumption (or cardiac risk) behaviour or that could promote the desired new energy or health-preserving behaviour. The amount and type of the public's information on the topic must be assessed: how well-informed people are about the amount of fuel or money saved by slower driving, by installing storm windows or attic insulation, etc.; and how informed they are about the effect of smoking (by itself and in conjunction with other practices such as oral contraceptive use) in increasing cardiac risk, or the extent of information on the danger and source of dietary sodium, etc. It may be found that the undesirable practice simply reflects lack of information so that the communication campaign need only inform rather than persuade. Or we may find that the behaviour is maintained by motives quite different from these assumed *a priori*.

A variety of techniques are available for mapping thoughts, feelings, and behaviour patterns that instigate and maintain the undesirable behaviour or could induce the desired new behaviour. One can use critical-incidents analysis by having drivers recall contrasting incidents where they were tempted to exceed 55 mph and did *vs.* did not speed; or getting descriptions of the decision processes from people who did decide to install storm windows *vs.* those who decided not to install them, etc. One can also give directed thinking tasks to speeding and non-speeding drivers, asking them to list antecedents and consequences of exceeding the 55 mph limit, or its desirable and undesirable aspects, and content analysing their responses to determine which related thoughts distinguish the speeding and non-speeding drivers and therefore would constitute promising campaign themes.

Step Five: selection of the campaign themes

This step involves examination of the sociocultural setting and psychological matrices that Steps Three and Four analyses have shown to surround the target behaviours. Here, in Step Five, one tries to tease out promising targets for change in the belief system and habit patterns that maintain the undesirable energy consumption or cardiac risk factor. One is guided in this selection by social influence principles, such as that it is easier to inform than persuade. For example, the Step Four information survey may show that to influence the installation of storm windows the campaign should be devoted to informing convinced people how they can have windows installed rather than by convincing opposed people that they ought to have them installed. Or one may find that people tend to exaggerate the health problems and underestimate the health benefits of lowering the thermostat setting; if so, it obviously would be more cost-effective to provide this health information than to persuade the people that health must to some extent be sacrificed in this time of national crisis. Again, people who exceed the 55 mph speed limit tend (relative to those who obey it) to underestimate the probability of being apprehended, the effect on frequency and seriousness of accidents, and the cost in fuel and car maintenance of speeding; hence, information about the likelihood of these consequences will induce more change than persuasive appeals about moral obligation to obey the law or conserve energy.

Another principle that one employs in theme-selection is that it is easier to change perceived instrumentalities than goal evaluation, and that it is easier to establish a missing instrumentality link than to change an existing one. Frequently non-compliers simply fail to perceive the connection between the energy conservation or cardiac risk reduction behaviour and some valued goal of their own, so that the campaign could effectively emphasize the missing connection rather than trying to change a connection that is already perceived. In selecting campaign themes one has to take into account both the cultural and psychological realities surrounding the target behaviour and also the principles developed in basic research on social influence.

Step Six: constructing the persuasive communication

Having selected the campaign themes in Step Five, Step Six calls for constructing communications which most effectively promote these themes. One chooses the input components mentioned earlier in the chapter (source, message, channel, receiver, and destination variables) that make up the communication, so as to maximize the communication's effect. By way of illustration, we shall describe a study indicating the persuasive effectiveness of a variable from each of the first three classes—source, message and channel.

As regards source variables, an ambiguity arises from the fact that communicator credibility derives from the perceived expertness of the source while communicator attractiveness arises from the source's perceived similarity to the recipient. But since recipients in the public audience tend to be rather ordinary people who are not themselves expert, the question arises whether the credibility or attractiveness of the source is more conducive to social influence: should the source be an expert who therefore is unlike the audience, or should the source be an ordinary inexpert person similar to the audience? A study by Brock (1965) suggests that the similar source is more effective than the expert: a temporary sales person in a paint store was represented to half of the customers as being an expert painter and to the other half as an ordinary person who like themselves occasionally does some painting around his house. In each case this clerk advocated a certain brand of paint, in half the cases a high-priced and in half a low-priced brand. More customers went along with the sales person's recommendation when he was perceived as an amateur like themselves than when he was thought to be an expert painter.

As an illustrative message variable, we shall consider speed of the persuasive speech. The Miller *et al.* (1976) study illustrates the danger of accepting common-sense beliefs about the social influence process without careful conceptual and empirical analysis. Miller and his colleagues recorded several versions of an interview (arguing on such topics as the danger of coffee drinking), differing only in the rate of delivery: in one version the source spoke at the ordinary rate of 140 words per minute, in another at a fast rate exceeding 190 words per minute and in a third, at the slower rate of 111 words per minute. Since there is a stereotype that buyers are very suspicious about the 'fast talking used-car salesman' it might be thought that the fast talkers would be perceived as less trustworthy. The results of the experiment were not at all in accord with the stereotype: when the audio-tapes of the speakers were played to randomly selected people at a shopping centre, it was found that the faster the source spoke the more persuasive the impact he had on the hearers, and the more expert and trustworthy he was perceived as being. Perhaps the unexpected association of trustworthiness with fast talking is due to its being perceived as a sign of a guileless and enthusiastic expression of what one really feels.

Research on how channel variables affect persuasive impact can be illustrated by a Chaiken and Eagly (1976) study which investigated how the effectiveness of a persuasive communication regarding a labour–management dispute was affected by whether it was presented in written, audio-taped, or video-taped modality. The written version has some advantage over the other two in that the recipients have more control over how they distribute their time studying its content, for example, they can spend more time reading and interpreting the difficult parts of the arguments; the audio-taped and video-taped presentations do not have the advantage of allowing a review but do gain in vividness and rapport with the source. In keeping with this analysis, the study showed that with the easy message, impact was greater with the audio- or video-taped presentations than with the written, but they had less impact than the written with the difficult version.

These three studies are simply illustrative of the many hundreds of experiments done each year by social psychologists to tease out principles of persuasion which can guide the Step Six construction of the communications. Other such principles are reviewed in the textbooks on attitude change research cited in the first section of this chapter.

Step Seven: evaluating the communication campaign's effectiveness

When one undertakes any significant activity, one should systematically monitor the various aspects of the communication campaign to determine if each is achieving the intended effect. Though we list evaluation as the last step (because there should be a final evaluation at the end of the campaign), it is an activity that should run parallel to the other steps, involving checks on the effectiveness of each aspect as it is carried out. When in the first step one establishes a priority list of targets (with a clarification of the actualities that were taken into consideration in drawing it up) one should submit it (along with the value-judgements made in Step Two) to various experts for their comments. After the sociocultural and psychological contexts surrounding these targets have been described by the Steps Three and Four open-ended mapping procedures, one's inferences should be subjected to more structured empirical tests, if time allows. The communications one constructs in Step Five should be copy-tested (Lipstein and McGuire, 1978), typically including alternatives, systematically varied forms of the message so that one can determine not only which is better but also why, thus allowing subsequent messages to incorporate the new insight. Those who are designing the campaign should be the ones who do this ongoing evaluation, since its purpose is to provide them with continuing feedback for improving the campaign.

The final evaluation that occurs at the end of the campaign, on the other hand, should be undertaken by outsiders who did not participate in the preceding six steps of designing and carrying out the social influence campaign, and so have more objectivity. The purpose of the final evaluation is to determine the cost of the campaign and its intended and unintended effects, both good and bad, along with an analysis of its strong and weak points and suggestions for how subsequent campaigns might be improved. This final evaluation should be communicated to those who design the campaign, those who sponsored it, appropriate regulatory and public interest groups, etc. Until recently this evaluation phase of social action campaigns was neglected but now a great deal of advice is available regarding it (Riecken and Boruch, 1974; Perloff *et al.*, 1976).

IMMUNIZATION AGAINST PERSUASION

In traditional warfare, more powerful offensive weapons tend to evoke stronger defensive devices, as when a larger-bore cannon evoked thicker town walls or battleship armour. Analogously in social influence research, advances in techniques of persuasion have evoked work on how the individual might be treated in advance to make her or him more resistant to subsequent persuasive attacks. It would hardly be desirable to make the person completely impervious to persuasion: turning him or her into a catatonic schizophrenic could accomplish this, but the individual ought not to be made impervious to all possibility of learning from others. It may, however, be desirable to protect certain beliefs that are likely to be attacked vigorously, so that people are given some degree of resistance to the persuasive communications aimed at weakening them. Five procedures for conferring resistance to persuasion on specific beliefs will be mentioned here with fuller descriptions elsewhere (McGuire, 1964).

Resistance through commitment

It has been shown that one holds more firmly to one's belief in the face of persuasive attack if one has taken some committing action on the basis of it. The commitment can take a form of active participation on the basis of the belief, or can be simply a public announcement of one's position prior to the persuasive attack. Indeed, a private decision also confers resistance to the attack. The person who is asked to think over his or her stand on the issue prior to being presented with a persuasive communication tends to be less influenced by it than the person who had not been asked to do this prior private thinking. Even 'external' commitment has an immunizing effect; that is, when another person tells us that he or she thinks that we entertain a certain belief, then we become more resistant to attacks on it than when the belief had not been attributed to us.

Resistance via anchoring

The person's belief can be made more resistant to change by having the believer engage in prior cognitive work which anchors it to other cognitions before the persuasive communication comes. The anchoring can take various forms such as active or passive linking of the belief to one's accepted values. Alternatively, the belief can be anchored by having the person think of other beliefs with which it is clustered. Resistance-conferring anchoring can also be achieved by making more salient to the person, just before the attack, the information that significant other persons and reference groups also adhere to that belief.

Inducing resistant emotional states

In so far as certain chronic emotional states are related to persisting individual differences in susceptibility to persuasion, one should be able to make any individual momentarily more resistant by putting him or her at the time of exposure to the attacking communication in a temporary emotional state which is similar to the chronic state of resistant individuals. However, a number of states sometimes thought to be associated with chronic resistance to persuasion such as aggressiveness, self-esteem, etc., prove to be more complexly related to susceptibility to social influence (McGuire, 1968); for example, increasing the person's self-esteem can make him or her more resistant or less resistant to persuasion, depending on such factors as issue complexity, the person's chronic self-esteem level, etc. Still a detailed knowledge of the correlates of susceptibility to social influence and of the particular situation under consideration should allow one to conclude fairly accurately whether, in a specified communication situation, a given change in motivational state would raise or lower resistance to persuasion.

Increased educational level

It has been claimed that increasing the person's general education will tend to make him or her more resistant to persuasion, since education will provide the person with more belief-supporting information, will sharpen her or his critical abilities, enhance self-confidence to allow maintaining a deviant view, etc. However, it must be recognized that with increasing education people also become more attentive to outside communications, better able to understand their arguments, etc., so that one's susceptibility to social influence goes up with education. For example, films were prepared during World War II by the US army to indoctrinate American soldiers with such purportedly morale-boosting beliefs as that their British and Soviet allies were bearing a large share of the effort needed to win the war against the Axis powers. In the research evaluating this programme, it was found that the more education the soldier had before coming into the army the more he was influenced by these films. Apparently the enhancement of comprehension associated with education more than compensated for the enhancement of critical ability, so that susceptibility to persuasion increased with educational level.

Resistance through pre-exposure to attacking material

It has been held that people typically maintain their beliefs in an ideologically asceptic environment by avoiding opposition views, particularly on issues where one's belief is widely shared by those within one's culture, with the result that these apparently robust overprotected beliefs often prove very vulnerable when exposed to a massive dose of attacking material. By analogy with biological inoculation procedures for people raised in a relatively germ-free environment, it should be possible to make such overprotected beliefs more resistant to persuasion by pre-exposing the person to a weakened dose of attacking material so as to build up his or her defences before exposure to the massive persuasive attack. Considerable support has been found (McGuire, 1964) for hypotheses derived from this position which suggests that the person's beliefs are more effectively immunized against persuasion if, instead of giving arguments supporting the beliefs in advance of the attack, one is pre-exposed to weakened forms of the attacking arguments themselves, thus stimulating the build-up of defences for the beliefs previously maintained in too germ-free an ideological environment.

CONCLUDING MORAL CONSIDERATIONS

The problems and crises in a person's life sometimes arise from conflicts within the person and at other times from conflicts between the person and society. While the problems which arise from the internal conflicts are often felt more poignantly by the person and tend to supply tragic themes of great drama, it is the external conflicts between the person and society that tend to become social problems and give rise to social influence attempts. When the impulses of the person comes into serious conflict with the demands of society, something has to give. Traditionally, the burden of change in these individual *vs.* society conflicts has been put on the individual. The deviant person whose behaviour and attitude become seriously out of tune with the expectations of the society tends to be labelled as sick, criminal, subversive, etc. and required to reform, be relegated to a deviant subculture, incarcerated, expelled from the society, or executed. As the affluence and peace of recent years have allowed some nations in Western Europe and North America to afford a more permissive stance to deviants, more tolerance has been extended to the nonconformist, and consideration has sometimes been given even to the proposition that in conflicts between the individual and society, perhaps it is society that should be changed.

The notion of social influence techniques as a mode of problem solution becomes particularly appropriate in cases where one is willing to entertain this latter tolerant possibility; once one admits that problem solution might involve changing the demands of society rather than the behaviour of the nonconformist individual, then there is more need for the techniques of mass persuasion that allow the single source to influence the many receivers. Persuasion is also of use in changing the individual, of course, but other pressures can more easily be brought by society on the individual than by the individual on society. That we shall continue to move towards a more permissive society is by no means certain: the trend may be cyclical rather than monotonic; but if permissiveness does increase, social influence processes are likely to become progressively more useful as a mode of problem solution.

While persuasive communication may be a relatively benign technique of manipulation and social influence, it does involve people exerting pressure on one another and is somewhat distasteful on that account. While part of the solution, persuasion is also part of the problem in the struggle of the weak against the strong, and for the improvement of social conditions. It is probably healthy to maintain one's distaste for the use of persuasive communication as a technique to manipulate other people, but also to moderate our disdain for this technique by an ambivalent attitude which paraphrases Winston Churchill's aphorism about democracy as a form of government: that persuasion is the worst possible mode of social control and conflict resolution except for all of the others.

REFERENCES

Abelson, R. P., Aronson, E., McGuire, W. J., Newcomb, T. M., Rosenberg, M. J., and Tannenbaum, P. H. (Eds.) (1968). *Theories of Cognitive Consistency*. (Chicago: Rand-McNally.)

Allen, V. L. (1975). Social support for nonconformity. In: L. Berkowitz (Ed.), *Advances in Experimental Social Psychology*, **8,** 1–43.

Asch, S. E. (1952). *Social Psychology*. (New York: Prentice Hall.)

Bandura, A. (1969). *Principles of Behavior Modification*. (New York: Holt, Rinehart, & Winston.)

Bandura, A. (1976). *Social Learning Theory*. (New York: Prentice Hall.)

Barber, T. X. (1969). *Hypnosis: a Scientific Approach*. (Princeton: Van Nostrand.)

Belson, W. (1979). *Television Violence and the Adolescent Boy*. (Farnborough, Hants.: Saxon House.)

Bernstein, D. A. and McAlister, A. (1976). The modification of smoking behavior: progress and problems. *Addictive Behavior*, **1,** 89–102.

Bettelheim, B. 1976. *The Uses of Enchantment: The Meaning and Importance of Fairy Tales*. (New York: Knopf.)

Brock, T. C. (1965). Communicator–recipient similarity and decision change. *Journal of Personality and Social Psychology*, **1,** 650–654.

Chaiken, S. and Eagly, A. H. (1976). Communication modality as a determinant of message persuasiveness and message comprehensibility. *Journal of Personality and Social Psychology*, **34,** 605–614.

Comstock, G. (1975). *Television and Human Behaviour: the Key Studies*. (Santa Monica: Rand.)

Eagly, A. H. and Himmelfarb, S. (1978). Attitudes and opinions. In: M. R. Rosenzweig and L. W. Porter (Eds.), *Annual Review of Psychology*, **29,** 517–554.

Evans, R. I., Rozelle, R. M., Lasale, F. M., Dembroski, T. M., and Allen, B. P. (1970). Fear arousal, persuasion, and actual versus implied behavioral change: new perspectives utilizing a real-life dental hygiene program. *Journal of Personality and Social Psychology*, **16,** 220–227.

Farquhar, W. J., Maccoby, N., *et al.* (1977). Community education for cardiovascular health. *Lancet*, 1192–1195.

Fishbein, M. and Ajzen, I. (1975). *Belief, Attitude, Intention, and Behavior*. (Reading, Mass.: Addison-Wesley.)

Frank, J. D. (1973). *Persuasion and Healing*. (Baltimore: John Hopkins University.)

Geen, R. G. and Quanty, M. B. (1977). The catharsis of aggression. In: L. Berkowitz, (Ed.), *Advances in Experimental Social Psychology*, **10,** 1–37.

Gray, H. H. (1963). Renaissance humanism: the pursuit of excellence. *Journal of the History of Ideas*, **24,** 497–514.

Janis, I. L. (1972). *Victims of Group Thinking*. (Boston: Houghton Mifflin.)

Jones, E. E. (Ed.) (1971). *Attribution: Perceiving the Causes of Behavior*. (Morristown, NJ: General Learning Press.)

Katz, D. (1960). The functional approach to the study of attitudes. *Public Opinion Quarterly*, **24,** 163–204.

Kennedy, G. (1972). *The Art of Rhetoric in the Roman World*. (Princeton: Princeton University Press.)

Lefkowitz, M. M., Eron, L. D., Walder, L. O., and Huesmann, L. R. (1972). Television violence and child aggression: a follow-up study. In G. Comstock and E. Rubinstein (Eds.), *Television and Social Behavior: Television and Adolescent Aggression*, pp. 35–135. (Washington, DC: DHEW.)

Leventhal, H. (1970). Findings and theory in the study of fear communications. In L. Berkowitz (Ed.), *Advances in Experimental Social Psychology*, **5,** 119–186. (New York: Academic Press.)

Lipstein, B. and McGuire, W. J. (1978). *Evaluating Advertising*. (New York: Advertising Research Foundation.)

Maccoby, N., Farguar, J. W., Wood, P. D. and Alexander, J. (1977). Reducing the risk of cardiovascular disease: effects of a community based campaign on knowledge and behavior. *Journal of Community Health*, **3,** 100–114.

Mahoney, M. J. (1974). *Cognitive and Behavior Modification*. (Cambridge, Mass.: Ballinger.)

Mahoney, M. J. (1975). The behavioral treatment of obesity. In: A. J. Enelow and J. B. Henderson (Eds.), *Applying Behavioral Science to Cardiovascular Risk*. (New York: American Heart Association.)

McGuire, W. J. (1964). Inducing resistance to persuasion. In: L. Berkowitz (Ed.), *Advances in Experimental Social Psychology*, **1,** 191–229. (New York: Academic Press.)

McGuire, W. J. (1968). Personality and susceptibility to social influence. In E. F. Borgatta and W. W. Lambert (Eds.), *Handbook of Personality Theory and Research*, pp. 1130–1187. (Chicago: Rand McNally.)

McGuire, W. J. (1974). Psychological motives and communication gratification. In: J. G. Blumler and E. Katz, (Eds.), *The Uses of Mass Communication*, pp. 167–196. (Beverley Hills: Sage.)

McGuire, W. J. (1976). Televised Over-the-counter Drug Advertising. Mimeo-ed report to FCC-FTC Panel, Washington, DC.
McGuire, W. J. (1978a). Retrieving the information from the literature. In: B. Lipstein and W. J. McGuire (Eds.), *Evaluating Advertising*, pp. xv–xxvi. (New York: Advertising Research Foundation.)
McGuire, W. J. (1978b). The communication/persuasion matrix. In: B. Lipstein and W. J. McGuire (Eds.), *Evaluating Advertising*, pp. xxvii–xxxv. (New York: Advertising Research Foundation.)
Milavsky, J. R., Pekowsky, B., and Stipp, H. (1976). TV drug advertising and proprietary and illicit drug use among teenage boys. *Public Opinion Quarterly*, **39,** 457–481.
Miller, N., Maruyama, G., Beaber, R. J., and Valone, K. (1976). Speed of speech and persuasion. *Journal of Personality and Social Psychology*, **34,** 615–624.
Moscovici, S. (1976). *Social Influence and Social Change*. (London: Academic Press.)
Oskamp, S. (1977). *Attitudes and Opinions*. (Englewood Cliffs, NJ: Prentice-Hall.)
Park, R. D., Berkowitz, L., Leyens, J. P., West, S. G., and Sebastian, R. J. (1977). Some effects of violent and nonviolent movies on the behavior of juvenile delinquents. In: L. Berkowitz, (Ed.), *Advances in Experimental Social Psychology*, **10,** 135–172.
Patterson, T. E. and McClure, R. D. (1976). *Picture Politics*. (New York: Putnam.)
Perloff, R., Perloff, E., and Sussna, E. (1976). Program evaluation. In: M. R. Rosenzweig and L. W. Porter (Eds.), *Annual Review of Psychology*, **27,** 569–594.
Riecken, H. W. and Boruch, R. F. (Eds.) (1974). *Social Experimentation: A Method for Planning and Evaluating Social Intervention*. (New York: Academic Press.)
Schein, E. H. (1961). *Coercive Persuasion*. (New York: Norton.)
Schwartz, S. H. (1977). Normative influence on altruism. In: L. Berkowitz, (Ed.), *Advances in Experimental Social Psychology*, **10,** 221–282.
Szalai, A. (Ed.) (1972). *The Use of Time*. (The Hague: Mouton.)
Triandis, H. C. (1977). *Interpersonal Behavior*. (Monterey: Brooks/Cole.)
Weigel, R. H. and Jessor, R. (1973). Television and adolescent conventionality: an exploration. *Public Opinion Quarterly*, **37,** 76–90.
Wicklund, R. A. and Brehm, J. W. (1976). *Perspectives on Cognitive Dissonance*. (Hillsdale, NJ: Erlbaum.)
Zimbardo, P. G., Ebbesen, E., and Maslach, C. (1977). *Influencing Attitudes and Changing Behavior*. (Reading, Mass.: Addison-Wesley.)

The Social Psychology of Psychological Problems
Edited by P. Feldman and J. Orford

13

Overview and Implications: Towards an Applied Social and Community Psychology

JIM ORFORD AND PHILIP FELDMAN

INTRODUCTION

The main focus of the first part of this book is on basic theory and research findings in social psychology which the authors consider to have actual or potential implications for the practical solution of psychological problems. The second is more concerned with actual attempts at changing behaviour or environment, emphasizing particularly the methods and findings of social and community psychology. In this final chapter we have attempted a selective overview of the findings, proceeding from a discussion of the more theoretical aspects to a consideration of individual and environmental modification, with particular emphasis on the prevention of psychological problems. We conclude with a section on social policy, which is partly concerned with issues raised by our contributors and partly with related matters not covered directly by them.

Each chapter author has, in his own way, written about the influence of the environment upon psychological problems or problem behaviour, or at least about the combined influence of the individual and the environment. In ordering these separate contributions, it may be useful to extend O'Donnell's division of relevant environments into micro- and macro-environments. Amongst the aspects covered in the various chapters, there exists a continuum ranging on the one hand from friendship between two people, the most micro of social environments, to, on the other hand, the total culture of which the individual is a part—the most macro of environments. In between, in ascending order from micro to macro, lie the nuclear family as a social group, the extended family or friendship social network, institutions and organizations, and local communities.

Social integration

The theme that recurs, despite these differences in scale, is that of social integration *vs.* social isolation. Time and again our contributors return to the conclusion, stated in different forms, that for the prevention or relief of psychological problems, people need people. In his chapter Shepherd argues that 'difficulties in social functioning' lie at the heart of many psychological difficulties. The framework for O'Donnell's chapter is a model which supposes that environmental design encourages or discourages frequent, accepting interactions between people, and that these promote attachments and responsibilities, which in turn aid the prevention or alleviation of many psychological problems. Duck, Orford, and Yule refer to social isolation amongst the elderly, amongst families containing a handicapped member or a member with a drinking problem, and in families where child-abuse occurs; and Argyle reports social isolation to be one of the most common problems encountered in clients of a social-skills training programme. Cochrane and Sobol in their chapter review the evidence suggesting that such factors as social integration, the strength of ties to others, and the availability of someone to confide in, moderate the influence of life stress upon psychological well-being.

Not all social interaction is health-enhancing, however. O'Donnell lays stress upon the way in which environmental design can promote the kinds of interactions that are friendly and accepting, and Duck finds evidence for the idea that it is an unsatisfied need for 'affectively positive interactions' that is involved in the causation of psychological problems. Consistent with these views is the mounting evidence, reviewed by Herbert, which suggests that it is the climate of the home which is most influential in promoting those qualities in children which give them the capacity to resist problems in childhood and in later life. The important influences may have more to do with the 'how?' of personal relationships in the family than with the 'what?'—in particular, long-standing discord, little affection, and much rejecting and critical behaviour towards offspring carries a bad prognosis for the latter's mental health. In similar vein Orford argues that the concept of family cohesion unites the findings of family research into a number of different psychological problems, and that for the most part low cohesion is predictive of the continuation of existing problems and the occurrence of new problems for family members. Argyle, Herbert, and Orford all consider some of the basic dimensions of interpersonal behaviour which may lie behind the general atmosphere or climate felt in a dyadic relationship or in a small group such as the family. Friendly acceptance or liking *vs.* criticism or rejection may have an unequivocal influence upon climate, but other basic dimensions concern dominance *vs.* submissiveness, dependence *vs.* independence, and laxness *vs.* strictness of control over children, and these have a less certain impact.

Herbert makes very clear that while early experience is important as a link in the continuing chain of human development, from conception to old age, it is only one link. Unfavourable childhood experiences can be made up for later, but it is a great deal easier to get things right initially by providing children with the appropriate adaptive behaviours. In addition to the detailed behaviour of the individual child and its social environment, such parent variables as attitudes towards the methods and objectives of child-rearing, and their feelings about the child, must be taken into account for the provision of the most effective help concerning child-rearing. The skills of the parents and their physical resources, as well as the 'temperament' of the child—all other things being equal, some are simply harder to train than others—are all limiting factors. 'Skills' refers to a combination of overtly expressed affection for the child and the effective application of specific training experiences. He reviews evidence suggesting that some balance of parental control and the allowing of autonomy, combined with basic acceptance, in general provides the climate for child-rearing from which children are most likely to mature into self-confident and competent adults. The optimum balance may be in different places, depending upon the structure and composition of the family group, but a similar type of balance may have to be struck by family members coping with psychological problems amongst their adult members. Training in positive, pro-social behaviours tends to be neglected in favour of waiting until a transgression occurs and then punishing it. The development of the former is particularly important for the prevention of undesirable behaviours by the anticipatory provision of desirable alternatives. The successful acquisition of positive behaviours is much assisted by systematic training in self-control and self-direction, rather than stopping at external control and direction.

Self-esteem and social competence

Self-esteem and social competence emerge as the two strongest contenders for the role of personal qualities intervening between positive socialization experiences on the one hand and psychological health or well-being on the other. Cook discusses the nature of self attitudes in detail, and Herbert discusses their development during childhood and their importance as basic ingredients of positive mental health. Basic self-esteem, the absence of self-denigrating attitudes, and the availability of normal defence mechanisms, play a vital part too in Cochrane and Sobol's hierarchical model of coping responses. In their view self attitudes form the basic first line of defence against life stress.

Social competence is considered in detail by Argyle in his chapter, by Shepherd, and by Duck in the context of friendship. Argyle itemizes the components of socially competent performance—such as accuracy of person perception, taking the role of the other, use of appropriate non-verbal signals—whilst Duck warns of the multidimensionality and complexity of the skills involved in acquainting, and Shepherd asks how important are feelings such as anxiety and cognitions in the process of acquiring social skills. Argyle estimates that problems such as social anxiety, lack of appropriate assertiveness, and heterosexual social problems, may occur in as many as 7 per cent of the population.

Duck points out the possibilities of analysing social relationships in terms of an overall theoretical framework such as equity theory, which then makes predictions from which practical tactics can be planned, rather than taking the ground-level approach of considering a specific skill for a specific situation. The distinction between general principles and particular techniques is an important one. Friendship formation and maintenance seems at least as important a part of 'preparation for life' as academic school subjects. The skills are complex and it may be helpful to train general principles of the accurate perception of others, the production of matching behaviours, and the disclosure of own attitudes, irrespective of particular contexts. Duck argues for training in friendship to be planned and systematic; the present casual approach is too likely to result in failures which have long-term and serious consequences for both work and leisure.

Cook collects together much recent work, particularly on attribution theory, which is concerned with what determines judgements of the causes of events. There are implications for a range of clinically relevant behaviours, from the aggressive actions of the 'mentally abnormal offender' to the use by many care agents of such typological descriptions as 'depressive' or 'schizophrenic'. Both relate to habitual attributions; the former to an attribution of hostility, the latter to an attribution that 'illness', once observed, is a permanent feature of the person concerned. An important future research task is to study how to teach care-agents, perhaps the general public also, about the variables which determine their judgements, to relate those judgements to the specifics of a given situation and to sample the full range of situations relevant to any particular judgemental task. Such skills could be used both to aid the effectiveness of social relationships and the identification and care of psychological problems.

Argyle and Duck both make mention of stereotyped and biased first impressions of people, as one aspect of relatively incompetent social behaviour, and Yule shows how the handicapped may suffer at the receiving end of such superficial judgements and how handicapped children, for example those with spina bifida, are particularly prone to worries about social–sexual peer relationships. He makes a point, as do several authors, of the crucial interaction between behaviour and environment. There is always a particular social setting with specific requirements which determines how severe, or trivial, are the consequences of the particular 'handicap' for a particular individual with a particular set of skills, and he cautions against categorizing people permanently and for all situations as 'normals' and the 'handicapped'. Thus handicap is to be understood in relation to specific goals and not in terms of handicapped people. A vital research task for the future is to define criteria for the performance of the behaviours of interest and the consequences for performance of particular assets and deficits.

Personal distress and distress to others

The importance of life events for psychological well-being and the probability that the direction of effect is causal—from events to subjective response—are discussed in detail by Cochrane and Sobol. They present a considerable body of evidence concerning the links between life events and psychological problems, as well as some provocative ideas concerning the processes which follow life events which cannot be coped with by the immediate social resources available to the individual—his own skills and those of family, friends, or neighbours. They suggest that people resort to professional help of some kind only when the more immediately available resources prove insufficient; even then they require both knowledge of professional services of an appropriate nature and access to them—conditions which are often not met in the field of psychological problems. Should the professional-help stage of the coping process be unavailable, or fail to succceed even if present, the next step is an attempt to secure hospitalization, or help of some kind; perhaps by means of self-injury.

There is an important distinction that has to be made between the problems experienced as such by people themselves and those caused to others. Feldman and O'Donnell consider the latter group, focusing on criminal behaviour. The task of the applied psychologist may be very different with offenders than with clients suffering from psychological problems, particularly in the areas of prevention and intervention (see below).

Feldman sets out the social influences and experiences which increase the probability that individuals will acquire and carry out criminal behaviours, including exposure to visible social models of successful criminal activity and to a general social setting in which such behaviours occur. Such social settings range from the informal groups, in which children play, to associations of business and professional men. Once carried out such behaviour is likely to be successful and hence repeated. Focusing on the positive acquisition of criminal behaviour is likely to be at least as important in the explanation of crime as the much more heavily researched failure to respond to parental training not to offend.

It is a paradox that the network of social agencies, from the police to the penal system, set up to prevent and restrain crime, may also contribute to its maintenance. Examples include the provocative behaviour of juveniles in encounters with police, which may be partially enhanced by police behaviour, and the 'training schools' for criminal loyalties and skills provided by prisons and other establishments. From the research point of view it is clear that the population available for study in penal institutions is an unsatisfactory sample of the total world of offenders, so that research should focus at least equally on groups obtained by the self-report method.

Environmental design

Both Yule and Shepherd write of the need to engineer the environments of residential care settings in order to facilitate the social functioning of the handicapped and those with social difficulties, and in order to prevent the decline in functioning associated with institutionalization. Large differences have been found in the degree to which staff are client-oriented as opposed to institution-oriented in their work, and in the sheer level of interaction with patients or clients, particularly warm, accepting interaction. The autonomy of staff, and their motivation and involvement in their work may be crucial variables (Shepherd).

O'Donnell, in his chapter, considers the design of institutional and small-group environments more generally, citing examples that include hospitals, schools, and places of work, amongst others. He suggests that the major components of environmental design are people and resources. Concerning the former, the essential message is that small is beautiful, for units of all kinds. The key concept is that of manning. The match between the number of people needed and available for social roles is likely to be better in small organizations. Resources may be as specific as toys and games in children's play groups. They are more available in small settings, both for group and solo play, the former enabling social contact, the latter productive solitude. Even the arrangement of furniture in group settings may encourage or hinder social interaction.

The same concept of manning may be relevant to human groups on a macro scale. O'Donnell has collected together a set of important findings which implicate, in the causation of illness and crime, such features of the urban environment as overmanning, zoning of different types of private and commercial property and resources, the physical design of housing, and the availability of play space and shared areas. Social interaction is reduced by high-rise buildings and promoted by single-family homes, nearby leisure areas and car-free pedestrian precincts. The most severe effects are experienced by non-working mothers with young children and little or no access to extended family contact, who live in the upper stories of high-rise buildings. To his list should be added features of particular importance to the rural dweller, for example transportation and access to centralized facilities.

O'Donnell also raises many important questions for future research, including the interaction of settings, social networks and psychological problems, and the effects of economic variables, which point to fruitful collaboration across the boundaries of disciplines such as psychology, architecture, and economics.

Some wider issues

Social class and unemployment are two aspects of the wider social and economic setting, the psychological implications of which receive attention in a number of other chapters. Cochrane and Sobol remind us of the powerful influences of social class on the results of studies such as the Mid-Town Manhattan Survey and the Camberwell Study of depression amongst women, carried out by Brown and his colleagues. Similarly Yule reminds us how strongly class-related is mild mental handicap. However, as Feldman argues forcefully in relation to criminal statistics, and as Orford points out with relation to child-abuse, relationships of psychological problems with social class may often be more apparent than real.

Yule stresses the importance of employment for handicapped school-leavers, and Cowen places similar emphasis on obtaining employment in community mental health programmes for delinquent and unemployed young people. In comparison with the recognition that has been given in recent years to the significance of the family for psychological health and well-being, comparatively little attention has been given to work and the work environment as sources of satisfaction and self-esteem, or alternatively to lack of work or to unsatisfactory aspects of work as sources of stress and psychological problems.

There is always the danger of limiting our vision to the preoccupations and fashions of the present time. A number of chapter authors have hinted at this possibility. Cochrane and Sobol in particular question whether the apparent increased prevalence of psychological problems may be attributed to certain broad social changes. Their own value-change model, for example, suggests that an increasing emphasis upon personal fulfilment may have resulted in a lower threshold to stress. Cowen too comments upon present higher expectations of psychological health, and a vastly increased scope for mental health concerns. Yule points out that the picture of mental handicap changes, often quite dramatically, with social and technical changes; for example the technological innovations which so dramatically increased the survival chances of children with spina bifida.

SOCIAL AND COMMUNITY APPLICATIONS

Introduction

To what extent can the practice of applied psychology borrow from the theoretical understanding outlined above, and to what extent can it hope to make an impact upon psychological problems which reside within social and community contexts? Clinical psychology, having outgrown its early psychometric image, has become, in many places where it is practised, largely a therapeutic enterprise. The limitations inherent in the therapeutic approach are outlined by a number of authors in this book, and they are little different from those limitations of individual patient-directed medicine which are now being recognized more clearly. Shepherd and O'Donnell refer to the central problems of the generalizability of treatment effects and to the durability of changes brought about by treatment. In the case of the psychological therapies there is the continuing problem of uncertainty over even the short-term effectiveness of treatment (Cowen), and there is continuing concern that such therapies may tend to be used with a biased selection of relatively higher socioeconomic status groups. Besides which, manpower is an overriding problem. With the increasing scope of mental health services to which Cowen refers in his chapter, the manpower crisis only intensifies. It is these criticisms—coupled with the hope that prevention may be more effective than a mode of working which involves waiting in a clinical setting for problems which may often by that time have reached an advanced stage, even an 'end-state' (Cowen)—which have led to the demand for a paradigm-shift towards an alternative way of working, which Cowen and others have called community psychology. The shift that is demanded is towards *pre*vention and away from individual treatment *inter*vention.

The term 'community psychology' has been used in a number of different but overlapping senses. Different definitions represent more or less radical departures from individual patient- or client-oriented work. Not everyone would agree with

Cowen's radical definition which confines community psychology to preventive work, and distinguishes it clearly from a variety of forms of applied psychological work which are 'in the community'. The latter, in the USA at least, would be subsumed under the general term 'community mental health'.

Parents and children

Many of the innovative ways in which psychologists are beginning to work in applied settings fall within the general area of CMH whilst still remaining largely interventionist in style. Herbert describes the 'triadic model' of working with disturbed children and their parents. As well as parents, siblings and peers have been involved and children are also trained to be their own behaviour therapists. The last development is particularly important both for children and adults, because skills learned by the client to deal with a particular problem may then be applied by him to other future problems, without the need for further professional help. Preferably successful coping behaviour should be applied to the requirements of particular life situations as they occur, thus avoiding problems in advance. Herbert also refers to work applying behavioural and other principles in the classroom.

Yule, too, makes reference to parents as treatment partners in the area of handicap, for example in overcoming the natural resistance to undertake painful exercise on the part of young people with rheumatoid arthritis. He describes the various stages of possible intervention following the birth of a handicapped child, at each of which psychological help may be of value, from breaking the news to the parents, through helping parents to help their children, to advising on the social and recreational needs of the older handicapped person. He writes too of helping both children and parents with impending death in the family, and rightly describes how a direct counselling approach in this and other matters, which treats parents as equal partners, has been associated with the much-maligned behaviour therapy approach.

Social difficulties

There is now a large literature in the field of intervention, both with clients seen specifically or largely for social skills training, and with those given social retraining following prolonged inpatient care for such severe problems as diagnosed schizophrenia (Shepherd). The more usual methods have involved therapeutic programmes, both psychodynamic and behaviourally based, within the hospital community. Both approaches suffer from the great difficulty in generalizing back to the outside world the experiences or behaviours achieved in hospital. The key issue always is whether the client can perform appropriately in the real-life setting. Whether generalization occurs depends largely on the number of elements common to the training and real-life situations, and the closeness of the skills required to those taught. It follows that training should be provided largely in the community itself, using such resources as families of clients—who then need to be prepared appropriately for their helping role. Prior to the stage of 're-entry' into the general community, albeit in a sheltered version of it, it is vital to avoid deterioration during what may be a lengthy hospital stay. This aim is assisted by an increase in staff–client interaction and by staff reinforcement of appropriate client behaviour. The achievement of such staff behaviours requires both special training for staff and staff involvement in the selection of desirable targets for clients to achieve. In turn, the attainment of targets depends upon the systematic analysis of such variables as the previous assets and deficits of clients and of specific individual differences relevant to each client.

Shepherd writes of the use of 'buddies' and volunteer workers as yet another means of attempting to overcome the treatment generalization problem. A dominant theme within the US literature on community psychology of recent years has been the employment of para-professionals or volunteers both as an extension of, and sometimes as a substitute for, the work of a person trained in one of the relevant mental health professions. Cowen mentions a number of such projects in his chapter—the use of 'teacher–counsellors' in the Re-Ed programme, 'teacher–moms' in the Elmont Project, indigenous para-professionals in New Careers programmes and the Neighbourhood Service Centre programme, as well as self-help on the part of former mental hospital patients illustrated by Fairweather's studies.

Employment and residential settings are important contexts for generalization (Shepherd). So-called intermediate or 'halfway' residential facilities such as hostels, lodges, and halfway houses, provide important settings for the stimulation of social competence and the prevention of institutionalization. However Shepherd warns us that institutionalization can occur as well in the community as in an institution, and Yule argues that community care needs to be *by* the community and not just in the community. It is fashionable to speak of the integration of the handicapped, but we should beware of underestimating the problems and resistances involved.

A further theme within both CMH and community psychology is the systematic planning and delivery of services based upon epidemiology as a tool (Yule). Amongst findings in the handicap field, which have clear implications for service provision, are high rates of handicap in children, high rates amongst the elderly, and in one study a three-fold difference between the high rate of backwardness in reading, found in an urban area in Britain, in comparison with the relatively low rate to be found in a provincial rural and small town area.

Reducing distress to others

Most people with handicaps or other psychological problems do not benefit from their 'problem' behaviours. Most offenders, on the other hand, do; it follows that the latter are much less likely to cooperate with change agents, both in the choice of targets for change and in carrying out the procedures to reach those targets. Feldman reviewed a number of methods of social response to convicted offenders which might help to reduce re-offending by them. They include the use of shorter custodial sentences, thus reducing exposure to criminalization, as well as such alternatives to custodial care as community-based reparation schemes. The latter are connected with the important shift to re-training in the natural environment rather than in the artificial setting of an institution. There are several recent examples of such community-based programmes and they show at least potential promise. Crucial requirements are the involvement of parents and other significant figures (which means giving them extensive pre-training) and a close contingency between the continued access to valued rewards and the avoidance by previous offenders of socially disapproved behaviours.

There are also a number of programmes, some of which, such as Achievement Place, are very well known, in which young people referred by the courts live in group homes but attend community-based activities such as school or work. Training programmes for offenders often face the serious difficulty of a lack of agreement about goals between staff and 'clients', and the associated problem of counter-control by the peer group. These problems make it vital that isolation from non-offending models be reduced as far as possible. Even with the best combination of psychological methods, success (measured by the absence of re-conviction) must be more difficult to achieve than with clients in general.

Prevention

Prevention represents the most clear-cut departure from previous, and most present, practice, and is the theme most central to the emergent field of community psychology. Despite its promise, there is as yet insufficient sound evidence of effective applied psychology in preventive work to convince everyone that resources should be redeployed on a large scale. Yule, Shepherd, and O'Donnell each find the results of attempts at primary prevention (efforts to prevent the occurrence of problems before they even begin to appear, and aimed at a whole population or subpopulation) disappointing. Others—Cowen, Herbert, Feldman and McGuire in particular—are more optimistic.

In the area of child socialization and primary prevention Herbert refers to recent developments in parent and teacher education and training in preventive mental health programmes. Such programmes are best delivered within the triadic model, whereby psychologists train other professionals (teachers, nurses, etc.) who then train parents so as to make maximum use of scarce resources. The context of training programmes should emphasize the skills which enable more effective coping in advance of problems, rather than waiting until they occur. They emphasize building positive, desired child behaviours, rather than eliminating undesired negative ones. Herbert cautions that training programmes must take into account the social context of training, the methods used, and the intrinsic attributes of the child. Being a parent must be seen as a systematic skill, needing and requiring effort, rather than something which is either 'instinctual' or learned by trial and error.

In the field of handicap the Milwaukee project, described by Cowen and Yule, represents an exceptional example of preventive work focusing upon a particular target group, in this case mothers of low intelligence known to be likely to raise children of low intelligence and poor educational attainment. Such programmes must be comprehensive and long-term. The efforts of psychologists seem less relevant to the primary prevention of severe mental handicap, except where the efforts of genetic counsellors and family planning advisers can be enhanced by the effective use of the social influence techniques described by McGuire.

In his particularly valuable chapter, McGuire reviews research into the major social influence situations, from 'suggestions' such as hypnotic induction, through to the mass media such as advertising (television is the more usual focus of research overviews). He provides a conceptual framework for all such situations, in terms of inputs (the components of communication such as the source and the receiver) and outputs (the process of being influenced from initial exposure to the post-behaviour cognitive consolidation). McGuire also covers a number of theories of social influence and sets out some predictions as to how to bring about actual compliance. For example, appeals should preferably be positive rather than fear-arousing and if the latter, should be at medium rather than high levels of fear. They should also emphasize ways of coping with the problem concerned, rather than merely evoking anxiety.

McGuire points out that individualized treatments, whether behavioural or psychodynamic, are costly; hence the attraction of large-scale field programmes using mass-media-based social influence findings. Many such programmes seem to contain elements of both prevention and intervention, for example one aimed at reducing smoking is likely to be delivered to a mixed audience of current smokers, those who have not yet begun, former smokers, and those who are well past the age at which most smokers begin. He sets out an exemplary seven-step public service communication campaign for two targets—energy conservation and the reduction of cardiac risk factors. The steps proceed from the analysis of 'environmental realities' through a description of the sociocultural context to the construction of the persuasive communication and the evaluation of its effectiveness.

The Stanford heart disease project is an outstanding example of the type of applied preventive work described in detail by McGuire in his chapter. This work is clearly in the public education and public health mode, persuasive communication is the means, and the whole population, or at least a large section of it, is the target. Such a mode of work becomes of central importance with the recognition that much present ill-health and psychological distress is caused by behaviours which are both widespread and within the control of citizens—for example smoking, excessive drinking, dangerous driving, excessive eating and inappropriate diet, and lack of exercise. In the Stanford project mass media presentation alone proved more cost-effective than mass media presentation supplemented by face-to-face intervention. However, it is possible that a two-stage approach might be the most cost-effective of all—beginning with mass media alone and then proceeding to individual interventions for those still unchanged.

In the crime and delinquency field, reviewed by Feldman, much the greatest amount of effort has gone into the prediction of future offenders with a view to providing them with suitable prophylactic experiences. Unfortunately, predictive instruments have failed to discriminate the majority who fall in the middle range of scores; even if successful discrimination has been achieved the methods of training to assist prevention are only just beginning to be developed. Such methods, which it is sensible to apply generally (primary prevention) rather than to selected subgroups, include training parents, or foster-parents, in effective child-rearing methods and particularly in the development of pro-social behaviours. In turn, the latter will be assisted by similar training in schools and by the provision of models of pro-social behaviours, particularly via the mass media. Next comes the availability of material and social rewards for carrying out socially approved behaviours, which thus become relevant and attractive alternatives to criminal behaviours. Training in job-related skills and friendship formation are both important here. Finally, police behaviour towards juveniles during the police–juvenile encounter might be modified by appropriate training so as to reduce the number of youngsters who enter the long tunnel which finally leads to incarceration for some of them.

Environmental design may also contribute to the prevention of offending, both by reducing the opportunities provided by visibly easy targets for crime, such as open doors and windows, and by distributing physical resources more evenly throughout a city, as O'Donnell indicates. For example, violent crime might be reduced by not concentrating in one area certain types of trading and leisure activities. In addition, environments which encourage a high level of everyday activities increase the surveillance of such illegal actions as thefts from parked cars.

O'Donnell emphasizes satisfactory environmental design in the prevention of psychological problems in general, by lowering the manning levels of overmanned settings through the breaking-up of larger units into smaller ones, for example in schools and housing projects. The effect is to increase opportunities for participation for those in the settings. The same result can also be achieved by increasing the number of roles and activities available.

Finally, the literatures concerning firstly, social skills and, secondly, life events are potentially of the utmost relevance to prevention. As Cochrane and Sobol state, it is perhaps easier to provide satisfactory experiences than to 'eliminate the inevitable stresses and strains of life'. Examples of supportive factors are social networks of kin, close personal friends, and a rewarding job. The former are assisted by skills in friendship formation and by physical access to potential friends. Argyle and Duck both argue for 'preparation for life', perhaps in the form of social-skills training, as a component of regular education. Aiding the development of social networks and self-help groups (O'Donnell) may also be included in the list of possible preventive exercises. Obtaining a rewarding job requires not only the appropriate job skills and the ability to perform effectively at interviews, but also political and economic policies which make available an adequate supply of appropriate jobs. Provided that friendships and jobs are both satisfactory they become key factors in helping people to tolerate inevitable stresses by providing alternative sources of personal satisfaction and hence of positive self-statements and self-regard.

TRAINING OF PSYCHOLOGISTS

Yule raises the question of implications for the training of applied psychologists, and it is to this question that we turn finally. Although a number of the practical applications outlined by these authors, and a number of the directions suggested by the more theoretical chapters, fall within the province of clinical psychology, there seems no good reason why the type of applied psychology towards which they collectively point should be confined to people trained in that particular branch of the discipline. Indeed as the mode of operation, in its style, target groups, and settings, moves further from the clinic, so it becomes increasingly obvious that other branches and aspects of psychology are equally relevant. For example the skills involved in the type of communicational work outlined by McGuire are specialized and are no more those of clinical psychology than of educational or academic psychology. Further, problems requiring psychological help arise in many contexts and need to be responded to in their own settings. For example, clinical psychologists have been used to seeing clients in medical settings, sometimes, greatly daring, in non-medical ones, but rarely at places of work. Yet most adults spend much of their lives at work and many of their psychological problems occur in work settings and should be dealt with there. It follows also that clinical psychologists should receive some training in occupational psychology and vice-versa. Exactly the same could be said for children's problems, educational settings, and educational psychology. The logical end-point is a single profession of applied psychology, with a basic training followed by specializations, which can draw on the full range of psychological research and applications.

The more theoretical contributions to this book equally raise questions about the necessary academic background for applied psychologists. We would argue that the appropriate base for the type of work suggested here must include not only a thorough grounding in social psychology but also a much greater appreciation of what can be borrowed from sociology, anthropology, economics, and social geography. At the same time we must be careful not to neglect the study of other aspects of psychology, particularly its biological components.

We are well aware that we are advocating what some will think an improperly grandiose brief for applied psychology; that we are proposing to take on too much without either an adequate understanding of the phenomena concerned or of the constraints that apply to our work. We are convinced, however, that if applied psychology is to make a significant impact on a range of personal problems, then one of the directions in which it must move is towards a much greater investment in the types of social and community studies and activities advocated by the authors of chapters in this volume.

Name Index

Subject Index